EDITION **5**

# Diagnosis and Improvement in Reading Instruction

**DOROTHY RUBIN**

*Professor Emeritus*
**The College of New Jersey**

**MICHAEL F. OPITZ**

**University of Northern Colorado**

PEARSON

Boston  San Francisco  New York
London  Toronto  Sydney  Tokyo  Singapore  Madrid
Mexico City  Munich  Paris  Cape Town  Hong Kong  Montreal

*Executive Editor:* Aurora Martínez Ramos
*Editorial Assistant:* Lynda Giles
*Executive Marketing Manager:* Krista Clark
*Production Editor:* Janet Domingo
*Editorial Production Service:* Nesbitt Graphics, Inc.
*Composition Buyer:* Linda Cox
*Manufacturing Buyer:* Linda Morris
*Electronic Composition:* Nesbitt Graphics, Inc.
*Interior Design:* Nesbitt Graphics, Inc.
*Photo Researcher:* Annie Pickert and Naomi Rudov
*Cover Administrator:* Joel Gendron

For related titles and support materials, visit our online catalog at www.ablongman.com.

Between the time website information is gathered and then published, it is not unusual for some sites to have closed. Also, the transcription of URLs can result in typographical errors. The publisher would appreciate notification where these errors occur so that they may be corrected in subsequent editions.

**Library of Congress Cataloging-in-Publication Data**

Rubin, Dorothy.

Diagnosis and improvement in reading instruction / Dorothy Rubin, Michael F. Opitz.—5th ed.
   p. cm.
Includes bibliographical references.
Contents: Pt. 1. Setting the stage for a diagnostic-reading and improvement program –
Pt. 2. Instruments and techniques for the assessment and diagnosis of reading
performance–Pt. 3. The diagnostic-reading and improvement program in action.
   ISBN 0-205-49845-0
   1. Reading.   2. Reading–Ability testing.   3. Reading–Remedial teaching.   I. Opitz,
Michael F. II. Title.

LB1050.42.R83 2006
372.43–dc22

2006048325

Photo credits appear on page xxiv, which constitutes a continuation of the copyright page.

Printed in the United States of America
10   9   8   7   6   5   4   3   2   1      [RRD-VA]      10   09   08   07   06

*With love to my understanding and very supportive husband, Artie;*
*my precious daughters, Carol and Sharon;*
*my delightful grandchildren, Jennifer, Andrew, Melissa, and Kelsey;*
*and my special sons-in-law, Seth and Dan.*
*D.R.*


*To Mom and Dad,*
*Two of my best teachers*
*M.F.O.*

# Brief Contents

# Contents

# 2 THE TEACHER'S ROLE IN THE DIAGNOSTIC-READING AND IMPROVEMENT PROGRAM  14

## PART 2   INSTRUMENTS AND TECHNIQUES FOR THE ASSESSMENT AND DIAGNOSIS OF READING PERFORMANCE   105

### 6   USING ALTERNATIVE ASSESSMENT TECHNIQUES ACROSS THE GRADES   107

Contents

**Chapter 11 Key Concepts**  353

**Suggestions for Thought Questions and Activities**  353

**Internet Activities**  353

**Selected Bibliography**  353

## 12 HELPING CHILDREN COMPREHEND  356

**Scenario: Assessing and Teaching Alan**  357

**Introduction**  358

**Chapter Objectives**  359

**Building Background about Comprehension**  359

Comprehension  359

Listening Comprehension  359

Reading Comprehension  361

Reading Comprehension Taxonomies  364

**Oral Reading and Reading Comprehension**  366

Guiding Principles  366

Oral Reading: Its Role in the Reading Lesson  367

**Comprehension Skills**  368

Main Idea of a Paragraph  368

Finding the Central Idea of a Group of Paragraphs  375

Drawing Inferences  378

**Comprehension Strategies**  383

**Teaching Comprehension**  383

The Directed Reading–Thinking Activity  384

Think Aloud  391

Repeated Reading  391

Reciprocal Reading Instruction  392

Literature Webbing  393

Questioning Strategies  394

Question–Answer Relationships (QARs)  395

**Noting Student Progress**  397

Questioning as a Diagnostic Technique  397

Cloze Procedure  398

Maze Procedure  402

## 14 TEACHERS AND PARENTS AS PARTNERS IN THE DIAGNOSTIC-READING AND IMPROVEMENT PROGRAM   437

## 15 PUTTING IT ALL TOGETHER   454

# Preface

*Diagnosis and Improvement in Reading Instruction*, Fifth Edition, as in the other four editions, is based on the premise that diagnosis and improvement are essential parts of reading instruction and are necessary parts of early intervention. If diagnosis and improvement are interwoven with reading instruction on a daily basis, there should be less need for remediation. We have designed this book to help preservice and in-service teachers acquire or add to their knowledge the skills necessary to make diagnosis and improvement an integral part of their reading program. To achieve this goal, *Diagnosis and Improvement in Reading Instruction* continues to combine theory, basic knowledge and skills, practical application, and hands-on material.

The new millennium continues to require knowledgeable teachers who know why they do what they do when teaching reading. Therefore, the first part of the book features the role of the teacher, the key person in the program. Teachers in the past few decades have become more autonomous. However, with autonomy comes a greater amount of responsibility. Teachers need as much information and knowledge as possible so that they can develop programs best suited to the needs and developmental levels of their diverse students.

In a viable diagnostic-reading and improvement program, teachers must be able to envision the totality of the reading program. They must fully understand basic developmental reading skills and strategies and be able to apply them, as well as various teaching strategies to help their students become proficient readers. They must recognize that reading is a thinking act and emphasize higher-order thinking. They must recognize that vocabulary is the foundation of reading, but, without comprehension, there is no reading. Good teachers must be knowledgeable of the many factors that affect the reading process and of authentic diagnostic assessment techniques and instruments, including how to administer and interpret them. They also must have a working knowledge of intervention techniques and understand the concept of early intervention. To help teachers to accomplish this kind of program, nothing should be taken for granted. In this book, nothing is.

Part I sets the stage for an effective diagnostic-reading and improvement program. We explain what a diagnostic-reading and improvement program is and define special terms, so there is no confusion when these terms are met later; then we present the teacher as the key person in the reading program, and his or her role is explored in four dimensions. We also present assessment terminology with which a classroom teacher should be familiar, and discuss various kinds of tests. There are many factors that affect reading performance, and we present a thorough explanation of them. Finally, we offer information and suggestions for identifying children most in need of accelerated reading instruction.

Part II presents various instruments and techniques for the assessment and diagnosis of students' reading performance. In this part, we explain and give examples of many kinds of diagnostic tests and techniques. We give special attention to assessing early literacy because we now know several ways of identifying children who appear to be finding reading acquisition difficult. We can provide early intervention for these children, making future reading successes more likely.

Part III, the last part of the book, presents the diagnostic-reading and improvement program in action. In Chapter 9 we explain why many texts need to be used and offer several suggestions for types of texts appropriate for various ages and stages of reading. Chapters 10, 11, and 12 consist of an explanation of phonics, vocabulary and comprehension and provide many diagnostic and teaching techniques that teachers can use to help children become proficient readers. This part also includes chapters on helping children acquire and apply study skills and on parents as partners in a diagnostic-reading and improvement program. The closing chapter provides readers with opportunities to apply what they have learned.

As a further aid to teachers, we include three appendixes. Appendix A offers suggestions for constructing an informal reading inventory. Appendix B contains a complete informal reading inventory. The instructions on how to administer it, mark it, and score it are presented in Chapter 8. Appendix C shows language transfer issues that impact reading. In addition, the book is accompanied by an Instructor's Manual with Tests that will facilitate your planning and use of *Diagnosis and Improvement in Reading Instruction*, Fifth Edition.

## NEW TO THIS EDITION

We have made substantial revisions to every chapter in this fifth edition in light of new discoveries related to reading and reading instruction. Chapters 5, 7, 9, and 15 are new to this edition. In Chapter 5, "Helping Children Achieve in Reading," we provide information about how to identify children most in need of additional reading instruction. Chapter 7, "Assessing and Teaching Early Literacy," is where we provide information about early literacy as well as ways to assess and teach children at this stage of literacy development. Using a variety of texts is our focus in Chapter 9, "Using Texts to Help Children Overcome Reading Difficulties." Our purpose in providing Chapter 15, "Putting It All Together," is to enable readers to review and synthesize the contents of the first fourteen chapters.

In *Diagnosis and Improvement in Reading Instruction*, Fifth Edition, we have made every effort to give principles in practical, comprehensible language, for a book overburdened with esoteric terminology tends to obscure rather than clarify concepts. Some explanations, however, cannot be given without specialized names, but when we use a technical term, we define the term and then use it. We trust readers will find that we have succeeded in minimalizing the number of new terms and that they will benefit from concentrating on practical principles.

# Acknowledgments

The number of individuals who work to make a book possible never ceases to amaze us. We are greatly indebted to all who helped us complete the fifth edition. We thank Dr. Harvey Rude, Director of Special Education at the University of Northern Colorado, for bringing us up to date on special education issues that pertain to this text; Dr. Yvonne Freeman and Dr. David Freeman, University of Texas at Brownsville, for providing us with current information about English Language Learners; Rachel Bates, fifth-grade teacher, for granting permission to use her anecdotal record. We would also like to thank the many individuals at Allyn & Bacon including our editor, Aurora Martínez Ramos, her editorial assistant, Lynda Giles, and production editor, Janet Domingo; and Jude Bucci, Kathy Smith, and Susan McNally from Nesbitt Graphics.

We are grateful to the following individuals for their careful review of the manuscript: Trisha Wies Long, Cleveland State University; Pam Matlock, Murray State University; and Willa Drue Narkon, University of Hawaii.

DR and MFO

---

I thank Dorothy Rubin for inviting me to revise this edition and for her support and encouragement; Dr. Michael Ford, University of Wisconsin, Oshkosh, for his coauthorship on professional writings cited in this text. Finally, I thank Sheryl Opitz, my wife, for making this project easier by taking care of day-to-day tasks.

MFO

## Photo Credits

Page 1, Robert Harbison; pp. 3, 311 Image 100; pp. 14, 61, 140, 239, 241, 266, 356, 454, Lindfors Photography; p. 39, Will Faller; p. 88, Brian Smith; p. 105, Will Hart; p. 107, Karen Mancinelli/Pearson Learning Photo Studio; p. 189, Pearson Learning Photo Studio; p. 410, Bob Daemmrich/The Image Works; and p. 437, Frank Siteman.

# PART 1

# Setting the Stage for a Diagnostic-Reading and Improvement Program

# 1

# Introduction to a Diagnostic-Reading and Improvement Program

**Scenario: A Diagnostic-Reading and Improvement Program in Action**

Whenever you walk into Ms. Johnson's third-grade classroom, you realize that something special is taking place; you can sense the excitement of learning. Often no one notices your arrival because the children are so engrossed in what they are doing.

Ms. Johnson's classroom is not a quiet one. It's a room in which children and teacher are involved in a dynamic, interactive teaching-learning program, which includes a diagnostic-reading and improvement program.

At various times on any one day, you can observe Ms. Johnson working with an individual child, a group of children, or a whole class. In Ms. Johnson's room, grouping is tailored to the needs of children and is very flexible. Children flow from one group to another depending on need. It's not unusual to find a child in more than one reading group, working individually, or working in a one-to-one relationship with Ms. Johnson. Ms. Johnson tries to correlate reading with all the other language arts and sees to it that she meets individually with each child in a special conference at least once during the week. She believes in "nipping problems in the bud," so she keeps very close tabs on her students. Whether children are reading from trade books or from their basal readers, she keeps records of their progress in word recognition and comprehension.

Ms. Johnson is always probing, questioning, and keeping a sharp eye out for what her students do well and for potential problems; she interweaves diagnosis with instruction. When she notices a problem, she talks to the child to try to determine whether the child recognizes that there is a problem. She then sets up a conference to meet and discuss the issue further.

At the conference, Ms. Johnson helps the child recognize that it's important to ask for help when needed. She also tries to elicit the child's perception of the problem. Ms. Johnson has at her fingertips various informal diagnostic strategies, which she readily employs to learn more about the child's reading abilities. If she feels it is necessary, she will use more formal techniques or contact the special reading teacher for suggestions.

Ms. Johnson also contacts the parents to discuss with them what is taking place and to solicit their help. She believes strongly that parents should be partners in their children's school learning and that their help and support are important and needed.

Ms. Johnson is a good teacher, and her abilities are improving with experience. Her students are fortunate to learn under her guidance.

# CHAPTER OBJECTIVES

After reading the chapter, you should be able to:

- Describe what is meant by a diagnostic-reading and improvement program.
- Discuss what is involved in diagnosis.
- State ten principles of diagnosis.
- Discuss the importance of a diagnostic-reading and improvement program.
- Discuss the definition of reading as described in this textbook.
- Describe what a total integrative reading program entails.

- Discuss how a definition of reading influences the diagnostic-reading program.
- Describe what is usually meant by remedial reading.
- Discuss what is usually meant by a balanced reading program.

# WHAT IS A DIAGNOSTIC-READING AND IMPROVEMENT PROGRAM?

**Diagnostic-reading and improvement program**
Reading instruction interwoven with diagnosis and intervention.

A *diagnostic-reading and improvement program* consists of reading instruction interwoven with diagnosis and intervention. The program is based on the premise that both ongoing diagnosis and intervention are integral parts of a daily developmental reading program (i.e., a program that addresses all reading skills and strategies that are systematically and sequentially developed to enable children to become readers) and that knowledgeable teachers can and should implement such a program once they have the necessary skills. It is also based on the premise that early intervention (i.e., identifying students' strengths and needs as early as kindergarten) is essential.

# WHAT IS DIAGNOSIS?

**Diagnosis**
The act, process, or result of identifying the nature of a disorder or disability through observation and examination. In education, it often includes the planning of instruction and an assessment of the strengths and weaknesses (i.e., needs) of the student.

Some educators are disturbed by the term *diagnosis* because it seems to connote illness or disease, and they do not like the analogies that are often made between medicine and education. *Diagnosis* is a term that has been borrowed from medicine. In the field of reading, it is used to discuss how to identify children's reading strengths and needs. The definition of *diagnosis* offered in *The Literacy Dictionary* (Harris & Hodges, 1995) is most often used:

> The act, process, or result of identifying the nature of a disorder or disability through observation and examination . . . As the term is used in education, it often includes the planning of instruction and an assessment of the strengths and weaknesses (i.e., needs) of the student. (p. 59)

Let us analyze the definition further.

1. The first step in diagnosis is the identification of strengths and needs by observing certain signs or symptoms as the child is reading throughout the day and by administering informal reading assessments. (See Chapters 6, 7, and 8.) Some examples of these signs or symptoms would be a child's ability or inability to read fluently, to decode words, or to comprehend.
2. The second step is to determine possible reasons for reading difficulties. This is accomplished by analyzing the results of assessments that are used to shed light on a child's reading performance. It may also include looking for some of the underlying factors, noneducative or educative, that could be contributing to the reading problem.

Note that in the first step, we look for both strengths and needs. Knowledge of what a child can do is often helpful in giving us an insight into a child's reading problem. We can also use what the child knows to teach new strategies. In the second step, we generally find that a reading problem is caused by a number of factors rather than just one. (See Chapter 4.)

## TEN PRINCIPLES OF DIAGNOSIS

Ten principles underlie the type of diagnosis and improvement we propose in this text. These principles are reflected in *Excellent Reading Teachers*, a position statement issued by the International Reading Association's board of directors (IRA, 2000).

1. Diagnosis underlies prevention.
2. Early diagnosis is essential in order to ameliorate reading problems from the start.
3. Diagnosis is continuous.
4. Diagnosis and instruction are interwoven.
5. Diagnosis is a *means* to improvement; it is not an end in itself.
6. Teacher-made as well as published reading assessment instruments are used in diagnosis.
7. Noneducative as well as educative factors are considered.
8. Diagnosis identifies strengths as well as needs.
9. Diagnosis is an individual process; that is, in diagnosis the teacher focuses on an individual child. (Diagnostic information can be obtained from various contexts: working in a one-to-one relationship with a child, observing a child in a group, or observing a child doing seatwork.)
10. The teacher is able to establish rapport and treats each student as an individual worthy of respect.

## DEFINING READING

The relationship of reading to diagnosis is important in a diagnostic-reading and improvement program. To fully understand this relationship it is first essential to define reading. Clearly, the definition that we choose will influence both the instructional and diagnostic components of the program. For example, if we see reading as a total integrative process, diagnosis will also be seen as a total integrative process.

There is no single, set definition of reading. A broad definition is that *reading* is a dynamic, complex act that involves the bringing to and the getting of meaning from the printed page. This definition implies that readers bring their backgrounds, their experiences, as well as their emotions, into play. It further implies that students who are upset or physically ill will bring these feelings into the act of reading, and the feelings will influence their interpretative processes. Yet another implication is that a person well versed in the reading subject matter at hand will gain more from the material than someone less

**Reading**
A dynamic, complex act that involves the bringing of meaning to and the getting of meaning from the written page.

knowledgeable. For example, a student who is a good critical thinker will gain more from a critical passage than one who is not. A student who has strong dislikes will come away with different feelings and understandings than those of a pupil with strong likings related to a given text. Under a global (i.e., integrative) definition, a diagnosis acknowledges that a reading problem is often caused by many different factors. Therefore, the diagnosis would include considerations of ecological (environmental), personal, and intellectual factors. Educative factors, as well as noneducative ones, are considered. A global definition also recognizes that not all children respond in the same way to either teachers or instruction. An atmosphere conducive to growth is important, as well as the maxim that success breeds success. Diagnosis is looked on as continuous, as underlying prevention as well as remediation, and as interwoven with instruction. The emphasis in diagnosis is on determining the child's reading problems and the conditions that contribute to them. This is the definition we advocate in this text. The following section further explains our view.

## READING AS A TOTAL INTEGRATIVE PROCESS

**Reading process**
Concerned with the affective, perceptual, and cognitive domains.

By using a broad or global definition of reading, we see reading as a total integrative process that starts with the reader and includes the affective, perceptual, and cognitive domains.

### The Affective Domain

**Affective domain**
Includes the feelings and emotional learnings that individuals acquire.

The *affective domain* includes our feelings and emotions. The way we feel greatly influences the way we look at stimuli on a field. It may distort our perception. For example, if we have adverse feelings about certain things, these feelings will influence how we interpret what we read. Our feelings will also influence what we decide to read. Attitudes exert a directive and dynamic influence on both our readiness to respond and our willingness to read a given text.

### The Perceptual Domain

**Perceptual domain**
Part of the reading process that depends on an individual's background of experiences and sensory receptors.

The *perceptual domain* involves giving meaning to sensations and the ability to organize stimuli on a field. *Perception* is a cumulative process based on an individual's background of experiences and sensory receptors. If, for example, an individual's eyes are organically defective, perceptions involving sight will be distorted. In the act of reading, visual perception is a most important factor. Children need to control their eyes so they move from left to right across the page. Eye movements influence what the reader perceives.[1]

Although what we observe is never in exact accord with the physical situation,[2] readers must be able to accurately decode the graphemic (written) representation. If however, readers have learned incorrect associations, it will affect their ability to read. For example, if a child reads the word gip for pig and

[1]Eric J. Paulson and Ann E. Freeman, *Insight from the Eyes* (Portsmouth, NH: Heinemann, 2003).

[2]Julian E. Hochberg, *Perception* (Englewood Cliffs, NJ: Prentice-Hall, 1964), p. 3.

is never shown the difference between these words, this may become part of his or her perceptions. Whether children perceive the word as a whole, in parts, or as individual letters will also determine whether they will be good or poor readers. More mature readers are able to perceive more complex and extensive graphemic patterns as units. They are also able to give meaning to mutilated words such as

**Perception**
A cumulative process based on an individual's background of experiences. It is defined as giving meaning to sensations or the ability to organize stimuli on a field.

As noted above, the perceptual process is influenced by physiological factors as well as affective ones. Therefore, a person's biases toward a topic may delete, add, or distort what is actually written.

*The Cognitive Domain*

**Cognitive domain**
Hierarchy of objectives ranging from simplistic thinking skills to the more complex ones.

The *cognitive domain* includes the areas involving thinking. Under this umbrella we place all the comprehension skills (see Chapter 12). Persons who have difficulty in thinking (the manipulation of symbolic representations) will have difficulty in reading. Although the cognitive domain goes beyond the perceptual domain, it builds and depends on a firm perceptual base. That is, if readers have faulty perceptions, they will also have faulty concepts. (See Chapter 7 for a discussion of concept development.)

Those who research the brain and cognitive processes have revealed findings that have implications for teaching and instruction. By regarding the brain as an active consumer of information, able to interpret information and draw inferences from it as well as ignore some information and selectively attend to other information, the learner is "given a new, more important active role and responsibility in learning from instruction and teaching."[3]

**Metacognition**
Thinking critically about thinking; refers to students' knowledge about their thinking processes and ability to control them.

Metacognition relates to the cognitive domain. The term *metacognition* is used "to refer to both students' knowledge about their own cognitive processes and their ability to control these processes."[4] It literally means thinking critically about thinking.

*Who Are Good Readers?*

Good readers are engaged in active learning strategies. They use good monitoring strategies whereby they establish learning goals for an instructional activity, determine the degree to which these are being met, and, if necessary, change the strategies being used to attain the goal.[5] Good readers know what

[3]Merlin C. Wittrock, "Education and the Cognitive Processes of the Brain," *The National Society for the Study of Education Seventy-seventh Yearbook*, Part II (1978): 101.

[4]Claire E. Weinstein and Richard E. Mayer, "The Teaching of Learning Strategies," *The Handbook of Research on Teaching*, 3rd ed. (1986): p. 323.

[5]Ibid.

to do, as well as how and when to do it; they have the metacognitive abilities that make them active consumers of information.

## READING THEORY AND TERMINOLOGY: A SPECIAL NOTE

**Top-down reading models**
Depend on the reader's background of experiences and language ability in constructing meaning from the text.

**Bottom-up reading models**
Models which consider the reading process as one of grapheme-phoneme correspondences; code emphasis or subskill models.

**Interactive reading models**
The top-down processing of information is dependent on the bottom-up processing, and vice versa.

The field of reading is replete with numerous theories, and different catch phrases are sometimes assigned to the same general theories, further confusing those who try to understand the proposed theories. One area that has caused much disagreement and debate among reading theorists is that of beginning reading. Controversy has centered on whether the reading process is a holistic one (emphasis on meaning), that is, a *top-down model;* a subskill process (code emphasis), that is, a *bottom-up model;* and, more recently, whether it is an *interactive model.* The interactive model is somewhat but not entirely a combination of both top-down and bottom-up models in that both processes take place simultaneously depending on the difficulty of the material for the individual reader. (See Fig 1.1.)

Practices in classrooms are based on the theories that teachers embrace. Those who believe in a bottom-up model will emphasize decoding to the exclusion of meaning; and those who believe primarily in a top-down model emphasize meaning. Those who believe in an interactive model will probably use a combination of both.

Reading theorists often tend to be exclusive; they promote their own theory and generally neglect others. The classroom teacher, however, need not accept an either-or dichotomy, but rather should seek a synthesis of all the elements that have proved to be workable; that is, the classroom teacher can take elements from each theory based on the individual needs of students. Good teachers realize that the reading process is a very complex one and that there are no simple answers.

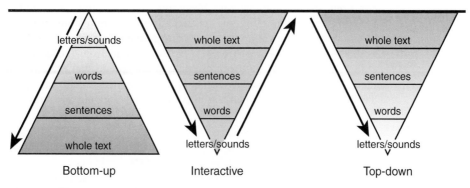

**FIGURE 1.1** Models of Reading

# OTHER TERMINOLOGY

Developmental reading, remedial reading, and balanced reading are terms associated with reading instruction. Each term has its own unique characteristics.

## WHAT IS A DEVELOPMENTAL READING PROGRAM?

**Developmental reading**
All those reading skills and strategies that are systematically and sequentially developed to help students become effective readers throughout their schooling.

In our view, *developmental reading* refers to all those reading skills and strategies that are systematically and sequentially developed to help students become effective readers throughout their schooling. "All those reading skills and strategies" refers to learning-to-read skills and strategies as well as reading-to-learn skills and strategies and reading for appreciation. Developmental reading is the major reading program, and the diagnostic-improvement program that takes place in the regular classroom is part of the developmental reading program; all other programs are adjuncts to the developmental program.

## WHAT IS REMEDIAL READING?

**Remedial reading program**
Takes place outside the regular classroom and is handled by special personnel.

*Remedial reading programs* can take place inside or outside the regular classroom and are handled by special personnel such as a special reading teacher, a therapist, or a clinician. The special reading teacher usually works with students who have severe reading problems that cannot be handled in the regular classroom. The students are usually referred for help by the regular classroom teacher. Regardless of where the remedial instruction occurs, it dovetails into the developmental reading program.

For example, the remedial reading program that takes place outside the regular classroom has as its prime purpose the task of helping students attain those developmental skills and strategies that they lack. This program is not a replacement for the student's classroom developmental instruction in reading; it is reading instruction that is given *in addition to* the reading instruction in the regular classroom, and therefore it must be related to or considered part of the developmental program. This is imperative because studies show that there is a consistent negative relationship between the time students spend in "pull-out" classes and reading.[6] Many times the "pull-out" program becomes the complete reading program for readers with severe reading problems, and rather than spending more time, the students spend less time in reading. Also, if the remedial program is looked on as separate from the developmental reading program, there is usually a lack of congruence between the teaching of the regular classroom teacher and that of the remedial reading teacher. This lack of congruence can confuse children who are already struggling.[7]

[6]G. V. Glass and M. L. Smith, *Pull-Out in Compensatory Education,* paper prepared for Office of the Commissioner, U.S. Office of Education, 1977.

[7]See R. L. Allington and M. C. Shake, "Remedial Reading: Achieving Curricular Congruence in Classroom and Clinic." *The Reading Teacher* (March, 1986): 648–654.

## WHAT IS BALANCED READING?

Balanced reading is defined in many different ways. We view it as a program that incorporates various philosophies, teaching strategies, and materials to achieve the best possible reading instruction for children.

Balanced reading programs are concerned with early intervention and with helping students gain the skills that they need to become effective readers as quickly as possible. Balanced reading programs are designed to help students to improve their higher-order thinking skills, as well as gain needed comprehension and word recognition skills and strategies. In addition, in these programs teachers nurture a love of books in their students to help them become lifelong readers. Clearly, a good diagnostic-reading and improvement program includes a balanced reading program that avoids extremes.

 ## Scenario: Balanced Reading

Ms. Hill has a balanced reading program in her classroom. Let's look at what she does.

Ms. Hill uses explicit teaching, that is, she presents an intentional program designed to teach skills and strategies. She realizes that just reading aloud to the children is not enough. She teaches phonics skills systematically because she believes in a sequential development of this skill. When appropriate, she also teaches spelling generalizations and vocabulary skills.

For those children who have difficulty with phonics, she uses a whole-word approach. Ms. Hill uses many different approaches. Her goal is to help her students become good, strategic readers; consequently, she presents them with word recognition and comprehension strategies. She incorporates a program that uses both oral and silent reading. She models oral reading for her students to help them gain and recognize good adult reading fluency.

A good balanced reading program helps her students become lifelong readers.

## A DIAGNOSTIC-READING AND IMPROVEMENT PROGRAM: A POINT OF VIEW

Ideally, a diagnostic reading and improvement program is the most helpful of all programs because in such a program all regular classroom teachers have the reading skills and strategies needed to present an effective reading program to their students. Teachers who embrace a diagnostic reading and improvement program focus on potential reading problems and try to prevent them. A diagnostic reading and improvement program is part of the ongoing reading program, and it takes place in the regular classroom under the leadership of the classroom teacher. The sooner an astute teacher recognizes a problem, the sooner the problem is diagnosed; and the sooner steps are taken to correct the problem, the less need there will be for later remediation.

A diagnostic-reading and improvement program can help to stop the "failure cycle." If children continually have reading difficulties, they begin to see themselves as failures; their self-concept is destroyed. The more they perceive themselves as failures, the more they fail. And so the cycle continues.

What we want instead is a success cycle (Cullinan, 2000). The basic idea is that the more a person reads, the more reading ability improves. This results in enjoyment of the reading experience. Because the reader enjoys the experience, more time will be spent reading.

## SUMMARY

Chapter 1 is an introduction to a diagnostic-reading and improvement program. Such a program consists of reading instruction interwoven with diagnosis and improvement. Since the definition that is chosen for reading will influence the diagnostic program, reading is defined in a global manner: Reading is a dynamic, complex act that involves the bringing to and the getting of meaning from the printed page. By using a broad definition, we look on reading as a total integrative process. Under a global definition when we make a diagnosis, we recognize that several factors can contribute to a reading problem.

## CHAPTER 1 KEY CONCEPTS

- A diagnostic-reading and improvement program consists of reading instruction interwoven with diagnosis and remediation.
- Diagnosis is the act of identifying students' reading strengths and needs from signs and symptoms and the analysis of the factors leading to a condition, situation, or problem.
- Reading in this text is defined as a dynamic, complex act that involves the bringing of meaning to and the taking of meaning from the printed page.
- Reading as a total integrative act begins with the reader and involves the affective, perceptual, and cognitive domains.
- Good strategic readers have good metacognitive ability; they know what to do, as well as how and when to do it.

- There are a number of reading theories that appear to be at odds with one another; however, the one most widely held is the interactive reading model, which embraces a balanced approach.
- Developmental reading encompasses all those reading skills and strategies that are sequentially developed to help students become effective readers throughout their schooling.
- A diagnostic-reading and improvement program takes place within the regular classroom and focuses on trying to prevent potential problems.
- A balanced reading program integrates the *best* of various theories, teaching strategies, and materials to achieve the best possible reading instruction for children.

## SUGGESTIONS FOR THOUGHT QUESTIONS AND ACTIVITIES

1. You have been assigned to a special committee to develop a reading program in your school that would help reduce the number of reading problems that now exist. You have decided to advocate the implementation of a diagnostic-reading and improvement program. Give your rationale for doing so. How would you go about implementing such a program?

2. Make a study of the ways that persons in a school district are defining *developmental reading*.
3. Make a study in your school district to see whether remedial reading is a "pull-out program" that is or is not integrated with the developmental reading program.
4. Ask a number of teachers how they define reading. Observe their classes and try to discern whether their reading program reflects their definition of reading.
5. Ask readers to reflect on how they became mature readers.

## INTERNET ACTIVITIES

Choose a search engine and search for websites related to the term *reading diagnosis*. Select one website from the search that helps you gain a good understanding of the term. Write a paragraph about the term. Include your understanding of the term and one example. (Be sure to identify both the search engine you used and the website you selected.)

## SELECTED BIBLIOGRAPHY

Allington, Richard L., and Mary C. Shake. "Remedial Reading: Achieving Curricular Congruence in Classroom and Clinic." *The Reading Teacher* (March, 1986): 648–654.

Anderson, Richard C., Elfrieda H. Hiebert, Judith A. Scott, and Ian A. G. Wilkinson. *Becoming a Nation of Readers*. Washington, DC: National Institute of Education, 1985.

Cullinan, Bernice. *Read to Me: Raising Kids Who Love to Read*. Rev. ed. New York: Scholastic, 2000.

Harris, Albert J., and Edward R. Sipay. *How to Increase Reading Ability*, 9th ed. New York: Longman, 1990.

Johnston, Peter H., Richard Allington, and Peter Afflerbach. "The Congruence of Classroom and Remedial Reading Instruction. *Elementary School Journal (85)* 4: 465–477.

Kamil, Michael L. et al., eds. *Handbook of Reading Research*, Vol. III. Mahwah, NJ: Lawrence Erlbaum, 2000.

Paulson, Eric J., and Ann E. Freeman. *Insight from the Eyes: The Science of Effective Reading Instruction*. Portsmouth, NH: Heinemann, 2003.

Pinnell, Gay Su, Mary D. Fried, and Rose Mary Estice. "Reading Recovery: Learning How to Make a Difference." *The Reading Teacher* 43 (January 1990): 282–95.

Snow, Catherine E. et al., eds. *Preventing Reading Difficulties in Young Children*. Washington, DC: National Academic Press, 1998.

Wittrock, Merlin C. "Learning and the Brain." In *The Brain and Psychology*, ed. Merlin C. Wittrock. New York: Academic Press, 1980.

# The Teacher's Role in the Diagnostic-Reading and Improvement Program

## Scenarios: Extremes Don't Work!

**1** Mrs. Brown, the mother of Lisa, a first grader in Ms. Clay's class, noticed that her daughter was bringing home books that she could not read independently. She told her child that she liked reading to her but that she wanted Lisa to read to her sometimes. She asked Lisa to bring home two books the next time—one that she wanted her mom to read to her and one that she could read on her own. The next week, Lisa brought home two books. When Lisa was reading her book aloud, Mrs. Brown noticed that it sounded as though Lisa had memorized the story. Mrs. Brown tested her theory by taking a number of the story's words out of the context of the book and asking Lisa to read them. What she suspected was true. Lisa had memorized the story, but was unable to identify the words out of context. Was this natural for beginning readers? Mrs. Brown didn't know, so she scheduled an appointment with Ms. Clay to discuss Lisa's reading program.

Ms. Clay told Mrs. Brown she believes strongly that if she immerses her first graders in lots of print, they will learn to read. She said that she first reads a story aloud to them and then has the whole class read the story aloud in unison, while she plays a tape of the story. She has her students do this many times. She uses trade books—that is, library books in class, and for independent reading, she allows children to choose whatever book they would like to read. She said that she didn't believe in explicit instruction. She felt that a teacher should be a guide or facilitator. "After all," she asked, "would you rather have 'beguiling stories' or 'drill'?" Ms. Clay assured Mrs. Brown that Lisa was learning to read.

Do you agree with the way Ms. Clay is teaching reading and her views on explicit instruction? Do you think she has an adequate understanding of explicit instruction? Here's another scenario of a teacher who uses extremes.

**2** Rachael started the third grade reading very well. According to her test scores, she was at grade level. Consequently, she was confused because she didn't understand why her teacher, Ms. Graves, kept having her read with children who appeared to be struggling. She started to dislike reading.

Toward the end of March, Rachael came home hysterical. Ms. Graves was sending her and her whole group to the "resource room" with a special reading teacher while the other groups stayed in the regular classroom and had reading with Ms. Graves. Rachael's mother phoned the teacher to find out what was happening.

Ms. Graves said that the children would be taking the standardized achievement tests soon and she feared that Rachael would not do well in reading, so she wanted her to go to the resource room for extra help with reading. Rachael's mother explained that her daughter was very upset about going out of the classroom and asked why Ms. Graves couldn't give her the help she needed in the regular classroom. Ms. Graves said that Rachael's whole group was going to the resource room and if Rachael didn't go, she'd be the only one left from her group. Obviously, she did not have the time to work with Rachael. Rachael's mother said that she would be happy to come in and work with her daughter if Ms. Graves would tell her what to do. She explained that her daughter was very, very upset and did not want to go out of the classroom to the "dummy" room. Ms. Graves said that under no circumstances could she come to class and work with Rachael.

Meanwhile, Rachael was becoming more and more upset. In the mornings she would have dreadful stomachaches. At times she would cry and beg her mother to let her stay home. She said that she felt like a dummy and she couldn't do the work. Rachael's mother wondered how a cheery, happy little girl who loved school and reading could change so radically.

Do you agree with the way Ms. Graves is handling Rachael and her mother? If you were Ms. Graves, would you have sent Rachael to the "resource room"? For that matter, would you have sent a whole group to the "resource room"? What insights can you draw from this scenario about Ms. Graves's ability as a reading teacher? How might Ms. Graves's attitude toward Rachael be affecting Rachael?

In this chapter we discuss the teacher's role in the diagnostic-reading and improvement program and focus on the characteristics of a good reading teacher in the regular classroom.

## CHAPTER OBJECTIVES

After reading the chapter you should be able to:

- Discuss the role of a teacher in a diagnostic-reading and improvement program.
- Describe the kinds of skills that teachers need to implement a diagnostic-reading and improvement program.
- Describe the characteristics of a good reading teacher.
- Discuss what is meant by *self-fulfilling prophecy.*
- Discuss teaching in the twenty-first century.
- Give some reasons why so many new teachers leave teaching after a few years.
- Describe *explicit instruction.*
- Discuss what a teacher should know about classroom management and organization.
- Explain how a teacher models thinking strategies for students.
- Discuss why and how a teacher can use self-assessment.

## THE TEACHER IN A DIAGNOSTIC-READING AND IMPROVEMENT PROGRAM

The role of a teacher in a diagnostic-reading and improvement program is complex. The teacher must observe individual children, understand individual differences and the factors that influence them, build readiness for reading at various reading levels, identify children who are having reading difficulties, combine diagnosis and improvement with everyday reading, and help children gain an appreciation of reading. Teachers must have knowledge of the various word recognition and comprehension skills and strategies at their fingertips and be able to teach them effectively. They must know observation techniques and be aware of the factors that influence children's reading behaviors.

Teachers must be able to administer and interpret a variety of assessments such as informal reading inventories and word analysis tests. If teachers are not able to construct their own informal diagnostic tests, they should be aware of those that are commercially available. Clearly, teachers in a diagnostic-reading and improvement program must be well prepared and well informed.

# THE TEACHER AS THE KEY TO A GOOD READING PROGRAM

Although a school may have the best equipment, the most advanced school plant, a superior curriculum, and children who want to learn, it is crucial that it has "good teachers" so that the desired kind of learning can take place. With today's emphasis on accountability, the spotlight is even more sharply focused on the teacher. Although there is no definitive agreement on how to evaluate teachers, researchers and educators agree that teachers influence students' behavior and learning.

Researchers have discovered that it is difficult to compare different methods or sets of materials and that students seem to learn to read from a variety of materials and methods.[1] More important, researchers consistently point to the teacher as the key to improving reading instruction. For example, the authors of *Becoming a Nation of Readers* state that "studies indicate that about 15 percent of the variation among children in reading achievement at the end of the school year is attributable to factors that relate to the skill and effectiveness of the teacher."[2] In contrast, "the largest study ever done comparing approaches to beginning reading found that about 3 percent of the variation in reading achievement at the end of the first grade was attributable to the overall approach of the program."[3] The teacher is the key to improving reading instruction:

> The main lesson, it seems to me, is that the teacher is of tremendous importance in preventing and treating children's reading and learning disabilities . . . good teaching is probably the best way to help children.[4]

Although most professional reading organizations, educators, and the public at large agree that the teacher is the key to improved instruction, there is no unanimity on the precise factors that affect teaching performance and students' learning or on the objective criteria for evaluating teacher performance.

---

[1]Guy L. Bond and Robert Dykstra, "The Cooperative Research Program in First-Grade Reading Instruction," *Reading Research Quarterly* 2 (Summer 1967): 1–142. Albert J. Harris and Coleman Morrison, "The CRAFT Project: A Final Report," *The Reading Teacher* 22 (January 1969): 335–40.

[2]Richard C. Anderson, Elfrieda H. Hiebert, Judith A. Scott, and Ian A. G. Wilkinson, *Becoming a Nation of Readers* (Washington, DC: National Institute of Education, 1985), p. 85.

[3]Ibid.

[4]Jeanne Chall, "A Decade of Research on Reading and Learning Disabilities," *What Research Has to Say About Reading Instruction* (Newark, DE: International Reading Association, 1978), pp. 39, 40.

This may be the result of the paucity of research in teacher education. For example, after an exhaustive search of the literature, the National Reading Panel found a very small number of experimental studies dedicated to this area.[5]

# SOME IMPORTANT CHARACTERISTICS AND PRACTICES OF GOOD READING TEACHERS

Although unanimity does not exist among educators as to which characteristics are the most salient in producing good teachers, most would agree that verbal ability; good educational background including such knowledge as the content of reading, ability to read with skill oneself, and ability to do higher-order thinking; good planning and organizing ability; instructional strategies; and positive teacher expectations and attitudes would be ones that reading teachers should possess. In fact, some researchers have identified practices and beliefs of teachers whose students demonstrated the highest achievement:

1. Coherent and thorough integration of skills with high-quality reading and writing experiences.
2. A high density of instruction (i.e., integration of multiple goals in a single lesson).
3. Extensive use of scaffolding (i.e., support).
4. Encouragement of student self-regulation (i.e., solving their own problems).
5. A thorough integration of reading and writing activities.
6. High expectations for all students.
7. Masterful classroom management.
8. An awareness of their practices and the goals underlying them.[6]

Some investigators suggest that teachers who have a good educational background and verbal ability are usually better teachers than those who do not.[7] This information makes sense and should come as no surprise. What is surprising is that there are some teachers who appear to lack necessary reading skills. A four-and-one-half-year study measuring the reading skills of almost 350 teachers led researchers to conclude that "many of the teachers tested demonstrated a wide range of deficiencies or discrepancies in their reading abilities."[8] Although researchers stated that care should be taken not to generalize

[5]Report of the National Reading Panel: Teaching Children to Read, "Teacher Education and Reading Instruction." (Bethesda, MD: National Institute of Child Health & Human Development, April 2000).

[6]R. Wharton-McDonald, M. Pressley, and J. Hampston. "Literacy Instruction in Nine First-grade Classrooms: Teacher Characteristics and Student Achievements," *The Elementary School Journal* (99, 1998): 101–128.

[7]Charles E. Bidwell and John D. Kasarda, "School District Organization and Student Achievement," *American Sociological Review* 40 (February 1975): 55–70. Eric Hanushek, "The Production of Education, Teacher Quality and Efficiency," paper presented at the Bureau of Educational Personnel Development Conference: "How Do Teachers Make a Difference?" Washington, DC.

[8]Lance M. Gentile and Merna McMillan, "Some of Our Students' Teachers Can't Read Either," *Journal of Reading* 21 (November 1977): 146.

from these results, teacher deficiencies in reading ability should warrant concern. Another researcher found that teachers scored low on tests of study skills intended for children completing elementary or junior high school.[9] If teachers feel insecure about a subject, they will tend to avoid teaching it, and when they do cover it, they may teach concepts and skills erroneously. If teachers lack a broad vocabulary, are unable to read critically, and have not acquired study skills, their students will suffer. How can teachers construct questions that challenge students' higher levels of thinking if they lack the ability to read at high levels of comprehension? They can't. How can teachers diagnose students' problems if they do not know what skills the students are supposed to have? They can't. How can teachers instill a love for books in students if they do not enjoy reading? They can't. If teachers are perceived by students as not placing a high value on reading, students may begin to feel likewise. The reverse is also true. (Chapters 9 to 13 present reading skills that teachers should have at their fingertips and help teachers learn how to interest their students in books.)

## TEACHER EXPECTATIONS

**Self-fulfilling prophecy**
Teacher assumptions about children become true, at least in part, because of the attitude of the teachers, which in turn becomes part of the children's self-concept.

The more teachers know about their students, the better able they are to plan for them. However, teachers must be cautioned about the *self-fulfilling prophecy*—where teachers' assumptions about children become true, at least in part, because of the attitude of the teachers, which in turn becomes part of the children's self-concept. Teachers' expectations about students' abilities to learn will influence students' learning.[10] For example, if a child comes from an environment not conducive to learning, the teacher may assume that this child cannot learn beyond a certain level and thus treat this child accordingly. If this happens, the teacher's assumptions could become part of the child's own self-concept, further reinforcing the teacher's original expectations.

Teachers who are aware of the effect that their expectations have on the learning behavior of students can use this to help their students. For example, teachers should assume that *all* their students are capable of learning to read, and they should use positive reinforcement whenever feasible to help students become and remain motivated.

## TEACHER STANDARDS

Accountability for teachers' performance is currently a very big issue and will probably increase in importance as the century progresses. Taxpayers across the country feel that they are beyond the talking point where educational accountability is concerned—they want action and they want it now. And many

[9]Eunice N. Askov, et al., "Study Skill Mastery among Elementary School Teachers," *The Reading Teacher* 30 (February 1977): 485–488.

[10]Robert Rosenthal and Lenore Jacobson, *Pygmalion in the Classroom* (New York: Holt, Rinehart and Winston, 1968). Douglas A. Pidgeon, *Expectation and Pupil Performance* (London: National Foundation for Educational Research, in England and Wales, 1970).

governors, ever mindful of polls that list education as a top priority among their constituents, are ready to comply. They want more rigorous standards for students, and they feel that the best way to achieve higher standards for students is to have equally high standards for teachers.

Teacher educators from numerous states have raised the grade-point average that those preparing to be teachers should have when graduating from college. Many require a 3.0 grade-point average (GPA), which is equivalent to a B.

Assuming that a high GPA translates into better instruction makes sense. Good teachers need many admirable traits, and among them is a strong knowledge base. Somehow, good grades signify that the student has the required knowledge. A strong knowledge base, however, does not guarantee that a teacher will be good, but without it, a teacher has little hope of being effective.

Even though grading is a complex topic, most instructors agree that the awarding of grades should be based on students' achievement in the course. And most would also concur that there should be many ways to assess students' accomplishment. However, the ultimate way to discern whether teachers should have received their degrees is their performance in the classroom. This is why their first year of on-the-job probation under a knowledgeable mentor is so important.

The National Council for Accreditation of Teacher Education (NCATE) in March 2002 announced new standards for accrediting schools of education that promise to revolutionize teacher education programs. The emphasis is on performance-based teacher-preparation programs, and the list of standards is comprehensive. For example, it requires teachers to demonstrate teaching effectiveness and the ability to diagnose students' needs. NCATE also expects teachers to be knowledgeable about research and to apply the research to their classrooms. In addition, teachers must be able to work with students who come from culturally diverse backgrounds, as well as students with special needs.

As mentioned in Chapter 1, the board of directors of the International Reading Association (IRA), a professional reading association, in January 2000 adopted a position statement enumerating the kinds of qualities excellent classroom reading teachers should possess.[11] Each quality is research-based.

## TEACHING IN THE TWENTY-FIRST CENTURY

The good news is that, in spite of the tougher teaching requirements being imposed on teachers today and the demands for greater accountability, those who choose teaching as their career seem to love it. Unfortunately, however, many of these same people claim that they feel that they have not been well prepared for the realities of the classroom.

[11]See "Excellent Reading Teachers: A Position Statement of the International Reading Association" (Newark, DE: International Reading Association, January 2000).

In the report "A Sense of Calling: Who Teaches and Why," the Public Agenda survey reported that 96% of new teachers say that "Teaching is work they love to do."[12] It is reassuring to know that teachers love what they are doing. The Public Agenda survey also reported that "most young teachers are highly motivated professionals who bring a strong sense of commitment and morale to their work. New teachers see themselves as talented, hardworking professionals who have responded to a calling."[13] However, it is devastating to learn that the same Public Agenda survey shows that "60% believe most new teachers take over classrooms without the requisite experience in how to actually run them"[14] and "more than half (56%) say there was too much education theory and not enough focus on practical classroom challenges."[15]

Today, with so many competing fields vying for job candidates, many capable people who might have chosen the teaching profession are instead choosing what they consider to be more lucrative professional fields. In addition, many of those who claim that they love teaching leave the field after a few years. Perhaps this would not be the case if the following fictitious scenario about what new teachers should experience was not so fictitious!

 ## Scenario of a New Teacher

Deidre Jackson had always wanted to be a teacher. As a small child, she played school with her dolls. And when she was a little older, she did the same with her friends and younger cousins.

When Deidre was in college, she majored in history with a minor in elementary education, and when she graduated, she got a position in a local elementary school. When her friends heard where she would be teaching, they tried to talk her out of it, but to no avail.

Deidre, or rather Dee as her friends called her, comes from the inner city herself. She is a very intelligent and articulate young woman who wants to make a difference. She feels she can accomplish her goal through teaching.

When school started in the fall, Dee arrived, filled with energy, excitement, idealism, and hope. She had a fifth-grade class that had a multicultural mix of students with limited English proficiency. She also had numerous mainstreamed students in some of her classes.

The first week of school was a learning period for her—she learned about her school and she got to know many of her students. She learned that many had trouble reading their history books, and many who could decode the words did not understand what they were reading. Very few read a newspaper and knew basic facts about their state or nation. Many students told Dee that they

---

[12]Farkas, Steve et al. "A Sense of Calling: Who Teaches and Why." New York: Public Agenda, 2000, p. 9.

[13]Ibid, p. 10.

[14]Ibid, p. 29.

[15]Ibid, p. 30.

were marking time until they were old enough to leave school. She also learned that many of the fifth graders were working at part-time jobs after school.

Dee was aware of the studies about at-risk students. She knew about the dismal results of the National Assessment of Educational Progress reports, especially among minority students. She knew that she would encounter difficulties among her students, but she had not expected the problems to be so overwhelming. In addition, she felt unprepared to cope with so many reading problems.

Dee came from a poor home herself, but she had always loved school and worked hard to learn and get the most she could from her classes. She had not expected that so many students would be so cynical, uncaring, and filled with despair.

After the first month of school, Dee was exhausted and disappointed, but she was not ready to give up. She felt that if she asked for help she would get the aid that she needed. Fortunately for Dee, her school system did provide mentors who were experienced expert teachers. These mentors met with Dee and not only gave her suggestions but also came to her classroom and presented demonstration lessons.

Dee also went back to her college and spoke to numerous professors to get suggestions about helping her students. She told her professors that she was grateful for all the clinical classroom experiences she had while at school and the good feedback that she got because it had helped her a lot. She also said that she remembers what they said about high-stake tests: "high-stake tests today might stop these kids from moving on, but if nothing is done to help them really early on, many will just do nothing until they're old enough to leave school."

At the middle of the school year, Dee received outstanding ratings from the principal and other supervisors. Dee is still teaching. Today, she is helping other new teachers. Let us hope she continues teaching.

Teaching is a complex behavior that requires teachers to perform different but related roles. We see the teacher as planner, explicit reading teacher, organizer and manager, and self-evaluator (see Figure 2.1). In this section we explain each role.

> **Commentary**
> Dee is one of the lucky teachers—she received help and support from her school system and her professors. However, what about those who do not receive any help or support? How long will they remain in their present field?

# TEACHER AS PLANNER

> **Diagnostic teaching**
> The practice of continuously trying a variety of instructional strategies and materials based on the needs of students.

Teachers in a diagnostic-reading and improvement program must also be good planners. Planning helps guide teachers in making choices about instruction; it helps them to clarify their thinking about objectives, students' needs, interests, and developmental levels, as well as to determine what motivating techniques to use.

The teacher in a diagnostic-reading and improvement program bases instruction on continuous analysis of students' strengths and needs. The teacher is flexible and is always alert to student feedback to determine whether to proceed with instruction, slow down instruction, or stop and correct or clarify some misconception. In other words, the teacher uses *diagnostic teaching*,

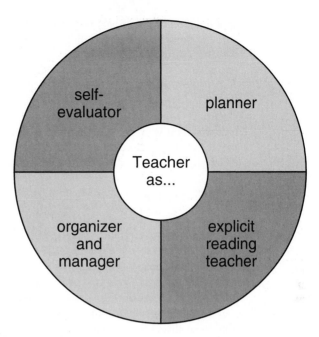

**FIGURE 2.1**  Teacher Roles

"the practice of systematic trial and evaluation of a variety of instructional strategies (including materials, methods of presentation, and methods of feedback) with individual students as part of their everyday educational program."[16] Teachers use a number of assessment instruments and techniques in such teaching, and they make whatever modifications they have to make on the basis of feedback from their students.

The teacher in a diagnostic-reading and improvement program must wisely plan time allotments for reading. And as Durkin (1993) noted well over a decade ago, there are different ways to do just that. Sometimes the instruction will be *planned and intentional.* This is the type of instruction in which the teacher has designed a lesson that focuses on a specific reading skill or strategy. The lesson includes a specific objective, teaching procedures that will enable students to attain the objective, and an individual assessment that will help the teacher to determine how well the students learned the objective of the lesson.

*Unplanned, intentional* instruction is another way to plan time. This type of planning requires teachers to be responsive to what students are doing and to think on their feet. For example, sometimes students might show a misunderstanding of a topic through their oral responses. As a result, the teacher may make the decision to clear up any misunderstandings; this requires on-the-

---

[16]John Salvia and James Ysseldyke, *Assessment in Special and Remedial Education,* 4th ed. (Boston: Houghton Mifflin, 1988), p. 525.

spot thinking of intentional ways to teach students to clear up their confusion. At other times, something might happen that will encourage the teacher to seize the moment to teach students. Take, for example, an experience I (Michael) encountered when the lights unexpectedly went out during the school day. The students lost all focus in the lesson I was conducting, so I decided to abandon the lesson altogether. Instead, I used the occasion to teach something about electricity. I first had students talk about everyday objects that use electricity. I recorded their words on a semantic map using "electricity fuels objects" as the defined center, and we read the chart together. I then read them a book about electricity and had them compare our chart to what was mentioned in the book.

# TEACHER AS EXPLICIT READING TEACHER

Most students need help in acquiring reading skills and strategies; they do not gain these through osmosis. The kind of instruction teachers use to explicitly teach reading will affect how well their students learn to read.

To help students become good readers, teachers must have metacognitive ability, so they know when to do what and how. In other words, they must know a number of teaching strategies and consistently monitor their teaching to help students become active consumers of information and good strategic readers.

Good teachers recognize that good readers interact with the text and bring their background of experiences to the reading act. Good teachers also become part of the interactive process by using explicit instruction.

**Explicit instruction**
Instruction guided by a teacher, who uses various strategies to help students understand what they are reading.

## WHAT IS EXPLICIT INSTRUCTION?

*Explicit instruction* is guided by a teacher, who uses different kinds of strategies to help students gain understanding of what they are reading. There are several instructional strategies that teachers can use to teach reading explicitly, and the techniques teachers employ transcend the kinds of materials they use. For example, in one class a teacher may use a published reading program, whereas in another, a teacher might use trade books, that is, library books. In yet another class, a teacher might use a combination of different printed matter including newspapers. All these teachers can still employ similar instructional strategies to help students achieve.

Explicit instruction in reading requires that teachers have goals and activities to accomplish these goals, as well as techniques that range from directly explaining some concepts to using inductive teaching strategies whereby teachers elicit generalizations from students based on the presentation of numerous examples or clues. In addition, explicit instruction requires that teachers provide immediate feedback to their students. As noted in the previous section, this instruction is most often planned and intentional. Consider the following scenario, which shows how a teacher uses a think-aloud activity to help his students gain understanding.

## Scenario: A Sample Explicit Reading Lesson

A teacher and five students in a fourth-grade class are engaged in a reading comprehension lesson. They are reading a trade book about the Civil War. They have been studying the Civil War, and this is a short novel depicting the lives of two different families during that period. Mr. Rojas, the teacher, prepares his students for the book by showing them a picture of President Lincoln reading the Gettysburg Address and uses this as a stimulus to discuss what they have learned about the Civil War. He then presents some key vocabulary words that he feels students may need to read the chapter. Next he tells them that they will be acting as investigative reporters. Even though they had previously discussed what investigative reporters do, he wants to review it with them because he wants them to read as if they are investigative reporters.

Today he will help them become better investigative reporters. He tells the students that before they return to their seats to read the first chapter silently, he wants to make sure they know how to collect information, especially if the information is not directly stated. Mr. Rojas hands out a short selection to each of the students and asks them to read it to try to determine how many soldiers had started out on the mission and in what direction they were headed. (None of the information is directly stated.) After the students finish reading the short selection, Mr. Rojas says that he will tell them how he figures out the answers. He tells them that he will "talk aloud" to give them his thoughts.

Mr. Rojas says that as he reads the selection to answer the first question, he notices some key information, namely, that the remaining one-third of the soldiers were exhausted. It also says that the nine remaining ones could not last much longer. From this information, he can determine that two-thirds have died or are missing. If 9 equals $\frac{1}{3}$ of the original number, then there were 27 soldiers at the beginning of the special mission. The selection also states that the soldiers were walking toward the mountain range, and in another sentence it states that the sun was setting behind the mountain range. He says that he knows the sun rises in the East and sets in the West. Since the soldiers are walking toward the mountain range and the sun is setting behind the mountain range, they are heading west.

Mr. Rojas has students read another selection and has them answer questions based on information that is not directly stated. He asks for volunteers to explain how they went about answering the questions.

He then tells them that he wants them to go back to their seats and read silently the first chapter in their books. While they are reading he wants them to collect evidence from this chapter to make some predictions about the two main characters who are introduced in the chapter and tells them to record their predictions. He also lets them know that tomorrow, they will discuss their predictions, and as they read the book, they will check to see how accurate these predictions were.

# TEACHER AS ORGANIZER AND MANAGER

Teachers in a diagnostic-reading and improvement program must be good organizers and managers. They must be able to work with large groups, small groups, the whole class, and individual students. As Table 2.1 shows, each type

**TABLE 2.1 Group Size for Guided Reading Experiences**

| Group Size | Description | Advantages | Disadvantages | When It Works |
|---|---|---|---|---|
| Whole Class | Teacher works with the whole class and everyone participates in similar activities. In one way or another, the same text is often read by all students. | • Builds a community of learners<br>• Provides a common knowledge base for all | • Differentiating instruction is more difficult<br>• Some students can get frustrated or bored depending on the level of instruction<br>• Students may not interact as planned | • Different learners are considered when planning instruction<br>• All members of the class are provided with a similar experience |
| Small Group | Groups of two to five students work together to accomplish a given task. | • Provides for focused instruction<br>• Engages more learners<br>• Students learn to work with one another | • Students may not interact<br>• Creates a higher noise level<br>• Students might be grouped together for too long<br>• Student perceptions of group can be negative | • Group membership changes on a regular basis<br>• Students are taught how to respond to one another |
| Partners | Students are paired up with one another to read text in one or more ways. | • Stays focused<br>• Enables relationships to develop<br>• Encourages independent learning so the teacher can help those who need it | • One of the two students may become too dependent on the other<br>• One of the two may dominate | • Partners are switched on a regular basis<br>• Procedures are clearly understood by both |
| Individual | Students work by themselves and each often reads a different text. | • Allows students to read at a comfortable level and to develop their own understandings<br>• Enables teacher to evaluate individual progress to determine what students know and need to know | • Can be hard to organize<br>• Students may become distracted and/or lose focus<br>• Little sense of community | • Reading is at the appropriate level<br>• Students understand procedures<br>• An effort is made to bring students back together either as a small or large group to discuss what they've learned |

of grouping has advantages and disadvantages. When thinking about grouping students, we need to think through what we are using as a basis for grouping them. Usually the basis for placement in reading groups is the student's achievement level. In this case, during the first few weeks of the term, teachers collect data concerning the achievement levels of each of the students in their classes through observation, teacher-made tests, and standardized tests. After evaluating the collected data, the teacher organizes tentative groups. The number of groups in a skill area depends on the amount of variability within the class. For some areas, there may be three or four groups; for some, there may only be two groups; for some, the teacher may decide to work with the whole class as a unit; and for some areas, the teacher may have a number of children working individually. The grouping pattern is a flexible one, and the groups themselves are recognized as flexible units; children can easily flow from one group to another. When the purpose for the group has been met, the group dissolves.

The teacher as a good manager is able to deal with more than one situation at a time. A teacher working with a group should be aware of what is going on not only in that group but also with the other children in the class. A teacher cannot "dismiss" the rest of the class because he or she is working with a particular group. Even though the children have been given challenging work based on their individual needs, the teacher must be alert to what is happening to ensure safety for all children and to keep children on task. The alert teacher is able to prevent problems. The following scenario presents an example of a good manager. Notice especially how Mr. Mills is able to manage a number of ongoing activities at the same time. Notice how he is always aware of what is going on in his class, and notice how he prevents problems from arising.

 ## Scenario: Mr. Mills—A Good Classroom Manager

One teacher and six children are engaged in reading at a round table. The rest of the class is involved in a variety of activities: A number of children are working individually at their seats or at learning centers; one child, sitting in a rocking chair, is reading; two children are working together; and a group of children are working together in the rear of the room.

The teacher says to his group at the round table, "We've talked about what inference means, and we've given examples of it. Who can tell us what we mean by inference?" A few children raise their hands. Mr. Mills calls on one, and he gives an explanation of inference. "Good," says Mr. Mills. "Now, I'd like you to read the paragraph about Mr. Brown and then tell us what inferences you can make about Mr. Brown. Be prepared to support your inferences with evidence from the paragraph."

Mr. Mills looks at each of the children as they are reading. He then glances around the room. He says, "Judy, may I see you for a moment?" Judy comes to Mr. Mills. The teacher asks Judy in a very quiet tone if he can help her. He says, "Judy, you look confused. What's wrong?" Judy says that she is having trouble figuring out a question. Mr. Mills tells Judy to work on something else for about ten minutes, and that then he will help her. As Judy goes back to her seat, Mr. Mills again quickly glances around the room. As his eyes meet those of some of the children, he smiles at them. Mr. Mills then looks at the children in his group. He sees that they are ready and asks them what inferences they can make about Mr. Brown. All raise their hands. Mr. Mills calls on one student, who makes an inference about Mr. Brown. Mr. Mills asks the rest of the group if they agree with the inference. Two students say that they do not agree. Mr. Mills asks everyone to skim the paragraph to find clues that would support their position. Mr. Mills again looks around the room. A child approaches and asks him a question. He answers the question and then goes back to the group. After a while, Mr. Mills and the group discuss whether they have accomplished what they were supposed to. They then discuss, for a moment, what they will be doing next time. They all go back to their seats. Before Mr. Mills calls another group, he checks off in his plan book the objectives that have been accomplished by the group. He also makes some remarks in his record book about the individual children in the group. Mr. Mills puts down his book and walks around the room to check on what the students are doing. He smiles at a number of the students, says "good" to some others, helps Judy with her problem, and listens in on the group that has been working together on a special project. Mr. Mills asks the group members how they are doing and how much more time they will need before they will be ready to report their progress to him and the class. Mr. Mills then goes back to the reading table and calls the next group.

## RECORD KEEPING

Since many of the students in Mr. Mills's class are working in different areas at different levels, he cannot rely on his memory to recall exactly what each student is doing and at what level each student is working. Mr. Mills, therefore, has established a record-keeping system. He has a folder for each student in the class. In the folder he keeps a record of each student's progress in each area. For example, Mr. Mills, after meeting with Judy, went back to his file drawer to pull Judy's folder. He wanted to record that Judy is attempting to accomplish answering questions.

Judy's folder contains a number of items: a checklist of activities, samples of Judy's work in various curriculum areas, a record of standardized achievement test scores, and criterion-referenced test information, as well as other diagnostic test information. In the folder there is also a sheet listing the particular objectives that Judy has attempted to accomplish. Next to each objective are the starting and completion dates.

### Students as Record Keepers

The students also keep records on what they are doing. As a matter of fact, Mr. Mills initiated the program by telling the children that they were all members of a company and as such they had certain responsibilities. He explained how companies are formed and organized. He also discussed with them that companies make agreements with suppliers and others by signing contracts. He then told them that they would operate somewhat like a company and that they would be drawing up and signing contracts for work that they will then be responsible for doing. He discussed with the class the importance of keeping up-to-date and accurate records on what they as members of the company were doing. Together they also decided that they would have periodic group meetings to discuss their progress and to determine whether any changes had to be made in their operation.

Thus the Fifth Grade Dynamo Company was born, and it flourished all year long.

# INDIVIDUALIZED INSTRUCTION

**Individualized instruction**
Students work at their own pace on material based on their needs, interests, and abilities.

The many different types of *individualized programs* range from informal ones, developed by teachers or teachers and students together, to commercially produced ones. A brief description of some of the characteristics of both informal and commercially produced individualized programs follows.

## TEACHER-MADE (INFORMAL) PROGRAMS

Informal programs can vary from teacher to teacher. However, most of the programs usually use instructional objectives, which are taken from curriculum guides, study guides, and instructors' manuals. To accomplish the objectives, the teachers usually select activities and materials from a number of sources, the teacher and student confer periodically, and the teacher keeps a check on the student's progress by maintaining adequate records.

## COMMERCIALLY PRODUCED OR PUBLISHED PROGRAMS

There are a variety of different commercial programs, and they have a number of things in common. Most of them use instructional objectives for each curriculum area. Usually each area is divided into small, discrete learning steps based on graduated levels of difficulty. A variety of activities and materials generally combined in a multimedia approach are used, and usually a system of record keeping, progress tests, and checklists is built into the commercial programs.

## SOME COMMON CHARACTERISTICS OF COMMERCIALLY PRODUCED AND TEACHER-MADE INDIVIDUALIZED PROGRAMS

In almost all individualized programs, students work at their own pace. Learning outcomes in individualized programs are based on the needs, interests, and ability levels of the students. Activities are interesting and challenging, and they usually employ a multimedia approach. The activities are based on desired outcomes, students work independently, and there is some system of record keeping.

## FOR WHOM DOES INDIVIDUALIZED INSTRUCTION WORK?

Students who have short attention spans, who have trouble following directions, and who have reading problems will find independent work challenging. Teachers will have to help these students set limited, short-range objectives that can be reached in a short period of time. For those students with reading problems, the teacher will have to rely very heavily on audiotapes to convey directions. Students with learning difficulties (see Chapter 5) will also need additional help; special programs will have to be devised for them. Students who have no discernible achievement problems but who have never worked in an individualized program before will also have difficulty unless they are properly oriented to the program. (Note: Do not confuse the need to work independently in an individualized program with the need to provide for the individual differences of each student in the class.)

## SOME COMMON SENSE ABOUT INDIVIDUAL PROGRAMS

Preparing individual outcomes and a specially tailored program for each student in each specific subject can be a monumental task. Therefore, what is generally done is to use outcomes and programs already prepared, either teacher-made or commercially made, and then match these to the needs of individual students. For such an individualized program to work effectively, teachers must have a variety of individualized programs available for their students, and they must know the individual needs of each student.

# LEARNING CENTERS

**Learning center**
An integral part of the instructional program and vital to a good individualized program. An area is usually set aside in the classroom for instruction in a specific curriculum area.

Good teachers have long recognized the importance of providing "interest centers" for their students based on their needs and ability levels. However, in the past, most of the science, art, library, listening, and fun centers were just "interest attractions"; they usually were marginally related to the ongoing teaching-learning program rather than an integral part of it.

As used today, learning centers are an important and integral part of the instructional program. They are generally more formalized and are recognized as vital to a good individualized program. A place is usually set aside in the classroom for instruction in a specific curriculum area. Aims for learning centers may be developed beforehand by teachers or cooperatively by teachers and students in the classroom. Some of the requirements for a good learning center include:

1. Is in an easily accessible area.
2. Is attractive.
3. Provides for students on different maturational levels.
4. Has clearly stated objectives so that students know what they are supposed to accomplish (outcomes).
5. Provides for group and team activities as well as individual activities.
6. Allows for student input.
7. Asks probing questions.
8. Has some humorous materials.
9. Provides activities that call for divergent thinking.
10. Uses a multimedia approach.
11. Has carefully worked out learning sequences to accomplish objectives.
12. Has provisions for evaluation and record keeping.

## DESIGNING A LEARNING CENTER

When designing a learning center, consider including the following steps.

1. Motivating technique: necessary to attract attention. This could be realia (real objects), pictures, humorous sayings, and so on.

   *Example:* Familiar commercials with pictures are listed on learning center bulletin board (propaganda learning center).

2. Objectives: necessary so that students know what they are supposed to accomplish (outcomes).

   *Example:* Propaganda learning center.
   a. Define *propaganda.*
   b. Define *bias.*
   c. Explain what is meant by a propaganda technique.
   d. List five propaganda techniques.
   e. Describe each of the five propaganda techniques you chose and give an example of each.
   f. Read ten commercials and identify the propaganda technique used in each.
   g. Read a political speech and state what propaganda techniques the politician uses.
   h. Team up with another student, and, using a propaganda technique, role play a commercial to be presented to the class.
   i. Using one or more propaganda techniques, write a commercial about an imaginary product.
   j. Record the commercial you have created on the imaginary product.

3. Directions to accomplish objectives: necessary so that students know what to do to accomplish objectives. Give step-by-step instructions so the students can accomplish the objectives. For example, tell students to:
   a. Read objectives so that you know what you are supposed to accomplish.
   b. Go to file drawer one, which contains the learning activities to accomplish objective one.
   c. Complete each learning activity and record your progress on each before you go on to the next objective. (This requirement depends on the learning center. In some learning centers, the students must accomplish the objectives in sequence; in others, it is not necessary to do so. For the propaganda learning center, some of the learning objectives must be accomplished in order. Obviously, before students can write a commercial using propaganda and bias, they must be able to define *propaganda* and *bias,* explain propaganda techniques, recognize various techniques, and give examples.)

*Summary of Steps in Preparing a Learning Center*

1. Select a topic.
2. State objectives.

3. Identify experiences.
4. Collect materials.
5. Prepare activities.
6. Make schedules (which children use the center and when).
7. Prepare record forms (each student using the center must have one).

## TEACHER AS SELF-EVALUATOR

Although the major goal of this text is to provide you with an understanding of the many ways to assess and evaluate children's reading growth, teacher self-assessment plays an important part in the diagnosis cycle. Taking time to reflect on lessons and how students perform can help you to measure the effectiveness of the lesson. Did all students attain the lesson objective? If not, why not? Asking questions such as these can illustrate that sometimes the problem resides with the teacher rather than with the student.

Consider the following example. A teacher decides to administer a word test to ascertain whether students have a store of words that they can identify instantaneously (i.e., sight words). When analyzing the results of the test, the teacher discovers that according to this measure, several students appear to have a limited store of words. The teacher decides to form a special needs group, placing all students who need to acquire more words into the group. He then designs a lesson to teach the words, but attempts to teach the words in isolation. Several of the students have difficulty with the lesson as indicated by their inability to identify the words at the conclusion of the lesson. A first glance might suggest that the source of this lack of performance resides with the students; they simply have a memory problem and they need to work harder. However, a second glance shows much more. The fact that *all* students had difficulty is the first sign that the source of the problem was more likely the teacher. Without a doubt, the lesson should have set students up for success and by the conclusion of it, all of the students should have been able to show that they accomplished the objective. Why didn't they? Another look helps us to see that the words the teacher is trying to teach NEED context because they are very abstract: *is, the, of, was*. Once students see how these words function to hold sentences together, they are more likely to be able to identify them out of context. Yet another look at the lesson shows us that students may likely be confused about how these words relate to reading books because they had no time to read books that could have been selected with these words in mind. As a result of this analysis, the teacher realizes that the lesson needs to be redesigned. Because the teacher can self-assess, then, he sees that his instruction plays a role in helping students to succeed. He revises the lesson and gives it another try.

There are many ways to self-evaluate. Videotaping and reviewing lessons using specific criteria is one. Evaluating student performance is another. In addition, a checklist can be designed to help evaluate the entire diagnostic reading and improvement program in general. Another checklist can be constructed to reflect on reading lessons. Another method is to write on the lesson itself either during the lesson or after the lesson. The underlying assumption is that there is a written plan for the lesson, which indicates that the teacher has thought

**FIGURE 2.2 All Children Survey**

**"All children can learn in a system that respects their abilities."**
**—C. Roller**

| Statement | Yes | No |
|---|---|---|
| 1. All children are provided the same amount of time to read authentic books and /or stories throughout the day. | | |
| 2. All children spend the same amount of time on skill/drill work. | | |
| 3. All children are permitted to read without interruptions. | | |
| 4. All children are expected to solve problems when reading. | | |
| 5. All children are provided time to solve problems when reading. | | |
| 6. All children are provided the same amount of time to read books during guided reading instruction. | | |
| 7. All children are provided many "just right" books. | | |
| 8. All children are engaged with high-level questions. | | |
| 9. All children preread silently before reading orally before a group. | | |
| 10. All children appear to enjoy reading. | | |
| 11. All children have the opportunity to self-select books. | | |
| 12. All children are provided time to read independently. | | |

From *Flexible Grouping in Reading* by Michael Opitz. Published by Scholastic Teaching Resources/Scholastic, Inc. Copyright © 1998 by Michael Opitz. Reprinted by permission.

through the lesson and the many associated considerations such as the students who will be receiving the lesson, the materials, and teaching strategies.

Figure 2.2 is an example of a checklist that can be used to look at the diagnostic reading and improvement program in general. Figure 2.3 shows a sample checklist that can be used to reflect on reading lessons. After reading each question, teachers using this checklist can rate themselves on a scale, with 1 being poor and 5 being excellent, and then write out any thoughts and/or ideas related to each question.

## ANOTHER LOOK AT LISA AND RACHAEL—EXTREMES DON'T WORK!

By now you should be able to answer the questions posed at the end of the introductory scenarios. Before reading our comments, take time to look at your answers. Then read our comments. Do you agree with them? Why or why not?

**FIGURE 2.3    Sample Checklist for Teacher Self-Assessment of a Reading Lesson**

Reading Lesson: _____    Date: _____

| Question | Rating Scale | Thoughts / Ideas |
|---|---|---|
| 1. Did I capitalize on students' interests? | 1  2  3  4  5 | |
| 2. Was I enthusiastic about the lesson? | 1  2  3  4  5 | |
| 3. Was I clear in presenting the lesson objective? | 1  2  3  4  5 | |
| 4. Did all activities relate to the objective and did they progress from concrete to abstract? | 1  2  3  4  5 | |
| 5. Did I provide for individual differences? | 1  2  3  4  5 | |
| 6. Did my assessment of students align with the objective for the lesson? | 1  2  3  4  5 | |
| 7. Did I allow enough time for students to complete the activities under my guidance? | 1  2  3  4  5 | |
| 8. Did I use positive reinforcement? | 1  2  3  4  5 | |
| 9. Did I give specific feedback so that students knew how well they were progressing? | 1  2  3  4  5 | |
| 10. Did I alter the lesson as needed? | 1  2  3  4  5 | |

Ms. Clay's belief that explicit instruction and drill are synonymous is a faulty one. As noted earlier in this chapter, explicit instruction calls on the teacher to show students how to do a given task. It is much more than simply giving children practice with a given skill or strategy. She needs to develop an understanding that most beginning readers need direct help in learning to read. She also needs to become aware of the many teaching strategies she can use to help students gain important word recognition, comprehension, and study skills. (See Chapters 10, 11, 12, and 13 for a review of these.)

To best help Lisa, Ms. Clay needs to use some explicit teaching. She should choose a few books at Lisa's independent reading level and then let

Lisa choose one for independent reading. In addition, Ms. Clay should make sure the trade books she is using for reading instruction are based on graduated levels of difficulty; that is, each subsequent trade book should be more challenging than the preceding one. She also needs to encourage Lisa to do a lot of easy reading when reading independently.

Ms. Graves is also a teacher who needs to further understand effective teaching. She is insensitive to Rachael's needs and appears to be incapable of helping her. If she had had a diagnostic-reading and improvement program in her classroom, she would have been able to "ascertain" Rachael's reading problems. Rather than send Rachael or her whole group to the "resource center," she would have worked with them in the regular classroom; she would understand the importance of making sure that all children feel that they are a part of one community. These children needed additional help and encouragement. She would have sought help from the special reading teacher and worked closely with Rachael's mother, as well as with the other parents. She would have created a nonthreatening atmosphere in which children feel they can learn and succeed—an atmosphere where the children are the center of the curriculum and tests are not used as ends in themselves.

## TEACHING: A POINT OF VIEW

Teachers are very important people, and all children deserve good teachers. However, not everyone is meant to be a teacher. Yet, for a long time, many persons have been allowed, even encouraged, to enter the classroom, even though they lack the requisite skills and knowledge to help students.

A specious philosophy has existed among numerous people that anyone can teach. So if you cannot do anything else, you go into teaching. This ridiculous view about teachers was promoted by George Bernard Shaw in 1903 in his work *Man and Superman* in which he says: "He who can, does. He who cannot, teaches."

With all due respect to George Bernard Shaw, he was wrong. Not everyone can teach. Teaching is exceedingly hard work that requires caring, sensitive, highly intelligent and perceptive individuals who want to make a difference and who are willing to give of themselves.

Unfortunately, many people agree with Shaw concerning teaching. All through the ages, teachers have been denigrated not only by students and parents but also by well-known persons. For example, Confucius, who lived from about 551 to 479 B.C., spoke disparagingly about teachers and blamed them for the failure of education in his day. He is reported to have said, "The teachers today just go about repeating in rigamarole fashion, annoy the students with constant questions, and repeat the same things over and over again. They do not try to find out what the students' natural inclinations are, so students are forced to pretend to like their studies; nor do they try to bring out the best in their talents." Peter Abelard, a famous French philosopher, who lived from about 1079 to 1142, made this much quoted remark: "When he [Abelard's teacher] lit the fire, he filled the house with smoke, not with light."

Respect for teachers is essential for them to be able to function effectively in the classroom. How can it be that teachers, who are such important people in the educational lives of our children, should be held in such low esteem?

The American Council on Education (ACE) states in its executive summary (1999), "Over the next decade, the nation will need to put into America's classrooms more than 2.5 million new teachers. They will be responsible for teaching the very children who, before the middle of the 21st century, will be the country's movers and shakers. . . . In sum, they will be preparing the citizens of America in the next century." The report goes on to state that "the single most important element in a child's success at learning—probably the element more important than all others put together—is the quality of the teacher." The ACE recommends that graduates of schools of education be "supported, monitored, and mentored." The goal is to make sure that schools have the best teachers possible. As the ACE claims, having poor teachers in the classroom is equivalent to educational malpractice.

The ACE's report about the importance of having good teachers in the classroom probably is not news to anyone. Almost everyone who has gone to school or who has children in school knows this. People want action—implementation. And they want it now. They want to know what can be done about getting the most effective teachers possible into classrooms.

The ACE report cites teacher education as the problem. And since colleges and universities are responsible for teachers' education, the ACE puts the blame squarely on the shoulders of these schools. The report states "it is colleges and universities that must take responsibility for the way teachers are taught, and ultimately the way children are taught."

The ACE also provides various recommendations for what students need to become effective teachers. For example, the ACE report states that all good teachers, regardless of the grade level at which they teach, must have "a firm command of their subject matter, receive sound professional preparation, and demonstrate a high overall achievement."

The recommendation that will probably be met with the greatest joy by the education profession is the one in which the ACE urges that "college and university presidents put the education of teachers at the center of the institutional agenda and accept the challenge and responsibility to lead constructive change." If schools of education do indeed become the center of institutions of higher learning, then it makes sense that "education faculty and courses are coordinated with arts and sciences faculty and courses."

Let us hope that, with the emphasis on higher standards for teachers and teacher programs, fewer teachers will opt to leave the profession and more qualified persons will choose to enter the field. All children deserve good teachers.

# SUMMARY

Chapter 2 focuses on the teacher as the key person in a diagnostic-reading and improvement program. The teacher is viewed as that person who should help children when they come to school regardless of their backgrounds. The role of a teacher in a diagnostic-reading and improvement program is viewed as multifaceted, so a teacher must be well prepared and well informed. A discussion of a number of studies shows that teachers influence students' behavior and learning and that the teacher is more important than the method of instruction or the materials used. Chapter 2 also discusses what characteristics a good teacher of reading should have: verbal ability, a good educational background including such knowledge as the content of reading, an ability to read, and positive expectations and attitudes. Teachers are cautioned about invoking the self-fulfilling prophecy. The stress on higher standards for students has brought a demand for higher standards for teachers. This demand has stimulated various professional teacher organizations to develop standards for prospective teachers. And concomitant with the push for teacher higher standards has come a greater emphasis on accountability and its by-product, pay-for-performance. Teacher planning, instructional time, and teacher instruction are also discussed, as well as the importance of teachers being good organizers and classroom managers.

## CHAPTER 2 KEY CONCEPTS

- The role of teachers in diagnostic-reading and improvement programs is complex.
- Good teachers in a diagnostic-reading and improvement program must be well prepared and well informed.
- The teacher is the key to improving students' reading instruction.
- Unanimity does not exist as to what factors affect teaching performance.
- Reading helps reading.
- Learning to read and reading to learn are not mutually exclusive.
- Most students need explicit instruction to help them acquire reading skills.
- A think-aloud is an effective explicit instructional technique whereby teachers think aloud; that is, they verbalize their thoughts about how they solve problems.
- Interactive instruction whereby teachers intervene at optimal times with optimal strategies to achieve desired learning is essential for good teaching.
- Higher student standards require higher teacher standards.
- Numerous professional organizations have developed standards for prospective teachers.
- Individualized instruction, learning centers, and record keeping are important considerations in a diagnostic-reading and improvement program.

## SUGGESTIONS FOR THOUGHT QUESTIONS AND ACTIVITIES

1. Make a list of all the characteristics you think a good teacher of reading should have in a diagnostic-reading and improvement program.
2. Think of one of the best teachers you have ever had. Write down the characteristics of the teacher you remember best.
3. Think of the worst teacher you have ever had. Write down the characteristics that you feel made him or her your worst teacher.
4. Observe a teacher during a reading lesson. Check off all the characteristics he or she exhibits that you listed in question 2.
5. Make a videotape recording of yourself teaching a reading lesson. Check off all the characteristics you exhibited that were in your list in question 2.
6. You have been assigned to a special committee that is concerned with teacher accountability. What are your views concerning teacher accountability? What suggestions would you have for the committee?
7. Videotape a lesson in which you use a think-aloud activity.

## INTERNET ACTIVITIES

Choose a search engine and search for websites related to the terms *teacher standards* or *teacher accountability*. Select one website from the search that helps you gain a good understanding of the term. Write three ideas you learn and why they are significant for you. (Be sure to identify both the search engine you used and the website you selected.)

## SELECTED BIBLIOGRAPHY

Ashton-Warner, Sylvia. *Teacher.* New York: Simon & Schuster, 1963.

Baumann, James F., and Ann M. Duffy-Hester. "Making Sense of Classroom Worlds: Methodology in Teacher Research," in *Handbook of Reading Reseacher,* Vol. III, Kamil, Michael L. et al., eds. Mahwah, N.J: Lawrence Erlbaum, 2000.

Durkin, Dolores. *Teaching Them To Read.* Boston: Allyn and Bacon, 1993.

Donahue, Patricia L. et al., eds. *NAEP 1998 Reading Report Card for the Nation and the States.* Washington, DC: U.S. Department of Education, March 1999. http://nces.ed.gov/naep.

*Do Teachers Make a Difference?* Department of Health, Education and Welfare Report No. OE 58042. Washington, DC: U.S. Government Printing Office, 1970.

Jackson, Phillip W. *Life in Classrooms.* New York: Teachers College Press, 1990.

Opitz, Michael. *Flexible Grouping in Reading: Practical Ways to Help All Students Become Better Readers.* New York: Scholastic, 1998.

Opitz, Michael, and Michael Ford. *Reaching Readers: Flexible and Innovative Strategies for Guided Reading.* Portsmouth, NH; Heinemann, 2001.

Report of the National Reading Panel: Teaching Children to Read. "Findings and Determinations of the National Reading Panel by Topic Areas," Bethesda, MD: National Institute of Child Health & Human Development, April 2000. www.nichd. nih.gov/publications/nrp/findings.htm.

Rosenthal, Robert, and Lenore Jacobson. *Pygmalion in the Classroom.* New York: Holt, Rinehart and Winston, 1968.

Woolfolk, Anita E. "Teachers, Teaching, and Educational Psychology," in *Educational Psychology,* 8th ed. Boston: Allyn and Bacon, 2001, pp. 2–21.

# 3

# Developing a Knowledge Base about Tests, Measurement, and Evaluation

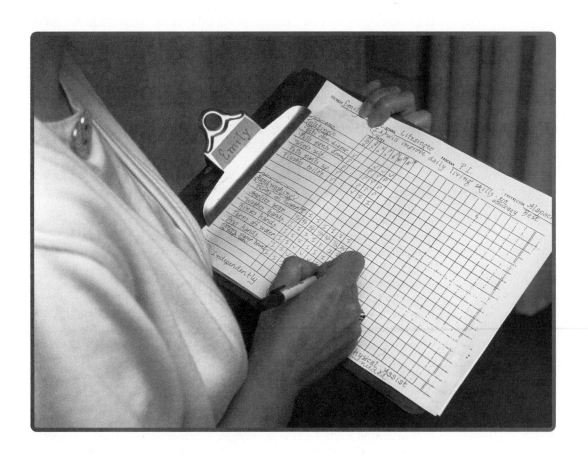

# ACCOUNTABILITY IN THE TWENTY-FIRST CENTURY

With the emphasis on more stringent standards, the upgrading of subject matter, and high-stakes tests, we would not be making an understatement if we were to call the present period in education the era of accountability. It also seems very likely that this will remain the state of affairs for some time.

The charge given to accountability and high-stakes testing is to make sure that students attain certain core curriculum standards. Using high-stakes tests and having the results reported in the media makes the educational situation stressful for administrators, teachers, parents, and students.

Imagine the amount of anxiety that children have when they are told that the standardized test that they are taking will dictate whether they will be promoted to the next grade and determine the overall ranking of their school. And imagine how frustrating this test could be if students have not been exposed to many of the skills that are measured by the test.

Student performance on tests can provide helpful information if used appropriately. They are a necessary part of a diagnostic-reading and improvement program. Often, however, tests are misused not so much by teachers but by those who oversee them. Expert test developers have stated many times that it is not necessarily the characteristics of the tests that are the problem, but that it is the "misuses of the tests in the hands of inadequately qualified users in education." Test users must know the tests' purposes and be qualified to administer and interpret test results. Likewise, those who mandate specific tests must also understand the purposes for the tests they are mandating.

Across the country, tests are being used to drive the curriculum and consequently raise standards. The assumption appears to be that teachers will teach to the test. Therefore, if the tests contain stringent content, teachers will present their students with more difficult material, thus raising standards for all students.

In the push for higher standards, we seem to be doing things backward. Rather than having the tests drive the curriculum to a higher level, it is the curriculum that should be driving the tests. It makes sense that the governing body of every state wants to raise standards for all their students. However, using and misusing tests as the means to raise standards will not work unless there are major changes in instructional practices.

Realistically, state proficiency tests required of all students can only assess the acquisition of minimum rather than maximum standards. For example, one state department staff developed a stringent standardized proficiency test to be used for promotion purposes. However, when 40,000 fourth graders failed the state proficiency test, there was such an uproar over the test and the retaining of so many children that state officials said that they would use their new more difficult proficiency test only as a goal to be reached. In the meantime, state officials said that they would use a lower score to determine students' proficiency. The latter news has also brought criticism from many.

It is good that school administrators across the country are trying to ensure that all students receive an excellent education. But using state proficiency tests to accomplish this can be a problem. As important as test information is, it is only one criterion that teachers and others should use in the evaluative process to determine a student's knowledge. It should not and cannot be determined by looking at performance on one test.

Students' test scores also are being used for teacher accountability. Doing so is causing some dedicated and ethical individuals to resort to unethical behaviors. For example, in some school districts across the country where students' test scores have been related to teacher and school scores—which in turn are used to determine the amount of funding for a given school—some teachers and even principals have been caught changing students' incorrect answers on standardized achievement tests.

Test mania has also produced some other suspect practices that cast doubt on the reported scores. For example, numerous school district officials exclude all "special needs" students from taking standardized tests so that their students will score higher on standardized proficiency assessments, making the entire student body appear to be well above average. In some school districts, students who have done very poorly on past standardized achievement tests may be erroneously classified as learning disabled and then be disqualified from taking any subsequent standardized tests.

One last point regarding test mania focuses on parents. As a result of observing how the results of high-stakes test results are used, some parents are opting out of the testing. That is, they will not permit their children to be tested. They are tired of watching their children experience test anxiety, and they are angry that their children's scores are used to determine the amount of funding provided to local schools. Do they want their children to progress in school and to see evidence that shows this progress? You bet they do. But they, like many teachers, realize that many different factors must be considered and that performance on one test simply cannot tell the whole story.

A good testing program does tell a larger part of the story. Such a program includes several measurements such as standardized tests, criterion-referenced tests, teacher-made tests, observation of students over time in different contexts, and student self-assessment. Reading is a complex behavior, and, as Ruth Strang noted years ago, "diagnosis is as complex as the reading process itself."[1] Without a doubt, a good testing program takes time, but it is time well spent when the goal is helping all children maximize their full reading potential. This is what a diagnostic and improvement reading program is all about—and a sound testing program that focuses on using a variety of measures is the vehicle that drives it.

 ## Scenario: Ms. Smith Learns about Assessment

Ms. Smith is a new teacher. She's excited about her job and wants to be the best teacher possible; however, she's a little overwhelmed and confused. At the orientation meeting at the beginning of the school term, the principal talked about the school district's testing program, and then the reading specialist talked about the various kinds of reading tests that the teachers were expected to give. They talked

[1]Ruth Strang, *Diagnostic Teaching of Reading, 2nd ed.* (New York: McGraw Hill, 1969.), p. 27.

about norm-referenced tests, informal tests, and criterion-referenced tests. They also talked about group and individual tests. In addition, they mentioned performance-based tests and said that their school district personnel were committed to authentic assessment and that teachers would be hearing much more about this during the school year.

Toward the end of the meeting, two teachers raised their hands and said that they felt all standardized reading tests should be outlawed. The silence that followed was deafening. Then, as if on cue, everyone started talking at once.

Ms. Smith listened carefully to the heated debate between those who felt there should be no standardized testing and those who disagreed. Most teachers spoke harshly against the use of standardized reading achievement tests as high-stakes tests. Others claimed that these tests did not measure the kinds of behaviors they are supposed to.

Taking his cue from the teachers' discussion, the principal said that he was aware of the testing controversy. He then told them that there would be more rather than less testing because of the increased emphasis on accountability. He went on to say that their school district administration was always open to new ideas and change if changes were warranted. He also said that regardless of an individual's teaching position, all teachers must know what is taking place and be knowledgeable about the various types of tests being used in the school. He reminded the teachers that in a diagnostic-reading and improvement program, they must know how to use various types of teacher-made and commercial tests to best assess their students' reading.

Ms. Smith recognized her lack of knowledge regarding assessment, but rather than lamenting this fact, she decided to gain as much background information as possible in this area. She agreed with the principal and reading specialist that a good teacher must be able to administer and interpret various types of tests, not only for evaluation but also for diagnostic purposes. She made a decision to learn how to do both in the coming year with the help of both the reading specialist and principal.

# CHAPTER OBJECTIVES

After reading the chapter, you should be able to:

- Discuss the differences among evaluation, tests, measurement, and assessment.
- Discuss the values of measurement.
- Describe some of the criteria of good tests.
- Define such terms as *standards, standard scores,* and *high-stakes tests.*
- Describe what is meant by *standardized tests.*
- Describe norm-referenced tests.
- Describe criterion-referenced tests.
- Describe teacher-made tests.
- Discuss some differences between group and individual tests.
- Discuss the variety of reading tests that is available.

# TESTING TERMINOLOGY: EVALUATION, TESTS, MEASUREMENT, AND ASSESSMENT

> Examinations are formidable, even to the best prepared, for the greatest fool may ask more than the wisest man can answer.
>
> *C. C. Colton*

The word *evaluation* seems to bring shudders to most people. Although some individuals may look on evaluation as necessary, it is often considered an intrusion on privacy and is avoided for as long as possible.

**Test**
An assigned set of tasks to be performed.

To some, the terms *evaluation, test,* and *measurement* are synonymous. But they are not. Test, which is the narrowest of the terms, is confined to "an assigned set of tasks to be performed."[2] It is the "instrument used to obtain the skill measure."[3] *Measurement*, which is broader, "refers to quantifying or assigning a number to express the degree to which a characteristic is present."[4]

**Measurement**
Part of the evaluative process; broader than test; involves quantitative descriptions.

*Evaluation*, which is the broadest of the terms and goes beyond test and measurement, "refers to all the means used in schools to formally measure student performance."[5] Evaluation has to do with the passing of personal judgment on the accuracy, truthfulness, and validity of something. Evaluation can be done with either qualitative (i.e., descriptive wording) or quantitative (i.e., numerical) data. Our own teaching experiences have helped us to understand that the more data that is considered, the better the chance that the evaluation will be accurate. Good evaluators need to avoid emotional bias in making their value judgments. Since humans do the evaluating, this objectivity is often hard to achieve. For this reason, ongoing evaluation is essential. Informally, it needs to occur daily. Formally, it needs to occur at the beginning, middle, and end of the school year. Evaluation also needs to be based on an adequate collection of data and be made in terms of desired objectives and standards.

**Evaluation**
A process of appraisal involving specific values and the use of a variety of instruments in order to form a value judgment; goes beyond test and measurement.

The positive values of measurement outweigh the negative connotations often associated with it. Measurement is useful for diagnostic, review, and predictive purposes. It can be used as a motivating technique for students, as well as a basis for grades. Through ongoing measurement, teachers are also able to reevaluate their own teaching methods.

In order for measurement to be an effective part of the evaluative process, teachers must acquire varied assessment techniques and be able to administer and interpret them. Such measurements include standardized tests and teacher-made tests. Direct observation of student behavior is also necessary in order to collect data for valid evaluations.

---

[2]Lou M. Carey, *Measuring and Evaluating School Learning,* 3rd ed. (Boston: Allyn and Bacon, 2001), p. 76.

[3]Ibid.

[4]Ibid.

[5]Robert E. Slavin, *Educational Psychology: Theory and Practice,* 6th ed. (Boston: Allyn and Bacon, 2000), p. 465.

---

**Assessment**
A broad term that encompasses a variety of tests and measurements.

*Assessment* is a broad term that encompasses a variety of tests and measurements.[6] One working definition of assessment is "educational assessment is a formal attempt to determine students' status with respect to educational variables of interest."[7] In this definition, *variables* refer to something that varies, and "variables of interest" are the many different areas that teachers would like to learn more about. These areas of interest can range from students' attitudes toward a subject (e.g., reading) to students' performance on a reading achievement test. The term *formal* refers to more than a teacher's or other individual's impression of the performance. It is the use of systematic techniques that helps teachers gain information about their students' reading behaviors. It also often refers to commercially produced (published) tests. *Informal* refers to the reverse—one teacher's impression and use of assessment that may or may not be commercially prepared.

*Standards* and *high-stakes tests* are two terms that we have been using. *Standards* describe or define what students should have learned in order to achieve certain levels of competency in various subjects.

*High-stakes tests* are created by expert committees or test developers. They are generally administered one time, are multiple-choice, and are given to whole groups. They are considered objective and are designed to measure how well students are doing compared to others in their same grade within their same state and/or across states. Many times, these assessments are produced by professionals within any given state to determine whether the content standards have been achieved. Tests such as these are considered high-stakes because the results are sometimes used to reward or penalize teachers, individually and/or collectively. The results are also sometimes used to retain students or, for students who are deemed not proficient, to develop a remediation plan. Sometimes the plan entails attending summer school.

## CRITERIA FOR GOOD TESTS

Anne Anastasi, a noted psychologist and psychometrician, once stated, "For practical purposes, the most effective tests are likely to be those developed for clearly defined purposes and for use within specified contexts."[7] We wholeheartedly agree. And, like Anastasi, we believe that test users must select a test that will help them to ascertain a specific aspect of the reading process. One way to ensure appropriate selection is to ask and answer three questions: What do I want to know? Why do I want to know? Which test will help me best discover this information? Test users must also be able to administer and interpret the results. After all, it is the test administrator and not the test itself that makes the diagnosis! Regardless of the tests they choose, there are four criteria that all good tests should meet:

---

[6]W. James Popham, *Classroom Assessment: What Teachers Need to Know,* 2nd ed. (Boston: Allyn and Bacon, 1999), p. 2.

[7]Anne Anastasi, "Mental Measurements: Some Emerging Trends," *The Ninth Mental Measurements Yearbook* (Lincoln, NB: Buros Institute of Mental Measurements, University of Nebraska, 1985), p. xxix.

**Objectivity**
The same score must result regardless of who marks the test.

**Validity**
The degree to which certain inferences can be made from test scores or other measurements; the degree to which a test instrument measures what it claims to measure (nontechnical definition).

**Reliability**
The extent to which a test instrument consistently produces similar results.

**Suitability**
The appropriateness of a test for a specific population of students.

1. *Objectivity:* The same score must result regardless of who marks the test. Since essay questions do not lend themselves to a high degree of objectivity, the developers of such tests should give specific directions for scoring and should make the essay questions as explicit as possible.

2. *Validity:* Educators often talk about the validity of a test and generally define validity as the degree to which a test measures what it purports to measure. However, technically we do not measure the test's validity but rather the validity of the inferences made from the test.

According to the *Standards for Educational and Psychological Testing,* "Validity is the most important consideration in test evaluation. The concept refers to the appropriateness, meaningfulness, and usefulness of the specific inferences made from test scores. Test validation is the process of accumulating evidence to support such inferences."[8]

The three categories of validity evidence are content-related, criterion-related, and construct-related evidence of validity. Reading teachers are concerned primarily with the content of a test. In order to determine the content aspect of validity, the test should be compared with instructional content.

3. *Reliability:* Reliability is concerned with consistency. A test's reliability depends on how consistent it is in measuring whatever it is measuring. Any test that is valid must be reliable, but reliability is not a sufficient condition for validity. It is possible to get a consistent measure of something, but consistency does not always mean that the measure is correct or truthful.

It is to be hoped that when a student takes a test, the score will remain consistent, even if conditions under which the test are taken change slightly, even if different scorers are used, or even if similar but not identical test items are used. There are a number of reasons why a student's test scores could vary. For example, the test may not be testing what it is supposed to measure, the student may not have a good rapport with the tester, the student may not be motivated, the student may be ill, or the student may be tired. Another reason may be that the student has good or bad luck in guessing or may be reluctant to guess at all. It is also possible that the student has acquired new knowledge between testings.

4. *Suitability:* In selecting or preparing a test, the teacher must determine not only whether it will yield the type of data desired but also whether the test is suitable for the age and type of students and for the locality in which they reside.

In Figure 3.1 we provide a diagram of the types of tests we introduce in this chapter. Use it as a guide by referring to it throughout your reading of this chapter.

---

[8]*Standards for Educational and Psychological Testing,* prepared by the Committee to Develop Standards for Educational and Psychological Testing of the American Educational Research Association, the American Psychological Association, and the National Council on Measurement in Education (Washington, DC: American Psychological Association, 1985), p. 9.

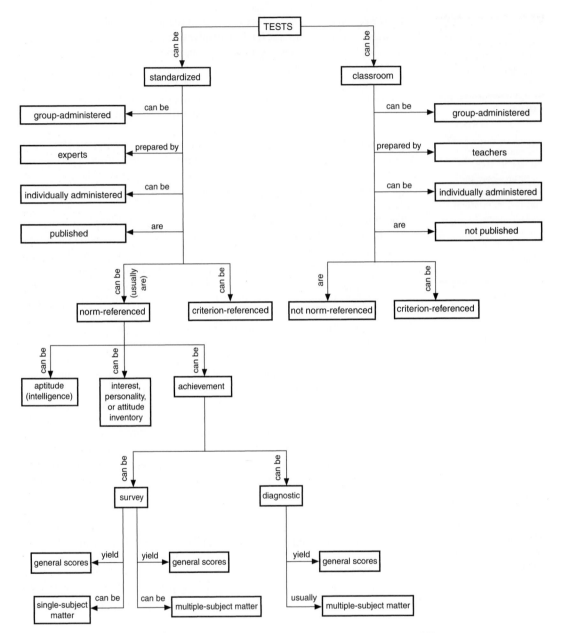

**FIGURE 3.1**   A Free Diagram of the Various Types of Tests.
This diagram is a simplification, showing the relationship of the tests.

# STANDARDIZED TESTS

**Standardized tests**
Tests that have been published by experts in the field and have precise instructions for administration and scoring.

Standardized tests are commercially published tests most often constructed by experts in the field. They are developed in a very precise fashion, and have specific instructions for both administration and scoring. These instructions are supposed to be followed by all who administer the tests.

Confusion may exist concerning the definition of standardized tests because of changes in the way the term is currently being used in comparison with how it was used in the past and is still being used by many, especially in the reading field. *Good's Dictionary of Education,* the *Penguin Dictionary of Psychology,* the *Dictionary of Behavioral Sciences,* and the *International Dictionary of Education* all include *norm-referenced* as one of the criteria for a standardized test; however, today the definition does not necessarily include that criterion. Today, a standardized test may or may not be a norm-referenced test. A test is considered to be a standardized test if it is a published test with specific instructions for administration and scoring.[9] Michael Zieky, executive director, Educational Testing Service, defines a standardized test "as any published test in which rules exist such that the test is administered and scored to all examinees under the same conditions (with the possible exceptions of individuals with certain disabilities)."[10] In this text, we consider any test that has been published and has precise instructions for administration and scoring to be standardized.

## NORM-REFERENCED TESTS

**Norms**
Average scores for a given group of students, which allow comparisons to be made for different students or groups of students.

Although not all standardized tests have norms, most usually do. Norms are average scores for a given group of students, which allow comparisons to be made among different students or groups of individuals. The norms are derived from a random sampling of a cross section of a large population of individuals.

**Norm-referenced tests**
Standardized tests with norms so that comparisons can be made to a sample population.

Norm-referenced tests are used to help teachers learn where their own students stand in relation to others in the class, school system, city, state, or nation. Although a child may be doing average work in a particular class, the child may be above average when compared to other norms. Similarly, it is possible for a child to be doing above average work in a third-grade class but to be below average for all third-graders in the nation.

Also keep in mind that norm-referenced tests have limitations. Identified by Otto (1973) and paraphrased by us, the limitations are listed in the following section.

[9]Teacher's Guide, *California Diagnostic Reading Tests Levels A and B* (Monterey, CA: CTB/McGraw-Hill, 1989), p. 7.

[10]Michael Zieky, Executive Director, Officers Division, Educational Testing Service (ETS), Princeton, NJ, 2001.

## LIMITATIONS OF NORM-REFERENCED MEASURES

1. The measure may be inappropriate for use with some groups or individuals. It might be too hard for some and not challenging enough for others.
2. Allocated time limits may be unrealistic, which means that the scores of students who work slowly but with precision are most likely not accurate.
3. Items may sample breadth of reading rather than depth, which results in a superficial view of the student's reading behaviors.
4. Administering the test in a group setting might invalidate the results in that children who fail to understand the directions may be unable to answer any of the items they actually know.
5. The test format limits the kinds of items used. Multiple-choice formats are often used and these do not measure some reading behaviors appropriately.
6. Norm-referenced tests generally provide an overestimate of the students' appropriate instructional reading level.[11]

Teachers must be cautious in their use of these tests. In addition to the limitations mentioned above, teachers must determine whether a test is appropriate for their students. If the class has not yet covered the information in the standardized test, the test obviously would not be valid.

Another important factor concerns the students themselves. Students who are overly anxious or upset by a test, who are tired or hungry, or who lack motivation, will not perform as well as others not burdened in this manner. Such factors will adversely affect test performance.

 ## Scenario: James Brown—A Teacher Who Knows the Purpose of Tests

James Brown, a sixth-grade teacher, loves to teach. He chose this profession over others because he likes to work with children, and he feels he can make a difference. He remembers his own sixth-grade teacher who helped him through rough times and feels good about being able to reciprocate. James is never defensive about having chosen teaching as his career and resents others who are. When he is asked, "And what do you do?" he proudly replies, "I am a teacher."

However, there is one period of time during the school year that bothers James; it probably disturbs many others also. In schools across the nation, you can always tell when it's time for the dreaded standardized achievement tests. A hush seems to envelop the school; it's as if everyone is walking on tiptoe. Doors are closed, and anxious students and teachers are captives within. Everyone waits with apprehension for the results. Will they be an embarrassment to the school district, or will the students score substantially above the national norms? It's a tense time for all involved.

It doesn't have to be. James is frustrated because he feels that tests should be used for more than comparative purposes; they should have instructional

---

[11]Wayne Otto, "Evaluating Instruments for Assessing Needs and Growth in Reading," in W. MacGinite, ed., *Assessment Problems in Reading* (Newark, DE: International Reading Association, 1973), pp. 14–20.

implications. If they were administered in the fall, close to the beginning of the school year, they could be used more for instructional purposes. (Most of the standardized test batteries are normed for the beginning and end of the school year, so this procedure would not be a problem; actually, some are normed for administration even more than twice a year.)

The standardized reading tests could be used as a screening device to identify students who have potential problems. At the end of the year, such tests seem almost counterproductive.

James has been pushing for a change in testing times because he feels that the fall results would be more indicative of the children's present developmental levels and more useful for grouping and teaching. What do you think?

## STANDARDIZED ACHIEVEMENT SURVEY TEST BATTERIES (MULTIPLE-SUBJECT MATTER TESTS) AND STANDARDIZED READING SURVEY TESTS (SINGLE-SUBJECT MATTER TESTS)

Some people differentiate between reading survey tests such as the *Gates-MacGinitie Reading Tests* and the reading subtest of an achievement survey test battery such as the *California Achievement Tests* now known as *TerraNova CAT*. As we show in Figure 3.2, the reading survey test and the reading subtest of an achievement survey test battery are quite similar and serve the same

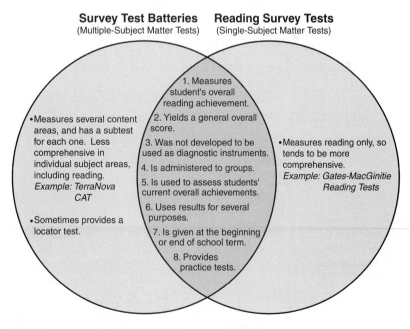

**FIGURE 3.2** Comparison of Standardized Tests: Survey Batteries and Reading Surveys

purposes. Both measure a student's overall reading achievement. The major difference between the two types of tests is that a standardized reading survey test, such as the *Gates-MacGinitie Reading Tests,* only measures reading and therefore can be somewhat more comprehensive. The reading achievement subtest of an achievement test, such as the *TerraNova CAT,* is part of a survey battery of achievement tests; that is, the reading achievement test is one of many tests that measure different curricula. For example, the *TerraNova CAT* is designed to measure achievement in the basic curricular areas of reading, spelling, language, mathematics, study skills, science, and social studies. Both reading survey tests and reading achievement tests from survey test batteries yield a general or overall score and were not developed to be used as diagnostic instruments; however, they play an essential role in any diagnostic program. These are group tests that are usually very easy to administer in a relatively short period of time, and they are useful for screening or identification, which is the first step in a diagnostic pattern. Standardized norm-referenced reading achievement or survey tests are used to assess the students' present achievement status. The results of these kinds of tests are used for a number of purposes. One use is usually to make comparisons among other schools in the district, state, or nation. Another use is to tell us which children are doing well, and it helps us to identify children who may need help. If the test is used to identify these children, the instrument is being used in a positive manner.

You are probably most familiar with standardized achievement tests such as the *Metropolitan Achievement Tests*, the *Stanford Achievement Tests*, and the *TerraNova CAT* because most schools employ these kind of tests. They are generally given either at the beginning or the end of the school year by the classroom teacher. It's usually a good idea to give the test at the same time that the test was given to the students who determined the norms for the test. For example, if you wish to give an achievement test in the fall to help you determine how to group for instruction, you should choose a test in which the norms were gathered in the fall. Standardized achievement tests that are given in the fall are usually used for instructional purposes and screening, whereas standardized achievement tests that are given at the end of the year are generally used for comparison purposes.

Before giving any tests, study the accompanying test manual. The manual usually contains information about the test, such as how norms were gathered, instructions on how to administer and score the test, and what the test measures.

## LOCATOR TESTS

**Locator test**
Used to determine at what level a student should begin testing.

Some of the achievement batteries supply a *locator test*, which is used to determine at which level a student should begin testing, when testing out-of-level, because the U.S. Office of Education for Title I testing recommends functional level testing. Locator tests are used to provide students with tests to which they can relate well. Students in sixth grade reading at a fourth-grade level will not relate well to a sixth-grade reading test. The locator test is used to determine the approximate functional level of these students, and it is recommended that those students who test out-of-level on the locator test be given the achievement test at the approximate functional level at which they tested on the locator test. Therefore, the sixth-grade students who score at the fourth-grade level on the locator test would be tested with a fourth-grade level test.

Locator tests may be individually or group administered. The developers of *Terra Nova* recommend that their Locator Tests be used with special education students.

## PRACTICE TESTS

> **Practice test**
> Ensures that the actual test measures what students know rather than their test-taking ability; it familiarizes students with the test.

Most standardized achievement tests provide a *practice test*. These are designed to ensure that students know how to mark an answer *before* they take the actual test. The practice tests are supposed to ensure that the actual test measures what students know and not their previous familiarity with test-taking procedures. Practice tests are supposed to help "level the test-taking playing field."

## CLASSIFICATION OF STANDARDIZED TESTS

Standardized tests can be classified in a number of ways, one of which is according to the *way* they are administered. For example, some tests are group administered and some are individually administered, so these tests would be considered group or individual tests. Some persons classify tests according to whether they have oral instructions or written instructions. Usually, however, tests are classified according to *what* is measured. Thus, standardized tests are generally divided into the following categories: aptitude (intelligence) tests; achievement tests, which include diagnostic, single subject-matter, and survey batteries; and interest, personality, and attitude inventories.

### Special Note

> **Survey batteries**
> A group of tests in different content areas.

*Survey batteries* consist of a group of tests in different content areas. These subtests have been standardized on the same population so that the results of the various components can be directly compared. Standardized achievement tests that yield a general score are usually called survey tests. They can be part of a survey battery, or they can be single-subject tests. ◼

## SELECTING A STANDARDIZED TEST

Like it or not, teachers are often left out of the loop when it comes to selecting a standardized test. Generally, these tests are selected by an elected body of administrators. Teachers are told rather than asked to administer the test.

There are times, however, when teachers are in a position to select a test with the three questions posed on page 44 at the forefront of their minds: What do I want to know? Why do I want to know? Which test will best help me to discover this information? Unfortunately, some teachers might feel a bit lost when it comes to answering the last question. Fortunately, there are references that provide much assistance.

The *Mental Measurements Yearbooks* are excellent resources for teachers intent on choosing standardized reading tests that best suit their purposes. The books help acquaint teachers with most tests in the field except the very recent ones. Frank critical evaluations of tests are written by authorities in the field.

Test users are also warned about the dangers of standardized tests and are told of their values. An essential contribution that the books make is to "impress test users with the desirability of suspecting all standardized tests—even though prepared by well-known authorities—unaccompanied by detailed data on their construction, validity, uses, and limitations.[12]

*The Ninth Mental Measurements Yearbook,* published in 1985 under a new editor, continues in the tradition of the others by giving individuals valuable information about tests. Other sources of test information that teachers would find helpful are *Tests in Print; Tests: A Comprehensive Reference for Assessments in Psychology, Education, and Business;* and *Test Critiques,* as well as journals such as *The Reading Teacher* and the *Journal of Adolescent & Adult Literacy* (formerly the *Journal of Reading*) that periodically review various tests.

## INTERPRETATION OF SOME ACHIEVEMENT TEST SCORE TERMS

Many teachers are often confused about the terms that test makers use in discussing standardized achievement tests. Following is a guide to some of the terms teachers will probably encounter at one time or another.[13]

### *Raw Score*

**Raw score**
The number of items that a student answers correctly on a test.

The *raw score* is the number of items that a student answers correctly on a test. (The number of test items, as well as the difficulty of the items, may vary from one section of a test to another; therefore, the weighting of the test items should vary.) The raw score is usually not reported because it does not convey meaningful information. Test makers use the raw scores to derive their scale scores.

### *Standard Scores*

**Standard Scores**
Used to compare test takers' assessment scores. Presented in terms of standard deviations.

Standard scores are used to compare test takers' assessment scores. They are presented in terms of standard deviations (measures that define a range of scores around the mean, that is, "how widely the scores vary from the mean."[14]). If the standard deviation is large, it means that the scores are more scattered in relation to the mean. Conversely, if the standard deviation is small, the scores are more clustered around the mean.[15]

### *Standard Deviation*

**Standard Deviation**
Deals with how widely scores vary from the mean.

Measurement experts like to work with *standard deviations* because they feel that they produce more accurate appraisals of a student's scores in relation to

---

[12]Oscar Buros, ed., *Reading: Tests and Reviews* (Highland Park, NJ: Gryphon Press, 1968), pp. xvi.

[13]Adapted from *Test Interpretation Guidelines, Comprehensive Tests of Basic Skills,* 4th ed. (Monterey, CA: CTB/McGraw-Hill, 1988). (*Comprehensive Tests of Basic Skills* now comes under the umbrella of *TerraNova.*)

[14]Anita E. Woolfolk, *Educational Psychology,* 10th ed. (Boston: Allyn and Bacon, 2007), p. 527.

[15]Ibid.

others, and they are exceptionally helpful in understanding test results. For example, on one test the standard deviation is 10, and the *mean* or average of all the scores is 100. On another test the standard deviation is 5, and the mean or average of all the scores is 100. Two students take the two different tests. Student A scores 110 on one test and Student B scores 105 on the other test. Even though both students have different scores, they both have scored one standard deviation above the mean. The 110 score is equivalent to the 105 score.

**Mean**
Arithmetical average.

The same logic would apply to tests with different means. It is beyond the scope of this book to discuss the various kinds of standard scores that exist. For more information on standard and scale scores, many excellent measurement textbooks are available.

### Special Note

Most standardized tests report students' results in terms of standard deviations (SD), so teachers should be familiar with the standard deviation of the test. Unless teachers know the standard deviation and means of the particular test, they will not know whether a score of 120 on one test is higher than a score of 110 on another. ■

**Normal curve**
Scores are symmetrically distributed around the mean.

### *Normal Curve*

Many teachers are familiar with the bell-shaped symmetrical curve in which the majority of scores falls near the mean (average) of the distribution, and the minority of scores appears above or below the mean. In Figure 3.3 we show a sample of a bell-shaped symmetrical curve.

### Special Note

The normal distribution in Figure 3.3 is presented in rounded off numbers for ease of interpretation. ■

**Grade equivalents**
Description of year and month of school for which a given student's level of performance is typical.

### *Grade Equivalent*

A *grade equivalent* is a description of the year and month of school for which a given student's level of performance is typical. A grade equivalent of 6.2 on the *TerraNova California Achievement Test (CAT)* is interpreted as the score that is typical of a group of students in the third month of the sixth grade.

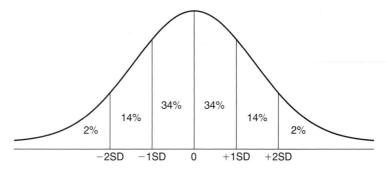

**FIGURE 3.3**   A Bell-Shaped Symmetrical Curve

(September is designated as month .0, October as .1, November as .2, December as .3, and so on up to June, which is .9.) These scores are useful in the elementary grades because fairly regular gains are expected in basic skill development at each grade level.

### Special Note

Extreme grade equivalents, those that are more than two years above or below grade level, must be interpreted with great caution because they are based on "extrapolations" rather than actual student performance. A very low or a very high score just means that the student scored far below or much above the national average. A grade equivalent score of 6.6 by a third-grader does not mean the third-grader is able to do sixth-grade work or should be in the sixth grade. It does mean that this student is scoring well above the average for third-grade students. ■

### Percentile

**Percentile**
A point on the distribution below which a certain percentage of the scores fall.

A *percentile* is a point on the distribution below which a certain percent of the scores fall. A test score equivalent to the 98th percentile means that the student did better, or the student's score is higher, than 98 percent of the test takers on that same test. Another way of looking at it is to say that only 2 percent of the students did better.

### Special Notes

1. The 50th percentile score is the middle score, which is also referred to as the median; it is the point above and below which half of the students scored.
2. Percentile and percent correct are not the same. A percentile score of 75 on an achievement test by a fifth-grader means that the fifth-grader obtained a score higher than 75 out of every 100 students in a representative sample of fifth-graders in the nation who took the test. ■

### Stanine

**Stanine**
A score in educational testing on a nine-point scale, ranging from a low of 1 to a high of 9, of normalized standard scores.

The *stanine* is a unit of a score scale that divides the scores of the norm population (representative sample) into nine groups, ranging from a low of 1 to a high of 9. There is a constant relationship between stanines and percentiles; that is, the range of percentiles included within each stanine is always the same (see Figure 3.4).[16]

Stanines 4, 5, and 6 are generally used to describe the "average" range of achievement. Stanines 1, 2, and 3 are used to describe below average, and 7, 8, and 9 usually describe above average.

As you can see, a major problem with stanine scores is that they are not very precise. For example, a stanine score of 5 could have a percentile score as low as 41 or as high as 59.

[16]Adapted from *Test Interpretation Guidelines Comprehensive Test of Basic Skills*, 4th ed. (Monterey, CA: CTB/McGraw-Hill, 1988.)

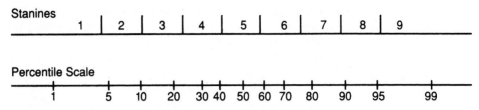

**FIGURE 3.4**    Stanines and Percentile Scale Conversion Table

# CRITERION-REFERENCED TESTS

Criterion-referenced tests are based on an extensive inventory of instructional objectives in a specific curriculum. The objectives are desired educational outcomes.

*Criterion-referenced tests* are designed to help teachers diagnose specific behaviors of individual students. They are used to gain more information about the students' various skill levels, and the elicited information is used to reinforce, supplement, or remediate the skill-development area being tested. The test results help the instructor plan specific learning sequences to help the students acquire the objective they missed.

Criterion-referenced tests are considered standardized if they are published tests that have been prepared by experts in the field and have precise instructions for administration and scoring. They can be administered individually or to a group, and they can be teacher-made or standardized. Criterion-referenced tests are concerned primarily with mastery of predetermined *objectives*, which are based on content material. On criterion-referenced tests, an individual is supposed to compete only with himself or herself. There can be very little difference in appearance between a norm-referenced test and a criterion-referenced test; however, differences do exist in the objectives of the tests.

For a criterion-referenced test to be valid, a *content domain* must be specified, and the test items must be representative of the content domain. Test makers identify various content-area domains and write measurable objectives within each domain; then they develop detailed item specifications that are supposed to ensure detailed coverage of the skills stated in the objectives. Usually, there are a number of items written for each objective to ensure reliable measurement.

There does not seem to be agreement on how specifically the content domain should be defined. A reasonable expectation is that the test designer specify with considerable detail the subject matter topics and pupil behaviors the test is designed to sample. Criterion-referenced tests are not norm-based; however, as odd as it may sound, "criterion-referenced tests and norm-referenced tests are no longer seen as a strict dichotomy."[17] Some tests are more useful for norm-referenced use than for criterion-referenced use, depending on the purpose

---

**Criterion-referenced tests**
Based on an extensive inventory of objectives in a specific curriculum area; they are used to help assess an individual student's performance with respect to his or her mastery of specified objectives in a given curriculum area.

**Objective**
Desired educational outcome.

**Content domain**
Term that refers to subject matter covered.

---

[17]Michael Zieky, Executive Director, Officers Division, Educational Testing Service (ETS), 2001.

for the test. Some tests have been prepared for use as both criterion-referenced and norm-referenced; that is, test users can compare a student's test results to a national norm or to a set of predetermined specific standards. When a criterion-referenced test has equated norms, it means that "the scores on one test have been statistically matched to the scores on a normed test."[18]

Some test makers are including a "cutoff or passing score" with criterion-referenced tests, perhaps because the term *criterion* implies this. "Whether there should be an implied standard of proficiency or cut-off score(s) is debatable. . . ." At any rate, everyone agrees that with a criterion-referenced interpretation of the scores, the focus is on what students can do and the comparison should be to a content domain. It has been suggested that criterion-referenced tests should be called *domain-referenced tests,* a term that is more accurate for the test. (Criterion-referenced tests are also referred to as *objective-referenced tests.*)

Not all criterion-referenced tests are published. Teachers can construct their own. Here is an example from a teacher-made criterion-referenced test. The test item is correlated to the objective for the specific skill. The important factor is whether we can infer that the test item does indeed measure what it is supposed to—in this case, the ability of the child to draw inferences. In other words, is the test item a valid representation of its content domain? Let's take a look.

> Content area: Reading comprehension (interpretation)
> Specific skill: Drawing inferences
> Objective: The student will draw inferences about the personality of the main character based on the content of reading material.

The child is asked to read a short story carefully. After finishing the reading, the child is asked to answer questions based on the story. An example of a question based on the given objective follows:

> What can you infer about the personality of Dennis?

The child is then asked to choose the best answer from the given statements. (Note that in criterion-referenced testing *every* test item is related to a corresponding objective.)

As with norm-referenced measures, criterion-referenced measures have limitations. These are listed in the following section.

## LIMITATIONS OF CRITERION-REFERENCED MEASURES

1. Some qualities such as appreciation or attitudes about reading are difficult to assess using objectives.
2. Stated objectives are sometimes considered mastered if the student can perform them one time. Retention and transfer of what the student has learned may not be considered as important.

[18]Ibid.

3. Determining specific instructional objectives to be taught and tested can be difficult.
4. Establishing the mastery standard can be difficult. Performance standards may need to fluctuate depending on the objective being assessed.

# TEACHER-MADE TESTS

**Teacher-made tests**
Tests prepared by the classroom teacher for a particular class and given by the classroom teacher under conditions of his or her own choosing.

*Teacher-made tests* are sometimes called *classroom tests* or *informal tests*. These are prepared by the classroom teacher for a particular class and given under conditions of the teacher's choosing. Usually, teacher-made tests are the primary basis for evaluating students' school progress. Teachers can get quick feedback on learning behaviors by constructing appropriate classroom tests. The tests with which you are probably the most familiar are those used to determine students' grades; these tests are generally classified into essay and objective tests and are mostly group-administered tests.

**Classroom tests**
Teacher-made tests; also called informal tests.

In the field of reading, classroom tests are generally used to help diagnose a student's reading problem or to learn more about a student's weaknesses and strengths. Many of the teacher-made tests used for diagnosis are individually administered. For example, the informal reading inventory, which can be commercially produced or teacher-made, is a valuable aid in helping a teacher to diagnose reading problems.

**Informal tests**
Teacher-made tests.

# GROUP AND INDIVIDUAL TESTS

**Group tests**
Administered to a group of people at the same time.

It seems evident that *group tests* are administered to a group of people at the same time, whereas *individual tests* are administered to one person at a time. It also should be obvious that it would be more time-consuming to give individual rather than group tests. What may not be as obvious are the reasons for administering an individual test. Individual tests in reading are usually given when the teacher feels that some inconsistency exists between the student's classroom behavior or reading potential and test scores on a group-administered standardized reading achievement test. Individual tests are also administered when teachers wish to learn more about a student's specific behavior, such as oral reading, and the only way to do so would be through an individual test. An individual test can also be given if the teacher suspects that a child has difficulty following directions. On an individual test, the tester can determine whether the student understands a question, or is tired, hungry, or not feeling well.

**Individual tests**
Administered to one person at a time.

There are two guiding principles to follow when administering an individual test. The first is privacy. When students are reading orally, for example, most often they will be encountering the text for the first time. They don't need the added pressure of performing for an audience. One suggestion for a way to adhere to this principle is to take students aside one at a time to a designated area of the room and have them read to you. This can be accomplished when students are completing independent activities, or when they are reading a given selection silently. As the rest of the students read to themselves, individuals can be taken aside to read a given segment of text privately for the teacher.

Another principle is to observe the children during the reading experience. Make notations of your observations on a copy of what the child is reading. Your notes can then be used for further analysis.

Group tests are more limited in their format than individual tests because they must be administered by the reading of simple directions and answered by some kind of mark on an answer sheet. Group tests are usually given by the classroom teacher, and there are as many different types of group tests as there are individual tests. For example, there are group and individual aptitude tests, group and individual achievement tests, group and individual personality inventories, group and individual attitude inventories, and so on. There are some individual tests, such as individual IQ tests, that must be administered by a specially trained clinician or psychologist; and there are some, such as individual diagnostic tests, that can be administered by the regular classroom teacher. Regardless of whether a teacher or a specially trained person administers an individual test, it is not given as often as a group test because it is more costly and more time-consuming. However, individual tests are generally more reliable than group tests; they are more useful with students who have reading difficulties because they usually require less reading than group tests; more can be learned about a student in a one-to-one testing situation than in a class; and they are usually more valid for those students who have difficulty taking tests in a group.

# DIAGNOSTIC READING TESTS

**Diagnostic reading tests**
Provide subscores discrete enough so that specific information about a student's reading behavior can be obtained and used for instruction.

A diagnostic reading test is designed to break down a complex skill into its component parts to help teachers gain information about a student's specific reading strengths and weaknesses. It is generally given after an analysis of a group standardized reading survey test. The analysis helps the teacher to determine which children seem to be reading below their ability. Unclear as to *why* a child appears to be struggling, the teacher decides to explore further through the use of a diagnostic reading test.

Diagnostic reading tests can be either standardized or teacher-made tests. Most reading diagnostic tests are individually administered and given by a special reading teacher rather than by the regular classroom teacher. However, many of these diagnostic tests can be given by the regular classroom teacher, and in a diagnostic-reading and improvement program, many should be. Informal reading inventories are examples of diagnostic tools that are indispensable to the classroom teacher (see Chapter 8).

Although agreement does not exist on how to define a diagnostic reading test and what tests to include under the umbrella of diagnostic tests, we believe that a test on a test battery that provides subscores discrete enough so that specific information about a student's reading behavior can be attained and used for instructional purposes should be included in this category. A reading diagnostic test or test battery may consist of oral reading, silent reading, comprehension, phonic analysis, structural analysis, sight vocabulary, phonemic awareness, visual and auditory discrimination, reading and study skills, or rate of reading.

The diagnostic test that is chosen should fulfill the criteria for all tests; that is, it should be valid, reliable, easy to administer in a reasonable period of time, and easy to score. Most importantly, the test should help the teacher diagnose a student's specific problem. Teachers should check the diagnostic test carefully before administering it to make sure that it does indeed identify the specific skill that the teacher wishes to have assessed. Once again, three questions can help to guide this selection: What do I want to know? Why do I want to know? Which test will help me discover this information?

## SUMMARY

Presenting general information about what teachers should know concerning tests, measurement, and evaluation was our focus in Chapter 3. Good evaluators use tests and other measurement techniques to avoid bias in their judgments. A discussion concerned the criteria that all good tests should have: objectivity, validity, reliability, and suitability. Because there is confusion concerning the term *standardized*, it was defined according to the way that it is currently being used in the field. A standardized test is a published test with specific instructions for administration and scoring. Even though a standardized test is usually norm-referenced, it doesn't necessarily have to be a norm-referenced test. The terms *norm-referenced* and *criterion-referenced* were also defined, and the ways that standardized tests may be classified were explored. Because there are so many standardized tests on the market, teachers need help in determining which ones to use. The *Mental Mea-surements Yearbooks* were cited as excellent resources. Teacher-made tests, which are also called classroom or informal tests, were discussed too. In this chapter, teachers were introduced to reading tests and the fact that many different kinds exist. We emphasized that teachers in a diagnostic-reading and improvement program must be knowledgeable of the various kinds of tests so that a wise selection can be made for the proper purpose. To that end, we proposed that teachers ask and answer three important questions: What do I want to know? Why do I want to know it? Which test will help me discover this information?

In addition, we presented information on terms such as standards, high-stakes tests, and state proficiency tests. Finally, we stated that with the emphasis on more stringent standards, the upgrading of subject matter, and high-stakes tests, this period in education could be referred to as the era of accountability.

## CHAPTER 3 KEY CONCEPTS

- The terms *evaluation, test,* and *measurement* do not have the same meaning.
- Assessment is a broad term that covers various types of tests and measurements.
- All good tests must be valid, reliable, suitable, and have objectivity in relation to scoring.
- A standardized test is published by experts and has precise instructions for administration and scoring.

- Norm-referenced tests are standardized tests with norms so that comparisons can be made to a sample population.
- There are a number of ways in which standardized tests may be classified.
- Teachers must be involved in the selection of standardized tests.
- Knowledge of terms such as *raw score, scale score, grade equivalents, percentile,* and *stanine* is important in interpreting students' standardized test results.

- Teacher-made tests are prepared by classroom teachers for a particular class and given under conditions of their own choosing.
- Criterion-referenced tests are based on instructional objectives and are primarily concerned with an individual student's achievement in relation to himself or herself.

- There are a number of different standardized and teacher-made reading tests that measure a variety of reading skills and abilities.
- A diagnostic reading test is designed to break down a complex skill into its component parts to help teachers gain information about a student's strengths and weaknesses.

## SUGGESTIONS FOR THOUGHT QUESTIONS AND ACTIVITIES

1. Your school is interested in using criterion-referenced tests. You have been appointed to explain the differences between criterion-referenced and norm-referenced tests. What will you say?
2. Many teachers in your school are confused about the many different types of tests that exist. You can help them by drawing a tree diagram showing the relationships among tests.
3. Discuss some of the important criteria that good tests must have.
4. Explain some of the differences between teacher-made tests and published or commercially produced tests.

## INTERNET ACTIVITIES

Choose a search engine and search for websites related to something in the chapter that you would like to research. Select one website from the search that helps you gain a good understanding of it. Write a five-sentence paragraph about the term. (Be sure to identify both the search engine you used and the website you selected.)

## SELECTED BIBLIOGRAPHY

McMillan, James H. *Classroom Assessment: Principles and Practice for Effective Instruction.*, 3rd ed. Boston: Allyn and Bacon, 2004.

Popham, James W. *Classroom Assessment: What Teachers Need to Know,* 2nd ed. Boston: Allyn and Bacon, 1999.

Salvia, John, James F. Ysseldyke, and Sara Bolt, *Assessment,* 10th ed. Boston: Houghton Mifflin, 2007.

*Standards for Educational and Psychological Testing.* Prepared by the Committee to Develop Standards for Educational and Psychological Testing of the American Educational Research Association, the American Psychological Association, and the National Council on Measurement in Education. Washington, DC: American Psychological Association, 1985, 1986.

Woolfolk, Anita E. "Standardized Testing," in *Educational Psychology,* 10th ed. Boston: Allyn and Bacon, 2007.

# 4

# Factors That Affect Reading Performance

## Scenario: Angelique and Sara: A Study in Contrast

Angelique and Sara are both in Mrs. Brown's first-grade class. Angelique is a bubbly, inquisitive, alert child who is excited about learning and looks upon every day as an adventure. She loves books and reads well. She asks good questions and likes to learn about things in depth. She talks about nocturnal birds and how she saw an owl one evening. She converses knowledgeably about wild animals and tame animals, and she is always eager to show anyone the stories she has written about different animals.

Angelique is quite verbal. She has an extensive vocabulary and uses words correctly. She can talk about animals, books she has read, books that have been read to her, other parts of the country, and many other things. She can give you opposites and words similar in meaning. She can tell if you are being "funny." In addition, she can relate present information or experiences to the past ones and make predictions about various things.

Angelique is an only child, and her college-educated parents adore her. They feel she is the joy of their lives. When she was born, her mother left her outside of the home job to stay home with Angelique until she started school. Her parents read to her, talk to her, and interact with her. They take trips together and have flown to various other parts of the country. She has eaten different kinds of food in various restaurants, gone to zoos, farms, museums, and so on.

Sara, on the other hand, comes from a home in which she is the oldest of six children. At seven years of age, she has had a great amount of responsibility thrust upon her. Her mother works outside of the home, and often Sara has to stay home to help take care of the other children. Her father does not live at home with them. Sara is a "put upon" child. She is very mature for her age and is gaining many experiences. However, she has never traveled, never been to a zoo, never been to a farm, never had anyone read to her. In short, Sara and Angelique's home environments and life experiences are quite different.

Here are composites of these two children. Which child would you predict will succeed in school? Why?

*Angelique L.*

Only child.

Upper socioeconomic status.

College-educated parents.

Standard English is dominant language.

Parents read to Angelique.

Many books are available for Angelique.

Newspapers, books, and magazines are available for parents.

Parents read for pleasure.

Angelique sees parents writing.

Television is supervised.

Parents discuss books and television shows with Angelique.

Family does many things together.

Angelique has pets.

Angelique helps take care of pets.

Family travels together to "fun" places.

Child has her own computer.

Time on computer and computer sites are supervised.

*Sara M.*

Oldest of six children.
Low socioeconomic status.
Mother has a seventh-grade education.
There is no father present.
Nonstandard English is spoken.
No newspapers, magazines, or books are visible.
Television is unsupervised.
No one reads to Sara.
Mother does not read for pleasure.
Sara is responsible for younger brothers and sisters.

You probably answered "Angelique," and if you did, you would probably be correct. You are also probably saying that the deck has been stacked in Angelique's favor. It has been; however, many children have backgrounds similar to those of Sara and Angelique. Most Angeliques do well in school because they have the background and experiences that seem to correlate well with school success. The Saras, who lack such backgrounds and experiences, are considered at-risk children. Unless these children are identified early and helped, they will remain at high risk of failing in school; some may eventually drop out of school altogether. Certainly there are many children who come from low socioeconomic home environments who do well both in school and in life. The portrait of Sara M. is not meant to imply that all children who live in disadvantaged areas will not do well in school. We provide it to raise the awareness of the possibility, to put teachers in a position so they can strive to narrow the gap between the "haves" and "have nots."

As Angelique and Sara's profiles help to illustrate, there are many factors associated with learning to read. In this chapter, we present several of these factors and explain how they affect reading performance. Although there may be some factors over which educators have little control (e.g., low-income home, little or no reading material in the home, lack of being read to), there are several over which teachers do have control (e.g., time spent reading at school, developing requisite background necessary for understanding a given concept, developing an ear for different ways to use language via a read-aloud and other forms of classroom communication). Understanding these factors puts teachers in better positions to set their students up for success. In other words, we can do much to help children overcome any shortcomings, and we are obligated to do so.

# CHAPTER OBJECTIVES

After reading the chapter, you should be able to:

- Differentiate between educational and noneducational factors.
- Discuss some factors that influence children's reading performance.
- Discuss how a child's home environment influences his or her reading ability.
- Discuss the relationship of intelligence to reading.
- Discuss the relationship of gender differences to reading.

- Discuss the relationship of birth order to language development.
- Discuss the relationship of language and dialect to the development of standard English.
- Discuss the relationship of physical health to reading.
- Describe who are considered educationally *at-risk* children.

# DIFFERENTIATING BETWEEN EDUCATIONAL AND NONEDUCATIONAL FACTORS

**Educational factors**

Those factors that come under the domain or control of the educational system and influence learning.

There are many ways to classify the many factors that affect children's reading performance. For purposes of this text, we classify the different factors as either *educational* or *noneducational* factors. In Table 4.1, we provide an overview of these categories, a definition of each category, and list the specific factors we present in this chapter. When people talk about *educational factors*, they generally are referring to those factors that come under the domain or control of the educational system and influence learning. In this category, we would usually include the various methods and materials that the child has been exposed to, the teacher, the instructional time, and the school environment. Under *noneducational factors*, we generally would include physical health (general), vision, hearing, personality, and gender. Noneducational factors are supposedly those that do not come under the domain or control of the educational system and cannot be influenced by it. Although the two categories appear distinct at first glance, a second look shows that they are not; some fac-

**TABLE 4.1    Factors Affecting Reading Performance**

| Category | Definition | Factors |
|---|---|---|
| Educational | Those factors that come under the domain or control of the educational system and influence learning | • Teaching methods<br>• Instructional materials<br>• The teacher<br>• Instructional time<br>• School environment |
| Noneducational | Those factors that do not come under the domain or control of the educational system and cannot be influenced by it | • Home environment<br>• Dialect and language differences<br>• Intelligence<br>• Gender<br>• Physical<br>    Illness<br>    Nutrition<br>• Perceptual<br>    Visual perception<br>    Auditory perception<br>• Emotional<br>    Self-concept<br>    Learned helplessness<br>    Motivation<br>    Attitude |

**Noneducational factors**
Supposedly those factors that do not come under the domain or control of the educational system and cannot be influenced by it.

tors overlap. For instance, although gender cannot be influenced by the schools, sex roles can. A case could even be made for general physical health as being influenced by educational practices. For example, children who are doing poorly in school may wish to avoid school to such an extent that they become ill every morning. The children's emotional health influences their physical health so that they actually get a stomachache, headache, or throw up. Their emotional state may so affect them that they cannot eat or sleep. The physical symptoms are real, even though the cause may not be a virus or bacterium.

A child's personality can also be affected by what takes place in school. Consider the scenario shown on page 84 at the end of this chapter. Larry had an undetected eye problem, and he was subjected to methods and materials in school that were not helping him learn to read. Larry soon changed from a happy, outgoing, and helpful young boy to a sullen, irritable, unhappy child who didn't like himself or anyone else.

Rather than spending time debating which factors belong in one category or the other, the important idea here is the interrelatedness of the many factors that affect reading performance. A child who has difficulty learning to read usually has concomitantly many emotional and social problems, and these are compounded as the child goes through school if he or she is not helped as soon as a problem is detected or suspected. Clearly, when using a diagnostic-reading and improvement program, many factors need to be considered in order to help all children advance in their ability to read.

# EDUCATIONAL FACTORS

Educational factors in learning come under the domain or control of the educational system. Examples are teaching methods, instructional materials, instructional time, teachers, and school environment. If a child is experiencing difficulty in reading, it's generally a good idea to check his or her school record to see if there is any information that might shed light on the child's problem. From the records, the teacher may be able to learn about the methods and materials the child has been exposed to in previous years. It may be that these were not effective, and something different should be tried. For example, a third-grade student might appear to have difficulty with decoding. An examination of school records reveals that this child has been taught phonics since kindergarten. Rather than use phonics as a primary mode of instruction, another approach (e.g., whole-word, language experience) seems warranted. In this case then, the *teaching method* could be a major contributing factor to the problem.

## Teaching Methods

Several methods can be used to teach reading (see Part III). And, while teachers might prefer one method over another, the one that works best to help children realize their full reading potential needs to be used. For example, if teachers subscribe to a top-down view of reading as mentioned in Chapter 1, they will be likely to use this approach when teaching students. Some students will learn and others will not. The same is true if a bottom-up view of reading is preferred. Some will learn and others will not. The good news is that, like other educational factors, we have control over the reading approach we use. If something isn't working, we can examine the lessons to determine why, and then alter the lesson. As mentioned in Chapter 2, students deserve nothing less.

## INSTRUCTIONAL MATERIALS

A former third-grade student of mine (MO) helped me to understand the importance of instructional materials—in this case the use of hardback books instead of softback books. We were provided multiple copies of the same text, some hardback and others softback. In the distribution, he was given a softcover text. Seeing this, he broke into loud sobs, saying that he couldn't read the book. In my effort to calm him, I assured him that of course he could read the book, and I pointed out the similarities of the versions. It didn't work. He kept crying, telling me I didn't understand. He was correct; I didn't understand, so I asked him to explain. He pointed out that in the softcover book, there wasn't as much space around the sides of the page and the lines were all squished together. Taking another look at the books, I saw what he was explaining and once again had to admit that he was correct. The hardcover book appeared much easier to read because of the extra space devoted to the margins and the line spacing. The problem was resolved by letting him read from a hardcover version—which he did with ease. The point here is that instructional materials matter more than we might think. We need to pay attention to this. Not only should the materials be in alignment with the teaching approach but also they should entice children to read. When given the choice, very rarely do students opt to read a page of print on poor quality paper over a trade book.

When students resist reading, we need to take a look at what we are putting before them to better understand if this resistance is a child problem or an instructional materials problem. We then need to make any necessary changes to keep the children reading.

## THE TEACHER

In the words of Albert Harris and Edward Sipay, "Teacher effectiveness has a strong influence on how well children learn to read."[1] We could not agree more. This is one reason that we devoted an entire chapter to the teacher's role in a diagnostic-reading and improvement program. In Chapter 2 we explain that teaching is a complex behavior, and show what needs to be done to facilitate reading progress rather than thwart it. Listed below are some teaching practices that reading educators believe contribute to reading problems:

1. Failing to ensure that students are prepared to learn the skill or strategy
2. Using materials that are too difficult
3. Pacing instruction either too fast or too slow

[1]Harris, Albert J. and Edward R. Sipay. *How to Increase Reading Ability*. (New York: Longman). 9th ed. 1990, p.355.

4. Ignoring unsatisfactory reading behaviors until they become habits
5. Rarely expecting any given child to perform tasks required of others
6. Asking questions, and then answering them without giving students time to respond
7. Failing to acknowledge students when they do try
8. Expressing disapproval or sarcasm when a mistake is made
9. Allowing other children to put down another child's efforts
10. Expecting a child to perform a task that he or she cannot do in front of others
11. Expecting a child to do poorly because older brothers and sisters did[2]

## Instructional Time

Sometimes research is needed to prove what common sense would tell us. The case in point is instructional time. As the result of Rosenshine's findings related to academic engaged time (i.e., the time students spend on academically relevant activities at the right level of difficulty), we now have proof that the more time students spend on the task, the higher their academic achievement will be.[3] And, as other researchers have reported, students spend more time on task when they are engaged with the teacher. So, as pointed out in Chapter 2, teachers need to know how to manage the class, communicate with students, use materials that reflect students abilities, provide instruction at a "just right" pace—one in which all students are set up to succeed, and give specific feedback. And let us not forget teacher enthusiasm! It can go a long way toward keeping students focused.[4]

## School Environment

Context matters. If children feel safe, they are more likely to take the necessary risks on their way to becoming proficient readers. In Chapter 2, we provide some guidelines for effective teaching that help to establish this safety net.

Beyond safety, though, the actual physical environment of the classroom has a great influence on learning. In order to become readers, children need to be exposed to a lot of print and in many forms. A classroom that is full of print and in which children are immersed in children's literature sends a powerful message to students. It says that print really is important and that there are many reasons to read (and write).

---

[2]Harris, Albert J. and Edward R. Sipay. *How to Increase Reading Ability: A Guide to Developmental and Remedial Methods* (New York: Longman, 1990, p. 356).

[3]Barak V. Rosenshine. 1978. "Academic Engaged Time, Content Covered, and Direct Instruction." *Journal of Education, 60:* 38–66.

[4]Edward M. Bettencourt, et al. 1983. "Effect of Teacher Enthusiasm on Student On-task Behavior and Achievement." *American Educational Research Journal 20:* 435–450.

# NON-EDUCATIONAL FACTORS

**Home environment**
Socioeconomic class,
parents' education,
and the neighborhood
in which children live
are some factors that
shape children's home
environments.

## HOME ENVIRONMENT

Socioeconomic class, parents' education, and the neighborhood in which children live are some of the factors that shape children's home environments. The results of studies have led researchers to conclude that the higher the socioeconomic status, the better the verbal ability of the child[5] and the better children usually achieve in school.[6]

Children who have good adult language models and are spoken to and encouraged to speak will have an advantage in the development of language and intelligence. Similarly children who come from homes where there are many opportunities to read; where there are many different types of text such as magazines, encyclopedias, books, and newspapers; and where they discuss what they read with their parents will be better readers than children without these advantages.[7] Parents who behave in a warm, democratic manner and provide their children with stimulating educationally oriented activities, challenge their children to think, encourage independence, and reinforce their children are preparing them very well for school. The National Assessment of Educational Progress reports have consistently shown that "parental education and student achievement are positively associated."[8]

Children who come from homes where parents have only an elementary-school education, where there are few reading materials available, where no one reads, where many people live in a few rooms, and where unemployment among the adults in the home is common will usually be at a disadvantage in learning language and in reading. (See Chapter 14 for more on the importance of parental involvement.)

The adult composition of the child's home environment also impacts the child. Whether a child is reared by both parents, a single parent, a nanny, grandparents, or foster parents will affect the child's attitudes and behavior. A child who is reared by a female single parent may behave differently from one reared by a male single parent, for instance. The death of one parent or of another family member will usually cause emotional stress in the child. Divorce can also be a traumatic experience for children.

How many children are born into a family and the order in which these children are born affects the achievement levels of individuals, at least to some degree? Studies are still being done on these factors, but several researchers have hypothesized that firstborn children do better both in school and in life

---

[5]Walter D. Loban, *Language Development: Kindergarten through Grade Twelve.* Urbana, IL. National Council of Teachers of English, 1976 (Research Report 18).

[6]Statement of Emerson J. Elliot, Commissioner of Education Statistics, at the Release of *National Assessment of Educational Progress 1994 Reading Assessment: A First Look,* April 27, 1995, p. 2.

[7]Patricia L. Donahue et al., *NAEP 1998 Reading Report Card for the Nation and the States,* National Assessment of Educational Progress (Washington, DC: Office of Educational Research and Improvement, U.S. Dept. of Education, 1999), p. 101.

[8]Ibid., p. 72.

than other children in the family. A child without siblings has been shown to be more articulate for the most part than a child who is a product of a multiple birth (like twins or triplets) or a singleton (one child born at a time) who has other brothers and sisters.[9]

Researchers have reported that the only child, who is more often in the company of adults, has more chances of being spoken to by the grown-ups around him or her than is the case when there are many children in the family. Then, too, twins seem to have less need to communicate with others because they usually have a close relationship with one another.

Singletons with siblings also have "interpreters" near at hand. Often, older siblings can understand a brother or sister's messages so well that the younger child need not attempt to express himself or herself more effectively.

All these factors form part of the learning climate in the home and influence the degree and amount of learning the child will do in school. Angelique, our child in the scenario, is off to a good start. But what about Sara?

## DIALECT AND LANGUAGE DIFFERENCES

**Standard English**
English in respect to spelling, grammar, vocabulary, and pronunciation that is substantially uniform, though not devoid of regional differences. It is well established by usage in the formal and informal speech and writing of the educated and is widely recognized as acceptable wherever English is spoken and understood.

Dialect and language differences are closely related to home environment because the home environment will determine whether the child will speak standard English, a dialect of English, or some other language. In a diagnostic-reading and improvement program, teachers must recognize that most classes will have a multicultural mix of children because we are a pluralistic society. The challenge teachers face is one of helping their students retain their cultural heritage while at the same time becoming accustomed to their new culture. This is an awesome task, but with help and commitment it can be done.

According to *Webster's Third New International Dictionary,* the term *standard English* is defined as "the English that with respect to spelling, grammar, pronunciation, and vocabulary is substantially uniform, though not devoid of regional differences, that is well established by usage in the formal and informal speech and writing of the educated, and that is widely recognized as acceptable wherever English is spoken and understood."

**Dialect**
A variation of language sufficiently different to be considered separate, but not different enough to be classified as a separate language.

The term *dialect* is more difficult to define, however. To some people, a dialect of English is any variation of standard English; to others, it is merely a means of expressing oneself; and to still others, it is a variety of language related to social class, educational level, geography, gender, and ethnicity. From these definitions, we can see that standard English could then be considered a dialect and that the definition of dialect is obviously intertwined with that of language. If we were to define dialect in a broad sense, we would be concerned with the language of a geographic area; if we were to define it in a specific sense, we would be looking at the language of a neighborhood, a family, or even an individual (idiolect). Generally, however, when we refer to dialect, we are talking about a structured subsystem of a language, with definite phonological and syntactic structures, that is spoken by a group of people

---

[9]Mildred A. Dawson and Miriam Zollinger, *Guiding Language Learning* (New York: Harcourt, 1957), pp. 36–37. Didi Moore, "The Only-Child Phenomenon," *The New York Times Magazine,* January 18, 1981, pp. 26–27, 45–48.

united not only by their speech but also by factors such as geographic location and/or social status.[10]

For some people the term *dialect* seems to have negative connotations associated with it. This is unfortunate because we all speak a dialect. "Dialects inevitably arise within all languages because all languages inevitably change."[11] If the geographical separation between groups of people is very great and the separation lasts long enough, "the dialects may diverge from each other so much that they become two distinct languages."[12] (Persons who speak different languages do not understand one another, whereas persons who speak different dialects usually do.)

In the United States, standard English is considered the "prestige" dialect, and where regional dialects differ very little from each other, perhaps almost exclusively in pronunciation, we would be more likely to speak of an "accent" than a "dialect."[13] In this book, whenever the term *nonstandard English* is used, it refers to a variation of standard English in the United States.

> **Nonstandard English**
> A variation of standard English in the United States.

Children who speak a variation or dialect of English or another language are not inferior to children speaking standard English, nor is their language inferior. Research by linguists has shown that many variations of English are highly structured systems and not accumulations of errors in standard English. Noted scholar William Labov states that "it is most important for the teacher to understand the relation between standard and nonstandard and to recognize that nonstandard English is a system of rules, different from the standard but not necessarily inferior as a means of communication."[14]

Children speaking in a dialect of English have no difficulty communicating with one another. However, any dialect that differs from standard English structure and usage may cause communication problems for children in school and in society at large. Many expressions used by children who speak a variation of English may be foreign to teachers, and many expressions used by teachers may have different connotations for the students. The similarities between the dialects of English and standard English can also cause misunderstandings between students and teachers because both groups may feel they "understand" what the others are saying when, in actuality, they may not.

> **Ebonics**
> A combination of *ebony* and *phonics*. A variation of standard English; in the class of nonstandard English.

These misunderstandings may be especially true for those students who speak *Ebonics* (a combination of the words *ebony* and *phonics*), which is another term for black English. Ebonics, which is in the class of nonstandard English, and standard English appear similar, but they are not. It may very well be that many minority children's difficulty in reading may be due to their speaking a form of nonstandard English. (See Appendix C for a sample summary of some language transfer issues among several languages that may impact reading.)

[10]Jean Malmstrom and Constance Weaver, *Transgrammar: English Structure, Style, and Dialects* (Glenview, IL: Scott, Foresman, 1973), p. 338.

[11]Peter Desberg, Dale E. Elliot, and George Marsh, "American Black English and Spelling," in *Cognitive Processes in Spelling,* ed. Uta Frith (New York: Academic Press, 1980), p. 70.

[12]Ibid., p. 71.

[13]John P. Hughes, *The Science of Language* (New York: Random House, 1962), p. 26.

[14]William Labov, *The Study of Nonstandard English* (Urbana, IL: National Council of Teachers of English, 1970), p. 14.

Children who come from homes where a language other than English is dominant may also have language difficulties when they enter school unless they are truly bilingual. Dictionaries usually define *bilingual* as being capable of using two languages equally effectively. However, many schoolchildren who speak a language other than standard English at home are not bilingual. These children may hear only "noises" when they first enter school, because the English sounds have little or no meaning for them. They will often confuse the language spoken at home with their newly acquired English and vice versa. It is not a question of one language being better than or preferred over another, but rather of helping children to get along in the dominant social, economic, and political culture and to become a part of it. In essence, we want children to be flexible language users—that is, we want to help them develop the understanding that every "club" has a language. To successfully communicate with members of any given club, one needs to speak the language of that club.

> **Bilingual**
> Using or capable of using two languages.

## STANDARD ENGLISH, AN IMPORTANT FACTOR FOR SCHOOL SUCCESS AND BEYOND: A POINT OF VIEW

Many factors determine how well students do in school. Unfortunately, many children come to school lacking the kinds of experiences needed to be successful in a school environment. One variable that is extremely important for school success is the ability to speak standard English.

Learning standard English for children who speak another language or a nonstandard form of English requires students to add another language, rather than to do away with their nonstandard form of English or language. They begin to understand that different forms of language are used in different contexts.

Even though everyone does not agree on how to help nonstandard English speakers learn standard English, almost all agree that students must attain standard English in order to succeed in school and the workplace. In 1995, an interviewer on a "60 Minutes" segment asked a personnel executive for a major corporation whether the way that a prospective employee speaks plays a role in hiring considerations. The executive, a person of color who speaks impeccable English, stated that he would not hire anyone who did not speak standard English well. He said further that it is one thing to speak in a certain dialect at home or with peers, and another when working with professionals. In this case, he noted that individuals in the firms he represents must speak standard English.

The bottom line is that to succeed in school and in the workplace, all students must be able to speak and write in standard English. To help achieve this objective, we need to begin or continue the process of helping students to use standard English as early as possible. This can be accomplished by making a concerted effort to use many different strategies. It can also be accomplished by employing knowedgeable teachers who are sensitive to the needs of their students and who speak standard English exceptionally well themselves.

## INTELLIGENCE

Intelligence includes problem-solving ability and the ability to do abstract reasoning. Since reading is a thinking process, it seems reasonable to assume that students who have the ability to think at high levels of abstraction and who have strategies for processing information should be good readers. To a large degree this assumption is true. However, investigators have reported that not all children deemed "highly able" become good readers. These findings suggest that there are factors besides intelligence, such as those we show in Table 4.1 on page 64 that contribute to success in reading and consequently to achievement in school.

Most intelligence tests are highly verbal, and persons who do well on vocabulary tests also seem to do well on intelligence tests. In addition, there is a research base that indicates a high positive correlation between reading achievement test scores and intelligence test scores.[15] Therefore, a child with a low IQ score would not be expected to do as well on a standardized reading achievement test as one with a high IQ score. Although intelligence is one factor to consider, reading educators Marjorie Lipson and Karen Wixson[16] note that there are several important points to keep in mind:

1. The components of intelligence cannot be observed, and there is disagreement about what components contribute to overall intelligence.
2. Intelligence has been expanded to include more than verbal skills. For example, Gardner's multiple intelligences theory posits that there are eight different kinds of intelligences.
3. Some researchers have reported that intelligence can be affected by experience and instruction.[17]
4. Culture impacts how children show their intelligence. Some, for example, teach students to provide more global answers rather than factual answers to posed questions.

## GENDER

There appear to be vast differences between males and females besides the obvious physical ones. Females seem to develop earlier than males from birth onward.[18] The skeletal development of girls is superior to that of boys at birth, and this physical superiority continues until maturity.[19] Males, however, give off more carbon dioxide than females;[20] therefore, boys need to take in more food and consequently produce more energy. Even though, on average, the male matures later than the female, his oxygen intake is greater and continues

---

[15]Keith Rayner and Alexander Pollatsek, *The Psychology of Reading* (Hillsdale, NJ: Erlbaum, 1994), p. 395.

[16]Marjorie Y. Lipson, and Karen K. Wixson, *Assessment and Instruction of Reading and Writing Difficulty: An Interactive Approach*, 3rd ed. (Boston: Allyn and Bacon, 2003).

[17]Carnegie Corporation, *Starting Points: Meeting the Needs of Our Youngest Students* (New York: Carnegie Corporation, 1994). Robert Slavin, *Educational Psychology* (Englewood Cliffs, NJ: Prentice Hall, 1991)

[18]Amram Scheinfeld, *Women and Men* (New York: Harcourt, 1944), pp. 58–71.

[19]J. M. Tanner, "Physical Growth," in *Carmichael's Manual of Child Psychology,* 3rd ed., ed. Paul H. Mussen (New York: Wiley, 1970), p. 109.

[20]Stanley M. Garn and Leland C. Clark, Jr., "The Sex Difference in the Basal Metabolic Rate," *Child Development* 24 (September-December 1953): 215–24.

so throughout life.[21] It has been hypothesized that sex differences in behavior may be due to these differences in metabolism.

These factors may affect the readiness levels of children in all areas of language arts, including listening, speaking, reading, writing, and viewing. Some primary-grade boys may not be as mature as some girls of the same chronological age. Consequently, they should not be expected to do equally well on tasks using specific hand muscles—such as handwriting. Similarly, many male students will be unable to sit still as long as some female students or to have a comparable attention span. Although cognitive psychologists report the results of studies that show no significant differences between males and females in general intelligence,[22] they continue to show differences in specific aptitudes.[23]

A review of research on gender differences shows that even though the data on gender differences studies are inconclusive and contradictory, there are a few generalizations that can be made. The reviewers report that "the largest differences appear in tests of mathematical or quantitative ability, where men tend to do better than women, particularly in secondary school and beyond. In recent years, there is some evidence that this gap may be narrowing. Women have tended to do better than men in many tests of verbal skills (particularly writing), but a number of studies indicate that this superiority has diminished since the early 1970s.[24] However, an extensive Educational Testing Service (ETS) study suggests that female superiority in writing and language skills still persists, and the investigators report that "research shows that females have closed the gap significantly on math and science scores."[25]

Investigators conducting the ETS gender study found that there are "many similarities and some genuine differences between how females and males perform in educational settings."[26] It seems that the "differences are the result of many factors, and they widen particularly between the 4th and 12th grades."[27]

So gender, like the other factors presented in this chapter, is but one factor that needs to be considered in terms of reading performance.

## PHYSICAL HEALTH

### Illness

A child who is ill is not able to do well in school. This statement is obvious; however, it may not be obvious that a child is ill. A teacher needs to be alert for certain symptoms that may suggest a child is not well or not getting enough

---

[21]Ibid., p. 222.

[22]Scottish Council for Research in Education, *The Intelligence of a Representative Group of Scottish Children* (London: University of London Press, 1939). Scottish Council for Research in Education, *The Trend of Scottish Intelligence* (London: University of London Press, 1949).

[23]Gita Z. Wilder and Kristin Powell, "Sex Differences in Test Performance: A Survey of the Literature," College Board Report No. 89–3 (Princeton, NJ: Educational Testing Service, 1989).

[24]"The Gender Gap in Education: How Early and How Large?" *ETS Policy Notes,* vol. 2, no. 1 (Princeton, NJ: Educational Testing Service, October 1989).

[25]Nancy S. Cole, *The ETS Gender Study: How Females and Males Perform in Educational Settings* (Executive Summary). (Princeton, NJ: Educational Testing Service, 1997), p. 26.

[26]Ibid.

[27]Ibid.

sleep. For example, a child who is listless, whose eyes are glazed, who seems sleepy, and who actually does fall asleep in class may need a physical checkup.

The reason a child who is ill does not usually do well in school is not necessarily the child's illness, but the child's frequent absence from school. Children who have illnesses that keep recurring are generally absent from school a lot. This lack of attendance can contribute to reading problems because it causes the child to miss important reading instruction. In fact, long absences, in first and second grade especially, is often the case with children who struggle with reading.[28]

### Nutrition

The effects of nutrition, and particularly malnutrition, on learning have been evident for a long time. It should come as no surprise that children who are hungry and malnourished have difficulty learning. They cannot concentrate on the task at hand; they also lack drive. They simply lack the energy to perform at their best. For several decades some researchers have suggested that severe malnutrition in infancy may lower children's IQ scores.[29] Several other researchers have found that the lack of protein in an infant's diet may adversely affect the child's ability to learn.[30] Still others have found that food additives may be a deterrent to learning for certain children.[31]

And consider the current state of affairs regarding nutrition. Childhood obesity is in the media spotlight; some even call it an epidemic and point to possible reasons why children are becoming obese in increasing numbers. Not surprisingly, nutrition is a major factor, as is the type of food that children consume. Is it any wonder that many children have trouble performing in school when they eat processed foods that contain a lot of sugar?

## PERCEPTUAL FACTORS

In Chapter 1 we noted the importance of perception (giving meaning to sensations) as part of the process of reading. We stated that a child who has problems in the perceptual domain will most assuredly encounter difficulty in concept development and consequently in reading. Vision and hearing are two important parts of perception.

### Visual Perception

Since reading requires the sense of sight, it seems almost absurd to say that a visual deficit will influence a child's ability to read. However, a visual problem is not always obvious and, as a result, is not always detected. Most schools have

---

[28]Albert J. Harris and Edward R. Sipay, *How to Increase Reading Ability: A Guide to Developmental and Remedial Methods* (New York: Longman, 1990).

[29]Merlin C. Wittrock, "Learning and the Brain," in Merlin C. Wittrock, ed. The *Brain and Psychology* (New York: Academic Press, 1980), pp. 376–77.

[30]Nevin S. Scrimshaw, "Infant Malnutrition and Adult Learning." *Saturday Review*, March 16, 1968, pp. 64–66, 84.

[31]Eleanor Chernick, "Effect of the Feingold Diet on Reading Achievement and Classroom Behavior," *The Reading Teacher* 34 (November 1980): 171–73.

some kind of visual screening that each child must undergo. If a school nurse is employed, the screening is generally done by the school nurse who often uses the Snellen chart. This chart uses line figures for young children and letters for those who can read letters; it tests acuity (keenness of vision). The test making use of the Snellen chart requires that the child stand twenty feet away from the chart with one eye covered. The child must identify letters of various sizes with each eye. A score of 20/20 is considered normal. A score of 20/40 or 20/60 means that a child has defective vision because the child with normal vision can see the letters at a distance of forty or sixty feet, whereas the child with defective vision can only see these letters at a distance of twenty feet.

The accuracy of the scores obtained from the Snellen chart has been questioned because the test does not detect moderate degrees of farsightedness (*hypermetropia*) or *astigmatism*, which causes blurred vision, and fails completely to detect even severe cases of poor fusion and eye-muscle imbalance.[32] The one defect it often discloses is nearsightedness (*myopia*). However, there are difficulties even with detecting nearsightedness because some children may memorize the chart and appear to have "normal" distance vision even though they do not.

Another problem with the Snellen chart is that school nurses are often unable to observe children's eye movements and features because the nurses usually have to point to the figures or letters they want the children to read.

A vision screening test that school nurses seem to like is the Insta-Line produced by the Good-Lite Company. They prefer this instrument over others because distance measurements are already done and it is portable. Its portability enables nurses to observe a child's eye movements and features. They can discern whether a child's eyes are crossed; whether the child is straining while reading; and whether the eyes are tearing, twitching, or squinting. They can also look for eye contractions, and so on.

The Titmus Vision Tester is another instrument that school nurses use; however, it has a major defect in that examiners cannot observe a child's eye behavior during the testing because the child is looking into a machine at slides. There are a number of more sophisticated eye survey tests available, but the function of the school nurse is to do preliminary screening for a possible problem rather than to diagnose, so the money spent on these more sophisticated instruments might not be warranted.

The school nurse is an important part of every school team and plays a major role in helping to detect possible vision problems that could contribute to reading difficulties. When a school nurse suspects a possible visual problem, she should speak to the parents and recommend that they take their child to an eye doctor for a thorough examination.

### Binocular Vision

A few years ago, I (DR) asked the students in my college-level class to take a simple test for *binocular vision*, the ability to focus both eyes on a similar point of reference and see one object. I asked them to hold up their forefinger at eye level at arm's length and then to look beyond the finger at some object.

**Hypermetropia**
Farsightedness; difficulty with close-up vision.

**Astigmatism**
A defect of vision that causes blurred vision.

**Myopia**
Nearsightedness; difficulty with distance vision.

**Binocular vision**
The ability to focus both eyes on a similar point of reference and see one object.

[32]Albert J. Harris and Edward R. Sipay, *How to Increase Reading Ability,* 9th ed. (New York: Longman, 1990), p. 347.

When they do so, they should see two fingers; that is, they will if they have done it correctly and if they have no problems with binocular vision. (The test proves that both eyes are in use.)

The farther the finger is placed away from the eyes, the less separation of the fingers they should see. If it were possible to place the finger on the object they were looking at, they would see only one finger if both eyes are working together properly.

One young man in the class who was an athlete had difficulty seeing two fingers at arm's length. He was disturbed by this result and went to an ophthalmologist (eye specialist) to find out whether he had a problem. Fortunately for him, the cause of his problem was easily treatable.

It is important that children be checked for binocular vision because there are some conditions that cannot be treated effectively after a child is a certain age.

Here is a listing of some symptoms that teachers should look for in order to detect a possible vision problem:

1. The child complains of constant headaches.
2. The child's eyes show some of the following: red rims, swollen lids, crusted lids, red eyes, frequent sties, watering eyes.
3. The child squints while reading.
4. The child asks to sit closer to the board.
5. The child can't seem to sit still while doing close-up tasks.
6. The child holds the reading material very close to his or her face while reading.
7. The child skips many words and/or sentences while reading.
8. The child makes many reversals while reading.
9. The child confuses letters.
10. The child avoids reading.
11. The child mouths the words or lip reads.
12. The child confuses similar words.
13. The child makes many repetitions while reading.
14. The child skips lines while reading.
15. The child has difficulty remembering what was read silently.

In Figure 4.1 we show these symptoms as a checklist that teachers can use while observing any given class.

If teachers notice some of these symptoms, they should speak to the child's parents or refer the child to the school nurse. As important as vision is to reading, keep in mind that the presence of one or more of the listed symptoms does not necessarily mean a child has an eye problem, nor does it mean that it is the only cause of the child's reading problem if one exists.

### Eye Movements

When we read, both our eyes are supposed to work together, but they do not go across the page in one smooth pattern. Instead, as we read we make stops for minutely small periods of time that are measured in milliseconds (*fixations*); we go back to reread text (*regressions*); and we make small, rapid, jerky jumps as we move from one spot in a text to another (*saccades*). It is during fixations that we gain visual information from text material.

**Eye movements**
How the eyes appear to move in the act of reading.

**Fixations**
Stops readers make in the act of reading continuous text.

**Regressions**
Eyes move backward; they move back to reread material while in the act of reading continuous text.

---

## FIGURE 4.1  Symptoms of Vision Problems

Child's Name: _____

Date of Observation: _____

*Symptoms*
*The child . . .*                                          **Yes**      **No**

| | Yes | No |
|---|---|---|
| 1. Complains of constant headaches | | |
| 2. Eyes show some of the following: red rims, swollen lids, crusted lids, red eyes, frequent sties, watering eyes | | |
| 3. Squints while reading | | |
| 4. Asks to sit closer to the board | | |
| 5. Can't seem to sit still while doing close-up tasks | | |
| 6. Holds reading material very close to face when reading | | |
| 7. Skips many words and/or sentences when reading | | |
| 8. Makes many reversals when reading | | |
| 9. Confuses letters | | |
| 10. Avoids reading | | |
| 11. Mouths words or lip reads | | |
| 12. Confuses similar words | | |
| 13. Makes many repetitions while reading | | |
| 14. Skips lines while reading | | |
| 15. Has difficulty remembering what was read silently | | |

**Saccades**
Quick, jerky movements of the eyes as they jump from one fixation to another in the reading of continuous text.

Mature readers have shorter fixations, longer and fewer saccades, and fewer regressions; the converse is true for beginning readers. Beginning readers "make more and longer fixations, shorter saccades, and more regressions than skilled readers."[33] Therefore, a beginning reader will have a slower reading rate than a more mature one. Also, it makes sense to say that a more difficult text will generally require more fixations, shorter saccades, and more regressions, especially if the reader has little background on the topic at hand.

[33]Keith Rayner and Alexander Pollatsek, *The Psychology of Reading* (Hillsdale, NJ: Erlbaum, 1994), p. 386.

**Visual discrimination**
The ability to distinguish differences and similarities between written symbols.

### Visual Discrimination

*Visual discrimination* is the ability to distinguish between written symbols. If pupils have difficulty discriminating between and among letters, they will experience difficulty when learning to read. In learning to read, children need to be able to make fine discriminations, and therefore need activities involving letters rather than geometric figures or pictures. Transfer of learning is greater if the written symbols children work with are similar to those they will meet in reading.[34]

A teacher-made visual discrimination test such as the following is one way to discover whether a child has some reversal problem:

*Directions:* Put a circle around the letters that are the same as the first in the line. (Read aloud the directions for children who cannot read.)

b   d   b   b   d   p   b
p   d   b   d   p   b   p

*Directions:* Put a circle around the words that are the same as the first in the line. (Read aloud the directions to children who cannot read.)

saw   was   saw   saw   was   won   now
won   now   won   won   now   not   won

Most pre-reading tests have a subtest on visual discrimination.

### Laterality

**Laterality**
Refers to sidedness.

**Crossed dominance**
The dominant hand on one side and the dominant eye on the other.

**Mixed dominance**
No consistent preference for an eye, hand, or foot.

Human perceptual-motor activity is usually initiated from the one dominant side of the body, even though humans are bilateral, or two-sided. By the time children enter school they generally show a fairly consistent preference for their right or left hand, as well as preferences in the use of eyes and feet. Such preferences concern *laterality* or sidedness. People are said to have a dominant side if their hand, eye, and foot preferences are similar. When people have a dominant hand on one side and a dominant eye on the other, they are said to have crossed dominance. Individuals who do not have a consistent preference for an eye, hand, or foot are said to have mixed dominance. (Often the term *mixed dominance* is used also for *crossed dominance*.) It has been hypothesized that children who have crossed or mixed dominance may tend to have *reversal* difficulties in reading and writing, but studies made in this area have not been definitive. Children with crossed dominance can perhaps shift from a left-handed orientation to a right-handed one in writing, but this change might cause difficulties for them.

In the past, no substantial evidence existed concerning cognitive deficits of left-handers.[35] The same is true today; however, a number of left-handers often have orientation problems in reading and writing. To better understand the left-handed child's problem in reading and writing we must refer to

[34]Albert Harris and Edward Sipay, *How to Increase Reading Ability.* 1975: New York: Longman. Marie Clay, *Early Detection of Reading Difficulties.* 1985 Portsmouth, NH: Heinemann.

[35]Merlin C. Wittrock, "Education and the Cognitive Processes of the Brain," *The National Society for the Study of Education 77th Yearbook,* Part II, 1978, p. 85.

**Reversals**
Confusion of letters
and words by
inverting them; for
example, *b* = *d*, *was* =
*saw,* and vice versa.

**Proximodistal
development**
Muscular
development from the
midpoint of the body
to the extremities.

*proximodistal development*—development from the midpoint of the body to the extremities. Right-handed children move their right hands from left to right naturally. Left-handed children find moving their left hand from left to right against their natural inclination.

Try this simple experiment to illustrate the point: Bring both hands to the center of your body. Now, move both hands out away from your body. The right hand will follow a left to right path corresponding to the English pattern of writing; the left hand follows a right to left path. Ask some left-handed persons to write a *t*. Observe carefully how they make the horizontal line. Most of them, unless they have been well conditioned, will draw the line from right to left.

Teaching reading is a complex task, and one of the things that the child learns is that in learning to read in English, he or she must read from left to right. This follows natural development for right-handed people. However, reading from left to right is not natural for left-handed children and we must be alert for possible reversal problems.

A teacher can easily test whether a child has crossed or mixed dominance. To determine hand dominance observe which hand the child uses to throw a ball, write, or open a door. The teacher can tell which eye is dominant by observing which eye the child uses to look through a microscope, telescope, or an open cylinder formed by a roll of paper. Foot dominance can be easily determined by observing which foot the child uses to kick a ball or stamp on the floor with.

Crossed or mixed dominance in a child does not mean that the child will have a problem, although the possibility exists. Be sure to give special attention to those children who are having reversal problems by emphasizing left-to-right orientation for reading and writing.

### Auditory Perception

Like visual perception, auditory perception involves several abilities. While auditory perception is important, we need to remember that it is just one factor that may affect reading performance. There are many children with hearing impairments who read quite well.

**Auditory acuity**
Physical response of
the ear to sound
vibrations.

### Auditory Acuity

Auditory acuity is concerned with the physical response of the ear to sound vibrations. If individuals have organic ear damage, they will not be able to hear properly, if at all, depending on the extent of the damage. Auditory acuity is the ability to respond to various frequencies (tones) at various intensities (levels of loudness).

Human speech comprises frequencies ranging from 125 to 8,000 hertz (Hz).[36] The intensity or loudness level found in everyday speech will range typically from 55 decibels (faint speech) to 85 decibels (loud conversation). When hearing is tested, a person's ability to hear is checked across the entire speech-frequency range. If more than the normal amount of volume (dB level) is required to hear sounds at certain frequencies, the individual is most probably exhibiting a hearing loss.

---

[36]*Hertz* is the accepted international scientific word for cycles per second, named after the great nineteenth-century German physicist who proved the existence of electromagnetic waves.

Many states and doctors are advocating that newborns' hearing be tested before they leave the hospital because hearing loss is so common. This makes sense, because a hearing loss that is undetected and therefore untreated usually will affect children's speech and all other language arts areas. This can be especially detrimental to children when learning to read.

It appears that children who have difficulty hearing high frequencies generally have problems discerning differences between and among consonants, whereas those who have problems hearing low frequencies usually have difficulties discriminating between and among vowels. Such problems with consonants and vowels could cause great difficulties for children learning to read.

**Audiometer**
An instrument used for measuring hearing acuity.

An *audiometer* is used by audiologists for precise measurement of hearing loss. But teachers can make a lot of informal measurements on their own. Teachers can observe if any of the following behaviors are present and refer the student for further testing if one or more are manifested:

1. Does the child appear to be straining to push himself or herself closer to the speaker?
2. Does the child speak either very softly or very loudly?
3. Does the child have difficulty following simple directions?
4. Does the child turn up the sound of the CD player or tape player?
5. Does the child have difficulty pronouncing words?
6. Does the child seem disoriented?

In Figure 4.2 we show these behaviors in a checklist format that teachers can use while observing a class.

According to William Jones, a well-known authority in audiology, it is possible for a child to have a normal result from auditory testing but still have significant difficulties processing and understanding sound symbols. The inability of a child to consistently follow directions when they are presented loud enough to be clearly understood is one sign that a child may have such a problem. These children should be referred to a specialist for further testing, including a complete audiological assessment.[37]

### Auditory Fatigue

**Auditory fatigue**
Temporary hearing loss due to a continuous or repeated exposure to sounds of certain frequencies.

*Auditory fatigue* is a temporary hearing loss caused by continuous or repeated exposure to sounds of certain frequencies. A monotonous tone or droning voice will have the effect of causing auditory fatigue. It has been shown that exposure to continuous loud noises over an extended period of time could be permanently harmful to an individual's hearing ability. Listening to music at a very high volume or being constantly exposed to cars and trucks rumbling through highway tunnels can have deleterious effects.

### Binaural Considerations

**Binaurality**
The ability of listeners to direct both ears to the same sound.

When individuals are in the presence of two or more conversations, they must be able to direct their attention to only one of the speakers in order to be able to get the essence of what is being said. The more readily listeners are able to separate the sound sources, the more they will be able to grasp messages cor-

---

[37]Dr. William O. Jones, Professor Emeritus, The College of New Jersey, 2001.

---

**FIGURE 4.2   Symptoms of Hearing Problems**

Child's Name: _____

Date of Observation: _____

| *Question* | *Yes* | *No* |
|---|---|---|
| 1. Does the child appear to be straining to push himself or herself closer to the speaker? | | |
| 2. Does the child speak either very softly or very loudly? | | |
| 3. Does the child have difficulty following simple directions? | | |
| 4. Does the child turn up the sound of the CD player or tape player? | | |
| 5. Does the child have difficulty pronouncing words? | | |
| 6. Does the child seem disoriented? | | |

---

rectly. *Binaurality* thus refers to the ability of listeners to increase their reception sensitivity by directing both ears to the same sound.

### Masking

**Masking**
Factor inhibiting hearing as sounds interfere with the spoken message.

*Masking* occurs when other sounds interfere with the message being spoken. Background noises drowning out a speaker, noisy classrooms, or simultaneous group discussions all retard hearing ability.

### Auditory Discrimination

**Auditory discrimination**
Ability to distinguish differences and similarities between sound symbols.

*Auditory discrimination*, which is the ability to distinguish among sounds, is important for the acquisition of language and for learning to read. Following is a summary of what speech clinicians have learned about auditory discrimination:

1. There is evidence that the more nearly alike two phonemes are in phonetic (relating to speech sounds) structure, the more likely they are to be misinterpreted.
2. Individuals differ in their ability to discriminate among sounds.
3. The ability to discriminate frequently matures as late as the end of the child's eighth year. A few individuals never develop this capacity to any great degree.
4. There is a strong positive relation between slow development of auditory discrimination and inaccurate pronunciation.
5. There is a positive relationship between poor discrimination and poor reading.
6. Although poor discrimination may be at the root of both speech and reading difficulties, it often affects only reading or speaking.

7. There is little if any relationship between the development of auditory discrimination and intelligence, as measured by most intelligence tests.[38]

For children who speak a nonstandard dialect of English or for whom English is a second language, it is good to bear in mind that the acquisition of speech sounds for any given dialect is learned very early in life and is usually established by the time the child starts school. These children especially need help in auditory discrimination if they are to learn standard English.

### Auditory Memory Span

**Auditory memory span**

Amount of information able to be stored in short-term memory for immediate use or reproduction.

*Auditory memory span* is essential for individuals who must judge whether two or more sounds are similar or different. In order to make such comparisons, the sounds must be kept in memory and retrieved for comparison. Auditory memory span is defined as "the number of discrete elements grasped in a given moment of attention and organized into a unity for purposes of immediate reproduction or immediate use."[39] A deficiency in memory span will hinder effective listening.

The *Wepman Auditory Discrimination Test,* which was developed by Joseph M. Wepman and published by Language Research Associates, is a norm-referenced test that teachers use to discern whether students have auditory discrimination problems. The teacher asks the student to turn around so that he or she cannot lip-read; then the teacher very distinctly pronounces each pair of words. The student must determine if the words are the same or different. There are two forms of the test, each one consisting of forty pairs of words.

Many of the reading diagnostic tests presented in Chapter 3 have subtests that test a child's auditory discrimination.

Individual intelligence tests, such as the *Stanford-Binet* and the *Wechsler,* have subtests that measure an individual's memory span. These tests are called *Digits Forward* and *Digits Backward.* The individual is told to listen carefully, and then the examiner says some numbers at the rate of one per second. After the entire series of numbers has been given, the individual must repeat them in the exact order. For the *Digits Backward,* the individual must repeat the digits in reverse order after the examiner has stopped.

## EMOTIONAL HEALTH

Self-concept, learned helplessness, motivation, and attitude are four aspects related to emotional health. Each needs to be considered when thinking about a child's emotional well-being and how it can affect reading performance.

### Self-Concept

Self-concept is the way an individual feels about himself or herself. Although the verdict is still out on specific origins of self-concept, our lives are testament to the fact that it exists and that it can change depending on the task at hand. For example, if we feel adequate, confident, and self-reliant about reading, we

[38]Joseph M. Wepman, "Auditory Discrimination, Speech and Reading," *Elementary School Journal* 60 (1960): 326.

[39]Virgil A. Anderson, "Auditory Memory Span as Tested by Speech Sounds," *American Journal of Psychology* 52 (1939): 95.

are more apt to be good readers. We would say that we have a positive self-concept as it relates to reading. However, if we are feeling less than adequate, have little confidence, and are not self-reliant about reading, we are more likely to be poor at reading and to have a negative self-concept about it. One factor to consider, then, is how children feel about themselves as readers. Asking students the following questions is one way to tap students' perceptions of themselves as readers:

1. Do you think you are a good reader? Why or why not?
2. How do you feel when you are expected to read?
3. Do you read at home?
4. Do you like to read?

### Learned Helplessness

Related to self-concept is learned helplessness. If we repeatedly experience failure at a task regardless of how hard we try, we are apt to develop the idea that we simply cannot perform the task; this is called *learned helplessness*. As a result, any time we are expected to perform the task, we become passive. This should come as no surprise, because few of us like to feel like failures! Avoidance is one way to block these feelings of failure. Thus, children who feel that they simply cannot perform well at reading are likely to show avoidance behaviors. Even if others, such as a well-meaning teacher, believe that a child can perform quite well, the important point to keep in mind is that learned helplessness is the child's viewpoint. The questions presented earlier can help to reveal children's perceptions of themselves as readers. Watching what children do when they are called on to read in various ways can also shed light on how they feel about reading. For example, during independent reading time, when children are to select a book of their choosing, those who feel less than adequate tend to roam around the room acting as if they are reading, when in fact they are doing everything they can to avoid it.

### Motivation

The factors that motivate any of us to do anything—including reading—are the subject of much debate. However, like Paris and Carpenter,[40] we believe that there are several components that facilitate *motivation* to read. These include how readers perceive their abilities to read, the text, the reason for reading, and the surrounding environment. Take, for example, children who attend a sleepover at school and are told to bring their favorite book for reading and sharing with others. Children who elect to attend the event are sure to be motivated to read. After all, they get to choose the text with the purpose in mind. Self-selection means that they are likely to pick out a text they feel they can read with ease. They need not be embarrassed when they share a part of it aloud with another person. Likewise, because everyone will be reading, the

---

[40]Scott G. Paris and Robert D. Carpenter, "Children's Motivation to Read," in James V. Hoffman and Diane L. Schallert, eds., *The Texts in Elementary Classrooms* (Mahwah, NJ: Erlbaum, 2004), p. 61–85.

environment encourages all children to do the same. The person who chooses not to follow suit will be odd one out and is likely to feel uncomfortable.

### *Attitude*

If we simply take a look at ourselves and our relationship to reading, we can fully understand what researchers have concluded over the years: *Attitude* is a major factor that affects reading performance.[41] In fact, a positive attitude can override missing skills,[42] enabling a reader to perform far better than one would expect when reviewing past reading performances. A former student of mine (MO) helped me to understand this. She selected a book that presented many challenges for her—too many from my perspective. As much as I tried to persuade her to read other easier texts, she kept returning to "her" book and simply would not give it up. For whatever reason, she wanted to read the book and, after continual assistance, she read it with ease. What seemed like a miracle was a positive attitude in action. Deep down, she wanted to read the book, felt that she could get it, and therefore she did. Excited about her newfound reading ability, I wondered whether she could read other texts at a similar level of complexity. My subsequent observations revealed that she could not. In fact, she often chose to read much easier books after she did a repeated reading of her more difficult book.

At the beginning of this chapter, we emphasized the interrelatedness of the many factors that can affect reading performance. Now that you have an understanding of these factors, we will conclude with a scenario about Larry, who is experiencing reading difficulties. As you read it, see how many factors you can identify that might be affecting Larry's reading performance. Which of the factors are educational? Which might be classified as noneducational?

 ## Scenario: The Profile of a First-Grade Failure

Larry came from an upper-middle-class home. His parents were highly educated and cared deeply about him. According to the statistics, Larry should be doing well in school. He was not, though, and there are many others just like him. Why? If children like Larry have problems, what hope is there for those who don't have Larry's social and economic advantages?

Larry's parents had spoken to me about their little boy and told me how unhappy they were with his situation. They told me that Larry had been left back in the first grade because he couldn't read. His first-grade teacher and the principal had recommended that Larry repeat the first grade, and the parents had not objected. They were told that by repeating the first grade, Larry would be happier and would do much better. Unfortunately, he was not happy, and he was not doing much better. Larry hated school. His personality was changing. He felt that he was dumb, and he didn't like himself very much. His parents

[41] Marjorie Y. Lipson and Karen K. Wixson. *Assessment and Instruction of Reading and Writing Difficulty: An Interactive Approach,* 3rd ed. (New York: Allyn & Bacon, 2003).

[42] Scott G. Paris, G. Olson, and H. Stevenson, eds. *Learning and Motivation in the Classroom.* (Hillsdale, NJ: Erlbaum, 1983).

spoke to the teacher, who said that Larry was having difficulty with the reading program, which was the only program the school was allowed to use. She was sure that Larry would adjust to it soon. The parents, not so sure, went to see the principal. The principal told them not to worry, that he and his staff were professionals, and they knew what they were doing. Larry would have to continue in the same program, and that the same method of instruction would be used.

Larry's parents were confused and bitter. They did worry. Private schools would not accept Larry because the school term had already begun, and their son was becoming more and more unhappy.

Larry's parents decided to go to outside sources for help. They asked me (DR) to test Larry, and I consented. When I met Larry, he said to me, "I'm the biggest one in my class because I was left back. Everyone knows that I was left back. I hate school." We talked for a little while, and I tried to learn about some of the things he liked to do. I discovered that he enjoyed looking through *National Geographic*, that he loved sports, that he went fishing and camping with his father and brother, and that he loved animals.

Even though Larry was only in the first grade, I decided to give him an informal reading inventory. When I asked him to state the words in the word recognition list, he picked up the sheet with the words and put it so close to his face that the paper was actually touching his nose. I asked Larry if he wore glasses. He said, "No." Larry had difficulty recognizing the words in isolation. I had him start at the lowest level in oral reading. Even at the preprimer level, he had trouble decoding words. His decoding problems were so pronounced that I decided to give Larry a listening capacity test because I felt his decoding problems would probably hinder his comprehension. I read aloud the passages to Larry and then asked him questions about them. Larry was able to answer the comprehension questions almost perfectly up to the fifth-grade level. He was able to tell me what a nocturnal bird was, as well as answer some very difficult and involved questions.

Larry was a highly able boy; he certainly was not "dumb." A crime had been perpetrated against him. Who was to blame? When Larry was retained, no one had given him any diagnostic reading tests. The parents should have noticed from Larry's behavior that he had some kind of vision problem. When the parents were asked about it, they claimed that the school nurse had tested Larry's eyes and that no vision problem had been noticed. From Larry's behavior, the teacher also should have noticed that Larry appeared to have some kind of vision problem and should have recommended that the parents have his eyes checked by an eye doctor, since the school nurse only tests for nearsightedness and farsightedness. Based on my suggestion, Larry was taken to an ophthalmologist. The eye specialist found that Larry had very severe astigmatism, which probably would account for his decoding problems. Larry had difficulty focusing on words. This does not excuse the school for insisting that Larry adjust to the program rather than adjusting the program to suit Larry. Regardless of who was to blame, Larry saw himself as a failure. At seven years of age, he couldn't wait to leave school. Damage had been done to Larry, and he is still suffering from it.

This profile of Larry, which is based on fact, was not written to portray the school personnel as being the devils and the author (DR) as the angel. It was presented to raise the consciousness level of teachers about the importance of early diagnosis.

# SUMMARY

In this chapter we presented a variety of educational and noneducational factors that can affect a child's reading performance. Educational factors, which are defined as those factors that come under the domain or control of the school, include teaching methods, instructional materials, the teacher, and the school environment.

Reading is a thinking act, and since intelligence measures a person's ability to reason abstractly, it seems logical that the more intelligent an individual is, the better reader he or she should be. However, researchers note that not all highly able students become good readers, and these results indicate that there are other noneducational factors beside intelligence that affect a student's ability to read.

Noneducational factors include home environment, dialect and language differences, gender, physical condition, visual and auditory perception, and emotional state. These factors were explored in depth in the chapter.

Teachers can do nothing about many of these individual differences, such as home environment, family makeup, and languages/dialects spoken. However, if teachers are aware that some of their children come from environments that may present obstacles to learning, they can provide experiences in school to help these children become successful readers. And for children with physical, perceptual, or emotional difficulties, teachers can also be ready to diagnose and provide remediation as soon as these difficulties become apparent.

# CHAPTER 4 KEY CONCEPTS

- Educational factors in learning include teaching methods, instructional materials, the teacher, instructional time, and the school environment.
- Noneducational factors in learning include home environment, dialect and language differences, intelligence, gender, physical health, perceptual factors, and emotional health.
- Socioeconomic class, parents' education, and the neighborhood in which children live are some factors that shape children's home environment.
- Dialect and language differences are closely related to home environment.
- Good thinkers have strategies for processing information.

- There is a high correlation between reading achievement test scores and intelligence test scores.
- Females, on the average, outperform their male counterparts in reading.
- The studies that try to answer the questions of gender differences in achievement are confusing and not definitive.
- Nutrition affects children's ability to do work in school.
- Both visual and auditory processes have an impact on reading ability.
- Emotional well being relates to reading ability.

# SUGGESTIONS FOR THOUGHT QUESTIONS AND ACTIVITIES

1. Explain why cultural factors have been suggested as an explanation for why there are more boys with reading disabilities than girls.
2. You have been asked to give a talk to your colleagues about why there are more reading disabilities among boys than among girls in the United States. What will you say?

3. Why may children who speak nonstandard English have more problems in school than children who speak a foreign language such as French or German?
4. Why would the community be considered an educational factor that could affect children's reading?

5. What is the relationship of intelligence to reading?
6. How can the physical health of a child affect his or her work at school?
7. Give examples of children who would be considered educationally at risk.

8. Discuss how emotional health relates to reading.
9. Explain how visual and auditory perception can assist readers.

## INTERNET ACTIVITIES

Select any term from this chapter about which you would like to learn more. Choose a search engine and search for websites related to the term. Select one website from the search and download an artifact that shows your findings. (Be sure to identify both the search engine you used and the website you selected in your paragraph.)

## SELECTED BIBLIOGRAPHY

Bennett, Christine I. *Comprehensive Multicultural Education: Theory and Practice,* 4th ed. Boston: Allyn and Bacon, 1999.

Cole, Nancy. *ETS Gender Study: How Females and Males Perform in Educational Settings.* Princeton, NJ: Educational Testing Service, 1997.

Grohens, Joe. "Nutrition and Reading Achievement." *The Reading Teacher* 41 (May 1988): 942–45.

Horgan, Dianne D. *Achieving Gender Equity: Strategies for the Classroom.* Boston: Allyn and Bacon, 1994.

Piaget, Jean. *The Language and Thought of the Child.* New York: Harcourt, 1926.

Rigg, Pat, and Virginia G. Allen, eds. *When They Don't All Speak English: Integrating the ESL Student into the Regular Classroom.* Urbana, IL.: National Council of Teachers of English, 1989.

Smith, Nila Banton. "Early Language Development: Foundation of Reading." *Elementary English* 52 (March 1975): 399–402; 418.

Sutton, Christine. "Helping the Nonnative English Speaker with Reading." *The Reading Teacher* 42 (May 1989): 684–88.

Tiedt, Pamela L., and Iris M. Tiedt. *Multicultural Teaching: A Handbook of Activities, Information, and Resources,* 5th ed. Boston: Allyn and Bacon, 1999.

Woolfolk, Anita E. "Cognitive Views of Learning," in *Educational Psychology,* 8th ed. Boston: Allyn and Bacon, 2001.

# Helping Children Achieve in Reading

# INTRODUCTION

You may recall that the first part of this book is about setting the stage for an effective reading program—one that focuses on helping children maximize their reading potential. So far, we have considered the philosophy of such a program (see Chapter 1); the teacher's role in such a program (see Chapter 2); terminology related to tests, measurement, and evaluation (see Chapter 3); and factors to consider in order to best help children (see Chapter 4). In this chapter we focus on the learners. In terms of setting the stage, we might view them as the performers on the stage, each with some similarities, but also unique differences that make for an interesting and challenging cast. Consider Mr. Brown's sixth-grade cast in the following scenario:

 ## Scenario: Mr. Brown—A Teacher Who Cares

Mr. Brown's self-contained sixth-grade class is composed of thirty children of approximately the same chronological age, but they are quite different. For example, according to his interpretation of reading achievement test scores and his informal observations, there are several children who are struggling with reading. Others are quite adept and appear to be reading well above grade level. In addition to these reading differences, some of Mr. Brown's students are English Language Learners. From the diversity his students display, Mr. Brown is beginning to wonder just what it means for a child to be "average."

Mr. Brown isn't interested in labeling children; he just wants to help them to the best of his ability. He recognizes that one way to do so is to learn as much as possible about them. He also recognizes that there are other professionals on the school staff who might be able to help him meet the learning needs of struggling students so that they can grow as readers.

Like Mr. Brown, we are more interested in helping children to maximize their full potential as readers than we are with labels, a view that is supported by the Council for Exceptional Children.[1] Remember that the goal of a diagnostic-reading and improvement program is to discover children's strengths and needs and to design appropriate instruction to address them. Put another way, children are always ready to learn something and our job as teachers is to figure out what that something is. Learning is what we're after. Let's be clear: "The success of education depends on adapting teaching to the individual differences among learners."

That being said, labels ARE applied to children. Being aware of these labels and how they are used is necessary for a better understanding of how to obtain support for children who need it. In this chapter, we examine and explain these labels. First, however, we take a look at the characteristics of children who carry the "good reader" label.

---

[1]Council for Exceptional Children. *What Every Special Educator Must Know: Ethics, Standards, and Guidelines for Special Educators,* 5th ed. (Upper Saddle River, NJ: Pearson/ Merrill/Prentice Hall, 2003.)

# CHAPTER OBJECTIVES

After reading this chapter, you should be able to . . .

- Discuss the differences between good and poor readers.
- Describe "good reader" attributes.
- Discuss reasons for determining a child's reading potential.
- Explain what is meant by *response to intervention.*
- Discuss problems associated with using intelligence test scores to determine reading potential.
- Describe listening capacity and how to assess for it.
- Describe ages and stages of literacy development.
- Describe English Language Learners.

# WHO ARE GOOD READERS?

We want all children to be good readers! However, this statement tells us little about what it is we want children to be able to do. What does it mean to be a "good" reader? Fortunately, there are specific characteristics we can use to answer this question. In Table 5.1, we provide a list of these behaviors and contrast them with those of "poor" readers.

## CHARACTERISTICS OF GOOD READERS

A close examination of this table shows that proficient readers have a large repertoire of strategies at their disposal that they use to help themselves better comprehend the text at hand. Therefore, the strategies they employ will shift depending on their background for the text and the manner in which the text is written. If they have read and heard stories, for instance, they most likely have an understanding of story structure (i.e., the pattern used to write stories). The text structure poses few if any difficulties, so they are able to read with greater ease.

In essence, then, good readers are active, purposeful, evaluative, thoughtful, strategic, persistent, and productive.[2] We explain each of these attributes in Table 5.2.

So now when you hear someone exclaim, "He is a good reader!" you will have a better understanding of what the exclamation means.

What do we do with the children who do not carry this label? Can we teach them the "good reader" characteristics so that they, too, can join the "good" reader club? Thanks to the work of several researchers who have designed metacognition training programs to explore this question, we can answer "yes." But the characteristics must be explicitly taught; for whatever reason, poor readers do not acquire them with little explicit instruction as do many of the good readers.

[2]Duke, N. K., and P. D. Pearson. Effective Practices for Developing Reading Comprehension. In *What Research Has to Say about Reading Instruction,* 3rd ed., eds. A.E. Fargstrup and S.J. Samuels. Newark, DE: International Reading Association, 2002. pp. 205–242.

**TABLE 5.1   Summary of Proficient and Less Proficient Reading Behaviors**

| *Proficient Reading Behaviors* | *Less Proficient Reading Behaviors* |
|---|---|
| Attempt to make what is read sound like language and make sense | Attempt to identify all of the words correctly |
| Monitor what is read for sense and coherence | Monitor what is read for correct letter/sound and word identification |
| Build meaning using the text, their purpose, and their background | Build meaning by attempting to identify the letters and words correctly |
| Utilize a variety of strategies when meaning breaks down: reread, rethink, read on and return if necessary, substitute, skip it, sound out, seek assistance, use text aids (pictures, graphs, charts), ignore it, stop reading | Utilize a limited range of strategies when meaning breaks down: sound out, skip it |
| Selectively sample the print; use a mixture of visual (print) and nonvisual (background) information | Utilize most of the visual (print) information |
| Use and integrate a variety of systems of language to create meaning | Rely heavily on graphemes, graphophonemics, and morphemes |
| Vary the manner in which texts are read based on purpose | Read all texts in a similar manner regardless of purpose |
| Typically correct one in three miscues | Typically correct one in twenty miscues |
| Attempt to correct miscues that affect meaning | Attempt to correct miscues that fail to resemble the word |
| "Chunk" what is read | Process letter-by-letter, which results in tunnel vision |

*Source:* Kucer, S. *Dimensions of Literacy: A Conceptual Base for Teaching Reading and Writing in School Settings,* 2nd ed. Mahwah, NJ: Erlbaum, 2005.

Another point that needs to be considered is one of potential. That is, children labeled good readers according to the characteristics cited above might not be performing to their potential. (See Chapter 4 for the many fac-

**TABLE 5.2    Explanations of Good Reader Attributes**

| Good Reader Attributes | Explanation |
| --- | --- |
| Active | Readers bring their own experiences to reading the text to construct meaning. They make predictions, make decisions such as what to read and reread, and when to slow down or speed up. |
| Purposeful | Readers have purposes in mind when they read a text. They then read with these purposes in mind. For example, they might choose to read for enjoyment or entertainment. At other times, they might read to discover specific details. |
| Evaluative | Readers evaluate what they are reading, asking themselves if the text is meeting their initial purposes for reading it. They also evaluate the quality of the text and whether it is of value. They react to the text both emotionally and intellectually. Readers also evaluate their interaction with others in different instructional groupings as well as their ability to function as both leaders and followers in the group. |
| Thoughtful | Readers think about the text selection before, during, and after reading. *Before reading*, they think about what they might already know. *During reading*, they think about how the current text relates to what they already know. *After reading*, they think about what the text offered and formulate their interpretations of it. |
| Strategic | Readers use specific strategies such as predicting, monitoring, and visualizing to ensure that they are comprehending the text. |
| Persistent | Readers keep reading a text even when it might be rather difficult if they feel that the text is helping them to accomplish a set purpose. |
| Productive | Readers are productive in more than one way. For instance, they bring their own experiences to the text at hand to construct or *produce* their understanding of it. Because they are engaged with reading, they are more productive in terms of the amount of reading they do. |

*Source*: Duke, N. K. and Pearson, P. D. "Effective Practices for Developing Reading Comprehension," in A. E. Fargstrup and S. J. Samuels, eds., *What Research Has to Say about Reading Instruction* 3rd ed., Newark, DE: International Reading Association, 2002. pp. 205–242.

tors that can affect reading performance.) Determining the student's reading potential now comes into focus, as do some labels. Reading disability is one such label. The definition provided in *The Literacy Dictionary* is commonly used to define reading disability: "reading achievement significantly below what could reasonably be expected of a person; a marked ability-achievement discrepancy."[3]

[3]Theodre L. Harris and Richard E. Hodges, eds. *The Literacy Dictionary*. (Newark, DE: International Reading Association), 1995, pp. 210.

# DYSLEXIA: A POINT OF VIEW

Learning to read requires much attention and practice. For some, learning to read appears effortless. For others, though, it requires tremendous effort! Those who struggle from the onset of instruction often lag behind their peers and, if their instruction is not accelerated, they frequently continue to find reading difficult in and out of school.

Given what we now know about the reading process and components of sound reading instruction, we find it disconcerting that many children seem to be having difficulty learning to read. Also unsettling is the fact that many of these same children are labeled "dyslexic."

According to Johnson, *dyslexia* originally "referred to the loss of ability to read following central nervous damage or dysfunction."[4] It was seen as a neurological problem. However, the term is sometimes used to describe just about any reading difficulty. The first drawback with using the term or label, then, is that so much ambiguity makes the term virtually useless.

A second complication with labeling children "dyslexic" is that many times assigning the label signifies the end of helping the child. In other words, the label serves as *the* reason the child is not succeeding—therefore all are relieved of responsibility! The result of this kind of thinking causes the third complication. That is, because the problem is seen to exist within the child rather than with the instruction being offered to the child, little if any accommodations that could potentially take care of the specific reading problem are provided. Yet the problem may reside with the instruction rather than with the child alone. If adaptations were made, the child just might succeed. There are early intervention programs such as Reading Recovery that appear to prove this point. As Marie Clay, the principal founder of Reading Recovery, once commented, "All we had to do was rearrange the teacher's talents, change the delivery conditions, and provide opportunities to succeed."[5]

Rather than labeling children with this or any other label, then, we believe, like Cathy Roller,[6] that we need to view children as unique individuals and accept the variability that their uniqueness brings about as normal. We then need to adjust instruction to make sure we are meeting the unique needs of students to the best of our abilities.

This is a tall order, indeed. Teaching is a complex behavior that requires knowledgeable, dedicated individuals willing to devote much time and energy on behalf of their students. Children deserve nothing less.

[4]Doris Johnson. *Dyslexia*. In *The Literacy Dictionary*, T. Harris & R. Hodges, eds. (Newark, DE: International Reading Association), 1995, pp. 64–65.

[5]Marie Clay, *Reading Recovery: A Guidebook for Teachers in Training*. (Portsmouth, NH: Heinemann 1993), pp. xiii–xiv.

[6]Cathy Roller, *Variability, not Disability: Struggling Readers in a Workshop Classroom,* (Newark, DE: International Reading Association, 1996).

# DETERMINING READING POTENTIAL

As we noted in Chapter 3, we can use three questions to guide our assessment and instruction: What do I want to know? Why do I want to know? How can I best discover this information? Let's take a look at each of these as they relate to assessing a student's reading potential.

> **What do I want to know?** In this instance, we want to know a student's reading potential, the level of proficiency a student should be achieving in reading if no problem exists.
>
> **Why do I want to know?** We want to make sure that the child is performing at his or her maximum ability and figure out why not if results show below-ability proficiency. Determining potential is a good first step. Those who are functioning below potential may have a reading disability and will need further diagnosis. Some of these children might need additional help from qualified specialists. Determining those who are eligible for additional instruction also helps teachers to fulfill legal requirements and to meet the rights of students and their families.[7]

### Special Note

In the past, we have said that eligible children are "reading disabled." However, given the current stance on labeling as established by the Council for Exceptional Children, we now understand that this label can be misleading and harmful. Here's what they have to say: "Words such as defective, disabled, retarded, impaired, disturbed, and disordered, when attached to children with special needs, are stigmatic labels that produce unfortunate results in both the children and in the community's attitudes toward the children."[8] Hence, saying "children who have reading disabilities" is more precise. ■

> **How can I best discover this information?** The question is easy, but the answer is a bit more complex. Here's why. Past practice has been to take a look at a student's achievement levels according to performance on a reading achievement test. This score was then compared to an intelligence test score, which most evaluators interpret to be an indication of the child's IQ. These two scores were then used to determine how large of a discrepancy existed by using one of many mathematical formulas developed by different reading researchers (e.g., Harris and Sipay, Bond and Tinker). The larger the discrepancy, the greater the need. However, this practice is now considered suspect for several reasons. McCormick lists the following four reasons:

1. There is a lack of agreement about what constitutes intelligence and the most appropriate ways for measuring it.
2. Some believe that the items on intelligence tests and the resultant scores

---

[7]John Venn. *Assessing Students with Special Needs*, 3rd ed. (Upper Saddle River, NJ: Merrill), 2004.

[8]Council for Exceptional Children, 2003.

only show how the individual is currently performing rather than the individual's potential intellectual functioning.

3. Not being able to read well appears to cause poor performance on IQ tests (even when little or no reading is required) because reading in and of itself is a cognitive process that calls on the learner to use various cognitive abilities.

4. Not all IQ tests are the same. Some require more verbal responses, whereas others require more nonverbal responses. Consequently, performance on different tests can yield disparate results. One might show a greater discrepancy than the other, yet this result might not be accurate.[9]

To this list we would add two additional reasons. First, the majority of intelligence tests call for a qualified examiner such as a school psychologist to administer, score, and interpret the results. Classroom teachers are not licensed to do so. Therefore, the use of an intelligence test score is beyond the classroom teacher's reach when trying to determine who might need specialized help with reading.

Second, the IQ discrepancy model is nearly obsolete. That is, the latest version of the Individuals with Disabilities Education Improvement Act (IDEIA), which was passed by Congress in 2004, specifies that it is no longer necessary to show a discrepancy in order to determine who has a learning problem (e.g., learning to read) that is severe enough to be classified as a learning disability. In its place is a process called *response to intervention*. Basically, this three-step process entails providing children who appear to be struggling with the best possible instruction and taking a look at how they perform under such conditions. This first round of instruction takes place in the classroom context and the classroom teacher provides the instruction. If the child makes little or no progress in comparison to his or her peers, the second step involves providing supplementary instruction, either individually or in a small group. The classroom teacher or another professional provides this instruction. If the child still makes little progress, additional tests are administered to determine if there is a specific learning disability. If there is, the child is placed in special education classes and given more intensive intervention.

*Intervention* is a key word here. Just as with the diagnostic-reading and improvement program we discuss in this text, identifying a problem early on and doing something to ameliorate it better ensures that students will continue to progress in reading. This is akin to what we call a *diagnostic pattern*. And, as you will see in Chapters 6, 7, and 8, there are numerous reading assessment techniques we can use to detect reading problems beginning in kindergarten. Each technique is accompanied by teaching suggestions that will assist you with planning instruction geared toward addressing the problem.

**Diagnostic pattern**
Consists of three steps: identification, appraisal, and diagnosis.

[9]Roller, C. *Variability, Not Disability: Struggling Readers in a Workshop Classroom.* Newark, DE: International Reading Association, 1996.

# WHAT IS A DIAGNOSTIC PATTERN?

**Identification**
Part of diagnostic pattern; the act of determining the student's present level of performance in word recognition and comprehension for screening purposes.

**Appraisal**
Part of diagnostic pattern; a student's present reading performance in relation to his or her potential.

Throughout this book we emphasize that appropriate instruction stems from and is interwoven with accurate and pertinent diagnostic information for each child in the regular classroom. We also stress that diagnosis is ongoing and is necessary for prevention as well as for improvement. In a diagnostic-reading and improvement program, the teacher is interested in determining the student's reading strengths and weaknesses, as well as the conditions causing them, as soon as possible so that any emerging reading difficulty can be nipped in the bud. To do this the teacher must first *identify* the student's present level of performance in word recognition and comprehension by using a variety of reading assessments. The teacher must then *appraise* the student's present level of reading performance in relation to his or her potential. The appraisal is done to determine if there is a discrepancy between the student's present reading performance and the student's reading potential. After appraisal, if a discrepancy exists between a student's present reading status and his or her reading expectancy, the teacher does extensive and intensive *diagnosis.* Step 3 is done to determine in detail the student's specific strengths and weaknesses, as well as to discover the specific conditions and abilities that underlie the student's performance in a particular reading area. Then the teacher must help that student to set attainable goals in the area. Identification, appraisal, and diagnosis are the three steps in a diagnostic pattern.[10]

# USING LISTENING CAPACITY TO ESTIMATE READING POTENTIAL

Early intervention makes a lot of sense, as do continuous assessment and excellent instruction. All of these are sure to help children read appropriate material for their age and ability. However, there might be some children who could do even better. That is, they have the potential to read at a higher level than their current performance indicates. And we really want them to perform to their highest potential. But if we are not going to use intelligence tests and the formulas mentioned above, how can we uncover this potential? We can use a listening comprehension measure (i.e., listening capacity), which is now considered the preferred way of assessing reading potential.[11] This measure provides a glance at what a student understands after listening to a text read aloud by the examiner. There are two distinct advantages for using this measure in place of an IQ test. First, classroom teachers can administer and score these assessments with relative ease. Second, listening comprehension is more directly

[10]The terms are adapted from Ruth Strang, *Diagnostic Teaching of Reading,* 2nd ed. (New York: McGraw-Hill, 1969).

[11]McCormick, S. *Instructing Students Who Have Literacy Problems,* 4th ed. Upper Saddle River, NJ: Pearson/Merrill/Prentice Hall, 2003.

related to reading than most IQ tests. A teacher can use the following steps to administer a listening comprehension test.

1. Secure an informal reading inventory such as the *Basic Reading Inventory.*[12] See Chapter 8 for further explanation regarding informal reading inventories. All inventories have graded passages you can use.
2. Read the directions about how to administer, score, and interpret the listening comprehension assessment.
3. Set aside the necessary time to individually administer the assessment to those you want to test. Provide as much privacy as possible so that the student can attend to your reading without distractions.
4. As directed by the author of the informal reading inventory you are using, select the starting passage and read it to the student. Ask the comprehension questions provided for the story or have the student retell the story. All of the student responses are oral rather than written.
5. Use the criteria specified in the informal reading inventory manual to determine the child's level of performance.
6. Continue reading passages that are increasingly difficult until you reach the point where the responses indicate a "just right" level. Again, the guidelines provided in the informal reading inventory will help you to establish cut-off points.
7. The last passage the student is able to respond to with relative ease denotes the child's potential.

Once the student's potential has been ascertained, the next step is to compare the score obtained on the listening capacity test with a score on a standardized achievement test. For example, Autumn is in third grade. Her reading test score leads us to conclude that she is reading at a third-grade level. This is material that she has read herself. However, when listening to another person read, she is able to perform well through the fifth-grade level. Our conclusion is that her potential reading level is fifth grade. As you can see, according to this measure, there is a two-year discrepancy between where she is actually reading and where she should be reading. Further testing is needed to determine why this is the case. She might have a reading disability even though she appears to be reading at grade level. There might be something getting in the way of Autumn's performing at her potential, and further testing will help us to determine what this might be. There are many different assessment techniques we can use to gain a better understanding (see Chapters 6, 7, and 8), which leads us back to asking our three ubiquitous questions: What do I want to know? Why do I want to know? Which test will help me discover this information?

An important consideration regarding potential as described above is that it is an estimate or an approximation of a person's potential. In a sense, we can never really ascertain hidden potential. We simply cannot know for certain how

---

[12]Johns, J. *Basic Reading Inventory,* 9th ed. Dubuque, IA: Kendall/Hunt, 2005.

far an individual might excel over a lifetime and we want to create an atmosphere that conveys this belief. We can, however, make an estimate based on our interpretation of student performance on different assessment measures, and this estimate can put us in a better position to help the child. Sometimes this help can come from classroom teachers and at other times, the help needs to come from a professional who has devoted specialized study in a given area (e.g., reading, learning disabilities, or gifted and talented).

 ## Scenario: Who Is Underachieving in Reading?

Ms. Nibur wants to find out as much as she can about her fourth-grade students. As a result, even though it was extremely time-consuming, she had each student read individually to her and she also administered a listening comprehension measure to each student. Now that she has all of this data, she is trying to figure out who might need further testing and who might need the most help. In other words, she wants to know if anyone is underachieving in reading. Based on what you have read so far, see if you can help Ms. Nibur determine which of her students listed below should concern her the most.

| Name | Instructional Reading Level | Listening Comprehension Level |
|------|------|------|
| Zach | 2nd grade | 6th grade |
| Ming | 4th grade | 4th grade |
| Sally | 3rd grade | 3rd grade |

## AGES AND STAGES OF LITERACY DEVELOPMENT

Reading ability continues to develop throughout life. For that matter, so do writing, speaking and, hopefully, listening abilities. In fact, we might say that reading ability grows with exposure to oral language and print. In general, children at given ages share common characteristics in terms of reading and writing abilities. Different reading researchers and educators cast these characteristics into stages of growth (e.g., Chall, 1983; International Reading Association and the National Association for the Education of Young Children, 1998; Cooper & Kiger, 2005) to help teachers like Mr. Brown featured in our opening scenario determine who is displaying age-appropriate reading behaviors.[13] Knowing some of these behaviors can also be extremely helpful in trying to determine who might need further assistance with learning to speak, listen, read, and write.

[13]Jean Chall. *Stages of Reading Development*. (New York: McGraw-Hill), 1983. International Reading Association and the National Association for the Education of Young Children. *Learning to Read and Write: Developmentally Appropriate Practices for Young Children. The Reading Teacher*, 52: 193–216, 1998. Cooper, J. D., and N. Kiger. *Literacy Assessment: Helping Teachers Plan Instruction,* 2nd ed. Boston: Houghton Mifflin, 2005.

Table 5.3 shows stages of literacy growth and some of their descriptors. Keep in mind that stages can overlap and that students rarely display every characteristic before they move into another stage. Many of the characteristics stay the same from stage to stage, but they become more sophisticated. Then, too, just like any of us learning something new, there can be plateaus. So, while the table shows a neat linear process that happens in a smooth waltz-like tempo, it is anything but that. Its tempo is more halting at times, similar to a cha-cha.

# ENGLISH LANGUAGE LEARNERS

As our society becomes increasingly diverse, so do our classrooms. And this diversity can sometimes take us by surprise. Janet, a fourth-grade teacher with a class of twenty-seven students, twelve of whom are English Language Learners, says it best:

> Before I had my own class, I had this abstract idea that all children will learn because I know how to teach. What I didn't know was that not only is each child different, but each child's social and learning situation is different. It is impossible for anyone who has never been in a teaching position to know how difficult, demanding, and rewarding teaching can be. As so many people sit back and judge teachers and teaching methods and programs, they don't have any idea of what it's like to look in children's eyes and see the confusion and dismay they face when learning English and trying to make sense of what they are reading.

**English language learners**
Children whose home language is not English.

*English Language Learners (ELL)* are those children whose home language is not English. Nonetheless, there are several terms that are often used when talking about children who speak languages other than English. These include English as a Second Language (ESL), English as a Foreign Language (EFL), Limited English Proficient (LEP), English for Speakers of Other Languages (ESOL), and Bilingual (i.e., use of two languages). We use the term ELL because it is more accurate. That is, in some cases, English might be their third or fourth language! So they really are English Language Learners.

There are three types of English Language Learners, so even within this group there is much diversity. In Table 5.4 we show the types of English Language Learners and provide the characteristics of each.

Many of the assessment techniques and teaching strategies noted throughout this book are appropriate for English Language Learners. However, because there are some differences among the way these children might use grammar and phonology (see Appendix C), some accommodations will need to be made. Instead of penalizing children for what might appear to be a mistake in oral reading, for example, you can consult the charts in Appendix C to gain a better understanding of why the child spoke as he or she did. Some researchers maintain that when children make a substitution using their native language, they are showing a very high level of learning. That is, they have actually looked at the English term and translated it into their own language and then read the word aloud.

**TABLE 5.3    Stages and Descriptors of Literacy Growth**

| *Stage* | *Brief Description* | *Sample Benchmarks* |
|---|---|---|
| *Early Emergent*<br><br>Typically before kindergarten | Viewed as a foundation on which children develop oral language and a curiosity about print. | • Attends to read-alouds<br>• Uses oral language for different purposes<br>• Likes playing with movable or magnetic letters<br>• Knows several nursery rhymes<br>• Uses paper and writing utensil to attempt writing |
| *Emergent Literacy*<br><br>Typically kindergarten; may overlap into the beginning of first grade | Children show more interest in all aspects of literacy. | • Retains oral directions<br>• Enjoys tongue twisters<br>• Knows some concepts about print such as book parts, word, how to handle a book<br>• Recognizes and names most letters<br>• Shows evidence of being phonemically aware<br>• Can write own name<br>• Uses some punctuation |
| *Beginning Reading and Writing*<br><br>Typically first grade; continues into second and third grade for some. | Oral language facility expands. Children develop word analysis skills, start to show fluency in reading, and increased understanding of many words. Their writing begins to follow print conventions. | • Uses increased oral vocabulary<br>• Participates in a discussion<br>• Recognizes and names all letters in any order<br>• Identifies many sight words<br>• Uses phonics to determine word pronunciation<br>• Uses a variety of comprehension strategies<br>• Reads and retells stories<br>• Enjoys writing<br>• Uses word processing |
| *Almost Fluent Reading and Writing*<br><br>Typically begins at end of second grade and continues into fourth or fifth grade | Children grow in their understanding of literacy. Oral language shows increased vocabulary, writing is more frequent, and silent reading increases. | • Grows in use of standard English<br>• Uses new oral vocabulary<br>• Uses context to determine word meaning<br>• Self-corrects<br>• Reads independently<br>• Reads for many purposes<br>• Begins learning research skills<br>• Writes for many purposes<br>• Writing conventions show growth<br>• Chooses to write in free time |

**TABLE 5.3** (*continued*)

| Stage | Brief Description | Sample Benchmarks |
|---|---|---|
| *Fluent Reading and Writing*<br><br>Typically begins in fourth grade and continues through life. | Children use reading and writing for a variety of purposes. The majority of skills are acquired and used as appropriate. | • Listens to presentations with understanding<br>• Uses oral language for a variety of purposes<br>• Seldom needs help with word recognition<br>• Uses several comprehension strategies<br>• Enjoys reading<br>• Writes for many purposes<br>• Edits own writing<br>• Experiments with different writing forms |

Adapted from Cooper & Kiger. *Literacy Assessment: Helping Teachers Plan Instruction.* Boston, MA: Houghton Mifflin, 2005.

**TABLE 5.4** **Types of English Language Learners**

| Type of English Language Learner | Characteristics |
|---|---|
| Newly arrived, with adequate schooling | • Recent arrivals (less than five years in United States)<br>• Adequate schooling in native country<br>• Will soon catch up academically<br>• May still score low on standardized tests given in English |
| Newly arrived, with limited formal schooling | • Recent arrivals (less than five years in United States)<br>• Interrupted or limited schooling in native country<br>• Limited native language literacy<br>• Below grade level in math<br>• Poor academic achievement |
| Long-term English learner | • Seven or more years in the United States<br>• Below grade level in reading and writing<br>• Mismatch between student perception of achievement and actual grades<br>• Some get adequate grades, but score low on tests<br>• Have had ESL or bilingual instruction, but no consistent program |

*Source:* Yvonne S. Freeman & David E. Freeman. *Closing the Achievement Gap: How to Reach Limited Formal Schooling and Long-Term English Learners.* Portsmouth, NH: Heineman, 2002. Used by permission.

As with any children you encounter, English Language Learners have strengths and needs and, as with all other students, we need to determine what these are so that we can better help them advance in their ability to acquire English—while at the same time valuing their other language(s). In fact, English Language Learners bring much with them, just like all students.

# UNDERACHIEVING IN SCHOOL: A POINT OF VIEW

Almost all reading standards begin with the phrase *all children will read at grade level* by the end of third or the beginning of fourth grade. The term *all* that most state education departments use in relation to their standards is troublesome. Not *all* children will read at, nor should they be reading at, grade level.

The confusion probably lies in the phrase "equal educational opportunity for all." Equal educational opportunity for all is good, but it doesn't mean that all children will achieve the same. If all students are expected to pass high-level reading achievement tests, then we should be looking at minimum-standard assessments, rather than high-level ones.

Students who are academically highly able will be underachieving if they are only at grade level; and if struggling readers, who normally score well below grade level were to score at grade level on reading achievement tests, they would not be considered struggling readers.

Not everyone is the same. Individual differences prevail. However, today many people act as if it is undemocratic or politically incorrect to recognize that individual differences exist among students. Consequently, the term *all* has been consistently used when speaking about students in relation to achievement.

For a while in the 1980s and 1990s, many educators and the public disparaged honors and advanced placement classes. The feeling was that all students should take these classes. Interestingly, the tide seems to have changed somewhat, because some school systems are actually beginning tracking at first grade. Based on a pre-reading assessment given at the end of kindergarten, children in some school systems are being placed in fast, medium, or slow reading classes.

Tracking in the primary grades does not make sense. It is too early to divide children according to ability levels based on a pre-reading test in kindergarten, even if it is combined with input from teachers. Tracking children at a very early age puts those who do poorly at an unfair disadvantage by labeling them too soon. On the other hand, within-class flexible grouping of students beginning in first grade is a very good practice. (See "Teacher as Organizer and Manager" in Chapter 2.) Also, student self-tracking in the upper grades when students, because of their precocious academic ability, opt to take honors classes and/or enroll in advanced placement classes, makes a great amount of sense.

## SUMMARY

In this chapter, we presented and explained characteristics of good readers. While labels are still used to categorize children, we pointed out that labels do nothing to help children learn to read. We need to figure out what they know and need to know to advance as readers. Another explanation had to do with why it can be important to determine reading potential, and how to best accomplish it. We cautioned that *estimate* is a key word when talking about reading potential because we can never truly know an individual's true potential. We also cautioned against using intelligence test scores when trying to ascertain a student's reading potential.

Response to intervention was explained, as was a diagnostic pattern. Both suggest guidelines that can be used to help students who struggle with reading. There are stages of literacy development that children seem to move through; these were shown along with some descriptors.

Teaching means working with diverse learners. Included in this mix are English Language Learners. We provided a definition of English Language Learners, along with some other terms that are used when talking about children who are learning English. A major point throughout the chapter was that each child is unique and we should think of this uniqueness as normal rather than as a disability.

## CHAPTER 5 KEY CONCEPTS

- Differences are sure to exist in classrooms, and they cannot be viewed as deficits.
- There are specific characteristics that can be used to define a "good reader."
- Proficient and less proficient readers exhibit different reading behaviors.
- Dyslexia is a term that causes much confusion. There are many problems associated with using the term when talking about the best ways to help children deal with reading problems.
- Determining a student's reading potential can help the teacher to see who might need additional reading help. However, because we can never truly know inner potential, the best we can do is make an estimate of it with the help of a listening capacity measure.
- There are many problems with using intelligence test scores to determine reading potential.
- A diagnostic pattern consists of identification, appraisal, and diagnosis.
- Children advance through different stages on their way to becoming proficient readers.
- English Language Learners are individuals whose home language is not English.

## SUGGESTIONS FOR THOUGHT QUESTIONS AND ACTIVITIES

1. The parents of one of your students wants to know if you consider their child to be a good reader. What will you say?
2. Explain the differences between proficient and less proficient reading behaviors to a group of fellow colleagues who have invited you to be a guest speaker.
3. The principal asks you to explain to a group of concerned citizens how the determination of reading potential has changed. Prepare your explanation.
4. Construct a workshop session focused on how children change as readers.
5. Some of the teachers you work with are having difficulty understanding the difference between the terms Second Language Learner and English Language Learner. How will you help to clear up the confusion?

# INTERNET ACTIVITIES

Choose a search engine and search for websites related to something in the chapter that you would like to research. Select one website from the search that helps you gain an understanding of it. Print out an artifact that helps to show your understanding. (Be sure to identify both the search engine you used and the website you selected.)

# SELECTED BIBLIOGRAPHY

Clay, M. *Reading Recovery: A Guidebook for Teachers in Training.* Portsmouth, NH: Heinemann, 1993.

# Instruments and Techniques for the Assessment and Diagnosis of Reading Performance

# 6

# Using Alternative Assessment Techniques across the Grades

## Scenario: Teachers Talking

Read the following conversation overheard in the faculty lounge:

*MS. ANDERSON:* I don't know what to do with Billy. His behavior is driving me crazy.

*MR. JOHNSON:* Why? What does he do?

*MS. ANDERSON:* What doesn't he do? He's forever getting up from his seat. He can't seem to sit still for a moment. He's always disturbing his neighbor. If there is any commotion or problem in the room, you can be sure that Billy is the cause of it.

*MR. JOHNSON:* Have you spoken to Billy's parents about his behavior?

*MS. ANDERSON:* Yes, but they say that they do not see the same kind of behavior at home, so they feel that it's something related to school. I've just about had it.

*MR. JOHNSON:* I've had Billy in my class, and I remember him as a pretty bright boy. I think that you should try to observe when Billy starts to act up. I know that I had a child who acted just as Billy does, and I thought that she was misbehaving all the time, just to make my life miserable. Fortunately, I had just finished a course in reading diagnosis, and the professor had discussed the uses of observation techniques to learn about the behavior of students. I decided to try it, and I was surprised at the results! Using observation techniques made me aware of how unfounded my statements about Susan were. Let's go to my room, and I'll show you what I did.

What do you think Mr. Johnson showed Ms. Anderson? Make a few guesses before continuing to read.

In Chapter 3 we explored many terms associated with tests, measurement, and evaluation. The primary focus was on different types of norm-referenced and criterion-referenced tests. We emphasized that teachers using a diagnostic-reading and improvement program must be knowledgeable about many different tests in order to better select a given test related to a specific purpose. We proposed three questions that teachers need to ask related to assessment: What do I want to know? Why do I want to know? How can I best discover the information?

These three questions remain relevant to this chapter. However, our focus is on using alternative ways to assess reading behaviors regardless of grade level. As you will see, there are several options that can be used across grade levels. Although they may appear to be less structured than those presented in Chapter 3, they are of value nonetheless. Once again, we emphasize that the specific purpose is what guides our choice of which reading assessment measures to use. In Table 6.1 we provide an overview of alternative assessment techniques.

# CHAPTER OBJECTIVES

After reading the chapter, you should be able to:

- Discuss the differences among alternative, authentic, and performance assessment.
- Describe portfolios.
- Explain how teachers can use portfolios as part of the diagnostic-reading and improvement program.
- Explain what is meant by *portfolio assessment.*
- Explain what is meant by *direct observation.*
- Discuss when teachers should make generalizations about students' behavior.
- Describe how observation can be made more objective.
- Discuss the kinds of behavior that teachers should record.
- Explain what checklists are.
- Describe some of the various kinds of checklists.
- Explain how a rating scale can be used with a checklist.
- Explain what is meant by an *anecdotal record.*
- Discuss the advantages of informal student interviews.
- Explain what is meant by *interest inventories.*
- Give some examples of interest inventories.
- Explain what is meant by *projective techniques.*
- Discuss the uses of projective techniques in the classroom.
- Describe the type of projective techniques suitable for teachers to use in the classroom.
- Explain some of the purposes of reading autobiographies.

**TABLE 6.1 Alternative Assessment Techniques**

| *What Do I Want to Know?* | *Why Do I Want to Know?* | *How Can I Best Discover?* |
|---|---|---|
| Do the children use what they know about reading regardless of what they read? | To show competence in reading, children need to show that they can use what they have learned. I need to see if they can do this, and if they cannot, I need to determine why. | Performance Assessment (p. 111)<br>Project (p. 111) |
| Do children show growth over time? | Children continue to grow as readers and I need to provide evidence of that growth. I want to be able to show the kind of progress the children are making. | Portfolio (pp. 113–115) |
| How do children perform in a variety of contexts? | Watching children as they perform a variety of reading-related tasks is an excellent way for me to see firsthand what they are able to do. I can also get a hunch of what they do well and what might need additional work. I can use these observations as a way of selecting additional reading assessments that will help me to better understand the children. | Direct Observation (pp. 115–116) |

*(continued)*

**TABLE 6.1**   *(continued)*

| *What Do I Want to Know?* | *Why Do I Want to Know?* | *How Can I Best Discover?* |
|---|---|---|
| How can I remember everything I see when observing? | Watching children can help me to learn more about them, but I simply cannot remember everything. I also need a way to document what I have actually observed as a way of proving to interested others that I have detected a pattern of behavior that sheds light on an given student's performance. | Anecdotal Record (pp. 116–119) |
| What specific behaviors do the children show when they complete reading tasks? | There are a variety of behaviors that children need to exhibit on their way to becoming accomplished readers. I need to determine which they show and those they need to learn, and be able to document this in a quick and clean way. I can then use the results to plan appropriate instruction. | Checklists (pp. 120–121) |
| How do the children view reading? | Faulty perceptions of what it means to read can inhibit reading growth. Uncovering these ideas can help me to see which are correct and those that need to be added to or altered. | Informal Student Interview (pp. 125–130) |
| What reading strategies do children think they use when they are reading? | Good readers use a variety of strategies to assist them as they try to comprehend a text. Relying on one or two strategies to the exclusion of others can prevent growth. I need to know those strategies that readers use and do not use so that I can help all children develop a full array of strategies. | Informal Student Interview (pp. 125–130) |
| What do children like to read? | We are more prone to read if we are interested in the reading material. Identifying the children's interests can help me to select texts for instruction and inclusion in the classroom library. I can also use interests to group children in different ways, making it possible for them to work with a variety of peers. | Interest Inventories (pp. 133–134) |
| How do children feel about themselves as readers? | Feelings of self-efficacy play a big part in reading success. I need to know how students feel about themselves as readers. Then I can identify children who view themselves as failures and work to help them gain confidence as competent readers. | Projective Strategies (p. 132) Reading Autobiography (pp. 137–138) |
| What kind of attitudes do the children have about reading? | Attitude has a big impact on reading. Identifying (attitudes) will help me see if I need to help a child develop a more positive outlook, which will make reading a more enjoyable experience. Children with a positive attitude are more likely to attempt reading. | Primary Reading Survey (p. 135) Reading Attitude Survey for Grades 3 and up (p. 136) |

# ALTERNATIVE, AUTHENTIC, AND PERFORMANCE ASSESSMENT: WHAT'S THE DIFFERENCE?

**Alternative assessment**
Def to come

**Authentic assessment**
Def to come

**Performance assessment**
Def to come

Three terms are often used to explain ways to assess reading: alternative, authentic, and performance assessment. *Alternative assessment* is the use of evaluations other than standardized tests to achieve "direct, 'authentic' assessment of student performance on important learning tasks."[1] This term is a very broad and includes both *authentic assessment* and *performance assessment*.

*Authentic assessment* (sometimes called *naturalistic assessment*) helps teachers to measure students' "important abilities using procedures that simulate the application of these abilities to real-life situations."[2] Therefore, a magazine article or a children's literature title might be used to assess how well students read different types of text. To assess students' ability to use phonics to decode words, individual students might be given a class roster such as the one shown in Chapter 7 and asked to read the names aloud while the examiner makes notes about what the child says in relation to the actual names.

*Performance assessment* is often used as a synonym for authentic assessment because it calls on the learner to show understanding by completing tasks like those "required in the instructional environment."[3] These demonstrations are sometimes documented in a *portfolio* (i.e., a selection of student's work meant to show learning progress) or by having students complete a project. For both portfolios and projects, a scoring system (i.e., rubric) is used to help teachers determine how well students have achieved specified standards. The *rubric* is a set of criteria that places a value on students' performance in certain areas. Students are usually given these rubrics—or invited to help construct one—in advance of the performance task so that they can see how they are going to be evaluated. They can use this rubric as a guide when preparing for the performance. Figure 6.1 shows a sample rubric. As you can see, certain criteria are established, but the teacher must still determine how well students have met the criteria. In other words, rubrics can help to reduce subjectivity, but they cannot completely do away with it. In fact, we would say that rubrics are "objective subjectivity."

As with norm-referenced and criterion-referenced measures, there are some limitations associated with performance assessments. First, they can be costly both in terms of time and human resources because performance assessments are individually administered. Teachers who videotape students' perfor-

---

[1]Barrentine, Shelby J., and Sandra M. Stokes, eds. *Reading Assessment: Principles and Practices for Elementary Teachers,* 2nd ed. Newark, DE: International Reading Association, 2005. Bratcher, Suzanne, with Linda Ryan. *Evaluating Children's Writing: A Handbook of Grading Choices for Classroom Teachers, 2nd ed.* Mahwah, NJ: Erlbaum, 2004.

[2]Slam, Robert E. *Educational Psychology: Theory & Practice,* 6th ed. (Boston: Allyn Bacon, 2000), p. 469.

[3]Easley, Shirley-Dale, and Kay Mitchell. *Portfolios Matter. What, Where, When, Why and How to Use Them.* Portland, ME: Stenhouse, 2003.

FIGURE 6.1 **Rubric for Writing to Learn**

| Criteria / Quality | 3 | 2 | 1 |
|---|---|---|---|
| Ideas & Content | Clear and focused. Provides several relevant examples from the text and own experiences. Shows own thinking about the topic. | Beginning to develop the paper. Some examples. Own thinking is starting to become evident but full explanation is lacking. | No real focus. Few examples are cited and original thinking is not evident. |
| Organization | Paper written with an introduction, body, and conclusion. Written in format as explained in class. | Paper has two of the three: introduction, body, conclusion. Written in the format as explained in class. | Paper has one of the three: introduction, body, conclusion. The format explained in class is not used. |
| Voice | Speaks to the reader; shows attention to audience. | Beginning to speak to the reader but still rather general; not always aware of audience. | Passive; writing appears distant; lack of attention to audience. |
| Print Conventions | Makes use of all print conventions: spelling, grammar, punctuation. | Most print conventions are used but occasional misspellings and incorrect grammar and/or punctuation are evident. | Little attention to print conventions as evidenced by misspelled words, incorrect grammar, and/or misuse of punctuation. |
| Legibility | Neat - easy to read. One side of paper is used and there are no crossouts. | Semi-legible - can be read but takes some effort. One side of paper is used; occasional crossouts. | Sloppy - hard to read. Both sides of the paper are used and there are several crossouts. |
| Totals | _____ | _____ | _____ |

_____ ÷5 = _____ (Total earned for this assignment)

mances for further analysis can spend enormous amounts of time on each assessment. Second, some students might not perform at their best when others are watching. Third, teachers must have excellent classroom management skills because the performance assessment activity can take the teacher away from the rest of the class. Students need to be able to function independently while the teacher is working on the assessments.

Nonetheless, like norm-referenced and criterion-referenced measures, performance assessments are an excellent way to learn about students' reading behaviors, and they must be used in the type of diagnostic-reading and improvement program we describe and explain in this text. They can inform instruction daily. As a result of watching students complete a task, we can note strengths and needs and design tomorrow's instruction accordingly. Like norm-referenced and criterion-referenced measures, performance assessment is based on a set of assumptions, which include:

1. Learners are active participants.
2. Ongoing evaluation and teacher guidance occur simultaneously.
3. Both the end product and the means of arriving there (i.e., process) are important.
4. Demonstrated growth and learning need to be applauded.
5. Many sources of evidence (i.e., a body of evidence) needs to be collected over time.
6. The performance must be interpreted to note students' strengths and needs and both should be used to plan appropriate instruction.
7. Performance assessment can be collaborative, which means that others, including students, can be informants on the learning process.

## PORTFOLIOS AND PORTFOLIO ASSESSMENT

**Portfolio**
A storage system that represents samples of students' reading and writing over a period of time.

**Portfolio assessment**
Material in a portfolio is evaluated in some way.

Many educators have promoted portfolios as a way to enhance students' reading and writing, and today portfolios are used for a variety of purposes. However, confusion sometimes exists concerning the concepts of portfolios and portfolio assessment.

*Portfolios* are primarily a storage system that represents samples of students' reading and writing over a period of time. *Portfolio assessment* deals with some form of evaluation. Portfolio assessment takes place when what has been stored in the portfolio is deemed ready for evaluation in some way. This evaluation is often initiated by the student and usually includes not only self-evaluation but also teacher and peer evaluation. For the evaluation to be effective, the students and teachers must be aware of the criteria used for the assessment.

Portfolios can be a powerful tool for reading diagnosis because they provide teachers with an ongoing record of their students' reading and writing behavior; however there are several questions that need to be asked and answered in order to get the most from using portfolios (see Figure 6.2).

Portfolios do not give students the reading and writing skills they need to become good readers and writers. They help teachers gain an idea of the kinds of skills students have and need. A close examination can help teachers to design appropriate instruction that will increase student learning.

The use of portfolios can give students more decision-making power. In this sense, they can give more "ownership" to students. They can also be a good way for students, teachers, and parents to see a progression of the students' learning over a period of time.

**FIGURE 6.2 Portfolio Checklist**

The following questions are those you may wish to pose to yourself as you go about implementing portfolios. Remember that more than one item may be "checked" to answer each question. Also note that your ideas are also important! These are **suggestions!**

**How will the portfolio be used?**
_____ for student self-reflection
_____ as part of regular school evaluation/report card
_____ at parent conferences
_____ in IEP meetings
_____ in communicating to next year's teacher(s)
_____ in curricular planning
_____ in acknowledging students' accomplishments

**How will the portfolio be organized?**
_____ for finished pieces only from several subject areas
_____ to show progress from first idea to final copy
_____ to show sample of a week/month/year's work
_____ "best" work only
_____ group work included

**How will the items in the portfolio be arranged?**
_____ chronologically
_____ by student: from worst to best (reasons stated for each)
_____ by teacher: from worst to best (reasons stated for each)
_____ from beginning of idea to final product
_____ by subject area

**What procedures will be used to place items in the portfolio?**
_____ select specific times for pulling student work
_____ show students how to select items
_____ pull items that meet established criteria
_____ random

**What will the portfolio look like?**
_____ two pieces of posterboard stapled or taped together
_____ box or other container (e.g., milk crate with a hanging file for each student)
_____ scrapbook
_____ manila folder or some other large envelope
_____ CD-ROM or DVD

**Who will do the evaluating?**
_____ teacher
_____ several teachers
_____ student self-evaluation
_____ peer evaluation
_____ parent evaluation

***How will the portfolio be evaluated?***    *(continued)*

\_\_\_\_\_ number of entries

\_\_\_\_\_ use of benchmarks or standards

\_\_\_\_\_ degree of self-reflection

\_\_\_\_\_ demonstrated improvement from past performances

\_\_\_\_\_ achievement of preset goals (student, teacher, and/or school)

\_\_\_\_\_ combination of products, perceptions, reflections

*Source:* Tom Armstrong. *Multiple Intelligence in the Classroom.* Alexandria, VA: Association for the Supervision of Curriculum Development (ASCD), 1994.

## THE USES OF OBSERVATION

Direct observation is an essential part of any reading program, and it is especially helpful in diagnosing reading strengths and needs. Observation is also useful for evaluation because it helps teachers become aware of students' attitudes and interests. It is one thing for students to say that they enjoy reading, but quite another to actually read. Through observation, teachers can observe many reading-related behaviors such as whether students are voluntarily choosing to read in their free time, and how they approach silent reading, oral reading, selecting books, completing assignments, and writing in response to reading. Most often, the best method to determine whether students have learned something is to observe whether they are actually using what they have been taught. Moreover, watching children in a variety of contexts reveals additional information not provided by other assessment measures.[4]

### MAKING OBSERVATIONS OBJECTIVE

**Observation**
A technique that helps teachers collect data about students' behavior.

*Observation* is a technique; it is a means for collecting data. For observations to be of value, teachers must be as objective as possible and avoid making premature generalizations about a student's behavior. For example, by observing that Sharon on one or two occasions is reading mystery stories, Sharon's teacher might conclude that Sharon likes mysteries. This may be so, but it may be that she is just trying them out. Sharon may actually like only a few mystery writers, and she may read only one or two a year. Here are some suggestions on how to make observations as objective and useful as possible:

1. Use checklists and anecdotal records (observed behavior without interpretations) to record observations (see next section).
2. Observe the student over an extended period of time before making any inferences about the student's behavior.
3. Avoid projecting feelings or attitudes onto the student's behavior.
4. Use observations in conjunction with other measurement techniques.

[4]J. Choate and L. Miller, "Curricular Assessment and Programming," in J. Choate, J. Bennett, B. Enright, L. Miller, J. Poteet, and T. Raledy, *Assessing and Programming Basic Curriculum Skills* (Boston: Allyn & Bacon, 1987), pp. 35–50.

5. Make sure that only observed behavior is recorded and record it immediately or as soon as possible.
6. Look for a pattern of behavior before making any inferences about behavior.
7. Recognize that checklists and anecdotal records do not reveal the cause(s) of the observed behavior(s); they only help to identify patterns of behavior from which one can try to deduce the existence of possible strengths and needs.
8. Do not oversimplify a student's observed behavior.
9. Date observations.

As valuable and powerful as observation is, it can seem overwhelming. There are so many skills needed to observe accurately that we hardly know where to begin. For example, oral reading can help us to observe much about a child's reading ability. Questions such as the following can guide the observation:

Does the child read for meaning?
What does the child do when meaning is not maintained?
How well can the child retell what was read?
Does the reader read with a sense of meaning, expression, and fluency?

But how can a teacher focus on all questions for all children in a class in one observation? It is no wonder that many teachers feel overwhelmed by the task.

Our suggestion is: Less is more. That is, rather than trying to use all questions at once, choose the question that best fits your purpose. What is it that you want to know? Once you have determined this, you can record your observations on a form such as the one shown in Figure 6.3

# ANECDOTAL RECORDS

**Anecdotal record**
A record of observed behavior over a period of time.

Another way to lessen any anxiety related to observation is to use *anecdotal records,* which record *observed behavior* as objectively as possible. When recording observed behavior, make every attempt to put down exactly what has taken place *as soon as possible.* The date and time of the incident should be recorded, and the interpretation of the observed behavior may be written; however, the teacher's interpretation or possible explanation for the student's behavior should be put in brackets or set off in some way to avoid confusion with the actual observed behavior. Recording the observed behavior and observing the student over an extended period of time before making any hypotheses about the cause or causes for the behavior is best. Observations over an extended period of time and an analysis of them are likely to reveal a pattern of behavior. Figure 6.4 shows one example of an anecdotal record.

## DETERMINING THE INFORMATION TO BE RECORDED

What information should be recorded? This is a difficult question to answer, and as already stated, is often overwhelming for the teacher. As a result, anecdotal information sometimes consists of unusual observed behavior. However, recording common behaviors can also be of help. Consider the following scenario.

## Scenario: Mr. Jackson Checks and Writes

Mr. Jackson has a reading checklist for each student, and after each reading lesson and at other appropriate times, he checks off what he has observed. To supplement his checklist, Mr. Jackson also employs anecdotal information. Whenever he notices anything unusual, he records the observed behavior. For example, yesterday, Joshua started a fight with his best friend, and then for the rest of the day, he refused to do any work. Mr. Jackson made note of this.

Mr. Jackson also observed and noted that Joshua rested his head on his desk during reading.

1/9 Joshua puts head on desk—reading period
1/13 Joshua puts head on desk—reading period
1/16 Joshua puts head on desk—reading period
1/20 Joshua puts head on desk—reading period
1/23 Joshua puts head on desk—reading period
1/27 Joshua puts head on desk—reading period

Joshua's behavior of putting his head on the desk has become such a normal occurrence that Mr. Jackson could have overlooked it. Only by recording when Joshua put his head on the desk could Mr. Jackson see that it was always during a reading period. By recording the dates, Mr. Jackson could check to see what kinds of reading lessons were involved. It may be that Joshua was tired or sleepy, but it is most unlikely. It is more probable that by checking further, Mr. Jackson will find that Joshua is bored because the work is too easy for him or that he is frustrated because the work is too hard for him. It may be that Joshua cannot do sustained silent reading because of an eye problem. Joshua's resting behavior may be related to many factors. The point is that Mr. Jackson would not be aware of these problems had he not recorded what appeared to be "common" behavior.

Exact guidelines cannot be given about what should or should not be recorded. The focus of observation should be: "What do I want to know?" However, alert teachers who are aware of the individual differences of the students in their classes will recognize those situations that warrant recording.

Here are some examples:

1. Susan always seems to want to go to the lavatory. Record when she goes and the frequency. It may be a physiological or emotional problem, or it may be that she wants to "escape" from a certain situation.
2. Michael is always causing disruptions in class. Record when Michael acts up to see whether there is a pattern. It may be that causing disruptions is Michael's way of avoiding reading. What is he avoiding? Is he bored or is he frustrated? Is something bothering him?
3. Maria starts walking around the room and chatting to other children who want to finish doing their reading. Record when Maria does this, and try to figure out why. Is she avoiding reading? If so, why?

**FIGURE 6.3   Observation Guide**

**Class Observation Form**

Focal Question: _____

Date: _____

| Name of Student | Notes |
|---|---|
|  |  |
|  |  |
|  |  |
|  |  |
|  |  |
|  |  |
|  |  |
|  |  |
|  |  |
|  |  |
|  |  |
|  |  |
|  |  |
|  |  |

Observations and the resultant anecdotal record do not explain the causes of behavior. Observation is a technique for gathering information; it helps teachers learn more about the behavior of students. When used with other assessment techniques and test data, it can help hypothesize possible causes for behavior. These hypotheses can be used to select additional assessment techniques.

---

### FIGURE 6.4   Rachael's Anecdotal Record

| *Strategies Implemented* | *Result* |
|---|---|
| **Spelling** | |
| 3/11 Start a list of trouble words and tape to desk. These become no excuse words. | 3/11 She refers to list and keeps it out. Because of CSAP we didn't do any writing. |
| 3/17 Go through published pieces and find words she wants to use as spelling words. (Find 5) | 3/17 She said in a conference "I was writing and noticed I spelled **her** and it didn't look right. I ment it to be **here.** The list helped and I know that her is **her** not **here.**" |
| 3/19 Do **look, say, cover, write,** and **check** practice. | 3/17 We added 3 words to her list (their, there, and white). |
| 3/23 Had her look through writing and check to see all no excuse words were spelled correctly. | 3/19 She was able to do the list she has on her desk. She is also working on definitions. |
| | 3/23 No words misspelled from her list. |

---

| | |
|---|---|
| **Sentence Starters** | |
| 3/17 Conference with her about past writings and discuss how authors start sentences in different ways. Ask her to try to vary her sentences as she writes today. | 3/17 I showed her examples of her writing, and we went over strengths and weaknesses. I had her read a past piece where she repeated the beginning. I had her identify and highlight what was repeating. We took 1 paragraph and rewrote to change the sentences. |
| 3/22 We focused on one sentence beginner and changed old sentences from past writing into new ones (used Writer's Express). | 3/22 Sample two shows how she was working on using introductory phrases. |
| | 3/23 Shared with me that she noticed an old piece was too repetitive. She changed the sentence beginning as she typed. |

---

### Special Note

Be extremely careful about what anecdotal information becomes part of a child's permanent records because federal legislation (Family Educational Rights and Privacy Act of 1974 [PL 93-380]) allows parents access to their children's records.[5] ■

5. See S.B. Baker, *School Counseling for the Twenty-First Century* (Englewood Cliffs, NJ: Prentice-Hall, 1996), p. 282.

# CHECKLISTS

**Checklist**
A means for systematically and quickly recording a student's behavior; it usually is a list that the observer records as present or absent.

*Checklists* usually consist of lists of behaviors that the observer selects as being present or absent. Checklists are a means for systematically and quickly recording a student's behavior. They are not tests, although it is possible to present or devise a test to enable the rapid filling out of a checklist of behaviors; in other words, the test is administered to get the result, which is the student's profile. For example, to ascertain students' reading interests, Michael administers a reading interest inventory to each student. He then compiles the results on a class profile, which is shown in Figure 6.5. At a glance, he can see who has common interests. He can use the results to group students when he has them do investigations. He can also use the list to make sure the classroom library reflects the interests of the class.

Checklist formats may vary: Some use rating scales, some are used for a whole class or group, and some are used for an individual child. The purpose for the checklist should determine the kind of checklist that is used. An example of a diagnostic checklist for a child's problems is shown in Figure 6.6.

## GROUP AND INDIVIDUAL CHECKLISTS

Checklists that are used to display the behavior of a whole class or of a group of students in a specific area are sometimes preferred by teachers because they can, at a glance, show who needs help in a specific area and who does not. A group checklist is helpful in planning instruction for the group as well as for the individual, whereas the individual checklist is useful in assessing the strengths and weaknesses of an individual student only.

Figure 6.7 shows a group checklist Michael used to record how his kindergarten students performed on a language concepts test. At a glance, he was able to see that some children understood the majority of concepts, whereas others did not. He used this chart to design lessons for the children who needed some explicit teaching. While the children were engaged with free exploration, Michael worked with those students who needed to learn a given concept. He also made sure that he used these terms when teaching the whole class as a way of reinforcing the language concept.

Both types of formats are helpful. A teacher who wishes to see a complete profile of a child may prefer the individual approach, whereas the teacher who wishes to see a profile of the strengths and weaknesses of the class in specific skills for instructional planning will probably prefer a group checklist. For example, when listening to a student read, Michael records notes and observations on a passage like the one the student reads from the text. Once all students in the class have read, he notes the scores on a class profile. Figure 6.8A shows the individual performance and Figure 6.8B shows the group performance.

Regardless of whether a group or individual checklist is used, it should contain an itemized list of behaviors in a particular area; there should be space for dates; and there should be space for special notes. An example of an individual diagnostic checklist for oral and silent reading is shown in Figure 6.9.

# FIGURE 6.5   Reading Interest Inventory

| Names \ Interests | animals | true stories | science fiction | fantasy | mysteries | stories about people | poetry | funny books | science topics | series books | magazines (sports) | magazines (computers) |
|---|---|---|---|---|---|---|---|---|---|---|---|---|
| Hank | ✔ | | | | | | | | | ✔ | ✔ | |
| Meredith | | | ✔ | | ✔ | | | | | | | ✔ |
| Brenda | ✔ | ✔ | | | | | ✔ | ✔ | | | | |
| Jay | ✔ | | ✔ | ✔ | | ✔ | | | | ✔ | | |
| Corey | | ✔ | | | | ✔ | | | | | | |
| Kamal | | | ✔ | | | | | | ✔ | | | |
| Jason | ✔ | | | | | | | | | | | |
| Joel | | | | | ✔ | | | ✔ | | | | ✔ |
| Holly | ✔ | | ✔ | | | | ✔ | | ✔ | | | |
| Marni | ✔ | | | | | ✔ | | | | | ✔ | |
| Sarah | | | | ✔ | | | ✔ | ✔ | | | | ✔ |
| Derrick | | ✔ | ✔ | ✔ | | | | | ✔ | | | |
| Ryan | | | | | | | | | | | | |
| John | | ✔ | | | ✔ | | | | | ✔ | | |
| Sandi | | | | | | | | | | ✔ | | |
| Robyn | ✔ | | | | | | | | | ✔ | | |
| Annie | | ✔ | | | | | | | | ✔ | | |
| Kurt | | | | ✔ | | | | | | ✔ | | |
| Jeff | | | | | | | | | | | | ✔ |
| Tina | | | ✔ | ✔ | | | | | | | | |
| Hailey | ✔ | | | | | | | | ✔ | | | |
| Bo | | | | | ✔ | | | ✔ | | | ✔ | |
| Jake | | | ✔ | | | | | ✔ | | | ✔ | |
| Shari | | | | | | | | ✔ | | | ✔ | |
| Jessie | ✔ | | | | | | | ✔ | | ✔ | | |

| **Rating scale** |
| --- |
| An evaluative instrument used to record estimates of particular aspects of a student's behavior. |

# CHECKLISTS AND RATING SCALES

A checklist that uses a *rating scale* is actually an assessment instrument. This type of checklist is different than one that records observed behavior. An assessment checklist can be used by the teacher at the end of a unit to help to determine a student's progress. It also can be used to make students aware of their progress in a specific area. When assessment checklists are used, checklists of observed behavior and anecdotal records should be used as supplementary information or as aids in verifying the student's rating.

If rating scales are used, it is important that criteria be set up beforehand to help teachers determine what rating to give to a particular student. For example, if a student consistently makes errors in recognizing words that begin with certain blends, that student would receive a rating of 3 on a scale of 1 to 3 in which 1 is the highest and 3 is the lowest. If the student almost never makes an error in recognizing words that begin with certain blends, that student should receive a rating of 1 on a scale of 1 to 3. If a student sometimes makes errors in recognizing words that begin with certain blends, the student would receive a rating of 2 on a scale of 1 to 3. Here is an example of a group checklist with a rating scale.

**Phonic Analysis Skills (Consonants) Rating Scale (Group)**

|  | *Maria 1 2 3* | *John 1 2 3* | *José 1 2 3* | *Susan 1 2 3* |
| --- | --- | --- | --- | --- |
| Single consonants |  |  |  |  |
|   Initial |  |  |  |  |
|   Medial |  |  |  |  |
|   Final |  |  |  |  |
| Consonant blends (clusters) |  |  |  |  |
| Consonant digraphs |  |  |  |  |
| Silent consonants |  |  |  |  |

**Special Note**

There are diagnostic checklists in a number of other chapters in this book. ■

# OTHER HELPFUL ALTERNATIVE ASSESSMENT TECHNIQUES

There are some important student characteristics that cannot be discerned through direct observation. Attitudes or feelings and interests are examples of essential characteristics that cannot be directly observed. Projective techniques, informal interviews, and inventory-type measures can help reveal those aspects of students that cannot be directly observed. The interpretation of achievement test performance can help teachers learn about the amount of students knowledge. Students also can be informants about their own learning.

In a diagnostic-reading and improvement program it is important for teachers to look at both the cognitive and affective characteristics of their stu-

**FIGURE 6.6   Diagnostic Checklist of Speech Problems**

Child's Name: _____

Grade: _____

Date: _____

|  | Yes | No |
|---|---|---|
| 1. Is child's voice | | |
| a. loud? | | |
| b. too low? | | |
| c. nasal? | | |
| d. hoarse? | | |
| e. monotonous? | | |
| f. pitched abnormally high? | | |
| g. pitched abnormally low? | | |
| 2. Is child's rate of speech | | |
| a. too slow? | | |
| b. too rapid? | | |
| 3. Is child's phrasing poor? | | |
| 4. Is child's speech hesitant? | | |
| 5. Does the child show evidence of articulatory difficulties such as | | |
| a. the distortion of sounds? | | |
| b. the substitution of one sound for another? | | |
| c. the omission of sounds? | | |
| 6. Does the child show evidence of vocabulary problems such as | | |
| a. the repetition of phrases? | | |
| b. a limited vocabulary? | | |
| 7. Does the child show evidence of negative attitudes toward oral communication such as | | |
| a. not engaging in discussions or conversations? | | |
| b. not volunteering to give a talk or oral report? | | |

dents, because students' attitudes and interests will affect what they learn and whether they learn. Reading helps reading; unfortunately, many students are not choosing to read. The reasons for this lack of interest in reading are varied and many. If they know their students' attitudes and interests, teachers can help motivate students and try to instill in them a positive attitude toward reading. For example, if a teacher has a student who is doing poorly in reading

**FIGURE 6.7   Whole Class Language Concepts Checklist**

| Names (Boehm Basic Language Concepts) | 1. top | 2. through | 3. away from | 4. next to | 5. inside | 6. same, not many | 7. middle | 8. few | 9. farthest | 10. around | 11. over | 12. widest | 13. most | 14. between | 15. whole | 16. nearest | 17. second | 18. corner | 19. several | 20. behind | 21. row | 22. different | 23. after |
|---|---|---|---|---|---|---|---|---|---|---|---|---|---|---|---|---|---|---|---|---|---|---|---|
| Vanessa | ✔ | ✔ | ✔ | ✔ | ✔ | ✔ | ✔ | ✔ | ✔ | ✔ | ○ | ✔ | ✔ | ✔ | ✔ | ✔ | ✔ | ✔ | ✔ | ✔ | ✔ | ✔ | ✔ |
| Jessica | ✔ | ✔ | ✔ | ✔ | ✔ | ✔ | ✔ | ✔ | ✔ | ✔ | ✔ | ✔ | ✔ | ✔ | ✔ | ✔ | ✔ | ✔ | ✔ | ✔ | ✔ | ✔ | ✔ |
| Diamond | ✔ | ✔ | ✔ | ✔ | ✔ | ✔ | ✔ | ✔ | ✔ | ✔ | ✔ | ✔ | ✔ | ✔ | ✔ | ✔ | ✔ | ✔ | ✔ | ✔ | ✔ | ✔ | ✔ |
| James | ✔ | ✔ | ✔ | ✔ | ✔ | ✔ | ✔ | ✔ | ✔ | ✔ | ○ | ✔ | ✔ | ✔ | ✔ | ✔ | ✔ | ✔ | ✔ | ✔ | ✔ | ○ | ✔ |
| Renee | ✔ | ✔ | ✔ | ✔ | ✔ | ✔ | ✔ | ✔ | ✔ | ✔ | ✔ | ○ | ✔ | ✔ | ✔ | ✔ | ✔ | ✔ | ✔ | ○ | ✔ | ○ | ○ |
| Victoria | ✔ | ✔ | ✔ | ✔ | ✔ | ○ | ○ | ○ | ○ | ✔ | ○ | ✔ | ✔ | ✔ | ✔ | ○ | ✔ | ○ | ✔ | ○ | ✔ | ○ | ✔ |
| Tatiana | ✔ | ✔ | ✔ | ✔ | ✔ | ✔ | ✔ | ✔ | ✔ | ✔ | ✔ | ✔ | ✔ | ✔ | ✔ | ✔ | ✔ | ✔ | ✔ | ✔ | ✔ | ✔ | ✔ |
| Kelly | ✔ | ✔ | ✔ | ✔ | ✔ | ✔ | ✔ | ✔ | ✔ | ✔ | ○ | ✔ | ✔ | ✔ | ✔ | ✔ | ✔ | ✔ | ✔ | ✔ | ✔ | ○ | ✔ |
| Rory | ✔ | ✔ | ✔ | ✔ | ✔ | ○ | ✔ | ○ | ✔ | ✔ | ✔ | ✔ | ✔ | ✔ | ✔ | ✔ | ✔ | ✔ | ✔ | ✔ | ✔ | ✔ | ✔ |
| Tiffany | ✔ | ✔ | ✔ | ✔ | ✔ | ✔ | ✔ | ✔ | ✔ | ✔ | ✔ | ✔ | ✔ | ✔ | ✔ | ✔ | ✔ | ✔ | ✔ | ✔ | ✔ | ○ | ○ |
| Ethan | ✔ | ✔ | ✔ | ✔ | ✔ | ✔ | ✔ | ✔ | ✔ | ✔ | ✔ | ✔ | ✔ | ✔ | ✔ | ✔ | ✔ | ✔ | ✔ | ✔ | ✔ | ✔ | ✔ |
| Genevieve | ✔ | ✔ | ✔ | ✔ | ✔ | ✔ | ✔ | ✔ | ✔ | ✔ | ✔ | ✔ | ✔ | ✔ | ✔ | ✔ | ✔ | ✔ | ✔ | ✔ | ✔ | ✔ | ✔ |
| Robert | ✔ | ✔ | ✔ | ✔ | ✔ | ✔ | ✔ | ✔ | ✔ | ✔ | ✔ | ○ | ✔ | ○ | ✔ | ○ | ✔ | ✔ | ✔ | ○ | ✔ | ✔ | ✔ |
| Marcelino | ○ | ✔ | ✔ | ✔ | ○ | ○ | ✔ | ✔ | ✔ | ✔ | ○ | ○ | ✔ | ✔ | ○ | ○ | ○ | ○ | ○ | ○ | ✔ | ○ | ○ |
| Christopher | ✔ | ✔ | ✔ | ✔ | ✔ | ✔ | ✔ | ✔ | ✔ | ✔ | ✔ | ✔ | ✔ | ✔ | ✔ | ✔ | ✔ | ✔ | ✔ | ✔ | ✔ | ✔ | ✔ |
| Margaret | ✔ | ✔ | ✔ | ✔ | ✔ | ✔ | ✔ | ✔ | ✔ | ✔ | ✔ | ✔ | ✔ | ○ | ✔ | ✔ | ✔ | ✔ | ✔ | ✔ | ✔ | ✔ | ✔ |
| Mindy | ✔ | ✔ | ✔ | ✔ | ✔ | ○ | ✔ | ○ | ✔ | ✔ | ✔ | ✔ | ✔ | ✔ | ✔ | ✔ | ✔ | ✔ | ✔ | ✔ | ✔ | ✔ | ✔ |
| Ben | ✔ | ✔ | ✔ | ✔ | ✔ | ✔ | ✔ | ✔ | ✔ | ✔ | ✔ | ✔ | ✔ | ✔ | ✔ | ✔ | ✔ | ✔ | ✔ | ✔ | ✔ | ✔ | ✔ |
| Megan | ✔ | ✔ | ✔ | ✔ | ✔ | ✔ | ✔ | ✔ | ○ | ✔ | ✔ | ✔ | ✔ | ✔ | ✔ | ✔ | ✔ | ✔ | ✔ | ✔ | ✔ | ✔ | ✔ |
| Natasha | ✔ | ✔ | ✔ | ✔ | ✔ | ○ | ✔ | ✔ | ✔ | ✔ | ○ | ✔ | ✔ | ○ | ✔ | ○ | ✔ | ✔ | ✔ | ✔ | ✔ | ✔ | ○ |
| Jack | ✔ | ✔ | ✔ | ✔ | ✔ | ✔ | ✔ | ✔ | ✔ | ✔ | ✔ | ✔ | ✔ | ✔ | ✔ | ✔ | ✔ | ✔ | ✔ | ✔ | ✔ | ✔ | ✔ |

and who never chooses to read voluntarily, and the teacher knows the child is interested in sports, the teacher can find books about sports to motivate the student to read.

**FIGURE 6.8A Individual Performance Checklist**

Name: *Brenda*

### *Pettranella*

Long ago in a country far away lived a little girl named Pettranella. She lived with her father and mother in the upstairs of her grandmother's tall, narrow house.

Other houses just like it lined the street on both sides, and at the end of the street was the mill. All day and all night smoke rose from its great smokestacks and lay like a grey blanket over the city. It hid the sun and choked the trees, and it ~~withered~~ the flowers that [*street* *hand* *un*] tried to grow in the window boxes. ‖

One dark winter night when the wind blew cold from the east, Pettranella's father came home with a letter. The family gathered around the table in the warm yellow circle of [*ow* *are*] I the lamp to read it; even the grandmother came from her rooms downstairs to listen.

"It's from Uncle ~~Cris~~ in America," began her father. "He has his homestead ~~there~~ now, [*goose* *through*] ‖ and is already clearing his land. Someday it will be a large farm growing many ~~crops~~ of [*claring* *cropes*] ‖ ~~grain~~." And then he read the letter aloud. [*gran*] I

When he had finished, Pettranella said, "I wish we could go there, too, and live on a homestead."

Her parents looked at each other, their eyes twinkling with a secret. "We *are* going," [*Here*] said her mother. "We are sailing on the very next ~~ships~~." [*sheep*] I

1.
2. } *couldn't remember anything for sure - even w/ prodding*
3.
4.

## INFORMAL STUDENT INTERVIEWS

**Informal interviews**
Teachers converse with students to learn about their interests and feelings.

The easiest way to learn about students' likes or dislikes is to ask them. Teachers have many opportunities during the school day to converse with their students and learn about their feelings and interests. Teachers can also set up special times during the school day to meet with students for a consultation in the form of an *informal interview*. This is a good technique because it helps to build rapport with students, as well as to gain information about them. This technique is especially helpful for the lower primary grades and for those students who have reading problems.

### FIGURE 6.8B   Group Performance Checklist

#### Level 1 — Pettranella

| Name | W. Rec. 0–12 | Comp 3–4 | P/F | Comments |
|---|---|---|---|---|
| Hank | 10 | +2 | F | because of comp. |
| Meredith | 4 | +4 | P | very fluent |
| Brenda | 9 | +0 | F | looks like comp. needs work but could be expressive voc. |
| Jay | 3 | +3 | P | fairly fluent; could retell a bit |
| Corey | 3 | +4 | P | fluent |
| Kamal | 1 | +4 | P | very fluent |
| Jason | 26 | +3 | F | applies knowledge of phonics |
| Jack | 4 | +0 | F | looks like comp. but most likely expression is what needs work |
| Holly | 7 | +2 | F | very fluent; comp. appears weak |
| Marni | 3 | +4 | P | very fluent |
| Sarah | 3 | +4 | P | |
| Derrick | 3 | +4 | P | |
| Ryan | 1 | +3 | P | fluent |
| John | 13 | +2 1/2 | P | —marginal |
| Sandi | 0 | +4 | P | |
| Robyn | 7 | +4 | P | fairly fluent |
| Annie | 0 | +4 | P | |
| Kristy | 1 | +4 | P | very fluent; good intonation |
| John | 4 | +4 | P | very fluent |
| Jeff | 0 | +4 | P | |
| Zack | 21 | +2 1/2 | F | will need curr. adap. to read this text successfully |
| Jeff | 11 | +3 | P | fairly fluent |
| Sara | 0 | +4 | P | |
| Haitley | 0 | +3 | P | |
| Tina | 0 | +4 | P | |
| Kyle | 1 | +4 | P | |

*Source* for Figures 6.8A and B: From *Flexible Grouping in Reading* by Michael Opitz. Published by Scholastic Teaching Resources/Scholastic, Inc. Copyright © 1998, by Michael Opitz. Reprinted by permission.

**FIGURE 6.9   Diagnostic Checklist for Oral and Silent Reading**

| Oral Reading | Yes | No | Specific Errors |
|---|---|---|---|
| 1. Word recognition errors.<br>The teacher listens to the child while he or she is reading orally and records whether the child makes any of the following errors: | | | |
| a. omissions | | | |
| b. insertions | | | |
| c. substitutions | | | |
| d. repetitions | | | |
| e. hesitations | | | |
| f. mispronunciations | | | |
| g. reversals | | | |
| 2. Manner of reading.<br>The teacher observes the child while he or she is reading aloud and records whether the child exhibits any of the following behaviors: | | | |
| a. word-by-word phrasing | | | |
| b. finger pointing | | | |
| c. head movement | | | |
| d. fidgeting | | | |
| e. voice characteristics<br>   high-pitched<br>   loud<br>   soft<br>   monotonous | | | |
| f. other | | | |

3. Comprehension.
(*See* Comprehension Diagnostic Checklist in Chapter 12.)

| Silent Reading | Yes | No |
|---|---|---|
| 1. Comprehension.<br>(*See* Comprehension Diagnostic Checklist in Chapter 12.) | | |
| 2. Manner of reading.<br>The teacher observes the child while he or she is reading silently and records whether the child exhibits any of the following behaviors: | | |
| a. lip movement | | |
| b. reads aloud | | |
| c. head movement | | |
| d. continually looks up | | |
| e. finger pointing | | |
| f. other | | |

Another purpose for interviewing students who are having difficulty with reading is to gain insight into how they perceive reading. Because perception determines behavior, a change in behavior follows rather than precedes implicit perceptions. In order to change reading behaviors, the students' perceptions of reading must first change. Thus, gaining an insight into students' existing perceptions assists the teacher in better understanding why students function as they do and knowing which, if any, additional aspects of the reading process students need to perceive and employ to increase their own reading ability.

A third purpose for interviewing students is to enable them to explore their own reading behaviors—to help them understand themselves. In talking about their reading, students become more aware of how they perceive and approach reading. Self-awareness is essential because it is the first step toward change. Thus, becoming aware of their perceptions about reading can help students realize whether their perceptions are accurate and, if not, which additional aspects need to be incorporated into their understanding of the reading process. In addition, becoming more conscious of the strategies that they presently use in reading may, with teacher guidance, lead students to see that there are additional strategies they can and may need to learn. Once aware of these options, students can decide which strategies to use and when to use them to ensure comprehension. In other words, they can exercise control over their cognitive actions.

Figure 6.10 is an example of a protocol that can elicit both perceptions of reading and strategies used in reading. The first four questions focus on perceptions of reading, whereas the last three are designed to elicit strategies used in reading.

The following are some suggestions for managing interviews:

1. Count on spending about ten minutes for each interview.
2. Because the interviews require one-to-one attention, plan independent activities for the other children to minimize interruptions.
3. Interview children more than once. You might consider interviewing them at the beginning, middle, and end of the year, making note of shifts in perceptions of reading and the repertoire of strategies on the form shown in Figure 6.11.
4. Interpret the responses. Do they primarily focus on reading as a meaning-seeking activity? Do the responses primarily focus on reading as being an act of calling words? Do the responses focus on something other than understanding of words? Do the responses show that the reader has a limited set of strategies?
5. Make a list of the strategies that students mention. Some they might mention are: sound it out, ask, use other words, break it into parts, skip it, use a dictionary, spell it, wait for the teacher, stop reading.

The following are some suggestions for using information revealed from the interviews:

1. Use what you discover to plan appropriate instruction. For example, if students comment that the purpose of reading is to say the words, prepare and

teach lessons that emphasize the meaning aspect. Such a lesson might begin like this: "Today I want to teach you another way of figuring out words. When you come to a word you cannot pronounce, say 'blank' and keep reading until the end of the sentence. When you get to the end of the sentence, go back to the word that caused you some problems and ask yourself what word might make sense that looks like the word that is actually printed."

2. Consider using a whole-class brainstorming session to create a chart showing what to do to gain pronunciation of a word and what to do to gain the meaning of a word when reading.

3. If the interviews as a whole seem to indicate that students lack understanding about what good readers do when they read, create a list and post it in the classroom.

## INTEREST INVENTORIES

**Interest inventory**
A statement or questionnaire method that helps teachers learn about likes and dislikes of students.

*Interest inventories* can be standardized or teacher-made. The purpose of an interest inventory is to help teachers learn about the likes and dislikes of their students. In this book, we are particularly invested in finding out about students' likes or dislikes so that we can use this information to help stimulate them to read.

Interest inventories usually employ statements, questions, or both to obtain information. The statement or questionnaire method enables the teacher to gain a great amount of information in a relatively short period of time, but there is a major difficulty with this method. When people fill out an inventory, they are not always truthful. Many times individuals give "expected responses"; that is, they answer with responses that they feel the tester expects or wants rather than ones based on what they actually do or how they feel. Students who wish to create a favorable impression on their teacher may especially answer in an expected direction. Teachers who have good rapport with their students and who have a good affective environment in their classrooms will be able to gain the trust of their students. Before administering the inventory, these teachers can discuss its purpose and try to stress to the students how important it is for them to put down exactly the way they feel rather than what they think they should feel. Doing so better ensures sincere responses.

Interest inventories can be individually administered, administered to a small group, or administered to the whole class. The interest inventory is usually used in a group, but it is individually administered if the student's reading problem prevents him or her from filling it out. In the lower primary grades teachers can use a checklist type of questionnaire, whereby they read the question to the children and the children mark the appropriate box. Figure 6.12 shows examples of some interest inventories that you can use with your students to determine their reading interests.

One way to collapse results of inventories was shown earlier (see p. 122). Using the results is essential.

---

**FIGURE 6.10    Student Interview Protocol**

Name: _____

*Student Interview*

1. What is the most important thing about reading?

   _____

   _____

2. When you are reading, what are you trying to do?

   _____

   _____

3. What is reading?

   _____

   _____

4. When you come to a word you don't know, what do you do?

   _____

   _____

5. Do you think it's important to read every word correctly? Why? Why not?

   _____

   _____

6. What makes a person a good reader?

   _____

   _____

7. Do you think good readers ever come to a word they don't know? If yes, what do you think they do?

   _____

   _____

---

*Source:* From *Flexible Grouping in Reading* by Michael Opitz. Published by Scholastic Teaching Resources/Scholastic, Inc. Copyright © 1998 by Michael Opitz. Reprinted by permission.

## READING ATTITUDE SURVEYS

Attitude has a significant impact on reading; this should come as no surprise if we take a minute to think about ourselves as readers. When we have a positive outlook on our ability to read, we are more likely to read because

**FIGURE 6.11   Student Interview Summary**

Name: _____         Interviewer: _____

Grade: _____   Age: _____   School: _____

**Beginning of School Year**                    **Date:** _____

Perceptions of Reading                          Strategies Used

**Middle of School Year**                        **Date:** _____

Perceptions of Reading                          Strategies Used

**End of School Year**                           **Date:** _____

Perceptions of Reading                          Strategies Used

we enjoy it and we are successful. We also are more likely to comprehend any given text when we have a positive attitude about it. The reverse is also true.

We can get at student attitudes by using an attitude survey. Figure 6.13 is a reading attitude survey intended for the primary grades, and Figure 6.14 is geared for grades 3 through 5.

## PROJECTIVE TECHNIQUES

**Projective technique**
A method in which the individual tends to put himself or herself into the situation and reveal how he or she feels.

*Projective techniques* are subtle procedures in which individuals put themselves into a situation and reveal how they feel. Projective techniques are more revealing than inventories because the student is less likely to fake an answer. The student does not know what the *correct* or *best* answer is, for there is no correct or best answer. On a projective test, students are more likely to give the answer that is natural for them, and as a result, reveal how they really feel.

As with any assessment technique, there are some limitations with projective techniques. The major limitation concerns the interpretation of the students' responses. Because of difficulty with interpretation, projective tests are not very trustworthy; however, they do have some definite benefits for teachers with students who have reading problems. They can help teachers gain some insights into the way students who have reading problems feel about themselves without the students realizing it. Teachers can also gain information about why the students think they have a reading problem. The teacher could then use this information to try to help the students.

Here are some examples of projective tests that can be either group- or individually administered.

### Special Note

Use projective tests with caution and try not to read too much into the responses. Also, avoid administering those tests that require clinical analysis by a psychologist. ■

### Sentence Completion Test

The sentence completion test is easy to administer in a relatively short period of time. Students are given some unfinished sentences that they are asked to complete as rapidly as possible. This test can be given orally to those students who have trouble reading or writing, or it can be given to a whole group at once. Here are some typical incomplete sentences:

Reading is . . .
I believe I can . . .
I prefer . . .
My favorite . . .

**FIGURE 6.12   Interest Inventories**

LOWER PRIMARY GRADES (Read aloud by teacher)

Name _____   Grade _____

1. Do you like to read?   Yes _____ No _____ Sometimes _____

2. What kinds of books do you like to read? Books about  a. animals _____ b. children _____
   c. sports _____ d. adventure _____ e. fairy tales _____

3. What do you like to do after school?  a. watch TV _____ b. read a book _____ c. play _____
   d. do schoolwork _____ e. work around the house _____ f. work on a hobby _____
   g. work with computer if available _____

4. What do you like to do when there is no school?  a. watch TV _____ b. read a book _____
   c. play _____ d. do schoolwork _____ e. work around the house _____
   f. go shopping with parents _____ g. visit the zoo _____
   h. work with computer if available _____

5. What are your favorite television shows?  a. cartoons _____ b. comedy shows _____
   c. movies _____ d. mysteries _____ e. musicals _____ f. game shows _____
   g. adventure _____

6. What are your favorite games? a. group games played outside _____ b. indoor games _____
   c. electronic (television) games _____ d. computer games _____

(For numbers 2 through 6, the child may check more than one.)


UPPER PRIMARY GRADES

Name _____   Grade _____

1. Do you like to read? _____

2. When do you like to read the best? _____
   _____

3. What is your favorite subject? _____

4. What is your favorite book? _____
   _____

5. What do you like to do after school? _____
   _____

6. What is your favorite game? _____
   _____

7. What is your favorite television show? _____
   _____

8. What kinds of books do you like to read? _____
   _____

*(continued)*

**FIGURE 6.12**   (*continued*)

9.   What is your hobby? _____

_____

10.   Do you take out books from the library?   _____

_____

INTERMEDIATE GRADES

Name _____   Grade _____

1.   Do you like to read? _____
2.   What kinds of books are your favorites?   _____

_____

3.   What do you like to do after school? _____

_____

4.   What are your favorite subjects?   _____

_____

5.   Name your favorite hobby. _____
6.   How often during the month do you go to the public library? _____
7.   How often during the week do you go to your school library? _____
8.   Name your favorite book. _____
9.   What do you enjoy doing the most?   _____
10.   What is your favorite television show? _____
11.   Name your favorite movie.   _____
12.   What is your favorite sport? _____
13.   If you could go anywhere in the world, where would you like to go?   _____
14.   If you could visit any book character you wanted to, whom would you like to visit?   _____

_____

15.   Name the magazines and newspapers that you read. _____
16.   What part of the newspaper do you like to read the best? _____
17.   What book is the most popular among you and your friends? _____
18.   What would you like to be when you grow up?   _____

*Wish Test*

The wish test is similar to the sentence completion test except that the phrase *I wish* precedes the incomplete sentence. Here are some typical examples:

I wish I were . . .
I wish I could . . .
I wish reading were . . .
I wish school were . . .
I wish my friends were . . .
I wish my teacher . . .

**FIGURE 6.13  Primary Reading Survey**

Name: _____

| How do you feel when: | 😊 | 😐 | ☹️ |
|---|---|---|---|
| 1. your teacher reads a story to you? | | | |
| 2. your class has reading time? | | | |
| 3. you can read with a friend? | | | |
| 4. you read out loud to your teacher? | | | |
| 5. you read out loud to someone at home? | | | |
| 6. someone reads to you at home? | | | |
| 7. someone gives you a book for a present? | | | |
| 8. you read a book to yourself at home? | | | |

**How do you think:**

| | | | |
|---|---|---|---|
| 9. your teacher feels when you read out loud? | | | |
| 10. your family feels when you read out loud? | | | |

**How Do You Feel About How Well You Can Read?**

Make this face look the way you feel.

**FIGURE 6.14   Reading Attitude Survey for Grades 3 and Up**

Name: _____

**Directions:** The 20 statements that follow will be read to you. After each statement is read, circle the letter that best describes how you feel about that statement. Your answers will not be graded because there are no right or wrong answers. Your feeling about each statement is what's important.

SA = Strongly Agree     A = Agree     U = Undecided
D = Disagree     SD = Strongly Disagree

SA  A  U  D  SD          1. Reading is for learning but not for enjoyment.

SA  A  U  D  SD          2. Money spent on books is well spent.

SA  A  U  D  SD          3. There is nothing to be gained from reading books.

SA  A  U  D  SD          4. Books are a bore.

SA  A  U  D  SD          5. Reading is a good way to spend spare time.

SA  A  U  D  SD          6. Sharing books in class is a waste of time.

SA  A  U  D  SD          7. Reading turns me on.

SA  A  U  D  SD          8. Reading is only for students seeking good grades.

SA  A  U  D  SD          9. Books aren't usually good enough to finish.

SA  A  U  D  SD          10. Reading is rewarding to me.

SA  A  U  D  SD          11. Reading becomes boring after about an hour.

SA  A  U  D  SD          12. Most books are too long and dull.

SA  A  U  D  SD          13. Free reading doesn't teach anything.

SA  A  U  D  SD          14. There should be more time for free reading during the school day.

SA  A  U  D  SD          15. There are many books that I hope to read.

SA  A  U  D  SD          16. Books should not be read except for class requirements.

SA  A  U  D  SD          17. Reading is something I can do without.

SA  A  U  D  SD          18. A certain amount of summer vacation should be set aside for reading.

SA  A  U  D  SD          19. Books make good presents.

SA  A  U  D  SD          20. Reading is dull.

From *Improving Reading: A Handbook of Strategies*, 2nd ed., by Jerry L. Johns and Susan Davis Lenski, Copyright © 1994, 1997 by Kendall/Hunt Publishing Company. Used with permission.

**Reading autobiography**
Students write or tell about their feelings and attempt to analyze their reading problems.

# READING AUTOBIOGRAPHY

The *reading autobiography* is not as subtle as a projective technique because the students are aware that they are writing or telling about their feelings and trying to analyze why they have a reading problem. It is a helpful technique, however, and probably more accurate than responses on an interest inventory because the students are partners in an attempt to analyze their reading difficulties. The reading autobiography is the student's own life story of his or her reading experiences. It can be presented in a number of ways, and it can be individually or group-administered.

### Open-Ended Reading Autobiography

One technique that could be used is simply to have the students write their reading autobiography. They are given the following instructions:

> Since this is the life story of your reading experiences, you must go back as far as you can remember. Try to recall your earliest reading experiences, what they were, and how you felt about them. Try to recall what books you liked when you were very small, and whether you still like those kinds of books. Try to remember when you first started to read. How did you feel? Try to recall how you first learned to read, and what you think helped you the most in learning to read. If you have a reading problem, try to remember when you think it first started and why it started. Put down anything that you feel is important in helping others to understand your reading problem if you think you have one.

> Students who have trouble writing could orally relate their autobiographies to the teacher, or they could tape-record them.

### Questionnaire Reading Autobiography

The questionnaire autobiography is also helpful in gaining information about a student's reading history, but it is more limiting than the open-ended reading autobiography. Also, it is only as good as the questions on it because students' responses are determined by the questions. Figure 6.15 provides an example:

---

**FIGURE 6.15**  **Reading Autobiography**

|  | Yes | No | Sometimes |
|---|---|---|---|
| 1. Do you like to read? | | | |
| 2. When do you like to read? | | | |
| 3. Do you like someone to read to you? | | | |
| 4. Do you feel you understand what you read? | | | |
| 5. Did anyone try to teach you to read before you came to school? | | | |
| 6. Did anyone read to you when you were younger? | | | |
| 7. Are there lots of books in your house? | | | |
| 8. Do you think you have a reading problem? | | | |

*(continued)*

**FIGURE 6.15** (*continued*)

If you answered *yes* to question 8, answer the following questions:

1. What do you think your reading problem is?

2. Why do you think you have a reading problem?

3. Has anyone tried to help you with your problem?

4. When do you feel your reading problem began?

5. Who do you think has helped you the most in reading?

6. What do you think has helped you the most in reading?

7. Have you ever left the class to attend a special reading class?

If you answered *yes* to question 7, answer questions 8 and 9.

8. How do you feel about being in a special reading class?

9. Do you think the special reading class has helped you?

10. Are your parents interested in helping you in reading?

11. Do you like to read to anyone?

12. What do you do when you come across a word you do not know?

13. What do you do when you do not understand something you are reading?

14. Do you have a library card?

15. If you have a library card, how often do you go to the library?

16. What kinds of books do you like to read?

## SUMMARY

In this chapter, we presented several alternative assessment techniques that can be used at any grade level. One major point that we emphasized is that three questions need to be asked and answered to select the best possible technique: What do I want to know? Why do I want to know? How can I best discover? We also pointed out that both cognitive and affective factors need to be considered when determining how to best help children with reading, and we provided a wealth of ideas about how to acquire insight into both types of factors. A third point we stressed is that observation, like the many other alternative assessment techniques, is a way of gathering information; it cannot explain the causes of any given behavior. A fourth major idea we presented was that alternative assessment techniques are viable techniques to help gain information about student characteristics that cannot be garnered from other sources.

## CHAPTER 6 KEY CONCEPTS

- Portfolios are primarily a storage system that provides teachers, students, and parents with an ongoing record of their students' reading and writing behavior.

- Portfolio assessment takes place when what is contained in the portfolio is deemed ready for evaluation in some way.

- Observation is an essential part of any reading program that helps teachers collect data about students' behavior.
- There are differences among the terms alternative, authentic, and performance assessment.
- Anecdotal records help teachers document their students' behavior by keeping a record over a period of time.

- Checklists and rating scales are helpful ways for teachers to gain information about students' behavior.
- Informal interviews, inventory-type measures, reading attitude surveys, and projective techniques can help teachers learn about aspects of students that cannot be directly observed.

## SUGGESTIONS FOR THOUGHT QUESTIONS AND ACTIVITIES

1. Construct a checklist for a reading skill to use for instruction.
2. Construct a reading checklist that uses a rating scale.
3. Construct an individual checklist that lists all the reading behaviors that you feel are important.
4. Use one of the checklists given either in this chapter or in another chapter to learn more about the behavior of a particular child.
5. Observe a child at various times in class. Record his or her behavior by using a checklist.
6. Observe a child at various times in class. Record his or her behavior by using an anecdotal record.
7. Discuss with various teachers how they use portfolios in their classes.
8. Develop a plan to use portfolios in your class. Discuss how the portfolios would help you diagnose your students' reading problems.

## INTERNET ACTIVITIES

Choose a search engine and search for websites related to an assessment technique mentioned in the chapter. Select one website from the search that helps you gain a good understanding of the technique. Download any forms related to the technique as well as any background information such as how to administer and score the assessment technique. (Be sure to identify both the search engine you used and the website you selected.)

## SELECTED BIBLIOGRAPHY

Barrentine, Shelby J., and Sandra M. Stokes, eds. *Reading Assessment: Principles and Practices for Elementary Teachers,* 2nd ed. Newark, DE: International Reading Association, 2005.

Bratcher, Suzanne, with Linda Ryan. *Evaluating Children's Writing: A Handbook of Grading Choices for Classroom Teachers,* 2nd ed. Mahwah, NJ: Erlbaum, 2004.

Cohen, Dorothy H., and Virginia Stern. *Observing and Recording the Behavior of Young Children.* New York: Teachers College Press, 1978.

Easley, Shirley-Dale, and Kay Mitchell. *Portfolios Matter. What, Where, When, Why and How to Use Them.* Portland, ME: Stenhouse, 2003.

Gillespie, Cindy S., et al. "Portfolio Assessment: Some Questions, Some Answers, Some Recommendations." *Journal of Adolescent & Adult Literacy* 39 (Mar 1996): 480–91.

Goodrich, Heidi. "Understanding Rubrics." *Educational Leadership* (Dec/Jan): 14–17.

Popham, James W. "Portfolio Assessment," in *Classroom Assessment: What Teachers Need to Know,* 2nd ed. Boston: Allyn and Bacon, 1999.

Salvia, John, and James E. Ysseldyke. "Assessing Behavior Through Observation," in *Assessment,* 8th ed. Boston: Houghton Mifflin, 2001.

# Assessing and Teaching Early Literacy

## Scenario: Helping Children Advance as Language Learners

Ms. Berger is a highly qualified early childhood teacher who believes that literacy is an ongoing, dynamic process and that children are often at different places in their literacy acquisition. Rather than waiting for children to show that they are ready for literacy instruction, she uses what she knows about her students to plan developmentally appropriate instruction. She wholeheartedly believes that assessment drives instruction, but she recognizes that she must use a variety of assessment measures, each designed to evaluate different aspects of early literacy. She can then interpret the results to plan lessons and to determine which children might need additional instructional time so that they can learn essential literacy skills.

As is often the case, Ms. Berger's students come from a variety of backgrounds. Some come from high-poverty areas, whereas others come from middle-class neighborhoods. When she looks at the results of the many different assessment measures she uses, she recognizes that some children perform poorly when compared to their peers. That is, some are lagging in oral vocabulary, print concepts, letter identification, and phonological awareness. She knows that she will be able to offer some children additional instruction in each of these areas, while others will be better served by teachers who are specially trained in early intervention. She fully understands that children who don't do well on the assessments need more rather than less help. Their progress must be accelerated in order for them to function at the same level of their peers.

Ms. Berger recognizes that there are noneducative factors such as parental support, socioeconomic status, and nutrition that affect school performance. She also knows that there are several educative factors such as teacher experience, curriculum rigor, and time on task that affect how children fare in school. Although all factors are important, she focuses on what she can control—the educative factors—and strives to teach children to the best of her ability.

Recent government mandates have Ms. Berger quite concerned. Even though she is an advocate of accountability, she also understands that the results of early literacy tests are not supposed to be used as high stakes tests in which children are labeled and sorted into various groups. Yet this is what she sees happening. She is concerned that too much time is being spent on labeling children and not enough time is being spent on helping them advance as language learners.

# INTRODUCTION

In this chapter, we focus on the different aspects of literacy that young children enrolled in kindergarten and first grade need to acquire. Our purpose is to explain these essential components and provide some ways to assess and teach each one. Whereas several of the assessment measures explained throughout this text are suitable for all ages, those in this chapter are especially appropriate for evaluating essential components related to early literacy.

## CHAPTER OBJECTIVES

After reading this chapter, you should be able to:

- Discuss the essential components of early literacy.
- Explain the difference between reading readiness and emergent literacy.
- Describe different assessment measures used to assess early literacy.
- Provide an example of a specific assessment measure and explain what it is designed to reveal.
- Discuss early intervention and provide an example of an early intervention program.
- Explain the pros and cons of three different ways to determine who is most in need of early intervention.

## BUILDING AN UNDERSTANDING OF EARLY LITERACY

**Emergent literacy**
The development of the association of print with meaning that begins early in a child's life and continues until the child reaches the stage of conventional reading and writing.

**Reading readiness**
Children demonstrate behavior that show they are ready for reading instruction.

Many terms are used to describe the beginning stages of literacy. One of the most common is *emergent literacy*, defined by Harris and Hodges as "the development of the association of print with meaning that begins early in a child's life and continues until the child reaches the stage of conventional reading and writing."[1] This definition suggests that children's involvement with language begins long before they come to school and that it continues to evolve over time. For example, what appears to be a young child's scribbling is really more than scribbling; it is the child's attempt at using written language. In the past, behaviors such as these were often thought of in terms of *reading readiness*. That is, children were showing that they were ready for reading instruction.

Although some may argue that emergent literacy and reading readiness are basically synonymous terms, they are not at all. Emergent literacy connotes an ongoing process that is developmental in nature. Reading readiness seems to connote a "waiting period." The notion of waiting in literacy development violates the spirit and essence of literacy as a developmental process.

Some make the distinction between emergent literacy and *beginning reading* by noting that once children show a certain amount of understanding about how print functions, they are no longer emergent but actually beginning to read in the formal sense. Therefore, they are beginning readers. But exactly how much do children have to know to move from being emergent to beginner? At what age does this shift happen?

Although kindergarten is usually considered to be the bridge between emergent and beginning reading, using kindergarten as a yardstick can be problematic for a couple of reasons. First, not all children attend kindergarten because it is not required in several states. Therefore, lack of exposure to a language-rich environment could mean that the children will not exhibit several emergent literacy behaviors until first grade.

[1]Harris, T., R. Hodges. *The Literacy Dictionary*. Newark, DE: International Reading Association, 1995.

Second, there are still differences of opinion about the purpose and curriculum of kindergarten. Those who believe that children will grow or mature into reading provide children with many opportunities to learn all areas of literacy (speaking, listening, reading, and writing), yet do very little explicit teaching. Others believe that children are continually developing and that they need some help as they develop. Consequently, like their counterparts, they provide children with a language-rich environment, but they also believe in offering children explicit instruction based on what they have discovered as a result of using several different assessment techniques and interpreting what they reveal.

We base our view, which we call "early literacy," on the latter opinion. We believe that children are always showing us what they know and what they need to learn. Children change over time in the way they think about literacy and the strategies they employ as they attempt to comprehend and/or produce text. Like Teale,[2] we believe that children are always trying to make sense of their world and that there is a logic behind what they do that drives their attempts to solve the literacy mystery. Once we understand this logic, we are in a better position to plan instruction that will foster their development toward conventional language use.

One of the best ways to take a look at children's attempts at using language in meaningful ways is to create a language-rich environment and observe what the children do. Such an environment needs to employ authentic language experiences and much support. Cambourne provides a useful way to think about such an environment. His conditions of learning are shown in Figure 7.1.

## AREAS OF EARLY LITERACY

In Chapter 5, we provided some sample benchmarks that show some specific behaviors that we would expect to see of children. Where as a number of the behaviors overlap and continue through different stages, many manifest themselves early on. In a broader sense, there are specific areas of emergent literacy that are viewed as the foundation for future reading and writing success. In Figure 7.1 we provide an overview of these components.

# ASSESSING EARLY LITERACY

## PRE-READING ASSESSMENT

Before the label *emergent literacy* surfaced and replaced *reading readiness,* most school systems administered whole-group reading readiness tests to their students, usually at the end of kindergarten, to determine if the children were "ready for reading." These tests were usually the first types of standardized tests that the children encountered in their lives at school.

Group-administered standardized tests are still being used. Most major standardized achievement assessment batteries still have some types of *pre-reading* tests that are usually administered to children some time in kindergarten. These tests are used by some school district personnel to predict

**Pre-reading**
Precursor to reading; before formal reading begins.

[2]Teale, W. "Emergent Literacy," in *The Literacy Dictionary,* T. Harris and R. Hodges, eds., pp. 71–72. Newark, DE: International Reading Association, 1995.

## FIGURE 7.1 Cambourne's Conditions of Learning

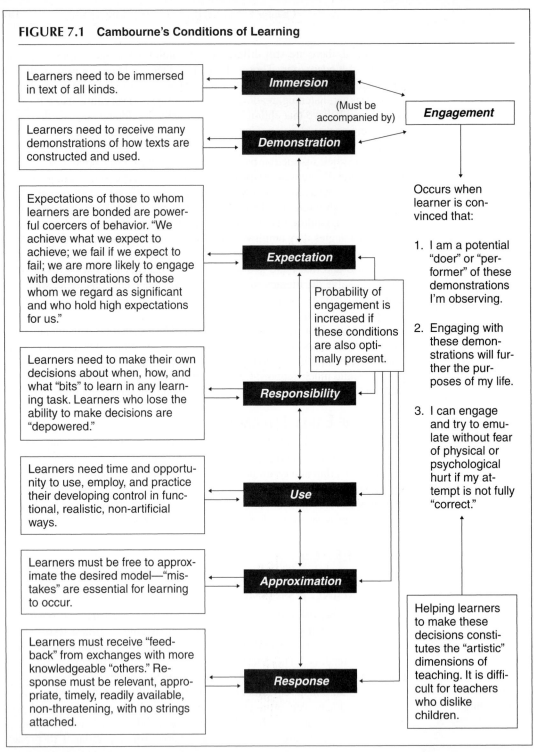

Source: Cambourne, B. "Towards an educationally relevant theory of Literacy Learning: Twenty years of inquiry." *The Reading Teacher,* 49 (3): 182–202. 1995.

reading success, as well as to determine those children who will be "at risk" in school. One example is the *Gates-MacGinitie Reading Test*, 4th edition (2000). This test is a group-administered standardized reading test. There is a pre-reading test (PR), which contains four subtests: literacy concepts, oral language concepts, letters and letter/sound correspondences, and listening comprehension, According to the authors, the purpose of the test is to determine "a student's background for reading instruction."[3] The authors also note that the test is designed to help teachers learn "what each student already knows about important background concepts on which beginning reading skills are built and which concepts students may need additional help with as they begin to receive reading instruction."[4] A close examination of the testing manual provides the authors' rationale for the subtests and other important information. A separate volume entitled *Linking Testing to Teaching: A Classroom Resource for Reading Assessment and Instruction* provides teachers with some ideas about interpreting test scores as well as teaching suggestions related to each subtest.

Unfortunately, there are some dangers attached to pre-reading tests if they are misused. One danger is a self-fulfilling prophecy. If a child does poorly on such a test, the teacher may feel that the child cannot benefit from reading instruction; the child is not expected to be able to learn to read, and as a result, the teacher defers instruction in reading. Eventually, the teacher's feelings concerning the inability of the child to read become part of the child's own self-concept (see "Teacher Expectations" in Chapter 2).

## USES OF GROUP-ADMINISTERED STANDARDIZED PRE-READING ASSESSMENTS

Studies have suggested that the predictive validity of pre-reading tests is not very high, that they could not predict with accuracy how well nonreaders would learn to read, and that teachers' ratings were as accurate in predicting reading success as were the tests.[5] On the other hand, there is a great amount of evidence available to support the relationship between young children's letter naming and their later reading achievement, as well as school achievements.[6] This is also true of phonological awareness. Studies have shown that the alphabet subtest of the *Metropolitan Readiness Tests* "has consistently been the best predictor of scholastic achievement."[7]

[3]Walter H. MacGinitie, Ruth MacGinitie, Katherine Maria, Lois G. Dreyer, Kay E. Hughes, *Gates-MacGinitie Reading Tests,* 4th ed. (Riverside Pub. Co., Itasca, IL., 2000).

[4]Ibid.

[5]Max Coltheart, "What Can Children Learn to Read—And When Should They Be Taught?" in *Reading Research: Advances in Theory and Practice,* vol. 1, eds. T. Gary Waller and G. E. MacKinnon (New York: Academic Press, 1979), p. 15.

[6]Daniel J. Walsh, Gary Glen Price, and Mark G. Gillingham, "The Critical but Transitory Importance of Letter Naming," *Reading Research Quarterly* 23 (winter 1988): 110; Marilyn Jager Adams, *Beginning to Read: Thinking and Learning about Print—A Summary* by Steven A. Stahl, Jean Osborn, and Fran Lehr (Urbana, IL: Center for the Study of Reading, 1990), p. 10.

[7]Ibid., p. 110.

**TABLE 7.1    Early Literacy Components and Their Definitions**

| *Early Literacy Component* | *Brief Definition* |
| --- | --- |
| Oral language concepts | Understanding concepts that are used in spoken language |
| Print concepts | Understanding written language related to books and some of the terms associated with it |
| Phonological awareness | Awareness that spoken language is made up of words, syllables, and phonemes |
| Letter identification | Understanding of the symbols used to form the alphabet |
| Alphabetic principle | Understanding that there is a systematic relationship among letters and sounds and that this code can be used to communicate with others |
| Story sense | Awareness of the structure used to create narrative stories; understanding that stories have to make sense and that books contain stories |

*Source*: Snow, C., S. M. Burns, and P. Griffin, eds. *Preventing Reading Difficulties in Young Children.* Washington, DC: National Academy Press, 1998.

It has been stated that "a great saving in testing time could well stem from using only the letters and numbers subtests or, perhaps, by not testing readiness at all. In either case, the sacrifice in information would be minimal."[8]

Such statements continue, and educators still decry the misuses of pre-reading tests.[9] Despite many expressions of concern, test makers continue to produce such tests, and many teachers are required to use them. It seems that some feel more secure with the results of commercially produced tests than with teachers' judgments, even though evidence weighs against such security.

Why is a test needed to predict future reading success? We already know from voluminous research that high-achieving readers usually come from homes with enriched verbal environments, whereas low-achieving readers usually come from homes in which little conversation takes place. We also know that a rich verbal environment is more likely to be found among middle and upper socioeconomic classes than in lower classes.

Pre-reading tests, like other assessment measures, have their problems. Here are three that come to mind:

[8]Robert L. Hillerich, *Reading Fundamentals for Preschool and Primary Children* (Columbus, OH: Merrill, 1977). p. 25.

[9]See "NAEYC Position Statement on Standardized Testing of Young Children 3–8 Years of Age," *Young Children* 43 (March 1988): 42–47; Sue Bredekamp and Lorrie Shepard, "How Best to Protect Children from Inappropriate School Expectations, Practices, and Policies," *Young Children* 44 (March 1989): 14–24; Constance Kamii (ed.), *Achievement Testing in the Early Grades* (Washington, DC: National Association for the Education of Young Children, 1990).

1. As any teacher who has ever tried to get a group of twenty kindergarten students all focused on the same item on the same page knows, actually administering the test can be extremely time-consuming. When test developers estimate how long it will take to administer the test, they do not take classroom management into account.

2. More often than not, there are too many prompts from the teacher. Therefore, a child's performance score may be inflated. Take, for example, a subtest that is designed to determine if students can identify words. There is a sentence with one word missing, and four choices are given below the sentences. The examiner's manual directs the test administrator to read the sentence *and* the words under the sentence. Students are then supposed to choose the word to complete the sentence so that the sentence will make sense. The problem? Although the test is designed to shed light on how well students can identify words, it does not do this at all because the teacher does all of the reading. All the students have to do is *recognize* a word, which is much easier than identifying it. The only conclusion that can be drawn about students who successfully complete a subtest such as this is that they appear able to recognize some words. But can they read them independently, as their performance on this test is supposed to indicate? We cannot say.

3. Yet another problem focuses on the lack of congruence between *emergent literacy* and the best way to assess it. Because children are constantly emerging and changing, it can be extremely difficult to obtain valid and reliable scores indicative of their development and learning from the one-time group-administered standardized test.

## SUGGESTIONS FOR CHOOSING AND USING MANDATED PRE-READING TESTS

Here are some suggestions on how to choose and use pre-reading tests if they are required in your school system:

1. Use a test that can provide you with information on a child's present level of literacy development.
2. Check the subtests to determine how directly the tasks required are related to reading. For example, some tests require children to match pictures and geometric figures rather than letters. Those children who do well in matching pictures and geometric figures may not do well in matching letters. Check to see if the subtests are similar to the activities presented in the beginning reading program.
3. Check the administration time of the test. Make sure that it is suited to the attention span of your students.
4. Make sure children comprehend the terminology used on the test and understand the directions.
5. Use the results of the test and your interpretation of them to gain information about the child's present level of development so that you can provide the best possible program for him or her.

6. Use the pre-reading test as one measure; also use informal assessments and your judgment to make decisions concerning the child's literacy development. (See Chapter 6.)

## Current Ways to Assess Early Literacy

One of the recommended policies set forth by the authors of the joint position statement of the International Reading Association (IRA) and the National Association for the Education of Young Children (NAEYC) calls for "appropriate assessment strategies that promote children's learning and development." Because children are constantly changing, it can be extremely difficult to obtain valid and reliable scores indicative of a child's development and learning from the one-time group-administered standardized test.

Does this mean that there is no place for standardized tests? Not necessarily. Standardization doesn't automatically make a test evil. Many times it is the *content* of these standardized tests juxtaposed with a teaching philosophy that causes upset. For example, one test that appears to be sweeping the nation is the *Dynamic Indicators of Basic Early Literacy Skills (DIBELS)* (2000).[10] This battery of tests was created by some individuals at the University of Oregon. (For more information, visit the web site at *dibels.oregon.edu.*) The tests begin in kindergarten and continue through third grade. The creators use the word "fluency" a lot when they really mean "proficiency." Thus, letter recognition is called "fluency of letter recognition." Students are given one minute to say the displayed letters. Their performance is then interpreted as a reading level. The problems we see with this battery of tests in general, and the letter recognition test in particular, stem from their lack of congruence with our view of what it means to be a reader (see Chapter 1). First, when assessing fluency, students need time to rehearse; a "cold" read tells us nothing about how fluently a child reads. Second, who cares how quickly a child can say letters of the alphabet? What we want to know is which letters does the child know and which need to be learned? Third, good readers adjust their rate of reading to their purpose for reading. But will students be left with this most important learning if they are constantly timed on all subtests? Not likely. Instead, tests such as these can potentially distort what it means to read, leaving children with many reading misconceptions. These misconceptions can prevent them from becoming willing and able readers.

And let's remember that most often teachers are told rather than asked about using standardized measures. Fortunately, there are several standardized measures that can be used to meaningfully and appropriately assess different aspects of early literacy. For example, the *Yopp-Singer Test of Phonemic Segmentation*[11] is a standardized useful tool to help ascertain how well children

---

[10]"Dynamic Indicators of Basic Early Literacy Skills (DIBELS)." Eugene, OR: University of Oregon. 2001.

[11]Yopp, H. "A Test for Assessing Phonemic Awareness in Young Children." *The Reading Teacher* 49 (1) (1995): 20–29.

can segment phonemes in spoken words. *Concepts About Print*[12] is another that is designed to tap students' understanding of books and terminology related to them. And the list goes on. (Rathvon[13] lists additional standardized measures.) The majority of these measures are individually administered and they can be given several times so that the teacher can note progress over time. When contrasted with group-administered tests, these individual assessment measures can also yield much more information because the examiner can watch what the child does on given tasks. For example, after reading a passage, a child might stop and talk about something that happened to him or her that is similar to what happened in the story. This type of response indicates that the child is making some self-to-text connections, that he is comprehending.

To standardize or not standardize is not the question. Instead, the pertinent question is "What are the children showing they know and what do they need to know to advance as language users?" Addressing these strengths and needs from the beginning is about preventing of problems rather than correcting them later on. Just as regular maintenance can prevent costly car repairs, so, too, does early intervention save resources, human as well as monetary.

Because there are different aspects of early literacy, we need to use a variety of measures to assess them. However, variety can be a bit overwhelming if we aren't sure what it is we're looking for. This leads us once again to ask three important questions: What do I want to know? Why do I want to know? How can I best discover? Table 7.2 provides some help in answering these questions.

# UNDERSTANDING, ASSESSING, AND TEACHING CONCEPTS

## WHAT IS A CONCEPT?

**Concept**
A group of stimuli with common characteristics.

A *concept* is a group of stimuli with common characteristics. These stimuli may be objects, events, or persons. Concepts are usually designated by their names, such as book, war, man, woman, animal, teacher, and so forth. All these concepts refer to classes (or categories) of stimuli. Some stimuli do not refer to concepts; Ms. Jones, the lawyer, Hemingway's "The Killers," World War II, and the Empire State Building are examples. These are specific (not classes of) people, stimuli, or happenings.

Concepts are needed to reduce the complexity of the world. When children learn that their shaggy pets are called dogs, they tend to label all other similar four-footed animals as "dogs." Young children overgeneralize, tending to group all animals together, and have not yet perceived the differences between and among various animals. Unless children learn to discern differences, the classes of words that they deal with will become exceptionally unwieldy and unmanageable. However, if children group each object in a class by itself, this

[12]Clay, M. *The Early Detection of Reading Difficulties,* 3rd ed. Portsmouth, NH: Heinemann, 1985.

[13]Rathvon, N. *Early Reading Assessment: A Practitioner's Handbook.* New York: Guilford, 2004.

**TABLE 7.2   What, Why, How of Early Literacy Assessment Techniques**

| *What Do I Want to Know?* | *Why Do I Want to Know?* | *How Can I Best Discover?* |
|---|---|---|
| Do the children have an understanding of basic language concepts? | Knowing the language concepts children understand and need to learn will better help me to explain instruction. | Informal Inventory of Concepts (pp. 153–155) |
| Do the children have an understanding of how print functions? | Understanding how print functions and knowing the terminology associated with reading are essential for effective reading. | Print Concepts (pp. 156–159) |
| Do children display phonological awareness? | Having phonological awareness can assist reading success. | Phonological Awareness Test (pp. 165–166) |
| Can children identify letters of the alphabet? | Knowing letters appears to be associated with competent reading. | Letter Identification (pp. 170–173) |
| To what degree do students write? | Understanding about the alphabetic principle and using other print conventions are essential for writing success. | Writing Vocabulary (p. 178) Message Writing (p. 179) |
| Do children understand how stories are structured, and do they show listening comprehension? | Understanding how stories are structured will facilitate future reading success. Showing listening comprehension indicates that students realize that understanding is essential for reading. | Wordless Picture Story (pp. 180–182) |

too will bring about difficulties in coping with environmental stimuli because it will also be such an unwieldy method.

The first step in acquiring concepts concerns oral vocabulary because concepts are based on word meanings: Without vocabulary there would be no base for concept development. The second step is gathering data, that is, specific information about the concept to be learned. In doing this, students use their strategies for processing information—they select data that are relevant, ignore irrelevant data, and categorize items that belong together. Concepts are formed when the data are organized into categories.

**Concept development**
Refers to development of thinking.

# HOW DO CONCEPTS DEVELOP?

*Concept development* is closely related to cognitive (thinking) development. Jean Piaget, a renowned Swiss psychologist, has written on children's cognitive development in terms of their ability to organize (which requires conceptualization), classify, and adapt to their environments.

According to Piaget,[14] the mind is capable of intellectual exercise because of its ability to categorize incoming stimuli adequately. *Schemata* (structured designs) are the cognitive arrangements by which this categorization takes place. As children develop and take in more and more information, it becomes necessary to have some way to categorize all the new information. At the same time, their ability to categorize by means of schemata grows too. That is, children should be able to differentiate, to become less dependent on sensory stimuli, and to gain more and more complex schemata. Children should be able to categorize a cat as distinct from a mouse or a rabbit. They should be able to group cat, dog, and cow together as animals. Piaget calls the processes that bring about these changes in children's thinking *assimilation* and *accommodation*.

Assimilation does not change an individual's concept, but allows it to grow. It is a continuous process that helps the individual to integrate new, incoming stimuli into existing schemata or concepts. For example, when children tend to label all similar four-footed animals as dogs, the children are assimilating. They have assimilated all four-footed animals into their existing schema.

If the child encounters stimuli that cannot fit into the existing schema, then the alternative is either to construct a new category or to change the existing one. Accommodation occurs when a new schema or concept is developed, or when an existing schema is changed.

Although both assimilation and accommodation are important processes that the child must attain in order to develop adequate cognition, a balance between the two processes is necessary. If children overassimilate, they will have categories that are too large to handle and, similarly, if they overaccommodate, they will have too many categories, as we have already seen. Piaget calls the balance between the two *equilibrium.* A person having equilibrium would be able to see similarities between stimuli and thus properly assimilate them, and would also be able to determine when new schemata are needed for adequate accommodation of a surplus of categories.

As children develop cognitively they proceed from more global (generalized) schemata to more particular ones. For the child there are usually no right or wrong placements, but only better or more effective ones. That is what good education is all about.

## HOW DOES CONCEPT DEVELOPMENT RELATE TO LANGUAGE AND READING?

Concept development is closely related to language development. Unless children attain the necessary concepts, they will be limited in reading as well as in all other aspects of the language arts (listening, speaking, writing, and viewing).

Knowledge of what concepts are and how children attain them is especially essential in a diagnostic-reading and improvement program. Teachers in

**Schemata**
These structured designs are the cognitive arrangements by which the mind is able to categorize incoming stimuli.

**Assimilation**
A continuous process which helps the individual to integrate new incoming stimuli to existing concepts—Piaget's cognitive development.

**Accommodation**
The developing of new categories by a child rather than integrating them into existing ones—Piaget's cognitive development.

**Equilibrium**
According to Piaget, a balance between assimilation and accommodation in cognitive development.

[14]Jean Piaget, *The Origins of Intelligence in Children* (New York: International Universities Press, 1952).

such a program must recognize early when a child is lacking certain concepts and help that child to attain them.

The quality of language development depends on the interrelationships of such factors as intelligence, home environment, sex differences, and family makeup. The factors that influence language development also influence concept development. As a result, children who are more advanced in language development are also usually more advanced in concept development, and these children tend to be better readers than those who are not as advanced.[15]

## How Can Oral Language Concepts Be Assessed?

Concepts are necessary to help students acquire increasing amounts of knowledge. For example, as students proceed through the grades in school, their learning becomes more abstract and is expressed in words, using verbal stimuli as labels for concepts. Many teachers take for granted that those spoken concept labels are understood by their students, but this is not always so. Young children's literal interpretation of oral and written discourse and their limited knowledge of the world around them affects their comprehension and ability to form correct concepts. If enough information is not given, concepts are often learned either incompletely or incorrectly.

When children enter school, the teacher must assess their concept-development level, and then help them to add the attributes necessary and relevant for the development of particular concepts. At the same time the teacher must help students to delete all those concepts that are faulty or irrelevant.

One way to assess language concepts is to use an informal inventory test of concepts, such as the one shown in Figure 7.2. It can be given orally to individual students.

Another method to determine whether children have the concepts such as opposites is to ask each child to give some opposites for words such as these:

| | | |
|---|---|---|
| no | good | fat |
| boy | mommy | go |
| happy | early | fast |

A third way to determine whether the children understand language concepts is to play games. For example, to see if children understand the concepts of left and right, play the game "Simon Says" with the children and use directions with the words *left* and *right.*

A fourth way to observe whether children understand specific language concepts is to use them as part of classroom routines. For example, the concepts of *first* and *last* can be assessed by asking children to name who is first or who is last in line.

---

[15]Walter D. Loban, *Language Development: Kindergarten through Grade Twelve*, Research Report #18 (Urbana, IL: National Council of Teachers of English, 1976).

---

**FIGURE 7.2**   **Example of an Informal Inventory Test of Concepts for Early Primary-Grade Students**

---

For each concept the teacher will orally state the tested term in the context of a sentence. The children will show they understand the concept by correctly checking or putting a circle around the picture that best describes the concept. Before beginning, the teacher should make sure that all children understand the symbol for a check (✓) and that they can draw a circle around an object.

    1. Concept *over.* Concept in sentence: The check (✓) is over the ball.

*Directions*

Put a circle around the picture that shows a ✓ is over a ball. (Again, the teacher should put a ✓ on the board to make sure children understand this term. The teacher should make a circle on the board to make sure children understand this concept as well.)

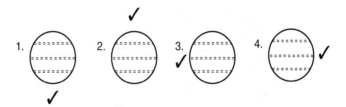

    2. Concept of *under.* Concept in sentence: The check (✓) is under the ball.

*Directions*

Put a circle around the picture that shows a ✓ is under a ball.

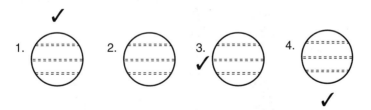

    3. Concept of *square.* Sentence: Which picture shows a square?

*Directions*

Put a check in the square.

(*continued*)

**FIGURE 7.2**   *(continued)*

4. Concept of *triangle.* Sentence: Which picture shows a triangle?
*Directions*
Put a check in the triangle.

5. Concept of *most.* Sentence: Which box has the most balls?
*Directions*
Draw a circle around the box that has the most balls.

1. 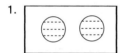  2. 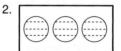  3.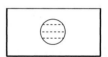

6. Concept of *least.* Sentence: Which box has the least number of balls?
*Directions*
Draw a circle around the box that has the least number of balls.

1. 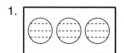  2. 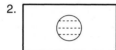  3.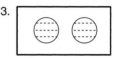

7. Concept of *smallest.* Sentence: Which ball is the smallest?
*Directions*
Draw a circle around the smallest ball.

1.   2.   3.   4.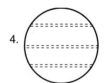

8. Concept of *largest.* Sentence: Which ball is the largest?
*Directions*
Draw a circle around the largest ball.

1.   2.   3.   4.

(*continued*)

9. Concept of *opposites.*

*Directions*

Draw a circle around the picture that is the opposite of the word that I am going to say. (For example, the teacher says, "What is the opposite of girl?")

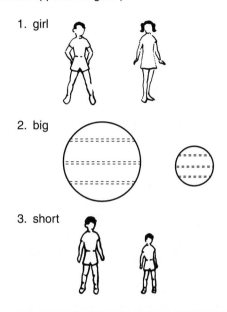

1. girl

2. big

3. short

A fifth, more formalized way of assessing oral language concepts is to use a standardized, norm-referenced test such as the *Boehm Test of Language Concepts,* 3rd edition (2000), which is published in both English and Spanish. The test is designed to help you see which of the 50 most frequently occurring concepts children know or need to learn.

## HOW CAN PRINT CONCEPTS BE ASSESSED?

Some concepts relate to print and books. Children's understanding of these concepts is important to their early reading success. These concepts include print carries a message, left-to-right progression, return sweep, and terms such as "word," "letter," "beginning," and "ending."

One way to assess for these print concepts is to use the *Print Concepts Test* shown in Figure 7.3. It is a modification of the original *Concepts About Print* test developed by Marie Clay.[16] The main difference between this version and Clay's is that it is not standardized. It also permits the examiner to use just about any children's literature selection.

[16]Clay, 1985.

## FIGURE 7.3  Print Concepts

Name: _____

**Directions:** Using the book that you have selected, give the following prompts to encourage the child to interact with it. Read the story aloud as you proceed. Place a ✔ next to each item answered correctly.

| Prompt | Response (✔ = correct) | Print Concept |
| --- | --- | --- |
| 1. Hand the child the book upside down, spine first, saying something like: "Show me the front of this book." Then read the title to the child. | | layout of book |
| 2. Say: "I would like to begin reading the story, but I need your help. Please open the book and point to the exact spot where I should begin reading." | | print conveys message |
| 3. Stay on the same page and say: "Point to where I need to start reading." | | directionality: where to begin |
| 4. Say: "Point to where I should go after I start reading." | | directionality: left-to-right progression |
| 5. Say: "Point to where I go next." Read the pair of pages. | | directionality: return sweep |
| 6. Turn the page and say: "Point to where I should begin reading on this page. Now point to where I should end." Read the page. | | terminology: beginning and end |
| 7. Turn the page and say: "Point to the bottom of this page. Point to the top of it. Now point to the middle of it." Read the page. | | terminology: top, bottom, middle |
| 8. Using the same page, say: "Point to one letter." | | terminology: letter |
| 9. Again using the same page, say: "Point to one word." | | terminology: word |
| 10. Turn the page. Make sure that this page contains words that have corresponding upper- and lowercase letters. Read the page. Then point to a capital letter and say: "Point to a little letter that is like this one." | | matching lower to uppercase letters |
| 11. Turn the page and say: "Let's read these pages together. I'll read and you point." Read the pages. | | speech to match print |
| 12. Finish reading the book. Then turn back to a page that has the punctuation marks you want to assess. Point to the punctuation mark and say: "What is this?" "What is it for?" | | punctuation: period, question mark, quotation marks |

*Print Concepts Administration Procedures*

1. Choose a book that is relatively short. *The Hungry Monster* by Phyllis Root (Candlewick, 1997) is one example.
2. Make a copy of the *Print Concepts* form for each child.
3. Read through the form to become familiar with what you will be asking and to make sure that the book you will be using has the appropriate examples as noted on the form.
4. Individually administer the *Print Concepts* assessment using the prompts shown on the *Print Concepts* form.

*Scoring Procedures*

1. Look at the responses that the child provides.
2. Record your observations on the *Summary of Print Concepts* form shown in Figure 7.4.
3. Use the results to plan instruction.

As noted in Chapter 6, compiling the results of individual assessment measures on a class matrix can be helpful in terms of seeing the class at a glance. The *Concepts About Print Class Profile* form shown in Figure 7.5 can be used for this purpose. The form is also helpful in that it shows which of the items related to directionality, terminology, and punctuation.

Those who need to use a norm-referenced standardized test will want to use Clay's *Concepts About Print* test. Standard prompts are used, as are the literature selections used to assess the print concepts.

## TEACHING ORAL LANGUAGE AND PRINT CONCEPTS

A rich oral language program is a necessary first step to prevent reading failure because it helps prepare children for reading. The closer the children's language is to the written symbols encountered in reading, the greater is their chance of success. Hearing English in the context of something meaningful with which they can identify helps children gain "facility in listening, attention span, narrative sense, recall of stretches of verbalization and the recognition of new words as they appear in other contexts."[17]

Teachers using a diagnostic-reading and improvement program understand that one main reason for assessing students is to determine what students know and what they need to learn. Teachers then can use the results to plan appropriate instruction. There are several ways to teach language and print concepts.

### Read Aloud to Children

Numerous researchers investigating the power of the read-aloud have arrived at the same findings: Reading aloud increases children's listening vocabularies.[18]

---

[17]Dorothy H. Cohen, "The Effect of Language on Vocabulary and Reading Achievement," *Elementary English* 45 (February 1968): 217; see also David B. Yaden, Jr., Deborah W. Rowe, and Laurie MacGillivray, "Emergent Literacy," *Handbook of Reading Research, III* (Mahwah, NJ: Lawrence Erlbaum Associates, Inc. 2000), p. 429.

[18]Warwick B. Elley, "Vocabulary Acquisition from Listening," *Reading Research Quarterly* 24 (Spring 1989): 174–87.

## FIGURE 7.4  Summary of Print Concepts

Title of Book: _____

***Directions:*** Use this form to summarize your observations of print concepts.

### Observations

The child demonstrates knowledge of the following print concepts (✔ the appropriate spaces)

_____ layout of books (item 1)

_____ print contains written message (item 2)

_____ directionality (items 3, 4, 5)

_____ terminology associated with reading (items 6, 7, 8, 9)

_____ uppercase letters (item 10)

_____ lowercase letters (item 10)

_____ speech to print match (item 11)

_____ punctuation (item 12)

### Comments/Notes

_____
_____
_____
_____
_____
_____
_____
_____
_____
_____
_____
_____
_____
_____
_____
_____
_____
_____

**FIGURE 7.5  Concepts about Print: Class Profile**

| Name | Directionality | | | | | Terminology | | | | Punctuation | | |
|---|---|---|---|---|---|---|---|---|---|---|---|---|
| | 1 layout of books | 2 print conveys message | 3 where to begin | 4 left-to-right progression | 5 return sweep | 6 beginning, end | 7 top, bottom, middle | 8 letter | 9 word | 10 upper- and lower-case matching | 11 speech-to-print match | 12 period, question mark, quotation marks |
| | | | | | | | | | | | | |
| | | | | | | | | | | | | |
| | | | | | | | | | | | | |
| | | | | | | | | | | | | |
| | | | | | | | | | | | | |
| | | | | | | | | | | | | |
| | | | | | | | | | | | | |
| | | | | | | | | | | | | |
| | | | | | | | | | | | | |
| | | | | | | | | | | | | |
| | | | | | | | | | | | | |
| | | | | | | | | | | | | |
| | | | | | | | | | | | | |
| | | | | | | | | | | | | |
| | | | | | | | | | | | | |
| | | | | | | | | | | | | |

From *Flexible Grouping in Reading* by Michael Opitz. Published by Scholastic Teaching Resources/Scholastic, Inc. Copyright © 1995 by Michael Opitz. Reprinted by permission.

Other researchers have discovered that children who speak nonstandard English make significant gains toward standard English when they are involved in a rich oral program, one that stresses the reading aloud of stories and the active involvement of the children in related activites. In terms of language and print concepts, the teacher can do much:

- Before reading, the teacher can emphasize "front" by saying something like, "The title of our book is on the front cover."
- The teacher can also point to the words while reading, which helps children to see that print carries the message and that there is a match between what is said and the print (i.e., speech-to-print match).
- Upon completion of the story, the teacher can emphasize language concepts such as "first" and "last" by using the terms as children tell what happened first and last.
- Concepts such as "pair" can be emphasized by telling students to pair up. Each pair can then be invited to chime in a rereading of the story at their designated time.

As you can see, there are many ways that language concepts can be reinforced through read-alouds. There are several children's literature titles that actually focus on language concepts that you can choose to use for read-aloud sessions. *A Pair of Protoceratops* by Bernard Most (Harcourt, 1998), *Parts* by Shelley Rotner (Walker, 2001), *Over, Under, Through* by Tana Hoban (Macmillan, 1973), and *What's Opposite?* by Stephen Swinburne (Boyds Mills, 2000) are a few of the many available titles.

Reading a story to children can be a rewarding, interactive learning experience if it is done properly. Here are some suggestions to ensure your success when reading aloud to children.

*Preparing for the Story*

1. Choose a short storybook that is at the attention, interest, and concept-development levels of the children and that has large pictures that can be easily seen.
2. Have the young children sit comfortably and in a position that allows them to see the pictures easily.
3. Make sure there are no distractions in the room.
4. State the title and show the book to the children. Ask them if they can figure out what the story will be about from the title.
5. Tell them to listen carefully for certain things. (Of course, this will be based on the story being read.)

*Reading the Story*

1. Read the story aloud to the children.
2. Stop at key points and have them predict what will happen or have them state the refrain if the story contains one.
3. State more questions for them to think about while they are listening to the story.

4. If children interject comments during the story, you should acknowledge these by saying "good thinking," if it shows they are thinking, and then continue reading.

*After the Story*

When the story is finished, have the children answer some of the unanswered questions and do some of the following based on their attention and interest levels:

1. Tell what the story is about.
2. Retell the story in sequence.
3. Discuss whether the story is based on fantasy or reality.
4. Act out the story.
5. Make up another ending for the story.

### *Play Games*

Learning language can and should be fun. Fun allows for a positive association with learning language. Games such as "Simon Says" are perfect for developing further understanding of specific language concepts. And playing the "Hokey Pokey" is a perfect way to help children to better understand specific language concepts.

### *Do Some Focused, Explicit Teaching*

You might decide that in addition to focused story reading, you want to design some lessons that teach specific language concepts. Looking at the class matrix described earlier can help you to see who needs some extra instruction in certain areas and you can teach them the needed concepts. In Chapter 6, we provide an example of a teacher who did just that.

### *Use Language in a Variety of Ways*

Several years ago, Halliday[19] identified seven distinct functions that children often use for language. However, some children appear to be limited language users. Knowing about these functions can help teachers to create situations in the classroom in which children need to use all seven functions, which will help them become flexible language users. In Table 7.3 we show these functions and provide sample classroom activities.

# UNDERSTANDING, ASSESSING, AND TEACHING PHONOLOGICAL AWARENESS

## WHAT IS PHONOLOGICAL AWARENESS?

Although the terms phonological awareness and phonemic awareness are sometimes used as synonyms, this is incorrect. *Phonological awareness* refers

---

[19]Halliday, M. *Explorations in the Functions of Language*. London: Arnold, 1975.

**TABLE 7.3    Halliday's Functions of Language and Sample Instructional Activities**

| Function of Language | Use | Sample Instructional Activities |
|---|---|---|
| Instrumental ("I want") | To satisfy needs or desires | Check out library books<br>Sign in for attendance<br>Provide directions for others |
| Regulatory ("Do as I tell you!") | To control behavior of others | Establish guidelines for taking care of classroom equipment<br>Play follow-the-leader type games |
| Interactional ("Me and You") | To establish and keep relationships | Write messages to one another<br>Have children share work areas and/or materials<br>Have children work together to plan a project |
| Personal ("Here I Come!") | To express one's personal feelings or thoughts | Provide time for students to talk with one another<br>Read stories and ask students to share their thoughts about the story |
| Heuristic ("Tell me why.") | To discover and find out why something happens | Create problems for students to solve<br>Conduct simple experiments |
| Imaginative ("Let's pretend.") | To create an imaginative world of one's own | Use puppets<br>Have a dress-up center |
| Informative ("I have something to tell you.") | To provide information to others | Provide time for students to share announcements<br>Provide time for students to tell current events |

From Halliday, M., *Exploration in the Functions of Language,* 1975.

to awareness of three aspects of spoken language: words, syllables within words, and sounds or phonemes within syllables and words. *Phonemic awareness* is the awareness that words are made up of individual sounds. It is one aspect of the larger category of phonological awareness. One way to remember the difference between the terms is to visualize an umbrella adorned with tassels. Phonological awareness would be the fabric and the frame holding the umbrella together. Phonemic awareness would be one of the tassels hanging from the end of one of the umbrella's sections. Both terms, however, refer to spoken language. A child who is phonologically and phonemically aware is not necessarily able to connect the sound units with written symbols.

Phonological awareness develops in stages. Learners first become aware that their spoken language is composed of words. They then progress to the stage in which they become aware that words are constructed of syllables. The last stage is the one in which learners become aware that words and syllables are made up of individual sounds (i.e., phonemes). Table 7.4 shows the different stages and sample tasks associated with each.

### Phonemic Awareness Tasks

There are many tasks associated with phonemic awareness; some are more difficult than others. When children can perform all of these tasks, they are considered to have phonemic awareness. Identifying and producing rhyme appears to be the least difficult. Another phonemic awareness task is *phoneme matching*, which calls for the learner to identify words that have a given sound or to generate a word that has a given sound. When children are expected to listen to a sentence and then state the sound that they hear at the beginning of a word or to state some words that begin like a given word, they are performing phoneme matching.

In a *phoneme blending* task, students are expected to put sounds together to form a given word. For example, the teacher might say, "I'm thinking of a word that names something we have at lunch. It's /m/ ilk. What's the word?" Children must blend the first sound with the rest of the sounds to state the word "milk."

In a *phoneme segmentation* task, children are given a word and asked to tell how many sounds they hear in it. They are also often expected to produce the actual sounds. For example, the teacher might say, "Tell me the sounds you hear in the word 'mom.'" Learners might be expected to drop a counter into a cup that represents the sounds heard in the word.

*Phoneme manipulation* entails manipulating the sounds within a given word in different ways. Sometimes, children are expected to substitute one

**TABLE 7.4   Stages of Phonological Awareness**

| *Phonological Awareness Level* | *Sample Activity* |
| --- | --- |
| Recognizing that words represent a sound unit—word awareness | Provide children with some sort of counter. After reading a story, select one sentence and say it aloud. Repeat the sentence slowly and instruct students to drop a counter into a cup every time they hear a word. |
| Detecting that words are made up of different parts—syllable awareness | After reading a story, select some words that have single and multiple syllables. Invite students to clap out the parts as words are read. |
| Recognizing that words are made up of individual sounds—phoneme awareness | State a given word from a story and ask students how many sounds they hear in the word. |

From *Rhymes and Reasons: Literature and Language Play for Phonological Awareness* by Michael Opitz. Copyright © 2000. Published by Heinemann.

sound for another as in "What word do we have if we change the /m/ in *man* to /p/?" Other times, children are asked to add sounds to a given word as in "Add /s/ to nail. What's the new word?" Another task requires children to delete a sound within a word such as when the teacher says, "Take away the first sound in gate. What's the new word?"

## HOW CAN PHONOLOGICAL AWARENESS BE ASSESSED?

Phonological awareness in general and phonemic awareness in particular appear to be important for reading success. Recently, the National Reading Panel[20] performed a meta-analysis of several studies and concluded that phonemic awareness is an important reading skill and that some children needed explicit instruction. Likewise, the Board of Directors of the International Reading Association published a position statement on phonemic awareness and the teaching of reading.[21] By posing several questions and answers in the statement, the group explains the intricacies of phonemic awareness.

There are both informal and formal ways of assessing the different levels of phonological awareness. The one shown in Figure 7.6 is an informal measure that Michael Opitz created for *Summer Success Reading*.[22] It is used here with permission.

*Administering the Phonological Awareness Test*

1. Make a copy of the score sheet shown in Figure 7.6 for each student to be assessed.
2. Individually administer the test following the prompts shown on the score sheet.

*Scoring the Phonological Awareness Test*

1. Write the number correct for each subtest in the Summary section shown on the form in Figure 7.6.
2. Write any pertinent comments in the space provided.

A second way to assess phonological awareness is to use a norm-referenced measure such as the Test of Phonological Awareness (TOPA),[23] which is a group-administered test.

## TEACHING PHONOLOGICAL AWARENESS

For most children, phonological awareness is more caught than taught. Children who come to kindergarten or first grade with this awareness have been

---

[20]National Institute of Child Health and Human Development. *Report of the National Reading Panel: Teaching Children to Read.* Washington, DC: NIH Publication 00-4654, 2000.

[21]"Phonemic Awareness and the Teaching of Reading: A Position Statement from the Board of Directors of the International Reading Association." Newark, DE: International Reading Association, 1998.

[22]Michael Opitz. *Summer Success Reading* (Boston, MA: Great Source Education Group, 2001.)

[23]Torgesen, J.K., and B. R. Bryant. *Test of Phonological Awareness.* Austin, TX: PRO-ED, 1994.

## FIGURE 7.6   PRETEST: Part A: Phonological Awareness Score Sheet

Name: _____ Date _____

For each item, circle + for each correct response and − for each incorrect response. Give one point for each +.

### 1. Word Level: Counting Words in Sentences

**Directions:** "I am going to say a sentence to you. I want you to clap every time you hear a word. Let's try one: 'I am here.'" (Pause for child to clap or repeat the sentence and clap.) "Good! You clapped three times! Now do the same for these sentences."

| *Sentence* | *Response* | |
|---|---|---|
| I like you. (3) | + | — |
| Summer is fun. (3) | + | — |
| The boy likes to read. (5) | + | — |
| Can you write? (3) | + | — |
| Tom drinks his milk. (4) | + | — | Score _____ |

### 2. Syllable Level: Counting Syllables in Words

**Directions:** "I am going to say some words to you, and this time I want you to tap on the table for each word part, for example, *cat* (tap once), *mother* (tap twice). Try some with me: *pig* (pause for response), *letter* (pause), *bunny* (pause). Good! Let's do some more words."

| *Word* | *Response* | |
|---|---|---|
| Dad (1) | + | — |
| funny (2) | + | — |
| animal (3) | + | — |
| toy (1) | + | — |
| sidewalk (2) | + | — | Score _____ |

### 3. Phoneme Level: Rhyming

**Directions:** "I am going to say two words. If they rhyme, say 'yes.' If they don't, say 'no.' Let's try a couple: *mat/cat* (pause for response). Yes! They rhyme. Now try another: *man/bet* (pause). Good! Let's do some more."

| *Word Pairs* | *Response* | |
|---|---|---|
| fish/wish (*yes*) | + | — |
| said/pet (*no*) | + | — |
| look/book (*yes*) | + | — |
| come/some (*yes*) | + | — |
| nine/name (*no*) | + | — | Score _____ |

*(continued)*

**FIGURE 7.6**    *(continued)*

**1. Phoneme Level: Matching**

***Directions:*** "Now let's think of words that begin with the same sound. For example, dad, dog, and door begin with /d/." (Be sure to state the sound rather than the name of the letter.) "Let's try one. I'll say a sound and you tell me a word that starts with that sound: /s/." (Accept any word that begins with /s/.) "Good! Let's do a few more."

| *Sound* | *Response* |   |
|---------|------------|---|
| /l/ | + — |   |
| /p/ | + — |   |
| /r/ | + — |   |
| /t/ | + — |   |
| /m/ | + — | Score _____ |

**Summary**

1. Word Level: Counting Words in Sentences       _____

2. Syllable Level: Counting Syllables in Words       _____

3. Phoneme Level: Rhyming       _____

4. Phoneme Level: Matching       _____

Total _____ /20

raised in a rich language environment where they were exposed to read-alouds, songs, nursery rhymes, poems, and other forms of language play. The reverse is true for those children who are lacking in phonological awareness. More than likely they have not been afforded with a rich language environment that facilitates an understanding of spoken language.

Here are six specific suggestions drawn from the work of many individuals who have shed light on how to best help children acquire phonological awareness.[24]

1. *Embed phonological awareness into everyday reading and writing experiences.* Doing so helps children understand how this awareness of sounds relates to reading and writing. Table 7.5 provides a list of typical reading and writing experiences, a sample activity for each, and an explanation of how the experience promotes phonological awareness.

[24]Opitz, M. *Rhymes and Reasons: Literature and Language Play for Phonological Awareness.* Portsmouth, NH: Heinemann, 2000.

**TABLE 7.5    Reading and Writing Experiences That Foster Phonological Awareness**

| Typical Reading/Writing Experiences | Sample Activity | Phonological Awareness |
| --- | --- | --- |
| Read-aloud | Reading books that emphasize language features such as rhyme and alliteration | Words are made up of sound elements that sometimes sound alike. |
| Shared reading | Reading a big book and asking children to clap every time they hear a word | Words are separate units in the speech stream. They can be used to create stories and sentences. |
| Guided reading | Providing children with a text to read and directing them to point to each word as they read | Stories are made up of words. Spaces show where the word starts and ends. |
| Independent reading | Providing time for children to read their own books | Stories are a written form of language. There are units of sound in the speech stream— including words, syllables, and sounds—that are used to write these stories. |
| Modeled writing | Inviting children to watch as words are written on a chart or the board, saying each slowly to stretch them out—either by syllable or by sound | Several word parts/ sounds can be used to create a word. These need to be put in a specific sequence. |
| Interactive writing | Encouraging children to participate in creating a message by stating their ideas | Speech can be written. It is written in chunks. |
| Independent writing | Providing time for children to write | Sounds are used to create words to communicate an idea to others. |

2. *Provide children with time to write using invented spelling.* Although it is true that phonological awareness is focused on sounds of language rather than its printed form, there is a wealth of research that points to the value of having children write to develop phonological awareness. As children write, they learn to represent spoken language with written symbols and hone their skills at segmenting phonemes.

3. *Read aloud books that utilize specific language features.* Texts such as these draw the learners' attention to given language features such as rhyme, alliteration, phoneme substitution, and phoneme segmentation. As a result of being exposed to books such as these, children become able to make distinctions among sounds and may develop phonological awareness in general and

phonemic awareness in particular in meaningful contexts. Fortunately, there are several such titles being written every year. *Clickety Clack* (Spence & Spence, 1999) is a rhyming story about what happens when many different kinds and numbers of animals decide they want to ride a train. Much initial consonant substitution is used to create the rhymes, making this an excellent book not only for exposing children to rhyme but also for providing some meaningful practice with phoneme substitution. *Pignic* (Miranda, 1996) is an example of alliterative text in which each member of the pig family brings to the pignic something that begins with the same sound that begins their name. Children can join in the fun by going on their own imaginary picnic and bringing along some item that begins with the same sound as their name. *Things That Are Most in the World* (Barrett, 1998) is a repetitive text that tells about some of the silliest, heaviest, and smelliest things in the world! Once they have finished reading the book, children can learn more about phoneme deletion by playing the take-away game. Using words from the text, children might be asked to "Take *-est* away from wiggliest. What's the new word?" *Earthsong* (Rogers, 1998) is a poetry text that includes a rhythmic, rhyming pattern in the dialogues between parents and their offspring. It is an excellent book to help children further understand rhyme.

Songs can also be used to further children's understanding of phonological awareness. Song picture books have been created to illustrate specific songs. For example, *Hush Little Baby* (Frazee, 1999) is true to the original song, but updated illustrations are used. Once children have sung the song, each word can be framed on a second reading to help children understand word boundaries.

Finally, texts that use language in humorous ways, such as those written by Dr. Seuss, help children to see that we often play with the sounds in our language. Along with this learning comes a heightened sense of phonological awareness. For example, in *Altoona Baboona* (Bynum, 1999), the author inserts a sound at the end of several words, making this a perfect book to help children further understand sound deletion or sound addition. Children can be directed to take the last sound off the word and say the remaining word (i.e., phoneme deletion), or add a sound to the end of their names (i.e., phoneme addition). Additional books that invite language play are listed in Table 7.6.

4. *Involve children in fun oral language activities.* Some children may need more explicit instruction to develop all levels of phonological awareness. These children need to be engaged with the three points listed above as well as activities that will stimulate their curiosity about and understanding of their spoken language. If children need to understand the concept that words represent a sound unit, then they can be provided with some sort of counter. Once a story has been read, students can be directed to pick up a counter for each word they hear. If children need to better understand that words are constructed of syllables, they can be invited to clap out the parts as words are read aloud. If students need additional practice with recognizing that words are made up of individual sounds (i.e., phonemes), they can be asked to tell the sounds they hear in given words from the story.

5. *Assess to see where children need the most help.* This can be accomplished through observing children as they participate in literacy-related activ-

**TABLE 7.6   Additional Books That Invite Language Play**

*Rhyme*

Downey, L. 2000.**The Flea's Sneeze.** Holt. 0-805-061037.

Marchank, S. 1999. **The Absentminded Fellow.** Farrar, Straus, & Giroux. 0-374-300135.

Martin, B. 1999. **A Beasty Story**. Harcourt. 0-15-201683-X.

*Alliteration*

Barron, R. 2000. **Fed Up! A Feast of Frazzled Foods**. Putnam. 0-399-234500.

Duncan, P. 1999. **The Wacky Wedding: A Book of Alphabet Antics**. Hyperion. 0-7868-2248-1.

*Repetition*

Bauer, M. 2002. **Sleep, Little One, Sleep.** Aladdin. 0-689-85269X.

Collicut, P. 1999. **This Train.** Farrar, Straus, & Giroux. 0-374-37493-7.

*Poetry*

Rylant, C. 1998. **Bless Us All: A Child's Yearbook of Blessings.** Simon & Schuster. 0-689-823703.

Stevenson, R. 1999. **My Shadow.** Harcourt. 0-7636-0923-4.

*Song*

Hoberman, M. 2000. **The Eensy-Weensy Spider.** Little, Brown. 0-316-363308.

Norworth, J. 1999. **Take Me Out to the Ballgame.** Aladdin. 0-689-82433-5.

*Goofy*

Bynum, J. 1999. **Altoona Baboona.** Harcourt. 0-15-201860-3.

London, J. 2001. **Crunch Munch.** Harcourt. 0-15-202603-7.

ities such as writing. Observations during writing could reveal those children whose writing shows spaces between words or words that have representative symbols for sounds. These would indicate that the child has developed a sense of all levels of phonological awareness. And the results of assessments such as those shown and mentioned above can be used to detect which children might need some additional help.

6. *Get families involved!* One way to accomplish this is to provide a book and a brief explanation that tells how to complete an accompanying activity. For example, if the book that is being sent home contains much alliteration, the letter can explain how to point out to the child that all of the words on a given page begin with a certain sound. The child can then be asked to listen for the sound and to state it after a page has been read. The parent can then be in-

structed to have the child think of other words that begin with the same sound. The letter must focus on exactly what the parent needs to do when working on the book with the child.

# UNDERSTANDING, ASSESSING, AND TEACHING LETTER IDENTIFICATION

## WHAT IS LETTER IDENTIFICATION?

Letter identification is just that—identifying the letters of the alphabet. Although common sense would tell us that being able to identify and name the letters of the alphabet is important for reading and writing tasks, there is also ample evidence that being able to name letters is a predictor of end-of-year achievement for kindergarten students.[25]

Letter identification also helps students learn letter–sound associations (i.e., alphabetic principle). This should come as no surprise because it would be pretty difficult to make any kind of association if one part of the equation is unknown! And, as Rathvon notes, "Only when children have developed the insight that written word forms are related to the sounds rather than the meaning of language can they learn the specific correspondences between letter and phonemes."[26]

## HOW CAN LETTER IDENTIFICATION BE ASSESSED?

Ask any kindergarten or first-grade teacher and he or she will tell you that a good way to assess letter identification ability is to individually ask children to name the letters in random order. Both uppercase and lowercase letters are assessed because knowing one form of the letter doesn't necessarily mean that a child knows the other form.

The protocol in Figure 7.7 shows one informal way of assessing letter identification.

*Administering the Letter Identification Test*

1. Place the letter identification page in front of the child. Say something like, "Here are some letters. Take a look at each one and tell me what it is. You may say 'pass' if you cannot remember the name of the letter."
2. Use index cards to cover everything but the lines being read. If necessary, point to each letter with your finger (or have the child point).
3. As the child responds, use your copy of the assessment to note correct responses (1) and incorrect responses (2). When responses are incorrect, record the actual response or "DK" (doesn't know) if the child doesn't

---

[25]Bond, G., and R. Dykstra. "The Cooperative Research Program in First-Grade Reading Instruction." *Reading Research Quarterly 2* (1967): 5–142.

[26]Rathvon, N. *Early Reading Assessment: A Practitioner's Handbook*. New York: Guilford, 2004.

FIGURE 7.7   PRETEST: Part A: Letter Identification, Student Copy

C  U  S  I  N  Q

Z  K  E  M  L  D  V

P  T  R  B  F  G

Y  X  W  O  H  A  J


d  w  e  t  f  p

j  u  h  k  n  r  i

x  b  o  y  c  a

g  m  v  l  q  z  s

know the specific letter. If the child self-corrects, write OK. Remember that self-corrections can be made at any time and should not be counted as errors.

*Scoring the Letter Identification Test*

1. Count the number of responses for the uppercase letters and lowercase letters.
2. Note the scores in the box on the scoring form in Figure 7.8.

Marie Clay's *Observation Survey* (Heinemann, 1985) provides a formal, norm-referenced standardized way of assessing letter identification. The assessment is similar to the one described above and it is individually administered. However, norms are provided, as are some additional assessment procedures.

## TEACHING LETTER IDENTIFICATION

Many children come to school already knowing the letters of the alphabet, so the suggestions given here simply enhance their understanding. However, there are some children who are just beginning to learn to identify letters. This is not to say that these children haven't already noticed letters. Few can escape environmental print and most understand at an intuitive level that certain marks are used to record their names. They simply cannot put a label with the squiggle. Here are a few suggestions for helping children to identify letters:

1. *Use their names!* Meaningful association is necessary for any of us to learn anything, and this also is true of children learning letters. That is why many kindergarten and first-grade teachers use children's names when thinking about which letters to teach first. In other words, the fact that children can identify their name is no guarantee that they know every letter in the name. Because names are meaningful, then, teachers often begin by having children learn these letters.

2. *Use alphabet books.* One sure way to help children see the connection between letters and reading is to share alphabet books with them. Different letters can be pointed out along the way. There are numerous alphabet books that would appeal to just about any interest. *ABC Disney* by Robert Sabuda (Hyperion, 1998) is a pop-up book that features different characters from Disney movies. Others include *The Accidental Zucchini* by Mary Grover (Harcourt, 1997), *Flora McDonnell's A B C* by Flora McDonnell (Candlewick, 1997), and *ABC Kids* by Laura Ellen Williams (Philomel, 2000).

3. *Create an Alphabet Book.* Staple enough pages together for each letter of the alphabet. You might print one letter on each page in alphabetical order or you may decide to have the children write the letters in the order they learn them. In either case, the letter can be written at the top of the page and children can find pictures associated with the letter. These pictures can be labeled and children can trace over the letter shown on the top of the page.

4. *Be newspaper detectives.* Tear pages of the local newspaper into four parts and give each child a part. Have them search out letters that match the ones they are learning. They can use a yellow marker to highlight the letter.

**FIGURE 7.8 PRETEST: Part A: Letter Identification, Score Sheet**

Name: ______________________ Date: ______________

## Capital Letters

C U S I N Q

Z K E M L D V

P T R B F G

Y X W O H A J

Number Correct ______

## Lowercase Letters

d w e t f p

j u h k n r i

x b o y c a

g m v l q z s

Number Correct ______

TOTAL CORRECT ____/152

From *Summer Success: Reading, Kindergarten* by James F. Baumann, Michael F. Opitz, Laura Robb. Text copyright

5. *Use objects*. Have children bring in toys or other objects whose names begin with letters they are learning. These could be put in a big tub and could be used for sorting into different pockets, each labeled with a different letter. Likewise, labels from cans and other food products can be brought into the classroom and students can identify the letters shown on the various labels.

# UNDERSTANDING, ASSESSING, AND TEACHING WRITING

## WHAT IS WRITING?

**Emergent writing**
Nonconventional writing that includes scribbling and nonphonetic letterings.

When young children of about two and one-half first put pencil or crayon to paper, they are in the initial, or emergent, stage of writing. Children in the *emergent writing* stage write in preconventional or emergent forms (scribbling, drawing, nonphonetic letterings, and phonetic spellings) before they write conventionally. The desire to create something of one's own is a very important and necessary first step.

Parents should create a stimulating environment for preschoolers, so that children can scribble and express themselves. After preschoolers have committed themselves on paper, they should be encouraged to tell about what they have drawn or "written." A number of preschoolers try their skills at writing stories, even though they do not have specific hand motor control. (See Figure 7.9.) Showing enthusiasm about the child's endeavors will reinforce continuance.

Parents should be good role models for their children. Parents who write will be more prone to have children who write. If parents react negatively to writing letters or "thank-you" notes, this will carry over to their children.

Children usually remain in the scribble stage until they master control of specific muscles. Three-year-olds are often able to make circles, showing that they are gaining control of specific hand muscles. By age five, many can construct other geometric figures, such as squares, which require more precision.

**FIGURE 7.9**   Melissa, who is 4, knows "M" is for "Mom."

**FIGURE 7.10**  Melissa at $4^1/_2$ includes Kelsey, her sister, in her stories. She also likes to draw and tell stories about her neighbor's kitten. (Melissa tells you that she is the one with the bow in her hair.)

Once the child can make figures such as circles, squares, triangles, and variations of these, his or her written expression takes on a "picture form." Kindergarten children may use these figures to "write a story." Some kindergarten children, who have the necessary hand coordination and mental ability, are able to construct letters or words. Some can print their names in some legible form and write a story about themselves or their families. See Figure 7.11 for an example of such a story.

As you can see, children attempt to use writing at a very young age and they progress through several stages on their way to becoming proficient writers. Taking a look at their writing enables us to identify these stages. We can also get a glimpse of the words a child has in his or her writing vocabulary—those words the child can write conventionally without any prompting from the teacher. Finally, we can see what the child understands about the alphabetic

**FIGURE 7.11**    A kindergarten child's story.

principle by noting the symbols the child uses to represent sounds in words; this indicates where the child is in terms of developmental spelling.

## WHAT IS DEVELOPMENTAL SPELLING?

**Developmental spelling**
Learning to spell is ongoing and based on the cognitive development of the child.

Learning to spell is a complex undertaking that entails more than the mere memorizing of words; it is developmental in nature and requires the acquiring and applying of knowledge of spoken and written language.[27] By *developmental, we mean that learning to spell is ongoing and based on the cognitive development of the child.* Correct spelling is learned gradually as the child proceeds

---

[27]Richard E, Hodges, "The Language Base of Spelling," in *Research in the Language Arts: Language and Schooling,* Victor Froese and Stanley B. Straw, eds. (Baltimore: University Park Press, 1981), p. 218.

through the grades, so the more information children have about their written and spoken language, the better spellers they are capable of being.

Young children's spelling is based on their limited knowledge of the language system, so when they spell, they may use *invented spelling.* When young children begin asking about the letters adults write because they want to write in this way too, they may be on their way to using invented spelling. The pattern of invented spelling will vary from one child to another. However, from an analysis of children's invented spelling, it appears that they seem to go through certain stages based on the way the individual child hears or pronounces the words. Some researchers in this area claim that children's spelling development parallels the earlier stages of language development. Investigators that hold this language-based hypothesis about how children learn to spell claim that children "internalize information about spoken and written words, organize that information, construct tentative rules based on that information, and apply these rules to the spelling of words.[28]

One researcher in this area has developed a model that shows the four stages children usually go through before they develop standard or correct spelling.[29] The first is called the *precommunicative stage* (formerly known as the deviant stage) because the appearance of the child's spelling attempts shows that the child has no knowledge of letter–sound correspondence. At the *semiphonetic stage* the child demonstrates some letter–sound correspondences; that is, the child is beginning to gain the concept that letters represent sounds and that these are used to write words. Semiphonetic spelling is abbreviated spelling in which one, two, or three letters usually represent the word; for example, U 5 *you,* B 5 *Be,* and LEFT 5 *elephant* show that the "speller represents words, sounds, or syllables with letters that match their letter name."[30] At this stage the child is also gaining the concept that letters are arranged in a left-right orientation, knows the alphabet, and can form the letters.

At the *phonetic stage,* the child's spelling is characterized by an almost perfect match between letters and sounds. The child's spelling includes all sound features as he or she hears and says them. As a result, the child's spelling at this stage does not resemble standard spelling, for example, "MONSTR" 5 *monster* and "DRAS" 5 *dress.* The *transitional stage,* which is the final stage in this model, precedes standard spelling. At this stage children are better acquainted with standard spelling, and words look like English, even though they are misspelled. The children are including vowels in every syllable, so phonetic "EGL" for *eagle* at this stage becomes "EGUL." It is at this stage that the child "moves from phonological to morphological and visual spelling (e.g., EIGHTEE instead of the phonetic ATE [*eighty*])[31] and begins to use more correctly spelled words in writing.

---

[28]James W. Beers, "Developmental Strategies of Spelling Competence in Primary-School Children," in *Developmental and Cognitive Aspects of Learning to Spell,* Edmund H. Henderson and James W. Beers, eds. (Newark, Del.: IRA, 1980), p. 36.

[29]J. Richard Gentry, "An Analysis of Developmental Spelling in GYNS at WRK," *The Reading Teacher* 36 (November 1982): 192–200.

[30]Ibid., p. 194.

[31]Ibid., p. 197.

# How Can Writing Be Assessed?

To find out whether children have a writing vocabulary, we can give them a blank sheet of paper and ask them to write all of the words they know.

To get a view of the children's understandings about the alphabetic principle, we can give them a blank piece of paper and tell them to write a message. We can then watch what they do and make note of our observations using a form such as the one shown in Figure 7.12.

Teachers who need a norm-referenced standardized writing test might want to use the writing assessments in Clay's *Diagnostic Survey* (Clay, 1993).[32] The writing vocabulary test is used to reveal a child's writing vocabulary, whereas the dictation test is used to shed light on a child's understanding of the alphabetic principle.

# Teaching Writing

In the first half of first grade, when children are learning to read and write, teachers should be careful that the children do not spend most of their time in merely imitative writing, that is, the copying of sentences and short stories that the teacher has written. Teachers should encourage children to try to express their own ideas. In this way, children will begin to gain confidence in themselves and feel that what they have to write is important and worth reading by others. When using the language experience approach, where the written stories are cooperatively developed based on the interests and experiences of the students, teachers should try to capture the children's unique self-expression.

Children love to create, and many have been creating their own stories and attempting to convey these in some written form as preschoolers. Teachers need to capitalize on the childrens' creativity. They can do this by giving children the time and opportunity to write and by respecting their ideas. Although the story may be only one or two sentences, it is the child's own creation. Then, by the latter half of first grade, when many students have acquired the specific hand motor control necessary for sustained writing, the children will often write longer stories.

As students go through school, they should be accumulating many first-hand as well as vicarious experiences, and the necessary skills they need for written self-expression.

### Writing Environment

The school plant, the curriculum, school materials, and books are all inert. They only become activated and part of the dynamic learning situation when the teacher and students use them in an effective manner. An attractive classroom, filled with books and children's "published" works, and well organized into a number of learning centers, may be a catalyst for students' writing. If the classroom is a place where exciting things are happening and where children are involved in reading, observing, manipulating, and experimenting, it will be a place where written self-expression goes on.

---

[32]Clay, M. *The Early Detection of Reading Difficulties.* Portsmouth, NH: Heineman, 2003.

## FIGURE 7.12   Writing Observation Form

**Brief Directions:** Give the student paper and pencil. Ask the student to do some writing. Record qualitative judgments, observations, and insights below.

| | Not Evident, Low, Seldom, Weak, Poor | | | Very Evident, High, Always, Strong, Excellent |
|---|---|---|---|---|

**Directionality**

Left to right

Top to bottom

**Writing**

Scribbles or "cursivelike" scribbles

Letterlike formations

Repeated letters, numbers, words

Variety of letters, numbers, words

Knowledge of first (F) and last (L) name

**Letter-Sound Relationships**

Represents sounds heard at word beginnings

Represents sounds heard at word endings

Represents sounds heard in middles of words

**Writing Conventions**

Use of word boundaries

Use of punctuation

**Overall Message Intent (check one)**

_____ Student indicated no message intent.

_____ Student talked about but did not read or pretend to read what was written.

_____ Student was able to read what was written.

Teacher could make sense of writing independently. _____ yes _____ no

### Observations, Comments, Notes, and Insights

The quality of the teacher–pupil and pupil–pupil relationships is important in setting the emotional climate of the classroom. If students and teachers are engaged in cooperative endeavors and students feel secure, they will want to write and share their written ideas with others.

Teachers can help establish a secure writing environment by doing some preplanning and by trying to anticipate a number of students' concerns. Children should know where supplies are, where they can go for help, what they can do when they are finished.

### Time for Writing

Students need time to express themselves in written form. Actually writing helps students to be better writers. Five or ten minutes before the lunch hour is not a good time for children to start writing. If teachers spend a great deal of time in preparation and motivational techniques to stimulate the desire to write in children, but allow little time for the writing activity itself, the spark, the excitement that has been ignited is hurriedly extinguished. The point to remember is that children should be allowed adequate time to write in class. After getting the proper start in class, many children will work on their own during free time and at home, finishing their compositions because they have become involved with the creative act and want to see the finished product. They should be given the option of working on compositions at home.

# UNDERTANDING, ASSESSING, AND TEACHING STORY SENSE

## WHAT IS STORY SENSE?

**Story sense**
The understanding that there is a structure used to tell stories and that stories are written to be understood.

*Story sense* is the understanding that there is a structure used to tell stories and that stories are written to be understood. In other words, not only does it involve understanding a simple story line but also it includes comprehension.

## HOW CAN STORY SENSE BE ASSESSED?

Probably the best way to assess story sense and story comprehension is to use a wordless picture book such as *Good Dog, Carl* by Alexandra Day (Green Tiger, 1985). As students tell the story, note whether they are able to tell the story with any kind of order that flows from one page to the next. This is the most authentic assessment, but it is time-consuming.

Another way to assess story sense and story comprehension is to use the wordless picture story shown in Figure 7.13. After giving the student time to preview the pictures, have him or her tell you the story. Follow the directions stated on the score sheet in Figure 7.14 to score the storytelling.

Likewise, to check comprehension, ask the questions shown on the score sheet in Figure 7.14 and score them as directed.

## TEACHING STORY SENSE AND STORY COMPREHENSION

Reading aloud to children is perhaps one of the best ways to help them develop a sense of story. Likewise, giving them time to share their thoughts

**FIGURE 7.13 PRETEST: Part B: Wordless Picture Story #1**

From *Summer Success: Reading, Kindergarten* by James F. Baumann, Michael F. Opitz, Laura Robb. Text copyright © 2001 by Great Source Education Group, a division of Houghton Mifflin Company. Reprinted by permission. All rights reserved.

**FIGURE 7.14   PRETEST: Part B: Wordless Picture Story #1 Score Sheet**

Name _____   Date _____

### Story Telling

Check the details the child mentions for each picture. Accept any logical interpretation. Give one (1) point for each detail the child includes. Make sure the student understands each picture before going on to the next.

#### Frame 1

1. a **man** (dad, brother, uncle, etc.)                              _____

2. is giving a **package** (box, present, gift, etc.)                 _____

3. to a **girl** (child, his daughter, etc.)                          _____

#### Frame 2

4. the **girl** (child . . .)                                         _____

5. is **tearing the paper off** (unwrapping)                          _____

6. the **package** (box . . .)                                        _____

#### Frame 3

7. the **girl**                                                       _____

8. **opens the box** (package . . .)                                  _____

9. **inside** the box                                                 _____

10. is a **ball** (basketball . . .)                                  _____

#### Frame 4

11. the **girl**                                                      _____

12. and the **man**                                                   _____

13. **play with the ball** (play catch, play basketball . . .)        _____

                                                     ***Score*** _____ /13

### Story Comprehension

Ask these questions. Give 1 point for each correct answer.

1. Who is this story about? *a girl (child . . .)*                    _____

2. What happens to the girl? *She gets a package with a ball in it.*  _____

3. What does the girl do with the ball? *plays with the man (her dad . . .)*   _____

4. How do you think the girl felt when she opened the package? How can you tell? *This response requires inferential thinking based on prior knowledge. Accept any reasonable opinion and explanation. Probably the girl is happy. She is smiling and she goes right out to play.*                     _____

                                                     ***Score*** _____ /4

about the story after the read-aloud can be a good way to check their comprehension.

What's really going on here has to do with listening comprehension, however, because students are listening to the text rather than reading it for themselves. Using the *Directed Listening/Thinking Activity* shown in Table 7.7 is an excellent way to teach students how to listen and to work on story sense and comprehension simultaneously.

*The Directed Listening/Thinking Approach*

The *directed listening/thinking approach* requires teachers to ask questions before, during, and after a talk. The steps in this approach are as follows:

Step 1: Preparation for talk, lecture, audiotape, or film. The teacher relates to students' past experiences, gives an overview of the talk and presents any special vocabulary and questions at various difficulty levels that students should try to answer while listening to the talk.

Step 2: Students listen to the presentation. During the presentation, the teacher stops, asks students to answer some of the previously given questions, and interjects some more thought-provoking questions to guide students.

Step 3: After the presentation. The children answer unanswered questions and are presented with some more challenging questions. In addition, the teacher asks for the central idea of the talk, as well as a short summary of it.

Step 4: The teacher asks students to devise some good questions that could be used as test questions.

**Directed listening/thinking approach**
Requires teachers to ask questions before, during, and after a talk; consists of a number of steps; requires students to be active participants.

**TABLE 7.7   Directed Listening/Thinking Approach (DLTA) Chart**

| What Teachers Do | What Children Do | What Teachers Need to Observe |
|---|---|---|
| Relate talk to children's past experiences | Listen carefully; relate to past experiences | Students' attentiveness and their interest level by the kinds of questions that students ask |
| Present motivating technique and vocabulary necessary to understand talk | | |
| Present questions as guide before, during, and after talk | Answer and ask questions | Students' responses to questions |

# PUTTING IT ALL TOGETHER: WHO IS IN MOST NEED OF EARLY INTERVENTION?

## WHAT IS EARLY INTERVENTION?

*Early intervention* is just what the term suggests: helping children to overcome reading problems as early as possible. Once their problem is identified, children receive specialized instruction that focuses on their needs. Because these children are behind when compared to their peers, they need additional instruction that will accelerate their progress so they can catch up. Teachers using a diagnostic reading and improvement program often will provide this instruction themselves, but they may also call on others to help them (see Chapter 5).

Extra reading help sometimes comes in the form of an early intervention program such as *Reading Recovery*.[33] The purpose of this program is to identify those children who are experiencing difficulty in their first year of reading instruction. In this short-term curriculum, children who are the lowest achieving readers in a given first-grade class receive daily individualized 30-minute lessons from a specially trained *Reading Recovery* teacher in addition to the regular classroom reading instruction. Every individualized lesson is tailored to engage children in authentic reading and writing activities that will help them catch up with peers.

## WHO IS IN MOST NEED OF EARLY INTERVENTION?

But how do we determine which children are the lowest achieving readers? The most obvious way is to make a class composite of each of the subtests shown in this chapter. The class composite will show how children performed relative to one another and can signal which children need the most help with a given aspect of early literacy.

A second way is to follow a process similar to the one used by *Reading Recovery* teachers. Children complete each test of Clay's *Diagnostic Survey*: letter identification, word test, concepts about print, writing vocabulary, dictation, and text reading. The examiner then adds the scores together to get an overall score. The children with the lowest scores receive the additional instruction.

As it relates to the measures we show in this chapter, teachers can use the form shown in Figure 7.15 to note scores for each test. As with the *Diagnostic Survey* noted above, the scores can be added together and the students with the lowest overall scores receive the individualized additional reading instruction designed to address their reading problems.

A word of caution is in order here. Combining scores to determine who is in most need can be a way to identify students. However, that's about all it can do. To design appropriate instruction, the teacher will need to take a look at the child's performance on each subtest. Doing so will help to reveal where the child needs some additional instruction.

---

[33]Clay, 1993.

**FIGURE 7.15  Summary of Early Literacy Test Results**

| Child's Name | Oral Language Concepts (9 possible) | Print Concepts (12 possible) | Phonological Awareness (20 possible) | Letter Identification (52 possible) | Story Sense (17 possible) | Total (110 possible) |
|---|---|---|---|---|---|---|
| | | | | | | |
| | | | | | | |
| | | | | | | |
| | | | | | | |
| | | | | | | |
| | | | | | | |
| | | | | | | |
| | | | | | | |
| | | | | | | |
| | | | | | | |
| | | | | | | |
| | | | | | | |
| | | | | | | |
| | | | | | | |
| | | | | | | |
| | | | | | | |
| | | | | | | |
| | | | | | | |
| | | | | | | |
| | | | | | | |
| | | | | | | |
| | | | | | | |
| | | | | | | |
| | | | | | | |
| | | | | | | |
| | | | | | | |
| | | | | | | |
| | | | | | | |

A third way to identify those children who need the most help is to use a rating tool such as the *Teacher Rating of Oral Language and Literacy (TROLL),*[34] which was created to guide observations of children's literacy skills in all areas of the language arts (speaking, listening, reading, and writing). This instrument provides a way for teachers to record what they see. The authors note that the TROLL also does something that a direct assessment cannot capture—it enables the teacher to observe children's interests in a variety of oral language and written language activities.

Another advantage of the TROLL is that teachers can use the results to inform instruction: to identify children who are showing evidence of serious language delay and who may need further testing to help pinpoint learning problems as well as those who are functioning well above average and therefore need additional stimulating activities.

Further explanation about TROLL and its development can be found by reviewing the article by Dickinson, McCabe, and Sprague. The authors include the entire instrument, along with an explanation about what the scores mean.

## SUMMARY

In this chapter we provided an overview of early literacy. We presented the different components of early literacy and discussed ways to assess each component. As part of this discussion, our explanation first focused on pre-reading assessment, discussed uses of group-administered standardized assessments, and gave suggestions for choosing and using mandated pre-reading tests. We then provided some background information about ways that early literacy is currently being assessed.

Our major focus in this chapter centered on how to best assess and teach various aspects of early literacy. After providing background for each component, we presented some assessment and teaching suggestions. The teaching suggestions were intended to give teachers a start on ways to teach the various components rather than to offer an exhaustive compendium of teaching strategies.

We concluded the chapter with three suggestions for determining who is most in need of early intervention. One suggestion focused on looking at children on each individual measure, whereas another suggestion focused on combining scores. A third suggestion offered an external instrument that could be used to assess how children use oral and written language.

## CHAPTER 7 KEY CONCEPTS

- Emergent literacy is a term used to describe the beginning stages of literacy.
- Emergent literacy and reading readiness are not the same.

- Cambourne's conditions of learning can be used to help teachers create an environment that promotes the authentic use of oral and written language.

[16]Dickinson, D., A. McCabe, and K. Sprague. "Teacher Rating of Oral Language and Literacy (TROLL): Individualizing Early Literacy Instruction with a Standards-Based Rating Tool." *The Reading Teacher,* 56 (6) (2003): 554–564.

- There are at least six essential areas of early literacy: oral language concepts, print concepts, phonological awareness, letter identification, alphabetic principle, and story sense.
- Letter identification and phonological awareness appear to predict reading success.
- There are many ways to assess early literacy. Asking three questions: What do I want to know? Why do I want to know? and How can I best discover? will help teachers to select the most relevant measure.

- Children must develop both oral language and print concepts to succeed in reading.
- Children use language in seven ways, and the classroom environment can be set up to facilitate these different uses of language.
- Early intervention means detecting problems as early as possible and doing something to address them.
- There are at least three ways to determine who is in most need of early intervention.

## SUGGESTIONS FOR THOUGHT QUESTIONS AND ACTIVITIES

1. Observe a kindergarten classroom, making note of the classroom environment. How many of Cambourne's conditions of learning do you see exemplified?
2. As a reading specialist, the principal wants you to give a presentation to parents of kindergarten children. She wants the presentation to highlight the different components of early literacy and what the parents can do at home to foster each one. Construct the presentation.
3. Create a list of alphabet books that could be used to help children learn more about the alphabet.

4. Using the guidelines stated on pages 166–170, develop a list of books that could be used to teach children about the different aspects of phonological awareness.
5. During your interview for a teaching position, the committee members ask you to explain how you would determine kindergarten students' strengths and needs. Construct your response.
6. The kindergarten and first-grade teachers want some ideas about how to get additional help for a few children. They recognize that they need to provide documentation, but feel lost as to how to organize all of their data. They have come to you for some suggestions. What will you suggest?

## INTERNET ACTIVITIES

There are several websites that offer information regarding early literacy. We have listed some of them here, along with their primary focus. Visit one or more of these websites and print out something that you find helpful.

| Website | What it provides |
|---|---|
| www.carolhurst.com/index.html | Children's literature titles |
| www.reading.org | Information about the International Reading Association |
| Pals.virginia.edu | A phonological awareness literacy screening |
| http://www.readingrecovery.org/ | Information about Reading Recovery, one of several early intervention programs |
| www.magickeys.com/books/ | Children's storybooks online |

## SELECTED BIBLIOGRAPHY

Elley, W. "Vocabulary Acquisition from Listening to Stories." *Reading Research Quarterly* 24 (1989): 174–87.

Johns, J. *The Basic Reading Inventory,* 9th ed. Dubuque, IA: Kendall/Hunt, 2005.

"Learning to Read and Write: Developmentally Appropriate Practices for Young Children: A Joint Position Statement of the International Reading Association and the National Association for the Education of Young Children." Newark, DE: International Reading Association, 1998.

O'Connor, R. E., and J. R. Jenkins. "Prediction of Reading Disabilities in Kindergarten and First Grade." *Scientific Studies of Reading* 3 (1999): 159–97.

Opitz, M. *Flexible Grouping in Reading: Practical Ways to Help All Students Become Better Readers.* New York: Scholastic, 1998.

Rubin, D. *Teaching Elementary Language Arts: A Balanced Approach,* 6th ed. Boston: Allyn and Bacon, 2000.

**Children's Literature Cited**

Barrett, Judi. *Things That Are Most in the World.* New York: Atheneum, 1998.

Barron, Rex. *Fed Up! A Feast of Frazzled Foods.* New York: Putnam, 2000.

Bauer, Marion. *Sleep, Little One, Sleep.* New York: Aladdin, 2002.

Bynum, Janie. *Altoona Baboona.* San Diego, CA: Harcourt, 1999.

Collicut, Paul. *This Train.* New York: Farrar, Straus, & Giroux, 1999.

Day, Alexandra. *Good Dog, Carl.* New York: Green Tiger, 1985.

Downey, Lynne. *The Flea's Sneeze.* New York: Holt, 2000.

Duncan, Pamela. *The Wacky Wedding: A Book of Alphabet Antics.* New York: Hyperion, 1999.

Frazee, Marla. *Hush, Little Baby.* San Diego: Browndeer/Harcourt, 1999.

Grover, Mary. *The Accidental Zucchini.* San Diego: Harcourt, 1997.

Hoban, Tana. *Over, Under, Through.* New York: Macmillan, 1973.

Hoberman, Mary. *The Eensy-Weensy Spider.* New York: Little, Brown, 2000.

London, Jonathan. *Crunch Munch.* San Diego: Harcourt, 2001.

McDonnell, Flora. *Flora McDonnell's ABC.* Cambridge, MA: Candlewick, 1997.

Marshak, Samuel. *The Absentminded Fellow.* New York: Farrar, Straus, & Giroux, 1999.

Martin, Bill. *A Beasty Story.* San Diego: Harcourt, 1999.

Miranda, Anne. *Pignic.* Honesdale, PA: Boyds Mills, 1996.

Most, Bernard. *A Pair of Protoceratops.* San Diego: Harcourt, 1998.

Norworth, Jack. *Take Me Out to the Ballgame.* New York: Aladdin, 1999.

Rogers, Sally. *Earthsong.* New York: Dutton, 1998.

Root, Phyllis. *The Hungry Monster.* Cambridge, MA: Candlewick, 1997.

Rotner, Shelley. *Parts.* New York: Walker, 2001.

Rylant, Cynthia. *Bless Us All: A Child's Yearbook of Blessings.* New York: Simon & Schuster, 1998.

Sabuda, Robert. *ABC Disney.* New York: Hyperion, 1998.

Spence, Rob, and Amy Spence. *Clickety Clack.* New York: Viking, 1999.

Stevenson, Robert. *My Shadow.* San Diego, CA: Harcourt, 1999.

Swinburne, Stephen. *What's Opposite?* Honesdale, PA: Boyds Mills, 2000.

Williams, Laura. *ABC Kids.* New York: Philomel, 2000.

# 8

# Listening in on Students' Oral Reading

## Scenario: Using Oral Reading to Learn More about Vicki

Vicki L is a new student in Ms. Mills's fifth-grade class. She and her family just moved into the school district. Ms. Mills is trying very hard to make Vicki feel at home because she knows how difficult it is for a young person to leave all her friends and come to a new school where she does not know anyone. Ms. Mills makes a point of speaking to Vicki informally during recess and at other times so that she can get to know her. During some of their conversations Ms. Mills tries to find out what Vicki's interests are and what kinds of books she likes to read. Ms. Mills also attempts to help Vicki adjust to her new environment by helping her choose books that deal with situations similar to hers. (Ms. Mills's wise use of bibliotherapy, which is the use of books to help individuals to cope better with their emotional and adjustment problems, has helped many children in her class.)

Vicki's records from her other school haven't arrived yet, so Ms. Mills has to do some informal testing to determine at what level Vicki is reading. Actually, Ms. Mills prefers to do her own informal testing before looking at a child's past records. She feels that often records can bias a teacher.

Ms. Mills chooses a passage from the middle of the basal reader, which is equivalent to a fifth-grade level. She tells Vicki that she wants her to read the passage aloud and that she should concentrate because she will be asked some questions about what she has read. She tells Vicki something about the story before Vicki begins to read. Vicki's voice is loud and clear, but she reads word by word, or rather syllable by syllable. She sounds out every word she comes to. It's as if she does not recognize any word or that she does not trust herself to say it correctly unless she first sounds it out. (Now Ms. Mills knows what people mean when they say that a child is "overphonicked." Ms. Mills believes in using phonics to help children become self-reliant and independent readers, but she stresses that phonics is only one part of the word recognition program and that the primary goal is comprehension.) When Ms. Mills asks Vicki questions on the passage, Vicki is able to answer most of the literal questions, but she has difficulty answering any at the interpretive level. Ms. Mills decides to choose another passage from the same basal reader and read it aloud to Vicki. She wants to see if Vicki would do better in comprehension if she did not have to concentrate so hard on sounding out the words. Ms. Mills tells Vicki to listen carefully and see how well she can answer questions on the selection. After Ms. Mills finishes reading the passage, she asks Vicki some questions. Again, Vicki is able to answer most of the literal questions but not the ones requiring a higher level of thinking.

Ms. Mills asks Vicki to tell her about her reading experiences. She asks Vicki how she learned to read. Vicki tells Ms. Mills that she had learned to sound out every word and that all they did at her other school was work with words. She says very proudly that she could figure out lots of words by herself. Ms. Mills says that she saw she could and that was very good, but she tells Vicki that she wants her to try to go beyond the words and concentrate more on the message that the words have. She also tells Vicki that she wants her to take a chance and not sound out every word. She gives Vicki another passage to read, and asks her to look at it first and then to try to read it in thought units. Ms. Mills reads the first two sentences aloud first, and then she asks Vicki to read the complete passage aloud. Ms. Mills praises Vicki for reading it with less sounding out of words. She asks Vicki if there are any words in the passage that she does not know. Vicki says that she knows all the words. "Good," says Ms. Mills.

"Let's put some in sentences." Ms. Mills asks Vicki to put a few of the words into sentences. Vicki was able to do this. Ms. Mills tells Vicki that she would like to work with her each day for a little while. She will also put her in one of the reading groups. Ms. Mills tells Vicki that her ability to sound out words is excellent, but she needs to concentrate more on understanding what she is reading and reading more smoothly. She says that she will arrange a meeting with her parents to see if they would work with her too.

Ms. Mills thinks that Vicki is a capable child who should be doing much better than she is. She believes that Vicki has not had any experiences in working with higher-level thinking skills, so she will plan a program for her that will help her to develop such skills. Ms. Mills also feels that Vicki needs practice in reading for meaning rather than for pronunciation and that she needs to gain confidence in herself. It could be that she has so overrelied on the sounding out of words that she did not pay attention to the whole word. As a result, each time she meets a word, it is as if she were meeting it for the first time. (Vicki appears to lose the whole because of the parts.) Ms. Mills decides that she will have Vicki look at the *whole* word and have her say it.

# INTRODUCTION

Fortunately for Vicki, Ms. Mills knows how to use oral reading to gain a better understanding of how children read. She also knows how to use the results of the reading to identify strengths and needs as well as to plan appropriate instruction.

Learning how to use oral reading to assess children's reading is the focus of this chapter. Oral reading can help teachers gain insight into both what students do well and what needs more attention. As with the assessment procedures mentioned in previous chapters, we need to ask and answer three important questions to guide selection of the most appropriate oral reading measure: What do I want to know? Why do I want to know? How can I best discover? In Table 8.1 we ask and answer these questions. The table also serves as an overview of the three assessment techniques we explain in this chapter: the Informal Reading Inventory, Modified Miscue Analysis, and Running Record.

# CHAPTER OBJECTIVES

After reading this chapter, you should be able to:

- Describe the components of an informal reading inventory.
- State the purposes of an informal reading inventory.
- Explain when a teacher should administer an informal reading inventory.
- Discuss to whom an informal reading inventory should be given.
- State Betts's reading levels on an informal reading inventory.
- Discuss how to compute the various reading levels of informal reading inventories.
- Discuss some controversial issues in relation to informal reading inventories.

**TABLE 8.1   What, Why, and How of Oral Reading Assessment**

| What Do I Want to Know? | Why Do I Want to Know? | How Can I Best Discover? |
|---|---|---|
| What are the children's functional reading levels? | All readers have three reading levels: independent, instructional, and frustration. I want to help children read books of varying difficulty if they are to become strong readers. A majority of what they read should be at their independent and instructional reading levels. | Informal Reading Inventory (pp. 204–209)<br><br>Running Record (pp. 228–235) |
| What strategies do children use when reading? | Using a variety of reading strategies rather than relying on one or two is a hallmark of a good reader. I need to discover which strategies students are using to determine other strategies that I should explicitly teach. | Modified Miscue Analysis (pp. 223–226)<br><br>Running Record) (pp. 228–235)<br><br>IRI (pp. 204–207) |
| How well do children comprehend? | Comprehension is the essence of reading. I need to make sure that children are comprehending at all levels and explicitly teach those children who are having difficulty. | IRI (pp. 204–207)<br><br>Retelling (p. 231) |
| Are students able to identify words when reading connected text? | Word identification is one part of successful reading. I need to determine if students have a large store of words to draw on when reading. | IRI (pp. 204–207)<br><br>Modified Miscue Analysis (pp. 223–226)<br><br>Running Record (pp. 228–235) |

- Describe how oral reading errors are coded and scored.
- Discuss some of the problems with scoring oral reading errors.
- Explain when a listening capacity test is usually administered.
- Explain the purposes for administering word lists as one part of an informal reading inventory.
- Explain a modified informal reading inventory.
- Discuss some points of caution concerning informal reading inventories.
- Explain miscue analysis.
- Explain Modified Miscue Analysis and discuss reasons for using it.
- Explain how to administer and score a Modified Miscue Analysis.
- Describe the Running Record.

- Discuss the similarities of and differences between the Running Record and IRI.
- Explain how to administer and score a Running Record.
- Discuss some advantages of using a Running Record.

# AN OVERVIEW OF THE INFORMAL READING INVENTORY

## WHAT IS AN INFORMAL READING INVENTORY?

**Informal Reading Inventory (IRI)**
A valuable aid in helping teachers determine a student's reading levels and his or her strengths and weaknesses. It usually consists of oral and silent reading passages selected from basal readers from the preprimer to the eighth-grade levels.

An *Informal Reading Inventory (IRI)* is individually administered and usually consists of oral and silent reading passages selected from basal readers from the preprimer to the eighth-grade levels (some exist up to the twelfth grade). Usually each selection has the following kinds of comprehension questions: factual, inferential, and word meanings. (A few may contain evaluative questions.)

Graded word lists, often taken from basal readers and consisting of approximately twenty or twenty-five words from each reader level, are used to determine at what grade level the student should begin reading the oral passages. The student begins the word list at two levels below his or her present grade level. The highest grade level at which the student has no errors on the graded word list is the grade level at which he or she begins reading the oral passage. The student reads aloud the oral passage, and the teacher records any omission, substitution, insertion, pronunciation, repetition, and hesitation errors. (Table 8.2 illustrates the code for marking and scoring errors.) If the student reads the oral passage at the independent or instructional level, he or she is asked the comprehension questions; the student then proceeds to read the silent passage at the same grade level and is asked the questions pertaining to the silent passage. The student then goes to the next reading grade level, continuing until he or she reaches or is rapidly approaching a frustration level. If the student makes so many word recognition errors in oral reading that he or she is reading at or close to a frustration level, the teacher begins to read the passages aloud to the student to determine his or her listening comprehension ability. This is called a listening capacity test.[1]

## WHAT ARE THE PURPOSES OF AN INFORMAL READING INVENTORY?

An informal reading inventory is probably one of the most valuable diagnostic aids because of the amount of information it can convey to perceptive teachers who know how to use it to its best advantages.

An essential function of an IRI is to help the teacher determine the child's levels of reading: independent, instructional, frustrational, functional. It is also used to get an estimate of a student's listening capacity. All are needed to make a proper match between the child and the books he or she reads.

---

[1]A listening capacity test may also be referred to as a listening comprehension test.

**TABLE 8.2   Code for Marking and Scoring Errors**

| Type of Error | Rule for Marking | Examples | Error Count |
|---|---|---|---|
| Omissions—leaves out a word, part of a word, or consecutive words | Put circle around omitted word or part of word. | She went in(to) the store.<br>The (big) black dog is here. | 1<br>1 |
| Substitutions— substitutes a whole word | Put line through substituted word, and insert word above. |         home<br>She went into the ~~house.~~<br>    along.<br>She went ~~alone.~~ | 1<br><br>1 |
| Insertions—adds a word, part of a word, or consecutive words | Put caret to show where word or word part was inserted, and write in inserted part of word or word(s). |   big<br>The ˄dog is black.<br><br>very big<br>The dog is black.<br>   ˄ | 1<br><br><br>1 |
| Mispronunciations— mispronounces a word to produce a nonsense word (unlike substitution where an actual word is substituted) | Put line through word that was mispronounced, and insert phonetically the word if possible. |    herz<br>A ~~horse~~ went into the barn.<br>      ka rōt′<br>It weighed a ~~carot.~~ | 1<br><br>1 |
| Words pronounced by examiner after four-second pause by child | Put *P* over word or words pronounced by tester. |       *P*<br>The anecdote was funny. | 1 |
| Hesitations—a pause of less than five seconds | Put an *H* above the word on which the hesitation occurs. |      *H*<br>She reiterated that she wouldn't go. | 0 |
| Repetitions—a word, part of a word, or a group of words repeated | Draw a wavy line under the part of word or word(s) repeated. | She mumbled her acceptance. We were reluctant to go. His probation would be up soon. | 0<br><br>0<br>0 |
| Reversals—word order is changed | Enclose words in a horizontal *S*. | The big black cat drinks milk. | 1 |
| Self-corrections— error is spontaneously corrected | Enclose incorrect word in parentheses. | (brought)<br>He bought something. | 0 |

Another important reason for administering and interpreting an IRI is to help a teacher learn about a student's reading strengths and needs so that the teacher can design appropriate instruction for the student. For example, if on giving a child an IRI the teacher observes that the child has difficulty answering inference comprehension questions, the teacher can develop lessons for the child to help build skill in this area. (See Chapter 12.) From listening to the student reading orally, the teacher can discover whether the student has word recognition problems that may be interfering with comprehension when the child is reading silently. (See Chapter 10.)

Yet another function of the IRI is to give the student feedback on his or her reading behavior. As the student reads passages at graduated levels of difficulty, he or she becomes aware of the reading level that is appropriate. It helps the student recognize his or her word recognition and comprehension strengths and needs. Being aware of a problem is a vital factor in helping the student overcome the difficulty. (See Chapter 6.)

The IRI is an excellent instrument for estimating students' reading levels and for helping teachers to diagnose their strengths and needs, but the IRI is only as good as the person administering it and interpreting its results. That is, the IRI does not diagnose; the teacher does!

### Special Note

The term *informal* implies that the inventory is teacher-made; however, many informal reading inventories are published (commercially produced) ones. In this chapter, information will be provided on how to administer, score, and analyze an informal reading inventory. In Appendix A, we provide suggestions for constructing an IRI based on the basal reader series in use in the class or any other reading program that is based on graduated levels of difficulty. Appendix B shows one commercially published IRI. ■

## DETERMINING READING AND LISTENING CAPACITY LEVELS

The IRI, which originated from the work of Emmett A. Betts and his doctoral student Patsy A. Killgallon, is used to determine three reading levels and a listening capacity level. The criteria for reading levels on the IRI were determined by Betts, and many informal reading inventories still use the same levels or modifications of them. The reason for this is that even though there is disagreement on what the quantitative reading levels should be, the research on determining reading levels is not conclusive.[2] Also, it is imperative to state again that "the valid and reliable use of IRIs must rely upon the accurate professional judgments of the person conducting the evaluation. The accurate use of IRIs requires judgment and interpretation, not the mechanical calculation or application of scores."[3]

The levels as determined by Betts and his percentages that designate the levels follow:

[2]Majorie Seddon Johnson, Roy A. Kress, and John Pikulski, *Informal Reading Inventories,* 2nd ed. (Newark, DE: International Reading Association, 1987), p. 13.

[3]Ibid.

**Betts Reading Levels**

| | | |
|---|---|---|
| Independent Level* | Children read on their own without any difficulty. | Word Recognition—99% or above Comprehension—90% or above |
| Instructional Level | Teaching level. | Word Recognition—95% or above Comprehension—75% or above |
| Frustration Level | This level is to be avoided. It is the lowest level of readability. | Word Recognition—90% or less Comprehension—50% or less |
| Listening Capacity Level* | Highest level at which a pupil can comprehend when someone reads to him or her. | Comprehension—75% or above |

*Betts also called the *independent level* the *basal level,* and the *listening capacity level* the *capacity level.*

In designating these levels Betts gave not only percentage determinants but also other criteria that teachers should look for at each level.[4]

*Independent Level*

**Independent reading level**
Level at which child reads successfully without any assistance.

The *independent reading level* "is the highest level at which an individual can read and satisfy all the criteria for desirable reading behavior in silent- and oral-reading situations."[5] At the independent level the child can read successfully without any assistance. When the student is reading orally or silently at this level, a minimum comprehension score on literal and interpretive questions of at least 90 percent should be achieved. The pupil should also be free from such observable evidence of tension as frowning, movements of feet and hands, finger pointing, and holding the book too close or too far.

For oral reading the student should have good rhythm with proper phrasing and attention to punctuation. The student's voice should be free from tension, and the student should have an accurate pronunciation of 99 percent or more of the words. The student's silent reading should be free from lip movement or subvocalizing.

The independent level is an important one for the child, teacher, parents, and librarian. It is at this level that the child will read library or trade books and other texts in school and at home. The reference books that children choose to read for a special project or assignment should also be at their independent level because they will be reading these on their own. If they choose books to read independently that are too hard for them, that will usually deter them from reading.

*Instructional Level*

**Instructional reading level**
The teaching level.

The *instructional reading level* is the one at which teaching is done. This level must not be so challenging that it frustrates the student nor so easy that the student becomes bored. At this level there should be a minimum comprehension score of at least 75 percent for both oral and silent reading on literal and

[4]Adapted from Emmett A. Betts, *Foundation of Reading Instruction* (New York: American Book Company, 1946), pp. 445–54.

[5]Ibid., p. 445.

interpretive questions, and in the oral reading there should be accurate pronunciation of at least 95 percent of the running words. As on the independent level, there should be no observable tensions or undue movements of feet and hands. There should be freedom from finger pointing, lip movements, and head movements; and there should be acceptable posture. Oral reading should be rhythmical with proper phrasing; there should be proper attention paid to punctuation; and the child's voice should be free from tension.

It is possible for students to have an instructional level that spans more than one, two, or even three reader levels. (When this happens, the instructional level is reported as a range; see "Reporting Students' Reading Levels.") A student may read at more than one instructional level for a number of reasons. For example, interests, background information, and experience play an essential role in how well a student may do in a particular content area. It is possible that a child may be at one instructional level in one subject and not in the same instructional level in another subject. It is therefore important that the IRI that is used to determine a student's reading ability levels has a variety of passages that represent different content areas and types of writing.

### Frustration Level

> **Frustration reading level**
> The child reads with many word recognition and comprehension errors. It is the lowest reading level and one to be avoided.

The *frustration reading level* should be avoided; however, for diagnostic purposes, it is helpful for teachers to know what this level is so that they can avoid giving students reading material at this level. A teacher can tell that a child has reached his or her frustration level when the child attains a comprehension score of 50 percent or less on literal and interpretive questions for oral and silent reading and is unable to pronounce 10 percent of the words on the oral reading passage.

At the frustration level, the child has difficulty anticipating meanings and is not familiar with the facts presented in the selection. The child shows frustration by frowning, constantly moving in a nervous fashion, finger pointing, blinking, or faulty breathing. The child may also be unwilling to read.

At this level, during silent reading, the child reads at a slow rate, uses lip movements, and makes low vocal utterances. During oral reading, the child does not observe punctuation, reads in a high-pitched voice, and reads with a lack of rhythm or word by word. The child's reading is further characterized by irregular breathing, meaningless word substitutions, insertion of words, repetition of words, partial and complete word reversals, omission of words, almost no eye-voice span, and an increased tendency to stutter.

Teacher judgment plays an important role in determining whether to continue testing. For example, it is possible to stop testing, even though a child has not reached his or her frustration level because the child is nervous or upset. (Be careful not to confuse tiredness with signs of frustration.) Also, even though minimum criteria are usually given for estimating the various reading levels of IRIs, these are actually general standards because of teacher judgment. Remember, the examiner is the final judge, not the "mechanical calculation or application of scores."

### Listening Capacity Level

> **Listening capacity level**
> The highest level at which a learner can understand material when it is read aloud to him or her.

The *listening capacity level*, as first determined by Betts, is the "highest level of readability of material which the learner can comprehend when the material is read to him."[6] Betts also established the minimum comprehension score of at least 75 percent, based on both factual and inferential questions for listening capacity, and he designated that the term "*level* refers to the grade level at which the material was prepared for use; for example, preprimer, primer, first reader, second reader, and so on."[7] (The listening capacity level may also be referred to as the *listening comprehension level,* the *capacity level,* and even the *potential level.*)

### The Buffer Zone of the IRI

**Buffer zone**
The area that falls between the instructional and frustration levels.

The *buffer zone* of the IRI is the area that falls between the instructional and frustration levels. For word recognition it is 94 percent to 91 percent, and for comprehension it is 74 percent to 51 percent (Betts's criteria). When a child's score falls in the buffer zone, the teacher must decide whether to continue testing, even though the child has not yet reached the frustration level. If the child appears interested in continuing, testing should continue. If, on the other hand, the child exhibits symptoms of frustration, testing should be stopped. Even though the decision of whether to continue testing is a subjective one, there are some factors that the teacher could take into consideration; for example, the types of errors the child has made, the personality of the student, the student's prior reading record, the health of the child, whether the child speaks another language at home, whether the child speaks nonstandard English, and so on.

A student who stays in the buffer zone for more than one reader level and does not exhibit signs of frustration will probably be able to gain the skills that he or she lacks more readily and quickly than a student who goes from the instructional level directly to the frustration level. It shows that the student has enough skills to be able to continue, as well as the interest and desire to do so.

## REPORTING STUDENTS' READING LEVELS

The independent level is reported as one level only: the highest level at which the child can read and satisfy the criteria for the independent level. If a child reads at an independent level at reader levels 1 (1st grade), $2^1$ (first semester of second grade), $2^2$ (second semester of second grade), and $3^1$ (first semester of third grade), the child's independent level is reported as reader level $3^1$.

The frustration level is also reported as one level only. The first reader level at which the child reaches frustration is reported as the frustration level. The examiner does not continue testing after the child reaches the frustration level.

The instructional level is often not reported as one level only. It is possible that a child's instructional level is a span of a number of reading levels. When that happens, the examiner reports the range. If a child reads at the instructional level at reader levels 4, 5, and 6 before going into the buffer zone or reaching the frustration level, the child's instructional level is reported as a 4–6 range.

To determine a student's independent and instructional reading levels, the criteria for both word recognition and comprehension should be met. For the

[6]Ibid., p. 452.

[7]Ibid., p. 439.

independent level, the student should meet the criteria of 99 percent accuracy in word recognition and 90 percent in comprehension. For the instructional level, the student should meet the criteria of 95–98 percent for word recognition and 75–89 percent in comprehension. For the frustration level, however, only one of the criteria has to be met, that is, 50 percent or less in comprehension or 90 percent or less in word recognition.

The examiner must use judgment in making these determinations. If a student has excellent comprehension at the independent level but, while reading aloud, makes a few minor word recognition errors that do not change the meaning or substance of what is being read, the comprehension level is probably more indicative of the student's reading level. The problem is in the subjectivity of determining minor errors and the ultimate consequence of possibly placing children in higher levels than they actually are. Be careful about giving students the "benefit of the doubt" when determining their reading levels. Remember, in diagnosis we want to uncover problems early and make sure we are not overlooking any possible difficulty.

### Special Note

Some examiners average the oral and silent reading comprehension scores to determine a student's reading comprehension level. This is not suggested because the oral and silent reading scores are indicative of different kinds of behavior. It is important that the examiner analyze independently both the oral and silent reading comprehension scores to gain insight into the student's reading comprehension behavior.

In addition, the averaging of the oral and silent reading comprehension scores is a violation of the spirit and intent of the IRI. A single score tends to rank students, which is not the purpose of the IRIs. "Informal reading inventories are typically not designed to rank student scores; for most, data have not been collected for this purpose nor have validation studies been conducted."[8]

The silent reading comprehension score on an informal reading inventory is more indicative of what a student does in a directed reading lesson than the oral reading comprehension score of an IRI; therefore examiners may use the silent reading comprehension score combined with the oral reading word recognition score to determine at what level students should read.

Again, we stress that an IRI gives a profile of a student's reading behavior, so it is important to look at the individual oral and silent reading comprehension scores, as well as the oral reading word recognition scores.

When a student does better on oral comprehension than on silent comprehension, it usually means that the student must hear the words in order to understand the message. These students are generally more immature readers, and this kind of behavior is usually more typical of younger readers. More mature readers generally do better on silent reading. If the silent reading is a level or two above the oral reading, this is usually not considered a problem.

Also, teachers should be aware that on informal reading inventories, students must rely heavily on their short-term memories, so those who have difficulties in this area will probably not do well when answering comprehension questions. ■

[8]Kalle Gerritz, senior examiner, Educational Testing Service, 2001.

## CODE FOR MARKING ORAL READING ERRORS

Becoming proficient in marking oral reading errors is beneficial so that you can focus on what the child is doing when reading. When you are listening to a child read, you must have overlearned to code so that you can quickly record the errors. The code is merely a shorthand method you can use to record information quickly; it is an aid. Table 8.2 on page 194 presents a marking code that you can use to administer the IRI in Appendix B. Most of the *terms* that are used to describe the errors and the symbols that represent them are used in many published IRIs, oral reading tests, and other diagnostic tests that have an oral reading subtest.

## SCORING ORAL READING ERRORS

The scoring scale, which is to be used with the IRI in Appendix B, is based on the philosophy that most good oral readers make some errors when they read. The counting of repetitions, hesitations of less than five seconds, and self-corrected words as errors would yield too low a score for the student. In the scoring scale of errors, multiple errors on the same word will only count as one error; mispronunciations due to dialect differences will not count as an error; mispronunciations of difficult proper nouns will not count as errors; hesitations of less than five seconds and repetitions will not count as errors; and an immediate self-correction will not count as an error. All other errors that are made will count one point. If a child meets the same word a few times in a selection and makes a substitution, omission, or mispronunciation error on it each time, it would count as *one error* the first time and as *one-half error* each subsequent time. After the third time, the teacher should pronounce the word for the child. In addition, the examiner should not count as errors words that are pronounced or substituted with dialectical equivalents (nonstandard dialects). For example, a child may say *rat* for *right*.

The teacher should keep a record of the errors made so that he or she can determine what kinds of strategies the student is using in figuring out words, whether a pattern exists among the errors made, and whether the student relies on graphic, semantic, or syntactic clues. The Summary Sheet in Figure 8.1 on page 201 has a checklist of possible errors, which should be helpful in recording a student's specific errors.

### Sample Markings of Oral IRI Passages

*Sample 1*

                         *H* polet
"What is making the lake polluted?" asked Jill.

                     s
"It could be @lot of things," said Mr. Brown.

"Let's go down to the lake and look at it."

                             big
Mr. Brown and the children went to the lake.

They looked into the water. It wasn't clean. They

         about                   was
walked ~~around~~ the lake. Then they ~~saw~~ why it wasn't clean.

**FIGURE 8.1   Diagnostic Checklist for Oral and Silent Reading**

| *Oral Reading* | *Yes* | *No* | *Specific Errors* |
|---|---|---|---|

1. Word recognition errors
   The teacher listens to the child while he or she is reading orally and records whether the child makes any of the following errors.

   a. omissions
   b. insertions
   c. substitutions
   d. repetitions
   e. hesitations
   f. mispronunciations
   g. reversals

2. Manner of reading
   The teacher observes the child while he or she is reading aloud and records whether the child exhibits any of the following behaviors:

   a. word-by-word phrasing
   b. finger pointing
   c. head movement
   d. fidgeting
   e. voice characteristics
      high-pitched
      loud
      soft
      monotonous
   f. other

3. Comprehension
   (*See* Comprehension Diagnostic Checklist in Chapter 12.)

| *Silent Reading* | *Yes* | *No* |
|---|---|---|

1. Comprehension
   (*See* Comprehension Diagnostic Checklist in Chapter 12.)

2. Manner of reading
   The teacher observes the child while he or she is reading silently and records whether the child exhibits any of the following behaviors.

   a. lip movement
   b. reads aloud
   c. head movement
   d. continually looks up
   e. finger pointing
   f. other

The error on *making* is actually a mispronunciation error. The omission symbol is used because it illustrates best what the child did.

*Total Error Count = 7*
*Polluted* counts for one error only.

The error on *saw* is shown as a substitution error, even though it actually is a reversal error. To simplify the marking, only inverted word order is shown as a reversal error (see Table 8.2) because it is easier to show this than to show letter reversals. When marking errors, it is easier to assume substitution errors than reversals because a reversal error requires analysis. However, after the testing, the teacher should review all substitution errors to determine whether they have been caused by possible reversal problems. In fact, all errors should be analyzed to determine whether a pattern exists. It is possible, also, that mispronunciation errors are caused by reversal problems.

*Sample 2*

Fritz and Anna lived on a farm. It was a small farm. It was also very dry, and things did not grow well. So Fritz and his wife, Anna, were poor.
One day there was a tap, tap, tap on the door. A woman had come to the farm. She had been walking most of the day, and she was hungry. She asked Fritz and Anna to give her something to eat. Fritz and Anna had a pot of soup. They let the woman come in to eat.

The error on *lived,* as in Sample 1, is actually a mispronunciation error; however, as in Sample 1, the omission symbol is being used because it shows what the student did.

*Total Error Count = 3*
The repetitions on *hungry* and *something* do not count as errors.

From analyzing this passage of 88 words, we can see that the three errors would put the student at the instructional level. We also see that the kinds of errors the student made would not interfere with her comprehension. However, her teacher should recognize that the student is unsure of some words, and that she tends to delete parts of words. This would detract from her reading fluently, so the teacher should try to determine whether this is due to the student's reading too rapidly or not looking at the whole sentence before she reads.

### Word Recognition Formula for Percent Correct

Here is a formula to help you to figure out the percent correct for word recognition:

$$\frac{\text{Number of words in passage } - \text{ number of errors}}{\text{number of words in passage}} \times 100\% = \text{percent correct}$$

**Example: 150 words in passage**

**7 errors**

$$\frac{150 - 7}{150} \times 100\% = 95\%$$

(This is at the instructional level using Betts's criteria.)

### *Word Recognition Formulas for Allowable Errors*

It is often easier to work with the number wrong rather than with the number correct because there are fewer errors than correct readings. In working with the number wrong, you are dealing with smaller numbers. Here is the formula for allowable errors for each level:

Independent level: allowable errors

= 0.01 × number of words in a passage

Instructional level: allowable errors

= 0.05 × number of words in a passage

Frustration level: allowable errors

= 0.10 × number of words in a passage

Examples: 150 words in passage

| *Level* | *Allowable Errors* |
|---|---|
| Independent | 1.5 = 2.0 rounded to nearest whole word |
| Instructional | 7.5 = 8 rounded to nearest whole word |
| Frustration | 15 |

From the above, you can see that a child who makes 7 errors in a 150-word passage would be at the instructional level using Betts's criteria.

## USING A DIAGNOSTIC CHECKLIST FOR ORAL AND SILENT READING

Coding is necessary if you are analyzing error patterns to determine a student's word recognition difficulties. If, however, you are only interested in quickly determining a student's reading level, you can simply check (✓) errors, because all you need is an error count. Diagnostic checklists are useful in recording errors, especially if you are only interested in an error count.

A checklist you can use is shown in Figure 8.1. Note that this checklist is helpful in recording a student's manner of reading, as well as his or her word recognition errors.

# ADMINISTERING AND SCORING THE IRI

## STEP 1: ESTABLISHING RAPPORT

Establishing rapport with the child who is to be tested is an important first step. Since you are the child's teacher, you should know this child quite well and should be able to allay any fears or apprehensions that the child may have about taking the test. Make sure the child understands that the IRI is not a test that will give him or her a grade; it is a test to help both of you learn more about the child's reading. The IRI will give more information so that you can work together to overcome the reading problem.

## STEP 2: THE WORD RECOGNITION INVENTORY

The Word Recognition Inventory (WRI), which is composed of the word lists selected from the basal reader series, is used to determine at what level to begin the oral reading passages of the IRI. It evaluates a student's ability to recognize (state) words in isolation and is administered to one student at a time.

*Preparation*

1. The WRI begins two grade levels below the student's grade level.
2. Duplicate the word lists for at least three grade levels above and below the grade level at which you will begin. (Note that the WRI in Appendix B has more than one reader level for each grade level up to grade 4.)
3. Decide how you will flash the words to the student and prepare the necessary materials. Here are two possible methods. Both require index cards.
   a. Cut out a rectangle no more than $3/_8$ inch by $1^1/_2$ inches in the center of an index card. Expose the words being tested, one at a time, through the rectangular opening.
   b. Use one index card to cover any printed matter that appears above the word the student is being asked to state. Use a second index card to cover all matter below the card. Continue this procedure for each word on the list.

*Administration*

1. Because you will be working with students on an individual basis, try to use a relatively isolated part of the classroom when administering the WRI.
2. Keep the word lists covered as you explain the method of presentation to the student.
3. Begin the WRI with a flash exposure of the first word. Be sure that the word is clearly and completely shown. The student should respond immediately.
   a. If the student's response is correct, place a check (✓) beside the word and proceed to the next word.
   b. If an initial response is incorrect but the student makes an immediate, independent correction, place a check with a plus sign (✓+) beside the word and proceed to the next word.

4. When the student's response is incorrect and is not independently corrected, reexpose the word. Allow a reasonable length of time for the student to study the word and to apply, without assistance, any word analysis skills he or she may have.

   a. If this untimed response is correct, place a check with a minus sign (✓–) beside the word and proceed to the next word.

   b. If the student is unable to decode the word correctly after an untimed exposure, record a zero (0) and proceed to the next word. For later reference, you may want to record the error made, for example, *run* for *ran.* To avoid confusion or the inaccurate reporting of results, it is important to record the responses immediately.

5. After the student has responded to all the list words for a particular level, record the total number of correct responses, including flash recognitions, independently corrected recognitions, and untimed recognitions. This total is the student's WRI score for that level.

6. Continue administering the WRI until the student misses four or more words at any level. Start the oral reading at the highest level at which the child has made 0 errors.

*Examples[9]*

1. Student: John X, fifth grade (the beginning)
   Begin WRI at third-grade reader level (beginning)

### Results

| Reader Level* | No. of Errors |
|:---:|:---:|
| $3^1$ | 4 |
| $2^2$ | 2 |
| $2^1$ | 1 |
| First | 0 |

*Refers to the grade level at which the material was prepared for use. For example, Readers $2^1$ and $2^2$ were prepared for use for the second grade; however, students should be reading in readers appropriate for their reading ability levels rather than those designated for their particular grade level. Also, note well that different reading programs have different ways of keying their book levels to reader grade levels. In one series *Level 7* is equivalent to $2^2$; whereas in another *Level 6* is equivalent to $2^2$.

*Interpretation of results:* Begin oral reading passages at first reader level.

[9]Examples are based on the WRI presented in Appendix B.

2. Student: Jane Y, fifth grade (middle)
   Begin WRI at third-grade reader level (middle)

**Results**

| Reader Level | No. of Errors |
|:---:|:---:|
| $3^2$ | 0 |
| 4 | 0 |
| 5 | 1 |
| 6 | 4 |

*Interpretation of results:* Begin oral reading passages at fourth-grade reader level.

3. Student: George Z, fourth grade (beginning)
   Begin WRI at second-grade reader level (beginning)

**Results**

| Reader Level | No. of Errors |
|:---:|:---:|
| $2^1$ | 0 |
| $2^2$ | 0 |
| $3^1$ | 1 |
| $3^2$ | 0 |
| 4 | 2 |
| 5 | 5 |

*Interpretation of results:* Begin oral reading passages at third-grade reader level (middle).

Note that each student is administered the WRI until he or she has made four or more errors so that you can see a pattern of the types of errors that the student has made.

## STEP 3: ORAL AND SILENT READING PASSAGES

The student begins to read the oral passage at sight at the highest reader level at which he or she has made zero errors on the Word Recognition Inventory (see examples given in Step 2). The teacher introduces the passage, asks the child to read aloud the passage and then answer questions on what was read. The child is asked to read aloud the passage without first looking at it.

While the child is reading aloud, the teacher records any oral reading errors the child makes (see Table 8.2). If the child's word recognition in oral reading is at the independent or instructional levels, the child is asked the comprehension questions. If the child's response is correct, the teacher puts a check

(✓) next to the question. If the answer is not correct, the teacher records the student's response. The child is then asked to read the silent passage. Again, the student is not given an opportunity to look over the passage before reading it. After finishing the silent reading passage, the child is asked the comprehension questions. If the response is correct, a check (✓) is put next to the response. If the answer is incorrect, the student's response is recorded next to the question.

The student then goes to the oral passage at the next reader level. The same procedure continues until the child reaches his or her frustration level.

If the student makes many word recognition errors while reading aloud, and the teacher feels the errors will interfere with the child's ability to answer the comprehension questions, the teacher usually does not have the child read the silent reading passage at the same reader level. The teacher administers a listening capacity test to the child; that is, the teacher reads aloud to the child and then asks the comprehension questions.

## STEP 4: THE LISTENING CAPACITY TEST

**Listening capacity test**
Given to determine a child's comprehension through listening. Teacher reads aloud to child and then asks questions about the selection.

A *listening capacity test* is given to determine a child's comprehension through listening. By determining a child's ability to comprehend material that is read aloud the teacher can gauge the child's ability to listen to instruction and oral reports. Also, a listening capacity test can help to identify those students who seem to gain information better through listening than through reading. This knowledge is important in planning proper modes of instruction for the child. (See Chapter 5 for more on listening capacity tests and for a discussion on how listening capacity tests help provide an estimate of a child's reading potential.)

The passages from the IRI are generally used to determine a child's listening capacity. The passages are evaluated in the same way that the oral and silent reading passages are evaluated except that the teacher reads aloud the selections to the child. If the passages that are to be read aloud have already been read by the child, alternate ones should be used. Some commercially produced IRIs have a separate set of selections for the listening capacity test for this reason.

## WHEN IS A LISTENING CAPACITY TEST GIVEN?

A listening capacity test is usually given when a child has reached or is rapidly approaching the frustration level in word recognition on the oral reading part of the IRI. If a child has difficulty decoding a large number of words in oral reading, this can interfere with his or her ability to answer comprehension questions. Also, if a child has difficulty with a large number of words at a certain reader level, the teacher usually does not use the silent reading passage at the same level because the decoding problems would probably interfere with the child's ability to answer comprehension questions. (See Example 1.) If a child does not have any extensive word recognition problems, the listening capacity test is usually given when the child is approaching or has reached his or her frustration level in silent reading on the IRI. (Although the student in Example 1, Jim X, had reached zero errors at the $2^2$ level [see chart on page 208], the WRI was continued until he reached four errors so that a pattern of the errors could better be seen.)

*Example 1[10]*

Student Jim X, fifth grade (beginning). Begin Word Recognition Inventory at $3^1$ level.

| Reader Level | Number of Errors |
|:---:|:---:|
| $3^1$ | 2 |
| $2^2$ | 0 |
| $3^2$ | 4 |

Jim begins oral reading at the $2^2$ level because he has zero errors at that level. The following chart shows his reading behavior.

| | Oral Reading | | | Silent Reading Comprehension | | Listening Capacity | |
|:---:|:---:|:---:|:---:|:---:|:---:|:---:|:---:|
| | Word Recognition | Comprehension | | | | | |
| Reader Level | No. Errors/ Total No. Words | % Errors | % Correct | % Errors | % Correct | % Errors | % Correct |
| $2^2$ | 4/131 | 0 | 100 | 0 | 100 | | |
| $3^1$ | 7/151 | 0 | 100 | 0 | 100 | | |
| $3^2$ | 10/171 | 20 | 80 | 25 | 75 | | |

**Listening Capacity**

| Reader Level | % Errors | % Correct |
|:---:|:---:|:---:|
| 4 | 0 | 100 |
| 5 | 0 | 100 |
| 6 | 0 | 100 |
| 7 | 20 | 80 |
| 8 | 40 | 60 |

At the $3^2$ level the teacher must decide whether to let Jim read silently or to give him a listening capacity test. His word recognition errors may be interfering with his ability to answer the comprehension questions. The teacher decides to let him read silently, even though he is in the "buffer" zone in word

[10]Examples are based on the IRI presented in Appendix B.

recognition, which is between the instructional and frustration levels, because she wants to see how well he uses context clues. Even though Jim has a word recognition problem, he seems to do quite well in comprehension. He scores 25 percent errors. The teacher has Jim read at the next level, which is the fourth-grade reader level, because he does not appear to be frustrated. At the next level, however, Jim makes 19 errors in oral reading, and he has difficulty answering the comprehension questions. The teacher decides to give him a listening capacity test. She starts to read aloud the silent reading passage at the fourth-grade reader level. Then she continues to read aloud one passage from each level. The chart on page 208 shows Jim's listening capacity scores. (It doesn't make any difference whether the passage was chosen from the oral or silent reading selections.) From the listening capacity test the teacher sees that Jim has excellent comprehension but his word recognition might be hindering him from working at his ability level. The teacher had decided to give Jim an IRI because his verbal behavior in class belied his reading achievement test scores.

The teacher continues administering the oral reading part of the IRI to determine Jim's independent oral reading level and to gain some more insight into the types of errors that he makes in word recognition so that she can develop a program to help him. (Jim reads the oral passage at the $2^1$ level. He makes one error out of 112 words. This is his independent oral reading level.) She will probably also give Jim another word analysis diagnostic test.

A summary sheet in Figure 8.2 shows a complete record of Jim's reading behavior on the IRI. The text continues on pages 212 and 213.

### *Example 2*

Student Susan Y, fifth grade (beginning). Begin WRI at $3^1$ level.

| Reader Level | No. of Errors |
|:---:|:---:|
| $3^1$ | 0 |
| $3^2$ | 0 |
| 4 | 0 |
| 5 | 0 |
| 6 | 4 |

Susan begins oral reading at the 5 level because that is her highest level of zero errors. She immediately reaches the frustration level in oral reading comprehension (see chart). Because of this, the teacher would be justified in not having her read the silent reading passage and start going down to lower grade levels to find her instructional and independent levels for comprehension. However, the teacher decides to have Susan read the silent reading passage because she wants to see if Susan was concentrating so hard on pronunciation that she didn't pay attention to what she was reading. Susan is asked to read the fifth-grade silent reading level passage. She makes 60 percent errors. The following chart shows Susan's reading behavior:

| | Oral Reading | | | Silent Reading Comprehension | | Listening Capacity | |
|---|---|---|---|---|---|---|---|
| | Word Recognition | Comprehension | | | | | |
| Reader Level | No. Errors/ Total No. Words | % Errors | % Correct | % Errors | % Correct | % Errors | % Correct |
| 5 | 2/208 | 60 | 40 | 60 | 40 | | |
| 4 | 2/187 | 60 | 40 | 60 | 40 | | |
| $3^2$ | 2/171 | 50 | 50 | 50 | 50 | | |
| $3^1$ | 2/151 | 40 | 60 | 50 | 50 | 50 | 50 |
| $2^2$ | 1/131 | 25 | 75 | 25 | 75 | 40 | 60 |
| $2^1$ | 1/112 | 10 | 90 | 10 | 90 | 25 | 75 |
| 6* | 9/252 | — | | — | | | |

*Susan was asked to read orally only at the sixth level to find her instructional oral reading word recognition level.

From the results, we can see that Susan has excellent word recognition, but she has severe difficulties in reading comprehension. A listening capacity test is given to determine the level at which she can listen to material and comprehend it at the instructional level. After looking at the results of Susan's reading performance, the teacher decides to start reading aloud to Susan at the $3^1$ level because this is the level at which she had reached frustration in silent reading. Since Susan is also at her frustration level on the listening capacity test at the $3^1$ level, the teacher moves to the $2^2$ level and reads aloud the passage. At this level Susan is approaching frustration. The teacher then reads the $2^1$ level passage and finds Susan's listening capacity level. (The selections read aloud to Susan to determine her listening capacity level were different from those in the IRI because Susan had already read those.) It is interesting to note that Susan's listening capacity score is lower than her oral and silent reading scores. She probably has more difficulty concentrating while listening than when reading silently or orally. Her oral and silent reading scores appear to be comparable. The teacher must analyze the kinds of comprehension errors that Susan made. It seems obvious that Susan's ability to read well orally has obscured her comprehension problems. Susan's teacher had decided to give her an IRI because she had noticed the discrepancy between Susan's verbalizing in class and her inability to answer even literal questions correctly. Susan can pronounce words very well, but she doesn't know the meanings for many of them. Even when she knows the meaning of the words used in a paragraph, she can't tell you what the paragraph is about. The IRI will give Susan's teacher some insights into Susan's comprehension difficulties; however, it may be that Susan is reading close to her reading ability (see Chapter 5). The listening capacity test that was administered to Susan indicates that Susan's reading potential may only be at a $2^1$ grade level. Susan's teacher will

**FIGURE 8.2 Summary Sheet***

Name ___Jim X___        Age ___10___

Grade ___5___        Teacher ___Mrs. Smith___

| Reader Level | Word Recognition in Isolation (No. of Errors) | Oral Reading | | | Silent Reading | | Listening Capacity | |
|---|---|---|---|---|---|---|---|---|
| | | W.R. | Comp. | | Comp. | | | |
| | | No. of Errors/ Total No. Wds† | % Errors | % Correct | % Errors | % Correct | % Errors | % Correct |
| Preprimer | | | | | | | | |
| Primer | | | | | | | | |
| First | | | | | | | | |
| 2¹ | | 1/112 | | | | | | |
| 2² | 0 | 4/131 | 0 | 100 | 0 | 100 | | |
| 3¹ | 2 | 7/151 | 0 | 100 | 0 | 100 | | |
| 3² | 4 | 10/171 | 20 | 80 | 25 | 75 | | |
| 4 | | 19/187 | 40 | 60 | | | 0 | 100 |
| 5 | | | | | | | 0 | 100 |
| 6 | | | | | | | 0 | 100 |
| 7 | | | | | | | 20 | 80 |
| 8 | | | | | | | 40 | 60 |

* For use with the IRI in Appendix B.

† Percentages can be easily calculated using the word recognition formula on pages 202–203, or see the IRI in Appendix B for corresponding reading levels, that is, independent, instructional, or frustration levels.

Level at which WRI was begun     $3^1$

Level at which oral reading was begun     $2^2$

Oral reading—word recognition

     Independent level     $2^1$

     Instructional level     $2^2$–$3^1$ (range)

     Frustration level     4

*(continued)*

**FIGURE 8.2**   *(continued)*

Oral reading—comprehension
  Independent level      $3^1$
  Instructional level      $3^2$
  Frustration level      _____
Silent reading—comprehension
  Independent level      $3^1$
  Instructional level      $3^2$
  Frustration level      _____
Listening capacity level      7

Word analysis
  Consonants—single
    initial
    medial
    final
  Consonants—double
    blends
    digraphs      *ch, sh, ph*
  Consonants—silent
  Vowels—single
    short      *ă, ĕ*
    long
  Vowels—double
    digraphs      *oa, ea*
    diphthongs      *ou in bough*
  Effect of final *e* on vowel
  Vowel controlled by *r*
  Structural analysis
    prefixes
    suffixes
    combining forms
    inflectional endings      *ignores most*
  Compound words
  Accent

*(continued)*

Special Notes on Strengths and Needs

*Jim has word recognition problems that are thwarting his comprehension ability. Jim doesn't attempt to use phonic clues. If he doesn't know the word as a sight word, and if he can't figure it out by using context clues, he skips over the word. His ability to use semantic and syntactic clues is excellent.*

Comments on Behavior During the Testing

*Jim seemed to like working in a one-to-one relationship. He said that he didn't like to read, but he liked to listen to others read aloud.*

Recommendations

*Give Jim a complete word recognition program stressing the use of graphic clues in combination with semantic and syntactic clues. Select books of low readability and high interest content.*

have to develop a program for Susan based on her needs. The first step seems to be concept development.

Figure 8.3 on pages 214–216 is a summary sheet, showing a complete record of Susan's reading behavior on the IRI.

## WHO SHOULD BE GIVEN AN IRI?

Some may say, "Why not give all students an IRI to be on the safe side?" Doing so is a good idea; however time constraints usually weigh against it. Here are some examples that show possible candidates for the IRI:

*Example 1.* The student answers questions that are posed orally in class very well, but he never raises his hand to read any printed material aloud. He has difficulty decoding many words that he uses with facility in his speaking vocabulary. Even though this child has scored on grade level on a standardized reading achievement test, he is a good candidate for an informal reading inventory.

**FIGURE 8.3    Summary Sheet***

Name _Susan Y_                                         Age _____10_____

Grade ____5_____                        Teacher _Mr. Jones_

| Reader Level | Word Recognition in Isolation (No. of Errors) | Oral Reading | | | Silent Reading | | Listening Capacity | |
|---|---|---|---|---|---|---|---|---|
| | | W.R. | Comp. | | Comp. | | | |
| | | No. of Errors/ Total No. Wds† | % Errors | % Correct | % Errors | % Correct | % Errors | % Correct |
| Preprimer | | | | | | | | |
| Primer | | | | | | | | |
| First | | | | | | | | |
| $2^1$ | | 1/112 | 10 | 90 | 10 | 90 | 25 | 75 |
| $2^2$ | | 1/131 | 25 | 75 | 25 | 75 | 40 | 60 |
| $3^1$ | 0 | 2/151 | 40 | 60 | 50 | 50 | 50 | 40 |
| $3^2$ | 0 | 2/171 | 50 | 50 | 50 | 50 | | |
| 4 | 0 | 2/187 | 60 | 40 | 60 | 40 | | |
| 5 | 0 | 2/208 | 60 | 40 | 60 | 40 | | |
| 6 | 4 | 9/252 | | | | | | |
| 7 | | | | | | | | |
| 8 | | | | | | | | |

* For use with the IRI in Appendix B.

† Percentages can be easily calculated using the word recognition formula on page 202–203, or see the IRI in Appendix B for corresponding reading levels, that is, independent, instructional, or frustration levels.

| | |
|---|---|
| Level at which WRI was begun | $3^1$ |
| Level at which oral reading was begun | 5 |
| Oral reading—word recognition | |
| Independent level | 5 |
| Instructional level | 6 |
| Frustration level | |

*(continued)*

Oral reading—comprehension

| | |
|---|---|
| Independent level | $2^1$ |
| Instructional level | $2^2$ |
| Frustration level | $3^2$ |

Silent reading—comprehension

| | |
|---|---|
| Independent level | $2^1$ |
| Instructional level | $2^2$ |
| Frustration level | $3^1$ |
| Listening capacity level | $2^1$ |

Word analysis

    Consonants—single

      initial           _____

      medial          _____

      final             _____

    Consonants—double

      blends         _____

      digraphs      _____

    Consonants—silent     _____

    Vowels—single

      short           _____

      long            _____

    Vowels—double

      digraphs      _____

      diphthongs    _____

    Effect of final *e* on vowel   _____

    Vowel controlled by *r*    _____

    Structural analysis

      prefixes        _____

      suffixes        _____

      combining forms   _____

      inflectional endings  _____

    Compound words     _____

    Accent             _____

*(continued)*

---

**FIGURE 8.3**    *(continued)*

---

Special Notes on Strengths and Needs

*Susan has excellent word recognition skills. She is weak in word meanings. She could not give the meanings of words that she could pronounce. She could not state the main idea of the paragraphs nor could she answer inferential questions. She was able to answer literal questions, but she even missed some of these.*

Comments on Behavior During the Testing

*She enjoyed reading aloud. She started squirming in her chair whenever comprehension questions were asked. She also squirmed in her chair when I was reading aloud to her.*

Recommendations

*Help Susan expand her vocabulary. Work on literal and interpretive comprehension skills. Give her a cloze test to further check her use of syntactic and semantic clues to figure out word meanings.*

---

*Example 2.* This student reads orally with excellent facility. However, whenever he is asked to answer comprehension questions on what he has read either orally or silently, he cannot. This child has scored below grade level on a standardized reading achievement test. He would be a good candidate for an IRI.

*Example 3.* The student stumbles on a number of words when she reads orally. She usually has no difficulty answering questions after she has read silently. She is very verbal and seems to know quite a bit of information on a number of different topics. She has scored a few months below her grade level, which is the fourth grade, on a standardized reading achievement test. She is a candidate for an IRI because her word recognition difficulties may be interfering with her ability to answer comprehension questions.

*Example 4.* This student has scored below grade level on a standardized reading achievement test; however, she does not seem to have any problems answering difficult reading comprehension questions at the literal, interpretive, and critical levels. The student also reads well orally. The teacher decides to give her an informal reading inventory to check at what grade level she is reading and also to determine whether she has reading difficulties that are not obvious. If the IRI does not point out any significant reading problem, this child should take another standardized reading achievement test. It is highly probable that the standardized reading achievement test score is not valid for this child.

## IRI SELECTION CRITERIA

A good IRI should have the following features:

1. There should be two forms, so that a pretest and a posttest can be given.
2. There should be different passages for oral and silent reading.
3. The comprehension questions should consist of a variety of literal and interpretive questions. (Critical reading questions are optional.)
4. All questions should be text-driven; that is, all questions including inferential and word meaning ones should be text-dependent.
5. The passage should be cohesive; it should be one for which it is possible to state the main or central idea.
6. The graded word lists should be representative of the grade level from which they have been taken.
7. The passages selected for oral and silent reading should be representative of the reading material in the book; that is, the readability level should not be higher or lower than the level from which the passages have been selected.
8. Specific directions should be given for administering and scoring the test.
9. There should be a separate set of passages and comprehension questions for the listening capacity test, if possible. These should also be representative of the reading material in the book.

## MODIFIED IRI APPROACHES: A CAUTION

Many teachers do not have the time to administer a complete IRI to their students, so they rely on a modified approach, whereby they use either oral reading in basal readers or trade books, or graded word lists to determine a student's placement. Teachers often use an approach in which a child is asked to read passages orally from various levels of a basal reader series. The level at which the child is able to read with some proficiency is the one that the teacher generally uses as the child's instructional reading level. The other technique frequently used is to expose the child to a graded list of words that has been selected from a basal reader series and have the child read aloud this list to determine his or her instructional reading level.

Word lists and on-the-spot oral reading without assessing comprehension are time-savers, but teachers must recognize the dangers of these techniques and realize that the information they are receiving may not be valid or reliable. If a teacher only uses a child's oral reading ability without assessing comprehension to determine reading level, many children may be provided inappropriate reading instruction. A child may have a word recognition problem but have excellent comprehension, and conversely, a child may have a comprehension problem but no word recognition problems. The latter child with no word recognition problem, who probably has a lower reading potential than the former child with the word recognition problem, would probably be placed in a higher reading group than the child with the word recognition problem.

For the on-the-spot oral reading approach to be effective, the teacher should devise some comprehension questions based on the material, or test understanding by having the child "retell" what he or she has read. The teacher could also determine comprehension by asking the student to give the main idea of what he or she has read.

The problem with the use of graded word lists to determine a student's reading level is similar to the one just discussed for the on-the-spot oral reading approach. From the graded word list, you are only getting an estimate of the student's ability to pronounce words; you are not getting any information about the child's comprehension, nor are you learning how the child reads the words in context. This limitation is dangerous because reading is a thinking act.

The on-the-spot approach is especially effective for students in the upper grades who are reading content material books and who are not involved in reading classes. Many times these students are having difficulty because the content books are at too high a readability level for them. The on-the-spot approach would be a viable method for these students. It is a good idea to choose a passage that is representative of the book; one from the middle of the book would probably be best for this purpose. In a one-on-one setting, have the student read aloud the passage, which should consist of a paragraph or two; then have the student answer some comprehension questions on it, or give a summary of what he or she has read.

Some people have used a group on-the-spot approach to test the readability of textbooks. There are a number of variations to this approach, but for it to be a group approach, all or a number of students must take it at the same time. In the group approach, the students usually read silently a passage close to the middle of the book, and then they write the answers to given questions on the passage, a summary of the passage, or the main idea of the passage, and so on. Be *cautious* in using such a test to determine whether the book is at the reading ability level of the student. It may be that the student has difficulty expressing himself or herself in writing. You may be testing a student's writing ability rather than his or her reading ability. From this type of test, you also are not learning whether the student has word recognition problems or comprehension problems.

## POINTS OF CAUTION CONCERNING IRIs

Recognize that an IRI can yield important information about a student's reading performance, but the results may vary from one IRI to another because of the following factors:

1. Criteria used to estimate reading levels.
2. Amount of information given before the student is asked to read aloud or silently.
3. Criteria used to record errors.

4. Type of comprehension questions asked and how scored.
5. Cut-off point for defining reading levels.
6. Readability of material.
7. Procedure for reading aloud. (Are students asked to look over material before they read aloud?)
8. Order of silent and oral reading passages. (Do students read orally first and then proceed to the silent reading passage, or do they read silently first and then proceed to the oral reading passage?)

Three of these factors warrant further discussion.

## CRITERIA FOR ESTIMATING READING LEVELS

The criteria as established by Betts for estimating reading levels were given earlier in the section "Determining Reading and Listening Capacity Levels." Although Betts's criteria are used by many, they are not universally accepted. One of the problems in using IRIs is that variability exists in the criteria for identifying reading levels. Two researchers summarized the criteria that various persons advocated for IRIs and illustrated the discrepancies among them.[11] They claim that differences exist in administrative procedures as well as in error classification; however, the researchers stated that the procedural differences are not enough to explain the discrepancies among the criteria put forth by authorities to estimate the instructional reading level.

Another researcher who reviewed the existing literature on informal reading inventories concludes that even though "the issues concerning IRI scoring are far from settled, several practical suggestions can be made. In general, the Betts criteria should be retained but not rigidly adhered to."[12]

Although there are a number of summaries of the literature, surprisingly, very little research exists to validate criteria for estimating reading levels. Of the studies that have been done, few agree on levels of criteria.

An issue since the 1970s that has been extensively discussed concerns whether the emphasis in determining reading levels should be on the number of errors or on the type of error that is made. It appears that both should be taken into consideration. For example, read the following sentence, and then read how three different children have read it:

The horse went into the stable.

*Student 1:* The horse went into the *store.*
*Student 2:* The *big* horse went *in* the *barn.*
*Student 3:* The horse went *in a* stable.

If we count all errors without consideration to type, Student 1 has the fewest errors, and Student 2 has the most. However, if we look at the readings of the three sentences, we would have to conclude that Student 3, with two errors, has a better understanding of the writer's message than Student 1, with

---

[11]William R. Powell and Colin G. Dunkeld, "Validity of the IRI Reading Levels," *Elementary English* 48 (October 1971): 637–42.

[12]Michael C. McKenna, "Informal Reading Inventories: A Review of the Issues," *The Reading Teacher* 36 (March 1983): 674.

one error; and Student 2, with three errors, is also a better reader than Student 1. The omission and insertion by Student 2 did not affect the meaning of the sentence, nor did the substitution of *barn* for *stable*; however, the substitution of *store* for *stable* did affect the meaning of the sentence. Student 1 made fewer errors and stuck closer to graphic cues than Student 2, but he sacrificed the meaning of the sentence. Student 1, with the fewest errors, has to be judged the poorest reader of the three.

Even though many authorities agree that both number and type of error should be taken into account, it is very difficult to devise a scoring procedure that incorporates these two concepts that would be easy and quick to use and that would eliminate subjectivity.

## How Should Oral Reading Errors Be Scored?

How to score word recognition ability on the graded oral passages is probably one of the biggest controversies concerning the use of IRIs. The way a child is scored will determine his or her placement in a reading level; different criteria for determining reading levels will result in different reading placements, and even if similar criteria are used, different methods of scoring will affect placements. In one study in which experienced examiners recorded the oral reading errors of an excellent-quality tape of one child slowly reading a 115-word passage, the examiners disagreed sharply on the error count. The error count of the fourteen examiners, who were reading specialists, ranged from one to fourteen.[13]

The problem seems to be twofold. It involves the classification or definition of errors and the scoring of them. There is no agreement on what should be considered an error and how the error should be scored, or even whether it should be scored. For example, some authorities note when a student has repeated a part of a word, a word, or words, but they do not count the repetitions as errors; others do. Some examiners count hesitations as errors; some do not. Some count every error made, even if it is on the same word; that is, it is possible to have multiple errors on one word, and rather than count them as one error, some testers will count each error on that word. If a student meets the same word five times in the oral reading, and each time makes an error, some examiners count this as five errors; however, some may count this as only one error. Some testers do not count errors on proper nouns; some do.

Examiners do not necessarily use similar categories of errors. Some include reversals; some do not. Some include help from the tester; some do not. Some include provisions for dialect differences; some do not; and so on it goes. Some examiners also include information about semantic, syntactic, and graphic cues and suggest that teachers should analyze their students' errors with these in mind so that they can distinguish between the trivial and the significant.

What does all this mean? It means that there is a lot of subjectivity in the scoring of errors, and you must be careful to choose a system that agrees with your philosophy and available research findings. It also suggests that the same scoring procedure needs to be used for all children.

---

[13]William D. Page, "Miscue Research and Diagnosis," *Findings of Research in Miscue Analysis: Classroom Implications,* ed. P. David Allen and Dorothy J. Watson (Urbana, IL: National Council of Teachers of English, 1976), pp. 140–41.

It is really only from the comprehension score that we can determine whether certain word recognition errors were indeed significant. Therefore, it is important that the student's word recognition behavior be accurately recorded to determine what kinds of errors may be interfering with comprehension. ■

### A Special Look at Repetitions

An oral reading error that has caused a great amount of discussion and confusion among users of IRIs is that of repetitions. As already stated, some recommend that repetitions be counted as errors, whereas a number of others do not. One research study using the polygraph to determine the frustration level of a student found that if repetitions are not counted as errors, a child will reach the frustration level before the examiner is able to count enough errors to designate it.[14] It must be remembered that each child in this study was monitored by a polygraph. It is possible that the polygraph, itself, may have caused anxiety.

We feel that it is unrealistic to count every repetition as an error for a number of reasons. Most normal reading aloud is subject to errors even by well-known excellent readers. There are a number of reasons why a student would repeat a word or words or make some short hesitations. The student may be nervous; he or she may be unused to reading aloud or unfamiliar with the type of material being read; the student may not have good rapport with the examiner; the student may be shy; and, more significantly, the student may be concentrating on the meaning of the reading because he or she either has been told that questions will be asked after the oral reading, or fully understands that comprehension is the essence of reading.

## ORAL AND SILENT READING COMPREHENSION

Betts, in developing the IRI, suggested that silent reading be given before oral reading. However, most authors of IRIs today present the oral reading passage before the silent one at the same level because the oral reading is used as a gauge to determine whether a student should read silently at the same level. If a student makes many oral reading errors, it is assumed that he or she will have difficulty reading silently at the same level. When the child is asked the questions after reading the silent passage, if he or she has not read orally at the same level, the teacher will not be able to determine whether the inability to answer the comprehension questions arose from a comprehension problem or a word recognition problem.

Most authors of IRIs instruct examiners to use the same criteria for scoring oral reading comprehension as for scoring silent reading comprehension, even though some persons have suggested that the former should be scored less stringently because readers concentrate more on word pronunciation during oral reading than on comprehension. Many people feel that students would score higher on comprehension after reading silently than after reading orally; however,

---

[14]Eldon E. Ekwall, "Should Repetitions Be Counted as Errors?" *The Reading Teacher* 27 (January 1974): 365–67.

this assumption has not been borne out by research. The comparative studies of silent and oral reading comprehension scores have been inconclusive.[15] As a result, the oral and silent comprehension criteria have remained the same.

It would appear that good readers would do better in comprehension after reading silently than after reading orally. However, there are some children who may do better in comprehension after reading orally because they need to hear the words in order to understand them. Their auditory modality may be more developed than their visual modality.

# AN OVERVIEW OF MISCUE ANALYSIS

**Miscue analysis**
A process that helps teachers learn how readers get meaning from language.

**Miscue**
Unexpected response to print.

## WHAT IS MISCUE ANALYSIS AND WHAT IS ITS PURPOSE?

Kenneth Goodman, the prime mover in miscue analysis research, feels that *miscue analysis* is a viable research process that goes beyond the "superficial behavior of readers" to learn how readers get meaning from language.[16] He objects to the use of the term *errors* because he feels that nothing the reader does in reading is accidental, and *error* implies randomness.[17] If teachers can understand how *miscues*, which are unexpected responses to print, relate to expected responses, they will better understand how the reader is using the reading process. Miscue analysis begins with observed behavior, but it tries to go beyond *through analysis*.

## HOW CAN MISCUE ANALYSIS BE USED?

To analyze readers' miscues, an analytic taxonomy was developed that considers the relationship between the reader's expected response (ER) with his or her observed response (OR). (This taxonomy has been and is continuously modified for new inputs from miscue studies.) The strength of this taxonomy is that it attempts to analyze the causes of a reader's miscues from a number of angles. However, its strengths are also its weaknesses for the classroom teacher. The Goodman Taxonomy of Reading Miscues consists of about nineteen questions, and each miscue is analyzed in terms of these nineteen questions. The Goodman Taxonomy of Reading Miscues "is a highly complex and sophisticated research instrument calling for considerable background on the part of the user."[18] This instrument may not be for the classroom teacher; however, evolving from the taxonomy is the Reading Miscue Inventory (RMI), which was designed to be used by the classroom teacher. The inventory has condensed the nineteen questions, which involved from four to fifteen possible responses for each, to nine questions involving three choices each.

[15]E. H. Rowell, "Do Elementary Students Read Better Orally or Silently?" *The Reading Teacher* 29 (January 1976): 367–70.

[16]Kenneth S. Goodman, "Miscues: Windows on the Reading Process," in *Miscue Analysis,* ed. Kenneth S. Goodman (Urbana, IL: National Council of Teachers of English, 1973), p. 5.

[17]The National Assessment of Educational Progress in its Reading Report Cards uses *deviation from text* in place of the term *error.*

[18]Carolyn Burke, "Preparing Elementary Teachers to Teach Reading," in *Miscue Analysis,* ed. Kenneth S. Goodman (Urbana, IL: National Council of Teachers of English, 1973), p. 24.

The miscue analysis studies, with the emphasis on reading as a process in which meaning is obtained, have greatly influenced many examiners' interpretations of students' reading behaviors. They have heightened the consciousness level of testers using the IRI so that many are now concerned not only with the number of errors that a student makes but also with the quality or kind of error. Most recognize that getting meaning is more important than absolute accuracy of word pronunciation.

Even less complex than the RMI is the modified miscue analysis procedure shown here, which is easily applied in the classroom and can be used with nearly any text.

# MODIFIED MISCUE ANALYSIS[19]

*Preparing for the Modified Miscue*

1. Choose an appropriate text. A passage of 150 words is acceptable for this assessment. The passage should be long enough to help you see if and how the reader uses reading strategies. You might want to use a passage from a book the child is reading.
2. Make a copy of the passage for the reader as well as for yourself. You can write on your copy while the reader reads from his or hers.
3. Make enough copies of the Modified Miscue Analysis Forms shown in Figure 8.4.

*Administering the Modified Miscue*

1. As with administering the IRI, you want to establish rapport with the child who will be reading.
2. Explain the procedure, saying something like, "I would like to listen to you read so that I can hear what you do when you read. I am going to take notes while you read."
3. Ask the child to begin reading from his or her copy.
4. Watch the reader. Do his or her body language or facial expressions note comfort or anxiety? How is the book held: too close? Too far?
5. As the child reads, make the following notations on your copy of the passage using the same notations as stated for coding the IRI (see Table 8.2).
6. After the reading, ask the child to retell what he or she remembers from the reading. Note how well the child recalls the main events from the passage and rank it as outstanding, adequate, or inadequate.

*Scoring the Modified Miscue*

Remember that the premise behind miscue analysis is that there is a logical reason for what the reader is doing when reading. The purpose of the analysis is to get a glimpse of this logic and to see which specific language cues the child uses when reading. The procedures listed here can help in this analysis.

1. Using the Miscue Analysis Form in Figure 8.4, write every word the child miscued and the actual word as it appears in the text.
2. As you attempt to figure out which cues the child used to miscue, you will need to look at the passage on which you recorded the child's reading behaviors.

[19]Opitz, M., and T. Rasinski. *Good-bye Round Robin.* Portsmouth, NH: Heinemann, 1998.

## FIGURE 8.4   Modified Miscue Analysis Form

Reader's Name: _____     Grade: _____

Title and pages: _____     Date: _____

Three important questions to ask for each miscue:
   M = meaning: Does the miscue make sense?
   S = structure: Does the sentence sound right?
   V = visual: Does the miscue resemble the printed word?

| *Student* | *Text* | *Cues Used* | | |
|---|---|---|---|---|
| | | M | S | V |
| | | M | S | V |
| | | M | S | V |
| | | M | S | V |
| | | M | S | V |
| | | M | S | V |
| | | M | S | V |
| | | M | S | V |
| | | M | S | V |
| | | M | S | V |
| | | M | S | V |
| | | M | S | V |
| | | M | S | V |
| | | M | S | V |
| | | M | S | V |
| | | M | S | V |
| | | M | S | V |
| | | M | S | V |

3. Ask yourself the three questions shown on the form *for every miscue*. If the answer is "yes," circle the appropriate letter(s): M, S, V.
4. Answer all questions and record any other observations on the Summary of Observations form shown in Figure 8.5.
5. Based on your analysis, make a decision about what you think the given child knows and what needs to be learned and design instruction accordingly.

# AN OVERVIEW OF THE RUNNING RECORD

**Running record**
Documentation of a child's reading.

## WHAT IS A RUNNING RECORD?

A running record is a documentation of a child's reading. Like the IRI, it is a systematic way of observing and chronicling a child's oral reading behavior. Introduced in the United States by Marie Clay[20], the running record was originally designed so that teachers could observe the reading behaviors children were using as they read a text in a naturally occurring context. With a blank piece of paper, a teacher could sit down next to a child and use a specific coding system to note what the child did when reading aloud to the teacher. The teacher could take these records "on the run" as he or she moved from student to student. The notes could then be further analyzed to assess what specific children were doing when reading.

## WHAT ARE THE PURPOSES OF A RUNNING RECORD?

Clay[21] lists and explains several reasons for running records. The one that most teachers are concerned with focuses on using the results of running records to inform instruction. As such, teachers can interpret children's performances and use them in several ways: to evaluate text difficulty; to group children; to adjust instruction, which might entail having children progress through texts at different rates; to note progress of individual children in a variety of reading-related behaviors such as use of different language cues; and to note specific difficulties that children may be having with reading.

## HOW ARE RUNNING RECORDS AND IRIS SIMILAR?

Running records and IRIs have several common aspects. Three of the most important are listed below.

First, they are based on similar beliefs about the value of having students read aloud as a way of showing what they are able to do as readers. Both require students to read orally so that the teacher can get a glimpse of how students are reading, the strategies they use in reading, and whether they self-correct any miscues. Both help the teacher to determine children's functional reading

---

[20]Clay, M. *The Early Detection of Reading Difficulties.* Portsmouth, NH: Heinemann, 1995.
[21]Ibid.

**FIGURE 8.5 Modified Miscue Analysis: Summary of Observations**

1. What did the reader do when unknown words were encountered? (Check all that apply.)

_____ made an attempt in these ways:

_____ used meaning cues      _____ used structure cues      _____ used letter/sound cues

_____ made repeated tries      _____ used pictures      _____ skipped it and read on

_____ used memory      _____ looked at another source

_____ other: _____

_____ made no attempt      _____ asked for help      _____ waited for teacher help

2. Which cues did the reader use most often? _____

_____

3. How often did the reader attempt to self-correct when meaning was not maintained?

(Circle one)      always      sometimes      seldom      never

Comments: _____

4. How often did the reader make repetitions?

(Circle one)      always      sometimes      seldom      never

Comments: _____

5. Did the reader read fluently?      _____ mostly      _____ somewhat      _____ little

Comments: _____

6. Did the reader attend to punctuation?      _____ mostly      _____ somewhat      _____ little

Comments: _____

*Comprehension*

Retelling was (Circle one):      outstanding      adequate      inadequate

Comments: _____

_____

Other observations: _____

_____

levels (i.e., independent, instructional, and frustrational) so that appropriate texts can be provided for both independent and instructional reading experiences.

Second, running records and IRIs use similar coding systems to mark the types of miscues that children make when reading. Consistency is important so that teachers can better interpret their markings when analyzing reading behaviors.

Third, both use connected text when assessing reading. That is, both are based on the philosophical premise that having children reading "real" text is reflective of what they actually do when reading. Therefore, it must be used to assess reading if we want to see what strategies children apply when they approach texts.

## HOW ARE RUNNING RECORDS AND IRIS DIFFERENT?

Although running records and IRIs have much in common, they also have some differences. The most notable difference is that as originally conceived, running records had no comprehension measure because more attention was paid to word accuracy and the way the child actually read the text. Self-corrections were viewed as evidence of comprehension. However, most teachers and reading specialists who use running records also recognize the importance of a separate comprehension measure and they have children do some sort of retelling or answering of questions, which brings the running record more in line with the IRI comprehension measures.

Another major difference between the two is that a running record can be completed with any text, whereas an IRI uses a set of graded passages. However, most teachers use a leveled set of books when using running records and chart children's progress relative to these levels. The text that is used resembles natural language patterns and is therefore seen as more authentic than the passages in an IRI. Depending on how passages are selected for an IRI, this may or may not be the case.

Yet another difference has to do with access. Although most IRI authors provide passages that are aimed at assessing first-grade children's reading, they rarely accomplish this task. Most often, the passages are too difficult, especially at the beginning of the year. The running record resolves this issue because teachers can use commercially prepared leveled texts that children are able to read. The *Developmental Reading Assessment (DRA)*[22] is often used by primary grade teachers because it offers leveled texts and accompanying materials that are easy to use.

A fourth major difference is that IRIs are most often used to get an estimate of a child's functional reading levels for placement purposes. This is not the case with running records. Running records are given to inform instruction, and many teachers frequently administer them to determine which texts children should be reading. Although there are some concerns about too much

[22]Beaver, J. *The Developmental Reading Assessment.* New York: Scott Foresman, 2001.

focus on the accuracy to select texts to the neglect of considering other factors such as the reader's background and the type of text to be read, the main point here is that running records are used much more frequently than IRIs.

# ADMINISTERING A RUNNING RECORD

Although running record administration and scoring procedures are similar to those used for IRIs, there are a few differences. You might want to take a look at the completed example on pages 234 and 235 before reading the following administration and scoring procedures.

1. Choose a text.
2. Make copies of both the Running Record Form (Figure 8.6) and the Running Record Summary (Figure 8.7). You might want to use the Running Record form as is or you might want to write the words from the text you will be using on each line like the one shown in the example in Figure 8.9 on page 233.
3. Assess children individually and begin by saying something like this: "I would like to listen to you read this book. While you are reading, I am going to take some notes so that I can remember how well you read." Sit next to the child so that you can watch his or her behavior rather than the reverse!
4. Have the child read the book while you record the reading on the Running Record form. If you are using a form with no text, use the following notations:

   - Make a check for each word read as shown in the book.
   - Write and circle any word that is omitted.
   - Add a caret for any word that the child inserts and write the word.
   - Write and draw a line through any word that is substituted and write what the child said in its place.
   - If the child repeats, draw an arrow to indicate where the child went back to reread.
   - Write SC when the child self-corrects.
   - If the child stops for more than 5 seconds, tell the student the word. Put a "T" for the stated word.
   - If the child loses his or her place or if the child begins reading text that is far different from the text, stop the child, point to where you want the child to start reading again, and say something like, "Try reading this again." Put brackets to indicate the problem section and write TTA inside the brackets.

   If you are using a form that includes the text the child is reading, use the following notations:
   - Place a check above each word as shown in the book.
   - Circle any word that is omitted.
   - If a child inserts a word, add a caret where the child inserts the word and write the word.

**FIGURE 8.6**  **Running Record**

Name: _____  Date: _____

Title of Book: _____  Author: _____

| Page | Reading Performance | Miscues<br>M  S  V | Self-Corrects<br>M  S  V |
|------|---------------------|--------------------|--------------------------|
|      |                     |                    |                          |
|      |                     |                    |                          |
|      |                     |                    |                          |
|      |                     |                    |                          |
|      |                     |                    |                          |
|      |                     |                    |                          |
|      |                     |                    |                          |
|      |                     |                    |                          |
|      |                     |                    |                          |
|      |                     |                    |                          |
|      |                     |                    |                          |
|      |                     |                    |                          |
|      |                     |                    |                          |
|      |                     |                    |                          |
|      |                     |                    |                          |
|      |                     |                    |                          |
|      |                     |                    |                          |
|      |                     |                    |                          |
|      |                     |                    |                          |
|      |                     |                    |                          |
|      |                     |                    |                          |
|      |                     |                    |                          |
|      |                     |                    |                          |
|      |                     |                    |                          |
|      |                     |                    |                          |
|      |                     |                    |                          |
|      | **Totals**          |                    |                          |

M = Meaning Cue    S = Structure Cue    V = Visual Cue

From *Reaching Readers* by M. Opitz and M. Ford, 2001. Portsmouth, NH: Heineman.

---

**FIGURE 8.7    Running Record Summary**

Name: _____    Date: _____

Title of Book: _____    Author: _____

**Summary of Reading Performance**

Total # of Words _____    Total # of Miscues _____    % of Accuracy _____

**Reading Level** (Circle the one that matches the % of accuracy.)

95% – 100% = Independent    90% – 94% = Instructional    89% or lower = Frustration

Total # of Self-Corrections _____    Self-Correction rate 1: _____

Note: Self-correction rates of 1:3, 1:4, or 1:5 are good. Each ratio shows that the reader is attending to discrepancies when reading.

---

**Summary of Observation**

1. What did the reader do when unknown words were encountered?

   _____ made an attempt

   The reader made an attempt in these ways:

   | | |
   |---|---|
   | _____ asked for help | _____ looked at pictures |
   | _____ used letter/sound knowledge | _____ used meaning |
   | _____ used structure (syntax) | _____ tried again |
   | _____ skipped it and continued reading | _____ looked at another source |

2. How often did the reader attempt to self-correct when meaning was not maintained?

   (Circle one)    always    frequently    sometimes    seldom    never

3. When the reader did self-correct, which cues were used? (✔ all that apply.)

   _____ letter/sound knowledge (visual)    _____ meaning    _____ syntax (structure)

**Calculating Accuracy Rate**

1. Subtract the total number of miscues from the total number of words in the text to determine the number of words that were correctly read.

2. Divide the number of words correctly read by the number of words in the passage to determine % of accuracy.

   Example:  58 total words – 12 miscues = 46 words read correctly
   46 words read correctly ÷ 58 total words = 79% accuracy

**Calculating Self-Correction Rate**

Use this formula:  $\dfrac{\text{self-correction} + \text{miscues}}{\text{self-corrections}} = 1:$ _____

## FIGURE 8.8   Retelling

Name: _____

**Directions:** Indicate with a check the extent to which the reader's retelling includes or provides evidence of the following information.

| Retelling | None | Low | Moderate | High |
|---|---|---|---|---|
| 1. Includes information directly stated in text. | | | | |
| 2. Includes information inferred directly or indirectly from text. | | | | |
| 3. Includes what is important to remember from text. | | | | |
| 4. Provides relevant content and concepts. | | | | |
| 5. Indicates attempt to connect background knowledge to text information. | | | | |
| 6. Indicated attempt to make summary statements or generalizations based on text that can be applied to the real world. | | | | |
| 7. Indicated highly individualistic and creative impressions of or reactions to the real world. | | | | |
| 8. Indicates effective involvement with the text. | | | | |
| 9. Demonstrates appropriate use of language (vocabulary, sentence structure, language conventions). | | | | |
| 10. Indicates ability to organize or compose the retelling. | | | | |
| 11. Demonstrates sense of audience or purpose. | | | | |
| 12. Indicates control of the mechanics of speaking or writing. | | | | |

**Interpretation:** Items 1–4 indicate the reader's comprehension of textual information; items 5–8 indicate metacognitive awareness, strategy use, and involvement with text; items 9–12 indicate facility with language and language development.

- If the child substitutes a word, draw a line through the word and write the word the child stated above it.
- If the child repeats, draw an arrow to indicate where the child went back to reread.
- Write SC on or above the word when the child self-corrects.
- If the child stops for more than 5 seconds, tell the student the word. Put a "T" for the stated word on or above the word.
- If the child loses his or her place or if the child begins reading text that is far different from the text, stop the child, point to where you want the child to start reading again, and say something like, "Try reading this again." Put brackets around the problem section and write TTA above the section.

5. To check comprehension, have the child do a retelling and note the degree to which the child was able to retell using a form similar to Figure 8.8.

## SCORING A RUNNING RECORD

The following are counted as errors:

- omissions
- insertions
- substitutions
- told words or told to try that again

### Special Note

All repeated errors are recorded. For example, if the child substitutes the word "a" for "the" two times, each time, this substitution would count as an error. Clay comments, "It is only when you go to the trouble of analyzing *all the errors* that you get quality information about the way the reader is working on print."[23]

As with miscue analysis, the running record can shed some light on the language cues the child may have used to read the text as he or she did. To get the most out of the running record, we need to go beyond simply counting the number of errors the child makes and look at why the child might have performed the way he or she did. In the short term, this analysis can help teachers to see which language cues the child uses as well as those that may need additional work. In the long term, the analysis of miscues over time can yield a pattern of behavior. Here are some suggestions for going beyond accuracy to look more closely at what the child did when reading:

1. Write M, S, and V for each error and self-corrections. Remember that a self-correction is not counted as an error, nor is a repetition.

---

[23] Clay, 1985/1995.

---

### FIGURE 8.9   A Running Record of Your Reading

Name: _Jesse_  Date: _Today_

Title of Book: _Summertime_  Author: _MacLeod, Skelton, & Strong_

| Page | The reading performance | Errors<br>M S V | Self-Corrects<br>M S V |
|------|------------------------|-----------------|------------------------|
| 1 | ✓ ✓ ✓   spring<br>I like the ~~summer~~. | (M)(S) V | |
| 1 | ✓   ✓   woke ✓ ✓<br>The birds ~~wake~~ me up. | (M)(S)(V) | |
| 2 | ✓✓  ✓   ✓  ✓ ✓  ✓<br>I like wearing shorts and a T-shirt. | | |
| 3 | ✓ ✓ to wear   ✓   ✓   ✓<br>I like ˄ ~~wearing~~ sandals without socks. | (M)(S) V<br>(M)(S)(V) | |
| 4 | ✓✓  ✓   ✓   ✓ ✓  ✓<br>I like playing outside in the sun. | | |
| 5 | ✓have sc ⌐R ✓  ✓  ✓   ✓<br>I ~~like~~ helping Mom in the garden | | (M)(S)(V) |
| 6 | ✓✓  ✓   ✓   ✓<br>I like climbing the (apple) tree. | (M)(S)(V) | |
| 7 | ✓ ✓  ✓  ✓ ✓   ✓<br>I like eating in the backyard. | | |
| 8 | ✓ ✓ ✓  ✓   ✓  ✓ ✓ when sc ✓  ✓<br>But, I don't like going to bed ~~before~~ it's dark! | | M S (V) |
| | | M S V<br>5 5 2 | M S V<br>1 1 2 |
| | **Totals** | 5 | 2 |

2. Read the sentence up to where each error was made and ask yourself these questions:
   - Does it make sense? If so, circle the M. This indicates that the child was attending to meaning when reading.
   - Does it sound right? If so, circle the S. This indicates that the child was attending to the grammatical structure.
   - Does it look like the actual word in the text? If so, circle the V. This indicates that the child was attending to the printed text.
3. For each self-correction, you need to ask yourself what made the reader go back to self-correct. Ask yourself these questions:

- Did the child self-correct because meaning was disrupted? If so, circle the M.
- Did the child self-correct because it didn't sound right? If so, circle the S.
- Did the child self-correct because the word didn't look like the one shown in the text? If so, circle the V.

4. Calculate the accuracy rate and the self-correction rate using the formula shown on the Running Record Summary Form in Figure 8.10
5. Record additional observations on the Running Record Summary form (Figure 8.7).
6. Take a look at the comprehension measure to determine how well the child appeared to comprehend the selection.
7. Use the results to design appropriate instruction. ■

# INTERPRETING A RUNNING RECORD

Taking a look at the summary, we are now in a position to interpret Jesse's reading behavior and make some inferences about what we need to do next. Let's first take a look at what Jesse appears to be doing well (his strengths). We'll then consider what he might need to learn (his needs) to advance as a reader.

*Strengths*

- Monitors self as evidenced by his self-corrections
- Uses all three language cues: letter/sound knowledge, syntax, meaning
- Attempts a word more than once when he senses that there is a problem
- Uses all three language cues to self-correct

In terms of comprehension, Jesse was able to retell the story with ease and also talked about what he likes to do in the spring. Neither literal nor inferential comprehension appeared to pose any problems with this particular text.

*Needs*

- Expand strategies to include cross-checking with pictures or looking back to see where he has seen a word before as ways of figuring out unknown words
- Increase sight word vocabulary. This might enable him to advance to a more sophisticated instructional level.
- Give additional attention to visual cues. Jesse uses all three language cues; however, according to the results of this running record, he relies most heavily on meaning and syntax.

**FIGURE 8.10   Running Record Summary**

Title of Book: *Summertime*                          Author: _____

**Summary of Reading Performance**

   Total # of Words _58_      Total # of Errors _5_      % of accuracy _91%_

**Reading Level** (Circle the one that matches the % of accuracy.)

   95% – 100% = Independent      (90% – 94% = Instructional)      89% or lower = Frustration

   Total # of Self-Corrections _2_      Self-Correction Rate 1: _3.5_

Note: Self-correction rates of 1:3, 1:4, or 1:5 are good. Each ratio shows that the reader is attending to discrepancies when reading.

----------------------------------------------------------------------------------------

**Summary of Observations**

1. What did the reader do when unknown words were encountered? (✔ all that apply)

   _____ made no attempt

   The reader made an attempt in these ways:

   _____ asked for help                    _____ looked at pictures

   _✓_ used letter/sound knowledge          _✓_ used meaning

   _✓_ used structure (syntax)              _✓_ tried again

   _____ skipped it and continued reading  _____ looked at another source

2. How often did the reader attempt to self-correct when meaning was not maintained?

   (Circle one)      always      frequently      (sometimes)      seldom      never

3. When the reader did self-correct, which cues were used? (✔ all that apply.)

   _✓_ letter/sound knowledge (visual)      _✓_ meaning      _✓_ syntax (structure)

**Calculating Accuracy Rate**

1. Subtract the total # of errors from the total # of words in the text to determine the number of words that were correctly read.

2. Divide the number of words correctly read by the number of words in the passage to determine % of accuracy.

   Example:  58 total words – 12 errors = 46 words read correctly
             46 words read correctly ÷ 58 total words = 79% accuracy

**Calculating Self-Correction Rate**

Use this formula:  $\dfrac{\text{self-corrections} + \text{errors}}{\text{self-corrections}} = 1:$ _____

# SUMMARY

In Chapter 8, we present a discussion of using oral reading to assess students' reading. An IRI is a valuable diagnostic aid because it can provide information about a student's reading levels as well as help the teacher gain insight into a child's reading strengths and needs. We also provide information on the IRI, its purposes, the criteria for estimating reading levels, how to administer one, how to mark oral reading errors, and how to score them. This chapter also presents information on research concerning IRIs and some information on word lists. Teachers are cautioned about the subjectivity of IRIs and are again reminded that any test, and especially the IRI, is only as good as the person administering and interpreting it. We also present miscue analysis and explain how research in this area has heightened the consciousness level of testers using the IRI so that many are now concerned not only with the number of errors a student makes but also with the quality of the errors that are made.

Finally, we examine the running record. We demonstrate how to use it and discuss how it is similar to and different from an IRI.

# CHAPTER 8 KEY CONCEPTS

- Oral reading is important for diagnostic purposes.
- There is a need for both oral and silent reading in a reading assessment.
- The informal reading inventory (IRI) is a valuable diagnostic tool if used properly.
- An IRI helps teachers determine students' independent, instructional, frustration, and listening capacity levels, which are needed to match students with appropriate-level books.
- An IRI helps teachers learn about a student's strengths and needs.
- Teachers can use adaptations of the IRI with both trade books and content-area textbooks.
- If teachers wish to construct an IRI using trade books or a reading program that only uses trade books, they must make sure that the books are based on graduated levels of difficulty.

- In order to administer an IRI, teachers must be aware of its subjectivity and be proficient in marking and scoring oral reading errors.
- IRIs are time-consuming to administer; therefore, an IRI is not usually given to every student.
- Most often, teachers' judgment plays the biggest role in determining who is a candidate for an IRI.
- Modified miscue analysis is a useful assessment technique that focuses on the types of miscues readers make.
- A running record is useful when assessing beginning readers' text readings.
- Much information can be gleaned from a running record.

# SUGGESTIONS FOR THOUGHT QUESTIONS AND ACTIVITIES

1. Administer an IRI, a modified miscue, or a running record to a child who has a reading problem.
2. Review three different commercially produced IRI tests.
3. Construct an IRI using a basal reader series.
4. Practice coding errors on an oral reading passage by listening to a tape of a child reading a passage.
5. Practice analyzing miscues using a child's taped reading and the forms shown in Figures 8.4 and 8.5.

6. You have been appointed to a committee to develop a coding and scoring system of oral reading that takes into account the research done on miscue analysis and the traditional coding and scoring system of most IRIs. What will you come up with?

7. Explain when you might choose to do a running record instead of an IRI.

8. Choose a story from a reading program and make up comprehension questions for it, including literal, interpretive, and critical reading questions.

## INTERNET ACTIVITIES

Choose a search engine and look up the term *miscue analysis*. Select one website from the search that helps you gain a good understanding of the term. Write a brief paragraph about the website's information. (Be sure to identify both the search engine you used and the website you selected.)

## SELECTED BIBLIOGRAPHY

Adams, Marilyn J. *Beginning to Read: Thinking and Learning about Print.* Cambridge, MA: The MIT Press, 1990.

Beaver, J. *The Developmental Reading Assessment.* New York: Scott Foresman, 2001.

Betts, Emmett A. *Foundations of Reading Instruction.* New York: American Book Company, 1946.

Burns, Paul C., and Betty D. Roe. *Informal Reading Inventory: Preprimer to Twelfth Grade,* 5th ed. Boston: Houghton Mifflin, 1999.

Clay, M. *The Early Detection of Reading Difficulties.* Portsmouth, NH: Heinemann, 1995.

Duffelmeyer, Frederick, and Barbara Blakely Duffelmeyer. "Are IRI Passages Suitable for Assessing Main Idea Comprehension?" *The Reading Teacher* 42 (February 1989): 358–63.

Duffelmeyer, Frederick, Susan R. Robinson, and Susan E. Squier. "Vocabulary Questions on Informal Reading Inventories." *The Reading Teacher* 43 (November 1989): 142–48.

Forell, Elizabeth. "The Case for Conservative Reader Placement." *The Reading Teacher* 38 (May 1985): 857–62.

Gillis, M. K., and Mary W. Olson. "Elementary IRIs: Do They Reflect What We Know about Text Type Structure and Comprehension?" *Reading Research and Instruction* 27 (Fall 1987): 36–44.

Johnson, Marjorie S., Roy A. Kress, and John J. Pikulski. *Informal Reading Inventories,* 2nd ed. Newark, DE: International Reading Association, 1987.

Martin-Lara, Susan G. "Reading Placement for Code Switchers." *The Reading Teacher* 42 (January 1989): 278–82.

Morris, Darrell, Criss Ervin, and Kim Conrad. "A Case Study of Middle School Reading Disability." *The Reading Teacher* 49 (February 1996): 368–377.

Opitz, M., and M. Ford. *Reaching Readers.* Portsmouth, NH: Heinemann, 2001.

Opitz, M., and T. Rasinski. *Good-bye Round Robin.* Portsmouth, NH: Heinemann, 1998.

Pikulski, John J. "Informal Reading Inventory," in Assessment Section. *The Reading Teacher* 43 (March 1990): 514–16.

Silvaroli, J. Nicholas, and Warren H. Wheelock. *Classroom Reading Inventory,* 9th ed. New York: McGraw-Hill, 2001.

# The Diagnostic-Reading and Improvement Program in Action

# 9

# Using Texts to Help Children Overcome Reading Difficulties

## Scenario: Imagining the Best Possible School

Let us imagine a mythical land where anything is possible. The inhabitants develop what they consider to be an ideal school system. The school is based on the philosophy that students are unique individuals who are capable of learning and who require instruction based on their developmental levels and needs.

The teachers in this mythical land are pragmatists—if something works, they use it to their advantage. They are also knowledgeable teachers who use a variety of materials and instructional strategies to directly help their students gain necessary skills and strategies in all subject-matter areas in relation to what they are reading and learning.

In this school system, teachers use various types of assessment instruments and believe in a diagnostic-reading and improvement program. They believe in the principle of equal educational opportunity but realize that this does not mean that all students will achieve at the same level at the same time. Teachers provide a challenging education for all students.

The students in this school system do very well because they are learning in authentic contexts. All this makes for extraordinarily good parent–school relations. Not only are parents happy but so are other taxpayers. All school bond issues are always passed.

By now, you should realize that this mythical school system isn't mythical at all. It's a description of some of the attributes a good school system has always possessed.

Reading is another important attribute of school systems in which students show high achievement. Children have access to many different texts for independent, self-selected reading as well as for reading instruction. When selecting texts for instructional purposes, Gates reminds us that "the use of a wide variety of reading materials and purposes has not been the result of chance but the outcome of a definite plan to develop various important phases of reading."[1] In this chapter, we describe many types of texts that can be used to teach reading. We begin with an overview about the value of spending time in reading.

## CHAPTER OBJECTIVES

After reading this chapter, you should be able to:

- Discuss the importance of providing students with time to read in school.
- Discuss reasons for using different types of texts.
- Explain how to use different types of texts for instruction.
- Explain the role of computers in a diagnostic-reading and improvement program.

[1]A. Gates. *New Methods in Primary Reading*. (New York: Teachers' College Press.), p. 225.

# TIME SPENT READING

Reading helps reading! Hardly anyone refutes this statement. However, according to the National Reading Panel's report in 2000, the studies that corroborate the finding are primarily correlational studies. Although the panel found very few studies that met the methodological quality required to prove that increasing independent reading results in better reading skills, our own teaching experiences have provided evidence that this is so. The National Reading Panel also wanted to make it clear that "these findings do not negate the positive influence that independent silent reading may have on reading fluency, nor do the findings negate the possibility that wide independent reading significantly influences vocabulary development and reading comprehension."[2]

Most people agree with the statement that children need to be helped to acquire comprehension skills; without the ability to comprehend, reading would not take place. The question is: How much time is spent on comprehension instruction in the schools? Durkin, a noted reading researcher, undertook a study to determine the answer to this question. She found that teachers spend very little time on comprehension instruction; they attend to written assignments; and none of the teachers in the study viewed social studies as a time to help with reading instruction.[3] In that part of the study dealing with fourth grade, the researcher reports that "less than 1 percent (28 minutes [out of 4,469 minutes]) went to comprehension instruction."[4] The results are startling; however, another researcher re-examined Durkin's data and found that by broadening the definition of comprehension instruction, she could state that "some teachers are attempting to teach reading comprehension approximately one-fourth of the time they are involved in teaching reading and social studies."[5] These findings seem more realistic.

*Learning to read* and *reading to learn* are not two mutually exclusive processes; they can and should take place together. Children in the lower grades as well as in the higher grades should be involved in both.

Not only is the amount of time spent in reading essential for success in reading but also the amount of actual reading accomplished is vital to reading achievement.[6] Researchers have found that differences exist between poor and good readers. One researcher found that poor readers do not complete equivalent amounts of reading in context generally, and have few opportunities to

---

[2]Report of the National Reading Panel: Teaching Children to Read, "Findings and Determinations of the National Reading Panel by Topic Areas—Independent Silent Reading." (Bethesda, MD: National Institute of Child Health & Human Development, April, 2000), p. 8. www.nichd.nih.gov/publications/nrp/findings.htm.

[3]Dolores Durkin, "What Classroom Observations Reveal About Reading Comprehension," *Reading Research Quarterly* 14, No. 4 (1978–1979): 533.

[4]Ibid., p. 497.

[5]Carol A. Hodges, "Toward a Broader Definition of Comprehension Instruction," *Reading Research Quarterly* 15, No. 2 (1980): 305.

[6]Richard L. Allington, *What Really Matters for Struggling Readers*, 2nd ed. Boston: Pearson Allyn & Bacon, 2005.

practice silent reading behaviors particularly.[7] Even though the teacher spends equal amounts of time with the two groups of students, the quality of the time is different. Teachers appear to have poorer readers spend more time on oral reading, and more time is spent correcting oral reading errors.[8]

The Nation's Report Cards have consistently found a positive relationship between achievement and exposure to intensive reading experiences.[9] In other words, those students who stated they read more frequently for fun on their own time, on the average, achieved better scores in reading than those who reported reading less frequently. Also, the 1998 report indicated that television viewing had a negative effect on reading.[10]

It is interesting to note that at all grade levels, those students who were involved in frequent discussions about their studies with friends or family had higher average reading proficiency than students who reported little or no such discussions.[11]

## REASONS FOR USING A VARIETY OF TEXTS IN A DIAGNOSTIC-READING AND IMPROVEMENT PROGRAM

In everyday life, we read several different types of texts. What we read depends on several factors, including interest and purpose. Using a variety of texts, then, is necessary to help students learn what it means to be a reader. Remember that we are teaching children to be readers rather than merely teaching them to read. Right from the start, children need to be reading books and other works written and illustrated by a variety of authors and illustrators. Here are six additional reasons for using many different kinds of texts.

1. *To help students understand that different texts are written in different ways.* Stories are written using a story grammar that includes setting, characters, problem, attempts to solve the problem, and resolution. Expository text (i.e., text written to inform) may encompass sequence of events, compare/contrast, and other text structures. Knowing about these different formats or structures that are used to write texts better ensures comprehension of them.[12]

2. *To expose children to content-specific vocabulary and new concepts.* As a result of reading a variety of texts, students acquire larger vocabularies. For example, when reading an informational article about spiders, students learn

---

[7]Richard L. Allington, "Poor Readers Don't Get to Read Much in Reading Groups," *Language Arts* 57 (November/ December 1980): 874.

[8]Ibid., pp. 872–76.

[9]Patricia L. Donahue et al., *NAEP 1998 Reading Report Card for the Nation and the States,* National Assessment of Educational Progress (Washington, DC: Office of Educational Research and Improvement, U.S. Department of Education, 1999), p. 109.

[10]Ibid., p. 110.

[11]Ibid., p. 103.

[12]Muth, K. D., ed. *Children's Comprehension of Text.* Newark, DE: International Reading Association, 1989.

words associated with spiders. An increase in knowledge assures that better reading comprehension will occur.[13]

3. *To capitalize on student interest.* Some students would rather read information texts than stories. They like learning about specific details related to given topics. Providing these children with texts they enjoy motivates them to read.[14]

4. *To address reading attitudes.* Attitudes exert a directive and dynamic influence on all our lives, and once they are set, they are difficult to change. It is often the concomitant learnings such as attitudes that will remain with us more than the subject matter itself. Therefore, using many different texts can help children develop a love of reading.

5. *To serve as a scaffold.* Because stories are generally easier for students to read than nonfiction, fiction and nonfiction can be paired so that when students are finished reading one book they have a better understanding of the content.[15] For example, as a way of helping children understand something about apples, children could first take a look at *Dappled Apples* (Carr, 2001) or *The Apple Pie Tree* (Hall, 1996) before they look at *Apples* (Robbins, 2002), which is a nonfiction selection. Having acquired an understanding of the material presented in these texts, the reader is more likely to comprehend information presented in other books such as textbooks. Reading texts that relate to a specific topic is another way to provide this scaffolding.

6. *To broaden students' knowledge base.* Good comprehension is dependent on knowledge. If we know something about the topic we are reading, we are more apt to understand what we have read and remember it longer. The reverse is also true. Exposing children to different ideas presented in different texts is a way of broadening a student's knowledge base.[16]

## USING TEXTS

There are many ways to use texts to help children learn to read better. Because there are so many different types of texts, we have divided them into three broad categories to better explain and describe them: commercial, trade, and other. *Commercial books* are texts that have been written for a given program. Three types of commercial books exist: little books, basal readers, and textbooks. *Little books*[17] are small books that can be easily held by young children.

---

[13]Alexander, P. A. "The Past, Present, and Future of Knowledge Research: A Re-examination of the Role of Knowledge in Learning and Instructing." *Educational Psychologist* 31 (1996): 89–92.

[14]Reed, J. H., and D. L. Schallert. "The Nature of Involvement in Academic Discourse." *Journal of Educational Psychology* 85: (1993) 253–66.

[15]Camp, D. "It Takes Two: Teaching with Twin Texts of Fact and Fiction." *The Reading Teacher* 53 (2000): 400–408.

[16]Alexander, 1996. Yopp, R. H., and H. K. Yopp. (2000) "Sharing Informational Text with Young Children." *The Reading Teacher* 53 (2000): 410–23.

[17]B. Peterson. "Selecting Books for Beginning Readers" in D. DeFord, C. Lyons, G. Pinnell (Eds). *Bridges to Literacy.* (Portsmouth, NH: Heinemann). 1991.

The books are usually the same size, have a paperback cover, and have few pages. *Basal readers* are grade-level anthologies accompanied by additional materials such as teacher guides, workbooks, and commercially created tests. *Textbooks* are written for specific content areas and are used primarily for instructional purposes. Most often these commercial texts have to be ordered directly from the publisher; they are not available in bookstores or public libraries.

*Trade books* can be found in bookstores and libraries. They are sometimes called *authentic literature* because they are primarily written to communicate a message to the reader. They are not created for a specific program. Authors that write these books are most interested in conveying their ideas, and they do so using a variety of words and illustrations. For the purposes of this book, children's literature, authentic literature, and trade books have the same meaning.

*Other* is used to list texts that don't fit neatly into either of the previous two categories. Magazines and newspapers are listed in this category.

Two points of confusion can surface when we talk about using different texts to teach children. One centers on how trade books are used in other programs. Sometimes the best of these trade books are selected for grade-level anthologies which, when taken together, comprise a reading program (i.e., a basal reader). Another point of confusion centers on the idea of "leveled" books. Basically, these are collections of books from two categories—commercial *and* trade—that are leveled according to difficulty.[18] As Figure 9.1 shows, specific features are used to determine the book's level of difficulty.

Table 9.1 illustrates the different texts that can be used for independent and small group reading instruction and shows the most appropriate grade levels in which the texts are used. Following Table 9.1 is additional information for each type of text that includes a description, examples, reasons for using the text, and teaching suggestions.

## COMMERCIAL BOOKS

### *Little Books*

**Description**

Little books are small books that are easily held by young children. They are usually the same size, have a paperback cover, and contain just a few pages. Many times, these books are written by different authors, yet all titles are leveled by the company that produces them. They are then assembled to create sets of readers that can be used for small group reading instruction.

**Examples**

Sets of little books are available from a number of publishers including the following:

- The Sunshine Series (Wright Group)
- Literacy by Design (Harcourt Archive)

---

[18]Ibid.

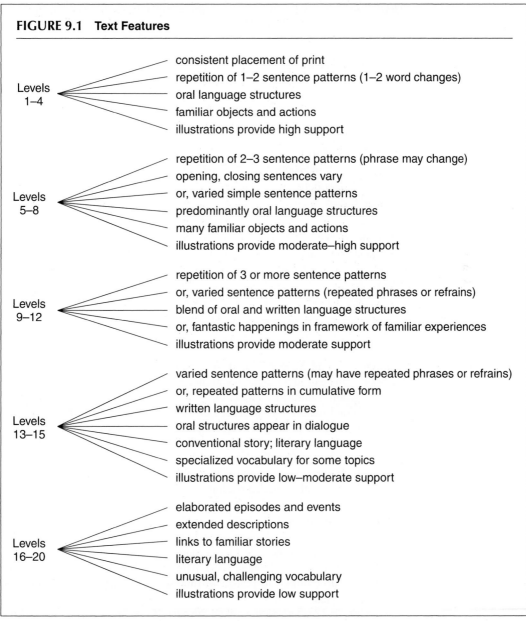

**FIGURE 9.1 Text Features**

**Levels 1–4**
- consistent placement of print
- repetition of 1–2 sentence patterns (1–2 word changes)
- oral language structures
- familiar objects and actions
- illustrations provide high support

**Levels 5–8**
- repetition of 2–3 sentence patterns (phrase may change)
- opening, closing sentences vary
- or, varied simple sentence patterns
- predominantly oral language structures
- many familiar objects and actions
- illustrations provide moderate–high support

**Levels 9–12**
- repetition of 3 or more sentence patterns
- or, varied sentence patterns (repeated phrases or refrains)
- blend of oral and written language structures
- or, fantastic happenings in framework of familiar experiences
- illustrations provide moderate support

**Levels 13–15**
- varied sentence patterns (may have repeated phrases or refrains)
- or, repeated patterns in cumulative form
- written language structures
- oral structures appear in dialogue
- conventional story; literary language
- specialized vocabulary for some topics
- illustrations provide low–moderate support

**Levels 16–20**
- elaborated episodes and events
- extended descriptions
- links to familiar stories
- literary language
- unusual, challenging vocabulary
- illustrations provide low support

*Source:* Barbara Peterson. *Characteristics of Text That Support Beginning Readers.* The Ohio State University. 1998.

- Windows on Literacy (National Geographic)
- People, Spaces & Places (Rand McNally)

**Why Use Them?**
Little books are especially designed for use with beginning readers starting in kindergarten and continuing through first grade. They are sometimes used with

**TABLE 9.1    Texts for Independent and Small Group Reading Instruction**

| Text Type/Grade Level | 1 | 2 | 3 | 4 | 5 | 6 |
|---|:---:|:---:|:---:|:---:|:---:|:---:|
| *Commercial books* | | | | | | |
| Little books | • | • | | | | |
| Basal readers | • | • | • | • | • | • |
| Textbooks | • | • | • | • | • | • |
| *Children's literature* | | | | | | |
| Predictable books | • | • | | | | |
| Information (nonfiction) | • | • | • | • | • | • |
| Multilevel literature | • | • | • | • | • | • |
| Series books | • | • | • | • | • | • |
| Poetry | • | • | • | • | • | • |
| Chapter books | | • | • | • | • | • |
| Multicultural literature | • | • | • | • | • | • |
| *Other* | | | | | | |
| Magazines | ? | • | • | • | • | • |
| Newspapers | • | • | • | • | • | • |

children in second grade as well. As leveled texts are packaged in multiple sets, the books can be used for demonstrations and interventions with young readers in small group settings. Likewise, the increasingly challenging texts facilitate the scaffolded instruction discussed earlier. They have the look and feel of real books, and their use more closely parallels reading experiences in which children's literature is used. They have a strong appeal to young readers because they convey a sense of reading whole books. Generally inexpensive, they can be used to create a classroom library of accessible books for use during independent reading time as well as guided reading.

**Teaching Suggestions**

- Select an appropriate title for a group of children who are reading at a similar general achievement level. After providing an introduction to the text, invite children to read it to themselves. After they have read the book, engage the children in one or more ways. They may first discuss the text and read a part they liked the best. If you are focusing on teaching different ways to figure out unknown words, select a word from the text that posed difficulty, write it and the sentence in which it appears on the board, and ask children how they can go about figuring out this unknown word.
- Using some common element such as story setting, select texts at different levels to represent the readers in the group. After children have had time to read their assigned books, teach them about story setting. Allow students time to share details about where their story took place.

*Basal Readers*

**Description**

Basal readers are the central components of commercially developed reading programs. They are often structured as anthologies of grade-leveled texts surrounded by a number of additional supportive materials such as teacher guides and student workbooks. Basal readers are most often selected and purchased to provide a cohesive, consistent, continuous reading curricula across and between grade levels throughout a school district or within individual schools. In most classrooms, each child is provided a copy of the anthology (i.e., reader) to use during guided reading.

**Examples**

- *Reading Street* (2005, Scott Foresman)
- Houghton Mifflin Reading, 2002

**Why Use Them?**

The use of basal readers is strongly encouraged and expected in many school districts. In fact, after these materials are purchased, little if any money is left over to purchase other materials that can be used to teach reading. One reason for using basal readers, then, has to do with district administrators' level of expectations. Another has to do with access. All students are provided with reading materials and teachers are provided with ample materials for instructional support. The selections are somewhat organized by increasingly sophisticated vocabulary, concepts, and text structures so that the selections within the anthologies can be used to scaffold instruction in much the same way as the "little books" discussed above.

**Teaching Suggestions**

- Choose individual selections within the basal anthology to use for a demonstration or intervention lesson.
- Newer basal reading anthologies have the added advantage of having selections organized by theme. Using these themed stories for common and shared-response activities with small groups of students is a natural. Assign all students within a group the same selection within a theme and then ask them to share something of interest. Another way to capitalize on the use of these themed stories is to have different students read different stories within the theme. Once finished, students could compare and contrast their stories and tell how their story relates to the overall theme.

*Textbooks*

**Description**

Besides the materials purchased for and used in the classroom reading/language arts program, a number of other commercially prepared texts are written for specific content areas such as science, social studies, and mathematics. Often, one series is selected for a school or school district. A series is most often composed of a set of common core texts, each containing grade-level appropriate presentations of increasingly sophisticated subject area content. Each student is provided a copy of the grade-level text.

### Examples

- Scholastic
- Prentice-Hall
- Silver/Burdett/Ginn

### Why Use Them?

As is the case with basal readers, both teachers and students usually have easy access to text books. They are often selected, purchased, and distributed by school district personnel as a foundation for content area curricula. As with basal readers, the use of textbooks is often strongly encouraged because often a great deal of money has been used to purchase them. Therefore, one reason to use textbooks is to meet externally mandated expectations. Another, perhaps more essential reason for using textbooks focuses on student success. As we all know, students will encounter textbook-based instruction in specific content areas. Students' success depends on their ability to handle the reading demands of these texts. The goal is to improve students' ability to negotiate their way through them with maximum comprehension. See Chapter 13 for additional suggestions on helping children read textbooks in content areas.

### Teaching Suggestions

- Choose a specific section of the textbook to show students how to do a preview as a warm-up for successful reading. After students have previewed the section, allow time for them to read the text to themselves. Once they have finished reading, have students relate information that they discovered.
- Most textbook chapters are divided by subheadings. Either assign or invite students to choose the section they would like to read; then, ask them to look for three specific ideas they can share with others in the group. Once they have finished reading, have students in the group create a note-taking guide to record information about the other sections of the chapter that they did not read.

## CHILDREN'S LITERATURE

### *Predictable Books*

### Description

Predictable books are written with specific features that enable children to read with ease. They share the following characteristics:

- *Pictures that support the text*. These pictures illustrate what the text says, so the child can use them to help read the text.
- *Repeated sentence or phrase*. The same sentence or phrase is repeated on nearly every page. The repetition helps the young reader use memory to read the sentence or phrase.
- *Rhyme and rhythm*. The use of both rhyme and rhythm enables the reader to use these language features to read the text.
- *Cumulative pattern*. As the story progresses, new lines are added, but previous lines are repeated, thus providing the reader with practice.
- *Familiar sequence*. Days of the week or counting are two examples of this feature. Students use what they know about both to successfully read the text at hand.

**Examples**

- *The Deep Blue Sea: A Book of Colors* (Wood, 2005)
- *Good Morning, Digger* (Rockwell, 2005)
- *Mommies Say Shhh!* (Poloacco, 2005)
- *Why Not?* (Wormell, 2000)
- *One Red Dot* (Carter, 2005)

**Why Use Them?**

Predictable books are advantageous for several reasons.[19] First, these books employ the language features listed above that enable children to read with greater ease. Second, they enable children to read authentic literature from the very beginning, thus helping children to see that they can read "real" books. Third, although they are most often used with beginning readers, predictable books provide a tremendous amount of support and success for those whose first language is not English and for older children who struggle with reading. Fourth, many predictable books are published as "big books," oversized versions of a book. They lend themselves to interactive sessions with a large group, which helps all students to see that they are a part of the classroom community.

**Teaching Suggestions**

- Select an appropriate title for a group of children who are reading at a similar general achievement level. After providing an introduction to the text, invite children to read it to themselves. After they have read the book, engage the children in one or more ways. They may first discuss the text and read a part they liked the best. If you are focusing on teaching different ways to figure out unknown words, select a word from the text that posed difficulty, write it and the sentence in which it appears on the board and ask children how they can go about figuring out this unknown word.

[19]Thogmartin, M. B. *Teach a Child to Read with Children's Books,* 2nd ed. Bloomington, IN: Educational Resource Center, 1998.

- Using some common element such as story setting, select texts at different levels to represent the readers in the group. After children have had time to read their assigned books, teach them about story setting. Allow students time to share details about where their story took place.
- When using a big book that contains a repetitive passage, think about pausing during the reading before coming to the passage to give children an opportunity to chime in. To help children develop a speech to print match, point to the words as they are read.

### *Information Books (Nonfiction)*

**Description**

Nonfiction books present factual information about a given topic. They are usually accompanied by photographs and illustrations to help students better understand the content.

**Examples**

- *Baby Sea Otter* (Tatham, 2005).
- *Into the Ice: The Story of the Arctic Exploration* (Curlee, 1998)
- *Liberty Rising: The Story of the Statue of Liberty* (Shea, 2005)
- *On Earth* (Karas, 2005)

**Why Use Them?**

There are two sound reasons for using information texts. First, they present facts about the world around us. Because many children are curious about their surroundings, these texts provide motivating and interesting reading material. Second, the text structures used to write information texts differ from those used to write fiction. Students need to learn how to read all of these different types of texts in order to become competent readers.

**Teaching Suggestions**

- Select a text with specific features that you want to teach students. For example, you might want to show them how to read a diagram and the way it relates to the written text. After providing instruction, have children read the text and follow up with a discussion in which children talk about how the diagram helped them read the text.
- Use a specific nonfiction selection to show students how to process the information presented: picture captions, subheadings, bold print, and other features. After providing this introduction, have students read the text. They can then report one or two ideas they learned from the text.

### *Multilevel Books*

**Description**

Multilevel books are written with multiple story lines. Books that have simple story lines and contain more information about specific features in the text at the end of the book are also considered multilevel. Although some of these books are fiction, the majority are nonfiction (informational). Still others combine fiction and nonfiction.

## Examples

- *A Subway for New York* (Weitzman, 2005) is a nonfiction selection containing two story lines. *Elephants Can Paint, Too* (Arnold, 2005) is another example.
- *This Rocket* (Collicut, 2005) is a nonfiction text that has a simple story line with accompanying information in the front and back of the text that gives a brief history of rockets (front) and tells about the Apollo 11 mission (back).
- *Sharks and Other Dangers of the Deep* (Mugford, 2005) is an example that contains three story lines.
- *Wise Guy: The Life and Philosophy of Socrates* (Usher, 2005) is an example that contains two story lines and information at the end of the text.

## Why Use Them?

Regardless of reading level or background, all children can read all or portions of these texts. Using these texts, then, is one way of showing students that they can all read a similar text and get something out of the experience; they are part of one community of learners.

The books are also rich in content; they contain much information about objects or situations that interest children. These texts also provide for meaningful repeated reading and a scaffold. That is, once children hear other parts of the story from either the teacher or classmates, they are more likely to be able to read the text themselves. Finally, in terms of a resource issue, a great deal of use can be gained with fewer dollars spent.

## Teaching Suggestions

- If students are grouped by similar level or background, different groups can read different parts of the text. For example, those who are just getting a handle on how print functions or those who have little background about the topic at hand could be invited to follow along as the teacher reads the given part of text. Once this has been accomplished, the teacher may have students choral read their part while he or she reads the additional text shown on the page, thus building children's background and knowledge base.
- After each group member has read through the text pertaining to the parts most appropriate for the given group, children can be grouped by twos (if the book has two story lines or parts) and threes (if the book has three story lines or parts). In turn, each person can read his or her part of the text while others listen. To emphasize listening comprehension, each group could be given one text that is passed from one person to the next as each part is read.
- In pair work, if the focus is on helping the less experienced reader attain a larger reading vocabulary and hear an example of fluent reading, each

child could be provided a copy of the text and the less experienced reader could follow along as the partner reads aloud. This particular way of reading provides the less experienced reader or the child with a limited background with a scaffold, enabling him or her to read a good portion of the text at a later time.

### *Series Books*

### Description

Series books share common elements such as characters, author's style, words, and format. Children can often follow the development of story characters and share in their adventures in each succeeding book in the series.

### Examples

- Mills, Claudia, *Gus and Grandpa* (grades 1–2)
- Reilly-Giff, Patricia, *Polk Street Kids* (grades 2–3)
- Adler, David, *Cam Jansen* (grades 2–3)
- Greenburg, Dan, *Zack Files* (grades 2–5)
- Erickson, John, *Hank, the Cowdog* (grades 3–4)
- Rowling, J. K., *Harry Potter* (grades 4–6)

### Why Use Them?

Series books can be very effective as a source of reading material for three reasons. First, they provide meaningful reading practice. Once children get hooked on a series, they have a desire to read additional books in the series. Because characters, plot structure, and words are common to all books in the series, students are provided with much meaningful practice. In other words, the natural redundancy of these features provides support for even the most novice readers, enabling children to read the texts. Much confidence results!

Second, series books provide opportunities for children to discuss and interpret events in the series. Students reading different titles in the series will make their own interpretations based on their own background. Talking with others broadens understanding.

Third, series books provide children with opportunities to make inferences. When reading the books out of order, especially, children must infer what has come before and how their book fits into the series. In effect, they get to solve a reading puzzle as they read different books in the series. Solving this puzzle can be very engaging for children and is even more challenging when the books in the series are numbered, but read out of order.

### Teaching Suggestions

- Group students according to who is reading the same series. Children can then discuss their books with teacher guidance. Several different teaching points could emerge, such as what all of the books have in common or how reading series books can increase comprehension.

- To help children experience being a part of a larger community of readers, provide each child in the class with a different book in the series. Children can then be grouped in a variety of ways for small group reading instruction. For example, those children who need to learn how to better use words to create visual images can be grouped together to learn this task. Those children who need to learn how to pay attention to meaning as well as visual cues can be grouped together as well. After they have been taught the given strategy, they can then practice it using their series book as the teacher provides guidance.

*Poetry*

**Description**

Poetry is writing in which rhythm, sound, and language are used to create images, thoughts, and emotional responses. Usually concise, poetry takes on many forms such as *narrative poetry*, which tells a story; *lyric poetry*, in which much rhythm is used; *humorous poetry*, in which everyday objects or events are portrayed in absurd ways; and *nonsense poetry*, which uses meaningless words and much exaggeration.[20]

**Examples**

- *In the Swim* (Florian, 1997)
- *School Supplies: A Book of Poems* (Hopkins, 1996)
- *Block City* (Stevenson, 2005)
- *Down to the Sea in Ships* (Sturges, 2005)
- *When I Heard the Learn'd Astronomer* (Whitman, 2004)

**Why Use It?**

As with other forms of writing, poetry is written using different forms. Exposing children to this form of writing, then, opens up this style of writing to them, making their comprehension of it more likely. Because many poems are succinct and are written with words that convey images, poems are excellent selections to use to help children learn to visualize. Likewise, because they are short, poems tend to be less intimidating for even the most novice reader. Finally, poetry helps students develop numerous reading skills such as phrasing, fluency, and comprehension.

**Teaching Suggestions**

- Select a poem to help students learn how to use words to create visual images. After modeling the process, provide students with another poem, giving them time to read it. Once they have read the poem, ask students to discuss specific lines and the images they saw when they read them.

---

[20]Goforth, F. *Literature and the Learner*. Belmont, CA: Wadsworth, 1998.

- To model fluency and reading poetry for enjoyment, select a poem and read it to the students. Point out how the phrases helped you know how to read the poem. Next, provide students with several poetry books. Invite them to choose and read a poem. Once they have read silently, have students read their poem aloud to the group.
- Students can also create materials to use during guided reading experiences once they become familiar with common core poems introduced during shared reading. Lines or stanzas from the poems can be printed on one side of a blank page. During independent work time, students can add illustrations to these pages, bind the pages, and create their own copy of a text. Then the teacher can invite students to bring their book to the guided reading table to use in demonstration and intervention lessons.

### *Chapter Books*

### Description
Chapter books are divided into different segments or chapters. They range in sophistication beginning with the very easiest in first grade and increase in difficulty throughout the grades.

### Examples

- Chapter books for novice readers
  *Henry and Mudge* series by Cynthia Rylant
  *Frog and Toad* series by Arnold Lobel
- Chapter books for older readers
  Recent Newberry award and honor books
  *Bud, Not Buddy* by Christopher Paul Curtis
  *Missing May* by Cynthia Rylant
  *The Giver* by Lois Lowry
  *Walk Two Moons* by Sharon Creech
  *Shiloh* by Phyllis Naylor

### Why Use Them?
Chapter books afford children with an opportunity to extend themselves into books that they will be reading in their everyday lives. Chapter books help students learn how a story is connected by individual sections. They also signal to children that they are becoming more competent readers. Chapter books also provide logical stopping points for instructional purposes.

### Teaching Suggestions

- Provide all students in the group with the same chapter book and give a structure for reading the book.
- Use chapter books to engage children in an author study. Different groups of children can read different chapter books by the same author. Author style across texts can become a focal point for instruction. Certain authors, such as Cynthia Rylant, Patricia Reilly Giff, Gary Paulsen, and William Steig, have written at all levels—picture books, simple chapter books,

complex young adult novels, and adult fiction and nonfiction. Studies of these authors allow teachers who work with a wide range of readers to match appropriate texts to their students' levels, while still engaging all students in a cohesive classroom conversation about the author.

### *Multicultural Books*

### Description

Multicultural literature refers to all genres that portray the likenesses and differences among all social, cultural, and ethnic groups. They are written to reflect our diverse society.

### Examples

- *Celia Cruz, Queen of Salsa* (Chambers, 2005)
- *Rosa* (Giovanni, 2005)
- *My Nana and Me* (Smalls, 2005)
- *Meow: Cat Stories from Around the World* (Yolen, 2005)
- *Beyond the Great Mountains* (Young, 2005)

### Why Use It?

All children need books that represent their cultural heritage. Reading multicultural books enables all children to have characters with whom they can identify. Multicultural literature also provides children with opportunities to learn about similarities and differences among people and to consider different points of view.

The importance of learning about other groups of people through literature is aptly expressed in the following:

> I never felt the world-wide importance of the children's heritage in literature more than on a day when I stood with Mrs. Ben Zvi, wife of the [then] President of Israel, in the midst of the book boxes she had filled for the centers in Jerusalem where refugee boys and girls were gathered for storytelling and reading of the world's great classics for children. "We want our boys and girls to be at home with the other children of the world," she said, "and I know of no better way than through mutual enjoyment of the world's great stories."[21]

"Young children find it easier to assimilate new information when this information is presented within the structure of a story."[22] The story acts as a bridge to help children "link their growing understanding of other cultures to their personal experience and background knowledge."[23]

The characteristics of "good" books are operative for all children regardless of background. Any book they read must help them to feel good about

---

[21]Dora V. Smith, "Children's Literature Today," *Elementary English* 47 (October 1970): 778.

[22]Jerry Y. Diakiw, "Children's Literature and Global Education: Understanding the Developing World," *The Reading Teacher* 43 (January 1990): 297.

[23]Ibid.

themselves. It must help them to view themselves in a positive light, to achieve a better self-concept, and to gain a feeling of worth.

A book that hinders a child from finding his or her identity, that portrays the child in a stereotyped role, is a book that would be considered poor reading for all children.

When selecting books for a class library, teachers should try to put themselves in the position of their students and ask, How would I feel if I read this book? Would this book make me come back for another one? Will this book interest me? Are these books on many readability levels? Does the book portray the black child or any other minority child as an individual? Are the adults portrayed in a nonchildlike manner? Are the characters supplied with traits and personalities that are positive? Would all children want to read the book?

If the answers are "yes," the teacher should choose the book, but even one "no" answer should disqualify it.

The importance of providing children with books that convey hope and with which children can identify, because they mirror their lives, cannot be overemphasized. Another factor, which is as important, concerns the image that children obtain when they read a book about people with different racial or ethnic backgrounds. Since children are greatly influenced by what they read, the way that people are portrayed in books will have a profound effect on children's perceptions of them.

### Teaching Suggestions

- Select a topic or theme that will encourage students to select multicultural books during reading instruction. For example, if the focus is on the impact of prejudice and discrimination, students can be exploring nonfiction and fiction titles at many different levels. Some might be reading picture books such as Robert Coles' *Ruby Bridges* and others might be reading novellas such as Mildred Taylor's *The Gold Cadillac*. The teacher brings small groups of students together to discuss the issues and ideas in their books related to the topic.
- Encourage critical literacy by selecting certain texts and then guiding students to look at those texts from perspectives other than their own. A teacher working on a frontier/pioneer theme may have small groups of students reading different tradebooks such as Laura Ingalls Wilder's *Little House in the Big Woods* and Carol Ryrie Brink's *Caddie Woodlawn*. Discussions can be structured by the teacher to ask students to respond to what was written by assuming various roles (Native Americans, pioneer children, modern women, etc.) to show how taking different perspectives helps readers to critically analyze texts. Introducing contrasting texts such as Michael Dorris's *Sees Behind Trees*, which focuses on a Native American perspective, allows the teacher to guide students through additional comparisons and contrasts as they look critically at historical events.

# OTHER TEXTS

*Magazines*

**Description**

Magazines are compilations of articles and stories designed to inform readers about many different topics. Columns of text, pictures with captions, short tidbits about different topics, diagrams, and advertisements are often used to create a magazine. Most magazines focus on a specific audience and feature articles that would appeal to this audience.

**Examples**

- *Sesame Street Magazine* (Ages 0–6)
- *Zoobooks* (Ages 6–14)
- *Cricket Magazine* (Ages 8–14)

**Why Use Them?**

Reading a magazine requires the reader to be "magazine literate." According to Stoll, being magazine literate means that the reader knows how the publication works—its organization, where to locate specific information, and how to maximize the potential of the magazine.[24] Using magazines for guided reading, then, is an excellent way to help students become magazine literate. Time can be devoted to teaching children how to read magazines and to explaining that magazines reflect many different personalities. Because some magazines include articles written by children and contain high-interest articles, they provide very motivating reading material. They can also serve as a catalyst for meaningful writing experiences; students can be encouraged to write their own articles for publication and to write letters to the editor. Finally, because columns of text, pictures with short captions, short blurbs about given topics, and diagrams are used to write magazines, much information can be accessed by all readers.

**Teaching Suggestions**

- Choose a specific magazine and devise a guided reading experience designed to show students the features of the magazine: how it's organized, the table of contents, the variety of articles, and so on. Students can then choose an article to read and share what they discovered with the rest of the group.
- Some magazines, such as *Zoobooks*, devote an entire issue to a given topic such as elephants. Provide a copy of the magazine for each student

[24]Stoll, D., ed. *Magazines for Kids and Teens*, Revised ed. Glassboro, NJ: Educational Press of America; Newark, DE: International Reading Association, 1997.

in the group. Show them how to skim the text, looking for facts about elephants. Then have students do the same searching for three facts about elephants that they want to share with others in the group. As they report their findings, make a chart that shows their ideas.

*Newspapers*

**Description**

Newspapers are collections of informational articles, advertisements, comics, and features that are written to inform the public of current events. Most are published daily, although some specifically written for classroom use are published weekly.

**Examples**

- *Weekly Reader* (preschool–grade 6)
- *Scholastic News* (grades 1–6)
- *Kids Page or Mini Page from Local Newspaper* (grades 1–3)
- *Local Newspaper* (grades 3–6)

**Why Use Them?**

Newspapers provide a wealth of reading material in everyday life. They supply information about current events at several levels. Like other reading materials, however, they are written with a specific format. Readers must learn how a newspaper is written so that they can get the information they need and successfully negotiate their way through it without feeling overwhelmed. Small group reading instruction is a perfect fit to do this. Specific newspapers and articles can be used to show students the variety of texts that are found in newspapers and teach how to read each one. Students can also learn how to read articles looking for the questions that most articles address: who, what, when, where, why, and how. Reading newspapers also helps students increase their world knowledge of given topics—thus enhancing their reading comprehension of these same topics when they are encountered in other texts. Finally, using newspapers helps students to see themselves as "real-life" readers. They see others reading newspapers outside of school and begin to recognize that they can do the same.

**Teaching Suggestions**

- Use the mini-page of the local newspaper to show students how it is organized. If the purpose of using the newspaper is to show students that articles focus on specific questions (who, what, when, where, why, how), list these key words on the board and then direct students to read a specific article searching for answers to these questions.
- As with other texts, news stories can present some challenging words for students to decipher. You may want to show students how to use context

clues to determine the meaning of an unknown word. Once you have modeled this, have students apply the strategy to an article they choose to read or one that you have chosen for them.

- Once students are familiar with the various parts of the paper, use it to teach critical thinking skills. For example, bring in different newspapers and have students read the same story as presented in the different papers. Students can discuss the headlines for the story and make up their own headlines using different voices—neutral, positive, or negative. You can also talk about how the tone of the headline influences readers.
- Discuss with students the differences between editorials and regular news stories. Then have them compare different editorials with news stories on the same topic. Next, invite students to discuss whether the news was adequately explained and whether the editor expressed his or her views. Finally, have students write their own editorials about a story they have been following for a number of days.
- Encourage children to be reporters and to cover school or community events. They can write about the events as both news stories and editorials.

## COMPUTERS AND READING IN A DIAGNOSTIC-READING AND IMPROVEMENT PROGRAM

The 1990s brought an influx of computers and computer programs into many classrooms. One great advantage of computers is their motivational value. Students usually enjoy working with them, and many become computer literate very quickly.

Some teachers find that the computer is an excellent management tool. For example, during a reading lesson, students read a passage, and then the computers question each student simultaneously. The students answer through menu selection or by composing their responses. The result to the teachers is immediate feedback of the responses of *all* the students. This type of questioning and feedback can be repeated for however much depth and breadth of coverage is desired. Teachers not only receive immediate feedback but can also look for a pattern in student responses. This pattern can give teachers insight into their students' strengths and needs. The computer can also show how an individual student has performed over an extended period of time. Teachers can use this information for evaluation and for grouping students.

The computer can be an exceptional help in individualizing instruction. For example, computers can be used in a one-to-one tutorial manner with students to either help them gain some needed skills and strategies or to diagnose some of their reading problems. Some students like receiving their results from an impersonal diagnostic tool because they feel that the computer is more private and more fair.

There is no dearth of computer programs on the market. There are a number of programs with voice synthesizers that can help those children whose listening modality is more developed than their reading ability. There are programs that stress higher order thinking and problem solving, as well as interactive programs whereby the student actually becomes part of the action.

As with all other instructional materials, teachers must carefully assess the worth of each computer program before bringing it into the classroom. Not all computer programs are high quality.

There are some software programs available on the market that show "valuable potential when used sensibly and critically by trained reading clinicians."[25] Some of these programs are computer-based informal reading inventories. Jay Blanchard's *Computer-Based Reading Assessment Inventory* has two forms with eight passages, word lists based on the passages, and comprehension questions. It is an untimed test that probes a student's reading behavior using a multiple-choice format rather than the usual recall method used on traditionally administered IRIs.[26]

Another program is the *Computer-Based Reading Assessment* by Jerry Johns, which is based on his *Advanced Reading Inventory;* however, as can be gleaned from the title, this program is for more advanced students in grades 7 through college.[27]

Another program, *Computer-Assisted Reading Achievement* by Michael McKenna, interprets general information concerning a student's background, analyzes a student's oral reading errors, and provides a miscue analysis. In addition, it determines a student's reading levels, as well as some inferences concerning a student's strengths and needs.

Good teachers recognize that there is a place for computers in the instructional program. Students and teachers have found that computers are a boon to literacy instruction, especially in writing. As aptly stated in the latest *Handbook of Reading Research*, "computers are the quintessential tool for process writing,"[28] that is, what people do when they are involved in writing. However, teacher judgment is still the critical factor in all diagnosis.

# DIAGNOSIS AND READING IMPROVEMENT IN CONTENT AREAS: A POINT OF VIEW

Diagnosis and improvement in reading should extend beyond the reading period. Reading is taking place all through the day at school, and teachers would be losing valuable opportunities to learn about students' reading strengths and needs if they did not observe their students' reading behavior in content areas. It's in these areas that teachers can observe whether students are applying what they have learned during the reading period.

A student's difficulties with mathematics may not be caused by an inability to do quantitative reasoning or basic mathematical operations; it may

---

[25]Renee Weisberg & Ernest Balajthy, "The Printout: Reading Diagnosis via the Micro computer," *Reading Teacher 42* April, 1989: 636.

[26]Ibid.

[27]Ibid.

[28]Michael L. Kamil et al. "The Effects of Other Technologies on Literacy and Literacy Learning," *Handbook of Reading Research Vol. III.* M. Kamil et al. (eds). Mahwah NJ: Lawrence Erlbaum, 2000, p. 773.

be a reading problem. Similarly, a problem in science or social studies may be a reading problem. The teacher should have students find the main idea of various paragraphs in their content books to discern whether they understand what they are reading. Teachers can also individually call students aside and listen to them read aloud from their books to determine whether the books are at the proper readability level for the students. (See "Modified IRI Approaches: A Caution" in Chapter 8.) Also, teachers should be alert to students' attitudes toward a subject. It may be that the student does not like the subject because he or she cannot read the textbook. A student who is not reading at grade level would probably have difficulty reading a social studies, science, or math textbook whose readability level is at the same grade level. If teachers cannot get books for their students at their reading ability levels, they will have to make special provisions such as providing a reading guide. The guide could list all those vocabulary words that the teachers feel would cause difficulty. Before the students are asked to read the material, teachers should review the vocabulary with the students. The words can be pronounced, presented in a sentence, and defined. After the students have read the material, the teachers should go over it with them in the same way that they would in a reading lesson. The emphasis, however, would be on gaining content concepts. (See Chapter 13 for strategies to use to help students read content material.)

## SUMMARY

In this chapter we present an explanation on the value of providing children with many opportunities to read. We also provide several reasons for exposing children to a variety of texts and emphasize that children need to develop a love of reading from a very young age. We discussed several different types of texts that can be used to help children develop this love for reading and to help children who are struggling with learning to read. Our explanation includes the type of text, reasons for using the given type of text, examples, and teaching suggestions. Cybertext is another important type of text and we explain some ways that computers can be used not only by children but also by teachers. A major point of the chapter is that knowledgeable teachers are the mainstay of a diagnostic-reading and improvement program and as such, they are the ones who make decisions about how to best help children advance as readers.

## CHAPTER 9 KEY CONCEPTS

- Children need time to read if they are to improve. That is, reading fosters reading.
- There are specific reasons for using many different texts in a diagnostic-reading and improvement program.
- One of the ways to remember the many different texts is to classify them into three categories: commercial, children's literature, and other.
- Computers have a place in a diagnostic-reading and improvement program. They can help both children and teachers.
- Knowledgeable teachers are essential in a diagnostic-reading and improvement program.

## SUGGESTIONS FOR THOUGHT QUESTIONS AND ACTIVITIES

1. You are thinking about the open house that is about to take place at your school and want to make sure that the parents of your students fully understand the importance of reading both in and out of school. To help get this point across, you have decided to provide parents with some suggested children's literature titles that they can use at home. Construct the list.

2. Your principal just discovered that you are a believer in using many different texts to help children read. Although the idea makes sense to her, she doesn't fully understand how first graders can read informational texts because she thinks they are way too hard for them. Besides, she thinks that children in first grade "learn to read" and it is only after doing so that they can "read to learn." What will you say to her?

3. Select one of the types of children's literature explained in this chapter and secure similar titles that would appeal to your students.

4. Find one website designed for children to use independently and explain how you would use it as a part of your diagnostic-reading and improvement program.

5. Although we provide several different types of texts that can be used to help children become lifelong readers, there may be other important texts that children find appealing. Construct a list that shows these texts and explain how they might be used to teach reading.

6. Construct a list of books based on one topic you will be teaching. Try to include as many types of texts as possible. Keep your students in mind as you construct this list. Which students will read which texts? How will the texts be assigned? Will you allow for student choice?

7. In being interviewed for a second-grade teaching position, the committee has asked you to explain how you would use both basal readers and children's literature titles to teach reading. They are very sensitive to diversity. Construct your response.

## INTERNET ACTIVITIES

Choose a search engine and search for websites related to texts that can be used to motivate reading. Print out one artifact that you find especially meaningful for your students. (Be sure to identify both the search engine you used and the website you selected.)

## SELECTED BIBLIOGRAPHY

Allen, Vernon L. *Children as Teachers: Theory and Research on Tutoring.* New York: Academic Press, 1976.

Allington, R. L. *What Really Matters for Struggling Readers,* 2nd ed. Boston: Pearson Allyn & Bacon, 2005.

Almasi, J. F., M. G. McKeown, and I. L. Beck. "The Return of Engaged Reading in Classroom Discussions of Literature." *Journal of Literary Research* 28 (1996): 107–46.

Charles, C. M. *Individualizing Instruction,* 2nd ed. St. Louis: C. V. Mosby, 1980.

Gates, A. *New Methods in Primary Reading.* New York: Teachers' College Press, 1928.

Geisert, Paul G., and Mynga K. Futrell. *Teachers, Computers, and Curriculum: Microcomputers in the Classroom,* 3rd ed. Boston: Allyn and Bacon, 2000.

Goldman, S. R., and J. A. Rakestraw Jr. "Structural Aspects of Constructing Meaning from Text." In *Handbook of Reading Research, Volume III,* ed. M. L. Kamil, P. B. Mosenthal, P. D. Pearson, and R. Barr. Mahwah, NJ: Erlbaum, 2000, pp. 311–35.

Jackobson, Julie, et al. "Cross-age Tutoring: A Literacy Improvement Approach for Stuggling Adolescent Readers." *Journal of Adolescent & Adult Literacy* 44 (March 2001): 528–536.

Opitz, M. *Getting the Most From Predictable Books*. New York: Scholastic, 1995.

Opitz, Michael F. *Learning Centers: Getting Them Started, Keeping Them Going*. New York: Scholastic, 1994.

Opitz, M., and M. Ford. *Reaching Readers*. Portsmouth, NH: Heinemann, 2001.

Opitz, M., M. Ford, with M. Zbarachi. *Books and Beyond: New Ways to Reach Readers*. Portsmouth, NH: Heinemann, 2006.

Peterson, B. "Selecting Books for Beginning Readers." In D. DeFord, C. Lyons, G. Pinnell, eds., *Bridges to Literacy*. Portsmouth, NH: Heinemann, 2001.

Reeves, Harriet Ramsey. "Individual Conferences—Diagnostic Tools." *The Reading Teacher* 24 (February 1971): 411–15.

## Children's Literature Cited

Adler, David. *Cam Jansen: The Catnapping Mystery*. New York: Putnam, 2005.

Arnold, Katya. *Elephants Can Paint, Too*. New York: Simon & Schuster, 2005.

Carr, Jan. *Dappled Apples*. New York: Holiday House, 2001.

Carter, David. *One Red Dot*. New York: Simon & Schuster, 2005.

Chambers, Veronica. *Celia Cruz, Queen of Salsa*. New York: Penguin, 2005.

Collicutt, Paul. *This Rocket*. New York: Farrar, Straus, Giroux, 2005.

Curlee, Lynn. *Into the Ice: The Story of Artic Exploration*. Boston, MA: Houghton Mifflin, 1998.

Erickson, John. *Hank, the Cowdog: The Secret Laundry Monster Files*. New York: Viking, 2002.

Florian, David. *In the Swim*. San Diego: Harcourt, 1997.

Giovanni, Nikki. *Rosa*. New York: Holt, 2005.

Greenburg, Dan. *The Boy Who Cried Big Foot (Zack Files)*. New York: Grosset & Dunlap, 2000.

Hall, Zoe. *The Apple Pie Tree*. New York: Scholastic, 1996.

Hopkins, Lee Bennett. *School Supplies: A Book of Poems*. New York: Simon & Schuster, 1996.

Karas, G. Brian. *On Earth*. New York: Putnam, 2005.

Mills, Claudia. *Gus and Grandpa*. New York: Farrar, Straus, & Giroux, 1997.

Mugford, Simon. *Sharks and Other Dangers of the Deep*. New York: St. Martin's Press, 2005.

Polacco, Patricia. *Mommies Say Shhh!* New York: Philomel, 2005.

Reilly-Giff, Patricia. *Meet the Polk Street Kids*. New York: Doubleday, 1988.

Robbins, Ken. *Apples*. New York: Simon & Schuster, 2002.

Rockwell, Anne. *Good Morning, Digger*. New York: Viking, 2005.

Rowling, J. K. *Harry Potter and the Sorcerer's Stone*. New York: Scholastic, 1996.

Shea, Pegi Deitz. *Liberty Rising: The Story of the Statue of Liberty*. New York: Holt, 2005.

Smalls, Irene. *My Nana and Me*. New York: Little, Brown, 2005.

Stevenson, Robert Louis. *Block City*. New York: Simon & Schuster, 2005.

Sturges, Philemon. *Down to the Sea in Ships*. New York: Putnam, 2005.

Tatham. Betty. *Baby Sea Otter*. New York: Holt, 2005.

Usher, M.D. *Wise Guy: The Life and Philosophy of Socrates*. New York: Farrar, Straus, & Giroux, 2005.

Weitzman, David. *A Subway for New York*. New York: Farrar, Straus, & Giroux, 2005.

Wood, Audrey. *The Deep Blue Sea: A Book of Colors*. New York: Scholastic, 2005.

Wormell, Mary. *Why Not?* New York: Farrar, Straus, & Giroux, 2000.

Yolen, Jane. *Meow: Cat Stories from Around the World*. New York: HarperCollins, 2005.

Young, Ed. *Beyond the Great Mountains: A Visual Poem About China*. San Francisco, CA: Chronicle, 2005.

# Helping Children Acquire and Apply Phonics Knowledge

## Scenario: Lack of Phonic Skills

George Y was a student in Ms. Mills's class who scored at a 4.2 level on the reading comprehension subtest of the *California Achievement Tests.** Ms. Mills was confused about this score because George was quite verbal; he always seemed to have a lot of information to contribute on many topics and he could answer nearly every question. To better understand George's reading, Ms. Mills decided to give him an informal reading inventory.

Ms. Mills started George two grade levels below his current grade level. George did not reach the zero level of errors for words in isolation until the first level. Therefore, George started oral reading at the first-grade level. Even at this level, he made one error, yet he had no problems with comprehension. George was able to answer all the comprehension questions for the oral and silent reading passages through the third level, even though he made a number of errors in the oral reading passages. At the fourth-grade level, the number of word recognition errors were at the frustration level, and Ms. Mills suspected that even with his superior comprehension, George would have some difficulty answering the questions; so she decided to give him a listening capacity test. She read aloud one passage from each level and asked George the questions. George was able to answer all the questions correctly up until the eighth level.

Ms. Mills realized that George's word recognition problems had masked his ability to answer many questions.

Ms. Mills decided to look at George's school records to see what methods and materials he was exposed to in learning to read. She also decided to discuss his word recognition problems with him.

In talking to George, Ms. Mills learned that George's parents were both professionals and well known in their fields, that George was an only child, and that George went everywhere with his parents and was included in their interesting conversations. George's background information certainly explained his high cognitive and language development, but it did not account for his decoding problems. Ms. Mills realized from the types of errors he made when he was reading orally that George probably used context clues to gain the information that he did get. Ms. Mills decided to give him an informal diagnostic word analysis test to see if she could pinpoint his word recognition problems.

Ms. Mills administered the *Informal Diagnostic Tests* (see pages 271–286). She wanted to test George's auditory discrimination because he had mentioned that he had had many ear infections when he was younger. She wanted to make sure that he was able to differentiate among various sounds. George had no difficulties with auditory discrimination; however, from the results of the word analysis tests, it was obvious that he had few phonic or structural analysis skills. When Ms. Mills asked George about this, he said that he couldn't remember having any instruction in phonics in the school that he had gone to.

Ms. Mills decided to set up an intensive word analysis program for George. She felt that George should have little difficulty gaining word analysis and synthesis skills and that he should acquire these skills in a relatively short period of time because he was highly motivated. Also, when she did some blending

*Now called *TerraNova CAT.*

activities to probe for his difficulties, she noticed how quickly George caught on and how he was able to apply what he learned; that is, his transfer of knowledge was excellent. George was also very excited when he saw, in his words, "how easy it was to figure out words by using graphic cues." What sorts of activities do you think Ms. Mills had George complete as a part of her instruction?

# INTRODUCTION

In this chapter we focus on helping you to better understand phonics. We also present a suggested developmental sequence of phonics skills. Understanding phonics, knowing how to assess students' ability to apply phonics as a reading strategy, and being able to teach students so that they will see the meaningful application of phonics are important ingredients of a word recognition program. They are especially important for teachers utilizing a diagnostic-reading and improvement program because they help teachers to determine what students should know and be able to do in terms of using phonics as one part of reading. As a result of acquiring this knowledge related to phonics, teachers are better able to help students who need additional assistance in acquiring this most important skill.

# CHAPTER OBJECTIVES

After reading the chapter, you should be able to:

- Discuss the importance of decoding in reading.
- Discuss the place of phonics in the reading program.
- Define word recognition.
- Discuss the relation of a diagnostic-reading and improvement program to teaching word recognition skills.
- Discuss the various word recognition strategies.
- Explain phonics terms: *consonant, vowel digraphs, diphthongs,* and *blends.*
- Give examples of some phonograms.
- Discuss the skills involved in a developmental sequence of phonics.
- Explain what is meant by *explicit phonics instruction.*
- Explain what is meant by *implicit phonics instruction.*

# THE IMPORTANCE OF DECODING IN READING

In Chapter 12, we discuss the importance of listening and the fact that children who have difficulty with listening will have a problem in both oral language and reading. Since reading is a process of interpreting printed symbols that are based on arbitrary speech sounds, it depends on a foundation of previously learned speech sounds. Usually, young children have a substantial oral vocabulary before and at the time they begin to read, when they learn that each word they speak or listen to has a printed symbol. Students who become effective readers must be able to automatically decode written symbols which represent speech sounds. Decoding is a vehicle for comprehension. Inability to decode will prevent readers from bringing anything to or getting any message from the printed page.

In order to read, most students must be able to decode words from the printed page. Phonics is an important pronunciation strategy because it helps students to decode words on the printed page, and it also helps many students become more self-reliant readers. However, phonics is not a magic bullet. Knowledge of phonics will not automatically make a child an excellent reader. Phonics is but one part of word recognition, which itself is one part of the reading process.

# PHONICS

**Phonics**
The study of the relationships between letter symbols of a written language and the sounds they represent.

*Phonics*, which is the study of relationships between the letter symbols (graphemes) of a written language and the sounds (phonemes) they represent, is a method used in teaching word recognition in reading. It is a pedagogical term. Phonics is used by readers as an aid to decoding words. It helps students gain independence and reliance in reading, but it is only one aspect of the reading process.

Phonics instruction in the early grades is important. However, it must be taught in conjunction with meaning and the emphasis should be on enabling children to apply what they know about phonics so that they become proficient readers as quickly as possible. Systematic phonics instruction coupled with reading connected texts and comprehension yields good readers.[1]

# A DEVELOPMENTAL SEQUENCE OF PHONICS

Although the teaching of phonics will vary according to the needs of the students, in a developmental sequence certain skills should be achieved before others. Surprisingly, very little research has been conducted to prove that a set sequence should be followed. What we offer here, then, is a suggested sequence. So that they can properly diagnose the needs of their students in phonics, teachers need to be proficient in this area and know the steps involved. First, the child usually learns a few sight words. Then, when the child learns that some words look alike and/or sound alike, the understanding of phonic word attack skills has begun. Said another way, because children can identify words by sight doesn't necessarily mean that they can identify the letters that form these words. A good place to begin, then, is to use words they can identify to teach them specific phonic skills. This task is complex!

Following is a suggested sequence for phonics instruction. For each area we provide a definition, an informal test related to that area, and some instructional suggestions.[2]

[1]C. Snow, M. Burns, & P. Griffin. *Reading Difficulties in Young Children.* (Washington, D.C.: National Academy Press, 1998).

[2]For ease of reading, the author has omitted slashes that are often used to enclose phonemic symbols.

1. Auditory discrimination.
2. Visual discrimination.
3. Consonants.[3]
   a. Initial consonants.
   b. Final consonants.
   c. Consonant clusters (blends) (*bl, st, str*).
   d. Initial consonant blends (clusters); final consonant blends (clusters).
   e. Initial consonant digraphs (*th, ch, sh*).
   f. Final consonant digraphs (*ng, gh*).
   g. Silent consonants (*kn, pn, wr*).
4. Vowel sounds.
   a. Long vowel sounds.
   b. Short vowel sounds.
   c. Effect of final *e* on vowel.
   d. Double vowels.
      (1) Digraphs.
      (2) Diphthongs.
   e. Vowel controlled by *r*.
5. Special letters and sounds.
6. Phonograms.
7. Syllabication.
   a. Meaning of syllable.
   b. Generalizations.
      (1) Double consonant vc/cv.
      (2) Vowel-consonant-vowel v/cv.
      (3) Consonant with special *le* c/cle or v/cle.
   c. Syllable phonics.
   d. Accent.

| Special Note |
| --- |

It is essential that teachers relate the skills that children are learning to what the students are working with and reading. The best way to determine if children have acquired a skill is to see if they are using it in their reading and writing. ■

## AUDITORY AND VISUAL DISCRIMINATION

Unless children are able to hear sounds correctly, they will not be able to say them correctly, read them, or write them. Not only must children be able to differentiate between auditory sounds and visual symbols in order to be ready for reading, they must also learn that the sounds they hear have written symbols.

Since they must have good auditory and visual discrimination, these samples of exercises should help in determining such discrimination.

**Auditory Discrimination**
Ability to detect differences and similarities in sound symbols.

### *Auditory Discrimination*
Auditory discrimination is the ability to detect differences and similarities in sound symbols.

---

[3]Consonants are usually taught before vowel sounds. In the English language, consonants carry the meaning. Vowels are simply fillers.

## SAMPLE INDIVIDUAL DIAGNOSTIC TEST

**Directions: Listen carefully. See if you can tell me which pair of words is the same.**

| | | | |
|---|---|---|---|
| sat | set | ball | bell |
| cap | cap | sing | singe |
| hand | hand | pan | pan |
| sail | sell | burn | but |

**Directions: Listen carefully. Give me another word that rhymes with**

can _____        fat _____

sail _____       day _____

**Directions: Listen carefully. Give me another word that begins like**

baby _____

door _____

can _____

fat _____

*Instructional Suggestions*

If a child has difficulty discriminating between or among various sound symbols, present the child with other words that have sounds similar to the ones that seem to be causing problems. This procedure will help you to determine whether the child "misheard" the original words. You should also model for the child what he or she is supposed to do, and then you should do some sample activities together. In addition, you should test the child's phonemic awareness (see Chapter 7).

Keep in mind that judging whether two or more sound symbols are similar or different is not easy for young children. The children must be able to keep a sound in memory and then retrieve it to make a comparison. Some five- or six-year-olds may not have developed this ability. These children need to be able to recognize that a word consists of a sequence of individual sounds and be able to produce the individual sound when presented with it auditorily. They then need practice in auditory discrimination. However, if after a large amount of practice the child still has difficulty, it is possible that the inability to discern similarities and differences in speech sounds may be a symptom that the child has an auditory problem.

In addition, if the child speaks nonstandard English or if standard English is not the child's dominant language, the child may not do well. For English Language Learners, certain sounds may be different or nonexistent in a student's native language (see Appendix C).

**Visual discrimination**
Ability to detect similarities and differences in written symbols.

*Visual Discrimination*

Visual discrimination is the ability to detect similarities and differences in written symbols.

## SAMPLE INDIVIDUAL DIAGNOSTIC TEST

**Directions: Draw a circle around the letter that is like the first letter.**

| | | | | | |
|---|---|---|---|---|---|
| s | c | p | c | e | s |
| p | d | p | b | r | q |
| l | t | k | h | l | d |
| b | p | d | b | o | u |
| d | s | b | p | d | q |
| m | n | m | s | h | w |

**Directions: Draw a circle around the word that is like the first word.**

| | | | | | |
|---|---|---|---|---|---|
| car | far | can | cap | car | fan |
| dear | bear | dark | deal | dear | bean |
| pail | sail | pail | bail | pain | pear |

### Instructional Suggestions

If a child has difficulty with the visual discrimination tests involving letters and words, make sure the child understands the directions. The best way to ensure understanding is to model an example for the child.

Some children need a large amount of practice to be able to make the fine discriminations necessary to read. If, however, a teacher has provided a child with several activities, and the child still has problems with recognizing similarities or differences in letters, the teacher might want to refer the child for an eye examination.

| **Consonants** |
|---|
| One speech sound represented by one letter. |

# CONSONANTS

### Initial Consonants

Initial consonants are single consonants (one speech sound represented by one letter). For example: *b* (bath), *c* (cake), *d* (damp), *f* (fat), *g* (girl).

## SAMPLE INDIVIDUAL DIAGNOSTIC TEST

**Directions: Listen carefully. What is the letter that stands for the first sound you hear in the following words?**

dog, mother, father, girl, boy, hat, cat, family

## SAMPLE GROUP DIAGNOSTIC TEST

**Directions: Listen carefully. Write the first letter of each word I say. Let's do one together. The word is *baby*. Again, the word is *baby*. Did you write a *b*? Good. Here are the words:**

| | |
|---|---|
| 1. girl | 6. log |
| 2. fan | 7. dog |
| 3. sit | 8. bat |
| 4. want | 9. pot |
| 5. tail | 10. light |

### *Instructional Suggestions*

The instructional technique used here is generally an implicit one. State a number of words beginning with the same initial consonant. Then ask the children to listen to the words *ball, book,* and *bee,* and write the words on the board in list form. Then ask how *ball, book,* and *bee* are similar. They all have the same beginning letter *b.* They all start with the same sound. You can then give more words that begin with *b* and ask students to state some others that start like *big, book,* and *balloon.*

For variety, give the children a series of words that begin with the same initial consonant and ask them to match these words with words in a second column that start with the same letter by drawing a line from one to the other. For example:

### Substitution of Initial Consonants

After children have learned to recognize single consonants and are able to state them, they are ready to substitute them in already learned words to generate new words. The new words must be in their listening vocabulary; that is, they must have heard the word and know the meaning of it in order to be able to *read* it. For example, children have learned the consonant letter *c* and they also know the word *man.* They should then be able to substitute *c* for *m* and come up with the word *can.*

### Special Notes

The sample group tests presented in this section require the children to write the letters that stand for the sounds they hear. This test should only be given if children have been exposed to the letter-sound combinations and have learned to write the letters. It would be a good idea to have a practice test first to go over the directions and make sure the children understand what they are being asked to do, as well as to review what will be on the test.

If children do poorly on the group-administered test, check the results by giving an oral individual test to determine whether the problem is one of letter-sound correspondence; that is, the child cannot associate a letter with the sound. Also, have the children read some of the words to check their letter-sound correspondence, to make sure the child knows what letters stand for what sounds.

It may also be that the instructions are too confusing for the children; it is possible that the concept of "the letter that stands for the sound" may confuse some children. Therefore, you might change your instructions to say "the sound of the letter," even though this usage is not linguistically correct because letters do not have sounds. However, our purpose is not to teach linguistic principles to the children. It is to help them see and hear patterns in words so they can decode them as quickly as possible when they meet the words in connected text.

The oral individual diagnostic test can be given at any time during the day to determine a child's phonic analysis ability. Good teachers interweave diagnosis with instruction throughout the day.

Be especially careful to pronounce all words very distinctly; your articulation must be excellent so as not to influence the test results. ▪

### Final Consonants

Final consonants are similar to the list given for the initial consonants, except that they appear at the end of the word. Examples of the most frequent single consonants are *b* (rob), *d* (road), *g* (pig), *k* (brook), *l* (tool), *m* (mom), *n* (hen), *p* (top), *r* (car), *s* (fuss), *s-z* (has), *t* (that).

## SAMPLE INDIVIDUAL DIAGNOSTIC TEST

(Same as for initial consonants, except children have to give the last letter in the word that stands for the last sound they hear.)

**Directions: Listen carefully. What is the letter that stands for the last sound you hear in the following words?**

cab, dog, man, hat, tap, drop

## SAMPLE GROUP DIAGNOSTIC TEST

**Directions: Listen carefully. Write the last letter of each word I say.**

| | |
|---|---|
| 1. rob | 6. pig |
| 2. pop | 7. hat |
| 3. ear | 8. sled |
| 4. hen | 9. tool |
| 5. miss | 10. head |

### Instructional Suggestions

Some teachers teach final consonants at the same time that they teach initial consonants. This approach is preferable, for teachers are working with a particular sound that they want children to "overlearn"; that is, they want students to be able to recognize and state the sound-letter combination over an extended period of time. When the initial and final consonants in words are emphasized, the children are gaining extra practice in both the particular sound and the letter that represents the sound being studied. As the children have learned that the letter *Gg* stands for a certain sound and can recognize this sound in *girl, go, game, get,* and so on, they should also be given words such as *pig, log, leg, tag,* and so on, to see whether they can recognize the same sound at the end of the word.

### Substitution of Final Consonants

In order to gain skill in the substitution of final consonants, give the children a list of words that they can already decode and recognize—such as *bat, pet, let, tan.* Then ask them to substitute the final letter *g* in all the words to make new words. For example, *bat* would become *bag, pet* would become *peg, let* would become *leg,* and *tan* would become *tag.* Pupils can also be asked to substitute other consonants to make new words. For example, *d* for *g* in *bag* to make *bad,* and *d* in *let* to make *led.*

**Consonant clusters (blends)**
A combination of consonant sounds blended together so that the identity of each sound is retained.

### Consonant Clusters (Blends)

Consonant clusters are simply a way of combining the consonant sounds of a language. Clusters are a blend of sounds. (In some reading programs, the term *consonant cluster* has replaced the term *consonant blend.*)

### Initial Consonant Blends (Clusters)

Consonant blends are a combination of sounds. They are two or more consonant sounds blended together so that each sound is retained. For example: *bl* (black), *br* (brown), *cl* (clap), *cr* (cross), *fr* (frame), *gl* (glass), *gr* (grass), *pr* (prize), *pl* (please), *sk* (skip), *sn* (snow).

## SAMPLE INDIVIDUAL DIAGNOSTIC TEST

**Directions: Listen carefully. What are the two letters that stand for the first two sounds you hear in the following words?**

blame, prune, flag, glove, glass, frog, snow, clear, break, crow

## SAMPLE GROUP DIAGNOSTIC TEST

**Directions: Listen carefully. Write the first two letters of each word I say.**

| | | | |
|---|---|---|---|
| 1. | clear | 6. | plane |
| 2. | grow | 7. | frog |
| 3. | train | 8. | brake |
| 4. | slow | 9. | steam |
| 5. | blow | 10. | floor |

### Instructional Suggestions

Consonant blends are generally introduced in the first grade. The teaching of the initial consonant blends depends on the developmental levels of the children, who may be at the stage where they can benefit from added instruction in order to help them more readily decode words. The children must be able to recognize, sound, and substitute initial consonants in words before proceeding to blends. Give them a list of sight words that have blends, such as *spin, snow, play, stop;* ask them to say these words; and then ask them to tell what sounds they hear at the beginning of the words. Also ask them to say a list of words such as *go, get, me,* and *mother* and then ask them what the difference between the two groups of words is. The children should be able to discern that in the group consisting of *play, stop,* and *spin,* they were able to hear two consonant sounds rather than one. Thus the concept of a blend is introduced. Then give the children exercises similar to those presented in the section on initial consonants. For example, you could choose a list of words that they may not necessarily know as sight words:

| 1 | 2 | 3 | 4 |
|---|---|---|---|
| black | big | mother | happy |
| ball | play | great | broom |
| blue | draw | farm | track |
| chain | down | spin | grow |
| train | go | run | help |

Then ask them to underline only those words you pronounce—such as *black, play, spin,* and *broom.*

This exercise can also be used to see how well children listen, follow directions, and recognize blends. For example, you can instruct the children to *listen carefully* and not to do anything until you have completed the sentence. Then, say, "Put a circle around *black* and a cross on *blue.* Put a circle around *draw* and a line under *play.* Put a line under *great* and a circle around *spin.* Put a cross on *track* and a circle around *broom.*"

Final consonant blends are usually taught after initial consonant blends, using similar techniques.

### Final Consonant Blends (Clusters)

Final consonant blends are similar to initial consonant blends except that they are at the end of the word and are composed of different combinations of blends. For example: *nd* (kind), *rk* (park), *mp* (stamp), *rt* (start), *sk* (mask), *rp* (harp), *nt* (ant).

## SAMPLE INDIVIDUAL DIAGNOSTIC TEST

**Directions: Listen carefully. What are the last two letters that stand for the last two sounds you hear in the following words?**

bump, cart, ask, park, sand, find

## SAMPLE GROUP DIAGNOSTIC TEST

**Directions: Listen carefully. Write the last two letters of each word I say.**

1. bark
2. mask
3. camp
4. Frank
5. cart
6. fist
7. sand
8. harp
9. slant
10. grasp

### Instructional Suggestions

Use techniques similar to those presented for initial consonant blends.

### Initial Consonant Digraphs

*Consonant digraphs* usually consist of two consonants that represent one speech sound. For example: *ch* (chair), *sh* (show), *th* (thank), *ph* (phone). Note that the sound normally associated with the consonant is replaced with a new speech sound.

**Consonant digraph**
Two consonants that represent one speech sound.

## SAMPLE INDIVIDUAL DIAGNOSTIC TEST

**Directions: Listen carefully. What are the two letters that stand for the first sound you hear in the following words?**

chain, thumb, shall, phone

## SAMPLE GROUP DIAGNOSTIC TEST

**Directions: Listen carefully. Write the first two letters of each word I say.**

1. phone
2. shame
3. chain
4. shall
5. child

6. chair
7. that
8. photo
9. thumb
10. shine

### Instructional Suggestions

These suggestions are similar to those given for initial consonant blends; however, you should help children recognize that combinations such as *ch, th,* and *sh* represent one sound rather than two. In addition make sure children understand that *ph* sounds like *f* in words such as *photo, phone,* and *phony.* Unless they have encountered these words and know how to spell them, they can write either the letter *f* or *fo* because you asked for the first two letters in the word. The children are writing what they hear.

### Final Consonant Digraphs

Examples of final consonant digraphs are *th* (booth), *ng* (sing), *sh* (mash), *ch* (cinch), *gh* (rough). Note: It is possible to have a digraph represent one of the sounds in a cluster. In the word *cinch, nch* represents a cluster (blend) because *nch* represents a blend of *two* sounds. The letter *n* represents a sound, and the digraph *ch* represents another sound.

## SAMPLE INDIVIDUAL DIAGNOSTIC TEST

**Directions: Listen carefully. What are the two letters that stand for the last sound you hear in the following words?**

flash, pinch, moth, ring, much

## SAMPLE GROUP DIAGNOSTIC TEST

**Directions: Listen carefully. Write the last two letters of each word I say.**

1. rash
2. touch
3. sing
4. mush
5. moth

6. cash
7. rich
8. push
9. teeth
10. bring

*Instructional Suggestions*
Use techniques similar to those given for initial consonant digraphs.

*Silent Consonants*

**Silent consonants**
Two adjacent consonants, one of which is silent, for example, *kn (know), pn (pneumonia).*

*Silent consonants* refer to two consonants in which one is silent. Examples are *kn* (know), *gh* (ghost), *wr* (wreck).

No special tests are being presented for silent consonants. Children learn these as they are exposed to them in print.

# VOWEL SOUNDS

*Long and Short Vowel Sounds and Effect of Final e*
The vowels are *a, e, i, o,* and *u,* and sometimes *y* and *w* act as vowels. A vowel is long when it says its name.

## SAMPLE INDIVIDUAL DIAGNOSTIC TEST

**Directions: Listen carefully. I will say a word. Tell me the vowel you hear in the word. Also tell me if you hear a long or short vowel sound.**

cat, note, make, mice, not, pet, but, cute

## SAMPLE GROUP DIAGNOSTIC TEST

**Directions: Listen carefully. I will say a word a few times. Write the vowel you hear in the word. Then write the word *short* or *long* next to it.**

| | |
|---|---|
| 1. cut | 6. hot |
| 2. cap | 7. cape |
| 3. mute | 8. time |
| 4. pen | 9. no |
| 5. Tim | 10. nut |

### Special Notes

It's a good idea to do a few examples orally together with the child before giving the group diagnostic test for long and short vowel sounds. For example, you can do the following:

"Let's do one together first. Listen carefully." Say, "Bat, bat," and ask, "What vowel did you hear?" If the child says *a,* ask the child to state whether the word *bat* has a long or short vowel sound. If the child has difficulty with the individual test, do not give the group test (see "Instructional Suggestions").

Also, the words *short* and *long* should be on the chalkboard and visible to all the children, and the children should know what each word stands for. We want to make sure we are assessing phonics rather than the understanding of the terms short and long. ▪

### Instructional Suggestions

Most children have encountered many of the vowel generalizations in sight words and have learned to pronounce the words properly before they are able to state the generalization. Vowel generalizations are usually introduced some time in the first grade and are taught throughout the primary grades. The timing of when to teach vowel generalizations depends on the developmental levels of the pupils in the class. The purpose of teaching vowel generalizations is to help students become more proficient in analyzing words, so that they can be more effective independent readers.

The emphasis, however, should be on enabling children to recognize certain word patterns. In other words, the children's attention should be on the spelling and sound structures of the word patterns they are learning.[4]

Should long or short vowels be taught first?[5] As the long vowel sound is the name of the vowel, children might have less difficulty in hearing this sound. Therefore, it would be better to start with long vowel sounds, even though there are more words with short vowel sounds.

Whichever kind of vowel is taught first, it is important to use the children's background of experiences to help them acquire new skills.

Be sure to familiarize children with the schwa sound, represented by (ə) of the phonetic alphabet. The schwa is important in phonics instruction because it frequently appears in the unstressed (unaccented) syllables of words with more than one syllable. (See "Special Letters and Sounds.")

### Long Vowel Sounds—a  e  i  o  u (and sometimes) y

In the teaching of this concept, draw attention to the sound element. Place on the board a number of sight words illustrating the long vowel sound:

| | | |
|---|---|---|
| āpe | bē | gō |
| āge | hē | nō |
| Āpril | ēven | ōpen |
| āte | mē | |

Ask the children to listen to the words as they are sounded. Can they hear the name of any of the vowels in the words? If they can, they can tell which ones they hear. After they correctly state the vowel they heard, "saying its name," explain that these vowels are called long vowels and they are marked with a bar over them, for example, *ā*.

---

[4]Adams, p. 80.

[5]Although some linguists frown at the use of the terms *long* and *short vowels,* because they claim there are only gradations of vowel sounds, it is helpful to use these terms in the teaching of phonics.

You can read a list of words containing long vowels to the children, and the students should then say which vowel is long in each word. Give them a list of words and ask them to mark all the vowels that are long after everyone has said the words aloud. For example:

| | | | |
|---|---|---|---|
| āble | gāme | hāte | mōst |
| boy | get | hid | nāme |
| cāke | girl | hīde | nō |
| come | gō | man | nōte |
| father | hat | mē | pet |

After children have had practice in recognizing long vowel sounds in spoken words, present written exercises in which the children work independently at marking the long vowel sound. The words in these exercises should all be sight vocabulary words—those the children have already encountered and are able to recognize. In this way, children use what they know to learn something new. Also give them appropriate-level passages to read that contain words with the long vowel sound.

*Y* represents a long vowel sound when it occurs at the end of a word or syllable and when all the other letters in the word or syllable are consonants. For example: *by, cry, baby, deny.* Note that *y* in these words represents different vowel sounds. It stands for a long *i* sound in one-syllable words containing no other vowels. (See "Special Letters and Sounds.")

**Short Vowel Sounds**

As the children have already had practice in long vowel sounds, place a list of words with short vowel sounds on the board and pronounce each one:

| | | |
|---|---|---|
| not | get | man |
| got | let | can |
| pin | put | mad |
| tin | cut | cap |
| met | hat | had |

Present the list containing long vowels so that children can hear the differences between long and short vowel sounds. Draw the children's attention to the *position* of the short vowel in such words as the following:

| | | | |
|---|---|---|---|
| fat | man | net | got |
| mat | mad | get | not |
| cat | can | let | |
| hat | | pet | |

Help children to notice the vowel generalization—*a single vowel in the middle of a word (or syllable) is usually short.* As this concept is usually introduced in the first grade, the presentation of the term *syllable* should be deferred. The concept of closed syllable is reviewed in the intermediate grades in conjunction with syllabication.

Be sure to note words like *gō, nō, mē,* and *hē.* The vowels are all long; there is only one vowel in the word; and *a vowel at the end of a one-vowel word (or syllable) usually has the long sound.*

Present the students with passages that contain words with the short vowel sound.

### Special note

When we are discussing words following certain patterns, the words *generalization* and *rule* surface. *Generalization* implies that the pattern sometimes applies and that the reader needs to give it a try, with the understanding that the attempt may not work because many words in the English language do not comply. *Rule,* on the other hand, implies consistency. We prefer the term generalization because it implies more flexibility. We also prefer the term because some children are very literal. They know that a rule is a rule and it cannot be broken. Consequently, they have great difficulty in being flexible phonics users because they are afraid of breaking the rule.

Generalizations should only be taught if enough cases warrant their teaching. Research on phoneme-grapheme relationships has been done with enumerated specific rule generalizations and the percentage of time that words followed the rule. Some investigators have claimed that a rule should not be taught unless it holds true at least 75 percent of the time.[6] However, the decision should depend on the words. There are some frequently used words that may conform to a rule pattern, whereas a number of less frequently used words may not conform to the same rule generalization. The percentage of these latter words that conform to a rule pattern may not be as high as 50 percent, even though the most often-used words almost always conform to the same pattern. For example, the "silent (final) *e*" rule, which is usually taught in the early primary grades, only has 63 percent applicability.[7] This 63 percent includes many frequently used words that conform to the same rule pattern. Therefore, the rule should be taught as a phonic generalization. ■

### *The Effect of the Final* e

List words that the children know as sight words on the board and pronounce them:

| | | |
|---|---|---|
| note | cake | cute |
| made | take | mile |

Ask children to listen to the vowel sound, and stress that in each of the sounded words the first vowel stands for a long sound. Then ask the children to notice what all the words have in common: all of the words have two vowels;

[6]Theodore Clymer, "The Utility of Phonic Generalizations in the Primary Grades," *The Reading Teacher* 16 (January 1963): 252–58; and Lillie Smith Davis, "The Applicability of Phonic Generalizations to Selected Spelling Programs," *Elementary English* 49 (May 1972): 706–12.

[7]Davis, p. 709.

one of the vowels is an *e,* which is always at the end of the word, and this *e* always has a consonant preceding it; the first vowel is long, and the final *e* is silent. List the following words on the board:

| | | |
|---|---|---|
| hat | cap | tub |
| kit | Tim | rob |
| can | not | hug |
| tap | cut | hop |

The students read the words and tell what the vowel is and what kind of vowel sound the word has. Ask children to put an *e* at the end of each of the words, so that the word list becomes the following:

| | | |
|---|---|---|
| hate | cape | tube |
| kite | time | robe |
| cane | note | huge |
| tape | cute | hope |

Invite the pupils to read the words aloud. If they need help, read the word. Again, ask the children to notice what all of the words have in common and what happened to the words when the final *e* was added to each of them.

Through observation and discussion, help the children to develop the silent (final) *e* generalization: *in words (or syllables) containing two vowels, separated by a consonant, and one of the vowels is a final* e, *the first vowel is usually long and the final* e *is silent.*[8]

Some practice exercises include a list of words to which children are instructed to add a final *e* to make a new word. The children then use both words in a sentence to show that they understand the difference in meaning between them. The following exercise also examines their ability to recognize differences between words:

*Directions: Put in the correct word.*

1. He _____ himself. (cut, cute)
2. She is _____. (cut, cute)
3. I _____ you like my pet. (hop, hope)
4. I like to _____ on my foot. (hop, hope)
5. My friend's name is _____. (Tim, time)
6. What _____ is it? (Tim, time)

**Vowel digraph**
Two vowels that represent one speech sound.

### Double Vowels: Digraphs

Two vowels adjacent to one another in a word (or syllable) stand for a single vowel sound and are called *vowel digraphs;* for example, *ea, oa, ai, ei, ie* in words like *beat, boat, hail, receive, believe.*

---

[8]When we say that a letter is silent, we mean that it does not add a sound to the syllable; however, it is just as important as any other letter in the syllable. It signals information about other letters, and it helps us to determine the sound represented by other letters.

**SAMPLE INDIVIDUAL DIAGNOSTIC TEST**

**Directions: Listen carefully. I will say a word. You tell me the two vowels that stand for the one vowel sound.**

boat, keep, pail, way, bean

**SAMPLE GROUP DIAGNOSTIC TEST**

**Directions: Listen carefully. I will say a word a few times. Write the two vowels that go together to make one sound. The two vowels are either *ea, oa, ee, ai,* or *ay.***

1. pain          6. say
2. boat          7. mail
3. load          8. may
4. keep          9. tray
5. mean          10. feet

*Instructional Suggestions*

In first grade, children typically learn the generalization that when two vowels appear together, the first is usually long and the second is silent. This generally holds true for a number of vowel combinations such as *ai, oa, ea, ay,* and *ee*; however, there are exceptions to this rule, such as *ae, uy, eo, ew.* These digraphs are sounded as a single sound, but not with the long sound of the first. Some examples are *sew, buy, yeoman, Caesar.* Note that in the word *believe,* it is the *second* vowel that is long. Some vowel digraphs combine to form one sound that is not the long sound of either vowel. For example, in the words *neighbor, weigh,* and *freight,* the digraph *ei* is sounded as a long *a,* and in the word *sew,* the digraph *ew* is sounded as a long *o,* with the *w* acting as a vowel. Note that in the word *rough,* the digraph *ou* is not sounded as a long vowel.

Spend time on those vowel combinations that are the most useful.[*] These are *ea, oa, ai, ay,* and *ee.*

Give students a set of words with one sound pattern at a time so that they can overlearn the letter–sound relationship. For example, the word *beat* can be put on the chalkboard and pronounced. Do the same for *team, meal,* and *bead.* After this, put other words on the board and ask children to pronounce them. At this time, you can elicit from the children what the *ea* combination in words such as *meat, meal,* and *tea* sounds like. (They should state the long *e* sound.) Then ask the children to generate words with the *ea* sound pattern. In addition, give them opportunities to meet words with the same *ea* sound combination in their reading.

[*](Based on Clymer, 1996.)

**Diphthongs**
Blends of vowel
sounds beginning
with the first and
gliding to the second.
The vowel blends are
represented by two
adjacent vowels, for
example, *oi*.

### Special Note

A child who gives *ea* as the vowel combination for *keep* is showing the understanding that the combination *ee* and *ea* have a similar sound in some words. ■

### *Double Vowels: Diphthongs*

*Diphthongs* are blends of vowel sounds beginning with the first and gliding to the second. The vowel blends are represented by two adjacent vowels. Examples include *ou, oi, oy, ow*. For syllabication purposes, diphthongs are considered to be one vowel sound.

## SAMPLE INDIVIDUAL DIAGNOSTIC TEST

**Directions: Listen carefully. I will say a word. You tell me the two vowels that go together in the word.**

boy, boil, how, cow, out

## SAMPLE GROUP DIAGNOSTIC TEST

**Directions: Listen carefully. I will say a word a few times. Write the two vowels that go together in the word. The two vowels are either *oi, oy, ou,* or *ow*.**

| | |
|---|---|
| 1. cow | 6. toy |
| 2. brown | 7. soil |
| 3. house | 8. town |
| 4. Roy | 9. mouse |
| 5. out | 10. gown |

### *Instructional Suggestions*

Digraphs usually are presented before diphthongs because they are easier to learn than diphthongs. Some of the diphthongs can be confusing to children. For example, the *ou* in *house* is a diphthong, but the *ou* in *rough* is a digraph. Also, the *ow* in *know* is a digraph, but the *ow* in *now* is a diphthong.

A good time to teach diphthongs is when children are reading stories or material that have a number of words with diphthongs. You can present these words as vocabulary words and discuss the most common diphthongs.

If children learn the representative sounds of the digraphs and diphthongs, when they meet them in words in context, their chances of being able to pronounce the words or gain an approximation of their pronunciation are good.

Emphasize to children that good readers use a combination of word recognition strategies rather than just one, and context clues help students determine which pronunciation is correct for the sentence.

---

**Special Note**

Note that in the word *how* the *w* acts as a vowel in the diphthong *ow.* (Even though a diphthong is a *blend* of two vowel sounds, for syllabication purposes you should consider it as one vowel sound.) ▪

### *Vowel Controlled by r*

A vowel followed by *r* in the same syllable is controlled by the *r.* As a result, the preceding vowel does not have its usual vowel sound. Examples are *car, fir, or, hurt, perch.* If a vowel is followed by *r,* but the *r* begins another syllable, the vowel is not influenced by the *r.* Examples: ī • rāte̸, tī • rāde̸.

Tests and practices similar to those for other types of vowel sounds can be developed for words that have the vowel controlled by *r.*

### *Review of Vowel Generalizations*

1. A long vowel is one that sounds like the name of the vowel.
2. A single vowel followed by a consonant in a word (or syllable) usually has a short vowel sound.
3. A single vowel at the end of a word (or syllable) usually has a long vowel sound.
4. A vowel digraph consists of two adjacent vowels with one vowel sound, as in *beat, coat,* and *maid.*
5. In words (or syllables) containing two vowels separated by a consonant, and one vowel is a final *e,* the first vowel is usually long and the final *e* is silent, as in *bāke̸.*
6. A vowel followed by *r* is controlled by the consonant *r.*
7. When *y* is at the end of a word containing no other vowels, the *y* represents the long sound of *i* as in *my, sky.*
8. Diphthongs are blends of vowel sounds beginning with the first and gliding to the second, as in *boy, boil, house.*

### *Review Exercise*

We have presented much phonics information thus far. Take a minute to review what you've been reading about related to vowel sounds.

### Clues to Vowel Sounds

Here are five clues that will help in determining which vowel sound you would expect to hear in a one-syllable word:

1. A single vowel letter at the beginning or in the middle is a clue to a short vowel sound—as in *hat, let, it, hot,* and *cup.*
2. A single vowel letter at the end of a word is a clue to a long vowel sound—as in *we, by,* and *go.*
3. Two vowel letters together are a clue to a long vowel sound—as in *rain, day, dream, feel,* and *boat.*

4. Two vowel letters separated by a consonant, and one vowel is a final *e*, are a clue to a long vowel sound—as in *age, ice, bone,* and *cube.*

5. A vowel letter followed by *r* in the same syllable is a clue to a vowel sound that is controlled by the *r*—as in *far, bird, her, horn, care,* and *hair.*

In the blank before each word, write the number of the statement in the list that would help you determine the vowel sound in the word.

| | | | |
|---|---|---|---|
| _____ | cut | _____ | cute |
| _____ | bean | _____ | me |
| _____ | cane | _____ | hurt |
| _____ | fine | _____ | note |
| _____ | not | _____ | coat |
| _____ | pain | _____ | my |
| _____ | far | _____ | lot |
| _____ | man | _____ | seen |
| _____ | say | _____ | go |
| _____ | get | _____ | cape |

### *Special Letters and Sounds*

#### Y

As already mentioned, *y* is used as both a consonant and a vowel. When *y* is at the beginning of a word or syllable, it is a consonant. Examples are *yes, yet, young, your, canyon, graveyard.* In the words *canyon* and *graveyard,* *y* begins the second syllable; therefore it is a consonant.

When *y* acts as a vowel, it represents the short *i* sound, the long *i* sound, or the long *e* sound. *Y* usually represents the short *i* sound when *y* is in the middle of a word or syllable that has no vowel letter. Examples are *hymn, gym, synonym, cymbal. Y* usually represents the long *i* sound when it is at the end of a single-syllable word that has no vowel letter. Examples are *by, try, why, dry, fly. Y* usually represents the long *e* sound when it is at the end of a multisyllabic word. Examples are *baby, candy, daddy, family.*

#### C and G

Some words beginning with *c* or *g* can cause problems because the letters *c* and *g* each stand for both a hard and a soft sound. The letter *g* in *gym, George, gentle,* and *generation* stands for a soft *g* sound. A soft *g* sounds like *j* in *Jack, jail,* and *justice.* The initial letter *c* in *cease, center, cent,* and *cite* stands for a soft *c* sound. A soft *c* sounds like *s* in *so, same,* and *sew.* The initial letter *g* in *go, get, game, gone,* and *garden* stands for a hard *g* sound. The initial letter *c* in *cat, came, cook, call,* and *carry* stands for a hard *c* sound. A hard *c* sounds like *k* in *key, king, kite, kettle.* Note that the letter *c* represents a sound that is either like the *s* in *see* or like the *k* in *kitten.*

#### Q

The letter *q* is always followed by the letter *u* in the English language. The *qu* combination represents either one speech sound or a blend of two sounds. At the beginning of a word, *qu* almost always represents a blend of two sounds, *kw.* Examples are *queen, quilt, quiet, queer, quack.* When *qu* appears at the end of a word in the *que* combination, it represents one sound, *k.* Examples are *unique, antique, clique.*

### The Schwa (ə)

**Schwa**

The sound often found in the unstressed (unaccented) syllables of words with more than one syllable. The schwa sound is represented by an upside-down e (ə) in the phonetic (speech) alphabet.

The *schwa* sound is symbolized by an upside down *e* (ə) in the phonetic (speech) alphabet. The schwa sound frequently appears in the unstressed (unaccented) syllables of words with more than one syllable. The schwa, which usually sounds like the short *u* in *but,* is represented by a number of different vowels. Examples are b*e*lieve (bə • lēvĕ), p*o*lice (pə • lēś), d*i*vide (də • vīdĕ), rob*u*st (rō̆ • bəst), Rom*a*n (rō̆ • mən). In the examples, the italicized vowels represent the schwa sound. Although the spelling of the unstressed syllable in each word is different, the sound remains the same for the different vowels. (Note: The pronunciations presented here come from *Webster's New Collegiate Dictionary,* but it should not be inferred that these are the only pronunciations for these words. Pronunciations may vary from dictionary to dictionary and from region to region.)

## PHONOGRAMS

**Phonogram**

A succession of graphemes that occurs with the same phonetic value in a number of words (*ight, ake, at, et,* and so on); word family.

*Phonograms,* which are successions of graphemes that occur with the same phonetic value in a number of words, are very helpful in both unlocking and building words.[9] Some examples of phonograms are *an, and, old, et, at, ate, eat, ap, ash, ump, ook, ad, ock, ame, ill, ink,* and so on. All phonograms begin with a vowel, and words that contain the same phonogram rhyme. For example: *bake, cake, rake, lake, take, make, fake,* and so on. (Phonograms may also be referred to as *word families.*)

Children can build many words using phonograms in the following manner:

1. Present children with the following phonograms.

   _____ et _____ an _____ ill _____ old

2. Have the children add different single consonants, consonant digraphs, and blends to the beginning of the phonograms to see how many words they can make.

Children can use phonograms to unlock words in the following manner:

1. The child meets the unfamiliar word *tank.*
2. The child recognizes *ank* as a phonogram he has met in *bank.*
3. The child substitutes *t* for *b.*
4. The child blends *t* and *ank* to get *tank.*

Likewise, as a result of knowing the most common phonograms (i.e., rime), children can create many different words. Figure 10.1 shows the most common phonograms, how frequently they occur, and example words.

[9]See Adams, pp. 84–85, for research studies that are very supportive of this technique.

**FIGURE 10.1**    **Most Common Phonograms in Rank Order Based on Frequency (Number of Uses in Monosyllabic Words)**[*]

| Frequency | Rime | Example words |
|---|---|---|
| 26 | -ay | jay say pay day play |
| 26 | -ill | hill Bill will fill spill |
| 22 | -ip | ship dip tip skip trip |
| 19 | -at | cat fat bat rat sat |
| 19 | -am | ham jam dam ram Sam |
| 19 | -ag | bag rag tag wag sag |
| 19 | -ack | back sack Jack black track |
| 19 | -ank | bank sank tank blank drank |
| 19 | -ick | sick Dick pick quick chick |
| 18 | -ell | bell sell fell tell yell |
| 18 | -ot | pot not hot dot got |
| 18 | -ing | ring sing king wing thing |
| 18 | -ap | cap map tap clap trap |
| 18 | -unk | sunk junk bunk flunk skunk |
| 17 | -ail | pail jail nail sail tail |
| 17 | -ain | rain pain main chain plain |
| 17 | -eed | feed seed weed need freed |
| 17 | -y | my by dry try fly |
| 17 | -out | pout trout scout shout spout |
| 17 | -ug | rug bug hug dug tug |
| 16 | -op | mop cop pop top hop |
| 16 | -in | pin tin win chin thin |
| 16 | -an | pan man ran tan Dan |
| 16 | -est | best nest pest rest test |
| 16 | -ink | pink sink rink link drink |
| 16 | -ow | low slow grow show snow |
| 16 | -ew | new few chew grew blew |
| 16 | -ore | more sore tore store score |
| 15 | -ed | bed red fed led Ted |
| 15 | -ab | cab dab jab lab crab |
| 15 | -ob | cob job rob Bob knob |
| 15 | -ock | sock rock lock dock block |
| 15 | -ake | care lake make take brake |
| 15 | -ine | line nine pine fine shine |
| 14 | -ight | knight light right night fight |
| 14 | -im | swim him Kim rim brim |
| 14 | -uck | duck luck suck truck buck |
| 14 | -um | gum bum hum drum plum |

From Fry, E. "The Most Common Phonograms." *The Reading Teacher, 51*(1998): 620–22.

## SYLLABICATION—INTERMEDIATE GRADES

**Syllable**
A vowel or a group of letters containing one vowel sound, for example, *blo*.

A *syllable* is a vowel or a group of letters containing one vowel sound. Syllabication of words is the process of breaking known and unknown multisyllabic words into single syllables. This is important in word recognition because in order to be able to pronounce the multisyllabic word, a child must first be able to syllabicate it. Knowledge of syllabication is also helpful in spelling and writing. In attacking multisyllabic words, the student must first analyze the word, determine the syllabic units, apply phonic analysis to the syllables, and then blend them into a whole word. For multisyllabic words the result will almost always be an approximation of the pronunciation. As for one-syllable words, the correct pronunciation will depend on the student's having heard the spoken word and whether it makes sense in the context of what is being read. Usually, students will have more success in applying phonics to monosyllabic words than to multisyllabic ones because the blending of the syllables into a whole word often changes the pronunciation from the syllable-by-syllable pronunciation. (See "Accenting Words" in this chapter.)

### Syllabication Generalizations

Because a multisyllabic word must be syllabicated before applying phonic analysis, syllabication generalizations will be given first. (The vowel generalizations that the students have learned since first grade should be reviewed because these same generalizations will be used in the application of phonic analysis.)

*Generalization 1:* Vowel followed by two consonants and a vowel (vc/cv). If the first vowel in a word is followed by two consonants and a vowel, the word is divided between the two consonants.

*Examples:* but/ter   can/dy   com/ment

*Generalization 2:* Vowel followed by a single consonant and a vowel (v/cv). If the first vowel is followed by one consonant and a vowel, the consonant usually goes with the second syllable.

*Examples:* be/gin   ti/ger   fe/ver   pu/pil

An exception to the v/cv syllabication generalization exists. If the letter *x* is between two vowels, the *x* goes with the first vowel rather than with the second one.

*Examples:* ex/it   ex/act   ox/en

*Generalization 3:* Vowel or consonant followed by a consonant plus *le* (v/cle) or (vc/cle). If a consonant comes just before *le* in a word of more than one syllable, the consonant goes with *le* to form the last syllable.

*Examples:* sam/ple   can/dle   an/kle   bun/dle   pur/ple   daz/zle
           bea/gle   ca/ble

*Generalization 4:* Compound words. Compound words are divided between the two words.

*Examples:* girl/friend   base/ball

*Generalization 5:* Prefixes and suffixes. Prefixes and suffixes usually stand as whole units.

*Examples:* re/turn   kind/ly

### Phonics Applied to Syllabicated Syllables

After the word has been divided into syllables, the student must determine how to pronounce the individual syllables. The pronunciation is determined by whether the syllable is open or closed, and whether it contains a vowel digraph or diphthong.

> *Open syllable*—one that contains one vowel and ends in a vowel. The vowel is usually sounded as long, as in *go.*
> *Closed syllable*—one that contains one vowel and ends in a consonant. The vowel is usually sounded as short, as in *mat.*

### Application of Vowel Generalization to Syllabication Generalization 1— Double Consonant Generalization (vc/cv)

The closed-syllable vowel generalization would apply to a syllable that contains one vowel and ends in a consonant. The vowel sound is usually short.

*Examples:* căn/dy   ăs/sĕt

### Application of Vowel Generalization to Syllabication Generalization 2— Vowel Consonant Vowel Generalization (v/cv)

The open-syllable generalization would apply to a syllable that contains one vowel and ends in a vowel. The vowel sound is usually long.

*Examples:* bē/gin   tī/ger   ō/ver   fā/tal   dē/tour

### Application of Vowel Generalization to Syllabication Generalization 3— Special Consonant *le* Generalization (v/cle) or (vc/cle)

If the syllable is closed as in the first syllable of *sad/dle* and in the first syllable of *can/dle,* then the vowel sound is usually short in the first syllable, for it ends in a consonant. If the syllable is open as in the first syllable of *fā/ble* and in the first syllable of *bū/gle,* then the vowel sound is usually long in the first syllable, for it ends in a vowel. The letter combinations containing *le*—such as *cle, ble, gle, tle,* and so on—usually stand as the final syllable. The final syllable is not accented; it is always an unstressed syllable containing the schwa sound.

*Examples:* sĭm/pəl   fā/bəl   săd/dəl   ăp/pəl   bū/gəl

## ACCENTING WORDS

Accenting is usually taught in conjunction with syllabication in the intermediate grades. To pronounce words of more than one syllable, students should syllabicate the word, apply phonic analysis, and then blend the syllables into one word. To blend the syllables into one word correctly, pupils should know something about accenting and how accents affect vowel sounds. They should know that unaccented syllables are usually softened, and if the syllable of a multisyllable word is an unstressed syllable, it will often contain the schwa sound. (Stressed syllables never contain the schwa sound.) Note: When syllables are blended together, the pronunciation is usually not the same as the syllable-by-syllable pronunciation.

*Example:* (kĭt)  (tĕn)  (kĭt'tən);  (bē)  (lĭēvé)  (bə • lĭēvé)

There may be differences between pronunciation of homographs (words that are spelled the same but have different meanings) because of a difference in accent.

*Example:* con´duct (noun)  con duct´ (verb)

**Procedures for Teaching Accenting**
The teacher places a number of two-syllable words on the board and syllabicates them:

| | | | |
|---|---|---|---|
| pi/lot | a/ble | ap/ple | va/cant |
| den/tist | rea/son | help/ful | bot/tle |
| sub/due | wi/zard | wis/dom | tai/lor |
| lo/cal | col/umn | jour/nal | |

The teacher explains that even though students are able to syllabicate the individual words and are able to apply the proper phonic analysis, in order to be able to pronounce the words correctly, they still must know something about accenting the words.

Students are asked to listen while the teacher pronounces each word, to determine which syllable is stressed. The teacher then asks individual students to volunteer to pronounce the words and explains that the syllable that is sounded with more stress in a two-syllable word is called the accented syllable. The teacher explains that the accent mark (´) is used to show which syllable is stressed, that is, spoken with greater intensity or loudness. This mark usually comes right after and slightly above the accented syllable. (Some dictionaries such as *Webster's Third New International Dictionary* have the accent mark come before the syllable that is stressed.) The teacher further explains that the dictionary has a key to pronunciation of words and that the marks that show how to pronounce words are called *diacritical marks*. The most frequent diacritical marks are the breve (˘) and the macron (¯), which pupils have already met as the symbols for the short and long vowel sounds. The accent (´) is also in the class of diacritical marks.

**Diacritical marks**
Marks that show how to pronounce words.

A list of words correctly syllabicated to put on the board:

| | | | |
|---|---|---|---|
| pi´lot | a´ble | ap´ple | pro´gram |
| rea´son | help´ful | bot´tle | jour´nal |
| wis´dom | tai´lor | lo´cal | den´tist |

The teacher then reviews syllabication and vowel rules. The two-syllable words in the preceding list are all accented on the first syllable. Another group of words in which the second syllable is stressed is then listed:

| | | |
|---|---|---|
| ap point´ | pro ceed´ | as tound´ |
| sub due´ | pa rade´ | po lite´ |
| re cede´ | com plain´ | pro vide´ |

Students are again asked to listen while each word is pronounced to determine which syllable is being stressed and to see if they notice any similarity among all the second syllables. They should notice that all stressed second syllables have two vowels. From their observations they should be able to state the following generalization: *In two-syllable words the first syllable is usually stressed, except when the second syllable contains two vowels.*

In three-syllable words it is usually the first or second syllable that is accented as in *an´ces tor, cap´i tal, ho ri´zon.*

These skills for decoding words are useful for all children. However, for English Language Learners, the teacher must be especially certain to utilize the aural-oral approach before attempting to teach reading. These children must have the words that are to be decoded in both their listening and speaking vocabularies in order to make the proper grapheme-phoneme associations.

# TEACHING PHONICS

## GUIDELINES FOR EXEMPLARY PHONICS INSTRUCTION

Phonics instruction needs to excite and stimulate language learning. Children need to understand the joy in being able to manipulate the sounds and letters of their language to create words. As you have seen, phonics instruction that is going to be most useful to children requires careful thought and planning. The instruction need not use worksheets, nor should it be a chore or a bore. Authors of many different commercial programs aim to help teachers with this thoughtful planning by providing them with scripted teacher manuals with accompanying student materials. But how can we be sure that these materials are the best to use?

Fortunately, there are some research-based guidelines for exemplary phonics instruction. These guidelines can provide a framework for designing phonics programs. If teachers must use a commercial phonics program, these guidelines can be helpful when examining the materials that comprise the program.

Exemplary phonics instruction:

1. Builds on what children already know about reading such as how print functions, what stories are and how they work, and the purpose for reading.

2. Builds on a foundation of phonological awareness (see Chapter 7).
3. Is clear and direct. That is, the explanations make sense, and the teacher uses demonstrations to help children better understand how to apply what they are learning.
4. Is integrated into a total reading program. In terms of explicit, formal instruction, this means that no more than 15–20 minutes per day is allotted to it. Likewise, children are provided with many reading and writing opportunities to apply their phonics knowledge.
5. Focuses on reading words rather than learning rules. To help children see that the purpose of phonics is to acquire words, children need to be taught how to look for patterns in words rather than how to memorize "rules."
6. Leads to automatic word identification. The purpose of phonics is to help children acquire a large store of words so that they can read with greater ease. They need much meaningful practice so that they can use these words instantaneously while reading.[10]

## EXPLICIT AND IMPLICIT PHONICS INSTRUCTION

**Explicit phonics instruction**
Each sound associated with a letter in the word is pronounced in isolation, and then the sounds are blended together.

As you have started to discover, there are many techniques for teaching phonics. All can be classified as either explicit or implicit depending on how the teacher designs the overall instruction. In *explicit phonics instruction*, each sound associated with a letter in the word is pronounced in isolation and then blended together. A problem with this method is that it is very difficult to produce pure speech sounds in isolation. As a result, what usually takes place in the classroom is the following: The teacher shows the children the word *cat,* points to the letter *c* and says that it stands for the sound *cuh.* The teacher then points to the letter *a* in the word *cat* and says it stands for the sound *ah* and then points to the letter *t* and says it stands for the sound *tuh.* The children are then told to blend *cuh ah tuh* together to get *cat.* Even though *cuh ah tuh* does not sound like *cat,* children are supposed to be able to recognize the word *cat* from this method.

**Implicit phonics instruction**
Does not present sounds associated with letters in isolation. Children listen to words that begin with a particular sound; then they state another word that begins with the same sound.

*Implicit phonics instruction*, on the other hand, does not present sounds associated with letters in isolation. The class is presented with a list of words that all begin with the same initial consonant such as the following:

girl   game   get

The teacher helps the children to recognize that all the words begin with the same letter *g.* Then the children are asked to listen carefully to the beginning sound of each word. The teacher pronounces each word and tells the children that the letter *g* stands for the sound at the beginning of the words *girl, game, get.* The children are then often asked to look around the room for other

---

[10]Stahl, S. "Saying the 'p' Word: Nine Guidelines for Exemplary Phonics Instruction." *The Reading Teacher 45*(1992): 618–25. Stahl, S., A. Duffy-Hester, & K. Stahl. "Everything You Wanted to Know About Phonics (but were afraid to ask). *Reading Research Quarterly, 33*(1998): 338–55.

words that begin with the letter *g* or like *game.* (Usually, the teacher has pictures of items around the room that begin with the letter *g*.)

It appears that many teachers use a combination of both explicit and implicit phonics instruction. The important thing to remember is that any method that helps children unlock words as quickly as possible should be used and that phonics instruction gives children the power and independence they need to pronounce unfamiliar words. The key, of course, is for children to overlearn words after they have sounded them out a number of times so that they will become part of their sight vocabulary. In other words, phonics is one way for children to develop a store of words.

### Special Note

Some writers use the terms *synthetic phonics* to refer to explicit phonics instruction and *analytic phonics* to refer to implicit phonics instructions.

As we show in Figure 10.2, we need to use either explicit or implicit instruction when we want children to know about a certain phonics element. This instruction needs to be coupled with demonstrations when we want children to actually use this knowledge when reading. That is, we need to model for them how they can use what they just acquired. ▪

## SEVEN TEACHING STRATEGIES

There are several ways to teach phonics. The instructional purpose is what guides the selection of the specific teaching strategy we choose for any given lesson. Here are seven suggestions:

### 1. Teach Word Recognition Strategies

It is important that teachers be aware of the different word recognition strategies and the purpose for each so that effective teaching can take place. For example, a teacher must realize that helping children to become proficient in phonics will not help them to be good readers unless they have developed a stock of vocabulary and have adequate concept development. A child may be able to decode all the words in a passage, but as stated in Chapter 1, this child would not be reading unless he or she could determine the meaning of the passage. A teacher not only should be aware of the different strategies for figuring out word pronunciation and meanings but also should recognize that some strategies work better with different children. This advice should not, however, preclude teachers from assisting children in becoming proficient in their use of all the strategies and from helping children to determine which strategy or strategies are best to use in a specific situation. Usually, a combination of strategies is used.

#### • *Word Recognition Strategies for Pronunciation*

When we read, we are intent on constructing the message and appear to do so automatically and in one step. We rarely notice the individual letters, groups of letters, or even every word if we are good readers. It isn't until we stumble on an unfamiliar word that we become aware of the individual letters that are

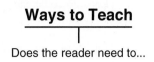

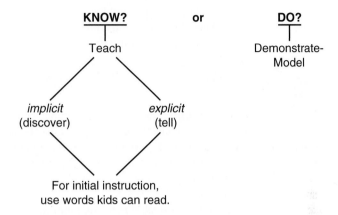

**Implicit = word to sound ⟶ no distortion**

**Explicit = sound to word ⟶ easier for some**

**FIGURE 10.2   Consideration for Teaching Phonics**
Based on D. Durkin, *Teaching Them to Read*, 6th ed. Boston: Allyn & Bacon, 1993.

grouped together to form a word. We stopped reading because the word we stumbled on has interfered with the message. The question is: Do you remember what you do when a word interferes with your understanding of what you are reading? Make a list before reading further.

*Word recognition* is necessary to be able to read. No one would disagree with that statement; however, people do disagree on what word recognition encompasses. We define word recognition as a twofold process that includes both the identification of printed symbols by some method so that the word can be pronounced and the attachment or association of meaning to the word. To understand better the concept that word recognition is a twofold process, there are a number of strategies that can be used to figure out how to pronounce a word as well as to determine its meaning, and these strategies are not necessarily the same.

Let's list those techniques that can help us to figure out the pronunciation of words:

1. Phonic analysis and synthesis
2. Whole word or "look and say"
3. Asking someone
4. Structural analysis and synthesis
5. Looking up the pronunciation in the dictionary

> **Word recognition**
> A twofold process that includes both the identification of printed symbols by some method so that the word can be pronounced and the association of meaning to the word can be applied.

Let's do some exercises containing nonsense and actual words. Read the following sentence:

I don't like *cland* food.

You should have stumbled on the nonsense word *cland.* Imagine that you do not know that *cland* is a nonsense word. Let's look at the kinds of strategies we could and could *not* use to help us pronounce a word *independently.*

**Phonic analysis**
The breaking down of a word into its component parts.

*Strategy 1:* *Phonic analysis* and *phonic synthesis*

*Definition:* Phonics is a decoding technique that depends on students' being able to make the proper grapheme (letter)–phoneme (sound) correspondences. *Analysis* has to do with the breaking down of something into its component parts. *Synthesis* has to do with the building up of the parts of something into a whole.

**Phonic synthesis**
The building up of the component parts of a word into a whole.

*Analysis:* Break down *cland* into the blend *cl* and the phonogram *and.*
We have met the blend *cl* before in such words as *climb* and *club.*
We have met the phonogram *and* before in such words as *sand* and *band.*
We therefore know the pronunciations of *cl* and *and.*

*Synthesis:* Blend together the *cl* and *and.*

Using this technique, we should be able to pronounce *cland* or at least gain an approximation of its pronunciation.

**Whole word or "look and say" method**
A word recognition technique in which a child's attention is directed to a word and then the word is said.

*Strategy 2:* *Whole word* or *"look and say"* method

*Definition:* The whole word or "look and say" method, which is also referred to as the sight method, has to do with the teacher's or any other individual's directing a student's attention to a word and then saying the word. The student must make an association between the oral word and the written word, and he or she shows this by actually saying the word.

This technique is a useful word recognition strategy that helps us to learn to pronounce words, but it will not help us to figure out the pronunciation of unfamiliar words independently.

*Strategy 3:* Ask someone to pronounce the word for you.

This request could be made, but doing so would be similar to using the "look and say" method, and it would not help us to figure out the word independently.

*Strategy 4: Structural* analysis and synthesis (word parts)

*Definition:* Structural analysis and synthesis have to do with the breaking down (analysis) and building up (synthesis) of word parts such as prefixes, suffixes, roots (bases), and combining forms.

Structural analysis is most often used in conjunction with phonic analysis. Knowledge of word parts such as prefixes, suffixes, and roots helps us to isolate the root of an unfamiliar word. After the root of a word is isolated, phonic analysis is applied. If the word parts are familiar ones, then we can blend them together to come up with the pronunciation of the word.

Structural analysis is a helpful word recognition technique that can aid with the pronunciation of words, but it will not help us to figure out the pronunciation of *cland* unless we apply phonic analysis because *cland* as a nonsense word is an unfamiliar root (base) word.

Let's see how we would go about figuring out how to pronounce the italicized word in the following sentence using structural analysis and synthesis.

The salesperson said that the goods were not *returnable.*

> **Structural analysis**
> A technique for the breaking down of a word into word parts such as prefixes, suffixes, roots, and combining forms.

*Structural Analysis:* Break down the word into its parts to isolate the root.

re   turn   able

If we had encountered *re* before and if we had encountered *able* before, we should know how to pronounce them. After we have isolated *turn,* we may recognize it as a familiar word and know how to pronounce it.

> **Structural synthesis**
> A technique for building up of word parts into a whole.

*Structural Synthesis:* Blend together *re, turn,* and *able.*

If *turn* is not a familiar root word for us, then we could apply phonic analysis to it and after that blend it together with the prefix *re* and the suffix *able.*

*Strategy 5:* Look up the pronunciation in the dictionary.

This is a viable method, but you may not have a dictionary handy, and by the time you look up the pronunciation of the word, you may have lost the gist of what you were reading.

### • *Word Recognition Strategies for Word Meaning*

Being able to pronounce a word is important, but this does not guarantee that we will thereby know its meaning. Word recognition is a twofold process: pronunciation and meaning. After we have pronounced a word, we have to associate the word with one in our listening vocabulary in order to determine the meaning of the word; that is, we need to have heard the word before and know what it means. Obviously, the larger our stock of listening vocabulary, the better able we will be to decipher the word. However, even though we can pronounce a word such as *misanthropic,* that doesn't mean that we can associate any meaning to it. If we have never heard the word before, it would not be in our listening vocabulary; therefore, the pronunciation would not act as a stimulus and trigger an association with a word that we have stored in our memory bank. Sometimes the process happens in the reverse, that is, we know the meaning of the word yet have difficulty pronouncing it. Sometimes pronunciation is not essential and other times it is. Let's see the techniques that we can use to help us unlock words that we have never encountered before.

---

**Context**
The words surrounding a particular word that can shed light on its meaning.

---

*Strategy 1:*   Context

By *context* we mean the words surrounding a particular word that can help shed light on its meaning. (Context clues can be very helpful in determining the meanings of words, especially words with multiple meanings, and because of their importance, special emphasis is given to this area in Chapter 11.) Read the following sentence:

Even though my *trank* was rather long, I wouldn't take out one word.

From the context of the sentence you know that the nonsense word *trank* must somehow refer to a sentence, paragraph, paper, or report of some kind. Even though you have never encountered *trank* before, the context of the sentence did throw light on it. You know from the word order or position of the word (syntax) that *trank* must be a noun, and words such as *word* and *long* give you meaning (semantic) clues to the word itself. There are times, however, when context is not too helpful and other strategies must be used.

*Strategy 2:*   Structural analysis and synthesis for word meaning

Read the following sentence:

We asked the *misanthrope* to leave.

From the position of the word *misanthrope* in the sentence, we know that it is a noun; however, there is not enough information to help us figure out the meaning of *misanthrope.* Structural analysis could be very useful in situations where there are insufficient context clues, and the word consists of a number of word parts.

*Analysis:*   Break down *misanthrope* into its word parts.

*Mis* means either "wrong" or "hate," and *anthropo* means "humankind."

*Synthesis:*   Put together the word parts. It doesn't make sense to say, "Wrong humankind," so it must be *hate* and *humankind.* Since *misanthrope* is a noun, the meaning of *misanthrope* would have to be "hater of humankind."

Structural analysis is a powerful tool, but it is dependent on your having knowledge of word parts and their meanings at your fingertips. If you do not have these available, you need another strategy.

***Strategy 3:*** Ask someone the meaning of the word.

This may be the most convenient if someone is available who knows the meaning of the word.

***Strategy 4:*** Look up the meaning in the dictionary.

If you cannot figure out the word independently rather quickly so that your train of thought is not completely broken, the dictionary is a valuable tool for word meanings.

Let's list those techniques that can help us figure out the meaning of words:

1. Context of a sentence
2. Structural analysis and synthesis
3. Asking someone
4. Looking up the meaning in the dictionary

There are times when it is possible for context clues to help with the correction of mispronounced words that are in the listening vocabulary of the reader but not yet in his or her reading vocabulary. Here is such an example. A student is asked to read the following sentence:

The child put on her coat.

He read the sentence as follows:

The *chilld* put on her coat.

He then self-corrected and reread the sentence correctly. What took place? The first pronunciation *chilld* was obtained from graphic clues. As the student continued to read, the context of the sentence indicated that the mispronounced word should be *child* rather than *chilld*. Since *child* was in the student's listening vocabulary, he was able to self-correct the mispronunciation. In this case, the context clues helped him to correct the mispronunciation of *child*.

It is important to state that he would not have been able to self-correct if the word *child* had not been in his listening vocabulary and if he had not heard it correctly pronounced.

Teachers should stress to their students that phonics usually only gives an approximation of the way a word is pronounced. Often readers must rely on sentence meaning and their familiarity with the spoken word to be able to pronounce it correctly.

**Special Note**

Many English Language Learners may pronounce a number of words incorrectly because they have heard them mispronounced or because they have difficulty producing the sounds. However, in spite of this, they may know the meanings of the words. Be careful to determine the cause of the child's mispronunciation; that is, is the mispronunciation due to a pronunciation problem or a comprehension problem? Using the pronunciation guide in Appendix C should prove helpful in making this determination. ▪

**Sample Lesson: Word Recognition Strategies**

One way to ascertain the strategies children use to gain both pronunciation and meaning of words is to provide a brainstorming session with the entire class. To prepare for the session, display two sheets of chart paper for all to see. Say something like, "Good readers sometimes see words that they do not know. When this happens, they try different ideas to figure out the word. What are some strategies you use when you see words you don't know?" As students share their ideas, write those that relate to pronunciation on one piece of chart paper and those that relate to meaning on the other. Remember that as the teacher, you always reserve the right to add to the lists. Therefore, if there are some strategies that students fail to mention, add them to the list. Once the lists have been created, see if students can figure out why you put the various strategies on different pieces of chart paper by saying something like, "All of the ideas on each of these charts are alike in some way. I think you might be able to tell me. Any volunteers?" If students cannot tell you, tell them! Write "Strategies for Gaining Pronunciation" and "Strategies for Gaining Meaning" as headings on the appropriate charts. Close the lesson by saying something like, "These are excellent reading strategies! I knew you were good readers and these charts show me that I was correct. You may have learned some new strategies to try when you come to a problem word. I am going to post these in our room as reminders. Make sure that when you are reading today you take a look at the charts to help yourself figure out any words you don't know."

**2. Teach from Whole to Part Using Nursery Rhymes and Children's Literature**

Getting a sense of the whole is often a sure way to help children understand the parts. There is much meaningful association because the learners see how the parts relate to the overall text. There are a couple of ways to implement whole-to-part instruction. These are as follows:

- *Whole-Part-Whole with Nursery Rhymes or Poems.*
  The inverted triangle shown in Figure 10.3 is one way we think about whole-to-part instruction. Using this diagram, then, a teacher might begin with a nursery rhyme such as Humpty Dumpty that is displayed on a chart large enough for all to see. After reading the entire text a few times, the teacher invites the children to read along. The children need to know the rhyme well in order to complete the other parts of the triangle.

  The second step involves writing each line of the rhyme on a sentence strip. Read the sentence strips to the children, placing them in a pocket holder for all to see. Ideally, the chart containing the nursery rhyme is next to the pocket chart. Point out (if no student tells you) that the two are the same. In turn, take each sentence strip out of the holder and place it on top of the one shown on the original chart. Reread the rhyme with the children, pointing to each word. Having modeled the process, ask the children to close their eyes while you take the sentence strips off the chart. Mix up the sentences and distribute them to some volunteers. In turn, each volunteer comes to the chart and places the sentence over the matching sentence on the chart. Reread the rhyme with the children.

The third step helps children to better understand wordness. Using a pair of scissors, cut each sentence strip apart and ask the children to count the number of words that fall on the floor. They can then reassemble the rhyme by placing the words over the matching words in the chart.

A fourth step involves helping children to understand that words are made of letters. Make word cards for some of the words shown in the rhyme, or use the words from the cut-apart sentences. Tell the children that you are going to cut apart a given word to show them how many letters make up that word. Then cut apart each word.

A fifth step involves phonic elements. Choose the words that focus on the phonic element you want them to notice and use these words to teach

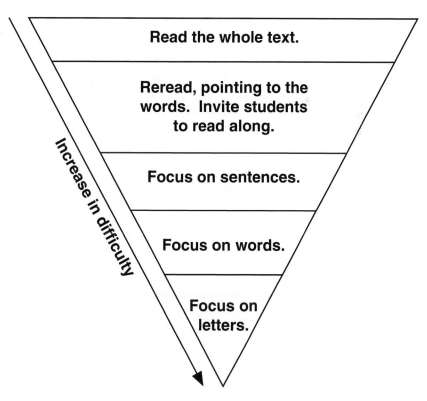

**FIGURE 10.3**   Whole-to-Part Phonics Instruction
*Source*: Opitz, 1995

the skill. For example, if you want children to learn about the initial consonant "h", select those words and use either explicit or implicit phonics instruction (described above) to teach them this initial consonant.

One important reminder is in order. Make sure that children reread the text every session. In this way, they will begin to see that all of the parts relate to the text.

- *Whole-Part-Whole with Children's Literature.*[11] Sometimes, using an entire children's literature selection to teach phonics is desirable. The procedures listed in Figure 10.4 will be of help in this process. Although phonics is the major focus, you will notice that experiencing the book for enjoyment is the first step.

Of utmost importance is identifying the specific phonic element you want to teach and rounding up the children's books that contain enough examples so that children can apply what they have learned when reading a text. The following list identifies some books that can be used to teach both long and short vowels.

*Children's Literature for Whole-Part-Whole Phonics Instruction*

> *Long a*: Cohen, C. L. *How Many Fish?* New York: HarperCollins, 1998.
> *Long e:* Milgrim, D. *See Pip Point.* New York: Atheneum, 2003.
> *Long i:* Ziefert, H. *A New House for Mole and Mouse.* New York: Puffin, 1987.
> *Long o:* Bauer, M.D. *Rain.* New York: Aladdin, 2004.
> *Long u:* Segal, L. *Tell Me a Trudy.* New York: Farrar, Straus, Giroux, 1977.
> *Short a:* Carle, E. *From Head to Toe.* New York: HarperCollins, 1997.
> *Short e:* Ets, M. *Elephant in a Well.* New York: Viking, 1972.
> *Short i:* Meister, C. *When Tiny was Tiny.* New York: Puffin, 1999.
> *Short o:* Foster, A. & Erickson, B. *A Mop for Pop.* New York: Barron's, 1991.
> *Short u:* Lewison, W.C. *Buzz Said the Bee.* New York: Scholastic, 1992.

### 3. Use Word Sorts

Sorting is a way of categorizing pictures or words with similar sound features. Pictures or words can be sorted into several categories such as those that rhyme, beginning sounds, phonograms, and vowel sounds. Sorting activities "enable children to make some connections about the ways they think about word elements."

There are two basic ways to have children sort. In a *closed sort*, you give students the categories and ask them to sort a given number of cards. This type of sort causes convergent thinking. In an *open sort*, you invite students to create the categories and tell you the names of the categories. This type of sort encourages divergent thinking. Both types of sorts are of value and will help you to see what students know about words. However, open sorts lend even more insight into what students are noticing on their own—what they have internalized.

---

[11]Trachtenberg, P. "Using Children's Literature to Enhance Phonics Instruction." *The Reading Teacher 43*: 1990. 648-654.

---

**FIGURE 10.4   Whole - Part - Whole Phonics Instruction**

---

*Whole*

---

- Read aloud.
- Model expressive reading.
- Promote enjoyment.
- Provide extension activities:
  - dramatization
  - compare/contrast

*Part*

---

- Focus on phonic element.
- Use portion from text.
- Children participate.
- Provide visual reminder.
- Word slotter: build words.

*Whole*

---

- Present new book, same phonic element.
- Children read the story:
  - choral reading
  - partner reading
  - individual reading

---

Based on Trachtenburg, 1990.

Here are some suggested steps when using word sorts:

1. Model what you expect students to do.
2. Give children several cards to sort into contrasting categories.
3. Provide practice with your guidance.
4. Have students work with one another to sort.

### 4. Teach Students How to Decode by Analogy

Basically, teaching students how to decode by analogy involves having them use a word they know to identify a word they do not know. For example, a child might know the word *cat*, yet not know the word *bat*. Assuming that both words are in the child's listening vocabulary, the teacher asks if *bat* looks like any word that the child knows. If not, the teacher writes the word the child does know, *cat*, right above *bat*. He has the child read *cat*. Most often, the child will see how the two words are the same and will read *bat* without additional help. Sometimes a prompt is provided such as, "If this word is *cat*, then this one has to be _____" to get the child to decode the word.

### 5. Use Writing

Perhaps one of the best ways for children to apply what they know about phonics and to learn more about it is for them to write. Regardless of what we *think* children know about phonics or what we *think* we taught them, their writing will show us what they have actually internalized to the point of being able to apply any given skill. For example, after learning about the "*ai*" spelling for long *a*, children may use it to spell all words having the long *a* sound. Just like when they are learning spoken language, they overgeneralize.

We suggest giving each student a blank book and using class time for writing at least once a day. The books serve as evidence of the children's performance and growth over time.

### 6. Construct Words

Making words is a manipulative word-building activity designed by Cunningham.[12] This activity involves having children put letter cards together to form words and it can be used to either teach or reinforce building words with phonograms. Figure 10.5 provides an example.

### 7. Use Prompts When Reading with Students

As expert readers, we know that there are several strategies we can employ to figure out unknown words. We want to pass this expertise along to students so that they, too, can be independent readers. We want to help them to develop what Clay calls a "self-extending system."[13] Prompting is one way to help them to develop this system.

Knowing the type of prompt to provide depends on what we know about both the student and the word that is posing difficulty. Table 10.1 gives some guidance.

## NOTING STUDENT PROGRESS

As we mention throughout this text, assessment drives instruction. This is as true for phonics as it is for any other aspect of reading. Three questions continually surface: What do I want to know? Why do I want to know? How can I best discover? In terms of phonics, then, we want to know if students are acquiring phonics skills and if they are applying them in their everyday reading experiences. We want to know this because application is the important part of phonics instruction. It shows that the children are making the connection with instruction and their reading, which is the purpose for the instruction. We can discover the degree to which they are using what they know by employing the brief informal tests presented earlier in this chapter. We can also use observation and the checklist shown in Figure 10.6 to document what we see. We can listen to children taking a running record (see Chapter 8) and analyze it to see how the reader used the visual cue when reading.

The *Tile Test*[14] is another meaningful way to assess children's phonics ability and metalinguistic awareness.

---

[12]P. Cunningham & J. Cunningham, "Making Words: Enhancing the Invented Spelling-decoding Connection." *The Reading Teacher, 46*: 106-115.

[13]M. Clay. *The Early Detection of Reading Difficulties.* (Portsmouth, NH: Heinemann.)

[14]Complete information including the actual test and recording sheet can be found in *The Reading Teacher, 58*: 42–52.

---

**FIGURE 10.5   Make Words Lesson**

---

Letters:  a   d   n   s   t
Words:  at   an   and   Dan   tan   ant   sat   sad   sand   stand

---

**Name letters and their common sounds:** Before beginning to make words, have the students hold up each letter, name it, and say its common sound. Have the students show both the lower-case and capital letters.

**Make words:** Have the students make these words, then send one student to make each word using the big letters. DO NOT wait for everyone to make the word before sending someone up. Keep the lesson fast-paced and the students will pay better attention. When the word is made with the big letters, ask everyone to check their words and fix them if necessary.

1. Take 2 letters and make **at**. We are **at** school.
2. Take the **t** away and add a different letter to make **an**. I ate **an** apple.
3. Add a letter to **an** and you can spell **and**. I like apples **and** bananas.
4. Now we are going to do a trick with **and**. Move the letters in **and** around so that they spell **Dan**. Stretch out **Dan** and listen for where you hear the **D** and the **a** and the **n**. (Look for a student who has **Dan** spelled with a capital letter **D**, and send that student to make **Dan** with big letters.) My cousin's name is **Dan**.
5. Take the **D** away and add a letter to spell **tan**. I got a **tan** at the beach.
6. Now let's do the "move the letters around" trick with **tan** to spell **ant**. Stretch out **ant** with me and listen for where you hear the sounds. The **ant** is tiny.
7. Let's start over and make another 3-letter word, **sat**. The boy **sat** down.
8. Take the **t** away, add another letter, and you can spell **sad**. He was very **sad**.
9. Now we are going to spell a 4-letter word. Add 1 letter to **sad** and you can spell **sand**. Let's all say **sand** and listen for the letter we need to add. She digs in the **sand**.
10. The last word in every lesson is the secret word. Add 1 letter to **sand** and you can spell another word. I am going to look and see if anyone has figured out the secret word. (Give them no more than a minute to try to figure it out and then say a sentence with the secret word. Everyone **stand** up.) Have someone make **stand** with the big letters.

**Sort:** Collect the letters, then read with the students all the words in the pocket chart. Next, have them sort the words into columns according to their first letter.

| at | sat | Dan | tan |
|----|-----|-----|-----|
| an | sad | | |
| and | sand | | |
| ant | stand | | |

**Transfer:** Say some words in sentences and have the students repeat the words and decide what letter they begin with.

| dog | top | sun | add | apple | teacher | doctor | sister |
|-----|-----|-----|-----|-------|---------|--------|--------|

From "Making Words: Enhancing the Inverted Spelling-Decoding Connection," by P. Cunningham and J. Cunningham. *The Reading Teacher,* 46: 106–115.

**TABLE 10.1    Word Analysis Prompts (based on Gunning, 2006)**

| Strategy | Use When | Example Prompt |
|---|---|---|
| Word part a student can pronounce | The unknown word has a part you know the student can pronounce | "There's a part of that word you can say. Find it and say it." |
| Analogy | The unknown word is similar to the word you know the student knows. | "This word is like another one you know." |
| Each sound | The student has difficulty with chunking words, yet can figure out the word using each sound. | "Say each sound in this word." |
| Context | The student is weak in using phonics clues | "Read to the end of the sentence and ask yourself what would make sense." |

---

**FIGURE 10.6    Diagnostic Checklist for Word Recognition Skills**

Student's Name: _____

Grade: _____

Teacher: _____

                                                                   Yes                No

1. The student uses
   a. context clues.
   b. picture clues (graphs, maps, charts).

2. The student asks someone to state the word.

3. The student uses the dictionary to try to unlock unknown words.

4. The student uses phonic analysis by recognizing
   a. consonants.
      (1) single consonants: initial, final.
      (2) consonant blends (clusters) (*br, sl, cl, st,* and so on).
      (3) consonant digraphs (*th, sh, ph, ch,* and so on).
      (4) silent consonants (*kn, gn, pn*).
   b. vowels.
      (1) short vowels (*cot, can, get,* and so on).
      (2) long vowels (*go, we, no,* and so on).
      (3) final silent *e* (*bake, tale, role*).

*(continued)*

Student's Name: _____

Grade: _____

Teacher: _____

|  | Yes | No |
|---|---|---|
| (4) vowel digraphs (*ea, oa, ee, ai,* and so on). | | |
| (5) diphthongs (*oi, oy*). | | |
| c. the effect of *r* on the preceding vowel. | | |
| d. special letters and sounds (*y, c, g,* and *q*). | | |
| e. known phonograms or graphemic bases (a succession of graphemes that occurs with the same phonetic value in a number of words [*ight, id, at, ad, ack*]). | | |

5. The student is able to apply the following syllabication generalizations to words:

| | Yes | No |
|---|---|---|
| a. vowel consonant/consonant vowel generalization (*vc/cv*) (*but/ter, can/dy*). | | |
| b. vowel/consonant vowel generalization (v/cv) (*na/tive, ca/bin*). | | |
| c. special consonant *le* generalization (vc/cle) or (v/cle) (*ca/ble, can/dle*). | | |

6. The student is able to apply phonic analysis to syllabicated words with

| | Yes | No |
|---|---|---|
| a. an open syllable (*no/ble*). | | |
| b. a closed syllable (*can/dy*). | | |
| c. a vowel digraph (*re/main*). | | |
| d. a diphthong (*foi/ble*). | | |

7. The student is able to apply the following accent generalization to two-syllable words:

*Accent falls on the first syllable except when the second syllable has two vowels (tailor, career).*

| | Yes | No |
|---|---|---|
| | | |

8. The student is able to use structural analysis to recognize

| | Yes | No |
|---|---|---|
| a. compound words (*grandmother, caretaker*). | | |
| b. the root or base of a word (*turn, state*). | | |
| c. suffixes (*tion, al, ic, y*). | | |
| d. prefixes (*re, un, non*). | | |
| e. combining forms (*bio, cardio, auto*). | | |
| f. derivatives. | | |
| (1) root plus prefix (*return*). | | |
| (2) root plus suffix (*turned*). | | |
| (3) root plus prefix and suffix (*returned*). | | |

Based on Gunning, 2006.

# SUMMARY

In this chapter we present information about helping children to acquire and apply phonics knowledge. We provide an explanation of the importance of decoding in reading along with a definition of phonics. Understanding terminology associated with phonics is important, which is why we discuss several phonics terms, provide an informal test for each, and give some teaching suggestions for each one. There are specific guidelines that should be followed when teaching phonics as well as two orientations toward phonics instruction and these are explained. We then list and describe eight teaching strategies to use when designing meaningful phonics lessons. As with other aspects of reading, assessing phonics is important and we offer some suggestions for how to do that. Throughout this chapter, we emphasize that phonics needs to be taught in conjunction with much emphasis on reading connected text and reading comprehension.

# CHAPTER 10 KEY CONCEPTS

- Word recognition includes both the identification of printed symbols by some method so the words can be pronounced and the association of meaning to the words.
- There are a number of different word recognition strategies.
- Word recognition strategies for pronunciation include phonic analysis and synthesis, whole word or look and say, asking someone, structural analysis, and the dictionary.
- Word recognition strategies for word meaning include context, structural analysis, asking someone, and the dictionary.
- Phonemic awareness is necessary for auditory discrimination and to decode words.
- Knowledge of phonics helps students to be able to decode words independently.

- Auditory and visual discrimination are necessary for phonics.
- Students should learn a sequential development of phonic skills in the early primary grades.
- Studies continue to stress the importance of teaching beginning readers systematic phonics development.
- Phonics helps students gain an approximation of the pronunciation of a word.
- There are specific guidelines for exemplary phonics programs.
- Both explicit and implicit approaches to teaching phonics are of value.
- There are many phonics teaching strategies.

# SUGGESTIONS FOR THOUGHT QUESTIONS AND ACTIVITIES

1. You have been appointed to a special primary-grade reading committee. Your task is to help teachers better understand the role that phonics plays in the word recognition process. How would you go about doing this?

2. You have been asked to give a workshop on creative activities that would help correct some students' word recognition problems. What are some activities you would present?

3. The administration in your school district has asked you to develop criterion-referenced tests for specific word recognition skills. What kind of tests would you construct for a primary grade? For an intermediate grade?

4. You have a child in your class who seems to have great difficulty retaining information. He needs extensive practice in order to overlearn his letters and words. You need to develop some activities that would be fun and

that would help this child in a primary grade overlearn his initial consonants. What kind of activities would you develop to help this child?

5. Present a lesson that would help a primary-grade student correct a word recognition problem.

6. Present a lesson that would help you to determine the syllabication skills of an intermediate-grade level student.

7. Your state legislators are proposing a bill to mandate the teaching of phonics in all schools. How do you feel about this? Prepare a talk expressing your views.

## INTERNET ACTIVITIES

Choose a search engine and search for websites related to phonics. Select one website from your search that provides you with some additional information about phonics instruction. Download and print out at least one meaningful teaching idea. (Be sure to identify both the search engine you used and the website you selected.)

## SELECTED BIBLIOGRAPHY

Adams, Marilyn Jager. *Beginning to Read: Thinking and Learning About Print.* Cambridge, MA: MIT Press, 1990.

Blachowicz, Camille L. Z., and Peter Fisher. "Vocabulary Instruction," in Michael L. Kamil et al., eds. *Handbook of Reading Research,* Vol. III. Mahwah, NJ: Lawrence Erlbaum, 2000.

Chall, Jeanne S. *Learning to Read: The Great Debate,* 2d ed. New York: McGraw-Hill, 1983.

_____. "Two Vocabularies for Reading: Recognition and Reading." *The Nature of Vocabulary Acquisition,* ed. M. G. McKeown and M. E. Curtis, pp. 7–17. Hillsdale, NJ: Erlbaum, 1987.

Cunningham, P. *Systematic Sequential Phonics They Use.* Greensboro, NC: Carson-Dellosa, 2000.

Durkin, D. *Teaching Them To Read,* 6th ed. Boston: Allyn & Bacon, 1993.

Durkin, Dolores. *The Decoding Ability of Elementary School Students.* Reading Education Report No. 49. Champaign, IL: Center for the Study of Reading, University of Illinois, 1984.

Fry, E. "The Most Common Phonograms." *The Reading Teacher, 51* (1998): 620–22.

Gruber, Barbara. "Boost Learning with Word Walls." Teaching Pre-K, 830 (1999): 64–5.

Gunning, T. *Assessing and Correcting Reading and Writing Difficulties,* 3rd ed. Boston: Allyn & Bacon, 2006.

Johnson, Dale D. *Vocabulary in the Elementary and Middle Grades.* Boston: Allyn and Bacon, 2001.

Nagy, William E., and Judith A. Scott. "Vocabulary Processes," in Michael L. Kamil et al., eds. *Handbook of Reading Research,* Vol. III. Mahwah, NJ: Lawrence Erlbaum, 2000.

Rubin, Dorothy. *Gaining Word Power,* 6th ed. Boston: Allyn and Bacon, 2000.

_____. *Phonics Skills & Strategies in a Balanced Reading Program* (Levels 1—4 series). Torrance, CA: Fearon Teacher Aids, 1998.

_____. "Vocabulary Development in the Language Arts Program," in *Elementary Language Arts,* 6th ed. Boston: Allyn and Bacon, 2000.

_____. *Vocabulary Skills & Strategies in a Balanced Reading Program.* Torrance, CA: Fearon Teacher Aids, 1998.

Stahl, S. "Saying the 'p' Word: Nine Guidelines for Exemplary Phonics Instruction." *The Reading Teacher 45* (1992): 618–25.

Stahl, S., A. Duffy-Hester, & K. Stahl. "Everything You Wanted to Know About Phonics (but were afraid to ask). *Reading Research Quarterly, 33*(1998): 338–55.

Trachtenberg, P. "Using Children's Literature to Enhance Phonics Instruction." *The Reading Teacher 43* (1990): 648–54.

**Children's Literature Cited**

Bauer, M. D. *Rain.* New York: Aladdin, 2004.

Carle, E. *From Head to Toe.* New York: HarperCollins, 1997.

Cohen, C. L. *How Many Fish?* New York: Harper-Collins, 1998.

Ets, M. *Elephant in a Well*. New York: Viking, 1972.

Foster, A., & Erickson, B. *A Mop for Pop*. New York: Barron's, 1991.

Lewison, W. C. *Buzz Said the Bee*. New York: Scholastic, 1992.

Meister, C. *When Tiny Was Tiny*. New York: Puffin, 1999.

Milgrim, D. *See Pip Point*. New York: Atheneum, 2003.

Segal, L. *Tell Me a Trudy*. New York: Farrar, Straus, Giroux, 1977.

Ziefert, H. *A New House for Mole and Mouse*. New York: Puffin, 1987.

# 11

# Helping Children Acquire and Apply Vocabulary

# Scenario: Mr. Jackson and Vocabulary Expansion

A number of years ago, Mr. Jackson had a student who taught him an important lesson. Mr. Jackson remembers feeling dismayed when one rather big, husky student in his sixth grade reading class said to him, "Mr. Jackson, I have a great amount of animosity toward you."

Mr. Jackson was upset because he thought that he had very good rapport with the student. He thought that the student enjoyed his reading class. Because the student's statement did not ring true, Mr. Jackson decided to question him.

"Craig," Mr. Jackson said, "Is anything wrong? Have I done anything to offend you in any way?"

Craig appeared perplexed. He looked Mr. Jackson straight in the eye and said, "No, I like your class. I look forward to coming to it."

"That is what I thought," said Mr. Jackson. "So why did you say that you disliked me?"

"I didn't," said Craig. "I said that I like you a lot. I said just the opposite."

It became clear to Mr. Jackson that Craig apparently did not know the meaning of *animosity*. When Mr. Jackson asked Craig why he used the word *animosity*, Craig replied, "I like the way it sounds, so I use it a lot."

Because Craig is such an imposing-looking young man, it could be that when he used the term *animosity* in relation to individuals, no one questioned him. It could also be that they, too, did not know the meaning of the word.

Mr. Jackson, who is an excellent teacher, always remembers his encounter with Craig. It helped him to realize that many students use words they can pronounce yet may not fully understand. Although Mr. Jackson knows that wide reading helps in vocabulary development, he feels that his students need more than this. He also knows that explicit instruction is necessary to help expand students' vocabulary.

As the scenario helps to illustrate, good vocabulary and good reading go hand in hand. Unless readers know the meanings of words, they will have difficulty understanding what they are reading. Simply knowing the meanings of the words will not ensure that individuals will be able to state the meanings of sentences, nor does knowing the meanings of sentences assure that readers can give the meanings of whole paragraphs. However, by not knowing the meanings of the words, the individual's chances of being able to read well are considerably lessened. Without an understanding of words, comprehension is impossible.

As children advance in concept development, their vocabulary development must also advance because the two are interrelated (see Chapter 7). Children who are deficient in vocabulary will usually be deficient in concept development. Years ago, one researcher noted that "vocabulary is a key variable in reading comprehension and is a major feature of most tests of academic aptitude."[1] Investigators continue to confirm earlier findings: "Numerous researchers have noted that poor readers have smaller vocabularies than good

[1]Walter M. MacGinitie, "Language Development," in *Encyclopedia of Educational Research*, 4th ed. (London: Collier-Macmillan, 1969), p. 693.

readers. Indeed, vocabulary knowledge is one of the best single predictors of reading comprehension."[2]

Given these findings, how can we help children to expand their vocabulary knowledge? This question provides the focus for this chapter. Our purpose is to provide you with some background related to reading vocabulary development and some specific suggestions for helping students to acquire a large vocabulary.

## CHAPTER OBJECTIVES

By the end of this chapter, you should be able to . . .

- Discuss what is involved in acquiring a reading vocabulary.
- Explain what is meant by *vocabulary consciousness.*
- Explain three levels of knowing a word.
- Provide examples of types of words.
- Explain the two categories of sight words.
- Define terms associated with word parts.
- Explain guidelines for effective vocabulary instruction.
- Demonstrate one of the many teaching strategies.
- Explain how to document student progress in attaining a reading vocabulary.

## VOCABULARY DEVELOPMENT

### ACQUIRING VOCABULARY

Just how is it that we acquire our reading vocabulary? Certainly, explicit instruction is one way. In fact, the development of vocabulary is too important to the success of a child in school to be left to chance. We need to provide children with a planned vocabulary expansion program when they first enter school. "Direct vocabulary instruction is generally shown to result in an increase in both word knowledge and reading comprehension."[3]

For a vocabulary program to be successful, the teacher must recognize that individual differences exist between the amount and kinds of words that kindergarten and first-grade children have in their listening vocabulary (ability to understand a word when it is spoken). Some children come to school with a

---

[2]Meredyth Daneman, "Individual Differences in Reading Skills," in *Handbook of Reading Research,* Vol. II. Rebecca Barr, Michael L. Kamil, Peter Mosenthal, and P. David Pearson, eds. (New York: Longman, 1991), p. 524.

[3]Adams, M. J. *Beginning to Read: Thinking and Learning about Print.* Cambridge, MA: MIT Press, 1990, p. 29. Hickman, P., S. Pollard-Durodola, and S. Vaughn. 2004. "Storybook Reading: Improving Vocabulary and Comprehension for English Language Learners." *Reading Teacher,* 57: 720–730. National Reading Panel, 2000. See p. 464.

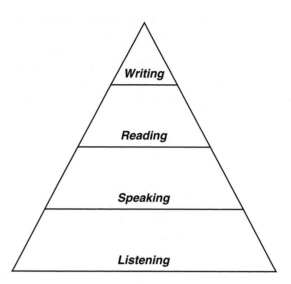

**FIGURE 11.1** Children's Vocabularies.

rich and varied vocabulary, whereas others have a more limited and narrow vocabulary.[4] This rich vocabulary can be used with their peers and at home, but it may not be useful in school. For example, some children may possess a large lexicon of street vocabulary and expressions, and some others may speak an English dialect that contains its own special expressions and vocabulary.

Young children's listening vocabulary is larger than their speaking vocabulary and much larger than their reading and writing vocabulary (see Figure 11.1). All four areas of vocabulary need to be developed. However, since children first learn language through the aural-oral approach, we need to make sure that we continue to expand their listening and speaking vocabularies.

If we learn 3000–4000 words each year, acquiring all of them via explicit instruction is impossible. Beyond instruction, then, there are three additional ways that we acquire words: wide reading, talking about words, and listening to others as they talk about words. Taken together, all of these routes to vocabulary acquisition help children to develop a vocabulary consciousness, the primary goal of a vocabulary program.

## VOCABULARY CONSCIOUSNESS

In the primary grades children are beginning to meet words that are spelled the same but have different meanings, based on their context in the sentence. Students learn that the word *saw* in "I saw Jennifer" does not carry the same

[4]Hart, B., and T. R. Risley (1995). *Meaningful Differences in the Everyday Experience of Young American Children.* Baltimore: Brookes.

**Vocabulary consciousness**
An awareness that words may have different meanings based on their context and a desire to increase one's vocabulary.

meaning as in "Andrew will help his uncle saw the tree." When primary-graders recognize that *saw, train, coat,* and many other words have different meanings based on surrounding words, they are beginning to build a *vocabulary consciousness*. This consciousness grows when they begin to ask about and look up the meanings of new words they come across in their everyday activities.

We can challenge primary-grade children's budding vocabulary consciousness in enjoyable ways. One way to do so is to use word riddles or fun-with-word activities. Some examples are:

1. From a six-letter word for what you put on bread, remove two letters to get what a goat does with his horns.
2. To a four-letter word for something liquid that falls from the sky, add two letters to make a kind of damage you can do by twisting a part of the body.
3. From a five-letter word for an animal with a shell, take one letter away to make a word for something that holds two pieces of wood together.
4. The plural of an insect, when you add a letter to it, becomes something you wear.

Answers: (1) butter, butt; (2) rain, sprain; (3) snail, nail; (4) ants, pants.

Another way to challenge primary-grade children and to help them to expand their vocabulary is through the learning of word parts. In the primary grades, children can learn about some prefixes, suffixes, and roots in order to expand their vocabulary.

As students become more advanced in reading in the intermediate grades, they encounter new contexts for words that previously only had one meaning. In the intermediate grades, students should be guided to a broadened understanding of vocabulary. If they are fascinated with words, they generally want to know the longest word in the dictionary, and many enjoy pronouncing funny or nonsense-sounding words such as *supercalifragilisticexpialidocious.* These students should be helped to:

1. Become aware of words they do not know.
2. Try to guess the meaning from the context and their knowledge of word parts.
3. Learn the most-used combining forms.
4. Jot down words that they do not know and look them up in the dictionary later.
5. Keep a notebook and write down the words they have yet to show understanding of in their vocabulary exercises. They can then continue to work on acquiring these words through additional study.
6. Learn to break words down into word parts in order to learn their meaning.
7. Maintain interest in wanting to expand vocabulary.

## LEVELS OF KNOWING A WORD

Some words are more difficult to acquire than others. We all appear to go through several levels of knowing a word. The first level is where we display no awareness of the word, neither recognizing it visually nor understanding it. Assuming that we continue to work to acquire the word, we then move into the

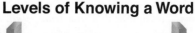

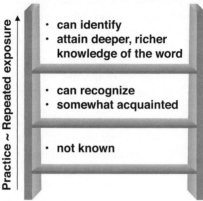

**FIGURE 11.2** Levels of Knowing a Word

second level, which is where we begin to be somewhat acquainted with the word. We can recognize it with some help. This is similar to being introduced to an individual and then seeing the person in another situation. If we are fortunate to be with someone who can give us a clue about who the person is, we can call the person by name and perhaps engage in a conversation. We *recognize* the person because we were prompted. The third level, and the one we strive to reach with words we feel are important, is the identification stage. At this level we can identify the word instantaneously, have a better understanding of it, and develop deeper meanings of the word. Take the word *catastrophe*, for example. While many of us are familiar with the word and can identify it without difficulty, 9/11 certainly helped us to develop a deeper meaning of the word. We show these levels in the ladder illustrated in Figure 11.2. Note that the way we move up the ladder is with much meaningful practice and repeated exposure.

## TYPES OF WORDS

When we think of teaching reading vocabulary, we need to remember that not all words are created equal. Try this exercise and see if you can determine which word in each group is the easiest for a reader to learn:

| *Group 1* | *Group 2* |
|---|---|
| ant | of |
| and | said |
| are | elephant |

Did you select *ant* from the first group and *elephant* from the second group? If so, you are correct because both are nouns. Nouns are easier to learn to read than other words because you can put an image with them. Even though elephant is a much longer word, it is much easier to picture than "of"! One reason so many young children can identify just about any name of any dinosaur, then, is that they are interested in knowing the dinosaur names and each name has a distinct image associated with it.

**Sight words**
Words we can identify instantaneously.

**High-frequency words**
Words that appear most often in children's texts.

**Prefix**
A letter or a sequence of letters added to the beginning of a root word.

**Suffix**
A letter or a sequence of letters added to the end of a root word.

**Affixes**
Prefixes and suffixes.

**Root**
Smallest unit of a word that can exist and retain its basic meaning.

**Derivatives**
Combinations of root words with either prefixes or suffixes or both.

## SIGHT VOCABULARY

*Sight words* are those words that we can identify without decoding; we know them instantaneously. All of us have our own personalized sight vocabulary because we have varied interests, which lead us to read texts associated with those interests. For example, an individual who is interested in sports would have a different personalized sight vocabulary than a person interested in music. This being said, when we talk of helping children to develop sight vocabulary, what we are referring to is *high-frequency* words. These are words that occur most often in children's books; hence, the label high-frequency. Different researchers have compiled high-frequency lists. Two of the most common lists are the Dolch list and the Fry Instant Word List. Because the Fry Instant Word List is more current, we provide a copy of the first 100 words in Figure 11.3.

## DEFINING WORD PART TERMS

There are many words in our language that combine with other words to form new words, for example, *grandfather* and *boardwalk* (compound words). You can also combine a root (base) word with a letter or a group of letters either at the beginning (*prefix*) or end (*suffix*) of the root word to form a new, related word, for example, *replay* and *played*. *Affix* is a term used to refer either to a prefix or a suffix.

In the words *replay* and *played, play* is a root or base, *re* is a prefix, and *ed* is a suffix. A *root* is the smallest unit of a word that can exist and retain its basic meaning. It cannot be subdivided any further. *Replay* is not a root word because it can be subdivided to *play*. *Play* is a root word because it cannot be divided further and still retain a meaning related to the root word.

*Derivatives* are combinations of root words with either prefixes or suffixes or both. *Combining forms* are usually defined as roots borrowed from another language that join together or that join with a prefix, a suffix, or both a prefix and a suffix to form a word. Many times the English combining forms are derived from Greek and Latin roots. In some vocabulary books, in which the major emphasis is on vocabulary expansion rather than on the naming of word parts, a *combining form* is defined in a more general sense to include any word part that can join with another word or word part to form a word or a new word.[5]

# TEACHING VOCABULARY

Learning vocabulary can be a fun and rewarding experience. Remember that the main goal of the vocabulary program is to help children develop a vocabulary consciousness. To do so, we need to remember to integrate vocabulary instruction across all content areas so that students can see the meaningful use of words in different contexts. We also need to provide them with enough repetition so that they can learn to identify many words. Finally, our instruction should be designed to use what students know to teach them something they

[5]Dorothy Rubin, *Gaining Word Power, 5th ed.* (Boston: Allyn & Bacon, 2000).

## FIGURE 11.3   The Instant Words* First Hundred

These are the most common words in English, ranked in frequency order. The first 25 make up about a third of all printed material. The first 100 make up about half of all written material. Is it any wonder that all students must learn to identify these words instantly and to spell them correctly also?

| Words 1–25 | Words 26–50 | Words 51–75 | Words 76–100 |
|---|---|---|---|
| the | or | will | number |
| of | one | up | no |
| and | had | other | way |
| a | by | about | could |
| to | word | out | people |
| in | but | many | my |
| is | not | then | than |
| you | what | them | first |
| that | all | these | water |
| it | were | so | been |
| he | we | some | call |
| was | when | her | who |
| for | your | would | oil |
| on | can | make | now |
| are | said | like | find |
| as | there | him | long |
| with | use | into | down |
| his | an | time | day |
| they | each | has | did |
| I | which | look | get |
| at | she | two | come |
| be | do | more | made |
| this | how | write | may |
| have | their | go | part |
| from | if | see | over |

**Common suffixes:** -s, -ing, -ed

*For additional instant words, see *The New Reading Teacher's Book of LIsts*. 1985 Prentice-Hall, Inc., Englewood Cliffs NJ. By E. Fry, D. Fountoukidis, and J. Polk. Reprinted with permission.

need to learn. For example, students might know *car* and we can use that word when teaching them *vehicle*, a broader category to which a car belongs.

Drawing upon the research of those that study vocabulary development enables us to provide some general guidelines for effective vocabulary instruction. Many of the teaching strategies that follow are ways to put these guidelines into action.

# GUIDELINES FOR EFFECTIVE VOCABULARY INSTRUCTION[6]

1: Create a word-rich environment.
   √ Promote wide reading.
   √ Provide time for discussion of new words and ideas.
   √ Intentionally focus on word learning in all content areas.
   √ Use time-effective strategies such as "word of the day."
   √ Be enthusiastic about acquiring new words.

2: Create independent word learners.
   √ Select and teach words that are central to the understanding of a topic.
   √ Show students how to use context clues.
   √ Show students how to use word parts.
   √ Allow for some self-selection.

3: Model good word-learning.
   √ active involvement
   √ graphic displays with discussion
   √ personalize words
   √ gather information from different sources
   √ play, experiment with words

## TEACHING STRATEGIES

There are several ways to teach vocabulary. Our purpose is what guides the selection of the specific teaching strategy we choose for any given lesson. Many of these strategies can be used when designing explicit vocabulary instruction focused on helping students understand key vocabulary. Remember, though, that we are teaching for independence; we want students to employ several of these strategies when they are on their own and come to unknown words. And remember the value of providing time for children to read books and other print sources. Wide reading is one sure way to help children acquire a large store of words.

When designing explicit instruction, you might find STAR[7] helpful. Here are the steps:

1. **S** (Select). Determine which words students need to know to better understand the text at hand. Keep the number limited to six words.
2. **T** (Teach). Select the appropriate strategy to help students learn the words. Some strategies work best before students read, whereas others work best during or after reading. For example, the *Knowledge Rating* (see page 346) is excellent to use before students actually begin reading. *Word Chain* (see page 346) is a perfect fit for review that takes place after reading. The *Context-Use* lesson (see page 329) is a natural strategy to use both before and during reading.

[6]Blachowicz, C., and P. Fisher. *Teaching Vocabulary in All Classrooms*, 2nd ed. Englewood Cliffs, NJ: Merrill, 2002.

[7]Blachowicz, C., and P. Fisher. "Vocabulary Lessons." *Educational Leadership* (March 2004):66–69.

3. **A** (Activate). Connect the words with students' writing. Think about creating a set of words that contain some of the words they are learning. In other words, give them many exposures to the words in different contexts to provide them with meaningful repetition that will better ensure their understanding of the word(s).
4. **R** (Revisit). Use review activities such as *Word Chain* to help students revisit words. You might also ask students to use their words to create games such as crossword puzzles.

### Context Clues: What Are They?

Students need to learn that words have multiple meanings and must understand how to determine the correct meanings from sentence context. Context clues are a vital aid in learning vocabulary and reading comprehension because there is such ambiguity in the English language.

### Context Clues (Definition, Explanation, and Description)

There are times when you can get the meaning of a word from context clues. By *context* we mean the words surrounding a word that can shed light on its meaning.

> **Context clue**
> An item of information from the surrounding words of a particular word in the form of a synonym, antonym, example, definition, description, explanation, and so on, that helps shed light on the particular word.

If the writer wants to make sure that you get the meaning of a word, he or she will define, explain, or describe the word in the sentence. The *context clue* in the form of definition, description, or explanation is the specific item of information that helps the reader to figure out the meaning of a particular word. For example, the word *context* has been defined because it is a key word in this section. The definition is the context clue. In the following examples the writer actually gives you the definition of a word. (Sentences such as these are generally found in textbooks or technical journals.)

*Examples*

1. An *axis* is a straight line, real or imaginary, that passes through the center of rotation in a revolving body at a right angle to the plane of rotation.
2. In geometry, a plane figure of six sides and six angles is called a *hexagon.*

Notice how the writer in the next example explains the meaning of the word by using a synonym. (A synonym is a word that has a similar meaning to another word. Notice also how this makes his writing more expressive and clear and avoids repetition.)

*Example* Although Senator Smith is *candid* about his drinking problem, he is less *frank* about his investments.

In the next examples, notice how the writers *describe* the words that they want you to know.

*Examples*

1. Although my *diligent* friend works from morning to night, he never complains.

2. Interior paints no longer contain *toxic* materials that might endanger the health of infants and small children.
3. The *cryptic* message—which looks as mysterious and secretive as it is—is difficult to decode.

Special Notes

The word *or* may be used by the writer when he uses another word or words with a similar meaning. Example: John said that he felt ill after having eaten *rancid* or *spoiled* butter.

The words *that is* and its abbreviation *i.e.* usually signal that an explanation will follow. Example: "A human is a biped, that is, an animal having only two feet," or "A human is a biped, i.e., an animal having only two feet." ◼

**Context Clues (Example and Comparison/Contrast)**

Many times an author helps you get the meaning of a word by giving you *examples* illustrating the use of the word. In the following sentence notice how the examples that the writer gives in his sentence help you determine the meaning of the word *illuminated.*

> **Example**  The lantern *illuminated* the cave so well that we were able to see the crystal formations and even spiders crawling on the rocks.

(From the sentence you can determine that *illuminated* means "lit up.")

| | |
|---|---|
| **Example** Something representative of a whole or a group. | |

Another technique writers employ that can help you gain the meaning of a word is *comparison.* Comparison usually shows the similarities between persons, ideas, things, and so on. For example, in the following sentence notice how you can determine the meaning of *passive* through the writer's comparison of Paul to a bear in winter.

> **Example**  Paul is as *passive* as a bear sleeping away the winter.

(From the sentence you can determine that *passive* means "inactive.")

| | |
|---|---|
| **Comparison** A demonstration of the similarities between persons, ideas, things, and so on. | |

*Contrast* is another method writers use that can help you to figure out word meanings. Contrast is usually used to show the differences between persons, ideas, things, and so on. In the following sentence you can determine the meaning of *optimist* because you know that *optimist* is somehow the opposite of *"one who is gloomy or one who expects the worst."*

| | |
|---|---|
| **Contrast** A demonstration of the differences between persons, ideas, things, and so on. | |

*Examples*
1. My sister Marie is an *optimist,* but her boyfriend is one who is always gloomy and expects the worst to happen.

(From the sentence you can determine that optimist means "one who expects the best" or "one who is cheerful.")

2. Frank, who is of average intelligence, appears slow in contrast to his *brilliant* cousin.

(From the sentence you can figure out that *brilliant* must mean "very smart" or "highly intelligent.")

The writer may use the words *for example* or the abbreviation *e.g.* to signal that examples are to follow. Example: *Condiments,* e.g., pepper, salt, and mustard, make food taste better. (From the examples of condiments you can determine that condiments are seasonings.)

An example is something that is representative of a whole or a group. It can be a particular single item, incident, fact, or situation that typifies the whole.

Many times such words as *but, yet, although, however,* and *rather than* signal that a contrast is being used. Example: My father thought he owned an authentic antique chest, but he was told recently that it was a fake. (From the sentence you can tell that authentic is the opposite of fake; therefore, authentic means "not false but genuine or real.") ■

**Context Clues (Synonyms and Antonyms)**

Often a word can be defined by another, more familiar word having basically the same meaning. For example, *void* is defined as *empty* and *corpulent* is defined as *fat. Void* and *empty,* and *corpulent* and *fat* are synonyms. *Synonyms* are different words that have the same or nearly the same meaning. Writers use synonyms to make their writing clearer and more expressive. Read the three sample sets of sentences. Don't you agree that the second sentence in each set is more descriptive than the first?

**Synonyms**
Words similar in meaning.

*Examples*

    a. (1)  The frightened child *looked* at the man.
       (2)  The frightened child *peered* at the man.
    b. (1)  We *walked* through the park.
       (2)  We *strolled* through the park.
    c. (1)  The *noise* brought the police to the scene.
       (2)  The *uproar* brought the police to the scene.

**Antonyms**
Words opposite in meaning.

*Antonyms* are words opposite in meaning to each other. Examples: tall—short; fat—thin; least—most; worst—best.

Earlier you learned that when a writer uses contrast in a sentence you can often figure out word meanings from the context. Antonyms, which are used to show contrast, help to make sentences clearer and more informative.

*Examples*

    1.  My biology professor gives *succinct* lectures, but his assistant is *verbose.*
    2.  My math professor claims that all the problems she gives us are *simple* ones, but we feel that they are *intricate* and hard to solve.

**Homographs**

Words that are spelled the same but have different meanings.

## Context Clues (Words with Multiple Meanings [Homographs])

Many words that are spelled the same have different meanings. These words are called *homographs.* The meaning of a homograph is determined by the way the word is used in the sentence. For example, the term *run* has many different meanings. (One dictionary gives 134 meanings for *run.*) In the sentences here notice how *run*'s placement in the sentence and the surrounding words help you to figure out the meaning of each use.

### *Examples*

1. Walk, don't *run.*
2. I have a *run* in my stocking.
3. Senator Jones said that he would not *run* for another term.
4. The trucker finished his *run* to Detroit.
5. She is going to *run* in a ten-mile race.
6. The play had a *run* of two years.

In sentence 1 *run* means "go quickly by moving the legs more rapidly than at a walk."

In sentence 2 *run* means "a tear or to cause stitches to unravel."

In sentence 3 *run* means "be or campaign as a candidate for election."

In sentence 4 *run* means "route."

In sentence 5 *run* means "take part in a race."

In sentence 6 *run* means "continuous course of performances."

### Special Notes

Some homographs are spelled the same but do not sound the same. For example, *refuse* means "trash"; *refuse* means "to decline to accept." In sentence 1 in the examples below *refuse* (ref´use) meaning "trash" is pronounced differently from the term *refuse* (re fuse´) meaning "to decline to accept" in sentence 2. In reading, you can determine the meaning of *refuse* from the way it is used in the sentence (context clues).

1. During the garbage strike there were tons of uncollected *refuse* on the streets of the city.
2. I *refuse* to go along with you in that project because it seems unethical to me. ■

Do not confuse *homonym* or *homophone* (terms to describe words that sound alike but have different spellings and meanings) with *homograph.* Here are some examples of homonyms or homophones:

| | |
|---|---|
| pear—pare; | to—two—too; |
| way—weigh; | fare—fair; |
| tow—toe; | plain—plane |

## Scenario: Ms. Johnson Uses a Modeling Strategy to Teach a Context Clue

Ms. Johnson takes two sentences from a story her first graders are reading. She puts them on the chalkboard:

Mrs. Brown grows vegetables on her farm.

She grows carrots, cabbage, peas, beets, corn, and beans.

Then Ms. Johnson says to her students, "Here is how I go about figuring out the meaning of the word *vegetables.* From reading the sentences, I see there are a number of clues to help me figure out the meaning of the word *vegetables.* The clues are *carrots, cabbage, peas, beets, corn,* and *beans.* The words *carrots, cabbage, peas, beets, corn,* and *beans* are examples of vegetables. I know that examples are not the meaning of a word. An example is something that shows what the rest are like. Examples may not be the meaning of a word, but they can help us figure out word meanings. From the examples, I see that vegetables are parts of plants that we eat."

Ms. Johnson then says, "Here are two other sentences. Let's see if we can figure out the meaning of the word *family,* using examples as clues." Ms. Johnson puts the following two sentences on the chalkboard:

There are six people in my family.

My grandmother, mother, father, two sisters, and I live in our house.

"See if you do the same things I do. First I look at the clues. The clues are *six people, grandmother, mother, father, two sisters,* and *I.* The sentences do not give me the meaning of the word *family,* but they give me examples. The words *grandmother, mother, father, two sisters,* and *I* are all examples and part of a family. Usually, families live together in the same home. From these examples, I see that these people are part of a family. They are all related and live together in the same home."

Ms. Johnson then tells her students that there are a number of different context clues and that she will present another one to them tomorrow. She then gives them some practice in using examples to figure out word meanings.

### Assessing Use of Context Clues

To get a feel as to whether your students use context clues, you can have them complete the appropriate sample informal assessment shown in Figure 11.4.

### Teaching Context Clues: Primary

Here are some techniques and instructional materials to help students recognize how context clues can help them figure out word meanings.

1. Present to your students the following sentence, which should have an unfamiliar word in it.

Mary is usually a prudent person.

Ask them if they can give you the meaning of *prudent.* If not, ask them what would help. Then present this sentence.

**FIGURE 11.4  Sample Informal Assessment**

*Upper Primary-Grade Level*
*Skill: Context Clues*

*Objective:* The students will use context clues to choose the word that best fits the sentence.

*Test*

*Directions:* Read each sentence carefully. Use context clues to help you choose the word that *best* fits the sentence. Put the word in the blank. A word may be used only once. All words are used as answers.

*Word List:* rose, point, suit, box, play

1. That was a good _____ she made in the game.

2. The batter stood in the batting _____.

3. We _____ late yesterday.

4. That color does not _____ you.

5. What is the _____ of the story?

Answers: 1. play  2. box  3. rose  4. suit  5. point
Tell students the results.

---

*Intermediate-Grade Level*
*Skill: Context Clues*

*Objective:* The students will use context clues to choose a word that makes sense in each sentence.

*Test*

*Directions:* Read each sentence carefully. Use context clues to help you choose the word that *best* fits the sentence. A word may only be used once. (More words are given in the word list than you need.) Insert the word in the blank.

*Word List:* buy, browse, pine, economy, suit, take, play, box, bore, pinch, coat, blade, post, rose, idle, work, iron, spectacles, posture, run, flowed, clothing, happy, fast, sell, dress

1. Good looks _____ in her family.

2. At the stadium the crowd _____ through the gate.

3. The soldier remained at his _____ all day.

4. At the library, I usually _____ through lots of books.

5. They said that they would try to _____ out their difficulties.

6. The children _____ for their dog who is missing.

7. During holidays, I usually feel the money _____.

8. Unless my mother wears her _____, she has difficulty seeing.

9. The senators surveyed the _____ of foreign affairs.

10. It is not good to allow your car motor to _____.

Answers: 1. run  2. flowed  3. post  4. browse  5. iron  6. pine  7. pinch  8. spectacles  9. posture  10. idle
Tell students the results.

However, yesterday she was very foolish.

Now ask them if they can figure out the meaning of *prudent.* Elicit from the children how the second sentence gave them a clue to the word *prudent.* From the second sentence, they should have realized that prudent must mean "wise," the opposite of *foolish.*

2. Put the following sentences on the chalkboard, and have the students use the context clues to help them figure out the meanings of each underlined word. Tell them that sometimes the clue to help them figure out the word meaning is in the next sentence. Go over each sentence with the students.

1. My kitten is very <u>tame.</u> She will not hurt anyone. _____
2. Everyone seems to know her. She must be a <u>famous</u> writer. _____
3. That is such an <u>enormous</u> ice-cream cone. You will have to get lots of people to help you eat some of it. _____
4. That street is so <u>broad</u> that we can all walk side by side. _____
5. The lion is a <u>fierce</u> animal. _____

Here are some instructional techniques and materials you can use with your students to help them recognize that words can have more than one meaning.

1. Hold up two pictures. The first picture is of a train, and the second picture shows a boy trying to train his dog. Ask the children what the two pictures have in common. Try to get them to make up sentences about what is taking place. Write the sentences about the two pictures on the board. Try to get them to use the word *train* for both pictures.

2. Hold up a number of pictures that depict the words *slip, root,* and *bark* in more than one way. Try to get the children to recognize that each set of pictures is different, but that the word telling what each picture in the set is about is the same. You can tell the students that words with more than one meaning are usually called *homographs.*

3. Put the following sentences on the chalkboard and have the students fill in the blanks with one word that fits all the blanks in each sentence. Go over the sentences with the children.

1. I _____ my father _____ the tree in the woods. (saw)
2. In the _____ our flowers look very pretty near our _____ (spring)
3. My mother says that I _____ help her _____ some vegetables from her garden. (can)
4. Don't you _____ when you change a flat _____ ? (tire)
5. After we drank water from the _____ , we did not feel _____. (well)

4. Challenge the children with riddles such as the following: I can make things brighter, I do not weigh a lot; and I'm the opposite of dark. What am I? Hint: One word fits all three things.

5. Ask the children to use their dictionaries to try to make up riddles to challenge their classmates.

### Teaching Context Clues: Upper Grades

Here are some instructional materials and techniques to use with your students.

1. Present your students with the following sentence that has an unfamiliar word.

Jim behaved in a very *rash* manner.

Ask your students why this sentence does not help them figure out the meaning of *rash.* Then present them with this sentence:

He rushed in too quickly and almost lost his life.

Now ask them to try to determine the meaning of *rash.* From the second sentence, they should recognize that *rash* refers to something that is done quickly and not very carefully.

2. Give them a sentence that uses comparison and ask them to see if they can figure out the meaning of an unfamiliar word.

Fred is as *obstinate* as a mule.

Ask the students to give you the meaning of *obstinate.* Since a mule is an animal that is considered stubborn, your students should get an idea of *obstinate* as meaning "stubborn."

Here are some techniques and instructional materials you can use to help students recognize that words can have more than one meaning.

1. Present students with a number of phrases. Tell them that the same word can fit in each set of phrases. The meaning of the word changes based on the words surrounding it (context). For example: a *brush* with the law; *brush* your teeth; a *brush* for your hair.

2. State a word such as *run.* Present sentences to your students and ask them to give the meaning of *run* in each sentence. Have them note that the meaning is different for each. Ask them to look up *run* in the dictionary. Have them write four other sentences using *run* in different ways.

3. Put the following sentences on the chalkboard and have the students fill in the blanks with one word that fits all the blanks in each sentence. Go over the sentences with the students.

1. My mind goes _____ every time I have to fill in any _____ .
   (blank)

2. In England, I paid two _____ for a book to help me shed some _____ . (pounds)
3. The lawyer knew that he had won his _____ when he produced the _____ containing the murder weapon. (case)
4. A certain _____ of dogs is easier to _____ than others. (breed)
5. Part of the _____ was to _____ a course that no one could follow after we hid the jewels in the chosen cemetery _____. (plot)

Here are two additional ideas that can be used across grades:

**Three-Day Lesson for Teaching Students to Use Context Clues[8]**

**Day 1:**
1. Read a riddle aloud and ask students to guess the answer:
   "I am a color which symbolizes wealth. I am often seen on the robes of queens and kings. I am also on petals of flowers. What am I?" (Answer: purple)
2. Have students point out any clues or cues that gave away the answer.
3. Have students create a riddle to share with others.

**Day 2:**
1. Provide time for students to share their riddles. As each is solved, ask students how the clues in each helped them find the answer.
2. Tell students that context clues, like clues in a riddle, are the clues in the text that can help them understand a word they might not know.
3. Provide students with a short passage and tell them to read and underline the unknown word.

   *Example:* "The *werbert* Sam brought for lunch looked delicious. It had layers of roast beef, cheese, lettuce, and tomato piled between two slices of bread."

4. Ask students to read the passage and underline the unknown word.
5. Ask students to look for clues in the text that help reveal the meaning of the word.
6. Using these clues, have students predict the meaning of the word.
7. Repeat the procedure with other passages.

*Day 3:*
1. Review the steps that can be used to find context clues in a passage.
2. Have students find an unknown word in the dictionary and write a short passage using it. Make sure they add clues to the meaning.
3. Have students exchange passages with others and use the process described on Day 2 to figure out unknown words.

[8]Nickerson, L. *Quick Activities to Build a Very Voluminous Vocabulary.* New York, NY: Scholastic, 1998.

### Context-Use Lesson[9]

1. Write a passage on a chart or on an overhead transparency and omit a contextually explained word.
2. Show students how they can use context using the following steps. Actually go through the process yourself and think aloud so that they can better understand how to use the process:

   (a) LOOK. Before, at, and after the word.
   (b) REASON. Connect what you know with what the author has written.
   (c) PREDICT A POSSIBLE MEANING.
   (d) RESOLVE OR REDO. Decide if you know enough or should stop.

3. Insert the omitted word.
4. Display another passage and have the students go through the process with your guidance.
5. Allow for discussion.
6. Reveal the author's word choice.

### *Using Word Parts*

**Combining forms**
Roots borrowed from another language that join together or that join with a prefix, a suffix, or both to form a word.

Vocabulary expansion instruction depends on the ability levels of students, their past experiences, and their interests. If students are curious about sea life and have an aquarium in the classroom, *combining forms* such as *aqua,* meaning "water," and *mare* meaning "sea" could help them develop a meaningful association with knowing word parts. The combining form *aqua* could generate such terms as *aquaplane, aqueduct,* and *aquanaut.* Since *mare* means "sea," students could be given the term *aquamarine* to define. Knowing the combining forms *aqua* and *mare,* many will probably respond with "seawater." The English term actually means "bluish-green." The students can be challenged as to why the English definition of aquamarine is bluish-green.

A terrarium can stimulate discussion of words made up of the combining form *terra.*

When discussing the prefix *bi,* children should be encouraged to generate other words that also contain *bi,* such as *bicycle, binary, bilateral,* and so on.

When presenting the combining forms *cardio, tele, graph,* and *gram,* place the following vocabulary words on the board:

cardiograph       telegraph
cardiogram       telegram

After students know that *cardio* means "heart" and *tele* means "from a distance," ask them to try to determine the meaning of *graph,* as used in *cardiograph* and *telegraph.* Have them try to figure out the meaning of *gram,* as used in *telegram* and *cardiogram.* Once students are able to define graph as an "instrument or machine," and *gram* as "message," they will hardly ever confuse a *cardiograph* with a *cardiogram.*

[9]Blachowicz and Fisher, 2002.

When students are exposed to such activities, they become more sensitive to their language. They come to realize that words are human-made, that language is living and changing, and that as people develop new concepts they need new words to identify them. *Astronaut* and *aquanaut* are good examples of words that came into being because of space and undersea exploration.

Children come to see the power of combining forms when they realize that by knowing a few combining forms they can unlock the meanings of many words. For example, if they know the following combining forms, students can define correctly many terms used in the metric system, as well as other words.

| | |
|---|---|
| *deca:* | ten |
| *deci:* | tenth |
| *cent, centi:* | hundred, hundredth |
| *milli:* | thousand, thousandth |
| *decameter:* | ten meters |
| *decimeter:* | 1/10 meter |
| *centimeter:* | 1/100 meter |
| *millimeter:* | 1/1000 meter |
| *decade:* | period of ten years |
| *century:* | period of one hundred years |
| *centennial:* | one-hundredth-year anniversary |
| *millennium:* | period of 1,000 years |
| *million:* | one thousand thousands |

(*Centi, milli, deci* are usually used to designate "part of.")

Here is a sample lesson on combining forms:

*Presentation of Combining Forms: A Sample Lesson*

1. State and write the combining form *bi* on the board.
2. Challenge the students to generate any words that they can think of that have this combining form, for example, *bicycle, bimonthly, biweekly.*
3. Since the most common word is *bicycle,* ask the students if they can figure out the meaning of *bi* from *bicycle.* Someone will probably volunteer *two* because a bicycle is a *two* wheeler.
4. Ask for volunteers to state other *bi* words and write them on the board. For example, *biped:* say, "We know that *bi* means *two*; let's see if we can figure out what *biped* means."
5. State two sentences using *biped*: *All humans are bipeds. However, all animals are not bipeds.* Ask, "Can anyone guess what *biped* means? Remember, you know what *bi* means."
6. To encourage and help students more, say, "Let me give you another word containing the combining form *ped.* Perhaps that will help you to get the meaning of *biped.*"
7. State and write *pedestrian* on the board and write the following sentence on the board: *Motorists must look out for pedestrians.* If the students still need help with the analysis, ask the students to state what they do when they ride a bicycle. It is to be hoped that someone will say "pedal." If not, suggest "pedal" and write the following sentence on the board: *People pedal hard when they want to go fast.* Students should at this point be able

to give the meaning of *ped* as "foot." *Biped* should be defined as "two-footed," and *pedestrian* as someone "who is on foot or a walker."
8. Tell students about how helpful combining forms can be in expanding vocabulary and in helping them figure out unknown words when reading.

### Vocabulary Expansion Instruction for Students Who Have a Limited Vocabulary

Working with upper-elementary-grade students who have a small vocabulary requires a relatively structured approach, one that emphasizes the systematic presentation of material at graduated levels of difficulty in ways somewhat similar to those used in the teaching of English Language Learners. Each day, present roots, combining forms, prefixes, and suffixes with a list of words made up from these word parts. Place emphasis on the meanings of the word parts and their combinations into words rather than on the naming of the word parts. For example, pronounce *auto, bio,* and *graph* and write them on the board. Give their meanings. When *autobiography* is put on the board, ask students if they can state its meaning.

Select terms for study that students will hear in school, on television, or on the radio, as well as those they will meet in their reading. Present the word parts in an interesting manner, and give those that combine to form a number of words. When students realize that they are seeing these words in their reading, they will be greatly reinforced in their learning.

To provide continuous reinforcement, give daily "nonthreatening" quizzes on the previous days' words. Give students the results of such quizzes immediately, so that any faulty concepts can be quickly corrected. Having students correct their own papers is one way to accomplish this task. The number of words that are presented would depend on individual students.

The possibilities for vocabulary experiences in the classroom are unlimited and there are a wealth of professional books that offer teaching suggestions. *50 Wonderful Word Games, Teaching Vocabulary in All Classrooms,* and *Building Academic Vocabulary* are two of these. Teachers must have the prefixes, suffixes, and combining forms at their fingertips in order to take advantage of the opportunities that present themselves daily. Here is a list of some often used word parts and vocabulary words derived from them:

| *Prefixes* | *Combining Forms* | *Vocabulary Words* |
|---|---|---|
| a—without | anthropo—man | anthropology, apodal |
| ante—before | astro—star | astronomy, astrology |
| arch—main, chief | audio—hearing | audiology, auditory, audition, audible |
| bi—two | auto—self | automatic, autocracy, binary, biped |
| cata—down | bene—good | benefit, catalog |
| circum—around | bio—life | biology, biography, autobiography |
| hyper—excessive | chrono—time | chronological, hypertension |
| hypo—under | cosmo—world | microcosm, cosmology |
| in—not | gamy—marriage | monogamy, bigamy, polygamy |
| inter—between, among | geo—earth | interdepartmental, geology |
| mis—wrong, bad | gram—written or drawn | telegram, mistake |
| mono—one, alone | graph—written or drawn, | telegraph, monarchy |
| post—after |     instrument | |

*(continued)*

re—backward, again
trans—across

*Suffixes*
able—able to
ible—able to
ology—the study of
tion—the act of

logo—speak
macro—large
micro—small
mis—hate
poly—many
retro—backward
ped, pod—foot, feet
scope—instrument for seeing
phobia—fear
theo—god
pseudo—false

theology, logical, catalog
macrocosm
microscope, transatlantic
misanthrope, misogamist
polyglot
retrorocket
pseudopod
microscope
monophobia
theocracy
pseudoscience

**Dictionary**
A very important reference tool that supplies word meanings, pronunciations, and a great amount of other useful information.

### The Dictionary as a Tool in Vocabulary Expansion

Although children use picture dictionaries in the primary grades more as an aid to writing than in vocabulary expansion, if young readers discover the wonders of the dictionary they can enrich their vocabulary. Primary-grade picture dictionaries consist of words that are generally in the children's listening, speaking, and reading vocabularies. They consist of alphabetized lists of words with pictures and can serve as the children's first reference tool, helping them to unlock words on their own and making them more independent and self-reliant. The children can also learn multiple meanings from a picture dictionary, when they see the word *saw,* for example, with two pictures which represent a tool and the act of seeing.

In the intermediate grades, dictionaries serve more varied purposes, and there is emphasis on vocabulary expansion. Children delight in learning new words. If properly encouraged by the teacher, vocabulary expansion can become an exciting hunting expedition, where the unexplored terrain is the vast territory of words.

At any grade level teachers can show by their actions that they value the dictionary as an important tool. If a word seems to need clarification, students can be asked to look it up in the dictionary. Although at times it may seem more expedient simply to supply the meaning, students should be encouraged to look up words for themselves. If pupils discover the meanings of the words on their own with teacher guidance they will be more apt to remember them.

In order to build a larger meaning vocabulary, the teacher can use a number of motivating techniques to stimulate vocabulary expansion. Each pupil can be encouraged to keep a paper bag attached to his or her desk, in which he or she puts index cards with words on one side and the meaning of the word he or she has looked up on the other. Sometime during the day students can be encouraged to challenge one another, with one student calling out the meanings of a word and another student supplying the word.

Here are two additional ways to help children use word parts:

### Decoding Words with Affixes[10]

1. Lay aside the prefix.
2. Lay aside each suffix, one at a time.

[10]Durkin, D. *Teaching Them To Read*. Boston: Allyn & Bacon, 1989.

3. If the root is unfamiliar, decode it.
4. Put back the suffix closest to the root.
5. If there is a second suffix, add it next.
6. Put back the prefix.
7. Read the word in the sentence to check meaning.

**Teaching Prefixes**[11]

1. Present a prefix in isolation and also attached to four words.

    *Example:* con- *construct, converge, conference, connect*

2. Define the prefix.

    *Example: Con-* means "to put together"

3. Use the whole words in sentences:

    *Example:* Builders *construct* houses.

4. Define the whole words.

    *Example:* To *construct* means to put or fit together.

5. After completing the above four steps with several prefixes, have students practice matching different prefixes to their meanings and root words to prefixes.
6. Have students identify the meanings of new words with familiar prefixes.

*Word Walls*

Most teachers recognize that children need direct instruction in vocabulary and that students enjoy various fun word activities that help them to develop needed skills. Word Walls, which are the most meaningful when they are created by students and their teacher, are versatile and their use is only limited by the teachers' creativity. Word Walls can be used for review, reinforcement, skill enhancement purposes, teaching a new skill, or as a writing reference.

Teachers can work with one specific category, such as contractions, or with a number of categories. What the teacher does is based on his or her objectives. The teacher can have the whole class involved or children can work in groups or teams.

World Walls are most often seen in the primary grades, but they can be used at any grade level. In the upper grades, teachers generally use Word Walls to expand the students' vocabulary.

---

[11]M. Graves, and H. Hammond "A validated procedure for teaching prefixes and its effect on students' ability to assign meanings to novel words," In M. Kamil & A. Moe (Eds) *Perspectives on Reading Research & Instruction* (pp. 184–188). Washington, D.C.: National Reading Conference, 1980.

In preparing to use a Word Wall, teachers must be clear about their purposes. For example, a teacher who is reviewing homophones, homographs, word families, and contractions can have available a box of representative word cards of similar size. At the top of the Wall Board, the four categories being reviewed are listed. In turn, children draw two cards from the box and place the words under the correct category. If one word is a contraction, the other card must have the two words that make up the contraction. If the two words are *red* and *read,* the words are placed under homophones. If the two words are *cake* and *bake,* the words would be listed under word families.

### Self-Selection Strategy[12]

1. Invite students to bring two words to class that they have found in reading or listening.
2. Allow students to present their words to the group.
3. Ask the group to vote on five to eight words to be learned for the week.
4. Lead a discussion of the class to clarify, elaborate, and extend word meanings.
5. Have students enter their words into personal word logs and ask them to create some sort of memory and meaning device (e.g., chart, diagram, picture, word map).
6. Ask students to use the words in various ways to provide practice with them.

### Yea/Nay[13]

1. Provide students with two different cards, one that says "Yea" and one that says "Nay."
2. Read a question with one or two words that students might or might not understand. *Example:* Would a *corpse* be a good *conversationalist*?
3. After reading the question, give students 5–10 seconds to think and then ask, "Yea or Nay? 1, 2, 3."
4. On the count of 3, students hold up their choices while you call on individuals to explain their choices.

### Create Word Riddles[14]

1. Pick a subject (e.g., *pig*).
2. Generate a list of related words (e.g., *ham, pen, hog*).
3. Pick a word (e.g., *ham*), drop the first letter(s) to get a shortened version (e.g., *am*), and find a list of words that begin the way the shortened version begins (e.g., *ambulance, amnesia*).

---

[12]M. Haggard. "The vocabulary self-selection strategy: An active approach to word learning." (*Journal of Reading, 26*: 203–207, 1982.)

[13]Beck, I., and McKeown, M. "Learning Words Well: A Program to Enhance Vocabulary and Comprehension." *The Reading Teacher, 36*(1983), 622–25.

[14]M. Thaler, "Reading, writing, and riddling." (*Learning*, pp. 58–59, 1988).

4. Put back the missing letter to create a new word (e.g., *hambulance*).
5. Make up a riddle for which this word is the answer (e.g., *What do you use to take a pig to the hospital?*).

**Semantic Feature Analysis[15]**

1. Select a category.
2. List words in the category.
3. List and add features.
4. Determine feature possession. Which words have which features?
5. Add more words and features.
6. Complete the grid.
7. Examine and discuss the grid.

*Categorizing*

**Categorizing**
A thinking skill involving the ability to classify items into general and specific categories.

**What Is It?**
The ability to divide items into categories is a very important thinking skill. As children advance through the grades they should be able to differentiate and group items into increasingly more complex categories. Primary-grade children should be able to categorize a cat as distinct from a mouse or a rabbit. They should be able to group cat, dog, and cow together as animals. As these children develop their thinking skills, they should be able to proceed from more generalized classifications to more specialized classifications.

**Assessing Students' Categorizing**
To get a feel as to whether or not your students categorize, you can have them complete the appropriate sample informal assessment shown in Figure 11.5.

**Teaching Categorizing: Primary Grades**
Young children tend to overgeneralize and need to learn how to make discriminations in order to classify. By the time children come to school, they are able to make many discriminations and are beginning to classify. Here are some suggested activities appropriate for children in different grade levels.

   1.  Five-year-olds can put things together that belong together—blocks of the same size in the same place; clothes for each doll in the right suitcase; parts of a puzzle in the right box; scissors, brushes, and paints in the spaces designated for these materials.

   2.  First-graders may separate things that magnets can pick up from things they do not pick up by using two boxes—one marked "yes" and the other marked "no." They can think of two kinds of stories—true and make-believe stories. They can make booklets representing homes, dividing the pictures they have cut from magazines into several categories—living rooms, dining rooms,

---

[15]Pittelman, S., Heimlich, J., Berglund, R., and French, M. *Semantic Feature Analysis: Classroom Applications.* Newark, DE: International Reading Association, 1991.

**FIGURE 11.5** **Categorizing: Informal Assessment**

LOWER PRIMARY-GRADE LEVEL

*SKILL: CATEGORIZING*

Objective: The students will categorize pictures of various objects into groups.

**Directions: The teacher will orally give directions to students. The children are given a page which consists of pictures of things that would be found in a house. Underneath each picture will appear the name of the object. These items are presented in random order on the page. The children are asked to cut out the pictures and paste them according to their groups on another sheet of paper, which has these headings: *Furniture, Appliances, and Eating Utensils.* The teacher reads these headings aloud to the children.**

The pictures on the page are as follows: sofa, bed, desk, dresser with mirror; iron, toaster, refrigerator, oven; fork, knife, plate, cup.

Tell students the results.

---

PRIMARY-GRADE LEVEL

*SKILL: CATEGORIZING*

Objective: The students will group a list of words in a number of different ways.

**Directions: First read the list of words. Then group them in at least seven different ways.**

| | |
|---|---|
| hen | dog |
| drake | turkey |
| sow | duck |
| mare | elephant |
| colt | ape |
| gander | tiger |
| puppy | goat |
| kitten | mule |
| goose | horse |
| pig | |

Answer:

Children will arrange the words into a number of different groups. Here are some:

Wild animals: elephant, ape, tiger

Tame animals: all the others

Fowl: hen, drake, gander, goose, turkey, duck

Female animals: hen, sow, mare

Male animals: drake, colt, gander

Pets: colt, mare, puppy, kitten, dog (many of the other animals can be pets)

Baby animals: puppy, kitten

Farm animals: hen, drake, sow, mare, colt, gander, and so on except for the elephant, ape, and tiger

Animals: all would be included

Tell students the results.

INTERMEDIATE-GRADE LEVEL

*SKILL: CATEGORIZING*

*Diagnostic Analysis*

Objective: The students will group items that belong together.

Test

**Directions: First find what the items in a group have in common, and then choose a word or phrase from the list below that *best* describes the group. There are more words and phrases than are needed. Put the word or phrase on the line after each group of words.**

**Words and Phrases:** books, fiction books, nonfiction books, fruit, vegetables, food, cooked food, desserts, dairy products, long books, writing, fowl, animals, tame animals, female animals, wood, wood products, meat, beef, pork, lamb.

1. pears, apples, bananas _____
2. meat, tomatoes, apples _____
3. milk, cheese, butter _____
4. jello, applesauce, ice cream _____
5. liver, pork chops, lamb chops _____
6. hen, mare, doe _____
7. biography, autobiography, novel _____
8. biography, autobiography, dictionary _____
9. novel, comics, fairy tales _____
10. paper, telephone pole, furniture _____

   Answers: 1. fruit  2. food  3. dairy products  4. desserts  5. meat  6. female animals
   7. books  8. nonfiction books  9. fiction books  10. wood products

   Tell students the results.

bedrooms, and so on. They can make two piles of magazines labeled "To Cut" and "To Read."[16]

3. Second-grade pupils continue to put things together that belong together—such as outdoor temperature readings and indoor temperature readings, valentines in individual mail boxes in the play post office, and flannel graph figures made to use in telling a story in the envelope with the title of the story. In addition, seven-year-olds begin to understand finer classifications under large headings; for example, in a study of the job of a florist, plants may be classified as "plants that grow indoors" and "plants that grow outdoors." Indoor plants may be further subdivided into "plants that grow from seeds,"

[16]Although grade designations are given, teachers must take the individual differences of students into account. Some first-graders may be at a third-grade level; others may be at a first-grade or lower skill-developmental level.

"plants that grow from cuttings," and "plants that grow from bulbs." After visiting the local bakery, second graders, who are writing stories and drawing pictures of their trip, can list the details in two columns—in one, "things we saw in the store," in the other, "things we saw in the kitchen."

4. Third-grade students have many opportunities to classify their ideas and arrange them in organized form. During a study of food in their community one group put up a bulletin board to answer the question "What parts of plants do we eat?" The pictures and captions followed this tabulation formulated by the third-graders:

| Leaves | Seeds | Fruits | Roots |
|---|---|---|---|
| cabbage | peas | apples | carrots |
| lettuce | beans | oranges | radishes |
| spinach | corn | plums | |

The file of "Games We Know" in one third grade was divided into two parts by the pupils—"indoor games" and "outdoor games." Each of these categories was further subdivided into "games with equipment" and "games without equipment." After a visit to the supermarket, a third-grade class made a book containing stories and pictures of the trip. The organization of the booklet with its numbered pages was shown in the Table of Contents:

OUR VISIT TO THE FOOD MARKET

Here are examples of some exercises you can present to your children.

1. Group these words: apple, peach, potato, rice, oats, cucumber, barley, peanuts, acorn, pecans, almonds, pear.
   Answer:
   *Nuts*          *Fruits*          *Vegetables*          *Grains*

| peanuts | apple | potato | rice |
| acorn | peach | cucumber | oats |
| pecans | pear | | barley |
| almonds | | | |

2. Circle the word that does not belong.

Airedale          Persian          Angora          Siamese

Answer: You should have circled *Airedale* because all the other words refer to *cats*.

### Teaching Categorizing: Intermediate Grades

Here are some instructional procedures and materials to use:

1. Present students with the following list of words and have them group them in as many ways as they can think of:

| chalk | book |
| checkers | library |
| pencil | auditorium |
| paper | science books |
| student | baseball |
| teacher | nurse |
| chalkboard | jump rope |
| desk | basketball |
| classroom | pen |
| principal | chess |
| history books | spelling books |

2. Present the following exercise to your students. Tell them here is a group of words. Put the words into five groups according to a common feature and state the common feature for each group. This activity is a more difficult one because students have to state the common feature. Have students look up any words they are not sure of in the dictionary.

After students have finished the exercise, go over it carefully, discussing why they did what they did.

wood, brass, round, silk, oil, wheat, tin, wool, satin, coal, nylon, iron, barley, oats, oval, cylindrical

1. _____

   _____ Common feature _____

2. _____

   _____ Common feature _____

3. _____

_____ Common feature _____

4. _____

_____ Common feature _____

5. _____

_____ Common feature _____

Answers: 1. wood, oil, coal—fuels 2. brass, tin, iron—metals 3. silk, wool, satin, nylon—fabrics 4. round, cylindrical, oval—shapes 5. wheat, barley, oats—grains

The Frayer Model and List-Group-Label are two additional ways to teach categorizing.

### Frayer Model[17]

| Step | Example Using the Word Treasurer |
| --- | --- |
| 1. Define the new concept, discriminating the attributes relevant to all instances of the concept. | The discriminating attributes of *treasurer* are membership in an organization and responsibility for the accounts. |
| 2. Discriminate the relevant from the irrelevant properties of the concept. | The amount of money the treasurer is responsible for is an irrelevant attribute. |
| 3. Provide an example of the concept. | The "treasurer of the school board" and the "treasurer of the school book club" |
| 4. Provide a nonexample of the concept. | The "chairman or secretary of the board" and a "banker" are nonexamples. |
| 5. Relate the concept to a subordinate concept. | Generic instances of a treasurer such as the treasurer of a country club or another club |
| 6. Relate the concept to a superordinate concept. | People who deal with money |
| 7. Relate the concept to a coordinate term. | Bookkeeper |

### List-Group-Label[18]

1. Provide students with a list of words related to a given subject. Keep the list to no more than 25 words.
2. Provide students with time to group them.
3. Ask students to label each group of words.
4. If you want, collect different categories of words and display them for the whole class. If some words do not fit, have a miscellaneous category or ask students to brainstorm additional words to go with them to form another category.

[17]D. Frayer, W. Frederick, and H. Klausmeier. *A Scheme for Testing the Level of Concept Mastery* (Working Paper no. 16) Madison: University of Wisconsin, 1969.

[18]J. Readence and L. Searfoss. "Teaching Strategies for Vocabulary Development" (*English Journal*, 69: 43–46, 1980).

| | |

**Analogies**
Relationships
between words or
ideas.

*Analogies*

**What Are They?**

Working with analogies requires high-level thinking skills. Students must have a good stock of vocabulary and the ability to see relationships. Students who are able to classify will usually have little difficulty working with analogies.

Some primary-grade children can be exposed to simple analogies based on relationships with which they are familiar.[19] Analogies are relationships between words or ideas. In order to be able to make the best use of analogies or to complete an analogy statement or proportion, the children must know the meanings of the words and the relationship of the pair of words. For example: *Sad is to happy as good is to _____.* Many primary-grade children know the meanings of *sad* and *happy* and that *sad* is the opposite of *happy;* consequently, they would be able to complete the analogy statement or proportion with the correct word—*bad.*

Some of the relationships that words may have to one another are similar meanings, opposite meanings, classification, going from particular to general, going from general to particular, degree of intensity, specialized labels, characteristics, cause-effect, effect-cause, function, whole-part, ratio, and many more. The preceding relationships do not have to be memorized. Tell your students that they will gain clues to these from the pairs making up the analogies; that is, the words express the relationship. For example: "*pretty* is to *beautiful*— the relationship is degree of intensity (the state of being stronger, greater, or more than); "*hot* is to *cold*"—the relationship is one of opposites; "*car* is to *vehicle*"—the relationship is classification.

To ensure students' success, review the word lists of the analogy exercises to determine whether students are familiar with the vocabulary. Encourage them to use dictionaries to look up any unfamiliar words.

Analogy activities can be done in small groups or with the entire class orally as well as individually. If children work individually, review the answers together in a group so that interaction and discussion can further enhance vocabulary development.

**Special Notes**

1. The term *word relationships* can be used with your primary-grade students rather than *analogies.*

2. In introducing some of the relationships that pairs of words can have to one another, use words that are in your students' listening vocabulary. ■

**Assessing Analogies**

To get a feel as to whether your students can use analogies, ask them to complete the appropriate sample informal assessment shown in Figure 11.6.

[19]See Sister Josephine, C.S.J., "An Analogy Test for Preschool Children," *Education* (December 1965): 235–37.

## FIGURE 11.6   Analogies: Informal Assessment

LOWER PRIMARY-GRADE LEVEL

*SKILL: PICTURE RELATIONSHIPS (ANALOGIES)*

Objective: The students will be able to choose a picture from the given pictures that will best complete the analogy.

Test

**Directions: (These will be given orally by the teacher.) Present the following picture sets to your children. Tell them that the sets of pictures belong together in some way. Each set has a missing picture. Have them look at the first pair of pictures in the set. Tell them to try to figure out how they belong together. Then have them choose a picture from the large box that would *best* complete the second pair in the set. Have them draw a line from the picture in the large box to where it belongs. *All the pictures in the box are used as answers.* Do the first set with the children.**

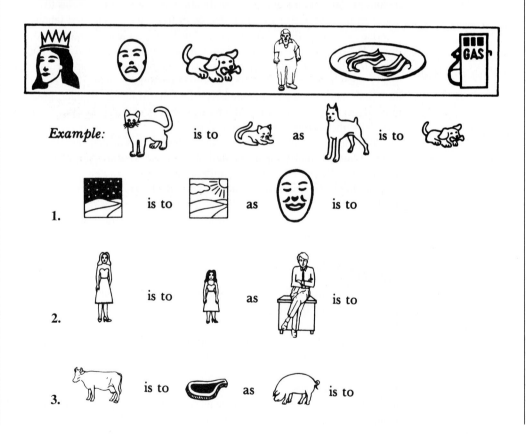

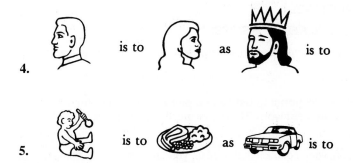

**4.**

**5.**

Tell students the results.

UPPER PRIMARY-GRADE LEVEL

*SKILL: WORD RELATIONSHIPS (ANALOGIES)*

Objective: The students will complete each analogy statement with the *best* word.

Test

> **Directions: Here are sets of words that have a certain relationship to one another. Each set has a missing word that you have to supply. Look at the first pair of words. Try to figure out what the relationship is. Then choose a word from the list that *best* completes the second pair in the set. (All words do not fit in.) The first is done for you.**

> **Word list:** hide, house, nice, proud, sire, hay, sow, stallion, ewe, gander, drake, stable, water, milk, drink, cruel, tired, great, hot.

1. *Bird* is to *nest* as *horse* is to _____**stable**_____ .
2. *Cool* is to *cold* as *warm* is to _____ .
3. *Cow* is to *bull* as *duck* is to _____ .
4. *Deer* is to *doe* as *pig* is to _____ .
5. *Hungry* is to *eat* as *thirsty* is to _____ .
6. *In* is to *out* as *kind* is to _____ .

> Answers: 1. stable 2. hot 3. drake 4. sow 5. drink 6. cruel
> Tell students the results.

*(continued)*

**FIGURE 11.6** (*continued*)

INTERMEDIATE-GRADE LEVEL

*SKILL: ANALOGIES (WORD RELATIONSHIPS)*

Objective: The students will complete each analogy statement with the *best* word.

Test

> **Directions: Find the relationship between a pair of words and then complete each analogy with the *best* word. There are more words given in the list than you need.**
>
> **Word list:** sun, moon, light, cold, kilometer, pour, year, rate, ship, day, compass, rain, cards, blizzard, doe, time, era, kind, drove, dame, ram, century, place, ewe, love, cub, binary, meter, ecstasy, chirp, moo, friend, hate, millimeter.
>
> 1. *Happy* is to *sad* as *night* is to _____ .
> 2. *Rain* is to *downpour* as *snow* is to _____ .
> 3. *Horse* is to *mare* as *deer* is to _____ .
> 4. *Chicken* is to *rooster* as *sheep* is to _____ .
> 5. *Sad* is to *miserable* as *joy* is to _____ .
> 6. *One* is to *thousand* as *meter* is to _____ .
> 7. *Hint* is to *disclose* as *drip* is to _____ .
> 8. *Distance* is to *odometer* as *direction* is to _____ .
>
> Answers: 1. day,  2. blizzard,  3. doe,  4. ram,  5. ecstasy,  6. kilometer,  7. pour, 8. compass
>
> Tell students the results.

### Teaching Analogies: Primary Grades

Here are some instructional procedures and materials that you can use to help primary-grade students understand analogies:

1. Present students with the words *hot* and *cold*. Ask them what the relationship between the two words is. Help them to recognize that *hot* and *cold* are opposites. Present students with the words *tall* and *short*. Ask them what the relationship between the words is. Again help them to recognize that they are opposites. Tell them that they are going to work with word relationships. The first relationship will be opposites. Put the following on the chalkboard:

> *Thin* is to *fat* as *little* is to _____ .

Ask them to give you a word that would fit the blank. Present a number of opposite relationships to your students.

2. Present students with the words *little* and *small*. Ask them what the relationship between the words is. Help them to recognize that these words have the same meaning; they are synonyms. Present students with the words *big* and *large*. Ask them what the relationship between the words is. Again help them to recognize that the words are similar in meaning. Tell the students that they are going to work with word relationships. Put the following on the chalkboard:

*Sad* is to *gloomy* as *happy* is to _____.

Ask them to give you a word that would fit the blank. Present a number of such relationships to your students.

3.  Do the same as above for different kinds of relationships.

Go over each analogy with the students. Have them explain why they chose the word that they did.

**Teaching Analogies: Upper Grades**

Here are some instructional procedures and materials that you can use to help upper-grade students understand analogies.

1.  Discuss the various relationships that words can have to one another and ask the students to give examples. Put the examples on large newsprint so that students can refer to them. As students learn new relationships, have them add to the list.

For example:

Opposites: *hot* is to *cold*
Similarities: *thin* is to *lean*
Degree of intensity: *pretty* is to *beautiful*
Classification: *boat* is to *vehicle*
Ratio: *5* is to *10*
Part is to whole: *finger* is to *hand*
Whole is to part: *foot* is to *toe*
Parent is to child: *bear* is to *cub*

2.  Have students construct their own analogies.

Here are some additional vocabulary activities that can help children to develop their vocabularies.

**Word Map[20]**

1.  Divide a piece of paper into four parts.
2.  Write a word in the center of the paper.
3.  Label each square with the following labels: synonym, antonym, example, nonexample.
4.  Have students write the distinguishing features for the word in the center.

| | |
|---|---|
| **Synonym:** Mad<br><br>*Angry* | **Antonym:** Happy |
| **Example:** My Dad when I do something wrong | **Nonexample:** When I score a home run |

[20]R. Schwartz and T. Raphael. "Concept of Definition: A Key to Improving Students' Vocabulary." (*Reading Teacher 39*: 198–205, 1985).

## Word Chain[21]

1. Identify a word associated with what you have been studying.
2. Write the word for all to see.
3. Tell students that they need to think of a second word that begins with the last letter of the displayed word. The word also has to relate to the displayed word in some way.
4. Continue building the chain until all possibilities have been exhausted.

*Note:* I have been very successful using this as a small group activity in college classes.

## Knowledge Rating[22]

1. Present students with a list of words in grid form as shown below.

| Word | Know Well | Seen/Heard It | Don't Know It |
|------|-----------|---------------|---------------|
| Apartment | √ | | |
| Villa | | √ | |
| Geodesic dome | | √ | |
| Yurt | | | √ |

2. Ask students to rate their understanding of each term by placing a √ in the appropriate column on the grid.
3. After students have rated themselves, invite them to share their ideas about the words and highlight the words that you feel need to be addressed.
4. Have students make predictions about what they will be reading based on these words. For example, you might say something like, "What do you think the topic of this chapter will be, based on our discussion of these words?"

## Book Aids[23]

Experienced readers know that authors use aids to signal important words, which helps the reader to comprehend. Most often, these aids and their functions have to be taught to students. Here are some examples:

1. *The use of boldface type and italics*
2. *Glossaries*
3. *Pronunciation guides*

[21]Trussell-Cullen, A. *50 Wonderful Word Games.* New York, NY: Scholastic, 1998.

[22]C. Blachowicz. "Problem-solving strategies for academic success." In G. P. Wallach and K. G. Butter (Eds.) *Language Learning Disabilities in School-Aged Children and Adolescents: Some Principles and Applications* (pp. 304–322). (Englewood Cliffs, NJ: Merrill/Prentice Hall, 1994).

[23]C. Blachowicz and P. Fisher. *Teaching Vocabulary in all Classrooms,* 2nd ed. Upper Saddle River, NJ: Merrill/Prentice Hall, 2002.

4. *Words defined contextually* (e.g., "pollution, the soiling of the air and water, is an increasing threat to wildlife in the Gulf region.")
5. *End of unit exercises.* (How important it is to look at these BEFORE reading to see what will be highlighted.)

### Children's Literature

Reading literature aloud to children is a viable means of increasing vocabulary and reading achievement.[24] Be sure to choose books that appeal to children. The authors of these books must be aware of what is important to a child and what is likely to be confusing so that they can build meaning out of words through the kind of imagery that makes sense to a child. For example, in *Mike Mulligan and His Steam Shovel,* the meaning of *steam shovel* is clarified by giving numerous examples in which a steam shovel is used. In Margaret Wise Brown's book *The Dead Bird,* the meaning of *dead* is given by a description of the bird's state.[25]

Here are some additional titles sure to assist vocabulary development:

Adler, David. *How Tall, How Short, How Far Away?* New York: Holiday House, 1999.
Adoff, Arnold. *Outside, Inside.* San Diego, CA: Harcourt, 1981.
Agee, Jon. *Palindromania.* New York: Farrar, Straus, Giroux, 2002.
————. *Elvis Lives! And Other Anagrams.* New York: Farrar, Straus, Giroux, 2000.
————. *Who Ordered the Jumbo Shrimp? And Other Oxymorons.* New York: Farrar, Straus, & Giroux, 1998.
Appelt, Kathi. *Piggies in a Polka.* San Diego, CA: Harcourt, 2003.
Arnold, Tedd. *More Parts.* New York: Dial, 2001.
Ballard, Robin. *Carnival.* New York; Greenwillow, 1995.
Bee, William. *Whatever.* Cambridge, MA: Candlewick, 1995.
Cohen, Peter. *Boris's Glasses.* New York: Farrar, Straus, & Giroux, 2003.
Crimi, Carolyn. *Outside, Inside.* New York: Simon & Schuster, 1995.
Crowther, Robert. *Colors.* Cambridge, MA: Candlewick, 2001.
DeGross, Monalisa. *Donovan's Word Jar.* New York: HarperCollins, 1998.
Dunphy, Madeline. *Here is the Southwestern Desert.* New York: Hyperion, 1995.
————. *Here is the Tropical Rain Forest.* New York: Hyperion, 1994.
————. *Here is the Artic Winter.* New York: Hyperion, 1993.
Elya, Susan. *Oh no, Gotta Go!* New York: Putnam, 2003.
Emberly, Ed. *Glad Monster, Sad Monster: A Book about Feelings.* New York; Little, Brown, 1997.

---

[24]Dorothy H. Cohen, "The Effect of Literature on Vocabulary and Reading Achievement," *Elementary English*, 45 (February 1968): 209–13, 217.

[25]D. Cohen, "Word Meaning and the Literary Experience in Early Childhood" *Elementary English 46* (Nov. 1969): 914–25.

Frasier, Debra. *Miss Alaineus: A Vocabulary Disaster*. San Diego, CA: Harcourt, 2000.

Glassman, Peter. *My Dad's Job*. New York: Simon & Schuster, 2003.

Grover, Max. *Max's Wacky Taxi Day*. San Diego, CA: Harcourt, 1997.

Hirschi, Ron. *Faces in the Forest*. New York: Cobblehill/Dutton, 1997.

Hoban, Tana. *So Many Circles, So Many Squares*. New York: Greenwillow, 1998.

————. *All About Where*. New York: Greenwillow, 1991.

————. *Shapes, Shapes, Shapes*. New York; Greenwillow, 1986.

————. *Is it Larger? Is it Smaller?* New York: Greenwillow, 1985.

Jeppson, Ann-Sofie. *Here Comes Pontus!* New York: Farrar, Straus, & Giroux, 2000.

Kalman, Maira. *What Pete Ate from A to Z*. New York: Putnam, 2001.

Kirk, Daniel. *Trash Trucks!* New York: Putnam, 1997.

Kiss, Andrew. *A Mountain Alphabet*. Toronto, Canada: Tundra, 1996.

Lasky, Kathryn. *Pond Year*. Cambridge, MA: Candlewick, 1995.

Levitt, Paul, Douglas Burger, and Elissa Guralnick. *The Weighty Word Book*. Boulder, CO: Manuscripts Ltd, 1985.

Lewin, Ted. *Fair!* New York: Lothrop, 1997.

Mitchell, Joyce Slayton. *Tractor-Trailer Trucker: A Powerful Truck Book*. Berkeley, CA: Tricycle Press, 2000.

Morris, Ann. *Shoes, Shoes, Shoes*. New York: Lothrop, 1995.

Reinhart, Matthew. *Animal Opposites: A Pop-Up Book of Opposites*. New York: Little Simon, 2002.

Rotner, Shelly, and Richard Olivo. *Close, Closer, Closest*. New York: Atheneum, 1997.

Samoyault, Tiphanie. *Alphabetical Order: How the Alphabet Began*. New York: Viking, 1998.

Siebert, Diane. *Truck Song*. New York: Harper Trophy, 1984.

Silverstein, Shel. *Runny Babbit: A Billy Sook*. New York: HarperCollins, 2005.

Smith, Charles R. Jr. *Short Takes*. New York: Dutton, 2001.

Sobel, June. *B is for Bulldozer: A Construction ABC*. San Diego: Harcourt, 2003.

Spires, Elizabeth. *Riddle Road: Puzzles in Poems and Pictures*. New York: McElderry, 1999.

Stojic, Manya. *Hello World! Greetings in 42 Languages Around the Globe!* New York: Scholastic, 2002.

Tobias, Tobi. *A World of Words: An ABC of Quotations*. New York: Lothrop, 1998.

Yoe, Craig. *Mighty Book of Jokes*. New York: Price, Stern, Sloan, 2001.

Yoe, Craig. *Mighty Book of Riddles*. New York: Price, Stern, Sloan, 2001.

### *Websites*

Websites provide a vehicle that can help students get excited about vocabulary study. Technology can be integrated into explicit teaching before, during, or after a reading experience. Likewise, students can use websites independently for meaningful vocabulary activities. Here are some they might want to visit:

www.vocabulary.com can be used by middle and high school students and teachers. It contains several different kinds of puzzles written at different levels. Emphasis is placed on definitions and root words. This is also a good site for those trying to improve their vocabularies in preparation for the SAT.

http://rhyme.lycos.com contains a rhyming dictionary and thesaurus. Visitors can type in a word and locate several words associated with it such as rhymes, synonyms, definitions, quotations, pictures, and words with similar spellings.

www.wordsmith.org/awad contains a word a day. Visitors can subscribe to it so that they receive a word each day through e-mail. They can also find additional words by searching the archives. An explanation of origin, a definition, a pronunciation guide, and at least one quote using the word are provided.

http://www.englishclub.net provides grammar and vocabulary activities, word games, and other activities. It also offers free handouts for ESL teachers.

www.m-w.com is a site from Merriam-Webster that offers several resources including an online dictionary and daily word games.

## NOTING STUDENT PROGRESS

As we mention throughout this text, assessment drives instruction. This is true for vocabulary instruction as well as for any other aspect of reading. Three questions continually surface: What do I want to know? Why do I want to know? How can I best discover? In terms of vocabulary, we want to know about several different dimensions. We can approach these questions in two main ways.

First, some of the assessment techniques we mention in earlier chapters are excellent tools for answering these questions. These include observation, talking with students, and using the word test of an informal reading inventory. The checklists shown in Figures 11.7 and 11.8 can provide documentation of our observations. We wish to underscore that these observations need to occur in a variety of contexts while students are reading a variety of texts.

Second, we can use teacher-created informal assessments such as the ones shown in this chapter. These can be used to help shed light on which students might need additional help learning a given aspect of vocabulary.

We provide the chart in Table 11.1 as a way of reminding you that purpose dictates the selection of the most appropriate assessment measure. These are intended as suggestions, not an all-inclusive list.

**FIGURE 11.7    Diagnostic Checklist for Vocabulary Development (Primary Grades)**

Student's Name: _____

Grade: _____

Teacher: _____

|  | Yes | No |
|---|---|---|
| 1. The child shows that he or she is developing a vocabulary consciousness by recognizing that some words have more than one meaning. | | |
| 2. The child uses context clues to figure out word meanings. | | |
| 3. The child can state the opposite of words such as *stop, tall, fat, long, happy, big.* | | |
| 4. The child can state the synonym of words such as *big, heavy, thin, mean, fast, hit.* | | |
| 5. The child can state different meanings for homographs (words that are spelled the same but have different meanings based on their use in a sentence). Examples: I did not *state* what *state* I live in. Do not *roll* the roll on the floor. *Train* your dog not to bark when he hears a *train.* | | |
| 6. The child is developing a vocabulary of the senses by being able to state words that describe various sounds, smells, signs, tastes, and touches. | | |
| 7. The child is expanding his or her vocabulary by combining two words to form compound words such as *grandfather, bedroom, cupcake, backyard, toothpick, buttercup, firefighter.* | | |
| 8. The child is expanding his or her vocabulary by combining roots of words with prefixes and suffixes. Examples: *return, friendly, unhappy, disagree, dirty, precook, unfriendly.* | | |
| 9. The child is able to give the answer to a number of word riddles. | | |
| 10. The child is able to make up a number of word riddles. | | |
| 11. The child is able to classify various objects such as fruits, animals, colors, pets, and so on. | | |
| 12. The child is able to give words that are associated with certain objects and ideas. Example: hospital—*nurse, doctor, beds, sick persons, medicine,* and so on. | | |
| 13. The child is able to complete some analogy proportions such as *Happy is to sad as fat is to* _____ . | | |
| 14. The child shows that he or she is developing a vocabulary consciousness by using the dictionary to look up unknown words. | | |

**FIGURE 11.8   Diagnostic Checklist for Vocabulary Development (Intermediate Grades)**

Student's Name:   _____

Grade:   _____

Teacher:   _____

| | Yes | No |
|---|---|---|
| 1. The student recognizes that many words have more than one meaning. | | |
| 2. The student uses context clues to figure out the meanings. | | |
| 3. The student can give synonyms for words such as *similar, secluded, passive, brief, old, cryptic, anxious.* | | |
| 4. The student can give antonyms for words such as *prior, most, less, best, optimist, rash, humble, content.* | | |
| 5. The student can state different meanings for homographs (words that are spelled the same but have different meanings based on their use in a sentence), for example:<br>It is against the law to *litter* the streets.<br>The man was placed on the *litter* in the ambulance.<br>My dog gave birth to a *litter* of puppies. | | |
| 6. The student is able to use word parts to figure out word meanings. | | |
| 7. The student is able to use word parts to build words. | | |
| 8. The student is able to complete analogy statements or proportions. | | |
| 9. The student is able to give the connotative meaning of a number of words. | | |
| 10. The student is able to work with word categories. | | |
| 11. The student is able to answer a number of word riddles. | | |
| 12. The student is able to make up a number of word riddles. | | |
| 13. The student uses the dictionary to find word meanings. | | |

**TABLE 11.1    Three Important Questions for Assessing Vocabulary**

| What Do I Want to Know? | Why Do I Want to Know? | How Can I Best Discover? |
| --- | --- | --- |
| Do students have a store of sight words? | Having a sight vocabulary is essential for reading. If a student is limited in this area, I need to provide several opportunities for the students to acquire and apply new words. | • Observation<br>• Word test from IRI |
| Are students developing a vocabulary consciousness? | Having a desire to learn words is a sure way for students to continue to expand their vocabularies, making comprehension of increasingly more complex texts possible. | • Self-selection strategy<br>• Talking with students<br>• Students' contributions to Word Wall |
| Are students able to apply what they know about word parts as one way to learn about new words? | The purpose for learning word parts is to use them when reading. I want to know if students are applying what they are learning and if not, why not. | • Talking with students<br>• Observation |
| How much time are students reading? | Wide reading is one way for students to acquire a large vocabulary. I need to ensure time in school for this reading, especially if students are not able to read after school for one reason or another. | • Independent Reading Record<br>• Observation |

# SUMMARY

In this chapter, we present information about helping children acquire an ever-expanding reading vocabulary. To this end, we provide an explanation about how vocabulary develops. This explanation includes vocabulary acquisition, vocabulary consciousness, levels of knowing a word, types of words, sight words, and word part terminology. We then provide some guidelines for teaching vocabulary effectively, along with several teaching suggestions. We continually stress that good vocabulary and good reading go hand in hand and that children who have a large vocabulary are more likely to be successful readers because they have an understanding of many words.

As with other aspects of reading, assessing vocabulary is necessary and we offer some assessment suggestions reminding you that three questions need to be asked and answered in order to select the most appropriate assessment technique: What do I want to know? Why do I want to know? How can I best discover? Finally, we underscore the importance of having students do much reading to increase their vocabularies. Many times this reading needs to take place during the school day so that all children are afforded the necessary texts, time, and space.

# CHAPTER 11 KEY CONCEPTS

- Knowledge of vocabulary is necessary to be a good reader.
- As children advance in concept development, their vocabulary must also increase.
- Children acquire a tremendous amount of words through wide reading.
- Children need to be explicitly taught some selected words in order to increase their reading vocabularies.
- Children need to talk about new words because discussion brings greater understanding.
- Children who have a vocabulary consciousness are interested in increasing their vocabu-

lary. Therefore, helping children to acquire a vocabulary consciousness is a major goal of teachers who want to have an effective vocabulary program.
- There are many tools students need to use to discover new words. The dictionary and combining forms are two of these tools.
- There are specific guidelines for effective vocabulary teaching.
- There are many teaching strategies that can be used to explicitly teach vocabulary.
- Assessment is an integral part of a good vocabulary program.

# SUGGESTIONS FOR THOUGHT QUESTIONS AND ACTIVITIES

1. You are interested in developing a vocabulary expansion program using combining forms. How would you go about doing it? What kinds of activities would you develop for students weak in vocabulary?
2. How important is vocabulary development? Explain.
3. How can you diagnose vocabulary problems in content areas?
4. Construct a pretest to determine whether your intermediate-grade students have knowledge of some often-used combining forms.
5. You have been asked to generate a number of diagnostic tests for intermediate-grade students in vocabulary development. What kind of diagnostic tests would you develop?
6. Develop a Word Wall activity to help your children learn to read and spell.

# INTERNET ACTIVITIES

Choose a search engine and search for websites related to vocabulary development. Select one web-site from the search and print out one artifact that you particularly want to add to your teaching ideas.

# SELECTED BIBLIOGRAPHY

Allen, J. *Words, Words, Words: Teaching Vocabulary in Grades 4–12.* York, ME: Stenhouse Publishers, 1999.

Baumann, J. F., and E. Kame'Enui, eds. *Vocabulary Instruction: Research to Practice.* New York: Guildford, 2004.

Blachowicz, C., and C. Obrochta. "Vocabulary Visits: Virtual Field Trips for Content Vocabulary Development." *The Reading Teacher, 59* (2005): 262–68.

Blachowicz, Camille L. Z., and Peter Fisher. "Vocabulary Instruction," in Michael L. Kamil et al., eds. *Handbook of Reading Research,* Vol. III. Mahwah, NJ: Lawrence Erlbaum, 2000.

Chall, Jeanne S. *Learning to Read: The Great Debate,* 2d ed. New York: McGraw-Hill, 1983.

———. "Two Vocabularies for Reading: Recognition and Reading," in M. G. McKeown and M. E. Curtis, eds., *The Nature of Vocabulary Acquisition,* pp. 7–17. Hillsdale, NJ: Erlbaum, 1987.

Hartill, M. *Fab Vocab!* New York, NY: Scholastic, 1998.

Johnson, B. *Wordworks: Exploring Language Play.* Golden, CO: Fulcrum, 1999.

Johnson, Dale D. *Vocabulary in the Elementary and Middle Grades.* Boston: Allyn and Bacon, 2001.

Mazano, R. and D. Pickering. *Building Academic Vocabulary.* Alexandria, VA: Association for Supervision and Curriculum Development, 2005.

Nagy, W. *Teaching Vocabulary to Improve Reading Comprehension.* Newark, DE: International Reading Association, 1988.

Nagy, William E., and Judith A. Scott. "Vocabulary Processes," in Michael L. Kamil et al., eds; *Handbook of Reading Research,* Vol. III. Mahwah, NJ: Lawrence Erlbaum, 2000.

Ohanian, S. *The Great Word Catalogue: Fundamental Activities for Building Vocabulary.* Portsmouth, NH: Heinemann, 2002.

Robb, L. *Easy Mini-Lessons for Building Vocabulary.* New York: Scholastic, 1999.

Rubin, Dorothy. *Gaining Word Power,* 6th ed. Boston: Allyn and Bacon, 2000.

———. *Phonics Skills & Strategies in a Balanced Reading Program* (Levels 1—4 series). Torrance, CA: Fearon Teacher Aids, 1998.

———. "Vocabulary Development in the Language Arts Program," in *Elementary Language Arts,* 6th ed. Boston: Allyn and Bacon, 2000.

———. *Vocabulary Skills & Strategies in a Balanced Reading Program.* Torrance, CA: Fearon Teacher Aids, 1998.

Schwartz, R., and T. Raphael, "Concept of Definition: A Key to Improving Students' Vocabulary". *The Reading Teacher,* (1985) 198–203.

Tompkins, G. E., and C. Blanchfield. *Teaching Vocabulary: 50 Creative Strategies, Grades K-12,* 2004.

## Children's Literature Cited

Adler, David. *How Tall, How Short, How Far Away?* New York: Holiday House, 1999.

Adoff, Arnold. *Outside, Inside.* San Diego, CA: Harcourt, 1981.

Agee, Jon. *Palindromania.* New York; Farrar, Straus, Giroux, 2002.

———. *Elvis Lives! And Other Anagrams.* New York: Farrar, Straus, Giroux, 2000.

———. *Who Ordered the Jumbo Shrimp? And Other Oxymorons.* New York: Farrar, Straus, & Giroux, 1998.

Appelt, Kathi. *Piggies in a Polka.* San Diego, CA: Harcourt, 2003.

Arnold, Tedd. *More Parts.* New York: Dial, 2001.

Ballard, Robin. *Carnival.* New York; Greenwillow, 1995.

Bee, William. *Whatever.* Cambridge, MA: Candlewick, 2005.

Cohen, Peter. *Boris's Glasses.* New York: Farrar, Straus, & Giroux, 2003.

Crimi, Carolyn. *Outside, Inside.* New York: Simon & Schuster, 1995.

Crowther, Robert. *Colors.* Cambridge, MA: Candlewick, 2001.

DeGross, Monalisa. *Donovan's Word Jar.* New York: HarperCollins, 1998.

Dunphy, Madeline. *Here Is the Southwestern Desert.* New York: Hyperion, 1995.

———. *Here Is the Tropical Rain Forest.* New York: Hyperion, 1994.

———. *Here Is the Arctic Winter.* New York: Hyperion, 1993.

Elya, Susan. *Oh no, Gotta Go!* New York: Putnam, 2003.

Emberly, Ed. *Glad Monster, Sad Monster: A Book about Feelings.* New York: Little, Brown, 1997.

Frasier, Debra. *Miss Alaineus: A Vocabulary Disaster.* San Diego, CA: Harcourt, 2000.

Glassman, Peter. *My Dad's Job.* New York: Simon & Schuster, 2003.

Grover, Max. *Max's Wacky Taxi Day.* San Diego, CA: Harcourt, 1997.

Hirschi, Ron. *Faces in the Forest.* New York; Cobblehill/Dutton, 1997.

Hoban, Tana. *So Many Circles, So Many Squares.* New York: Greenwillow, 1998.

———. *All About Where.* New York: Greenwillow, 1991.

———. *Shapes, Shapes, Shapes.* New York; Greenwillow, 1986.

———. *Is It Larger? Is It Smaller?* New York: Greenwillow, 1985.

Jeppson, Ann-Sofie. *Here Comes Pontus!* New York: Farrar, Straus, & Giroux, 2000.

Kalman, Maira. *What Pete Ate from A to Z.* New York: Putnam, 2001.

Kirk, Daniel. *Trash Trucks!* New York: Putnam, 1997.

Kiss, Andrew. *A Mountain Alphabet.* Toronto, Canada: Tundra, 1996.

Lasky, Kathryn. *Pond Year.* Cambridge, MA: Candlewick, 1995.

Levitt, Paul, Douglas Burger, and Elissa Guralnick. *The Weighty Word Book.* Boulder, CO: Manuscripts Ltd., 1985.

Lewin, Ted. *Fair!* New York: Lothrop, 1997.

Mitchell, Joyce Slayton. *Tractor-Trailer Trucker: A Powerful Truck Book.* Berkeley, CA: Tricycle Press, 2000.

Morris, Ann. *Shoes, Shoes, Shoes.* New York: Lothrop, 1995.

Reinhart, Matthew. *Animal Opposites: A Pop-Up Book of Opposites.* New York: Little Simon, 2002.

Rotner, Shelly, and Richard Olivo. *Close, Closer, Closest.* New York: Atheneum, 1997.

Samoyault, Tiphanie. *Alphabetical Order: How the Alphabet Began.* New York: Viking, 1998.

Siebert, Diane. *Truck Song.* New York: Harper Trophy, 1984.

Silverstein, Shel. *Runny Babbit: A Billy Sook.* New York: HarperCollins, 2005.

Smith, Charles R. Jr. *Short Takes.* New York: Dutton, 2001.

Sobel, June. *B is for Bulldozer: A Construction ABC.* San Diego: Harcourt, 2003.

Spires, Elizabeth. *Riddle Road: Puzzles in Poems and Pictures.* New York: McElderry, 1999.

Stojic, Manya. *Hello World! Greetings in 42 Languages Around the Globe!* New York: Scholastic, 2002.

Tobias, Tobi. *A World of Words: An ABC of Quotations.* New York: Lothrop, 1998.

Yoe, Craig. *Mighty Book of Jokes.* New York: Price, Stern, Sloan, 2001.

Yoe, Craig. *Mighty Book of Riddles.* New York: Price, Stern, Sloan, 2001.

# 12

# Helping Children Comprehend

## Scenario: Assessing and Teaching Alan

Alan Y is a fifth-grader who scored at a 4.2 level on the reading comprehension subtest of the *California Achievement Tests,*[*] which is given in the fall of the school year and is used as a screening device for instructional purposes. Ms. Mills knows that Alan appears to have a problem in comprehension, but she does not know why. Therefore, Ms. Mills chooses a comprehension assessment measure that will help her learn more about Alan's specific comprehension strengths and problems. From observing Alan in his reading group and from individual sessions, Ms. Mills knows that Alan appears to be strong at the literal comprehension level. His problem appears to be at the interpretive and critical reading levels. Ms. Mills administers a criterion-referenced test to Alan to determine what specific interpretive and critical reading skills he uses and those that need explicit instruction. The criterion-referenced test she uses reveals a number of difficulties in specific skills that appear to be causing problems for Alan, one of which is finding the main idea. Ms. Mills decides that she will probe further to find out what strategies Alan is using to find the main idea of paragraphs. She chooses a few paragraphs at Alan's independent reading level so that he can read with ease. Alan reads the first paragraph silently and then attempts to state its main idea. He then reads the second paragraph silently and states its main idea. Ms. Mills notices that Alan gives the topic as the main idea. She asks Alan what he thinks the main idea of any paragraph should tell him. Alan answers, "What the paragraph is about." Ms. Mills says, "Good, but that is only part of it. What the paragraph is about is the topic of the paragraph. No wonder you keep giving the topic as the main idea."

Ms. Mills proceeds to tell Alan that there is a technique that can help him find the main idea of paragraphs. She says, "Every paragraph is written about something or someone. The something or someone is the topic of the paragraph. To find the main idea of the paragraph, you must determine what the topic of the paragraph is and what the author is saying about it that is special. Once you have found these two things, you should have the main idea. Let's try one together."

### Modeling: An Instructional Technique

Ms. Mills decides to model (think out loud) for Alan to show him how she would go about finding the main idea, so she says the following:

"Here is a paragraph from one of the books you are reading. Let's go through the various steps to get the main idea of it. Remember, to find the main idea, we must first find the topic of the paragraph and then what is special or unique about it. All the details should develop the main idea."

"Let's both read the paragraph." Here is the paragraph they both read:

Paul Smith wasn't a liar; he just exaggerated a lot. Paul exaggerated so much that people always expected him to exaggerate. Paul never disappointed them. Here are some examples of Paul's exaggerations. If Paul ate three pancakes, he'd say, "I ate fifty pancakes." Also, if he walked a mile, he'd say, "I walked a hundred miles today."

*Now called *TerraNova* CAT.

After reading the paragraph, Ms. Mills says: "First I ask myself what is the topic of the paragraph? Asking the question who or what can help me get the topic, so I'll try that. Alan, you try it too. I know you're good at doing this.

"Here are our choices:

a. Lying
b. Paul's lying
c. Paul's exaggeration
d. Exaggeration

"What did you choose? Good, I chose—Paul's exaggeration, also. I chose it because it best answers what the paragraph is about, but I know that this is not the main idea; it is only part of it. I have to go on and ask myself some other questions. Listen carefully to what I do next. Now, I have to decide what the author is saying about Paul's exaggeration that is special and helps tie all the details together. Here are our choices:

a. It is bad.
b. It is not believed.
c. It is a problem.
d. It applies to everything he does.
e. It should not be allowed.

"I chose d. The topic is Paul's exaggeration, and what is special about it is that it applies to everything he does. Therefore, the main idea is 'Paul's exaggeration applies to everything he does.'"

"When I check to see if all the details support this, I find that they do."

Ms. Mills tells Alan that she knows finding the main idea can be challenging, but with more practice, she is sure he will improve.

# INTRODUCTION

Ms. Mills is a knowledgeable teacher. She knows that assessment drives instruction, and this is the main reason that she assessed Alan before doing any explicit teaching. Before she gave the assessment, she had developed some "hunches" about Alan's comprehension, but she needed to further evaluate how to best help him.

Ms. Mills also invited Alan to be an informant on his own reading by asking him for his thoughts about main idea. She was checking his metacognition, his ability to talk about what he was doing relative to identifying main idea. She discovered that he had a limited understanding of main idea and that this limited view was part of the problem. She provided him with appropriate instruction, which included much guidance. Once Alan embraced this new understanding, he was better able to ascertain the main idea.

In this chapter, we elaborate on what transpired in this scenario. Our purpose is to provide you with some background related to reading comprehension and some specific assessment and teaching suggestions for helping students to better comprehend.

# CHAPTER OBJECTIVES

After reading the chapter, you should be able to:

- Define what is meant by *comprehension.*
- Discuss how listening comprehension relates to reading comprehension.
- Define what is meant by *reading comprehension.*
- Explain what is meant by explicit instruction in comprehension.
- Explain how oral reading can be used to enhance comprehension.
- Explain the difference between comprehension skills and comprehension strategies.
- Discuss similarities and differences between cloze and maze.
- Explain how teachers can help students to develop various comprehension skills and strategies.
- Discuss different ways to document student progress.

# BUILDING BACKGROUND ABOUT COMPREHENSION

## COMPREHENSION

**Comprehension**
Understanding; the ability to get the meaning of something.

Comprehension is a construct; that is, it cannot be directly observed or directly measured. We can only infer from overt behavior that someone "understands." *Webster's Third New International Dictionary* defines *comprehension* as "the act or action of grasping (as an act or process) with the intellect," and *intellect* is defined as "the capacity for rational or intelligent thought especially when highly developed." The more intelligent an individual is, the more able he or she is to comprehend. What may not be so obvious is that persons who have difficulty understanding may have this difficulty because they have not had certain experiences that require higher levels of thinking; thus, they may not have learned how to do high-level thinking.

## LISTENING COMPREHENSION

To be able to recognize expressions in print, students must have heard these phrases correctly in the past; they must be in the students' listening vocabulary. Reading comprehension depends on comprehension of the spoken language. Students who are sensitive to the arrangement of words in oral language are more sensitive to the same idea in written language. Listening helps to enlarge a student's vocabulary. It is through listening that children learn many expressions they will eventually see in print. Listening takes place all the time. Teachers orally explain word meanings and discuss what the text says. Students listen to other children read orally, talk about books, and explain their contents.

In the elementary grades, when children are learning to read, many students prefer to listen rather than to read independently. These children gain more comprehension and retention from listening because of the important added cues they receive from the speaker, such as stress given to words or phrases and facial expressions.[1] Other children prefer to read because they can set their own rate of reading for maximum comprehension and retention. They do not wish to be constrained by the fixed oral rate of the teacher. Both listening and reading are important. We want students to feel comfortable in both situations.

Sometimes, a student can understand a passage when it is orally read, but cannot understand it when reading it alone. This indicates that the words are in the student's listening vocabulary but that the student may not have gained the skills necessary for decoding words from their written forms. It could also be that the student has some kind of visual problem.

It may be that some words are in the children's listening vocabulary (for example, they know the meaning of the individual words when they are said aloud), but they still might not be able to assimilate the words into a meaningful concept. The instructor will have to help these children in concept development and in gaining the necessary reading comprehension and listening skills.

A person who does not do well in listening comprehension skills will usually not do well in reading comprehension skills. Help in one area usually enhances the other because both listening and reading contain some important similar skills,[2] as researchers going as far back as the 1930s have noted. For example, an investigation made in 1936 found that children who did poorly in comprehension through listening were also poor in reading comprehension.[3] Research in 1955 on the relationship between reading and listening found that practice in listening for detail will produce a significant gain in reading for the same purpose.[4] Others have also found that training in listening comprehension skills will produce significant gains in reading comprehension[5] and that reading and listening have similar thinking skills.[6]

A number of other studies have been done that strongly support the link between reading and listening comprehension. In one such study, a researcher asked whether some good decoders in reading are poor comprehenders because of an overemphasis with word accuracy when decoding or because of a lack of

> **Listening vocabulary**
> The number of different words one knows the meaning of when they are said aloud.

---

[1]Robert Ruddell, "Oral Language and the Development of Other Language Skills," *Elementary English* 43 (May 1966): 489–98.

[2]Thomas Jolly, "Listen My Children and You Shall Read," *Language Arts* 57 (February 1980): 214–17.

[3]William E. Young, "The Relation of Reading Comprehension and Retention to Hearing Comprehension and Retention," *Journal of Experimental Education* 5 (September 1936): 30–39.

[4]Annette P. Kelty, "An Experimental Study to Determine the Effect of Listening for Certain Purposes upon Achievement in Reading for Those Purposes," *Abstracts of Field Studies for the Degree of Doctor of Education* 15 (Greeley: Colorado State College of Education, 1955): 82–95.

[5]Sybil M. Hoffman, "The Effect of a Listening Skills Program on the Reading Comprehension of Fourth Grade Students," Ph.D. dissertation, Walden University, 1978. Janice A. Dole and Virginia Simon Feldman, "The Development and Validation of a Listening Comprehension Test As a Predictor of Reading Comprehension: Preliminary Results," *Educational Research Quarterly* 9 (1984–1985): 40–46.

[6]Thomas Sticht et al., *Auding and Reading: A Developmental Model* (Alexandria, VA.: Human Resources Research Organization, 1974). Walter Kintsch and Ely Kozminsky, "Summarizing Stories After Reading and Listening," *Journal of Educational Psychology* 69 (1977): 491–99.

listening comprehension; that is, the decoders are "word callers" who do not have the words in their listening vocabulary. The results of the study suggest that the students' "listening vocabulary was not better than their reading comprehension. So, decoding does not seem to distract or otherwise interfere with comprehension among children whose decoding skills are well developed. [Instead, according to the investigator,] once a child has become a good decoder, differences in reading ability will reflect differences in listening ability."[7]

Although there are many common factors involved in the decoding of reading and listening—which would account for the relationship between the two areas—listening and reading are, nonetheless, separated by unique factors. The most obvious is that listening calls for *hearing,* whereas reading calls for *seeing.* As has already been stated, in the area of listening, the speakers are doing much of the interpretation for the listeners by their expressions, inflections, stresses, and pauses. Similarly, the listeners do not have to make the proper *grapheme (letter)-phoneme (sound) correspondences* because these have already been done for them by the speakers. It is possible for students to achieve excellent listening comprehension but not to do as well in reading comprehension.

> **Grapheme-phoneme correspondences**
> Letter-sound relationships.

In reading we must first make the proper grapheme-phoneme correspondences and must then organize these into the proper units to gain the author's intended meaning. Readers must also be able to determine the shades of meaning implied by the words, to recognize any special figures of speech, and finally to synthesize the unique ideas expressed by the passage.

In Table 12.1 we show some of the similarities between listening comprehension skills and reading comprehension skills. We also show the different levels of listening and offer a brief definition of each level.

**Special Note**

Given the similarities, using listening comprehension to help students with reading comprehension appears obvious. That is, when teaching students about recalling details, focus first on listening comprehension so that the students are only concerned with that specific skill. Then teach the same skill, but have students do the reading, which places emphasis on reading comprehension. ■

## READING COMPREHENSION

> **Reading comprehension**
> A complex intellectual process involving a number of abilities. The two major abilities involve word meanings and reasoning with verbal concepts.

*Reading comprehension* is a complex intellectual process involving a number of abilities. The two major abilities involve word meanings and verbal reasoning. Without word meanings and verbal reasoning, there would be no reading comprehension; and without reading comprehension, there is no reading. Most people would agree with these statements; however, disagreement surfaces when we ask, "How does an individual achieve comprehension while reading?" In 1917, Edward Thorndike put forth his statement that "reading is a very elaborate procedure, involving a weighing of each of many elements in a sentence,

---

[7]Susan Dymock, "Reading But Not Understanding," *Journal of Reading* 37 (October 1993): 90.

**TABLE 12.1    Comparison of Listening Comprehension and Reading Comprehension**

| Listening Levels | Listening Comprehension Skills | Reading Comprehension Skills |
|---|---|---|
| **Discriminative Listening:** Knowing which sounds to attend to and which to ignore; distinguishing verbal and nonverbal cues | | |
| •Phonological awareness | X | |
| •Vocal expression | X | |
| •Onomatopoeia | X | |
| **Precise Listening:** Paying attention and ascertaining details | | |
| •Associating words with meanings | X | X |
| •Deducing meaning of words from context | X | X |
| •Recalling details and sequences | X | X |
| •Following directions | X | X |
| •Recognizing multiple characters | X | X |
| **Strategic Listening:** Listening to gain understanding of the intended meaning of the message | | |
| •Connecting prior knowledge | X | X |
| •Summarizing | X | X |
| •Predicting | X | X |
| •Asking questions | X | X |
| •Inferencing | X | X |
| •Identifying main ideas | X | X |
| **Critical Listening:** Analyzing the message and evaluating it | | |
| •Recognizing emotive language | X | X |
| •Recognizing bias | X | X |
| •Distinguishing between fact and opinion | X | X |
| •Evaluating sources | X | X |
| •Detecting propaganda devices | X | X |
| **Appreciative Listening:** Listening to appreciate oral style | | |
| •Recognizing the power of language | X | X |
| •Appreciating oral interpretations | X | |
| •Understanding the power of imagination | X | X |

*Source:* Opitz, M., and M. Zbaracki. *Listen Hear! 25 Effective Listening Comprehension Strategies.* Portsmouth, NH: Heinemann, 2004.

their organization in the proper relations to one another, and the cooperation of many forces to determine final response."[8] He stated further that even the act of answering simple questions includes all the features characteristic of typical reasoning. Today investigators are still exploring reading comprehension in attempts to understand it better, and through the years many have expounded and expanded upon Thorndike's theories.[9]

For more than a quarter of a century, research into the process of understanding has been influenced by the fields of psycholinguistics and cognitive psychology. As a result, terms such as *surface structure*, *deep structure*, *microstructure*, *macrostructure*, *semantic networks*, *schemata*, *story grammar*, *story structure*, and *metacognition* are used by authors who provide their explanations about comprehension.

Although it is difficult to state definitively how persons achieve comprehension while reading, researchers report that good comprehenders appear to have certain characteristics.[10] Good comprehenders are able to do inferential reasoning; they can state the main or central ideas of information; they can assimilate, categorize, compare, make relationships, analyze, synthesize, and evaluate information. They engage in meaningful learning by assimilating new material to concepts already existing in their cognitive structures;[11] that is, good comprehenders relate their new learning to what they already know. Also, good comprehenders are able to think beyond the information given; they are able to come up with new or alternate solutions. In addition, they seem to know what information to attend to and what to ignore. Clearly those persons who have good strategies for processing information are able to bring more to and gain more from what they are reading or listening to than those who do not have these strategies. As we explain in Chapter 5, good comprehenders are active, purposeful, evaluative, thoughtful, strategic, persistent, and productive.

### Special Note

**Schema theory**
Deals with relations between prior knowledge and comprehension.

*Schema theory* deals with the relations between prior knowledge and comprehension. "According to schema theory, the reader's background knowledge serves as scaffolding to aid in encoding information from the text."[12] A person with more background knowledge for a given text will comprehend better than

---

[8]Edward L. Thorndike, "Reading as Reasoning: A Study of Mistakes in Paragraph Reading," *Journal of Educational Psychology* 8, No. 6 (June 1917): 323.

[9]Cathy Collins Black and Michael Pressley, eds., *Comprehension Instruction Research-Based Best Practices.* Guilford, 2002, New York.

[10]Barbara M. Taylor, "Children's Memory for Expository Text After Reading," *Reading Research Quarterly* 15:3 (1980): 399–411; B. J. Bartlett, "Top-level Structure as an Organizational Strategy for Recall of Classroom Text," unpublished doctoral dissertation, Arizona State University, 1978; and John P. Richards and Catherine W. Hatcher, "Interspersed Meaningful Learning Questions as Semantic Cues for Poor Comprehenders," *Reading Research Quarterly* 13, No. 4 (1977–1978): 551–52.

[11]Richards and Hatcher, p. 552.

[12]Steven Stahl, Michael G. Jacobson, Charlotte E. Davis, and Robin L. Davis, "Prior Knowledge and Difficult Vocabulary in the Comprehension of Unfamiliar Text," *Reading Research Quarterly* 24 (Winter 1989): 29.

one with less background. Preparing readers for what they will be reading "by actively building topic knowledge prior to reading will facilitate learning from text."[13] ■

## READING COMPREHENSION TAXONOMIES

**Reading comprehension taxonomy**
A hierarchy of reading comprehension skills ranging from the more simplistic to the more complex ones; a classification of these skills.

A number of *reading comprehension taxonomies* exist, and many appear similar to one another. This similarity is not surprising. Usually the individuals who develop a new taxonomy do so because they are unhappy with an existing one for some reason and want to improve upon it. As a result they may change category headings, but keep similar descriptions of the categories, or they may change the order of the hierarchy. Most of the existing taxonomies are adaptations in one way or another of Bloom's taxonomy of educational objectives in the cognitive domain, which is concerned with the thinking that students should achieve in any discipline. Bloom's taxonomy is based on an ordered set of objectives ranging from the more simplistic skills to the more complex ones. Bloom's objectives are cumulative in that each one includes the one preceding it.[14] And most taxonomies that have been evolved are also cumulative.[15]

In this text we use an adaptation of Nila Banton Smith's model.[15] In her original model, she presented literal-level reading skills as requiring no thinking. We believe that literal-type questions do require thinking, even though it is a low-level type of thinking. In our model, we divide the comprehension skills into four categories. Each category is cumulative in building on the others. The four comprehension categories are (1) literal comprehension, (2) interpretation, (3) critical reading, and (4) creative reading.

Two cautions are in order here. Grade level and age have little to do with the taxonomy. That is, children of all ages can engage at all levels of the taxonomy. Second, we need to guard against a strict linear type of thinking. Our own teaching experiences have shown us that there are some children who are able to answer higher-level comprehension questions, yet have difficulty answering literal questions. We offer the taxonomy as a way of helping you to think about the variety of questions that need to be used to better ensure thoughtful learners.

**Literal comprehension**
The ability to obtain a low-level type of understanding by using only information that is explicitly stated.

### Literal Comprehension

*Literal comprehension* represents the ability to obtain a low-level type of understanding by using only explicitly stated information. This category requires a lower level of thinking skills than the other three levels. Answers to literal questions simply demand that the pupil recall from memory what the book says.

[13]Ibid., p. 30.

[14]Benjamin Bloom, *Taxonomy of Educational Objectives Handbook 1: The Cognitive Domain.* New York: David McKay Co. Inc. 1956.

[15]Nila Banton Smith, "The Many Faces of Reading Comprehension," *The Reading Teacher* 23 (December 1969): 249–59, 291.

Although literal-type questions are considered a low-level type of thinking, it should *not* be construed that reading for details to gain facts that are explicitly stated is unimportant. A fund of knowledge is important and necessary in order to read texts in many different content areas. It is also the foundation for high-level thinking. If we want students to graduate to higher levels of thinking, we need to make sure that we ask more than literal questions.

### Interpretation

*Interpretation* is the next step in the hierarchy. This category demands a higher level of thinking because the questions are concerned with answers that are suggested or implied by the text, but not directly stated. To answer questions at the interpretive level, readers must have problem-solving ability and be able to work at various levels of abstraction. Obviously, children with learning difficulties will have trouble working at this level as well as in the next two categories.

The interpretive level is the one at which the most confusion exists when it comes to categorizing skills. The confusion concerns the term *inference*. *Inference* can be defined as something derived by reasoning; something that is not directly stated but suggested in the statement; a logical conclusion that is drawn from statements; a deduction; an induction. From the definitions we can see that inference is a broad reasoning skill and that there are many different kinds of inferences. All the reading skills in interpretation rely on the reader's ability to "infer" the answer in one way or another. However, by grouping all the interpretive reading skills under inference, "Some of the most distinctive and desirable skills would become smothered and obscured."[16]

Some of the reading skills that are usually found in interpretation are as follows:

- determining word meanings from context
- finding main ideas
- "reading between the lines" or drawing inferences[17]
- drawing conclusions
- making generalizations
- recognizing cause-and-effect reasoning
- recognizing analogies

### Critical Reading

*Critical reading* is at a higher level than the other two categories because it involves evaluation, the making of a personal judgment on the accuracy, value, and truthfulness of what is read. To be able to make judgments, a reader must be able to collect, interpret, apply, analyze, and synthesize the information. Critical reading includes such skills as the ability to differentiate between fact and opinion and fantasy and reality, as well as the ability to discern propaganda

**Interpretation**
A reading level that demands a higher level of thinking ability because the material it involves is not directly stated in the text but only suggested or implied.

**Critical reading**
A high-level reading skill that involves evaluation, making a personal judgment on the accuracy, value, and truthfulness of what is read.

---

[16]Ibid., pp. 255–56.

[17]Although, as already stated, all the interpretive skills depend on the ability of the reader to infer meanings, the specific skill of "reading between the lines" is the one that teachers usually refer to when they say they are teaching *inference*.

techniques. Critical reading is related to critical listening because they both require critical thinking.

**Creative reading**
Uses divergent thinking skills to go beyond the literal comprehension, interpretation, and critical reading levels.

### Creative Reading

*Creative reading* uses divergent thinking skills to go beyond the literal comprehension, interpretation, and critical reading levels. In creative reading, the reader tries to come up with new or alternate solutions to those presented by the writer.

## ORAL READING AND READING COMPREHENSION

Oral reading is another consideration related to reading comprehension. Although it is true that we most often read silently, oral reading is necessary as well, especially as it relates to reading comprehension. Through oral reading, students can further develop reading comprehension strategies such as making connections, predicting, visualizing, questioning, using prior knowledge, monitoring while reading, summarizing, and making inferences. Some students may need to learn how to visualize when reading, whereas others may need to learn how to use signals provided by the author to convey an idea (i.e., typographical signals).

Another reason for using oral reading is to teach children how to read with fluency, which appears to be associated with competent readers. That is, according to the reported results of the 2002 National Assessment of Educational Progress (NAEP), "Students who can read text passages aloud accurately and fluently at an appropriate pace are more likely to understand what they are reading, both silently and orally."[18] However, there also seems to be evidence from the same study that many of those tested need additional instruction to enhance their ability to comprehend. So, although reading fluency (i.e., "an effortless, smooth, and coherent oral production of a given passage . . . in terms of phrasing, adherence to the author's syntax, and expressiveness"[19]) appears to be a contributing factor to reading, we have to guard against thinking of it as the missing link that will help all students better comprehend. Instead, we need to focus on explicitly teaching reading comprehension. Said another way, beautiful oral reading is not a guarantee of reading comprehension.

### GUIDING PRINCIPLES

At least three guiding principles must be adhered to for effective use of these and other oral reading strategies that are meant to enhance comprehension. First, the specific strategy must be identified. Do students need to learn to visualize? Then induced imagery would be a good choice. Do students need to

---

[18]Manzo, K. "More Focus on Reading Fluency Needed, Study Suggests." *Education Week (2005) 25*:11.

[19]Ibid.

learn to attend to features such as enlarged print to see how doing so helps with understanding text? If so, then using a strategy such as "look for the signals"[20] would be a good choice.

Second, specific examples from children's literature selections should be provided. Using authentic examples is essential, for it shows children how authors actually use words and other typographic symbols to convey their ideas. Using children's literature also helps students connect the exercise with actual reading experiences. In other words, they can see the connection between the lesson and everyday reading.

Third, students need to be provided with meaningful practice. This practice provides students with time to actually use the skill that has just been taught as they read, making their internalization of it more likely. Books such as *Maniac Magee* (Spinelli, 1990), *Dear Mr. Henshaw* (Cleary, 1983), *Alligator Baby* (Munsch, 1997), and *When Papa Snores* (Long, 2000) are just a few examples that provide students with meaningful practice. Students can be reminded to use visualizing or attend to typographical cues as they read throughout the day. Students might also be encouraged to share examples of what they discovered.

## ORAL READING: ITS ROLE IN THE READING LESSON

Reading aloud to children is important for reading development. However, some teachers have gone overboard with oral reading. In numerous classrooms, the reading lesson consists primarily of a whole class of children of varying ability reading aloud together or with a tape—and silent reading is nonexistent. After the children learn a stock of vocabulary words, we need to incorporate silent reading into the reading lesson. And this silent reading needs to occur before oral reading in a guided reading lesson. In fact, oral reading may or may not be used depending on the purpose for the lesson. Unfortunately, some teachers have ignored silent reading and cite several reasons for this.[21]

Whether we use trade books or commercially produced reading programs, we need to set purposes for silent reading and oral reading. For example, children read silently to answer a question. After the children answer the question in their own words, they can act as detectives to find the clues that answer the question. Volunteers can then read aloud the answer. The National Reading Panel (NRP) did an extensive analysis of the available research that met their standards in the area of guided oral reading. Their investigation "concluded that guided repeated oral reading procedures that included guidance from teachers, peers, or parents had a significant and positive impact on word recognition, fluency, and comprehension across a range of grade levels."[22] The NRP also claimed that their research applies to good readers as well as those who have reading difficulties.

---

[20]Opitz, M., and T. Raskinski. *Good-bye Round Robin*. Portsmouth, NH: Heinemann, 1998.

[21]Ibid.

[22]National Reading Panel 2000. *Teaching Children to Read: An Evidence-Based Assessment of the Scientific Research Literature on Reading and its Implications for Reading Instruction.* Washington DC: US Department of Health and Human Services, National Institute of Health.

# COMPREHENSION SKILLS

The comprehension taxonomy we explain on pages 364–366 contains several comprehension skills for each level. Identifying the main idea of a paragraph, identifying the central idea of a passage, using visuals, and making inferences are just four skills. All of these are interpretive level reading skills and we present them here for both primary and intermediate grade children as examples of how skills can be assessed and taught.

## MAIN IDEA OF A PARAGRAPH

### *Background*

The main idea is probably the skill with which teachers and students spend the most time; this is good because it seems to pose difficulty for some students. Students have more difficulty coming up with the main idea themselves than choosing one from a given list of choices. In fact, identifying the main idea is much more difficult, even if it is directly stated.[23]

Because of the difficulty of the main idea construction (identification) task, sufficient time must be allotted to provide the needed "think time." In addition, researchers have reported "that if readers' prior knowledge for the text topic is not sufficient, the difficulty of main idea construction is compounded."[24] Also, if the paragraph is not a well-constructed cohesive one, it would be difficult to come up with its main idea.

Confusion in finding the main idea may exist because it seems to mean different things to different people. One researcher investigating the literature found that "educators have increasingly given attention to main idea comprehension, but with no concomitant increase in the clarity of what is meant by main or important ideas. The exact nature of main ideas and the teaching practices intended to help students grasp main ideas vary considerably."[25]

Even though the concept of main idea is nebulous to some researchers and the "notion that different readers can (and should) construct identical main ideas for the same text has been questioned,"[26] the teaching of main idea is a very important skill for reading, writing, and studying that can and should be taught. It is possible that the skepticism concerning the ability to teach main idea may result from "the failure to teach students to transfer their main idea skills to texts other than those found in their readers."[27] Some studies have found that "students who have been taught to identify main ideas using only contrived texts

---

[23]Peter P. Afflerbach, "The Influence of Prior Knowledge on Expert Readers' Main Idea Construction Strategies," *Reading Research Quarterly* 25 (Winter 1990): 44.

[24]Ibid.

[25]James W. Cunningham and David W. Moore, "The Confused World of Main Idea," *Teaching Main Idea Comprehension,* James Baumann (ed.). Newark, DE: International Reading Association, 1986, p. 2.

[26]Afflerbach, p. 45.

[27]Victoria Chou Hare, Mitchell Rabinowitz, and Karen Magnus Schieble, "Text Effects on Main Idea Comprehension," *Reading Research Quarterly* 24 (Winter 1989): 72.

such as those found in basal reader skills lessons will have difficulty transferring their main idea skills to naturally occurring texts."[28] (The majority of reading programs in the recent past and present time have been literature-based that use whole pieces of literature rather than "contrived texts," which should counter the former criticism.)

In reading and writing, finding the main idea is very useful. In reading, the main idea helps readers to remember and understand what they have read. In writing, the main idea gives unity and order to a paragraph.

> **Main idea**
> The central thought of a paragraph. All the sentences in the paragraph develop the main idea.

The *main idea* of a paragraph is the central thought of the paragraph. It is what the paragraph is about. Without a main idea, the paragraph would just be a confusion of sentences. All the sentences in the paragraph should develop the main idea.

### Finding the Main Idea of a Paragraph

To find the main idea of a paragraph, you must find what common element the sentences share. Some textbook writers place the main idea at the beginning of a paragraph and may actually put the topic of the paragraph in bold print in order to emphasize it. However, in literature this is not a common practice. In some paragraphs the main idea is indirectly stated, or implied, and you have to find it from the clues given by the author.

Although there is no foolproof method for finding the main idea, there is a widely used procedure that has proved to be helpful. In order to use this procedure you should know that a paragraph is always written about something or someone. The something or someone is the topic of the paragraph. The writer is interested in telling his or her readers something about the topic of the paragraph. To find the main idea of a paragraph, you must determine what the topic of the paragraph is and what the author is trying to say about the topic that is special or unique. Once you have found these two things, you should have the main idea. This procedure is useful in finding the main idea of various types of paragraphs.

Reread the preceding paragraph and state its main idea. *Answer:* A procedure helpful in finding the main idea of a paragraph is described.

Now read the following paragraph. After you have read the passage, choose the statement that *best* states the main idea.

> Frank Yano looked like an old man, but he was only thirty. Born to parents who were alcoholics, Frank himself started drinking when he was only eight. He actually had tasted alcohol earlier, but it wasn't until he was eight or nine that he became a habitual drinker. His whole life since then has been dedicated to seeking the bottle.

1. Frank Yano looks old, but he's not.
2. Frank Yano enjoys being an alcoholic.
3. Frank Yano was a child alcoholic.
4. Frank Yano has been an alcoholic since childhood.

[28]Ibid.

5. Frank Yano would like to change his life of drinking, but he can't.
6. Frank Yano's parents helped him become an alcoholic.

Answer #4

Numbers 1 and 3 are too specific because they each relate to only one detail in the paragraph. Numbers 2 and 5 are not found in the paragraph; that is, no clues are given about Frank Yano's wanting to change his life or about his enjoying his life as an alcoholic. Number 6 is also too specific to be the main idea because it relates to only one detail. Number 4 is the answer because what is special about Frank Yano is that he has been an alcoholic since early childhood. All the details in the paragraph support this main idea.

## Special Note

The main idea of a paragraph is a general statement of the content of a paragraph. You must be careful, however, that your main idea statement is not so general that it suggests information that is not given in the paragraph.

Textbook authors usually see to it that their paragraphs have clear-cut main ideas. The main ideas of paragraphs in other books may be less obvious. The literary author is usually more concerned with writing expressively than with explicitly stating the main ideas. The main idea may be indirectly given. If this is the case, the steps presented earlier are especially helpful. Let's look again at the steps involved in finding the main idea.

1. Find the topic of the paragraph.
2. Find what is special about the topic. To do this, gather clues from the paragraph, find out what all the clues have in common, and make a general statement about the clues. ■

## Special Notes

**Supporting details**
Additional information that supports, explains, or illustrates the main idea. Some of the ways that supporting details may be arranged are as cause and effect, examples, sequence of events, descriptions, definitions, comparisons, or contrasts.

1. The topic sentence is usually the first sentence in a paragraph, and it states what the paragraph will be about by naming the topic. From the topic sentence you can usually anticipate certain events. You can usually determine that the following sentences will supply *supporting details* as examples, contrasts, similarities, sequence of events, cause-and-effect situations, and so on to support the main idea.
2. The main idea can be developed in many different ways. Whatever technique is used to develop the main idea, it must support and add meaning to the main idea.
3. A topic sentence may or may not contain the main idea.
4. It is possible for any sentence in the paragraph to be the topic sentence.
5. Some paragraphs may not have a topic sentence.
6. Do not confuse the topic sentence with the main idea. The topic sentence usually anticipates both the main idea and the development of the main idea.
7. Even though the topic sentence is stated explicitly (fully and clearly) in a paragraph, the main idea may not be stated explicitly. ■

---

**FIGURE 12.1  Informal Assessment of Main Idea**

---

PRIMARY-GRADE LEVEL

*ASSESSING FOR MAIN IDEA*

Objective 1: The students will choose a statement that best states the main idea of a short one-paragraph story.

Objective 2: The students will state a title for a story that gives an idea of what the story is about.

**Directions: Read the short story. Then read the statements that follow the story. Choose the one that *best* states the main idea of the story. Also, state a title for the story. Then write the title in the blank.**

Tom and Jim are not feeling very happy. They have just had their first fight. Tom and Jim have never had a fight before. Tom thought about the fight. Jim thought about the fight. They both felt sad.

1. Tom and Jim are sad.
2. Tom and Jim have never fought before.
3. Tom and Jim's first fight makes them feel sad.
4. Tom and Jim fight.
5. Tom and Jim feel ill.

    Answers: Number 3. *Sample title:* Tom and Jim's First Fight
    Tell students the results.

Some students may already know how to identify main idea and others may not. In Figure 12.1, we provide a sample informal assessment for teachers to use to determine who can and cannot identify main ideas.

### *Instructional Suggestions: Primary Grades*
Here are some instructional techniques and materials to use with your students who need some additional explicit instruction.

1.  Present the following paragraph to your students:

Sharon was sad. She felt like crying. She still couldn't believe it. Her best friend, Jane, had moved away. Her best friend had left her. What would she do?

Ask your students what the topic of the paragraph is or about whom or what the paragraph is written.

*Answer:* Sharon

Ask your students what the writer is saying that is special about Sharon.

*Answer:* Sharon is sad because her best friend moved away.

Tell your students that the main idea of the story is finding who or what the story is about and what is special about the who or what of the story.

2. Present your students with exercises such as the following. Ask your students to read the short story. Ask them also to read the statements that follow the short story, and choose the one that best states the main idea of the story. Then ask your students to write a title for the story that gives readers an idea of what the story is about.

Tom and Jim live on the moon. They spend a lot of time in their house. They have to because it is very hot when the sun is out. It is also very cold when the sun is not out. On the moon, daylight lasts for fourteen earth days. Darkness or nighttime lasts for fourteen earth days, too.

1. It's cold on the moon.
2. Tom and Jim stay in their house a lot.
3. The moon's weather.
4. Tom and Jim's house.
5. The moon's weather forces Tom and Jim to stay in their house.
6. Tom and Jim like to stay in their house.

Answers: Number 5. Sample title: The Moon's Weather

3. Discuss with the children the difference between the title and the main idea. Help them to see that the title and the main idea are not necessarily the same, and that the main idea is usually more fully stated than the title.

4. Another way of teaching main idea involves your hand. Trace a figure of your hand on an overhead transparency. Provide children with a statement (the main idea), which you write in the palm of the hand. For example, write the sentence, "We are having fun at school today." Next, ask children to volunteer some ideas that prove they are having fun at school. As they volunteer their ideas, write each one in a finger. These are actually the supporting details, but students do not need to know this at this point in the lesson. Now invite the class to read the entire "hand" with you. Once finished, tell students that they have just learned about main idea and supporting details. Just like the palm of your hand holds your fingers together, so too, the main idea holds the details together. You may also want to show them how to rewrite the statements on the hand into paragraph form. See Figure 12.2 for a sample completed hand.

As with primary students, some intermediate students may already know how to identify the main idea and others may not. In Figure 12.3, we provide a sample informal assessment for the intermediate-grade level.

### *Instructional Suggestions for Intermediate Grades*

Here are some instructional techniques and materials that you can use with your students who need additional explicit instruction:

1. Have your students read the following two paragraphs. After they read them, try to elicit from them which is a better paragraph and why. You should tell them that the first one makes sense because it is well organized. You can tell what the author is trying to say because there is only one main idea and all the

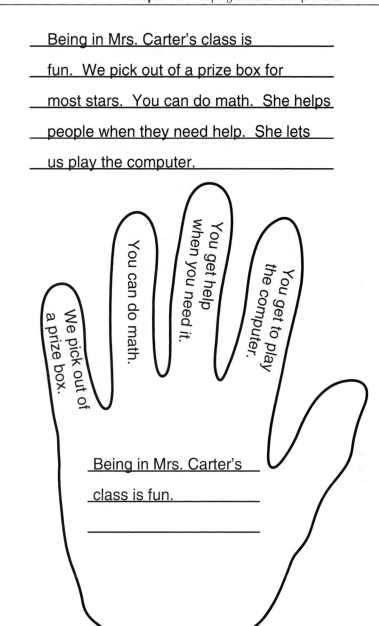

Being in Mrs. Carter's class is
fun.  We pick out of a prize box for
most stars.  You can do math.  She helps
people when they need help.  She lets
us play the computer.

You get to play
the computer.

You get help
when you need it.

You can do math.

We pick out of
a prize box.

Being in Mrs. Carter's
class is fun.

**FIGURE 12.2**   Main Idea/Supporting Details Hand

sentences in the paragraph expand on the main idea. Notice how disorganized
the second paragraph is and how difficult it is to discover what the main idea is
because each sentence seems to be about a different topic.

---

### FIGURE 12.3   Informal Assessment of Main Idea

---

INTERMEDIATE-GRADE LEVEL

*SKILL: MAIN IDEA OF A PARAGRAPH*

Objective: The students will state the main idea of a paragraph.

> **Directions: Read the paragraph carefully. Write the main idea of it in the space below.**
>
> Jim and his friends planned to go on a camping trip. For weeks, he and his friends talked about nothing else. They planned every detail of the trip. They studied maps and read books on camping. Everything was set. Everything, that is, except for asking their parents to let them go. Jim and his friends had planned everything. They had not planned on their parents not letting them go. However, that is what happened. Jim's and his friends' parents did not allow them to go.

Answer: Jim and his friends' plans to go camping are blocked by their parents.
Tell students the results.

---

### Organized Paragraph

All through school, John's one goal was athletic success so that he could be in the Olympics. John's goal to be in the Olympics became such an obsession that he could not do anything that did not directly or indirectly relate to achieving his goal. He practiced for hours every day. He exercised, ate well, and slept at least eight hours every night. Throughout school, John allowed nothing and no one to deter him from his goal.

### Disorganized Paragraph

All through school, John's one goal was to be the best so that he could be in the Olympics. He practiced for hours every day. John's family was unhappy about John's obsession to be in the Olympics. John's social life was more like a monk's than that of a star athlete. John's coach was a difficult man to please.

2. Have your students reread the organized paragraph. After they read the paragraph, have them choose the word or words that *best* answer the two questions that follow.

    a. What is the topic of the paragraph?
        (1) exercise and practice
        (2) work
        (3) Olympics
        (4) John's goal
        (5) athletic success
        (6) attempts

Answer: 4

    b. What is the author saying about John's goal to be in the Olympics (the topic) that is special and that helps tie the details together?

(1)  That it needed time and patience.
(2)  That it was a good one.
(3)  That it was not a reasonable one.
(4)  That it was the most important thing in John's life.
(5)  That it required good health.
(6)  That it was too much for John.

Answer: 4

Tell your students that if they put the two answers together, they should have the main idea of the paragraph. Main idea: The goal, being in the Olympics, was the most important thing in John's life.

3.  Choose a number of paragraphs from the students' social studies or science books. First have them find the topic of each paragraph and then have them state the main idea of each paragraph. Go over the procedure for finding the main idea with them.

## FINDING THE CENTRAL IDEA OF A GROUP OF PARAGRAPHS

**Central idea**
The main idea of a larger chunk of text.

*Background*
We generally use the term *central idea* rather than *main idea* when we refer to a *group* of paragraphs, a story, or an article. The procedure, however, for finding the main idea and for finding the central idea is the same.

The central idea of a story is the central thought of the story. All the paragraphs of the story should develop the central idea. To find the central idea of a story, students must find what common element the paragraphs in the story share. The introductory paragraph is usually helpful because it either contains or anticipates what the central idea is and how it will be developed. The procedure for finding the central idea of a story is similar to that for finding the main idea of a paragraph.

It is important to help your students recognize that the title of a story and the central idea are not necessarily the same. The ability to state the title of a story is related to the skill of finding the central idea; however, many times the title merely gives the topic of the story. The central idea is usually more fully stated than the title.

You may wish to use the informal assessment for central idea that we show in Figure 12.4 to determine those students who might need some instruction. The informal assessment in Figure 12.5 is intended for intermediate grade students.

*Instructional Suggestions for Upper-Primary Grades*
Here are some instructional techniques you can use with your students who need additional explicit instruction.

1.  Choose a short story the children know and enjoy reading. Have them state what the topic of the story is. Then have them go over the story and try to state what is the most important thing about the topic. Have them put the two together.

---

**FIGURE 12.4   Informal Assessment: Central Idea**

---

UPPER PRIMARY-GRADE LEVEL

*SKILL: CENTRAL IDEA OF A SHORT STORY*

Objective 1: The students will state the central idea of a short story.

Objective 2: The students will state a title for a story.

**Directions: Read the story. Write the central idea of the story. Then write a title for the story that gives readers an idea of what the story is about.**

Once upon a time in the deep green jungle of Africa, there lived a cruel lion. This lion frightened all the animals in the jungle. No animal was safe from this lion. One day the animals met and came up with a plan. The plan was not a very good one, but it was the best they could think of. Each day one animal would go to the lion to be eaten by him. That way the other animals would know that they were safe for a little while. The lion agreed to the plan and that is how they lived for a time.

One day it was the sly fox's turn to be eaten by the lion. Mr. Fox, however, had other plans. Mr. Fox went to the lion's cave an hour late. The lion was very angry. "Why are you so late? I am hungry," he said. Mr. Fox answered, "Oh, I am so sorry to be late, but another very, very big lion tried to catch me. I ran away from him so that you could eat me." When the lion heard about the other lion, he became more angry. "Another lion?" he asked. "I want to see him." The fox told the lion that he would take him to see the other lion. The fox led the lion through the jungle. When they came to a well, the fox stopped. "Look in there," said the fox. "The other lion is in there." The lion looked in the well, and he did indeed see a lion. He got so angry that he jumped in the well to fight the lion. That was, of course, the end of the lion.

Answers: *Central idea:* A clever fox outsmarts a cruel lion.

*Sample title:* The Clever Fox and the Cruel Lion or A Fox Outsmarts a Lion.

Tell students the results.

---

2. Have the children write their own short stories. Have them state the central idea of their short story. Have them go over each of their paragraphs to see if it helps develop their central idea. Have them write a title for their story.

### Instructional Suggestions for Intermediate-Grade Level

Here are some instructional techniques you can use with your students who need additional explicit instruction.

1. Choose a story the students have read. Ask them to state the topic of the story. Then have them reread the story to state what is the most important thing about the topic. Ask them to put these together. Then have them review the story to determine whether everything in the story is related to their central idea.

2. Ask students to write their own stories. Have them state the central idea and write a title for their stories.

3. Choose some short stories and follow the same procedure for finding the central idea. Present the short stories without the titles. Ask the students to make up a title for each short story. Discuss the fact that the title and the central idea are not necessarily the same, and explore what the differences are.

---

**FIGURE 12.5  Informal Assessment: Central Idea**

---

INTERMEDIATE-GRADE LEVEL

*SKILL: CENTRAL IDEA OF A SHORT STORY*

Objective 1: The students will state the central idea of a short story.

Objective 2: The students will be able to state a title for a story.

**Directions: Read carefully the following short story to determine the central idea of the story. After you have found the central idea of the story, choose a title for the story that gives readers an idea of what the story is about.**

A man and his son went to the market one morning. They took along a donkey to bring back whatever they would buy.

As they walked down the road, they met a woman who looked at them with a sour face.

"Are you not ashamed," she called to the father, "to let your little boy walk in the hot sun, when he should be riding on the donkey?"

The father stopped and lifted his boy to the donkey's back. So they went on.

After a little while they met an old man. He began at once to scold the boy. "You ungrateful son!" he shouted. "You let your poor old father walk while you sit there on the donkey like a lazy good-for-nothing!"

When the old man had passed, the father took his frightened son from the donkey and got onto the animal himself.

Further on they met another man who looked at them angrily. "How can you let your child walk in the dusty road?" he asked. "And you sit up there by yourself!"

The father was troubled, but he reached down and lifted his son up where he could sit on the donkey in front of him.

A little later they met a man and his wife, each of them riding a donkey. The husband called out, "You cruel man! How can you let the poor donkey carry such a heavy load? Get off at once! You are big enough and strong enough to carry the little animal instead of making it carry two of you."

The poor man was now really perplexed. He got off the donkey and took his son off, too.

Then he cut down a young tree for a pole and trimmed it. He tied the donkey's four feet to the pole. Then he and his son lifted the pole. They trudged along, carrying the donkey between them.

As they were crossing a bridge over a stream, they met with a crowd of young men. Seeing the donkey being carried on a pole, they started to laugh and shout. Their noise startled the poor donkey who started to kick violently and broke the ropes holding his feet. As he frisked about, he tumbled off the bridge and was drowned.

The man looked sadly into the stream and shook his head.

"My son," he said to the boy, "you cannot please everybody."

Answers: *Central idea:* A man and his son learn that you cannot please everyone.

*Sample title:* You Can't Please Everyone

Tell students the results.

### *Visual Representations and Main Idea*

It is difficult to read a textbook, magazine, or newspaper without finding a variety of visual representations in the form of graphs, diagrams, and charts. Visuals provide relief from print, and a graphic representation is often worth 1,000 words. Graphs, diagrams, and charts grab your attention, and pack a great amount of information in a short space. *USA Today* uses pictorial representations every day in each section of its newspaper for these reasons.

Writers use graphs, diagrams, and charts to convey information, and each one, like a paragraph, has a main idea. To understand the charts, diagrams, and graphs, you must be able to get the main idea of them. Not surprisingly, the technique we use to do this is similar to that for finding the main idea of a paragraph.

Figure 12.6 is a graph from *Health Behaviors* by Rosalind Reed and Thomas A. Lang.[29] Let's go through the various steps to get the main idea of it. Remember, to find the main idea, we must first find the topic of the chart, diagram, or graph and then note what is special or unique about it. All the details should develop the main idea. (Note that writers also usually give clues to the topic of their graphs, diagrams, and charts.) Here are the steps we would go through:

1.  We look carefully at the graph to determine its topic. We notice it deals with smokers and nonsmokers and their mortality rates for selected diseases. Therefore, the topic is

The mortality rates of smokers and nonsmokers for selected diseases.

2.  Next, we need to find what is special about the topic. In looking at the graph again, we note that the writer is obviously making a comparison between smokers and nonsmokers. The comparison is about various types of diseases. In addition and what is most crucial is that the smokers have consistently higher mortality rates for all presented diseases. Therefore, the main idea must be

The mortality rates for smokers are consistently higher than for nonsmokers for all selected diseases.

**Inference**
Understanding that is not derived from a direct statement but from an indirect suggestion in what is stated; understanding that is implied.

## DRAWING INFERENCES

Many times writers do not directly state what they mean, but present ideas in a more indirect, roundabout way. That is why inference is called the ability to "read between the lines." *Inference* is defined as *understanding that is not derived from a direct statement but from an indirect suggestion in what is stated.* Readers draw inferences from writings; authors make implications or imply meanings.

The ability to draw inferences is especially important in reading fiction, but it is necessary for nonfiction, also. Authors rely on inferences to make their sto-

---

[29]Rosalind Reed and Thomas A. Lang, *Health Behaviors* (St. Paul, MN: West Publication, 1988), p. 328.

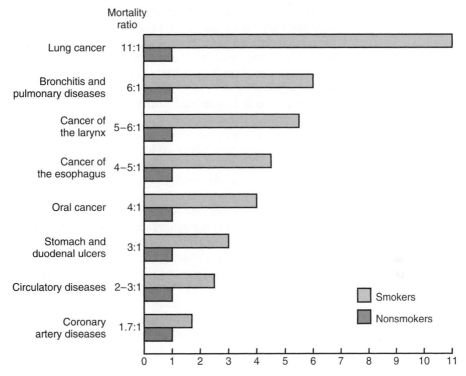

**FIGURE 12.6** Mortality Rates for Smokers and Nonsmokers for Selected Diseases.
*Source:* From *Health Behaviors* by Rosalind Reed and Thomas a. Lang. St. Paul, MN: West Publications, 1988, p. 328.

ries more interesting and enjoyable. Mystery writers find inference essential to the maintenance of suspense. For example, Sherlock Holmes and Encyclopedia Brown mysteries are based on the ability of the sleuth to uncover evidence in the form of clues that are not obvious to others around them.

Inference is an important process that authors rely on. Good readers must be alert to the various ways that authors encourage inference.

### *Implied Statements*

As has been said already, writers count on inference to make their writing more interesting and enjoyable. Rather than directly stating something, they present it indirectly. To understand the writing, the reader must be alert and be able to detect the clues that the author gives. For example, in the sentence *Things are always popping and alive when the twins Herb and Jack are around,* you are given some clues to Herb's and Jack's personalities, even though the author has not directly said anything about them. From the statement you could make the inference that the twins are lively and lots of fun to be around.

You must be careful, however, that you *do not read more* into some statements than is intended. For example, read the following statements and put a circle around the correct answer. *Example:* Mary got out of bed and looked out of the window. She saw that the ground had something white on it. What season of the year was it? (a) winter, (b) summer, (c) spring, (d) fall, (e) can't tell.

The answer is "(e) can't tell." Many persons choose "(a) winter" for the answer. However, the answer is (e) because the "something white" could be anything; there isn't enough evidence to choose (a). Even if the something white was snow, in some parts of the world, including the United States, it can snow in the spring or fall.

Good readers, while reading, try to gather clues to draw inferences about what they read. Although effective readers do this, they are not usually aware of it. As Sherlock Holmes says in *A Study in Scarlet,* "From long habit the train of thought ran so swiftly through my mind that I arrived at the conclusions without being conscious of intermediate steps."

In Figures 12.7 and 12.8 we provide an informal assessment procedure that you can use to assess inference at the primary grade level and intermediate grade level.

### *Instructional Suggestions for Primary-Grade Level*

Here are some instructional procedures and materials to use with your students who need additional explicit instruction.

1. Present the following short selection to your students:

   Sharon and Carol are going out to play. They are dressed very warmly.

   Ask your students what they can say about the weather outside. They should say that it must be cold outside because the children are dressed very warmly. Even though it didn't say that it was cold outside, there was enough evidence to make this inference.

   Now ask the children to tell you what season of the year it is. They should say that you can't tell because there is not enough evidence. It could be cold in the fall and spring. Some children might be able to state that you can't tell because different places of the country and the world have different climates.

2. Give your students a number of opportunities to make inferences from stories they are reading if enough evidence exists.

### *Instructional Suggestions for Intermediate-Grade Level*

Here are some instructional procedures and materials that you can use with your students who need additional explicit instruction.

1. Present your students with the following statements:

   Jack looks out of the train window. All he sees are miles and miles of leafless trees.

**FIGURE 12.7    Informal Assessment: Inference**

PRIMARY-GRADE LEVEL

*SKILL: INFERENCE OR "READING BETWEEN THE LINES"*

Objective: The students will read a short story and answer inference questions about it.

**Directions: Read the short story. Then answer the questions.**

Zip and Zap are a cat and rat. They are good friends. They live on the moon. Zip and Zap love to ride in space. Their school goes on a space trip every month. Zip and Zap must wear their space clothes and their air masks in the spaceship. All the other moon cats and rats must wear them, too. Zip and Zap want to be spaceship pilots. This is the same spaceship that brought Zip and Zap to the moon. The spaceship has its own landing place. It is well taken care of. Special cats and rats take care of the spaceship. Zip and Zap are happy that they can ride in the spaceship.

1. Is there air in the spaceship? Explain.

2. Were Zip and Zap born on the moon? Explain.

3. Is the spaceship important to the moon cats and rats? Explain.

4. Is travel an important part of school learning? Explain.

5. Do Zip and Zap know what they want to do when they grow up? Explain.

Answers:

1. No. Zip and Zap wear their space clothes and their air masks in the spaceship.
2. No. It is stated that the spaceship is the same one that brought Zip and Zap to the moon.
3. Yes. It is their means of travel. It is stated that there are special cats and rats who take care of the spaceship and that the spaceship is well taken care of.
4. Yes. Every month the school goes on a space trip.
5. Yes. It is stated that they want to be spaceship pilots.

Tell students the results.

**FIGURE 12.8 Informal Assessment: Inference**

INTERMEDIATE-GRADE LEVEL

*SKILL: INFERENCE OR "READING BETWEEN THE LINES"*

Objective: The students will make inferences about short selections if enough evidence exists for the inferences.

**Directions: Read the following selection *very carefully.* Without looking back at the selection, try to answer the questions.**

The two men looked at each other. They would have to make the decision that might cost many lives. They kept rubbing their hands together to keep warm. Although they were dressed in furs and every part of them was covered except for their faces, they could still feel the cold. The fire that had been made for them from pine trees was subsiding. It was getting light. They had promised their men a decision at dawn. Should they go forward or should they retreat? So many lives had already been lost.

a. Did this take place at the North Pole or South Pole? _____

   How do you know? _____

   _____

   _____

   _____

b. Circle the word that best fits the two men. The two men were: (1) trappers (2) officers (3) soldiers (4) guides. Explain why you made your choice.

   **Explain:** _____

   _____

   _____

c. What inference can you draw from this short passage? Circle the answer.
   (1) The men were on a hunting trip.
   (2) The men were at war with a foreign nation.
   (3) The decision that the two men had to make concerned whether to take an offensive or defensive position in some kind of battle.
   (4) The men were on a hunting trip, but they got caught in a bad storm.

   **Explain:** _____

   _____

   _____

Answers:

(a) No. There are no pine trees at the North or South Pole. (b) Officers. Guides would not talk about *their* men. Guides usually act as advisers. They do not make decisions. Trappers trap animals for fur. Also, it is stated that the fire had been made for them. Officers do not usually prepare the camp. (c) The term *retreat* would be a commander's term. Nothing was stated about a storm nor was anything stated or suggested about a foreign nation. Hunters would not usually hunt under such adverse conditions. It was too cold to hunt big game, and hunters would very rarely lose so many lives.

Tell students the results.

Ask them whether Jack just began to look out of the window. The students should answer "no." Ask them how they know this. They should say because it says that he saw miles and miles of trees. He couldn't see "miles and miles of trees" unless he had been looking out the window for a while.

Ask them whether Jack is traveling through a densely populated or sparsely populated area. They should say that Jack is traveling through a sparsely populated area. Ask them how they know this. They should say because the area has so many trees. Ask them what kind of area it is. The students should say that it could be a forest or a park or a preserve. Enough evidence isn't given to determine this. Ask them if they can determine what season of the year it is since there are leafless trees. They should say "no." It could be any season of the year. It is not stated in what part of the country or world Jack is traveling. The trees could be leafless as a result of a forest fire, disease, drought, or some other cause.

2. Have students read a number of stories and see what inferences they can draw from them. Help them to recognize that enough evidence should exist to make an inference. Tell them that many times people "jump to conclusions" before they have enough evidence. This can cause problems. Taking an educated guess is helpful in scientific activities and in searching for the answers to difficult questions. Students should be encouraged to make educated guesses, but they need to recognize when they do not have enough evidence to do so.

## COMPREHENSION STRATEGIES

In addition to specific comprehension skills, there are strategies (i.e., mental processes) that may require some explicit comprehension instruction. As with the skills noted above, remember that students need plenty of time to read in order to actually apply these skills and strategies. The six strategies we show in Figure 12.9, making connections, making predictions, monitoring understanding, visualizing, questioning, and retelling/summarizing, are research-based. Each sample lesson includes a brief overview of the particular strategy, some teaching suggestions, and some ideas for providing students with meaningful practice.

## TEACHING COMPREHENSION

Time spent in reading seems to be an important variable for success in reading, whether it is direct instructional time or time spent reading independently. However, we cannot count on students reading outside school because of the many other enjoyable activities, as well as responsibilities, that compete for their time and attention. Therefore, we must plan for students to have time to read as well as time for explicit instruction in reading comprehension.

There are various teaching strategies that can be used with explicit instruction; some are less structured than others. Explicit instruction requires teachers to present strategies to help their students comprehend the material being read; this is done in addition to asking children questions before, during, and after they read. "Direct [explicit] instruction in comprehension means explaining the steps in a thought process that gives birth to comprehension."[30] The instructional pattern that teachers use to help students gain comprehension will vary based on the concept being learned, the composition of the class, and the ability of the teacher.

Providing instruction before, during, and after the reading activity is a way to design supportive instruction. Before reading, prepare the students for the reading activity by doing some of the following: previewing the reading selection, going over the new vocabulary or difficult words, teaching any strategies that students will need to read the material, as well as actively building topic knowledge.

During reading, give students a number of questions to think about as they read or encourage students to ask questions about the text material. Challenge students to act as investigative reporters while they are reading.

After reading, students can answer their own questions or the teacher's questions, state the main idea of the selection, summarize it, discuss their feelings toward the material, or tell how they used a specific comprehension strategy such as visualizing. There are numerous comprehension teaching strategies that can be used as a part of an explicit reading lesson. Purpose is what guides the selection of the specific teaching strategy we choose for any given lesson. The following sections provide seven suggestions for teaching strategies.

**Directed Reading–Thinking Activity** (DRTA) Requires teachers to nurture the inquiry process and students to be active participants and questioners; includes prediction and verification.

## THE DIRECTED READING–THINKING ACTIVITY

The *Directed Reading–Thinking Activity* (DRTA) can be an especially effective approach in the hands of good teachers, whether they use a basal reader series or trade books.

DRTA requires that students be active participants. "The reading-thinking process must begin in the mind of the reader. He must raise the questions and to him belongs the challenge and the responsibility of a judgment. The teacher keeps the process active and changes the amount of data to be processed."[31] Here is an outline of the process:[32]

I. Pupil actions
   A. Predict (set purposes)
   B. Read (process ideas)
   C. Prove (test answers)
II. Teacher actions
   A. What do you think? (activate thought)
   B. Why do you think so? (agitate thought)
   C. Prove it. (require evidence)

---

[30]Richard C. Anderson, et al., *Becoming a Nation of Readers: The Report of the Commission on Reading* (Washington, DC: National Institute of Education, 1985), p. 72.

[31]Russell G. Stauffer, *Directing the Reading-Thinking Process* (New York: Harper & Row, 1975), p. 37.

[32]Ibid.

**FIGURE 12.9    Comprehension Strategy: Making Connections**

*What is Making Connections?*

This strategy has readers (a) connect their knowledge to a selection, (b) connect other texts to a selection, and (c) connect their responses to a selection.

*How do I teach Making Connections?*

1. **Introduction:** Present a short selection to students and have them tell what they *know* about the topic, if the selection makes them think of other *stories*, and how they might *respond* to the selection. State that these are different kinds of *connections* a reader can make to a selection. Explain that making connections helps readers understand stories better and enjoy them more.

2. **Instruction:** Write on the board, a chart, or a transparency three different kinds of connections a reader can make to a selection:

 • Connections to what a reader *knows*.
 • Connections to other *stories*.
 • Connections to story *responses*.

Model how to make connections by using a poster selection, a selection from a read-aloud book, or one of the magazines. Model connecting by reading a part of the story and then thinking aloud as you make connections for students by asking and answering questions such as the following: (1) Connections to what a reader *knows*. "What do I know about this topic? Can I say or write down those ideas?" (2) Connections to other *stories*. "Does this story remind me of another story? Do I know other stories by this same author or illustrator? How are they alike and different?" (3) Connections to story *responses*. "Did I enjoy this story? Was it interesting or funny? What do I think about the characters or what happened?"

3. **Guided Practice:** Have students practice making connections by reading the next section of the selection and asking themselves *know*, *story*, and *response* connection questions like those above. Provide support and extra modeling as necessary to guide students through the process of making connections.

*How can students practice Making Connections?*

Have students complete a connection chart as a group, with a partner, or individually. Have students discuss and write *know*, *story*, and *response* connections before, during, and after reading the selection.

| Making connections to . . . | | |
|---|---|---|
| what I **know**. | other **stories**. | story **responses**. |
| | | |

FIGURE 12.9   **Comprehension Strategy: Making Predicitons**

*What is Making Predictions?*

This strategy requires students to (a) use prior knowledge and information in a selection to make logical guesses or predictions about events in the selection, (b) read on to check (verify) their predictions, and (c) change or make new predictions from the new information in the selection.

*How do I teach Making Predictions?*

1. **Introduction:** Present a picture or read a short selection to students and have them guess what might happen next. Tell them that these guesses are ***predictions***. Explain that making predictions helps readers think about the story and look for ideas the writer might tell them later. State also that making and checking predictions gives readers a purpose for reading and helps them understand what they read.

2. **Instruction:** Write the four steps for making predictions on the board, a chart, or a transparency:

   Step 1. ***Read*** a part of the story.
   Step 2. ***Predict*** what will happen next.
   Step 3. Read on and ***Check*** predictions (**T** = True, **F** = False, **CT** = Can't Tell Yet.)
   Step 4. ***Change*** or make new predictions.

   Model how to follow these steps using a poster selection, a selection from a read-aloud book, or one of the magazines: (1) ***Read*** aloud part of the selection. (2) Think aloud as you make several ***predictions*** and write them down. (3) Read more of the selection and think aloud as you ***check*** the predictions by writing **T** (**T**rue), **F** (**F**alse), or **CT** (**C**an't **T**ell Yet) after each. (4) ***Change*** the predictions or make new ones from new ideas in the selection.

3. **Guided Practice:** Have students follow the four steps on the next portion of the selection by having them ***read***, ***predict***, ***check*** predictions, and ***change*** or make new ones. Provide support and reteaching as necessary to guide students through the prediction process.

*How can students practice Making Predictions?*

Have students complete a prediction equation as a group, with a partner, or individually. Ask students to write ***clues*** from the story and ideas they ***know*** that lead them to a ***prediction***. Then have students ***check*** their prediction and either change them or make new ones.

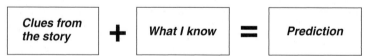

Check your prediction. Was it (circle one)   **T**   **F**   **CT** ?

Change your prediction or make a new one: _____

**FIGURE 12.9  Comprehension Strategy: Monitoring Understanding**

*What is Monitoring Understanding?*

This strategy has readers (a) develop the ability to recognize comprehension breakdowns when they occur, and (b) apply fix-up strategies to correct comprehension difficulties.

*How do I teach Monitoring Understanding?*

1. **Introduction:** Read aloud a short selection to students, but insert several words or short sentences that do not make sense within the overall passage. Ask students "Did that story make sense? Why not?" State that what they did was to check or *monitor* their reading comprehension. Explain that *monitoring* reading comprehension is important so that readers can tell when a selection is not making sense. They can then correct, or fix up, their understanding.

2. **Instruction:** Write on the board, a chart, or a transparency the two steps for monitoring comprehension:

   Step 1.  Read part of a selection, stop, and ask "Is this selection making sense?"
   Step 2.  If you answer "No," then try one or more of these fix-up strategies:
   • Read the sentence or paragraph again.
   • Retell the sentence or paragraph in your own words.
   • Ask a question or make a prediction.
   • Read on and see if the selection makes sense.

Model how to monitor comprehension by selecting a challenging selection from a poster, a read-aloud book, or one of the magazines. Model monitoring by reading a paragraph, stopping, and asking "Is this making sense?" Answer "No," and indicate what has you confused such as a main idea, a character's motive, a cause/effect relationship, or a word referent, is not clear. Then select one or more of the "fix-up" strategies and model how to apply each by thinking aloud as you clarify the confusing part of the selection.

3. **Guided Practice:** Have students practice monitoring by inviting volunteers to read the next section of the selection, asking "Is this making sense?", and then applying one or more of the fix-up strategies to help them comprehend. Provide support and extra modeling as necessary to guide students through the process of monitoring.

*How can students practice Monitoring Understanding?*

Make comprehension monitoring "Stop Signs" as below. Have students use them as they read, stopping at the end of each paragraph or page, putting down the stop sign with Side 1 up, and asking "Is this making sense?" If they answer "No," then have them turn the sign to Side 2 and try one or more of the fix-up strategies.

**Stop!**
Is this making sense?

**To Fix Up**
reread, retell, question, predict, or read on.

## FIGURE 12.9   Comprehension Strategy: Visualizing

### *What is Visualizing?*

This strategy has readers create pictures in their minds to promote their understanding, recall, and appreciation of a selection.

### *How do I teach Visualizing?*

1. **Introduction:** Ask students to close their eyes and listen carefully while you read aloud a short, descriptive selection. When you have finished, have students open their eyes, and ask "What was the selection about? Did anyone see a picture of what you heard? Can you tell us about the picture you drew in your mind?" Explain that making a mental picture, or **visualizing**, is a powerful way to help listeners and readers understand, remember, and enjoy a selection.

2. **Instruction:** Write on the board, a chart, or a transparency the following ideas to help students visualize as they are reading:

   - Read a selection carefully.
   - Look for words that tell about **settings**, **actions**, **colors**, **characters**, or **sounds**.
   - Use the writer's words to **visualize**, or make a mental picture of, the selection.

   Model how to visualize by using a selection from a poster, a read-aloud book, or a magazine. Think aloud as you (1) read part of the story and look for words to help you visualize; (2) comment on words that tell about actions, colors, characters, sounds, or settings; and (3) use the writer's words to paint a verbal picture of the scene or events in the selection.

3. **Guided Practice:** Practice visualizing by inviting volunteers to read the next portion of the selection and talk about the words that help them form mental pictures. Then have them describe the pictures they drew in their minds as they read. Invite students to compare how their visualizations were alike and different, noting how readers paint different pictures for the same selection. Discuss how visualizing might help them understand, remember, or enjoy a selection.

### *How can students practice Visualizing?*

Complete a visualizing chart as students read a selection. Have them write words the author uses to help them visualize. Then have them draw pictures that show their visualizations.

| To visualize while I read, I can . . . | |
|---|---|
| write words that help me make mental pictures. | draw a picture of what I saw in my mind. |
| | |

## FIGURE 12.9   Comprehension Strategy: Questioning

### *What is Questioning?*

With this strategy, readers learn to generate questions as they read. Self-questioning promotes active, engaged reading and enhances students' literal, inferential, and critical comprehension.

### *How do I teach Questioning?*

1. **Introduction:** Read aloud a short selection that requires some interpretation. Stop occasionally and ask questions like "Who is the main character? I wonder when this story takes place? What's the writer's main point here? What will happen next?" Ask the students what you were doing. State that you were asking yourself questions about the selection as you read. Explain that *questioning*—readers asking themselves about the selection—is a useful way to better understand, remember, and enjoy what one reads.

2. **Instruction:** Write on the board, a chart, or a transparency different categories and examples of questions readers might ask themselves as they try to understand a selection:

   - *Setting:* Who are the characters? When and where is this taking place?
   - *Events:* What happened? What caused it to happen? What did the author leave out and expect me to figure out? What was the result of these events?
   - *Content:* What do I know about this topic? What's the main idea here? How does one event lead to another? What conclusion can I draw?
   - *Response:* What would I do? Do I agree with the character's actions? What was funny, sad, or interesting? Does this remind me of something else I have read?

   Model how to self-question when reading a selection from a poster, read-aloud book, or a magazine. Think aloud by asking setting, event, content, and response questions. Help students realize that there are no "right" questions but only those that help them understand and appreciate what they are reading.

3. **Guided Practice:** Invite students to engage in self-questioning as they read subsequent sections of the selection. Encourage them to ask a variety of setting, event, content, and response questions. Help students realize that there are no "right" questions but only those that help them understand and appreciate what they are reading.

### *How can students practice Questioning?*

Create a self-questioning map. Use the map to help students self-question as they read fiction, nonfiction, and other genres. Write setting, event, content, and response questions on the map.

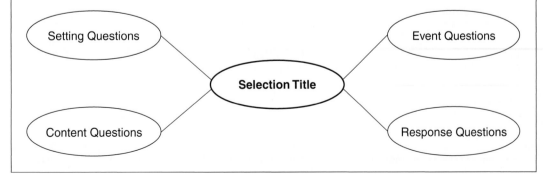

---

FIGURE 12.9    **Comprehension Strategy: Retelling/Summarizing**

*What is Retelling/Summarizing?*

These strategies have readers identify and work with the main ideas and supporting details of a selection. Retelling requires students to restate the major events and supporting details in a selection. Summarizing requires students to extract only the main ideas from a selection.

*How do I teach Retelling/Summarizing?*

1. **Introduction:** Read aloud a short selection. Then retell the selection by restating the main events in order, and summarize the selection by constructing a statement that tells the main ideas of the selection. Ask students whether they can describe the two things you just did and how they were alike and different. Explain that the first was a ***retelling*** (saying the events in a selection in the order in which they happened) and the second was a ***summary*** (saying just the main ideas of a selection).

2. **Instruction:** Write on the board, a chart, or a transparency the following descriptions:

| *To retell a selection . . .* | *To summarize a selection . . .* |
|---|---|
| • say or write the main events and important details.<br>• say or write them in the order in which they happened. | • figure out the most important ideas or events in the selection.<br>• say or write them in a brief statement. |

Model how to retell and summarize by selecting a short item from a poster, read-aloud book, or magazine. Read the selection and then retell it, including the main events and important details in the order in which they happened. Next, summarize the selection, thinking aloud to show how you figured out the main ideas and then constructed a short statement to express them. Invite students to explain how your retelling differed from your summary (for example, retelling is longer, includes more detail, uses many words from the selection; summary is shorter and includes only the main ideas from the selection).

3. **Guided Practice:** Select and read another short passage and invite students to offer first a retelling of it and then a summary of it. Refer them to the chart as needed. Ask students to compare and contrast the retelling and summary for similarities and differences.

*How can students practice Retelling/Summarizing?*

Select a short passage and have students generate both a retelling and a summary and write them on a chart. Have them consider how their retelling and summary are alike and different. Ask how they both are helpful for understanding and remembering important ideas in selections.

| Retelling of _____ | Summary of _____ |
|---|---|

From *Summer Success Reading* by James F. Baumann, Michael F. Opitz, Laura Robb. Text copyright © 2001 Great Source Education Group, a division of Houghton Mifflin Company. Reprinted by permission. All rights reserved.

In order to use DRTA effectively, teachers must know how to encourage students to ask questions that stimulate higher-level thinking; teachers must be well-versed in facilitating the inquiry process.

## THINK ALOUD

Many good teachers have probably used this approach, but may not have been aware of it. Often when a teacher has students who have difficulty understanding something that is being explained, the teacher may "model" the skill for them. That is, the teacher "thinks aloud" or verbalizes thoughts to give the students insight into the process. The teacher literally states out loud exactly the steps that he or she goes through to solve the problem or gain an understanding of a concept. Many reading program authors are including modeling as part of their instructional plans.

Here are some suggested teaching procedures:[33]

1. Choose a passage to read aloud. The passage should have some areas that will pose some difficulties such as unknown words. It could also contain an excellent description that would be perfect if you want to teach students something about visualizing.
2. Begin reading the passage orally while students follow. When you come to a trouble spot, stop and think through it aloud while students listen to what you say.
3. When you have finished reading, invite students to add any thoughts to yours.
4. Partner-up the students and have them practice.
5. Remind students to use the strategy when they are reading silently. A self-evaluation form such as the one shown in Figure 12.10 might help students evaluate how well they read.

## REPEATED READING

**Repeated reading**

Similar to paired reading; child reads along (assisted reading with model or tape) until he or she gains confidence to read alone.

*Repeated reading* is a technique that has gained favor among a number of teachers to help students who have poor oral reading to achieve fluency in reading. A suggested procedure for repeated readings follows:[34]

*Passage length:* Short; about 50 to 100 words
*Types of passages:* Any reading materials that will be of interest to the child
*Readability level of passage:* Start at independent level; proceed to more difficult passages as the child gains confidence in oral reading; controlled vocabulary is not imperative.

---

[33]Davey, B. "Think Aloud: Modeling the Cognitive Processes of Reading Comprehension." *Journal of Reading* 27(1983): 44–47.

[34]Adapted from Sarah L. Dowhower, "Repeated Reading: Research into Practice," *The Reading Teacher* 42 (March 1989): 504–506.

---

**FIGURE 12.10   Analyzing My Reading**

Name _____   Date _____

What I read: _____

Here's what I did and how well I think I did it:

|  | *Little* | *Some* | *Much* |
|---|---|---|---|
| 1. I formed questions before reading. |  |  |  |
| 2. I tried to make pictures using the author's words. |  |  |  |
| 3. I made some connections with other books. |  |  |  |
| 4. I knew when I was having a problem and I did something to fix the problem so that I could continue reading with understanding. |  |  |  |
| 5. I was able to comprehend this text. |  |  |  |

---

*Assisted reading:* Use the read-along approach (assisted reading with a model or tape) to help with phrasing and speed; use when speed is below 45 words per minute (WPM), even though the child makes few errors. *Unassisted reading:* Use when the child reaches 60 WPM.

**Special Note**

Repeated reading, which is at times called assisted reading, is supposed to be used to help students who need to become fluent readers. Those who can read fluently need not participate in this activity. ■

**Reciprocal Reading Instruction**

A teacher-directed technique consisting of four steps: summarizing, questioning, clarifying, and predicting.

## RECIPROCAL READING INSTRUCTION

*Reciprocal reading instruction*, which is used in a group setting to help students gain comprehension skills,[35] is a teacher-directed technique because it requires the teacher to first model the various four steps for students before having them perform the task. Also, like all techniques, reciprocal reading instruction is only as good as the teacher presenting it.

---

[35]*See* Ann L. Brown, Annemarie Sullivan Palincsar, and Bonnie B. Armbruster, "Instructing Comprehension-Fostering Activities in Interactive Learning Situations," in Heinz Mandl et al., eds., *Learning and Comprehension of Text* (Hillsdale, NJ: Lawrence Erlbaum, 1984).

The four steps involved in this technique are summarizing, questioning, clarifying, and predicting. When the students in the group have all read a specified passage, the teacher models the four steps for them. After the teacher has modeled the passage using all four steps, he or she has the students do the same. Of course, the amount of help and the number of times that the teacher will model how to use the procedure for the children will vary depending on the individual needs of the children.

## LITERATURE WEBBING

**Literature webbing**

A story map technique to help guide children in using predictable trade books.

Success breeds success! If children have good experiences in reading at an early age, these experiences will help instill good attitudes about reading in them. Predictable books appear to be one way to provide these experiences.[36] *Literature webbing* is a story map or graphic illustration that teachers can use as one approach to guide them in using predictable trade books with their children.

The literature webbing strategy lesson (LWSL), which is an adaptation by Reutzel and Fawson of Watson and Crowley's Story Schema Lessons to "provide support for early readers,"[37] includes a six-step process. The preliminary preparation includes the teacher's reading of the text and excerpting a number of samples from it that are large enough so that children can make predictions about them. (The excerpts can be accompanied by enlarged illustrations if this procedure is used early in the year.) After the excerpts are chosen, the title of the book is placed in the center of the board with various web strands projecting from the title. (There are three more strands than needed for the number of excerpts. These strands, which are used for discussion purposes, are personal responses to the book, other books we've read like this one, and language extension activities.) Then the children follow these six steps:[38]

1. Sample the book by reading the randomly ordered illustrations and text excerpts that are placed on the chalk tray below the literature web.
2. Predict the pattern or order of the book by placing the excerpts in clockwise order around the literature web.
3. Read the predictable book straight through. (It may be a big book or a number of copies of the normal-sized text.)
4. Confirm or correct their predictions.
5. Discuss the remaining three strands that are on the board for discussion purposes.
6. Participate in independent or supported reading activities.

---

[36]D. Ray Reutzel and Parker C. Fawson, "Using a Literature Webbing Strategy Lesson with Predictable Books," *The Reading Teacher* 43 (December 1989): 208.

[37]Ibid., p. 209

[38]Ibid.

## QUESTIONING STRATEGIES

Most children need help in developing higher-level reading comprehension skills. Asking many types of questions that demand higher-level skills will better ensure that students become thoughtful and insightful readers.

The kinds of questions the teacher asks will determine the kinds of answers he or she will receive. In addition to asking a question that calls for a literal response, use questions that call for higher levels of thinking. This process can begin as early as kindergarten and first grade. For example, suppose the children are looking at a picture in which a few children are dressed in hats, snow pants, jackets, and scarves. After asking the children what kind of clothes the children in the picture are wearing, try to elicit from students the answers to the following questions: "What kind of day do you think it is?" "What do you think the children are going to do?"

This type of inference question is very simple because it is geared to the cognitive development level of the children. As the children progress to higher levels of thinking they should be confronted with more complex interpretation or inference problems. Work with children according to their individual levels. Expect all the children to be able to perform, but avoid putting students in situations that frustrate rather than stimulate them.

Critical reading skills are essential for good readers. Use primary-graders' love of folktales to begin to develop some critical reading skills. For example, after the children have read "The Little Red Hen," ask questions such as the following:

1. Should the Little Red Hen have shared the bread with the other animals? Explain.
2. Would you have shared the bread with the other animals? Explain.
3. Do you think animals can talk? Explain.
4. Do you feel sorry for the other animals? Explain.
5. Do you think this story is true? Explain.

**Divergent thinking**
The many different ways to solve problems or to look at things.

Creative reading questions are probably the most ignored. To help children in this area, learn how to ask questions that require divergent rather than convergent answers. Some questions that should stimulate *divergent thinking* on the part of the reader would be the following:

1. After reading "The Little Red Hen," try to come up with another ending for the story.
2. Try to add another animal to the story of "The Little Red Hen."
3. Try to add another part to the story of "The Little Red Hen."

Divergent answers require more time than convergent answers. Also, there is no one correct answer.

Following are a short reading selection and examples of the four different types of comprehension questions. Read both as practice in recognizing the different types of questions at the four levels.

One day in the summer, some of my friends and I decided to go on an overnight hiking trip. We all started out fresh and full of energy. About halfway to our destination, when the sun was almost directly overhead, one-third of my friends decided to return home. The remaining four of us, however, continued on our hike. Our plan was to reach our destination by sunset. About six hours later as the four of us, exhausted and famished, were slowly edging ourselves in the direction of the setting sun, we saw a sight that astonished us. There, at the camping site, were our friends who had claimed that they were returning home. It seems that they did indeed go home, but only to pick up a car and drive out to the campsite.

The following are the four different types of comprehension questions:

*Literal comprehension:* What season of the year was it in the story? What kind of trip were the people going on?

*Interpretation:* About what time of day was it when some of the people decided to return home? How many persons were there when they first started out on the trip? In what direction were the hikers heading when they saw a sight that astonished them? At about what time did the sun set?

*Critical reading:* How do you think the hikers felt when they reached their destination? Do you feel that the persons who went home did the right thing by driving back to the site rather than hiking? Explain.

*Creative reading:* What do you think the exhausted hikers did and said when they saw the two who had supposedly gone home?

## QUESTION–ANSWER RELATIONSHIPS (QARs)

**Question–Answer Relationships (QARs)**
Helps students distinguish between "what they have in their heads" and information that is in the text.

The more children understand what they do when they are in the act of answering questions, the better question solvers they can be. Raphael has designed an instructional strategy, Question–Answer Relationships (QARs), that teachers can use to help their students gain insights into how they go about reading text and answering questions. It helps students "realize the need to consider both information in the text and information from their own knowledge background."[39]

In the QAR technique students learn to distinguish between information that "they have in their heads" and information that is in the text. The steps that can help children gain facility in QAR are presented in the following paragraphs. Note that the amount of time children spend at each step is determined by the individual differences of the students.

**Step 1.** Students gain help in understanding differences between what is in their heads and what is in the text. Ask children to read a passage, and then present questions that guide them to gain the needed understandings. Here is a short sample:

[39]Taffy E. Raphael, "Teaching Question Answer Relationships, Revisited," *The Reading Teacher* 39 (February 1986): 517.

Mike and his father went to the ball game.
They were lucky to get tickets for the game.
They saw many people they knew.
At the game Mike and his father ate hot dogs.
They also drank soda.

Ask the students the following questions:

1. Where did Mike and his father go? (To the ball game)
2. Where did they see the people? (At the ball game)

Help the children see that the first answer is directly stated, whereas the second is not; it is "in their heads."

***Step 2.*** The "In the Book" category is divided into two parts. The first deals with information that is directly stated in a single sentence in the passage, and the second deals with the piecing together of the answer from different parts of the passage. (Raphael calls this step "Think and Search" or "Putting it Together.")[40]

Give the children practice in doing this.

***Step 3.*** This is similar to Step 2 except that now the "In My Head" category is divided into two parts. They are "Author and You" and "On My Own."[41] Help students recognize whether the question is text-dependent or independent. For example, the answer to the first question would require the student to read the text to be able to answer it, even though the answer would come from the student's background of experiences. However, the student can answer the second without reading the passage.

1. How else do you think the cat could have escaped?
2. How would you feel if you were lost?

The QAR approach can be very useful in introducing children to inferential reasoning; it helps them understand better what information is directly stated and what is implied. Teachers can modify the QAR approach to suit their students' needs.

[40]Ibid., p. 518.

[41]Ibid.

# NOTING STUDENT PROGRESS

As we mention throughout this text, assessment drives instruction. This is true for comprehension instruction as well as any other aspect of reading. Three questions reveal themselves when thinking about comprehension assessment: What do I want to know? Why do I want to know? How can I best discover? (See Table 12.2) In terms of comprehension, there is much we want to know. There are four ways we can get at these questions.

First, some of the assessment techniques we mention in earlier chapters are excellent tools for answering the questions. These include retelling, asking questions representative of the different comprehension levels (such as those used in the informal reading inventory), observation, and interviewing students. Additional ways to use questioning are shown in the next section.

Second, we can use teacher-created informal assessments such as those shown in this chapter. We can use student performance on these assessments to determine who might need additional explicit comprehension instruction.

Third, we can take a look at how students perform on comprehension-related tasks that they perform across all content areas. That is, we want students to see that they need to use comprehension skills and strategies any time they read. For example, if we expect students to summarize, we can provide a summarizing activity related to a social studies reading assignment and note whether they are able to use what they know about summarizing in social studies.

Fourth, we can use a cloze or maze procedure. Both of these are described in the following sections.

## QUESTIONING AS A DIAGNOSTIC TECHNIQUE

Asking questions is not only an important part of teaching and learning, it is also very useful in diagnosis. Teachers' questions, which can stimulate students to either low- or high-level thinking, give insight into students' ability to comprehend information. Student responses can help a teacher to see whether students need help; whether they are able to see relationships and make comparisons; and whether the materials the students are reading or listening to is too difficult or too easy.

Students' questions are an important part of their learning, and they are essential diagnostic aids in giving teachers feedback on the students' ability to understand information. In order to ask good questions, students must know their material. As a result, those students who ask the best questions usually are those who know the material best. Confusing questions are a signal that the teacher needs to slow down or reteach certain material.

Teachers can use questioning as a diagnostic technique to learn about their students' thinking ability. Here are some examples.

The teacher has the children read a short story. The story is about a boy who wants to go to school, but he can't because he is too young. The teacher tells the children that she is going to make up some questions about the story, and the children have to tell her whether the questions that she makes up are capable of being answered. If a question is able to be answered, the student should answer it; if a question is not able to be answered, the student must tell why. The teacher makes up the following questions:

1. What are the names of Ben's sister and brother who go to school?
2. Why does Ben want to go to school?
3. Make up an adventure for Ben.
4. Why can't Ben go to school?
5. What are the names of the bus driver's children?
6. What does Ben do in the summer?

This technique can help the teacher learn which children are able to concentrate, as well as which children are able to do different kinds of thinking. Questions 1 and 4 are literal questions; question 2 is an inferential question; question 3 is a creative question; and questions 5 and 6 are not able to be answered because no such information was given in the story either directly or indirectly.

A more difficult questioning technique that the teacher could use with children is to have them make up questions for a selection that they have read.

After students have read a selection, the teacher can ask them to make up three different questions. The first question should be one for which the information is directly stated in the passage. The second question should be one for which the answer is not directly stated in the passage. The third question should be one that requires an answer that goes beyond the text.

In early primary grades the teacher can use pictures as the stimuli for questions, or the teacher can relate a short story to the children and have them devise questions for it.

Here are some questions that a group of fourth-grade children made up after reading a story about Melissa and her friend Fred, who were always getting into trouble.

1. Who is Melissa's best friend? (literal)
2. What is the main idea of the story? (inferential)
3. From the story what can we infer about the main character's personality? (inferential)
4. Relate an episode that you think Melissa could get into. (creative)

The children who made up the questions challenged their classmates with their questions and then they were responsible for determining whether their classmates had answered them correctly.

## CLOZE PROCEDURE

**Cloze procedure**
A technique that helps teachers gain information about a variety of language facility and comprehension ability skills.

Can you supply the _____ that fits this sentence? When you came to the missing word in this sentence, did you try to gain closure by supplying a term such as *word* to complete the incomplete sentence? If you did, you were engaged in the process of *closure,* which involves the ability of the reader to use context clues to determine the needed word.

The *cloze procedure* was primarily developed by Wilson Taylor in 1953 as a measure of readability, that is, to test the difficulty of instructional materials and to evaluate their suitability for students. It has since been used for a number of other purposes, especially as a measure of a student's comprehension.

**Cloze test**

Reader must supply words which have been systematically deleted from a passage.

Cloze procedure is not a comprehension skill; it is a technique that helps teachers gain information about a variety of language facility and comprehension skills. A *cloze test* or exercise is one in which the reader must supply words that have been systematically deleted from a text at a particular grade level.

There is no set procedure for determining the length of the passage or the number of deletions that a passage should have. However, if you wish to apply the criteria for reading levels that have been used in research with the traditional cloze procedure, you should follow these procedures. First, only words must be deleted, and the replacements for each word must be the *exact* word, not a synonym. Second, the words must be deleted in a systematic manner. The researchers who have developed the criteria for scoring cloze tests state that "any departure from these rules leaves the teacher with uninterpretable results."[42]

The traditional cloze procedure consists of deleting every fifth word of a passage that is representative of the material being tested. The passage that is chosen should be able to stand alone. Usually the first and last sentences of the passage remain intact. Then beginning with either the first, second, third, fourth, or fifth word of the second sentence, every fifth word of a 250–260 word passage should be deleted.

At the intermediate-grade levels and higher, the passage is usually 250 words, and every fifth word is deleted. For maximum reliability, a passage should have at least fifty deletions. At the primary-grade level, the passage is usually shorter, and every eighth or tenth word is deleted. A cloze technique would not yield as reliable a score for the primary-grade level as for the intermediate-grade level because passages for the former are shorter and have fewer deletions.

Teachers can use cloze exercises for diagnosis, review, instruction, and testing. In constructing the exercise, the main point to remember is its *purpose*. If the purpose is to test a student's retention of some concepts in a specific area, the exact term is usually necessary; however, if the purpose is to gain information about a student's language facility, ability to use context clues, vocabulary development, or comprehension, the exact term is not as important because often many words will make sense in a passage.

### *Scoring the Cloze Test*

If you have deleted fifty words, the procedure for scoring the cloze test is very easy. All you have to do is multiply the number of correct insertions by two and add a percentage symbol. For example, twenty-five correct insertions would be equal to 50 percent. If you have not deleted exactly fifty words, use the following formula, in which the number of correct insertions is divided by the number of blanks and multiplied by 100 percent.

$$\text{Formula:} \quad \frac{\text{Number of Correct Insertions}}{\text{Number of Blanks}} \times 100\%$$

[42]John R. Bormuth, "The Cloze Procedure: Literacy in the Classroom," in *Help for the Reading Teacher: New Directions in Research,* William D. Page, ed. (Urbana, IL: National Conference on Research in English, 1975), p. 67.

$$\text{Example: } \frac{40 \text{ Correct Insertions}}{60 \text{ Blanks}} \times 100\%$$

$$\frac{40}{60} \times 100\% = (40 \div 60) \times 100\%$$

$$= 67\% \text{ (rounded to nearest digit)}$$

For a traditional cloze test in which only exact words are counted as correct and every fifth word has been deleted, a score below 44 percent would indicate a frustration level. A score between 44 and 57 percent would indicate the instructional level, and scores above 57 percent would indicate the independent level. It is important to note that these criteria should be used only if the exact words are used and if every fifth word has been deleted from the passage. These levels are indicative of the text that was used to design the test. In other words, they tell how the student matches up to the text to be used for instruction.

*Reading Levels Scale for Cloze Procedure*

| | |
|---|---|
| Independent level | 58% and above |
| Instructional level | 44% through 57% |
| Frustration level | 43% and below |

***Variations of the Traditional Cloze Procedure: An Emphasis on Diagnosis***
Variations of the cloze technique are sometimes used. For example, rather than deleting every fifth or tenth word, every noun or verb is deleted, or every function or structure word (definite and indefinite articles, conjunctions, prepositions, and so on) is deleted. This technique is used when the teacher wishes to gain information about a student's sentence sense. For example:

Jane threw _____ ball _____ Mary. (the, to)

Another variation of the cloze technique is to delete key words in the passage. This technique is useful for determining whether students have retained certain information. For example:

A technique in which the reader must supply words is called the _____ procedure. (cloze)

Cloze technique can also be adapted for other uses. Students can be presented with a passage in which they must complete the incomplete words. For example:

Dick r_____ his bike every day. (rides)

Another adaptation is to present the students with a passage in which every nth word is deleted. They must then choose words from a given word list that *best* fit the blanks.

Here is an example of an exercise using the cloze technique for an upper primary grade. Notice how explicitly the instructions are stated for the students, and also notice that the first and last sentences of the passage are given intact.

In addition, note that the deletion pattern is not the same throughout the passage.

*Directions: Read the first and last sentences that have no missing words in them to get a clue to what the story is about. Then read very carefully each sentence that has a missing word or words in it. Using context clues, figure out a word that would make sense in the story and put it in the blank.*

In the forest live a kind old man and woman. (1) _____ have been living in (2) _____ forest for almost ten (3) _____. They had decided to (4) _____ to the forest because they (5) _____ nature.

The kind old (6) _____ and woman make their (7) _____ by baking breads and cakes and (8) _____ them to the people who (9) _____ the forest. Everyone who (10) _____ the forest usually buys (11) _____ bread or cake from the old (12) _____. The kind old man and woman are happy in the forest.

Answers: 1. They, 2. the, 3. years, 4. move, 5. love, like, 6. man, 7. living, 8. selling, 9. visit, 10. visits, 11. some, 12. couple.

Here is an example of an exercise using cloze technique for an intermediate grade.

*Directions: Read the first and last sentences of the story to get a clue to what the story is about. Then read each sentence that has a missing word or words very carefully. Using context clues, insert a word in each blank so that the story makes sense.*

Everyone was looking forward to Friday night because that was the night of the big basketball game. This (1) _____ would determine the championship (2) _____ Deerville High and Yorktown (3) _____. For years Deerville High and (4) _____ High have been rivals. This (5) _____ was very (6) _____ because so far (7) _____ school had won (8) _____ equal number of games. (9) _____ game on Friday night would break the (10) _____.

Friday night finally arrived. The game (11) _____ the championship title (12) _____ being played in the Deerville High (13) _____ because the game (14) _____ year had been played (15) _____ the Yorktown High gym. (16)

_____ gym was so (17) _____ that many spectators were without (18) _____ . When the two teams (19) _____ the gym from the dressing areas, (20) _____ were thunderous (21) _____ and whistles from the (22) _____ . Each team went through (23) _____ warm-up drills of (24) _____ baskets and passing. Then the buzzer (25) _____ . The game would begin (26) _____ a moment. Just as the referee (27) _____ the ball in the (28) _____ for the starting jumpball, the lights (29) _____ the gym went (30) _____ . There was complete darkness. Everyone (31) _____ taken by surprise. Almost immediately a (32) _____ on the loudspeaker (33) _____ that the game would have (34) _____ be postponed because of a (35) _____ failure. The game would take (36) _____ next Friday. All were (37) _____ to remain where they (38) _____ until someone with a flashlight came to help them. Everyone was disappointed that the game had to be cancelled.

Answers: (1) game, (2) between, (3) High, (4) Yorktown, (5) game, (6) important, (7) each, (8) an, (9) The, (10) tie, (11) for, (12) was, (13) gym, (14) last, (15) in, (16) The, (17) crowded, (18) seats, (19) entered, (20) there, (21) cheers, (22) spectators, audience, *or* crowd, (23) its, (24) shooting, (25) sounded *or* rang, (26) in, (27) threw, (28) air, (29) in, (30) out, (31) was, (32) voice, (33) announced, (34) to, (35) power, (36) place, (37) told, (38) were

## Maze Procedure

**Maze Test**
Reader must choose the correct word from three choices for words which have been systematically selected from a passage.

Some teachers prefer to use a maze instead of a cloze procedure because they find it easier for students to use. Because words are added rather than deleted every fifth word, they believe that it gives students more support. To compensate for this ease, the scoring is a little different. That is, students have to achieve at higher levels to reach independent, instructional, and frustrational levels.

Basically, the maze is the same as the cloze with the exception of adding words and establishing cut-off scores. The Venn diagram shown in Figure 12.11 shows how the two are alike and different.

The checklists shown in Figures 12.12 and 12.13 can provide a means of documenting observations, which need to take place in a variety of contexts. As we state in this chapter and throughout this text, students need to read a great deal, and they need to read many different kinds of texts if they are to become accomplished readers. Note that one of the checklists focuses on documenting students' listening comprehension.

We provide the chart in Table 12.2 as a reminder that purpose dictates the selection of the most appropriate comprehension assessment technique. These are intended as suggestions, rather than an all-inclusive list.

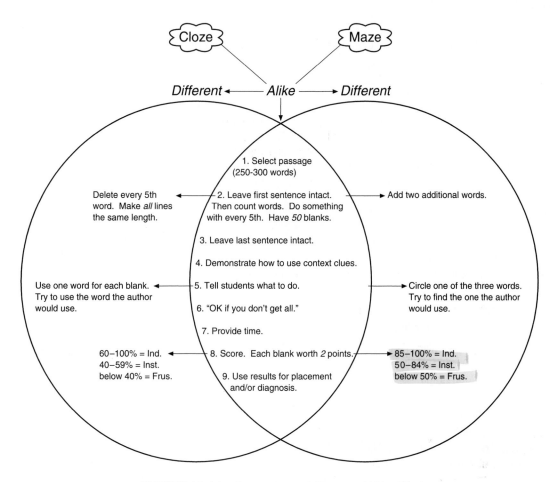

**FIGURE 12.11**   Comparison of Cloze and Maze Testing Procedure

**Special Note**

The *Meta-Comprehension Strategy Index* (Schmitt, 1990) is another meaning-full way to assess students' awareness of the strategies they use in reading. Complete information including the test, administration and scoring procedures, and suggested instructional techniques can be found in *The Reading Teacher, (March)*: 454–461.   ■

## FIGURE 12.12    Diagnostic Checklist for Listening Comprehension*

Student's Name: _____

Grade: _____

Teacher: _____

|  | Yes | No |
|---|---|---|
| 1. Precise listening. The child, after listening to a passage, can answer questions that relate to information explicitly stated in the passage. |  |  |
| 2. Strategic listening. The child, after listening to a passage, can answer questions dealing with |  |  |
| a. finding the main idea. |  |  |
| b. generalization. |  |  |
| c. "reading between the lines." |  |  |
| d. conclusions. |  |  |
| e. cause-effect relationships. |  |  |
| f. multiple meanings. |  |  |
| 3. Critical listening. The child, after listening to a passage, can answer questions dealing with |  |  |
| a. propaganda. |  |  |
| b. fact or opinion. |  |  |
| c. bias. |  |  |
| d. emotive language. |  |  |
| 4. Appreciative listening. The child voluntarily chooses to listen to various tapes. |  |  |

*The length and difficulty of the selection used are determined by the grade level and the developmental level of the individual child. Also, this is not an inclusive list of listening comprehension skills.

**FIGURE 12.13   Diagnostic Checklist for Selected Reading Comprehension Skills**

Student's Name: _____

Grade: _____

Teacher: _____

| | Yes | No |
|---|---|---|
| 1. The student is able to state the meaning of a word in context. | | |
| 2. The student is able to give the meaning of a phrase or a clause in a sentence. | | |
| 3. The student is able to give variations of meanings for homographs (words spelled the same but with more than one meaning, for example, *train, mean, saw, sole,* and so on). | | |
| 4. The student is able to give the meaning of a sentence in a paragraph. | | |
| 5. The student is able to recall information that is explicitly stated in the passage (literal questions). | | |
| 6. The student is able to state the main idea of a paragraph. | | |
| 7. The student is able to state details to support the main idea of a paragraph. | | |
| 8. The student is able to summarize a paragraph. | | |
| 9. The student is able to answer a question that requires reading between the lines. | | |
| 10. The student is able to draw a conclusion from what is read. | | |
| 11. The student can hypothesize the author's purpose for writing the selection. | | |
| 12. The student can differentiate between fact and opinion. | | |
| 13. The student can differentiate between fantasy and reality. | | |
| 14. The student can detect bias in a story. | | |
| 15. The student can detect various propaganda tactics that are used in a story. | | |
| 16. The student can go beyond the text to come up with alternate solutions or ways to end a story or solve a problem in the selection. | | |
| 17. The student shows that he or she enjoys reading by voluntarily choosing to read. | | |
| 18. The student shows the ability to use a variety of comprehension strategies when reading (e.g., visualizing, predicting, monitoring, asking questions). | | |

**TABLE 12.2   Selecting Appropriate Comprehension Measures**

| What Do I Want to Know? | Why Do I Want to Know? | How Can I Best Discover? |
|---|---|---|
| Are students acquiring and applying specific comprehension skills and strategies when reading? | Good readers have many skills and strategies at their disposal and they use those they find most appropriate when reading given texts. I want to make sure that all students are acquiring and applying comprehension skills and strategies because both will help them become able readers. | • Observation<br>• Performance on daily comprehension tasks<br>• Cloze<br>• Maze |
| Are students able to comprehend at different levels? | Many different levels of comprehension are necessary for excellent comprehension. I want to make sure that students are using higher-level comprehension as well as literal comprehension. | • Retelling<br>• Comprehension test from IRI<br>• Talking with students<br>• Questioning (pages 379–398) |
| Are students aware of the strategies they use to comprehend text? | Metacognition is an important part of comprehension. If students are aware of the strategies they use in reading, they are more likely to use them. I can also help students to expand their repertoire of strategies if necessary. | • Student Interview<br>• Student self-assessment |

## SUMMARY

In Chapter 12 we are concerned with helping you better understand reading comprehension, as well as with helping you gain techniques for the diagnosis and teaching of comprehension. Reading comprehension is a complex intellectual process involving a number of abilities. The two major processes involve word meanings and reasoning with verbal concepts. We emphasize that comprehension involves thinking, and as there are various levels of thinking, so are there various levels of comprehension. Reading comprehension is categorized into a hierarchy of four levels: literal comprehension, interpretation, critical reading, and creative reading. We also address listening comprehension as a segue to reading comprehension. We then provide some information about how oral reading can facilitate reading comprehension. There are many compre-

hension skills and four of them are highlighted: finding the main idea of a paragraph, describing the central idea of a group of paragraphs, finding the main idea of visual representations, and drawing inferences. For each, we provide an explanation and examples, as well as informal assessment measures and instructional suggestions.

Comprehension strategies are also important and we present background and lessons related to six of them.

There are a number of instructional strategies that teachers can use to help students acquire comprehension ability. We list and describe seven of them.

We conclude the chapter by offering some suggestions for ways to note student progress.

# CHAPTER 12 KEY CONCEPTS

- Reading comprehension cannot be directly observed or directly measured; one can only infer that someone "understands."
- Reading comprehension is a complex intellectual process involving a number of abilities.
- Although it is difficult to state definitively how persons achieve comprehension while reading, studies suggest that good comprehenders have certain characteristics.
- A person with background information related to what one is reading will comprehend better than one with less such information.
- The ability to relate present information to past information and experiences will enhance understanding.
- Reading taxonomies deal with a hierarchy of reading comprehension skills ranging from the more simplistic ones to the more complex ones.
- Comprehension involves thinking, and higher levels of comprehension include higher levels of thinking.
- Listening comprehension is related to reading comprehension.
- Oral reading can help with comprehension.
- Time spent in reading is important for success in reading.
- Teachers must plan for their students to have explicit instruction, as well as independent reading.
- Repeated reading helps poor oral readers gain fluency in reading.
- Teachers can use questioning techniques for diagnostic purposes.
- Teachers should use a diagnostic-reading and improvement approach to help their students acquire important comprehension skills at all levels.
- Diagnosis and improvement in reading should take place throughout the school day.
- Teachers should be aware that a student may dislike a subject because he or she cannot read the textbook.
- A good reading program should manifest itself in the literature program.
- Cloze procedure is a technique that helps teachers gain information about a variety of language facility and comprehension skills.
- Variations of the cloze procedure have usually been used.
- A maze procedure is similar to a cloze procedure.
- Comprehension strategies as well as skills need explicit attention.

# SUGGESTIONS FOR THOUGHT QUESTIONS AND ACTIVITIES

1. State the four levels of comprehension presented in this chapter. State one skill for each level. Then prepare an objective and a test for the objective for each skill you have chosen (primary grades).
2. Do the same for the intermediate grades.
3. You have been appointed to a special reading curriculum committee at your school. The committee is interested in revamping their primary reading program. What suggestions would you make?
4. You are appointed to a committee that is charged with developing assessments for reading comprehension. What suggestions would you make to the committee to proceed?
5. Generate reading comprehension questions for a selection that would elicit high-level reading/thinking responses.
6. Present a reading comprehension lesson and record it. Note the kinds of questions you ask. Critique your lesson and state some ways in which you can improve it.
7. Compare your students' reading behavior in the content areas to their behavior when reading in reading groups. Try to determine whether interest in a subject affects the students' reading performance.

8. Choose a fairy tale. Construct questions at the literal, interpretive, critical, and creative levels for the fairy tale.
9. Use one of the strategies presented in this chapter to teach a reading lesson.
10. Choose five predictable books that would lend themselves to being used in a webbing reading lesson.
11. Suggest three ways to encourage students to read voluntarily.

12. You have a student in your class who has difficulty answering comprehension questions. How would you go about determining what his or her problems are? What can you do to help this student?
13. How would you develop a recreational reading program in your classroom? What techniques and procedures would you use?

## INTERNET ACTIVITIES

Choose a search engine and search for websites related to something you read about in the chapter about which you would like to know more. Select one website from the search that helps you gain a good understanding of the term. Write a brief paragraph about what you discover. (Be sure to identify both the search engine you used and the website you selected.)

## SELECTED BIBLIOGRAPHY

Blachowicz, C., and Ogle, D. *Reading Comprehension: Strategies for Independent Learners.* New York: Guilford, 2001.

Block, C. C., L. L. Rodgers, and R. B. Johnson. *Comprehension Process Instruction.* New York: Guilford, 2004.

Boyles, N. N. *Constructing Meaning Through Kid-Friendly Comprehension Strategy Instruction.* Gainesville, FL: Maupin House, 2004.

Buss, Kathleen, and Leslie McClain-Ruelle, eds. *Creating a Classroom Newspaper.* Newark, DE: International Reading Association, 2000.

Cianciolo, Patricia J. *Informational Picture Books for Children.* Chicago: American Library Association, 2000.

Cole, A. *Knee to Knee, Eye to Eye: Circling in on Comprehension.* Portsmouth, NH: Heinemann, 2003.

Cramer Eugene H. and Marrietta Castle, eds. *Fostering the Love of Reading: The Affective Domain in Reading Education.* Newark, DE: International Reading Association, 1994.

Dorn, L. J., and C. Soffos. *Teaching for Deep Comprehension: A Reading Workshop Approach.* Portland, ME: Stenhouse, 2005.

Galda, Lee, et al. "Children's Literature," in *Handbook of Reading Research,* Michael L. Kamil et al., eds., Vol. III. Mahwah, NJ: Lawrence Erlbaum, 2000.

Hoyt, L. et al. *Spotlight on Comprehension: Building a Literacy of Thoughtfulness.* Portsmouth, NH: Heinemann, 2005.

Mantione, R., and Smead, S. *Weaving Through Words: Using the Arts to Teach Reading Comprehension Strategies.* Newark, DE: International Reading Association, 2003.

Marriott, D. *Comprehension Right from The Start.* Portsmouth, NH: Heinemann, 2003.

Oczkus, L. *Reciprocal Teaching at Work: Strategies for Improving Reading Comprehension.* Newark, DE: International Reading Association, 2003.

Outsen, N., and Yulga, S. *Teaching Comprehension Strategies All Readers Need.* New York: Scholastic, 2002.

Owocki, G. *Comprehension: Strategic Instruction for K-3 Students.* Portsmouth, NH: Heinemann, 2003.

Pierce, Cathryn M., ed. *Adventuring with Books: A Booklet for PreK–Grade 6,* 12th ed. Urbana, Ill: National Council of Teachers of English, 2000.

Post, Arden Ruth, et al. *Celebrating Children's Choices: 25 Years of Children's Favorite Books.* Newark, DE: International Reading Association, 2000.

Pressley, Michael. "What Should Comprehension Instruction Be the Instruction Of?" Michael L. Kamil et al., eds. in *Handbook of Reading Research,* Vol. III. Mahwah, NJ: Lawrence Erlbaum, 2000.

Rubin, Dorothy. *Comprehension Skills & Strategies in a Balanced Reading Program.* Torrance, CA: Fearon Teacher Aids, 1998.

————. *Elementary Language Arts,* 6th ed. Boston: Allyn and Bacon, 2000.

————. *Word Meaning & Reasoning Strategies,* (a three-book series). Torrance, CA: Good Apple, 1996.

Sadler, C. *Comprehension Strategies for Middle Grade Learners: A Handbook for Content Area Teachers.* Newark, DE: International Reading Association, 2001.

Shaw, D. *Retelling Strategies to Improve Reading Comprehension.* New York: Scholastic, 2005.

Spiegel, D. *Classroom Discussion.* New York: Scholastic, 2005.

Sweet, A., and Snow, C., eds. *Rethinking Reading Comprehension.* New York: Guilford, 2003.

Wilhelm, J. *Action Strategies for Deepening Comprehension.* New York: Scholastic, 2002.

**Children's Literature Cited**

Cleary, Beverly. *Dear Mr. Henshaw.* New York: Dell, 1983.

Munsch, Robert. *Alligator Baby.* New York: Scholastic, 1997.

Long, Melinda. *When Papa Snores.* New York: Simon & Schuster, 2000.

Spinelli, Jerry. *Maniac Magee.* New York: Little, Brown, 1990.

# 13

# Learning Strategies and Study Skills in a Diagnostic-Reading and Improvement Program

# INTRODUCTION

How many times have you heard students make the following statements?

"I spent all night studying, but I did very poorly on my exams."
"I reread the chapter ten times, but I still don't understand it."
"I always listen to music when I study."
"I like to be relaxed when I study."
"I don't need to study."
"I don't know how to study."

Many students do poorly in school because they have never learned how to study. Often, elementary-school teachers spend little time helping children acquire study skills because they may lack the skills themselves,[1] or because they feel that this is the job of high school teachers. Many high school teachers spend little instructional time in this area because they make the assumption that their students have already acquired the study skills they need. As a result, many students go through school without ever being helped to acquire study skills. Most children need help in acquiring good study habits as soon as possible before they develop either poor study habits or erroneous concepts about studying. Children need to understand that with good study habits, they can spend less time studying yet learn much.

In this chapter we offer some information and skills that are necessary for you to help your students become better learners. Helping students to be better learners is important in a diagnostic-reading and improvement program where the emphasis is on the *prevention* of reading and learning problems.

# CHAPTER OBJECTIVES

After reading the chapter, you should be able to:

- Describe what is involved in building good study habits.
- Explain how teachers can help students to combine SQ3R and notetaking.
- Discuss how attitudes influence studying.
- Describe what is meant by *skimming*.
- Explain the role of skimming in studying.
- Explain how reading and writing are used as modes of learning.
- Discuss the place of graphic organizers in studying.
- Explain how teachers can help students to be better notetakers.
- Describe how to summarize a passage.
- Explain how teachers can help students to be better test takers.
- Discuss why children should be good question askers.
- Discuss the role of concentration in studying.

---

[1] Eunice N. Askov et al., "Study Skill Mastery Among Elementary Teachers," *The Reading Teacher* 30 (February 1977): 485–88.

# WHAT ARE SOME GOOD STUDY PROCEDURES?

Although there is no simple formula that will apply to all students, educational psychologists have found that some *study procedures* help all students. The key is in building good habits, devising a system that works for the individual student, and keeping at it.

A person cannot relax and study at the same time. Studying requires a certain amount of tension, concentration, and effort in a specific direction. The amount of tension varies with different individuals. The point is that studying is most often difficult and students who are prepared to make a proper effort can maximize their learning time.

## Building Good Study Habits

The first step in building good study habits is to determine *when to study*. Some students study only just before an announced test. Some may even stay up until all hours and cram. All of us have probably done this once or twice. However, if this is a student's normal way of doing things, he or she will not do well in school. Cramming does not bring about sustained learning. It can be justified only as a last resort. To be a good student, a student must plan study time and spread it out over a period of time. Students must realize that a regular plan will prevent confusion and help them retain what they are studying. Students, even in the elementary grades, need to be shown how to plan an overall time schedule in which they allow for social and physical activities. Recreational reading should also be included in the schedule. Students must recognize that a rhythm of activities is important. Regardless of whether they study in the evening, before or after dinner, or right after class during free periods, following a schedule and spreading out the studying over the week is what's important.

The second step in building good study habits is to determine *where to study*. Some students are able to study well in a school or public library, but there are others who cannot. Most elementary-school students study at home. Regardless of where students study, they should choose a place that is comfortable and convenient, has enough light, and is *free from distractions*. Consistency is important.

To help children establish a comfortable, convenient, and suitable place for study at home, the teacher and the children can design such a place in the classroom. A special area can be set aside as a study area. It should be as free from distractions as possible, comfortable, and well lighted. Students should be free to go to this area whenever they wish to study. If a student is in this area, other students should recognize that it is "off bounds"; that is, other students should respect the student's desire to study and not interrupt or bother the student.

Teachers must recognize that there are some students in class who may not have a place at home to study. There may be many children in the house and not enough rooms, so that the only place to study may be the kitchen. However, the kitchen is not very good because it usually has too many distractions. Teachers should be aware of the home situations of their students and try to help them as much as possible without embarrassing them. The teacher could discuss with the student the possibility of studying at the library or at a friend's house.

If these are not feasible, and if the student does not have to ride a bus to school, the teacher might make some arrangements that permit the student to study in the school. A teacher must be sensitive to the fact that students who do not have a place to do homework or study at home are actually being penalized twice—once, because they do not have a place to study, and again, because they will probably be penalized for not doing the homework.

The third step in building good study habits is to determine the *amount of time* to spend in studying. You must help students recognize that the amount of time they spend will depend on the subject and how well they know it. It is unrealistic to set up a hard-and-fast rule about the amount of time to study in a specific subject because the amount of time will vary. In some subjects a student may need to spend a lot of time studying because he or she is weak in that area, whereas in others the student may only have to spend a short time studying. You should help students understand the concept of *overlearning* because some students feel that if they know something, they do not have to study it at all. Overlearning helps persons retain information over a long period of time. Overlearning happens when individuals continue to practice even after they think they have learned the material.

**Overlearning**
Helps persons retain information over a long period of time; occurs when individuals continue to practice even after they think they have learned the material.

## HOW TO STUDY

**SQ3R**
A widely used study technique that involves five steps: survey, question, read, recite or recall, and review.

**Survey**
To gain an overview of the text material.

**Recite or recall**
The process of finding the answer to a question in one's memory without rereading the text or notes.

After you have helped students attain positive attitudes toward their learning tasks and helped them recognize that they must exert effort to study, find a suitable place to study, and spend time in studying, you must still help them learn *how to study*. There are a number of study techniques and *SQ3R*[2] is one of them. It is a widely used technique developed by a well-known psychologist that has proved helpful to many students. Here are the five steps in this technique:

1. *Survey*—Students should get an overall sense of their learning task before proceeding to details. They should skim the whole assignment to obtain some idea(s) about the material and how it is organized.
2. *Question*—Students should check section headings and change these to questions to set their purposes for reading.
3. *Read*—Students should read to answer the questions that they have formulated for themselves. While reading they should notice how the paragraphs are organized because this knowledge will help them remember the answer.
4. *Recite or recall—This step is very important.* Without referring to their book, students should try to answer the questions that they have formulated for themselves. (Writing down key ideas will provide necessary notes for future review. See the section on notetaking.)
5. *Review*—Students should take a few moments to review the major headings and subheadings of the material they have just finished studying.

[2]Adapted from Francis P. Robinson, *Effective Study,* 4th ed., (New York: Harper & Row, 1970).

You should recommend to your students that it's also a good idea to try to relate what they just finished studying to the previous assignment on the same topic. (Their ability to relate their new learning with previous learning will determine how well they will remember the new material.)

Make sure students understand that they can survey a reading assignment to determine its organization and to obtain some ideas about it, but they cannot study unfamiliar material by skimming or reading rapidly. Help your students to recognize that one of the key factors in remembering information is recall or recitation and not the immediate rereading of their assignment. The time they spend answering the questions that they have formulated is crucial in learning.

The following scenario provides an example of how you can help your students adapt the SQ3R technique to suit their personal needs:

## Scenario: Modeling the SQ3R Approach for Fourth Grade Students

Ms. Mills tells her fourth grade students that she is taking courses at the local college, and she has lots of reading to do. If she didn't know how to study, she would be in trouble. She tells them that she was very fortunate to have a teacher who taught her how to study, and she wants to do the same for them. She will show them what she does when she has to study something.

*Step 1:* Ms. Mills chooses a chapter from the students' history textbook and has her students turn to the chapter. She then says, "I always quickly skim through an assignment first to get an idea of what it's about and what it covers. So that's what I'm going to do. I also want you to do the same."

Ms. Mills then says, "As I skim through the chapter, I look at some of the section heads to see if I should break the chapter up into parts to study. I do this if it's an area I don't know anything about. Why don't you do the same?"

*Step 2:* Ms. Mills says, "I try to be honest with myself. If the chapter has a great amount of new material, I know I should break it up into parts. Also, I know my concentration ability. I don't feel I can study the whole chapter all at once, so I will break this chapter into parts for study purposes and choose a few sections to study at a time. Would you have done the same? Remember, it depends on your background of experiences."

*Step 3:* Ms. Mills says, "I look over the first part of the chapter I have decided to study. I check the section heads and use these to make up questions. If there were no section heads, I would look for other clues such as words in margins, words in bold print, or words in italics. If the material doesn't have any of these, then I survey or skim it more slowly and also read the first sentence to get an idea of what the selection is about.

*Step 4:* "Now, I read the part I chose to study and try to answer my questions. As I do this, I try to determine how the writer has organized his paragraphs because that will help me remember the material better," says Ms. Mills. In addition, she tells her students that she makes sure she studies in an area where she will not have any distractions. When she studies, she really tries to concentrate very hard; otherwise, it's a waste of time, and she might as well be doing something else.

*Step 5:* "This step is the most important for me. I stop to think about the material I have read and answer my questions. If I can't answer my questions, then I go back and reread that part.

*Step 6:* "Since I divided the chapter into parts, I take a few moments to go over the main points of the part I just finished studying before going on to a new part," says Ms. Mills.

*Step 7:* Ms. Mills tells her students that she then goes through the same steps in the next part. When she has completed the whole assignment, she reviews everything she has studied by going back to the beginning, looking at each section heading, and trying to state the main idea of each paragraph or central idea of each section. She emphasizes to her students that they should always try to relate their new learning to their past learning because doing so will help them remember the information.

Ms. Mills also tells her students that there are no shortcuts to studying. "You have to exert effort. When you do, the rewards are great!"

## ACTIVITIES

Here are some sample activities to give your students practice in using the SQ3R technique:

1. Like Ms. Mills, model the strategy.
2. Choose a selection your students have not read before, and have them do the following:
   a. Survey the selection to determine what it's about.
   b. Prepare six questions that can be used to set purposes for reading and that students can answer. (Use the given six questions to set purposes for reading.)
   c. Read the selection carefully.
   d. Without looking back at the selection, try to answer the six questions.
3. Choose a selection that your students have not read before, and have them formulate questions that could help them in studying.

### Special Note

PQ4R, which is similar to SQ3R and is a modification of it, is also widely used. PQ4R stands for Preview, Question, Read, Reflect, Recite, Review. In SQ3R, "reflect" is implied in the recall stage. However, the "mulling" of material (reflecting) is certainly important in studying. PQ4R is more explicit in designating the stage. ■

One way to help students become aware of their own study habits is to provide them with a checklist such as the one we show in Figure 13.1. Students can also use this checklist to self-evaluate their growth over a period of time.

## KNOWING YOUR TEXTBOOK

Helping children to learn about the various parts of their textbooks is an important study skill that can save valuable time and effort. Here are some reading activities that students can do after they have acquired their textbooks:

FIGURE 13.1   **Student Checklist of Study Habits and Strategies**

|  | Always | Sometimes | Never |
|---|---|---|---|
| 1. I have a special study place. | | | |
| 2. My study place is quiet. | | | |
| 3. I set goals for myself. | | | |
| 4. I make good use of my time. | | | |
| 5. I first look over my reading assignment to get an overview of it. | | | |
| 6. I look for writers' aids such as words in italics or bold and words in margins. | | | |
| 7. I break up my reading assignment into manageable sections. | | | |
| 8. I set questions for my reading material. | | | |
| 9. After reading each section, I stop to answer my questions. | | | |
| 10. I also try to state the central idea of each passage. | | | |
| 11. I relate my present reading to past assignments. | | | |
| 12. I review my present reading assignment before going on to something else. | | | |
| 13. In reviewing, I state generalizations about what I have read. | | | |

1. *Survey the textbook.* Surveying helps students see how the author presents the material. Students should observe whether the author presents topic headings in bold print or in the margins. Students should also notice if there are diagrams, charts, cartoons, pictures, and other features.
2. *Read the preface.* In the preface or foreword, the author presents the purpose and plan for writing the book. Here the author usually describes the organization of the book and explains how the book either is different from others in the field or is a further contribution to the field of knowledge.
3. *Read the table of contents.* The table of contents provides a good idea of what to expect from the book. Then when students begin to study they will know how each section they are reading relates to the rest of the book.
4. *Skim the index.* The index indicates in detail what material students will find in the book. It is an invaluable aid because it helps students find specific information that they need by giving them the page on which it appears.
5. *Check for a glossary.* Not all books have a glossary; however, a glossary is helpful because it gives students the meanings of specialized words or phrases used in the book.

*Activities*

Have the students skim to answer the following:

1. Using the index of one of their textbooks, the students state the pages on which they would find various topics.
2. Using one of their textbooks, the students give the meaning(s) of some of the terms that are presented in the glossary.
3. Using the table of contents of one of their textbooks, the students state the pages on which given chapters begin.

# CONCENTRATION

**Concentration**

Sustained attention. It is essential for both studying and listening to lectures.

You need to help your students recognize that even though they are acquiring some good study habits, they may still have difficulty studying because they cannot *concentrate.* Concentration is necessary not only for studying but also for listening in class. *Concentration* is sustained attention. If you are not feeling well, if you are hungry or tired, if you are in a room that is too hot or cold, if your chair is uncomfortable, if the lighting is poor or if there is a glare, if there are visual or auditory distractions, you will not be able to concentrate well.

Concentration demands a mental set or attitude, a determination that you will block everything out except what you are reading or listening to. For example, how many times have you looked up a phone number in the telephone directory and forgotten the number almost immediately? How many times have you had to look up the *same* number that you had previously dialed a number of times before? Probably very often. The reason for your not remembering is that you did not fully *concentrate.* In order to remember information, you must concentrate. Concentration requires active involvement from wide-awake and alert individuals. It also demands persons who have a positive frame of mind toward the task at hand. Establishing a good affective classroom environment and encouraging students will greatly influence how well they will perform. This means lectures and assignments should be as interesting as possible to better ensure concentration.

Without concentration, there is little hope of understanding the information. The following types of activities will help your students develop their concentration.

*Activities*

**Activity 1: Word Concentration (Listening)**

In playing this game, just two persons are needed—a speaker and a listener. It can also be played with teams. The speaker says, "Listen carefully. I am going to say some words and when I am through, I want you to repeat them. I will state the words only once and at a rate of one per second. Remember. Listen carefully and wait until I am finished to say them. I'll start with two words and then I'll keep adding one word. Let's do one together."

*Example:*   Speaker says, "Train, nail." The listener repeats, "Train, nail." And the speaker says, "Good," if the words are repeated correctly.

Set 1: can/dog . . . red/map . . .
Set 2: mail/milk/book . . . cake/pen/sad . . .
Set 3: sad/none/in/may . . . chair/help/two/six . . .
Set 4: name/sail/bike/pen/man . . . worm/boat/sick/has/more . . .
Set 5: chair/name/key/same/hop/note . . . leg/rope/teach/dance/dog/name . . .
Set 6: witch/rob/sleep/some/read/check/nuts . . . ball/ape/mind/sleep/dog/king/hair . . .
Set 7: spoon/mate/can/man/all/book/sad/show . . . love/rode/room/all/door/can/girl/pad . . .
Set 8: boat/lamp/paint/long/dock/teach/knife/win/chair . . . draw/food/pat/car/sand/pan/size/spring/farm . . .

In this game, the words that are presented are not related to one another, so that the listener must concentrate in order to be able to repeat them immediately. This game can be played each day or a few times during the week. Children enjoy playing this game and are delighted when they find that they are able to pay attention for longer periods of time and are, therefore, able to repeat more and more of the words.

**Activity 2: Digit-Span Concentration (Listening)**
Digit-span exercises based on a graduated level of difficulty are helpful in developing concentration. The instructions for the digits are similar to those in Activity 1 for words; however, in place of words the term *numbers* is inserted.

**Activity 3: Adding Word Concentration (Listening)**
The teacher says, "I'm going to say two sets of words. The second set has all the words from Set 1 but it also has a new word. You have to write what the new word is. Example: *Set 1*: pen, dog, tall. *Set 2:* tall, dog, pen, snow. (The new word is *snow.*)"

*Set 1:* stamp, week, red
*Set 2:* week, stamp, red, (smoke)
*Set 1:* child, help, dark, nice
*Set 2:* child, (grow), help, nice, dark
*Set 1:* sun, spoon, mouth, five, bet
*Set 2:* spoon, mouth, five, (game), bet, sun
*Set 1:* wild, rose, bread, couch, pill, cup
*Set 2:* rose, bread, couch, pill, (crumb), cup, wild
*Set 1:* pin, fat, net, pine, wind, swing, dog
*Set 2:* fat, net, pine, wind, (damp), swing, pin, dog

# FOLLOWING DIRECTIONS

Being able to follow directions is an important skill that we use all our lives. Scarcely a day goes by without the need to follow directions. Cooking, baking, taking medication, driving, traveling, repairing, building, planning, taking examinations, doing assignments, filling out applications, and a hundred other common activities require the ability to follow directions.

You can help your students to be better at following directions through practice and by having them heed the following pointers:

1. Read the directions *carefully*. Read all words.
2. If you do not understand any directions, ask for help.
3. Concentrate! People who follow directions well tend also to have the ability to concentrate well.
4. Follow the directions that *are* given, not the ones you think ought to be given.
5. Reread the directions if you need to, and refer to them as you follow them.
6. Remember that some directions should be followed step by step.
7. Practice following directions. Try this activity, which will give you experience in following directions.

*Directions:* Read carefully the entire list of directions that follows before doing anything. You have four minutes to complete this activity.

1. Put your name in the upper right-hand corner of this paper.
2. Put your address under your name.
3. Put your telephone number in the upper left-hand corner of this paper.
4. Add 9370 and 5641.
5. Subtract 453 from 671.
6. Raise your hand and say, "I'm the first."
7. Draw two squares, one triangle, and three circles.
8. Write the opposite of *hot.*
9. Stand up and stamp your feet.
10. Give three meanings for *spring.*
11. Write the numbers from one to ten backward.
12. Write the even numbers from two to twenty.
13. Write the odd numbers from one to twenty-one.
14. Write seven words that rhyme with *fat.*
15. Call out, "I have followed directions."
16. If you have read the directions carefully, you should have done nothing until now. Do only directions 1 and 2.

*Answer:* The directions stated that you should read the entire list of directions carefully *before doing anything.* You should have done only directions 1 and 2. When you take timed tests, you usually do *not* read the directions as carefully as you should.

Here is another activity in following directions:

*Directions:* Read each numbered instruction once only, and then carry out the instructions on the boxed material. (This activity requires a great amount of concentration.)

| 1 | 7 | 3 | 4 | play | dog | man | M | N | O |
|---|---|---|---|------|-----|-----|---|---|---|
| P | Q | 35 | 32 | 63 | 15 | 10 | stop | under | big |

*Instructions*

1. If there are two numbers that added together equal 7 and a word that rhymes with *may*, put a line under the rhyming word.
2. If there is a word that means the same as *large,* a word opposite to *go,* and a word that rhymes with *fan,* put a circle around the three words.
3. If there are two numbers that added together equal 8, two numbers that added together equal 67, and a word the opposite of *over,* underline the two numbers that added together equal 8.
4. If there are five consecutive letters, four words that each contain a different vowel, and at least four odd numbers, put a cross on the five consecutive letters.
5. If there are six words, three even numbers, two numbers that added together equal 45, and three numbers that added together equal 16, circle the word *dog.*
6. If there are two numbers that added together equal 25, two numbers that added together equal 95, and three numbers that added together equal 79, put a circle around the three numbers that added together equal 79.

# SKIMMING

Setting purposes for reading is a crucial factor for reading comprehension. It is important that students learn that they read for different purposes and that they need to adjust their rate of reading to their purpose. If they are reading for pleasure, they can read either quickly or slowly based on the way they feel. If they are studying or reading information that is new to them, they will probably read very slowly. If, however, they are looking up a telephone number, a name, a date, or looking over a paragraph for its topic, they will read much more rapidly. Reading rapidly to find or locate information is called *skimming.* All skimming involves fast reading; however, there are different kinds of skimming. Skimming for a number, a date, or a name can usually be done much more quickly than skimming for the topic of a paragraph or to answer specific questions. (Some persons call the most rapid reading *scanning* and the less rapid reading skimming.) Teachers can also help students recognize that they read rapidly to locate some specific information, but that once they have located what they want, they should read the surrounding information more slowly.

**Skimming**
Reading rapidly to find or locate information.

Make sure that students understand the difference between skimming and studying. Although skimming is used as part of the SQ3R technique when students survey a passage, skimming material is not the same as studying. Studying requires much slower and more concentrated reading.

Skimming is an important skill because it is used so often throughout one's life, and it is many times the only way to get a job done in a reasonable amount of time. Some skimming activities for intermediate-grade students include:

1. Skim newspaper headlines for a particular news item.
2. Skim movie ads for a particular movie.

3. Skim tape catalogs for a specific title.
4. Skim the Yellow Pages of the phone book for some help.
5. Skim the television guide to find a particular show.

# ASKING QUESTIONS

**Questions**
A good way for students to gain a better insight into a subject; questioning also gives the instructor feedback.

Asking questions is an important part of learning, and we want all children to recognize this. A nonthreatening environment is necessary for students to feel comfortable asking questions. Knowing how and when to ask questions helps students to gain a better insight into a subject and gives the teacher feedback. This also helps the teacher monitor the pace of a lesson. However, some students are afraid to ask questions for one reason or another. Students may not know how to formulate the question or may be "afraid of looking like a fool."

Here are some pointers to communicate to students:

1. Students who ask the best questions are usually those who know the material best.
2. Asking questions is not a substitute for studying the material.
3. Questions help to clarify the material for students.
4. Teachers usually want and encourage questions.
5. The questions students ask will probably help a number of other students.

Here are suggestions on the kind of questions students should ask about examinations:

1. What kind of test will it be? Will it be an objective or a subjective test?
2. How long will the test be? (This will help the students to know whether it's a quiz (a minor exam) or a test (one that usually counts more than a quiz).
3. Will dates, names, formulas, and other such specifics be stressed? (Whether these things are stressed is important for the student to know because it will influence the type of studying that he or she will do.)
4. Will it be an open-book or closed-book exam? (This option is important because it will influence the type of studying a student will do.)
5. What chapters will be covered?

Here are some suggestions on other kinds of questions students should ask:

1. In going over an examination, students should ask general questions or those that relate to everyone's papers. Tell students that if they have specific questions on their papers, they should ask the teacher their questions in private.
2. Tell students that they should not hesitate to ask questions about the grading of their papers if they do not understand it. They should especially ask the teacher about comments on their papers that they do not understand. Help them to recognize that they learn from knowing the results and understanding their mistakes.

Here are some suggestions on how students should ask questions:

1. They should be as specific as possible.
2. They should state the question clearly.
3. They should not say, "I have a question," and then go into a long discourse before asking it. (The question may be forgotten.)
4. They should make sure that the question is related to the material.

Students should know that questioning is an important part of SQ3R and that questions help them set purposes for their reading. Questions help give direction and organization to reading and guide students to be actively involved while reading. Good readers usually ask questions before, during, and after the reading. The questions they ask are triggered in a number of ways. For example, they may have found some inconsistency in their reading or feel that the writer is being biased, or they may feel that what they are reading is confusing. Students who are good critical readers ask many questions of the text they are reading.

# READING AND WRITING AS MODES OF LEARNING

There are several reading and writing strategies that can help students learn better. Notetaking, graphic organizers and summaries are three strategies. Each calls for explicit instruction.

## NOTETAKING FOR STUDYING

**Notetaking**
A useful study and paper-writing tool.

*Notetaking* is a very important tool; it is useful not only in writing long papers but also in studying. Students are usually concerned with notetaking when they begin writing long reports or papers.

Students need to understand that notes consist of words and phrases that help persons remember important material. They do not have to be complete sentences; however, unless an individual's notes are clear and organized, the notes will be difficult to study from later.

In the following scenario, Ms. Mills helps students develop these understandings.

 ## Scenario: Notetaking, Studying, and SQ3R

Ms. Mills presents the following notes to her students on a transparency. (She tells the students that the notes do not belong to anyone in the class. Nevertheless, the notes are on a topic they have been studying.) She asks her students to examine the notes carefully.

*Notes*

1. influenced by age
2. influenced by gender
3. skin
4. thin

5. outer layer
6. several layers
7. epidermis
8. dermis
9. tough
10. stores fat
11. thicker than epidermis

*List of Main Topics*

I. Age of skin
II. Layers of skin
III. Skin

She asks her students what they think about the notes. Are the notes "jogging their memories" about what they had studied? Refreshing memories is the main purpose of notes for studying. She then discusses with her students why the notes were not very helpful. Here are the things they stated:

It is difficult to make sense of these notes because the main topics are either vaguely stated, too general, or too specific.
The items in the list of notes can fit under more than one main topic; they are not precise enough; that is, they do not contain enough information to unmistakably identify or distinguish them.

Ms. Mills then tells her students that notetaking for study can be incorporated in the SQ3R study technique. Here is a suggested procedure combining SQ3R and notetaking that she presents to her students:

1. Read the whole selection to get an overview of what you have to study. A preliminary reading provides an overview of the organization of the material.
2. Choose a part of the selection to study, basing the choice on ability to concentrate.
3. Survey the part chosen and note the topic of the individual paragraph or group of paragraphs. Write the topic(s) in your notebook instead of the questions you would write in a normal SQ3R procedure.
4. Read the part.
5. After finishing each paragraph, state its main idea. Put down *only* important supporting details under the main idea.

   a. Although a formal outline for notes is not necessary, *indent* the listing so that the relation of supporting material to main ideas is clear.
   b. Try not to take any notes until after reading the whole paragraph. Remember that *recall* is the essential step in the SQ3R technique. By not taking notes until finishing reading, you are more actively involved in thinking about the material while constructing notes.

Good notes are very helpful for review, and they can save students a great amount of time. Remind students that for study, if the material is new to them, it is usually a good idea to write the topic for each paragraph unless the paragraph is a transitional one. Also tell your students that textbook writers sometimes list the topics of their paragraphs in the margins and the students should be on the lookout for these helpful clues.

A number of students find that a visual representation of the material helps them to remember information they have studied. The following scenario presents the *semantic mapping* technique Ms. Mills uses to help her students.

 ## Scenario: Semantic Mapping and Studying

---

**Semantic mapping (graphic organizer)**

A graphic represen-
tation used to
illustrate concepts
and relationships
among concepts such
as classes, properties,
and examples.

---

Ms. Mills tells her students that rather than taking notes using an informal outline, they could make a graphic illustration of what they are studying. She then enumerates these steps for her students:

*Step 1:*  Again, as in SQ3R, choose the amount of information we will be studying. (This is usually more than a paragraph.)

*Step 2:*  Set our purposes for reading.

*Step 3:*  Read the material.

*Step 4:*  Determine the central idea of what we have read and place it in the center of a blank sheet of paper.

*Step 5:* Reread each paragraph, state the main topic of each, and append it to the central idea.

*Step 6:* Review the material once again and append the important supporting details to its main topic. (Figure 13.2 is an example of a semantic map that Ms. Mills did with her class.)

## SUMMARIES AS A MODE OF LEARNING

Many teachers are helping intermediate- and higher-grade level students learn how to summarize passages because they recognize summaries as a viable means of gaining the essential information. Summarizing material helps

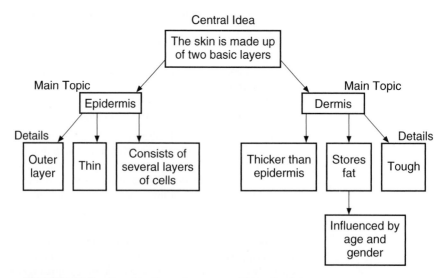

**FIGURE 13.2**    Graphic Organizer as an Aid to Studying.

students retain the most important facts in a long passage, and if the summary is a written summary, it helps integrate the reading and writing process.

Beginning with paragraphs and working up to longer passages is one way to help students learn how to summarize. Children need to be shown that a good *summary* is brief and includes only essential information. The main idea of the paragraph (if only a paragraph is being summarized) or the central idea of an article and the important facts should be stated but not necessarily in the sequence presented in the article. Students also need to see that they can include only the information stated in the paragraph or article.

Many times, students confuse retelling with summarizing. Although the two are related, retelling involves more details than does a summary. We suggest using a lesson similar to the one shown in Figure 13.3 to help students better understand both retelling and summarizing.

**Summary**
A brief statement of the essential information in a longer piece.

# TEST TAKING

The term *test* can make some students shudder. However, tests are a part of life and students need to learn how to use them to their best advantage.

The more students know about tests, the better they can do on them. The general test-taking principles that follow can be taught to students and posted in the classroom in a chart so that children have a visual reminder. The principles you present to your students will depend on the grade level you are teaching as well as the students with whom you are working. Many intermediate-grade students are ready to learn about test-taking techniques and how to study for tests. As a matter of fact, so are some primary-grade children.

Explicitly teaching students test-taking principles will make their success more likely. In fact, research has shown that people do better on tests if they know certain test-taking techniques and are familiar with the various types of tests.

Here are some general test-taking principles:

*Before*

1. Plan to do well. Have a positive attitude.
2. Be well rested.
3. Be prepared. The better prepared you are, the less nervous and anxious you will be.
4. Look upon tests as a learning experience.
5. Look over the whole test before you begin. Notice the types of questions asked and the points allotted for each question. (Students have to learn not to spend a long time on a one- to five-point question that they know a lot about. They should answer it and go on.)
6. Allot your time wisely and check the time.
7. Concentrate!

*During*

8. Read instructions very carefully. (Some students need to be taught to answer each question appropriately. For example, if a question asks for a

## FIGURE 13.3    Student Checklist of Study Habits and Strategies

*What is Retelling/Summarizing?*

These strategies have readers identify and work with the main ideas and supporting details of a selection. Retelling requires students to restate the major events and supporting details in a selection. Summarizing requires students to extract only the main ideas from a selection.

*How do I teach Retelling/Summarizing?*

1. **Introduction:** Read aloud a short selection. Then retell the selection by restating the main events in order, and summarize the selection by constructing a statement that tells the main ideas of the selection. Ask students whether they can describe the two things you just did and how they were alike and different. Explain that the first was a *retelling* (saying the events in a selection in the order in which they happened) and the second was a *summary* (saying just the main ideas of a selection).

2. **Instruction:** Write on the board, a chart, or a transparency the following descriptions:

| *To retell a selection . . .* | *To summarize a selection . . .* |
|---|---|
| • say or write the main events and important details. <br> • say or write them in the order in which they happened. | • figure out the most important ideas or events in the selection. <br> • say or write them in a brief statement. |

Model how to retell and summarize by selecting a short item from a poster, read-aloud book, or magazine. Read the selection and then retell it, including the main events and important details in the order in which they happened. Next, summarize the selection, thinking aloud to show how you figured out the main ideas and then constructed a short statement to express them. Invite students to explain how your retelling differed from your summary (for example, retelling is longer, includes more detail, uses many words from the selection; summary is shorter and includes only the main ideas from the selection).

3. **Guided Practice:** Select and read another short passage and invite students to offer first a retelling of it and then a summary of it. Refer them to the chart as needed. Ask students to compare and contrast the retelling and summary for similarities and differences.

*How can students practice Retelling/Summarizing?*

Select a short passage and have students generate both a retelling and a summary and write them on a chart. Have them consider how their retelling and summary are alike and different. Ask how they both are helpful for understanding and remembering important ideas in selections.

| Retelling of _____ | Summary of _____ |
|---|---|

From *Summer Success Reading* by James F. Baumann, Michael F. Opitz, Laura Robb. Text copyright © Great Source Education Group, a division of Houghton Mifflin Company. Reprinted by permission. All rights reserved.

description and *examples,* be sure to give examples.) If you do not under-stand the instructions, you should ask the teacher to clarify them.

9. Begin with the questions you know you can successfully answer. This will give you a feeling of confidence and success.

10. If you do not know an answer, make an intelligent guess. As long as the penalty for a wrong answer is the same as for no answer, it pays to take a calculated guess.

11. Work on the questions that are worth the greatest number of points.

12. Allow for time to review your test responses. Check to see that you have an-swered all the questions. Be leery about changing a response unless you have found a particular reason to while reviewing the test. For example, you may have misread the question, you may have misinterpreted the question, or you may not have realized that it was a "tricky" question. If the question is a straightforward one, it's probably better to leave your first response.

*After*

13. After the test has been graded and returned, review it with your teacher. Doing so will help you to learn from the testing experience. You want to understand why your responses were graded as correct or incorrect.

14. Examine the test after you get it back to determine what your teacher emphasizes.

# THE SCHOOL LIBRARY AND LIBRARY SKILLS

The school library should be an integrated part of the students' schooling expe-rience. A number of school architects have designed their physical plants so that the library is in the center of the building, easily accessible to all classrooms. The library, properly utilized, becomes the students' storehouse of information and a reservoir of endless delight. The library is the heart of the school.

The atmosphere in the library should be one that makes children feel wel-come, invited, and wanted. The media specialist is the individual who is re-sponsible for setting this tone. A friendly, warm person who loves children and books will usually have a library which has similar characteristics. Children should feel free to visit the library at all times, not just during their regularly scheduled periods.

An enthusiastic and inventive media specialist will, by various means, act as an invitation to children to come to the library. Some media specialists en-gage in weekly storytelling for all grade levels. Media specialists should en-courage teachers and children to make suggestions for storytelling, as well as to share the kinds of books they enjoy and would like. The media specialist should also act as a resource person in helping the classroom teacher develop children's library skills. Once students gain the "library habit," it is hard to break, and it will remain with them throughout life.

Following are some of the library skills appropriate for elementary school children.

## PRIMARY GRADES

In the primary grades children are ready to acquire some library skills that will help them become independent library users. Teachers can help primary-grade children learn the kinds of books that are available in the library, for example, fiction and nonfiction books. Providing the name of different types of books (e.g., fiction or nonfiction) with accompanying text examples will help children better understand the terms and how they relate to books. Using familiar books, for example, is a sure way to help students understand.

## INTERMEDIATE AND UPPER-ELEMENTARY GRADES

By the fourth grade children can learn about other categories of books in the library, such as reference books.

### Reference Books

Children in the elementary grades ask many questions about many different topics. Using some of these questions to help children learn about reference sources is extremely meaningful. Children need to understand that we live in an information age and that knowing how to access information is more important than trying to know everything, an impossible task. Reference books can help all students in their attempts to learn about any given topic. For example, the *Readers' Guide to Periodical Literature* will help a student to find magazine articles written on almost any subject of interest. There are reference books on language and usage, such as Roget's *Thesaurus of English Words and Phrases,* which help upper-grade students find synonyms and less trite words to use in writing.

The dictionary, which is a very important reference book, is probably the one with which the students are the most familiar. It is helpful in supplying the following information:

1. Spelling.
2. Correct usage.
3. Derivations and inflected forms.
4. Accents and other diacritical markings.
5. Antonyms.
6. Synonyms.
7. Syllabication.
8. Definitions.
9. Parts of speech.
10. Idiomatic phrases.

The most often used reference book in elementary school, besides the dictionary, is the encyclopedia. Children need to learn how to use the encyclopedia as a tool and as an aid, rather than as an end in itself. That is, children should be shown how to extract and paraphrase information from the encyclopedia rather than copying the article verbatim. The same is true when children use an online reference.

In the upper elementary grades children should learn that there are many reference books available in the library which can supply information about a famous writer, baseball player, scientist, celebrity, and others. The key factor is being aware that these reference sources exist and knowing which book to go to for the needed information.

Providing thought-provoking assignments that call on children to seek out different reference books is one way to help them become familiar with the many different reference texts.

In Chapter 6, we present several ways to assess and document student progress. A checklist is one technique that can provide much information at a glance. The purpose of Figure 13.4 is to document students' progress in attaining reading and study skills.

# CONCENTRATION AND STUDYING: A POINT OF VIEW

A parent said that when she was a volunteer in her daughter's third-grade class, the teacher, before giving students their spelling test, put a tape in her player and out boomed loud music. The parent said that she was surprised that the children could make out the spelling words. It seemed as if the teacher's voice was competing with the music emanating from the boom box.

When the parent asked the teacher about this practice, the instructor said, "Oh, I do this all the time, especially when students are taking tests. It's important to use various types of media when teaching children."

The concept of using multimedia to enhance children's learning makes sense; however, what this teacher is doing does not make sense. Playing music while students are taking tests could cause a sensory overload for most of them. When the third graders are concentrating on listening for the spelling words and trying to spell them correctly, they are tuning out the music because it is interfering with their concentration.

Helping children gain information by using multimedia is fine. It gives "unique learning opportunities for those learners whose educational needs might not be sufficiently met through more traditional modes of instruction."[3] However, according to investigators, there appears to be a "paucity of research on the differential learning effects of multimedia instruction."[4]

Some investigators have found that students look on multimedia information as fun; it makes learning more exciting and easier to remember than monomedia information. The researchers, however, also claim that multimedia does not always lead to improved information and knowledge transfer.[5]

In addition, using multimedia does not mean that teachers should have different media vying for children's attention. Teachers should use various media to appeal to children's different senses, but the different media should be used

---

[3]Michael L. Kamil et al., "The Effects of Other Technologies on Literacy and Literacy Learning," in *Handbook of Reading Research,* Vol. III, Michael L. Kamil, et al., eds. (Mahwah, NJ: Lawrence Erlbaum, 2000), p. 775.

[4]Ibid.

[5]See Martijn Hoogeveen, "Towards a Theory of Effectiveness of Multimedia Systems" *International Journal of Human Computer Interactions* 9(2) (1997): 151–168 (martijn@cyber-ventures.com.).

**FIGURE 13.4  Diagnostic Checklist for Reading and Study Skills**

Student's Name: _____

Grade: _____

Teacher: _____

|     1. Dictionary | Yes | No | Sometimes |
|---|---|---|---|

### A. GRADES 1, 2

The student is able to

|  |  |  |  |
|---|---|---|---|
| 1. supply missing letters of the alphabet. |  |  |  |
| 2. arrange words none of which begin with the same letter in alphabetical order. |  |  |  |
| 3. list words several of which begin with the same letter. |  |  |  |
| 4. list words according to first and second letters. |  |  |  |
| 5. list words according to the third letter. |  |  |  |
| 6. find the meaning of a word. |  |  |  |
| 7. find the correct spelling of a word. |  |  |  |

### B. GRADES 3, 4, 5, 6

The student is able to

|  |  |  |  |
|---|---|---|---|
| 1. locate words halfway in the dictionary. |  |  |  |
| 2. open the dictionary by quarters and state the letters with which words begin. |  |  |  |
| 3. open the dictionary by thirds and state the letters with which words begin. |  |  |  |
| 4. open the dictionary at certain initial letters. |  |  |  |
| 5. use key words at the head of each page as a guide to finding words. |  |  |  |
| 6. use the dictionary to select meanings to fit the context (homographs). |  |  |  |
| 7. use the dictionary to build up a vocabulary of synonyms. |  |  |  |
| 8. use the dictionary to build up a vocabulary of antonyms. |  |  |  |
| 9. answer questions about the derivation of a word. |  |  |  |
| 10. use the dictionary to learn to pronounce a word. |  |  |  |
| 11. use the dictionary to correctly syllabicate a word. |  |  |  |
| 12. use the dictionary to get the correct usage of a word. |  |  |  |
| 13. use the dictionary to determine the part(s) of speech of the word. |  |  |  |
| 14. use the dictionary to gain the meanings of idiomatic phrases. |  |  |  |

*(continued)*

Student's Name: _____

Grade: _____

Teacher: _____

| 2. Library Skills | Yes | No | Sometimes |
|---|---|---|---|

**A. PRIMARY GRADES**

The student is able to

| | Yes | No | Sometimes |
|---|---|---|---|
| 1. find books in the library. | | | |
| 2. state the kinds of books that are found in the library. | | | |

**B. INTERMEDIATE GRADES**

The student is able to

| | Yes | No | Sometimes |
|---|---|---|---|
| 1. state the kinds of reference materials that are found in the library. | | | |
| 2. use the encyclopedia as an aid to gaining needed information. | | | |
| 3. find books in the school library. | | | |

| 3. Building Good Study Habits | Yes | No | Sometimes |
|---|---|---|---|

**INTERMEDIATE GRADES**

The student is able to

| | Yes | No | Sometimes |
|---|---|---|---|
| 1. plan his or her studying time. | | | |
| 2. choose a place to study that is free from distractions. | | | |
| 3. recognize that he or she needs to study. | | | |

| 4. Study Procedures | Yes | No | Sometimes |
|---|---|---|---|

**INTERMEDIATE GRADES**

The student is able to

| | Yes | No | Sometimes |
|---|---|---|---|
| 1. use the SQ3R technique when studying. | | | |
| 2. apply the SQ3R technique when studying a chapter in a textbook. | | | |

| 5. Concentration and Following Directions | Yes | No | Sometimes |
|---|---|---|---|

**A. PRIMARY GRADES**

The student is able to

| | Yes | No | Sometimes |
|---|---|---|---|
| 1. listen carefully and follow directions. | | | |
| 2. read directions and follow them carefully. | | | |
| 3. show that concentration is increasing by being able to pay attention for longer periods of time. | | | |

*(continued)*

**FIGURE 13.4**    *(continued)*

Student's Name: _____

Grade: _____

Teacher: _____

| 5. Concentration and Following Directions | Yes | No | Sometimes |
|---|---|---|---|

**B. INTERMEDIATE GRADES**

The student is able to

| | Yes | No | Sometimes |
|---|---|---|---|
| 1. listen carefully and follow directions. | | | |
| 2. read directions and follow them correctly. | | | |
| 3. fill out some application forms. | | | |

| 6. Skimming | Yes | No | Sometimes |
|---|---|---|---|

**A. PRIMARY GRADES**

The student is able to

| | Yes | No | Sometimes |
|---|---|---|---|
| 1. find some information quickly by skimming. | | | |
| 2. skim a paragraph and state its topic. | | | |

**B. INTERMEDIATE GRADES**

The student is able to

| | Yes | No | Sometimes |
|---|---|---|---|
| 1. differentiate between skimming and studying. | | | |
| 2. recognize the role that skimming plays in studying. | | | |
| 3. locate information such as the departure time of trains by skimming train schedules. | | | |

| 7. Knowing Your Textbook | Yes | No | Sometimes |
|---|---|---|---|

**A. PRIMARY GRADES**

The student is able to

| | Yes | No | Sometimes |
|---|---|---|---|
| 1. use the table of contents to find chapter headings. | | | |
| 2. use the glossary to gain the meaning of a word. | | | |
| 3. list the parts of a textbook. | | | |

**B. INTERMEDIATE GRADES**

The student is able to

| | Yes | No | Sometimes |
|---|---|---|---|
| 1. read the preface to learn about the author's purpose in writing the book. | | | |
| 2. skim the index to learn about the material that will be found in the book. | | | |
| 3. skim the index to find the page on which a specific topic is found. | | | |

*(continued)*

Student's Name: _____

Grade: _____

Teacher: _____

| 8. Asking Questions | Yes | No | Sometimes |
|---|---|---|---|

A. PRIMARY GRADES

The student is able to

1. formulate questions that will obtain the wanted information.
2. ask questions that are pertinent to the topic under discussion.

B. INTERMEDIATE GRADES

The student will be able to

1. ask questions that will help in studying for a test.
2. ask questions that will help in learning about what to study.

| 9. Test Taking | Yes | No | Sometimes |
|---|---|---|---|

A. PRIMARY GRADES

The student is able to

1. read questions very carefully so that they are answered correctly.
2. follow directions in taking a test.

B. INTERMEDIATE GRADES

The student is able to

1. recognize that he or she studies differently for objective and essay tests.
2. take objective tests.
3. take essay tests.
4. go over the test to learn why he or she did or did not do well.
5. ask questions about a test to learn from the mistakes.

| 10. Summaries | Yes | No | Sometimes |
|---|---|---|---|

INTERMEDIATE GRADES

The student is able to

1. summarize a passage.
2. use a summary for study.

*(continued)*

**FIGURE 13.4   (*continued*)**

Student's Name: _____

Grade: _____

Teacher: _____

| 11. Notetaking | Yes | No | Sometimes |
|---|---|---|---|

**INTERMEDIATE GRADES**

The student is able to

1. explain why notetaking is a useful study tool.

2. explain why notetaking is helpful in writing long papers.

3. take notes while listening to a talk.

4. take notes while reading to help remember important information.

separately. For example, if students are watching a film that has subtitles, when they are busy reading the subtitles, they are usually concentrating more on the reading than on the viewing of the action, and vice versa.

Concentration is sustained attention. It demands a mental set or attitude, the determination to block out everything except what the individual is reading or listening to.

Paying attention does not guarantee that students will do well in school or that they will understand what they are reading or listening to; however, concentration is an important first step. Without concentration, there is little hope that students will understand the information or concepts being presented or read. Teachers must help their students to understand this.

Students usually cannot listen to music or watch television while doing intensive studying; the combination of these activities generally tends to overload the brain's central processing capacity, that is, its ability to take in information. Researchers have found that human central processing resources are limited and that extra demands on attention, such as watching TV or having the television on when students are involved in tasks that require concentration, such as reading or studying, may interfere with their getting the most from their primary task. This is certainly logical, and it should not be surprising that background television or music could have adverse effects on activities such as reading comprehension, complex problem solving, and creative thinking.

Some individuals insist that they cannot study unless they are watching television or listening to music. What these students are probably doing is what I call "variable time sharing"; that is, they are fluctuating between watching TV or listening to music and studying. But, what kind of studying are they doing? How effective is it? And how long will it take with or without any background interference?

Concentration demands active involvement. It is a contradiction to say that students can concentrate and be relaxed at the same time because concentration is hard work. Concentration requires wide-awake, alert individuals who have a positive frame of mind. If a room is too hot or cold, if students are hungry, if they are tired or sleepy, if the chairs that students are sitting in are uncomfortable, if the lighting is poor or if there is glare, if there are auditory or visual distractions, most students will not be able to concentrate.

Teachers can help to develop their children's concentration ability by presenting them with suitable concentration activities. Unless teachers recognize the important role that concentration plays in the process of learning, this essential area will be neglected.

## SUMMARY

In Chapter 13 we provide information and teaching procedures to help students learn necessary study skills. The importance of building good study habits, which includes when to study, where to study, and the amount of time to spend in studying, is discussed. In discussing how to study, the SQ3R technique is explored. Examples of how to use this technique and activities are also given. In addition, a scenario is presented in which a teacher models the use of the SQ3R approach in studying. We also offer teaching suggestions to help your students gain competence in concentration and questioning. Skimming—reading rapidly to find information—is discussed, as well as summarizing passages to help students retain information. Reading and writing strategies as modes of learning are presented in scenarios, as was semantic mapping (graphic organizer). Both are suggested as ways to help students retain information they have studied. "Knowing Your Textbook" and "Test Taking" are also presented, as is a diagnostic checklist that can be used to rate students' progress relative to reading and study skills.

## CHAPTER 13 KEY CONCEPTS

- Building good study habits is important.
- Good study habits include when to study, where to study, and the amount of time to spend in studying.
- Overlearning helps persons retain information over an extended period of time.
- Students need to be helped to gain positive attitudes toward their learning tasks.
- Teachers need to help students learn about their textbooks.
- Concentration and following directions are essential ingredients for studying.
- Students need to learn that they read for different purposes and that it's important to set purposes for reading and to adjust their rate of reading to their purpose for reading.
- Questioning is a good way for students to gain insight into a subject.
- Reading and writing are modes of learning.
- Notetaking is a useful study tool.
- Graphic representations can help students see relationships among concepts.
- Summaries can be a good method of learning.
- Students can become better test takers by learning certain principles of test taking.
- The school library should be an integral part of the student's education experience.

# SUGGESTIONS FOR THOUGHT QUESTIONS AND ACTIVITIES

1. You have been appointed to a special committee to help develop a study skills program for your elementary school. What suggestions would you make? What kinds of skills and activities would you recommend for the primary grades? For the intermediate grades?
2. Develop some concentration activities for primary-grade children.
3. Develop some concentration activities for intermediate-grade students.
4. What would you do to help students become better test takers?
5. What kind of program would you develop to help your students become better notetakers?
6. Some teachers in your school system feel that elementary-grade children are too immature to learn study skill techniques. How would you convince these teachers that this is not so?
7. How can reading and writing be used as modes of learning?
8. What is the role of graphic representations such as semantic maps in learning information?

# INTERNET ACTIVITIES

Choose a search engine and search the terms *notetaking* and *test taking*. Choose a website that helps you gain a good understanding of each term. Write three new ideas you learned about each term.

# SELECTED BIBLIOGRAPHY

Irvin, Judith L., and Elaine D. Rose. *Starting Early with Study Skills: A Week by Week Guide for Elementary Students.* Boston: Allyn and Bacon, 1995.

Luckie, William R., and Wood Smethurst. *Study Power: Study Skills to Improve Your Learning and Your Grades.* Cambridge, MA: Brookline Books, 1997.

Rubin, Dorothy. *Comprehension Skills & Strategies in a Balanced Reading Program.* Torrance, CA: Fearon Teacher Aids, 1998.

———. *Gaining Word Power,* 5th ed. Boston: Allyn and Bacon, 2000.

———. *Word Meaning and Reasoning Strategies* (a three book series). Torrance, CA: Good Apple, 2001.

———. *Writing & Thinking Skills: Paragraphs and Composition.* Torrance, CA: Good Apple, 2000.

———. *Writing & Thinking Skills: Sentence Writing.* Torrance, CA: Good Apple, 2000.

———. *Writing & Thinking Skills: Fun with Writing.* Torrance, CA: Good Apple, 2001.

# Teachers and Parents as Partners in the Diagnostic-Reading and Improvement Program

# INTRODUCTION

"Mommy, what's the name of this book?" asks Jennifer.

"The name of the book is *The Cat in the Hat,*" replies her mother.

"Daddy, what does this say?" asks Johnny.

"It says 'Don't touch,'" replies his father.

"Mommy, what is this word on the cereal box?" asks Paul.

"The word is 'yummy,'" replies his mother.

"Mommy, what does the sign say?" asks Sharon.

"The sign says 'Stop,'" replies Sharon's mother.

"Daddy, what's this word in the book?" asks Carol.

"The word is 'happy,'" replies Carol's father.

And on it goes. Many young children are curious about words, and they see them everywhere. The people they go to for help in learning these words are their families. Family members are their first teachers. This is natural, and hardly anyone would question family members' desire to help children satisfy their thirst for learning and desire to read. As a matter of fact, today reading program authors, test makers, and various professional journals such as *The Reading Teacher* include materials for caregivers.

In this chapter we will discuss active parental involvement and we will look at the role that parents can and should be playing in the reading program.

# CHAPTER OBJECTIVES

After reading the chapter, you should be able to:

- Discuss why educators' attitudes toward parental involvement in the schools have changed.
- Discuss the kinds of reading programs in which parents are involved.
- Discuss parents' role in emergent literacy.
- Discuss the success of parental involvement programs.
- Discuss the role of parents in preschool programs.
- Describe some ways parents can help their children.
- Explain what is meant by *reality time.*
- Explain the role of the parent-teacher conference.
- Describe factors that help make a good parent-teacher conference.

# PARENTAL INVOLVEMENT IN THE SCHOOLS

Parental involvement in the schools is ever present. Parents sit on the boards of education; they are involved in parent-teacher associations, parent councils, and parent clubs. Parents help formulate school policy, have a say in curriculum, and even help to choose textbooks. Parents definitely have a voice in school matters. However, until rather recently, parents have been encouraged to take more of a passive role in working with their own children, particularly in reading. Teaching was considered the sole domain of the educator, and parents who wanted to teach their children were sometimes viewed as meddlers, troublemakers, and outsiders. At best they were looked on as well-meaning but unknowledgeable, and until the late 1950s, parents were admonished not to teach their children to read at home. Today in many school districts across the country parents are seen as partners and potential resources. What caused the pendulum to swing in favor of active parental involvement?

## SOME POSSIBLE CAUSES FOR A CHANGE IN ATTITUDE TOWARD PARENTAL INVOLVEMENT

A number of events have happened not only in changing educators' attitudes toward parental involvement in reading instruction but also in changing parents' attitudes about their role in helping their children to read. One contributing factor is that parents began to lose confidence in the schools because of the great number of reading failures found there. With this loss of confidence came the desire for more direct involvement.

Second, Rudolf Flesch's book *Why Johnny Can't Read—And What You Can Do About It,* written in 1955, probably helped to raise the consciousness level of parents concerning the role they should be playing in helping their children learn to read. Flesch's book was addressed to parents, and it was written primarily to help parents assist their children in learning to read by using a phonic method. Whether one agrees with the views expressed in the book is not as important as the impact that the book made. Parents wanted to know more about what their children were doing in reading, and many wanted to be more directly involved.

Third, the increase of reading problems in the schools probably helped to change educators' attitudes as well as parents' attitudes. Searching for causes of any given reading problem may have caused educators to take another look at parents because many began to feel that they could use all the help they could get. They also recognized that parents could provide information about their children's reading habits at home. Perhaps one of the best ways to obtain information from parents is by interviewing them. Interviews can yield information about the reading habits of the family such as the parents' view of reading, parent-child relationships, parents' attitudes about their child's reading, any pertinent information about the child's health, and information about the child's previous school experiences.

Fourth, and perhaps the greatest impetus for parental involvement probably came from the influx of federal monies to fund programs related to the improvement of children's reading skills. Almost all these programs in the United States have usually required mandated parental involvement. Head Start, initiated in the summer of 1965, is one such program. Its target audience is preschoolers and kindergartners. Follow Through, another such program, was first initiated as a pilot project in 1967 and became nationwide in 1968. Its audience is the children who participated in the Head Start program. Probably the passage of Title I in 1965 had the greatest effect on parental involvement because its programs continue to cover a much larger population of children than Head Start.

It wasn't until 1983 when *A Nation at Risk* knocked us out of our complacency that parents of all children again began to realize that we appeared to be on the road to mediocrity. The National Assessment of Educational Progress reports continue to show that students need help with higher level thinking and that those who achieve the best come from homes where parents read and where there are diverse reading materials available.

Today, the trend is to definitely welcome parental involvement. The irony is that now, more than ever, there are more single parents and families where both parents are working; as a result, time for parental involvement is limited. For example, two-parent wage earners and single working parents often find volunteering during the day difficult. And what about single parents who have to work more than one job to provide for their children? They, too, find volunteering difficult. Without a doubt, a major problem facing educators today is that parental involvement in the schools is not evenly distributed among various types of schools and school locations. For example, parental participation in the majority of middle-class suburban school districts is higher than in many inner-city school districts, especially in high-poverty districts. And this huge parental involvement gap between inner-city and suburban school students has often been cited as exacerbating the achievement gap between the haves and have-nots.

Finally, most agree that parental involvement in school helps students to achieve better. In addition, studies also suggest that school officials and teachers usually pay more attention to children whose parents volunteer to help out in their children's classrooms or schools.

## EMERGENT LITERACY AND PARENTS

In Chapter 7, we define emergent literacy as all those language and reading and writing activities that children engage in before coming to school or before conventional or formal reading and writing begin. Acquiring literacy is developmental and parents play an essential role in this literacy development.

Parents who spend time with their young children, who are good role models, who read aloud to them and ask them questions that encourage higher order thinking, who listen and interact with them, and who invite them to be involved in planning and some decision making are preparing their children very well for school. Researchers consistently suggest that parents who expect their children to do well and encourage them are enhancing their young children's literacy development.

Parents can be involved with their children's development of literacy in one of four ways:

1. *Observation*—Being read to or seeing adults model reading and writing behavior.
2. *Collaboration*—Having an individual interact with the child to provide encouragement, motivation, and help.
3. *Practice*—Trying out what has been learned; for example, the child writes a story or retells it to another child, stuffed animal, or doll without any help or without being supervised by an adult.

**FIGURE 14.1   A Parent Checklist for Preschoolers and Early-Primary-Grade Children**

|  | *Often* | *Seldom* |
|---|---|---|
| I listen to my child. |  |  |
| I read aloud to my child every day. |  |  |
| I discuss ideas with my child. |  |  |
| I explain concepts to my child. |  |  |
| I spend time with my child. |  |  |
| I ask my child good questions. |  |  |
| I ask my child to read picture books to me. |  |  |
| I watch special TV shows with my child. |  |  |
| I encourage my child. |  |  |
| I am patient with my child. |  |  |
| I take my child to interesting places. |  |  |
| I do not pressure my child. |  |  |
| I read and write in the presence of my child. |  |  |
| I am a good role model for my child. |  |  |

4. *Performance*—Sharing what has been learned with an adult who shows interest and support and gives positive reinforcement.[1]

The parent checklist shown here can be a valuable aid for parents interested in helping their young children. The International Reading Association publishes several pamphlets related to many of the attributes shown on the checklist in Figure 14.1. These can be accessed online by visiting IRA's website, www.reading.org. Likewise, the Irvine Unified School District provides several ideas such as "phrases that encourage" on their website www.iusd.k12 .ca.us/parent_resources/helping.htm.

# RESEARCH ON PARENTAL INVOLVEMENT IN THEIR CHILDREN'S EDUCATION

According to the researchers who conduct studies on parental involvement, many parents are involved in their children's education in the early grades in elementary school. As children progress through the grades, however, parents usually become less involved.

---

[1]Lesley Mandel Morrow and Jeffrey K. Smith (eds.), *Assessment for Instruction in Early Literacy* (Boston: Allyn and Bacon, 1990), p. 3.

Home support is a major factor in fostering higher achievement; in fact, "one of the clearest predictors of early reading ability is the amount of time spent reading with parents."[2] Researchers also consistently suggest that parents who expect their children to do well and encourage them are enhancing their young children's literacy development.[3]

A research report released in 1994 by the then Secretary of Education Richard W. Riley found that "nearly three-quarters of students aged 10 to 13 would like to talk to their parents more about schoolwork."[4] In the same report, it was also noted that "40 percent of parents believe they are not devoting enough time to their children's education."[5] In addition, the report stated that 90 percent of the difference in performance between high- and low-achieving students is due to "three factors over which parents exercise authority—student absenteeism, variety of reading materials in the home, and excessive television watching."[6]

The conclusion concerning the importance of parental involvement in children's education is confirmed by the National Assessment of Education Progress (NAEP) reports. The NAEP studies have continuously reported that those students who have home support for literacy usually have higher average reading achievement than those students without such home support.[7]

*The Basic School: A Community for Learning,* written by the late Ernest Boyer, former president of the Carnegie Foundation for the Advancement of Teaching, stresses that what elementary schools need most is a greater bond between parents and teachers. Boyer, in an interview, stated that "school is a partnership. If education is in trouble, it's not the school that has failed. It's the partnership that has failed." He also stated that "at many schools, parents still feel that they are on the edges. If parents are going to be made partners, schools are going to have to be the ones to reach out. They control the gates."

In *The Basic School,* Boyer presents examples of schools that give parents realistic ways to become involved. He also shows how employers are getting into the act by giving employees paid time off to volunteer in schools.

In 1986, a federal judge ruled that the Missouri taxpayers had to spend as much money as necessary in Kansas City to desegregate the schools and put them on a par with the surrounding suburban schools. After spending $1.2 billion, desegregation was the same as before, and the students' achievement scores, especially at the high school level, were as low as ever, and their scores

---

[2]Scott G. Paris, Barbara A. Wasik, and Julianne C. Turner, "The Development of Strategic Readers," in *Handbook of Reading Research,* Vol II, Rebecca Barr, Michael L. Kamil, Peter Mosenthal, and P. David Pearson, eds. (New York, Longman, 1991), p. 628.

[3]Ibid.

[4]*United States Department of Education News* (Washington, DC: Dept. of Education, September 7, 1994).

[5]Ibid.

[6]Ibid.

[7]Patricia L. Donahue et al., *NAEP 1998 Reading Report Card for the Nation and the States,* (Washington, DC: United States Department of Education, 1999), p. 101.

in reading, writing, and mathematics were lower than any other inner-city school in the nation. The only school that achieved well was the Martin Luther King School, which had been the worst school in the district. This school staff required parental involvement; parents had to sign a contract and had to make sure that their children did their homework. Clearly, parental involvement can make a tremendous difference!

Many schools supply after-school homework help and homework hotlines that both children and parents can access. In a number of schools, parents can dial a special number or look on the school's website to learn what students' assignments are. Regardless of all these aids, there is still a lot of stress associated with children's homework. Some of the stress may come from the parents themselves, because they may feel that they are the ones being judged. It is not unusual in some schools to have parents staying up all night to finish a child's project, as if they are vying with one another as to whose child's project is the best.

Parental involvement is good, but when it gets out of hand, it can become a hindrance. Parents want to help their children, but there must be limits. Parents should not be expected to assume the responsibility of completing their children's assignments nor of teaching them concepts that they should be learning in school.

## PARENTAL INVOLVEMENT IN SCHOOL PROGRAMS

Programs that involve parents vary from school to school; some have significant parental involvement programs, and some do not. Beyond the initial open night that is usually presented at the beginning of the school year to acquaint parents with the school staff, program, and teachers, some parents feel unwelcome in their children's school, which is unfortunate, because parents are an extraordinary resource. But there are numerous schools that employ those who welcome and encourage parental involvement.

On the surface parents and teachers report cordial relationships. However, the findings of a major study on parental involvement in the schools led investigators to suggest that teachers are not happy with parents' overall performance. Many teachers feel that parents are "not living up to their end of the deal."[8]

According to the findings, "neither parents nor teachers want parents more heavily involved in public schools or making decisions about staffing or curriculum."[9] It seems that both teachers and parents endorse what might be called the "bake sale" model of parental involvement—parents as volunteers and helpmates."[10]

---

[8]Steve Farkas et al., *Playing Their Parts: Parents and Teachers Talk About Parental Involvement in Public Schools* (New York: Public Agenda, 1999), p. 9.

[9]Ibid., p.12.

[10]Ibid., p.16.

# PARENTAL INVOLVEMENT IN REGULAR SCHOOL READING PROGRAMS

Parents sometimes become more involved in school programs when their children have a specific reading problem; however, the trend appears to be for increasing parental involvement for those without reading problems.

The participation of parents in many school districts is often dependent on how aggressive the educators and parents are in demanding such involvement. The presence of the parents in the regular reading program seems to vary from district to district, and even in some school districts, from school to school. In one school system, you will find an organized program, and in another you will find that the program is up to the individual teacher in each individual class. The programs that do exist usually are similar in format; they generally include workshops, instructional materials, and book suggestions. What is presented, however, will vary from district to district. Here are some examples:

### Example 1: New Jersey

The following is an example of a program that was developed by employees in a New Jersey school system to incorporate parental involvement in its regular reading program for all children in grades one through five. The program consists of instructional packets, book suggestions, and three workshops. At the first workshop, a reading specialist explains the reading program that is in use in the school system. The parents are acquainted with the reading program and its corresponding terminology. At the second workshop, the parents watch a reading lesson, which shows a teacher and children engaged in a Directed Reading Lesson. The third session, "A Book Talk," provides parents with appropriate children's books at different readability and interest levels. They are also given several suggestions for how to involve their children in reading them.

Another part of the program concerns instructional materials. For those children who have reading problems, teachers construct parent packets that consist of activities based on the skills and strategies that children are learning. Different parent packets are available for different grade levels. For those children who have few reading problems, the packets contain suggestions for ways to extend learning. Yet another packet which emphasizes more complex books such as several Newberry award winners, is available for parents of children who are able to read such material.

### Example 2: Junior Great Books

A program of special interest is aimed at highly able readers in grades two through six, their teachers, and parents. The program, called the "Junior Great Books Program," includes twelve volunteer parents and twelve teachers. A parent and a teacher are paired off to work together as a team. The parents who volunteer have to take the two-day training session, which is conducted by a special person from the Great Books Foundation, located in Chicago. The sessions consist primarily of helping parents learn about the kinds of questions they should ask, as well as how to conduct the discussions. The children who participate in the program are considered "good readers" by their teachers. (See Chapter 5 for a list of qualities of good readers.) The parent-teacher team

---

**Newberry award books**
Those books that have received the Newberry Medal, which is given annually to the book in the United States that has been voted "the most distinguished literature" for children.

**Junior Great Books Program**
Program in which parent-teacher teams work together to plan reading discussion sessions for students; sessions take place in regular classrooms during the reading period and are led by both parent and teacher.

meets every week to plan for the reading discussion, which takes place in the regular classroom during the regularly scheduled 45-minute reading period. Both the parent and the teacher lead the discussion with a particular group of children.

**Reading Olympics programs**
Programs vary; however, most challenge students to read the most books they can and to share them in some way with parents.

### Example 3: Reading Olympics

The structure of these programs varies from school system to school system, from school to school, and even from one class to another; however, all include reading books and sharing them in some way with parents. Here is how one such program works in the middle part of the year in a first-grade class.

Children are challenged to read as many books as they can. They must read these books aloud to one of their parents, and after they finish reading the book aloud, the parent asks them questions about the story or has them retell it. Completed books are recorded on a reading record form similar to the one shown in Figure 14.2. Children compete to see who can read the most books. The rewards are manifold. Andrew, the child who won the Read-Aloud Olympics contest in his first-grade class, read 120 books aloud to his parents.

**Paired reading**
The child reads aloud simultaneously with another person, usually the parent.

### Example 4: Paired Reading

Another practice that seems to be gaining favor is that of paired reading. This is a method whereby parents and children read aloud simultaneously. This technique is generally used with children who have reading difficulties but can be used with just about any child. At any time during the simultaneous reading, the child can signal that he or she wishes to read alone. The parent should praise the child's desire to do so, and allow the child to read alone. "The child is encouraged to read alone by lack of criticism and by frequent praise for any independent reading."[11] This technique is powerful because it keeps the focus on reading for enjoyment. Parents need not be concerned with helping their children learn specific reading strategies. They can leave this most important aspect of reading instruction to the knowledgeable teacher.

Paired reading was also originally designed for parents to use with their children[12] and the growth that children showed in both reading vocabulary and reading comprehension was so startling that it is now used by individuals who provide tutoring to those who need to learn how to become better readers. A demonstration video with accompanying printed information is available from the International Reading Association.

Here are some suggested procedures:[13]

1. Agree on a time that the reading will regularly occur.
2. Provide time for the reader to select the material to be read. This material can be changed from one session to another. That is, if a child selects reading material and decides at the end of the session that he really does

---

[11]Kathy Johnston, "Parents and Reading: A U.K. Perspective," *The Reading Teacher* 42 (February 1989): 355.

[12]Topping, K. "Paired Reading: A Powerful Technique for Parent Use." *The Reading Teacher,* 40 (1987): 604–14.

[13]Ibid.

**FIGURE 14.2    Reading Record**

| Day | Title of reading material | Amount of time spent reading / Number of pages read | Comments |
|---|---|---|---|
| Sunday | | | |
| Monday | | | |
| Tuesday | | | |
| Wednesday | | | |
| Thursday | | | |
| Friday | | | |
| Saturday | | | |

not want to continue with it at the next session, he or she can bring another text to the next session.

3. Sit side by side because you will both want to see the text with ease.
   Make sure that you select a place that is free of all distractions.

4. Agree on a starting signal such as 1, 2, 3. Begin reading together. Also establish a signal for when the reader wants to read solo. A tap on the shoul-
   der is often used. When the reader chooses to read solo, reinforce the
   reader for taking this risk by saying something such as "Good!"

5. Stop at logical points to talk about the meaning of what is being read.

6. If the reader makes a miscue, wait to see if the reader self-corrects. If not, and the miscue alters the author's intended meaning, point to the word, say it for the child, and have the child repeat it. Continue reading aloud with the child until the solo signal is again given.

### *Example 5: Family Literacy Project*

Many school district personnel are so interested in parental involvement that they design specific programs for parents. The Family Literacy Project is one such program. Developed by Irvine Unified School District educators, the project aims to provide parents with both encouragement and support in their efforts to instill lifelong reading habits in their children. To accomplish this purpose, they provide numerous tips such as "Tips for Reading to Your Child," "Ten Tips: Helping Your Child Read Effectively," and "Helping Children Develop Oral-Language Skills." All of this information is easily accessible both in hard copy form, which is available at the school district's child resource center, and at their website, www.iusd.12.ca.us/parent_resources/helping.htm.

All of these examples show that involving parents goes far beyond the usual letters that are sent home several times a year. Publishers have developed a package that includes the suggestions and activities that are needed to implement a "Parents as Partners" program. Some test publishers also provide material to help parents understand their assessment program and what their child's scores indicate. Some also provide instructional activities for parents.

### Special Note

Educators conducting parent-involvement programs need to help parents recognize that there is a place for "reality time" with children as well as "quality time."

Parents' involvement with children is good, and young children especially benefit from being with their parents. However, parents should not get into a frenzy if every moment they spend with their child is not "quality time." Teachers should help all parents recognize that "reality time" is just as important, especially for young children. Reality time is the time that parents spend with their children while making a bed, cooking, baking, going for a walk, swimming, talking, or just quiet time. When children and parents are together, every moment does not have to be filled with "pearls of wisdom."

If children perceive that the only times they spend together with parents are related to trying to teach them something so they can do better in school, they may begin to react negatively to both their parents and school. They may feel that if they do not do well in school, their parents will not love them. ◾

## HOW SUCCESSFUL ARE PARENTAL INVOLVEMENT PROGRAMS?

The success of any program that demands voluntary participation has to be based on turnout—not initial turnout, but continuous turnout. The programs reported in the literature and those we surveyed had a great deal of parent participation. Most of the reading coordinators claimed that parent turnout had grown and that verbal feedback had been very good. The parents participating in the programs claimed that since their involvement in the program their children were more interested in reading, and the parents of children who had reading difficulties claimed that their children's reading skills and attitude toward reading had improved.

The interest of parents in their children's schooling is exceedingly important and cannot he overstated, especially since the findings of numerous studies suggest that "the potential for parents to help their children in learning to read is tremendous."[14] It is good that the trend toward parental involvement seems to be getting stronger because children reap the benefits.

For parents to be partners in learning with educators there has to be equal "give and take." If parents are looked on as parent-educators, this viewpoint "acknowledges the home-school relationship as a rich potential shared among equals, equals who bring important and divergent experiences to bear upon individual and often limited perspectives."[15]

# TELEVISION, COMPUTERS, PARENTS, CHILDREN, AND READING

## TELEVISION

In a chapter on parental involvement in their children's school experiences, we would be remiss if we did not discuss the impact of television on children's reading, because most television viewing is done at home. We would also be negligent if we did not consider the computer's impact on children's reading.

The question of the influence of television viewing on children's reading skills has been debated since television was first introduced. The findings have not been definitive. Some studies suggest that "television viewing has a considerable negative impact on reading achievement only for children who watch for relatively many hours—more than 4 to 6 hours a day."[16] Television also seems to affect different groups of children in different ways. The reading achievement of children of high socioeconomic status decreased when they watched greater amounts of television, whereas the converse appeared to be true for low socioeconomic status children; that is, heavier viewing for these children increased their reading achievement.[17]

Although we want children to be engaged with a variety of texts and to develop a habit of reading for a variety of purposes, we need to remember that we live in an information age and as such, there are several ways to obtain information. Television can be used to stimulate children's reading habits rather than take away from them. Using television to its best advantage can help children to see that there is room for a variety of activities in their lives and that just because they read does not mean that they cannot watch television. The reverse is also true.

[14]Timothy Rasinski and Anthony Fredericks, "Working With Parents: Can Parents Make a Difference?" *The Reading Teacher* 43 (October 1989): 84.

[15]Gayle Goodman, "Worlds Within Worlds: Reflections on an Encounter with Parents," *Language Arts* 66 (January 1989): 20.

[16]Johannes W. J. Beentjes and Tom H. A. Van Der Voort, "Television's Impact on Children's Reading Skills: A Review of Research," *Reading Research Quarterly* 23 (Fall 1988): 401.

[17]Ibid.

**TABLE 14.1  Using Television to Spur Reading**

| Statement | Rating (1 = low degree, 5 = high degree) |
|---|---|
| 1. My child uses good judgment when selecting programs to watch. | 1  2  3  4  5 |
| 2. My child talks to me about some of the ideas gained from television shows. | 1  2  3  4  5 |
| 3. Television is one of several of my child's free time activities. | 1  2  3  4  5 |
| 4. My child appears to be motivated to read about some of the ideas presented on the viewed television shows. | 1  2  3  4  5 |
| 5. My children see me both reading and watching television. | 1  2  3  4  5 |
| 6. Many different kinds of reading materials are available in my home and they are easy for my children to access. | 1  2  3  4  5 |
| 7. Reading gets as much time as television watching. | 1  2  3  4  5 |

Fortunately for parents and teachers alike, there is quite a bit of information about the wise use of television. One source of information is a brochure published by the International Reading Association entitled, "You Can Use Television To Stimulate Your Child's Reading Habits." Among several practical suggestions, the authors of the brochure also provide a simple checklist that parents can use to determine whether they are teaching their children how to be wise television watchers. Our version of this checklist is shown in Table 14.1.

### Captioned Television

The captions used on television appear to impact students' learning.[18] Watching television shows with accompanying captions appears to improve students' reading. Listening to the script on the television while simultaneously reading the script reinforces the effect on student's word recognition and reading fluency. We can encourage parents to turn on the captioning feature when their children watch television. The volume can be lowered several decibels so that children have to take a close look at the text to better understand what is happening on the show.

## COMPUTERS

In Chapter 9, we offer information about using computers to assist children's reading. The focus here is to provide some information about several websites that both children and parents can use to assist reading development.

[18]Koskinen, P., R. Wilson, L. Gambrell, and S. Neuman. "Captioned Video and Vocabulary Learning: An Innovative Practice in Literacy Instruction." *The Reading Teacher, 47*(1993): 36–43.

Many websites are now available for parents and children. Some of these are created by educators employed in specific school districts (e.g., Irvine Unified School District), whereas others are created by professional organizations and publishers. Several of these are listed here.

### *Websites for Parents:*

- Professional organizations:

  www.nea.org/parents/index.html (National Education Association)
  www.reading.org (International Reading Association)

  Both of these websites offer numerous suggestions for ways that parents can get involved in their children's reading education. Specific book titles for different ages and interests are also provided. Information can be downloaded for future reference.

- Publishers:

  www.scholastic.com/families/index.asp (Scholastic)
  www.sfreading.com/ (Scott Foresman)

  Both of these provide grade-level appropriate books and activities sure to be helpful to most families.

- Government:

  www.ed.gov/print/parents/academic/help/reader/part1.html
  www.ed.gov/pubs/parents/writing/index.html

  Both offer several ideas and publications for all ages and stages of growth.

- Other:

  www.rif.org/ (Reading Is Fundamental)
  www.familyeducation.com/home/ (Family Education)
  www.vsarts.org (Visual Arts)

  As with those noted above, these websites offer suggestions for reading-related activities as well as other important information.

### *Websites for Children:*

www.umass.edu/Aesop (offers Aesop's fables)
pbskids.org/arthur/ (Marc Brown's Arthur is featured here.)
www.magickeys.com/books/ (offers a children's storybook online)
www.guysread.com (offers suggestions especially appealing to boys)
www.dustbunny.com (offers astronomy for children)

Several children's authors such as Mem Fox, Jan Brett, Eric Carle, and Janet Stevens also have websites that children might find interesting.

## TELEVISION AND COMPUTERS: A FINAL WORD

In relation to both working with computers and television viewing, *excessive* is the operative term. Moderation is the key. Here's where parents come in. It is they who are the final arbiters as to whether their children are spending too much time in front of the television or computer.

# PARENT-TEACHER CONFERENCES

In some schools the only parent-teacher involvement may be through the parent-teacher conference. This conference is an excellent opportunity for parents and teachers to learn to feel more comfortable with one another, as well as to exchange information. Also, the parent-teacher conference may be the only way for parents to learn about the reading program and the specifics of how their children are doing.

For parent-teacher conferences to be effective, teachers must be well-prepared, friendly, interested, and allow for an exchange of ideas. It is also important for teachers to recognize that although they may have twenty-five or thirty students in the class, each conference focuses on a different child and each one is important. Most importantly, since this conference is primarily an exchange of ideas, teachers should encourage parents to give some insights into their children that would be helpful in teaching them. Remember, parents know their children better than anyone else. If the children need any special help, teachers should point this out to parents and explain precisely what they can do.

Parent-teacher conferences need not take place only during the reporting period. Whenever a need for a conference arises, that is the right time to call for one. Indeed, sometimes parents initiate the conference. However, teachers should remember that successful parent-teacher conferences require careful planning and effort.

# SUMMARY

In this chapter we focused on parental involvement. In the 1950s, many parents were discouraged from attempting to help their children to learn to read; however, beginning in the 1970s, and continuing in the new century, the trend has definitely moved toward more parental involvement. Parents are looked on as partners in education, and many parents are taking a more active role. The amount of parental involvement depends on the school district in which their children are enrolled. Parental involvement has been triggered by a number of factors. Two salient factors are loss of confidence in the schools and the input of federal funds that mandate parental involvement.

The reading programs that include parental involvement vary from district to district and even from school to school in the same school district; however, more and more school district personnel are developing programs that involve parents. Publishing companies are including special materials for their reading series specifically for parents and children, and so are test publishers. The parent-teacher conference was discussed as an excellent means for parents and teachers to get to know more about each other and to exchange information about an individual child. In addition, suggestions were given to help teachers guide parents in activities that would help their children attain literacy abilities.

# CHAPTER 14 KEY CONCEPTS

- Parents are children's first teachers.
- Parents who encourage their children and expect them to do well are enhancing their children's literacy development.
- Today the trend is to involve parents in their children's school work.
- Studies show that parent-school partnerships are effective ways to help students do better in school.
- Parents usually become involved in school programs when their children have a specific reading problem.
- The participation in a school district is usually dependent on how aggressive the parents and educators are in demanding involvement.

- As children go through the grades, parental involvement usually decreases.
- The key term in discussing computers' and television's effect on children's reading habits is *excessive.*
- The parent-teacher conference is a good way for parents and teachers to learn to feel more comfortable with one another and to exchange information.
- For parent-teacher conferences to be effective, teachers must be well-prepared, friendly, interested, and allow for an exchange of ideas.
- The success of any program that requires voluntary participation has to be based on continuous turnout.

# SUGGESTIONS FOR THOUGHT QUESTIONS AND ACTIVITIES

1. You have been put on a special committee in your school district to represent your school. The committee was formed to try to learn how parents can be more involved in the schools' reading programs. What suggestions would you make?
2. If you were asked to conduct an opinion poll concerning parents' attitudes about school and in particular about the reading program, what kinds of questions would you ask?

3. Survey school district administrators to determine the kinds of federally funded programs that it has. Then try to find out about the ways in which parents are involved.
4. Choose a school in your area. Schedule an appointment with an administrator to learn how that school involves parents in its reading programs.

# INTERNET ACTIVITIES

Choose a search engine and search for websites related to parental involvement. Select one website from the search that helps you gain a good understanding of the term. Write a brief paragraph about the website's information. (Be sure to identify both the search engine you used and the website you selected.)

## SELECTED BIBLIOGRAPHY

Boyer, Ernest L. *The Basic School: A Community for Learning.* Princeton, NJ: Carnegie Foundation for the Advancement of Learning, 1995.

Farkas, Steve, et al. *Playing Their Parts: Parents and Teachers Talk about Parental Involvement in Public Schools.* New York: Public Agenda, 1999.

Guest-edited Issue. Family Literacy. *The Reading Teacher* 48 (April 1995).

Koskinen, P., R. Wilson, L. Gambrell, and S. Neuman. "Captioned Video and Vocabulary Learning: An Innovative Practice in Literacy Instruction." *The Reading Teacher* 47 (1993): 36–43.

Purcell-Gates, Victoria. "Family Literacy," in Michael L. Kamil et al., eds., *Handbook of Reading Research,* Vol. III Mahwah, NJ: Lawrence Erlbaum, 2000.

Rubin, Dorothy. *Your Child Can Succeed in School: 100 Common-Sense Answers to Frequently Asked Questions.* Torrance, CA: Fearon Teacher Aids, 1999.

Thomas, Adele, et al. *Families at School.* Newark, DE: International Reading Association, 1999.

Topping, K. "Paired Reading: A Powerful Technique for Parent Use." *The Reading Teacher* 40 (1987): 604–14.

# 15

# Putting It All Together

## Scenario: Case Report of Child

Jason, a student in Mr. Jones's second-grade class, is having a great amount of difficulty in all his class work. Mr. Jones believes Jason has a word recognition problem that is interfering with his comprehension of printed material, so he decides to administer some diagnostic assessments to determine exactly what Jason's word recognition problems are. What follows are some of the diagnostic techniques and procedures he administered to Jason over a week's time, as well as an analysis of his word recognition difficulties.[1]

*Graded Word List*—To gain information of Jason's sight vocabulary.

*Description*

The Fry Instant Word List is a good gauge of a child's sight vocabulary. The first 300 words and their common variants represent 65% of the words used in textbooks in the lower elementary grades. If children have difficulty recognizing these words as sight words, they will have difficulty reading running text with any degree of fluency. Jason missed the following words: *they, his, from, or, word, what, were, when, can, each, which, their, other, them, these, her, would, make, into, time, two, more, write, number, way, could, than, first, been, call, now, find, long, come, part.*

*Informal Reading Inventory* (IRI)

*Description*

The purposes of the IRI are to determine a student's reading and listening capacity levels, as well as strengths and weaknesses in word recognition, oral reading comprehension, and silent reading comprehension.

*Analysis of Data*

Jason started the Word List at the Preprimer Level; he made four errors. Therefore Mr. Jones had Jason start the oral reading passages also at the Preprimer Level.

| Reader Level | Oral Reading WR Errors | Comprehension | Silent Reading Comprehension |
|---|---|---|---|
| PP | 6 (Frust.) | 85% (Instr.) | 85% (Instr.) |
| P | 14 (Frust.) | 25% (Frust.) | |

Listening Capacity = $3^2$ (Reader Level)

*General Analysis of IRI*

From an analysis of the IRI, we can see that Jason's word recognition problems are interfering with his comprehension. His word recognition problems are also causing him to read hesitantly.

*Qualitative Analysis of IRI*

Jason's errors were analyzed using the following five criteria:

[1]Case report adapted from Dr. Dallas Cheek, Professor, The College of New Jersey, 2001.

Initial Sound:     Does the error have the same beginning sound as the text word?

Medial Sound:   Does the error have the same middle sound as the text word?

Final Sound:      Does the error have the same ending sound as the text word?

Syntax:             Is the error the same part of speech as the text word?

Semantic:         Does the error make sense in the text?

| Text Word | Error | Initial | Medial | Final | Syntax | Semantic |
|-----------|-------|---------|--------|-------|--------|----------|
| Bob | p | no | no | no | no | no |
| came | got | no | no | no | yes | yes |
| who | how | yes | no | no | no | no |
| a lot | lots | no | yes | no | yes | yes |
| mountain | p | no | no | no | no | no |
| who | how | yes | no | no | no | no |
| sat | asked | no | no | no | no | no |
| her | their | no | no | yes | yes | no |
| string | thing | no | no | yes | yes | no |
| here | p | no | no | no | no | no |
| red | already | yes | no | no | no | no |
| hair | p | no | no | no | no | no |
| saw | was | no | no | no | no | no |
| that | with | no | no | no | no | no |
| father | friends | yes | no | no | yes | no |

*Informal Phonics Inventory*
*Description*

Mr. Jones developed a phonics survey inventory based on what phonic information students should have at the primary grades. From this inventory he found that Jason had not mastered the following elements.

| 1st Grade Elements (Not Mastered) | | |
|---|---|---|
| *Initial Consonants* | *Initial Consonant Clusters* | *Short Vowels* |
| t | st | i |
| w | fr | e |
| h | bl | o |
| f | tr | u |
| j   (hard) | gr | |
| g   (hard) | br | |
| y | | |
| v | | |

Now that you have read this entire text and have an expanded knowledge base about reading and reading instruction, take some time to answer these questions:

1. What conclusions would you draw from looking at the results of the case report?
2. What would you consider to be this child's strengths and needs?
3. Which instructional strategies would you use to help this child?
4. What type of texts would you use?
5. How would you involve parents?

Without a doubt, teachers who subscribe to a diagnostic-reading and improvement program have their work cut out for them! There are many considerations to think through when it comes to trying to help children become proficient readers, and this thought process takes time and energy. But with practice, the process becomes second nature. This is not to say that figuring out just what might be getting in a child's way of reading becomes any less of a mystery. Nonetheless, as a result of knowing how to select, administer, score, and interpret a variety of reading measures and knowing several instructional strategies, we become more confident because we know where to start. Once started, we have to take our cues from the child to determine the next step.

The purpose of this chapter is to provide you with some simulated experiences aimed at helping you to become more skillful in determining children's reading strengths and needs and in designing appropriate instruction that will help children to become more proficient.

## CHAPTER OBJECTIVES

After reading this chapter, you should be able to . . .

- Examine and analyze scenarios.
- Design a plan that shows a child's strengths, needs, and evidence of determining both.
- Develop an instructional plan that shows how you would address each need.
- Articulate why you acted the way you did.

## SCENARIO EXPLANATION

In this section, we show five scenarios. Select at least one scenario and do the following:

1. After reading the scenario, create a list of strengths and needs. You are really forming some hypotheses; you are making your best guess based on the limited information and your background knowledge.
2. Review the different assessment techniques we present in this text.

**FIGURE 15.1    Strengths, Needs, and Assessment Techniques to Validate Them**

| Strength | Need | Assessment Technique |
|---|---|---|
|  |  |  |
|  |  |  |
|  |  |  |
|  |  |  |
|  |  |  |
|  |  |  |
|  |  |  |
|  |  |  |
|  |  |  |
|  |  |  |
|  |  |  |
|  |  |  |

3. Construct a chart that shows each strength, need, and the assessment techniques you will use to test your hypotheses. You might want to use a form such as the one shown in Figure 15.1.
4. Create a chart that shows each need listed on your previous chart and instructional suggestions and appropriate texts you would use to address each need. Indicate where in this textbook you located each teaching suggestion and text. You might want to use the form shown in Figure 15.2.
5. State how you would involve parents or primary caregivers. Again, reference the text to show where you located the specific idea(s).

# FIVE SCENARIOS

### Sally, a First Grader, Age 6

Sally entered first grade knowing letters and sounds in isolation very well and her teacher thought she was going to make very good progress. Now it is the middle of the school year and Sally's teacher is concerned because Sally has not made the anticipated progress. The teacher can't seem to determine Sally's reading levels. Sally can read predictable books very well, yet she has a limited sight vocabulary. Although she can state all consonant sounds and can state the names of the letters, Sally doesn't appear to apply what she knows when she comes to unknown words. Her listening comprehension is very good as is evidenced by her ability to retell stories. She enjoys being read to and chooses to read during her free time.

### Bob, a Sixth Grader, Age 12

Bob had little trouble with reading throughout his elementary schooling but he always seemed to lag behind others when reading and it took him much longer to write answers to comprehension questions. Now that Bob is in sixth grade, he appears to be struggling with several subjects even though he spends several hours studying each evening. He seems to have trouble remembering what he has read, regardless of the subject. He also gets stomachaches when tests are approaching and usually does not perform well. His instructional level is approximately fifth grade when it comes to reading fiction but it really drops when reading nonfiction. At one time Bob read for pleasure but now he spends so much time on his homework that the last thing he wants to do is read during his free time.

### Mary Beth, a Fourth Grader, Age 9

Mary Beth is intensely competitive and sees every reading activity as a race. She reads aloud at grade level fairly fluently but when faced with an unfamiliar word appears to guess wildly and go right on. She rarely pauses, repeats, or corrects an attempt. In silent reading she always tries to be the first one done and appears to read only parts of each page. Her comprehension is poor; she appears to make little attempt to predict what might occur next or apply what she already knows to a subject. Consequently her instructional level is barely at grade level, with an independent level of early second. She urgently desires to be "right" and gets upset with herself when she makes an error, but seems to have

**FIGURE 15.2** **Student Needs and Instructional Techniques**

| Need | Instructional Suggestions | Appropriate Texts |
|------|---------------------------|-------------------|
|      |                           |                   |
|      |                           |                   |
|      |                           |                   |
|      |                           |                   |
|      |                           |                   |
|      |                           |                   |
|      |                           |                   |
|      |                           |                   |
|      |                           |                   |
|      |                           |                   |
|      |                           |                   |

few dependable strategies in word recognition or comprehension. She does almost no pleasure reading.

### *Alan, an Eighth Grader, Age 14*

Alan had little difficulty with reading in elementary school, although teachers remarked on his slow reading and dogged effort at comprehension. However, in seventh and eighth grades his subject area work has suffered and his grades are slipping. He is achievement-oriented and conscientious, spending hours every night reading and rereading his assignments. But he has trouble remembering what he reads, panics when faced with a test, and relies on memorization, which usually fails him under pressure. As he experiences more difficulty, he begins to read more and more slowly, trying to remember everything. In ordinary fiction his instructional level is solid at eighth grade, but in nonfiction of similar difficulty he can barely manage. His word recognition and decoding skills are good but he often lacks meanings for words he can accurately identify. He spends so much time trying to keep up with required reading that he does little or no reading for pleasure, and shows signs of increasing anxiety and fear of failure.

### *Matt, a Second Grader, Age 7*

Reading has been a struggle for Matt since the very beginning. He now has an instructional level of mid-first grade, no independent level, and a late-first frustration level. Both oral and silent reading are painfully slow, and oral reading is halting with many substitutions, repetitions, and long pauses. Most miscues are significant and reflect attempts to sound out words. Sounding out is Matt's primary strategy when uncertain of any word. His comprehension is fairly good, at least in getting the gist of what he reads, given his lack of fluency. He is a conscientious boy but avoids reading, especially orally, as much as possible. His self-esteem is suffering badly and he is beginning to show dislike toward school in general. He does enjoy being read to.

# Appendix A

# Constructing an IRI

## CONSTRUCTING YOUR OWN
## INFORMAL READING INVENTORY

Although it is time-consuming to construct your own IRI, there are some teachers who would like to do so. This section will present more specific information on the parts of an IRI as well as information on how to construct and score one.

Usually an IRI consists of word lists at varying levels, which have been selected from a traditional basal reader series; passages which are based on graduated levels of difficulty that have also been selected from a basal reader series for oral and silent reading; and comprehension questions for both the oral and silent reading passages. A separate set of passages and comprehension questions at graduated levels of difficulty are also usually included to determine the listening capacity level. (The instructions are given for a traditional basal reader program; you can, however, adapt these instructions for use with any reading program that is based on graduated levels of difficulty.)

### GRADED WORD LISTS

The graded word lists usually consist of twenty or twenty-five words. There is a word list for every reader level of the basal series. The list usually starts at the preprimer level and proceeds to the highest level book available. If the IRI begins at the preprimer level and ends at the eighth-grade level, there would be a word list for each level up to the eighth. (Many traditional basal reader series have two reader levels for certain grades, and some have three or more preprimer reader levels. If there are three or more preprimer reader levels, it's a good idea to use the second one as representative of the three. The IRI in this Appendix B is based on a traditional basal reader series.)

The words for the word lists are selected from those introduced in the basal reader for each book level. (At the back of each basal reader there is usually a list of words that have been introduced in the book.) Words for the word lists are based on a random sampling, so that each word introduced at a particular level has an equal and independent chance of being chosen.

If you are constructing your own IRI, an easy way to get a random sampling of the words for the word lists, if there are fewer than 100 words, is to put each word on a slip of paper and put the slips in a small box or hat. (Make sure the slips of paper are well mixed.) Pull 20 words from the hat. (If there are only 20 words that have been introduced at a particular reader level, you obviously would use all the words.) However, at the upper-grade levels, where there are more than 100 words presented at each level, you need a method different from the cumbersome "old hat" random sampling method. You need a formula to help you determine the number of random samples of the required sample size for a given word list. The formula for this is as follows:

$$\frac{\text{Word List}}{\text{Sample Size}} = \text{Number of Samples}$$

The number of words you want on your word list is your sample size, and the word list is the total number of words. For example, if you want to select 20 words from a 100-word list, first apply the formula

$$N = \frac{100}{20} = 5$$

Since the number of samples is 5, number the total amount of words sequentially up to 5, that is, 1, 2, 3, 4, 5. To get the 20 words from the 100-word list, select all those words that are numbered either 1, 2, 3, 4, or 5. (Select which number you will use by any method you wish, and then choose all words that have that number.) This procedure will give you a sample of 20 words from the 100-word list covering the entire alphabetical range, if the words are presented alphabetically.

## GRADED ORAL AND SILENT READING PASSAGES

To randomly draw sample passages for your IRI, note the number of pages in each basal reader, and then choose any one of the numbers. For example, if there are 200 pages, choose any number from 1 to 200. Open the book to the number you have chosen. Choose a selection on that page that can be easily excerpted; that is, it can stand alone and make sense. The first sentence of the selection should not have any pronouns that have antecedents in the previous paragraph. If there are no paragraphs on that page that can be easily excerpted, go to the previous page. It may be that you will have to go to the beginning of the story to get a selection that can stand alone.

The sample selections should contain approximately the following sample sizes:

Preprimer level, approximately 40 to 70 words
Primer level, approximately 50 to 85

First-grade level, approximately 70 to 100
Second-grade level, approximately 100 to 150
Third-grade level, approximately 125 to 175
Fourth-grade level, approximately 150 to 200
Fifth-grade level, approximately 175 to 225
Sixth-grade level and up, approximately 175 to 275

The paragraphs that are chosen to comprise your IRI should be representative of the readability level of the basal reader from which they were taken. There are times when this is not so; it's a good idea to double-check the chosen paragraphs with a readability formula. If your selection does not pass the readability formula criterion, repeat the process to choose a different passage. Each selection chosen for the IRI should have a short statement telling something about it.

There is disagreement in the field as to whether the oral and silent reading passages should be from the same or different selections. We prefer to use oral and silent reading passages from the same selection to ensure a greater chance of having a similar difficulty level of concepts and vocabulary. Dissimilarity can be a problem because most basal reader series are literature based or consist completely of trade books. These kinds of reading programs seem to have a greater variation in vocabulary load between different selections at the same level in the same program than previous basal reader series. It is important to have vocabulary and concepts at the same difficulty level for both oral and silent reading passages because the teacher uses the oral reading passage to determine whether the child should read the silent reading passage.

In addition, we have found that there appears to be a much greater variation in vocabulary load and difficulty among the present literature-based reading programs than in previous series. Often there may be only a few similar words in the glossaries of different reading programs at the same reader grade level. Be aware of these differences if you use selections from different reading programs to construct your IRIs.

## THE COMPREHENSION QUESTIONS

Both the oral and the silent reading passages must have questions based on each passage, and the questions must be text-dependent. These are usually literal comprehension questions, interpretive questions, and word meaning questions. (Some IRIs may contain critical reading questions. These may present a problem because a number of these questions are usually not text-dependent; that is, the student may be able to answer them independently of the text.) Examples of the types of questions that can be asked to assess selected comprehension skills at each level follow.

### *Literal Comprehension Questions*
Literal questions are the easiest to construct, and they are generally the ones most often asked. The answers for literal questions are directly stated in the

selection. Here is an example of a selection and some literal comprehension questions based on it:

> Sharon and Carol are sisters.
> They like to play together.
> They play lots of games.
> Their favorite game is Monopoly.

*Literal Questions*

1. Who are sisters? (story detail)
2. What do the sisters like to do? (story detail)
3. What do the sisters play? (story detail)
4. What is their favorite game? (story detail)

### Interpretive Questions

Interpretive questions are more difficult to answer because the answers are not directly stated in the selection; they are implied. Interpretive questions are also usually more difficult to construct and are usually not asked as often as literal comprehension questions. Here is an example of a selection and some interpretive questions based on it:

> Do you ever think of the right thing to say too late? I always do, but my friend George always has the right words and answers at the snap of his fingers. Whenever you see George, there's always a crowd around him, and they are always laughing at his jokes. He is never serious about anything. I'm always serious about everything. There's an old saying that definitely explains our friendship.

*Interpretive Questions*

1. What is the main idea of the selection? (main idea)
2. What can you infer about the speaker in the selection? (inference or "reading between the lines")
3. State the old saying that explains the friendship between the two persons in the selection and then tell why it explains their relationship. (figurative language; making comparisons)
4. Choose the row with ideas from the story that belong together. (association)

   a. George, unfriendly, crowds
   b. George's friend, friendly, witty
   c. George, witty, crowds
   d. George's friend, serious, witty

5. Choose the word that best completes this analogy: George's friend is to somber as George is to _____ (analogy)

   a.  people.
   b.  happiness.
   c.  grave.
   d.  cheerful.

### *Critical Reading Questions*

Critical reading questions are those that involve evaluation, which is the making of a personal judgment on the accuracy, value, and truthfulness of what is read. The critical thinking questions should be text-dependent. Here is an example of a selection and some critical reading questions based on it:

> Fortunately, the school election will be over soon. I don't think that I can stand another week such as the last one. First, there was John, who told me that I was the only one not voting for his candidate, "True-Blue Tim." Then there was Mary, who told me that if I were a student with lots of school spirit, I'd be out campaigning for her candidate, "Clever Jane." Mary says that the majority of students are supporting her candidate. She says that even the famous local star thinks that Jane is the best person. Personally, I think that both their candidates are creeps, and I don't intend to vote for either one. I'm going to vote for Jennifer because she is so democratic and fair.

*Critical Comprehension Questions*

1. State at least five propaganda techniques that are used in the selection, and give examples of them. (propaganda techniques)
2. Determine whether each of the following statements are facts or opinions. (fact or opinion)

   a. The speaker in the selection doesn't think much of the candidates.
   b. The majority of students are voting for Jane.
   c. Jane is clever.

# Appendix B

# Informal Reading Inventory*

**Summary Sheet**

Name _____     Age _____

Grade _____     Teacher _____

| Reader Level | Word Recognition in Isolation (No. of Errors) | Oral Reading | | | Silent Reading | | Listening Capacity | |
|---|---|---|---|---|---|---|---|---|
| | | W.R. | Comp. | | Comp. | | | |
| | | No. of Errors/ Total No. Wds | % Errors | % Correct | % Errors | % Correct | % Errors | % Correct |
| Preprimer | | | | | | | | |
| Primer | | | | | | | | |
| First | | | | | | | | |
| $2^1$ | | | | | | | | |
| $2^2$ | | | | | | | | |
| $3^1$ | | | | | | | | |
| $3^2$ | | | | | | | | |
| 4 | | | | | | | | |
| 5 | | | | | | | | |
| 6 | | | | | | | | |
| 7 | | | | | | | | |
| 8 | | | | | | | | |

*The Informal Reading Inventory is based on the Silver Burdett & Ginn series *World of Reading,* 1989.

Level at which Word Recognition Inventory
(WRI) was begun                                    _____

Level at which oral reading was begun              _____

Oral reading—word recognition
   Independent level                               _____

   Instructional level                             _____

   Frustration level                               _____

Oral reading—comprehension
   Independent level                               _____

   Instructional level                             _____

   Frustration level                               _____

Silent reading—comprehension
   Independent level                               _____

   Instructional level                             _____

   Frustration level                               _____

Listening capacity level                           _____

Word analysis
   Consonants—single
     initial                                     _____

     medial                                      _____

     final                                       _____

   Consonants—double
     blends                                      _____

     digraphs                                    _____

   Consonants—silent                               _____

   Vowels—single
     short                                       _____

     long                                        _____

   Vowels—double
     digraphs                                    _____

     diphthongs                                  _____

Effect of final *e* on vowel                       _____

Vowel controlled by *r*                            _____

Structural analysis

    prefixes                                      _____

    suffixes                                      _____

    combining forms                       _____

    inflectional endings                 _____

Compound words                       _____

Accent                                         _____

Special Notes on Strengths and Weaknesses

Comments on Behavior During the Testing

Recommendations

## SPECIAL NOTES

Information on the following is given in the body of Chapter 8:

1. Code for marking oral reading errors (p. 200)
2. The scoring of oral reading errors (p. 200)
3. Criteria for estimating the reading levels (p. 219)
4. Administering the IRI (p. 204)
5. Examples (pp. 208–216)

Partial credit may be given for comprehension questions if an answer consists of more than one part. For example, if the answer to a question consists of three names, and the student has named only one, the student should get one-third credit. If the answer to a question consists of two things, and the student gives one only, the student should receive half credit.

Do not count mispronunciations of difficult proper nouns in the oral reading passages as errors. You may pronounce these for the children if necessary. Also, do not count as errors dialectical equivalents (nonstandard dialects); however, these should be noted.

In addition, the term *main idea* is used rather than *central idea*, even though the oral and silent passages are usually more than one paragraph. (See "Finding the Central Idea of a Group of Paragraphs" in Chapter 12.)

## Word Recognition Inventory (WRI)

| *Preprimer* | | *Primer* | | *First* | |
|---|---|---|---|---|---|
| 1. water | _____ | 1. blow | _____ | 1. soup | _____ |
| 2. play | _____ | 2. little | _____ | 2. tents | _____ |
| 3. sand | _____ | 3. many | _____ | 3. afternoon | _____ |
| 4. look | _____ | 4. bright | _____ | 4. baked | _____ |
| 5. wind | _____ | 5. old | _____ | 5. family | _____ |
| 6. jump | _____ | 6. won | _____ | 6. alone | _____ |
| 7. cave | _____ | 7. things | _____ | 7. great | _____ |
| 8. make | _____ | 8. yellow | _____ | 8. white | _____ |
| 9. put | _____ | 9. farm | _____ | 9. soft | _____ |
| 10. bear | _____ | 10. friend | _____ | 10. boy | _____ |
| 11. over | _____ | 11. more | _____ | 11. dinner | _____ |
| 12. out | _____ | 12. thanks | _____ | 12. does | _____ |
| 13. cap | _____ | 13. snow | _____ | 13. wife | _____ |
| 14. could | _____ | 14. some | _____ | 14. horse | _____ |
| 15. down | _____ | 15. cows | _____ | 15. head | _____ |
| 16. sun | _____ | 16. game | _____ | 16. sorry | _____ |
| 17. have | _____ | 17. please | _____ | 17. summer | _____ |
| 18. side | _____ | 18. leaves | _____ | 18. hungry | _____ |
| 19. top | _____ | 19. draw | _____ | 19. drank | _____ |
| 20. surprise | _____ | 20. work | _____ | 20. enough | _____ |

# Word Recognition Inventory (WRI) (*Cont.*)

| 2¹ | 2² | 3¹ |
|---|---|---|

| 2¹ | 2² | 3¹ |
|---|---|---|
| 1. brave _____ | 1. office _____ | 1. plow _____ |
| 2. noon _____ | 2. perfect _____ | 2. horn _____ |
| 3. park _____ | 3. patient _____ | 3. hesitate _____ |
| 4. strange _____ | 4. enemy _____ | 4. neglect _____ |
| 5. November _____ | 5. donkey _____ | 5. deaf _____ |
| 6. money _____ | 6. dirt _____ | 6. language _____ |
| 7. library _____ | 7. clever _____ | 7. attention _____ |
| 8. join _____ | 8. company _____ | 8. drawn _____ |
| 9. angry _____ | 9. candle _____ | 9. complain _____ |
| 10. apple _____ | 10. beard _____ | 10. fame _____ |
| 11. carrots _____ | 11. bundle _____ | 11. goal _____ |
| 12. class _____ | 12. address _____ | 12. familiar _____ |
| 13. answer _____ | 13. snowflake _____ | 13. elevator _____ |
| 14. loud _____ | 14. sailors _____ | 14. plunge _____ |
| 15. mouth _____ | 15. score _____ | 15. nature _____ |
| 16. matter _____ | 16. tune _____ | 16. poem _____ |
| 17. hurry _____ | 17. thirsty _____ | 17. stall _____ |
| 18. idea _____ | 18. unload _____ | 18. talent _____ |
| 19. carve _____ | 19. view _____ | 19. worthy _____ |
| 20. clothes _____ | 20. trouble _____ | 20. lung _____ |
| 21. delicious _____ | 21. south _____ | 21. medal _____ |
| 22. below _____ | 22. shy _____ | 22. mistake _____ |
| 23. boil _____ | 23. ambulance _____ | 23. customer _____ |
| 24. built _____ | 24. tiny _____ | 24. courage _____ |
| 25. dragons _____ | 25. hobby _____ | 25. announce _____ |

# Word Recognition Inventory (WRI) (*Cont.*)

| $3^2$ | 4 | 5 |
|---|---|---|
| 1. petal _____ | 1. gracious _____ | 1. tragedy _____ |
| 2. rein _____ | 2. imitate _____ | 2. applause _____ |
| 3. furious _____ | 3. defense _____ | 3. amazement _____ |
| 4. popular _____ | 4. declare _____ | 4. harvest _____ |
| 5. identify _____ | 5. electronics _____ | 5. thaw _____ |
| 6. forecast _____ | 6. punishment _____ | 6. original _____ |
| 7. attach _____ | 7. robot _____ | 7. balcony _____ |
| 8. bought _____ | 8. uniform _____ | 8. marvel _____ |
| 9. admire _____ | 9. twilight _____ | 9. mileage _____ |
| 10. noble _____ | 10. tragedy _____ | 10. cluster _____ |
| 11. migrate _____ | 11. stranger _____ | 11. architect _____ |
| 12. patient _____ | 12. tame _____ | 12. heroine _____ |
| 13. novel _____ | 13. technique _____ | 13. audition _____ |
| 14. ruin _____ | 14. suspect _____ | 14. interrupt _____ |
| 15. rescue _____ | 15. ordinary _____ | 15. landscape _____ |
| 16. unusual _____ | 16. native _____ | 16. petition _____ |
| 17. x-ray _____ | 17. haughty _____ | 17. permission _____ |
| 18. wisdom _____ | 18. hostile _____ | 18. vessel _____ |
| 19. rough _____ | 19. entire _____ | 19. promotion _____ |
| 20. protest _____ | 20. errand _____ | 20. violence _____ |
| 21. persuade _____ | 21. average _____ | 21. voyage _____ |
| 22. influence _____ | 22. appetite _____ | 22. vast _____ |
| 23. prince _____ | 23. radiant _____ | 23. nuisance _____ |
| 24. bandage _____ | 24. prowl _____ | 24. luxury _____ |
| 25. bridge _____ | 25. caution _____ | 25. lonely _____ |

# Word Recognition Inventory (WRI) (*Cont.*)

| 6 | 7 | 8 |
|---|---|---|
| 1. tenement ____ | 1. sham ____ | 1. prospect ____ |
| 2. rebel ____ | 2. scrutiny ____ | 2. quest ____ |
| 3. ease ____ | 3. refuge ____ | 3. scoop ____ |
| 4. exhibit ____ | 4. prestigious ____ | 4. journalism ____ |
| 5. appoint ____ | 5. quarrel ____ | 5. invincible ____ |
| 6. shuttle ____ | 6. nomad ____ | 6. listless ____ |
| 7. unwilling ____ | 7. fault ____ | 7. mirror ____ |
| 8. recede ____ | 8. flattery ____ | 8. circuit ____ |
| 9. wizard ____ | 9. hindrance ____ | 9. defy ____ |
| 10. wrench ____ | 10. imperative ____ | 10. anguish ____ |
| 11. revenge ____ | 11. colleague ____ | 11. augment ____ |
| 12. tiresome ____ | 12. trifle ____ | 12. aristocratic ____ |
| 13. spout ____ | 13. souvenir ____ | 13. formidable ____ |
| 14. strategy ____ | 14. chore ____ | 14. faculty ____ |
| 15. pamphlet ____ | 15. aggressive ____ | 15. seizure ____ |
| 16. persist ____ | 16. barometer ____ | 16. terrace ____ |
| 17. heritage ____ | 17. emigrate ____ | 17. scrabble ____ |
| 18. conquer ____ | 18. verdict ____ | 18. undermine ____ |
| 19. humble ____ | 19. zodiac ____ | 19. sphere ____ |
| 20. arrogant ____ | 20. wrench ____ | 20. naive ____ |
| 21. astronomy ____ | 21. probe ____ | 21. plateau ____ |
| 22. distinguish ____ | 22. momentum ____ | 22. recitation ____ |
| 23. gratitude ____ | 23. mortal ____ | 23. jaunt ____ |
| 24. guarantee ____ | 24. exile ____ | 24. frugal ____ |
| 25. legacy ____ | 25. imitation ____ | 25. hysteria ____ |

## Preprimer

*ORAL READING (64)*[1]

**Introduction: Read this story aloud to find out what a little boy can make. Then I will ask you questions about the story.**

The sun came out.
Bob and Mom came out to play.
Bob said, "Who can play with me?"
Mom said, "Do you see what I see?"
Bob said, "All I see is sand.
I see a lot of sand.
I can make a mountain
with all the sand I see."
Mom said, "Make a sand mountain!
You will see who will come to play."

### Comprehension Questions

| | | Points |
|---|---|---|
| (Literal) | 1. Who came out to play? (Bob and Mom) | 20 |
| (Inference) | 2. What did Mom see? (Sand) | 16 |
| (Literal) | 3. How much sand was there? (A lot) | 16 |
| (Literal) | 4. What did Bob say he could make with the sand? (A sand mountain) | 16 |
| (Inference) | 5. What kind of day is it? (Sunny, warm, nice) | 16 |
| (Inference) | 6. What did Mom think the sand mountain would do? (Bring other children to play) | 16 |

### Scoring Scale

| Levels | Word Recognition Errors | Comprehension Errors |
|---|---|---|
| Independent | 0–1 | 0–10 points |
| Instructional | 2–3 | 11–25 points |
| Frustration | 6 or more | 50 points or more |

[1]Level 2, "The Sand Mountain," *Out Came the Sun* (Needham, MA: Silver Burdett & Ginn, 1989), pp. 38–39.

*SILENT READING*[2]

**Introduction: Read this story to find out what Bob and his friends do. Then I will ask you questions about the story. Read it carefully.**

Jane said, "Can I help make it a
big mountain?"
Bob said, "I can put sand here.
You can put sand on the other side."
Fran said, "I came to play.
Can I help make the sand mountain?"
Bob said, "Come on, you can play.
You can help Jane and me."
Jane said, "Will you get water?
The wind is blowing the sand off the mountain."

Comprehension Questions

|  |  | Points |
|---|---|---|
| (Inference) | 1. Who came to play first? (Jane) | 16 |
| (Literal) | 2. What did Jane want to do? (Help Bob make a big mountain) | 16 |
| (Literal) | 3. What did Bob tell Jane she could do? (Put sand on the other side of the mountain) | 16 |
| (Literal) | 4. Whom did Bob say Fran could help? (Jane and him) | 20 |
| (Literal) | 5. Who said, "Will you get water?" (Jane) | 16 |
| (Inference) | 6. Why did Jane want water? (To make the sand wet so that the wind would not blow it away) | 16 |

Scoring Scale

| Levels | Comprehension Errors |
|---|---|
| Independent | 0–10 points |
| Instructional | 11–20 points |
| Frustration | 50 points or more |

[2]Ibid., pp. 40–42.

## Primer

*ORAL READING (76)*[3]

**Introduction: Read this story aloud to find out what Sara wants. Then I will ask you questions about the story.**

Sara sat and sat, looking out at the
big tree. She looked at her mother and asked,
"Mom, do you have some string?"
   "Yes, here is some red string,"
said Sara's mother. "Is it for your hair?"
   "No," said Sara, "It's not for my hair."
   "I know," said Mother. "You
are going to fix something with it."
   "No," said Sara. "You'll see."
   Sara saw that her father had
some string, too. She asked him for it.

### Comprehension Questions

|  |  | Points |
|---|---|---|
| (Literal) | 1. What was Sara looking at? (The big tree) | 12.5 |
| (Literal) | 2. What did Sara want from her mother? (String) | 12.5 |
| (Literal) | 3. What color string did her mother have? (Red) | 12.5 |
| (Literal) | 4. What did Sara's mother first think the string was for? (Sara's hair) | 12.5 |
| (Inference) | 5. Who thought something was broken? (Sara's mother) | 12.5 |
| (Inference) | 6. How do we know Sara's mother thought something was broken? (She thought the string was to fix something.) | 12.5 |
| (Literal) | 7. Who else had string? (Her father) | 12.5 |
| (Literal) | 8. What did Sara do when she saw her father had some string? (She asked him for it.) | 12.5 |

### Scoring Scale

| Levels | Word Recognition Errors | Comprehension Errors |
|---|---|---|
| Independent | 0–1 | 0–10 points |
| Instructional | 2–4 | 11–25 points |
| Frustration | 8 or more | 50 points or more |

---

[3]Jane Mechling, "A Rainbow for Sara," Level 4, *Make a Wish* (Needham, MA: Silver Burdett & Ginn, 1989), pp. 32–34.

*SILENT READING*[4]

**Introduction: Read this story to find out more about Sara and her string. Then I will ask you questions about the story. Read it carefully.**

Sara ran outside to play with Peter
and Anna.
   "I am keeping string in a box,"
said Sara.
   "I have some green string in my
pocket. You may have it," said Peter.
   "You are keeping string?"
said Anna. "What are you going
to do with all that string? Will
you and your cat play with it?"
   "No," said Sara. "You'll see."
Soon Sara had all the string she needed.
She had red string, orange string,
green string, and yellow string.

Comprehension Questions

|  |  | Points |
|---|---|---|
| (Literal) | 1. Where did Sara go? (Outside) | 12.5 |
| (Literal) | 2. Why did Sara go outside? (To play with Peter and Anna) | 12.5 |
| (Literal) | 3. Where was Sara keeping her string? (In a box) | 12.5 |
| (Inference) | 4. Who else was saving string? (Peter) | 12.5 |
| (Literal) | 5. What color string did Peter have? (Green) | 12.5 |
| (Literal) | 6. Where did Peter keep his string? (In his pocket) | 12.5 |
| (Inference) | 7. Does Sara have a pet? If she does, what is it? (Yes; a cat) | 12.5 |
| (Literal) | 8. What were the colors of the string Sara had? (Red, orange, green, and yellow) | 12.5 |

Scoring Scale

| Levels | Comprehension Errors |
|---|---|
| Independent | 0–10 points |
| Instructional | 11–25 points |
| Frustration | 50 points or more |

[4]Ibid., pp. 35–36.

# First Reader

*ORAL READING (88)*[5]

**Introduction: Read this story aloud to find out about Fritz and Anna. Then I will ask you questions about the story.**

Fritz and Anna lived on a farm. It was a small farm. It was also very dry, and things did not grow well. So Fritz and his wife, Anna, were poor.

One day there was a tap, tap, tap on the door. A woman had come to the farm. She had been walking most of the day, and she was hungry. She asked Fritz and Anna to give her something to eat. Fritz and Anna had a pot of soup. They let the woman come in to eat.

## Comprehension Questions

|  |  |  | *Points* |
|---|---|---|---|
| (Literal) | 1. | Where did Fritz and Anna live? (On a farm) | 10 |
| (Literal) | 2. | What kind of farm was it? (Small, dry) | 10 |
| (Inference) | 3. | Why were Fritz and Anna poor? (Things didn't grow well on their farm.) | 10 |
| (Inference) | 4. | Why didn't things grow well? (It was too dry.) | 10 |
| (Word meaning) | 5. | What does poor mean? (Not having money; not having much food to eat) | 10 |
| (Inference) | 6. | Who knocked on Fritz and Anna's door? (A woman) | 10 |
| (Literal) | 7. | What had the woman been doing? (Walking all day) | 10 |
| (Literal) | 8. | How did the woman feel? (Hungry) | 10 |
| (Literal) | 9. | What did Fritz and Anna have? (A pot of soup) | 10 |
| (Inference) | 10. | How do we know Fritz and Anna are kind people? (Even though they are poor, they share their soup with the woman.) | 10 |

## Scoring Scale

| Levels | Word Recognition Errors | Comprehension Errors |
|---|---|---|
| Independent | 0–1 | 0–10 points |
| Instructional | 2–4 | 11–25 points |
| Frustration | 9 or more | 50 points or more |

[5]Verna Aardema, "The Three Wishes," Level 5, *A New Day* (Needham, MA: Silver Burdett & Ginn, 1989), p. 160.

*SILENT READING*[6]

**Introduction: Fritz and Anna are given some wishes by the woman. Read to find out what Fritz and Anna do with one of the wishes. Then I will ask you questions about the story. Read it carefully.**

For most of the day, Fritz and Anna
talked about the three wishes they
would make. They talked long after it was
time to eat again, and they forgot to cook.
They began to get hungry.

By the time Anna and Fritz made soup,
they were both very, very hungry.
As they sat down to eat, Fritz said,
"I wish we had a sausage to go with this soup."

And there on the table was a great big
brown sausage!

Comprehension Questions

|  |  | Points |
|---|---|---|
| (Literal) | 1. How many wishes were Fritz and Anna given? (Three) | 10 |
| (Literal) | 2. How long did they talk about the wishes? (For most of the day) | 10 |
| (Literal) | 3. What did they forget to do? (Cook) | 10 |
| (Inference) | 4. Why did they forget to cook? (They were excited about the three wishes; they were busy talking about them.) | 10 |
| (Inference) | 5. How did they know they hadn't eaten? (They became hungry.) | 10 |
| (Literal) | 6. What did they make to eat? (Soup) | 10 |
| (Literal) | 7. How did they feel when the soup was ready? (Very, very hungry) | 10 |
| (Literal) | 8. Who wished for something? (Fritz) | 10 |
| (Literal) | 9. What did Fritz wish for? (A sausage to go with the soup) | 10 |
| (Literal) | 10. What did the wish bring? (A great big brown sausage) | 10 |

Scoring Scale

| Levels | Comprehension Errors |
|---|---|
| Independent | 0–10 points |
| Instructional | 11–25 points |
| Frustration | 50 points or more |

[6]Ibid., p. 163.

## Level 2[1]

*ORAL READING (112)*[7]

> **Introduction: Read this story aloud to find out why a farmer needs help. Then I will ask you questions about the story.**

Once there was a farmer who went to the town wise man because he had a problem, and he did not know what to do. "How can I help you?" the wise man asked.

"I have a house with one small room," sighed the farmer.

"That is not a problem," the wise man said.

"It is a problem," the farmer sighed. "I live in this one small room with my wife and my seven children. We are always in one another's way, and we are always talking at the same time. It is so loud that I can hardly hear myself think. I cannot stand it any longer. Can you help me?"

### Comprehension Questions

|  |  | Points |
|---|---|---|
| (Literal) | 1. To whom did the farmer go? (To the town wise man) | 10 |
| (Word meaning) | 2. What is a town wise man? (A person who can help others; a man who knows lots of things; he can answer many questions.) | 10 |
| (Literal) | 3. Why did the farmer go to the town wise man? (He had a problem.) | 10 |
| (Literal) | 4. Where does the farmer live? (In a house with one small room) | 10 |
| (Inference) | 5. How many people live in the house? (Nine: seven children, the farmer, and his wife) | 10 |
| (Inference) | 6. Explain whether you think the farmer is rich or poor. (Poor, because he lives in one room with such a large family) | 10 |
| (Inference) | 7. What is the farmer's problem? (It is too noisy in his house.) | 10 |
| (Literal) | 8. What does everyone in the house do at the same time? (Talk) | 10 |
| (Literal) | 9. What is the noise stopping the farmer from doing? (Thinking) | 10 |
| (Inference) | 10. What does the farmer want the town wise man to do? (Help the farmer solve his problem) | 10 |

### Scoring Scale

| Levels | Word Recognition Errors | Comprehension Errors |
|---|---|---|
| Independent | 0–1 | 0–10 points |
| Instructional | 2–6 | 11–25 points |
| Frustration | 11 or more | 50 points or more |

---

[7]Michael Patrick Hearn, "Not So Wise as You Suppose," Level 6, *Garden Gates* (Needham, MA: Silver Burdett & Ginn, 1989), pp. 94–95.

*SILENT READING*[8]

**Introduction: Read this story to find out what the farmer does to solve his problem. Then I will ask you questions about the story. Read it carefully.**

The wise man stroked his chin and thought.
"Do you have a horse?" the wise man asked.
"Yes, I have a horse," the farmer said.
"Then the answer is simple," the wise man said,
"but you must do as I tell you. Tonight you must bring
the horse into your house to stay with you,
your wife, and your seven children." The farmer was
surprised to hear such a plan, but he did as he was told.
The next morning he returned to the wise man.
He was quite upset.
"You are not so wise as you suppose!" the farmer said,
"Now my house is even louder. The horse just kicks
and neighs morning, noon, and night!
I cannot stand it any longer."

Comprehension Questions

| | | Points |
|---|---|---|
| (Literal) | 1. What did the wise man stroke? (His chin) | 10 |
| (Literal) | 2. What was the wise man doing when he stroked his chin? (Thinking) | 10 |
| (Literal) | 3. What did the wise man ask the farmer? (If he had a horse) | 10 |
| (Word meaning) | 4. What does "simple" mean? (Easy) | 10 |
| (Literal) | 5. What did the wise man say was simple? (The answer to the farmer's problem) | 10 |
| (Literal) | 6. What did the wise man want the farmer to do? (To bring the horse into the house to stay with the farmer and his family) | 10 |
| (Literal) | 7. When was the farmer supposed to bring the horse into the house? (That night) | 10 |
| (Inference) | 8. Explain how you know whether the wise man's plan worked. (It didn't work because the farmer came in very upset.) | 10 |
| (Literal) | 9. What did the horse do in the house? (Kicked and neighed) | 10 |
| (Literal) | 10. What did the farmer think about the wise man now? (That the wise man was not as wise as he thought he was) | 10 |

Scoring Scale

| Levels | Comprehension Errors |
|---|---|
| Independent | 0–10 points |
| Instructional | 11–25 points |
| Frustration | 50 points or more |

[8]Ibid., p. 96.

## Level 2[2]

*ORAL READING (131)*[9]

> **Introduction: Read this story aloud to find out what the children's surprise is. Then I will ask you questions about the story.**

The children sat down in a big circle on the ground. Everyone was excited. Mr. Ortero (or-te'-rō) had promised them a surprise.

Mr. Ortero walked into the middle of the circle. He ran the after-school program in the park.

"I have a mystery today," Mr. Ortero said. "A treasure is hidden somewhere in the park. Your job is to solve the mystery and find the treasure."

Marita (mä-rē'-ta) raised her hand. "What is the treasure?" she asked.

"That's part of the mystery," Mr. Ortero answered.

Marita laughed with everyone else. Mr. Ortero liked to tease them.

"Each of you gets one clue," Mr. Ortero said.

He started around the circle, handing out the clues. Marita was sitting between Jenny and Mike.

"I'm really a good detective," Mike said. "I bet I'll find the treasure."

### Comprehension Questions

| | | Points |
|---|---|---|
| (Literal) | 1. How were the children sitting? (In a big circle on the ground) | 10 |
| (Literal) | 2. Why were they excited? (Mr. Ortero had promised them a surprise.) | 10 |

[9]Judith Stamper, "The Treasure Hunt," Level 7, *Going Places* (Needham, MA: Silver Burdett & Ginn, 1989), p. 197.

| | | |
|---|---|---|
| (Literal) | 3. Who was Mr. Ortero? (The person who ran the after-school program in the park) | 10 |
| (Literal) | 4. What did Mr. Ortero have for the children? (A mystery) | 10 |
| (Word meaning) | 5. What is a mystery? (Something that is not known; a secret; a puzzle that has to be solved or figured out) | 10 |
| (Literal) | 6. What is the mystery Mr. Ortero has for the children? (He has hidden a treasure in the park and wants the children to find it.) | 10 |
| (Literal) | 7. What did Marita want to know? (What the treasure is) | 10 |
| (Inference) | 8. Why didn't Mr. Ortero tell the children what the treasure is? (The treasure is part of the mystery and therefore might give the mystery away; it might make it too easy to solve the mystery.) | 10 |
| (Literal) | 9. What did Mr. Ortero do to help the children find the treasure? (He gave each child a clue.) | 10 |
| (Inference) | 10. Why does Mike think he will find the treasure? (Because he thinks he's a good detective) | 10 |

Scoring Scale

| Levels | Word Recognition Errors | Comprehension Errors |
|---|---|---|
| Independent | 0–1 | 0–10 points |
| Instructional | 2–7 | 11–25 points |
| Frustration | 13 or more | 50 points or more |

*SILENT READING*[10]

**Introduction: Read this story to find out more about the treasure hunt. Then I will ask you questions about the story. Read it carefully.**

Jenny looked at Marita and smiled. They both liked Mike, but he bragged a lot.

Mr. Ortero gave Jenny her clue. Marita was next, and then Mike. Soon, each child had a clue to open and read. Mr. Ortero stepped back into the middle of the circle.

"Listen to the rules," he said. "First, stay inside the park. The treasure is hidden here. Second, don't harm any plants or trees. Third, you must find the treasure in twenty minutes. Meet me back here in twenty minutes. Good luck!"

The children jumped to their feet and ran in different directions. Marita read her clue over and over. It said:

*Thirsty, tired, and very hot?*
*I'm near what's cool and hits the spot.*

"Near something to drink," Marita thought. She ran to find the nearest water fountain. She looked all around the fountain, but there was no treasure.

Comprehension Questions

|  |  | Points |
|---|---|---|
| (Literal) | 1. How did Jenny and Marita feel toward Mike? (They liked him.) | 10 |
| (Word meaning) | 2. What does "brag" mean? (To boast) | 10 |
| (Inference) | 3. Why did Jenny smile at Marita? (Because Mike is probably always bragging; they were used to his bragging.) | 10 |
| (Literal) | 4. What did Mr. Ortero do after he gave each child a clue? (He gave them rules.) | 10 |

[10]Ibid., p. 198.

| | | |
|---|---|---|
| (Word meaning) | 5. What is a rule? (Something you have to follow) | 10 |
| (Literal) | 6. What were the three rules he gave the children? (Stay inside the park; don't harm any plants or trees; they must find the treasure in twenty minutes.) | 10 |
| (Inference) | 7. How do we know Mr. Ortero is concerned about the park? (He tells children not to harm the plants or trees.) | 10 |
| (Literal) | 8. What did Marita run to find? (The water fountain) | 10 |
| (Inference) | 9. Why did Marita run to the water fountain? (Because of her clue) | 10 |
| (Inference) | 10. What did Marita expect to find at the water fountain? (The treasure) | 10 |

## Scoring Scale

| Levels | Comprehension Errors |
|---|---|
| Independent | 0–10 points |
| Instructional | 11–25 points |
| Frustration | 50 points or more |

# Level 3[1]

*ORAL READING (151)*[11]

> **Introduction: Read this story aloud to find out what Jason wants. Then I will ask you questions about the story.**

Every time ten-year-old Jason Hardman wanted a book from a library, he borrowed his sister's bike and pedaled six miles to the next town, Monroe. Since Jason's favorite thing to do was to read books, he spent hours pedaling.

Jason's town of Elsinore, Utah, had only 650 people, too tiny for a library of its own. Elsinore was so small that the children even went to school in Monroe.

One night, Jason said to his parents, "I want to start a library in Elsinore." They were pleased but told him that he would have to talk with the town council.

"What is a town council?" Jason asked.

"It's a group of about eight elected members and the mayor. They run all the town's business," his mom said. "Elsinore, like all towns, collects taxes from its citizens and uses the money for public services, such as fire and police protection," she explained.

## Comprehension Questions

| | | Points |
|---|---|---|
| (Literal) | 1. How old is Jason Hardman? (Ten years old) | 10 |
| (Word meaning) | 2. What does "borrow" mean? (To use something that belongs to someone else after agreeing to return it) | 10 |
| (Literal) | 3. What did Jason borrow? (His sister's bike) | 10 |
| (Inference) | 4. Where did Jason spend a lot of time? (In the Monroe library) | 10 |
| (Literal) | 5. What was Jason's favorite thing? (Reading) | 10 |
| (Literal) | 6. Why didn't Jason's town have a library? (It was too small.) | 10 |
| (Literal) | 7. What did Jason want to do? (Start a library) | 10 |
| (Inference) | 8. Why did Jason want to start a library? (Because he loved to read and didn't want to keep pedaling to Monroe to get library books) | 10 |
| (Literal) | 9. What is a town council? (A group of about eight elected members and a mayor, who run the town's business) | 10 |
| (Main idea) | 10. What is the main idea of the story? (Jason Hardman wants to start a library.) | 10 |

[11]Margaret Tuley Patton, "Jason Wants a Library," Level 8, *Castles of Sand* (Needham, MA: Silver Burdett & Ginn, 1989), pp. 184–85.

Scoring Scale

| Levels | Word Recognition Errors | Comprehension Errors |
|---|---|---|
| Independent | 0–2 | 0–10 points |
| Instructional | 3–8 | 11–25 points |
| Frustration | 15 or more | 50 points or more |

*SILENT READING*[12]

> **Introduction: Jason meets with the town council and tells them he wants to start a library. Read the story to find out more about Jason and his library. Then I will ask you questions about the story. Read it carefully.**

Another week passed. Every day when Jason came off the school bus, he'd ask his mother: "Did the mayor phone?" Each day, the answer was, "No." Jason phoned the mayor every night for two weeks. Each night, the same answer was given: "The council is still thinking about it." Jason grew tired of waiting. Why can't I use the town hall basement for my library? he thought to himself.

During those weeks, Jason pedaled often to Monroe for library books. "I wonder if I will be biking these six miles forever for a book?" he asked himself sadly. He began to doubt that he would ever get a library for Elsinore.

At last it happened. When he phoned the mayor, Jason was invited to the council's next meeting. The mayor told him they might find space in the town hall basement. It was just too good to be true.

Comprehension Questions

|  |  | Points |
|---|---|---|
| (Literal) | 1. What did Jason ask his mother when he came home from school? (Did the mayor phone?) | 10 |
| (Inference) | 2. Explain how you know whether Jason lived close or far from his school. (He didn't live close because he rode a bus to school.) | 10 |
| (Literal) | 3. What did Jason do every night? (He phoned the mayor every night.) | 10 |
| (Literal) | 4. What answer was he always given? (The council is still thinking about it.) | 10 |
| (Literal) | 5. Where did Jason want to have his library? (In the town hall basement) | 10 |
| (Literal) | 6. What did Jason do while he was waiting? (Pedaled often to the library in Monroe) | 10 |
| (Word meaning) | 7. What does forever mean? (Always) | 10 |
| (Literal) | 8. What finally happened? (Jason was invited to the council's next meeting. They told him they might find space in the town hall basement for his library.) | 10 |
| (Inference) | 9. How do we know Jason could hardly believe his ears. (In the story it says, "It was too good to be true.") | 10 |

[12]Ibid., p. 187.

(Main idea)  10. What is the main idea of the story? (After Jason waits a few weeks,   10
the mayor finally tells Jason that he might be able to use the town hall
basement for his library.)

Scoring Scale

| Levels | Comprehension Errors |
|---|---|
| Independent | 0–10 points |
| Instructional | 11–25 points |
| Frustration | 50 points or more |

# Level 3[2]

*ORAL READING (171)*[13]

> **Introduction: Read this story aloud to find out what King Midas loves. Then I will ask you questions about the story.**

Once upon a time there was a very rich king named Midas. He lived in a fine castle with his daughter, Marygold.
The two things he loved best in life were gold and Marygold.
He loved to go into his treasure room and count his coins.
No one, not even Marygold, was allowed into the king's treasure room.

One day Midas was sitting in the treasure room dreaming about his gold. In his dream, he saw a shadow fall across
the piles of valuable gold coins. He looked up and saw
a stranger standing near him. Since no one was allowed into his treasure room, Midas was surprised. The stranger looked kind, however, so Midas wasn't afraid. He greeted the man, and they began to talk of gold.

"You certainly have a lot of gold," said the stranger.

"It's not so much," said Midas.

The stranger smiled. "Do you want even more gold
than this?" he asked.

"If I had my way, everything I touched would turn
into gold," Midas replied.

## Comprehension Questions

|  |  | Points |
|---|---|---|
| (Literal) | 1. What were the two things that Midas loved best in the world? (Gold and his daughter, Marygold) | 10 |
| (Word meaning) | 2. What is the meaning of "valuable"? (Worth a lot such as gold, money, or jewelry) | 10 |
| (Literal) | 3. Where was no one allowed to go? (In the king's treasure room) | 10 |
| (Literal) | 4. What did King Midas love to do in his treasure room? (Count his coins) | 10 |
| (Inference) | 5. How do we know Midas loves gold very much? (He spends a lot of time sitting in the treasure room counting the coins. He also dreams about the gold.) | 10 |

---

[13]"King Midas and the Golden Touch," retold by Judy Rosenbaum, Level 9, *On the Horizon* (Needham, MA: Silver Burdett & Ginn, 1989), pp. 130–31.

| (Word meaning) | 6. What is a stranger? (A person who is unknown to you; someone you don't know) | 10 |
| (Literal) | 7. Where did Midas see a stranger? (In his dream while sitting in the treasure room) | 10 |
| (Literal) | 8. Why was Midas surprised when he saw a stranger in his treasure room? (Because no one was allowed in the room) | 10 |
| (Inference) | 9. How do we know Midas is not satisfied with what he has? (Even though he is very rich and has so much gold, he says that it's not so much. He also says he'd like everything he touched to turn into gold.) | 10 |
| (Main idea) | 10. What is the main idea of the story? (Even though King Midas is very rich and has lots of gold, he thinks it's not so much.) | 10 |

## Scoring Scale

| Levels | Word Recognition Errors | Comprehension Errors |
|---|---|---|
| Independent | 0–2 | 0–10 points |
| Instructional | 3–9 | 11–25 points |
| Frustration | 17 or more | 50 points or more |

*SILENT READING*[14]

> **Introduction: The stranger tells King Midas that he will give him the Golden Touch. Everything he touches will turn to gold. Read the story to find out what happens. Then I will ask you questions about the story. Read it carefully.**

Midas was so excited that he could hardly wait until morning. At last the sun rose. Still dreaming, Midas sat up and reached for the water jug by his bed. At once it became gold. Midas was so overjoyed, he got up and danced around the room, touching everything within his reach. Soon he had a room full of gleaming gold objects. When he reached for his clothes, they turned into heavy golden cloth. "Now I shall really look like a king," he said. He got dressed and admired himself in the mirror. Midas was impressed by his golden clothes, though they were so heavy he could hardly move.

His looking glass was more of a problem. He tried to use it to see his new treasures better. To his surprise, he could not see anything through it. He put it on the table and found that it was now gold, but Midas was too excited to worry. He said, "I can see well enough without it. Besides, it is much more valuable now."

Comprehension Questions

|  |  | Points |
|---|---|---|
| (Literal) | 1. What did Midas first do after the sun rose? (He reached for the water jug.) | 10 |
| (Literal) | 2. What happened to the water jug after he touched it? (It turned to gold.) | 10 |
| (Literal) | 3. What did Midas do after the water jug turned to gold? (He got up and danced around the room, touching everything within his reach.) | 10 |
| (Literal) | 4. What happened to everything he touched? (It turned to gold.) | 10 |
| (Inference) | 5. Why were his clothes so heavy? (They too had turned to gold because he had to touch them to put them on.) | 10 |
| (Inference) | 6. Why had his looking glass become gold? (He had touched it.) | 10 |
| (Inference) | 7. Were all these things really happening to Midas? Explain. (No, Midas was dreaming it all.) | 10 |
| (Word meaning) | 8. What does "admire" mean? (To think of someone with approval and respect) | 10 |
| (Literal) | 9. What did Midas say when his looking glass turned to gold? (I can see well enough without it. Besides, it is much more valuable now.) | 10 |
| (Main idea) | 10. What is the main idea of the story? (In his dream, King Midas is very excited because everything he touches turns to gold.) | 10 |

[14]Ibid., p. 132.

Scoring Scale

| Levels | Comprehension Errors |
|---|---|
| Independent | 0–10 points |
| Instructional | 11–25 points |
| Frustration | 50 points or more |

# Level 4

*ORAL READING (187)*[15]

> **Introduction: Read this story aloud to find out how a writer begins a book for young people. Then I will ask you questions about the story.**

How does a writer such as Mr. Pinkwater begin a novel for young readers? How does he work? "When I'm beginning a new book," he states, "I am almost like an actor getting into character. I listen to music. I watch television. I talk to people. I turn up at a K-Mart store and go through all the motions of being an ordinary citizen.

"When I start a novel, all I'm really doing is waiting for the characters to show up. It's like the movie *Close Encounters of the Third Kind.* The people who have been 'selected' to be in this story show up. It is a very interesting experience."

He does not sit down and write every day. "It would be terrible if I had to work that way. I show up at my office every day in the event that something may want to happen, but if nothing happens, I don't feel that I have failed to perform. If something gets started, fair enough. If it doesn't, and I feel I've given it enough time, I go to K-Mart. I showed up, the story didn't!"

## Comprehension Questions

|  |  | Points |
|---|---|---|
| (Literal) | 1. To whom does Mr. Pinkwater compare himself when he first begins to write? (An actor) | 10 |
| (Literal) | 2. State three things Mr. Pinkwater does when he begins to write? (Listen to music, watch television, talk to people) | 10 |
| (Inference) | 3. What does listening to music, watching television, and talking to people help him do? (Get into character for his book) | 10 |
| (Literal) | 4. When he first starts writing what is he waiting for? (For his characters to show up) | 10 |
| (Literal) | 5. What place does Mr. Pinkwater visit? (K-Mart) | 10 |
| (Word meaning) | 6. What does "ordinary" mean? (not special; usual; normal) | 10 |
| (Inference) | 7. What does Mr. Pinkwater mean when he says he goes through the motions of being an ordinary person? (He is acting; he is trying to act like the people who go shopping at K-Mart, so he can learn what it feels like.) | 10 |

---

[15]Lee Bennett Hopkins, "Daniel Manus Pinkwater," Level 10, *Silver Secrets* (Needham, MA: Silver Burdett & Ginn, 1989), p. 56.

(Literal)                          8. What movie does Mr. Pinkwater refer to? (*Close Encounters of the*   10
                                       *Third Kind*)
(Inference)                        9. What are Mr. Pinkwater's feelings about writing every day? (He    10
                                       doesn't feel he has to. He doesn't feel he is a failure if he doesn't
                                       perform every day.)
(Main idea)                       10. What is the main idea of the story? (Mr. Pinkwater describes what he  10
                                       does in beginning to write a book.)

### Scoring Scale

| Levels | Word Recognition Errors | Comprehension Errors |
| --- | --- | --- |
| Independent | 0–2 | 0–10 points |
| Instructional | 3–9 | 11–25 points |
| Frustration | 19 or more | 50 points or more |

*SILENT READING*[16]

**Introduction: Read this story to find out how Daniel Pinkwater feels while he is writing his books. Then I will ask you questions about the story. Read it carefully.**

"I love the story as it is being written. Sometimes it's as though it were happening without my doing it. I'll go to bed, excited about what's going to happen tomorrow. I know something's got to happen because I've only got 175 pages done and I've got to do more.

"To me, the beauty in writing is making the words come out as clear as a pane of glass. That I can do, and I'm rather pleased because it took me years to learn how.

"Writing for girls and boys has helped me to remember my own childhood. And since I'm writing books for a specific reader, namely myself at different ages, I've gotten more and more expert at revisiting that person within me at different ages."

He sometimes uses a computer. "The computer allows me to think in a different way. It helps me to be a better, more daring writer. Using a computer was a breakthrough for me."

### Comprehension Questions

|  |  | Points |
|---|---|---|
| (Literal) | 1. What does Mr. Pinkwater love? (The story as it is being written) | 10 |
| (Literal) | 2. How does Mr. Pinkwater feel when he goes to bed after working on a story? (Excited) | 10 |
| (Inference) | 3. Why is Mr. Pinkwater excited when he goes to bed after working on his story? (He can't wait to see what will happen or how his story will turn out.) | 10 |
| (Literal) | 4. How does Mr. Pinkwater know something has to happen? (Because he only has 175 pages done and he has to do more.) | 10 |
| (Inference) | 5. What is the beauty in writing for Mr. Pinkwater? (His being able to make words come out as clear as a pane of glass) | 10 |
| (Inference) | 6. What does it mean when he says that his words are as clear as a pane of glass? (That it is easy to understand what he is saying; he gets his ideas across; his words help bring pictures to your mind.) | 10 |

[16]Ibid., pp. 56–57.

| (Inference) | 7. How do we know it wasn't always easy for him to make his words as clear as a pane of glass? (He said it took him years to learn how.) | 10 |
| (Literal) | 8. What has writing for children helped him to do? (Remember his own childhood) | 10 |
| (Literal) | 9. How does the computer help Mr. Pinkwater? (It allows him to think in a different way; it helps him to be a better, more daring writer.) | 10 |
| (Main idea) | 10. What is the main idea of the story? (Mr. Pinkwater describes what he does and how he feels while writing a story.) | 10 |

Scoring Scale

| *Levels* | *Comprehension Errors* |
|---|---|
| Independent | 0–10 points |
| Instructional | 11–25 points |
| Frustration | 50 points or more |

## Level 5

*ORAL READING (208)*[17]

> **Introduction: Read this story aloud to find out about how the Davidsons lived years ago. Then I will ask you questions about the story.**

Early in April of 1872, the Davidsons' covered wagon rolled onto their 160-acre land claim in eastern Nebraska. There was no shelter waiting for them. Like most settlers on the Great Plains, the Davidsons had to build their own shelter. At first, the family lived in the covered wagon. That was all right for a while. But by fall, they needed more protection from Nebraska's cold and windy climate.

Back east, the Davidsons had lived in a wooden farmhouse. They would have liked to build a wooden house on the Plains, too. But there wasn't a tree in sight. Lumber for building wasn't available in Nebraska, even if the family had been able to afford it.

There wasn't time for building, anyway. As farmers, the Davidsons knew they had to get on with the all-important work of plowing and planting. Only then would their new land provide enough harvest to see them through the winter.

Rabbits and foxes dig their burrows and dens in hillsides, and that's what the Davidsons did too. The settlers chose the streambank location because it was conveniently close to water. There were no building materials to buy or skilled workers to hire. After two days of digging, the Davidsons' new home was ready.

### Comprehension Questions

| | | Points |
|---|---|---|
| (Literal) | 1. When did the Davidsons arrive at their destination? (In April of 1872) | 10 |
| (Literal) | 2. What was their destination? (A 160-acre land claim in eastern Nebraska) | 10 |
| (Literal) | 3. Where did they live when they first arrived? (In their covered wagon) | 10 |

---

[17]Duncan Searl, "A Sea of Grass," Level 11, *Dream Chasers* (Needham, MA: Silver Burdett & Ginn, 1989), pp. 423–24.

| | | |
|---|---|---|
| (Literal) | 4. Why did they live in a covered wagon? (There was no shelter waiting for them.) | 10 |
| (Inference) | 5. How do we know that the Davidsons weren't wealthy? (The story said that lumber wasn't available, even if the Davidsons could afford it. Also, they needed the harvest to see them through the winter.) | 10 |
| (Inference) | 6. During what season or seasons of the year did the Davidsons live in their covered wagon? (During the spring and summer; a student may include the beginning of fall as part of the answer. Accept this also.) | 10 |
| (Inference) | 7. What was the Davidsons' highest priority? (Plowing and planting) | 10 |
| (Inference) | 8. The Davidsons' home was compared to homes built by what two animals? (Rabbits and foxes) | 10 |
| (Word meaning) | 9. What is a burrow? (A hole that an animal digs in the ground) | 10 |
| (Main idea) | 10. What is the main idea of the story? (The Davidsons' only choice to survive the cold and windy climate was for them, themselves, to dig a home in the hillside like the rabbits and foxes.) | 10 |

Scoring Scale

| Levels | Word Recognition Errors | Comprehension Errors |
|---|---|---|
| Independent | 0–2 | 0–10 points |
| Instructional | 3–10 | 11–25 points |
| Frustration | 21 or more | 50 points or more |

*SILENT READING*[18]

> **Introduction: Read this story to find out more about how the Davidsons lived years ago. Then I will ask you questions about the story. Read it carefully.**

Most people believe in the old saying, "There's no place like home." The Davidsons, however, might not have felt that way about their dugout. The cramped dwelling was damp and dark, even on sunny days. Dirt from the roof sifted down into bedding and food. Insects and snakes were constant house guests.

Hoping their new shelter would be a temporary one, the Davidsons began to plow and plant. But this wasn't as easy as they had expected. In the early 1870s, more than a foot of thick sod covered almost every inch of the territory. Held together by a mass of tangled roots, this sod was almost impossible to cut through. It could take weeks to plow a single acre. Settlers like the Davidsons became known as "sodbusters."

The sod's toughness gave the settlers an idea. Why not build with it? The new fields were covered with long ribbons of sod that had been plowed up. It would be a simple matter to cut these into smaller pieces and use them as building blocks. The settlers even had a nickname for this unusual building material—"Nebraska marble."

Comprehension Questions

|  |  | Points |
|---|---|---|
| (Literal) | 1. What is the saying that most people believe in? (There's no place like home.) | 10 |
| (Inference) | 2. How would the Davidsons feel about the saying "There's no place like home"? (They would not agree because they lived in a dugout that was not very comfortable.) | 10 |
| (Literal) | 3. State three problems with their dugout. (It was cramped, damp, and dark; dirt from the roof sifted down into bedding and food; and so on.) | 10 |
| (Literal) | 4. Who were the Davidsons' constant guests? (Insects and snakes) | 10 |

[18]Ibid., p. 425.

(Inference)      5. How long had the Davidsons planned on staying in their dugout?    10
(Not long; they hoped their new shelter would be a temporary one.)

(Word meaning)      6. What is the meaning of "temporary"? (Lasting for a short time; not    10
permanent)

(Literal)      7. What covered almost every inch of the Davidsons' territory?    10
(More than a foot of thick sod)

(Inference)      8. Why were the settlers known as "sodbusters"? (Because it was very    10
hard to cut through the sod; however, they did, even though it could
take weeks to plow one acre.)

(Literal)      9. What idea did the sod's toughness give the settlers? (To build with it)    10

(Main idea)      10. What is the main idea of the story? (The Davidsons, unhappy with    10
their dugout, come up with the idea to use the tough sod for building
material.)

### Scoring Scale

| Levels | Comprehension Errors |
|---|---|
| Independent | 0–10 points |
| Instructional | 11–25 points |
| Frustration | 50 points or more |

# Level 6

*ORAL READING (252)*[19]

**Introduction: Read this story aloud to find out what is special about the Monterey Bay Aquarium. Then I will ask you questions about the story.**

You walk through the door—and immediately freeze. Overhead, to your left, a thresher shark whips its tail. To your right are three huge killer whales. Have you wandered into a nightmare? Hardly. You've just entered the Monterey Bay Aquarium.

The shark and whales, lifesize and hanging from the ceiling, are fiberglass. The other 6,000 creatures you'll meet are not. On a visit to the aquarium, on the shores of California's Monterey Bay, you'll have a chance not only to see them swim, scurry, hunt, and court, but to pick up and handle a few as well.

One of the aquarium's most spectacular exhibits is the three-story-high kelp forest—the world's only kelp forest growing indoors. Clinging to the bottom with a rootlike "holdfast," the yellow-brown kelp reaches up through 28 feet of water, spreading out on the tank's sunlit surface. With "stipes" instead of trunks, and "blades" in place of leaves, the kelp forest resembles an underwater redwood grove. Sunbeams slant down from above, while the kelp sways gently back and forth. With a patient eye, you will begin to spot some of the many creatures that call the kelp forest home.

Long-legged brittle stars and crabs can be seen within the tangled holdfast. Watch for turban snails higher up. The fish of the kelp forest aren't as fast as those of the open ocean, but they're better at playing hide-and-seek. Special air sacs allow some of them to hover in hiding within the maze of blades. Many are completely camouflaged.

## Comprehension Questions

|  |  | *Points* |
|---|---|---|
| (Literal) | 1. What do you first see when you walk through the door of the Monterey Bay Aquarium? (Overhead to your left a thresher shark and to your right three huge killer whales) | 10 |
| (Inference) | 2. Why would you immediately freeze when you first walk through the door? (Because the thresher shark and three killer whales must look very real, but they aren't.) | 10 |
| (Literal) | 3. How many real creatures are there in the aquarium? (6,000) | 10 |
| (Word meaning) | 4. What does "spectacular" mean? (Of or like a remarkable sight; showy; striking) | 10 |
| (Literal) | 5. What is one of the aquarium's most remarkable exhibits? (The three-story-high kelp forest) | 10 |
| (Inference) | 6. Why is the kelp forest so remarkable? (It's the world's only indoor kelp forest.) | 10 |
| (Literal) | 7. What does the kelp forest resemble? (An underwater redwood grove) | 10 |

---

[19]Paul Fleischman, "The Monterey Bay Aquarium," Level 12, *Wind by the Sea* (Needham, MA: Silver Burdett & Ginn, 1989), pp. 395–96.

| | | |
|---|---|---|
| (Inference) | 8. Why are the fish in the kelp forest better at playing hide-and-seek? (They can hover in hiding within the maze of blades so that they blend in with the blades; they are completely camouflaged.) | 10 |
| (Literal) | 9. What allows some of the fish to hover in hiding? (Special air sacs) | 10 |
| (Main idea) | 10. What is the main idea of the story? (The Monterey Sea Aquarium is a very unusual aquarium that houses the world's only kelp forest growing indoors.) | 10 |

Scoring Scale

| Levels | Word Recognition Errors | Comprehension Errors |
|---|---|---|
| Independent | 0–3 | 0–10 points |
| Instructional | 4–13 | 11–25 points |
| Frustration | 25 or more | 50 points or more |

*SILENT READING*[20]

**Introduction: Read this story to find out about one of the Monterey Bay Aquarium's residents. Then I will ask you questions about the story. Read it carefully.**

Among the animals who depend on the kelp are the aquarium's most playful residents, the sea otters. Floating on their backs, doing somersaults in the water, taking part in high-speed games of tag, these smallest of the marine mammals charm every audience.

Their two-story tank lets you view them from above as well as from below the water's surface. In the wild, though, their home is the kelp beds. They live on creatures who live on the kelp. They depend on it for shelter during storms. Before sleeping, they wrap themselves in it to keep from drifting out to sea.

Why are otters so playful? No one knows, though part of the answer might lie in the fact that their constant motion helps to keep them warm. Unlike the whales and other marine mammals, otters have no layer of blubber between their warm-blooded insides and the cold water outside. So they move around a lot, which requires a lot of energy, which in turn requires a lot of eating. Could you eat 25 hamburgers a day? That's the equivalent of what an otter swallows, eating up to one-quarter of its body weight daily. If you're present at feeding time, you'll be amazed at how much fish, squid, and abalone an otter can eat. Wild otters eat so many purple sea urchins that their bones eventually turn purplish as well.

Otters have another defense against the cold—their coats. When you touch the soft sample of fur on the wall by their tank, you'll understand why they were hunted until they were nearly extinct.

Comprehension Questions

|  |  | Points |
|---|---|---|
| (Literal) | 1. What animals are the aquarium's most playful residents? (The sea otters) | 10 |
| (Literal) | 2. How do the sea otters charm audiences? (They float on their backs, do somersaults, and play high-speed games of tag.) | 10 |
| (Literal) | 3. Where do the otters live in the aquarium? (In a two-story tank) | 10 |
| (Literal) | 4. Where do the otters live in the wild? (In the kelp beds) | 10 |
| (Literal) | 5. What is the reason given for the otter's playfulness? (Their constant motion keeps them warm.) | 10 |
| (Inference) | 6. Why do the otters have to move around a lot to keep warm? (The otters have no layer of blubber between their warm-blooded insides and the cold water outside.) | 10 |
| (Inference) | 7. What is the effect of the great amount of movement? (The otters have to eat a lot because they use up a lot of energy; they eat one-quarter of their body weight daily.) | 10 |
| (Word meaning) | 8. What does "extinct" mean? (No longer existing; no longer living; having died out) | 10 |
| (Inference) | 9. Why were otters hunted until they almost didn't exist anymore? (For their fur; it is very soft.) | 10 |

[20]Ibid., p. 397.

(Main idea)          10. What is the main idea of the story? (The sea otters are the most          10
                          playful aquarium residents because they need to move around a lot
                          to keep warm.)

Scoring Scale

| *Levels* | *Comprehension Errors* |
|----------|------------------------|
| Independent | 0–10 points |
| Instructional | 11–25 points |
| Frustration | 50 points or more |

# Level 7

*ORAL READING (263)*[21]

> **Introduction: Read this story aloud to find out what some courageous children do. (Etienne is pronounced ā-tyen′.) Then I will ask you questions about the story.**

The voice came from out of the sky, "Hey fellows, quick, grab those ropes and pull me into the wind as if I were a kite. Hurry!"

Looking up, the young people were startled to see a man waving wildly at them from a strange banana-shaped flying balloon—a balloon that was about to crash!

Sara reacted quickly and grabbed one of the ropes that dangled near her. But Sara could not even stop the flying contraption, let alone pull it in the other direction. As she attempted to dig her heels into the ground, the balloon nearly toppled her.

"Boys, don't just stand there. Help her," the man in the balloon shouted at Etienne and Louis.

Rushing to help their sister, the boys grabbed other ropes trailing from the balloon and frantically tugged at the runaway flying machine. Finally, the three of them were able to change the direction of the balloon, carrying it into the wind as the aeronaut had requested. The flying machine bobbed up like a kite.

As the young people pulled the balloon down, following the aeronaut's instructions, a crowd began to gather. The moment the flier was safe on the ground, he was surrounded by a large crowd of curious people, all talking at once.

Sara realized that the man she had rescued was the famous Monsieur Santos-Dumont, the wealthy Brazilian inventor and daredevil who predicted people would someday fly like birds.

"Where are the young people? They are the real heroes of this escape from the jaws of death," she heard him shout over the crowd.

## Comprehension Questions

|  |  | Points |
|---|---|---|
| (Literal) | 1. Describe what the children saw when they looked up in the sky. (A strange banana-shaped balloon that was about to crash) | 10 |
| (Inference) | 2. How do we know the person in the balloon didn't expect the girl to help him? (He called out to the fellows.) | 10 |
| (Literal) | 3. What did he want the fellows to do? (To grab the ropes and pull him into the wind as if he were a kite) | 10 |
| (Literal) | 4. What happened when Sara tried to help? (She couldn't stop the balloon, let alone pull it in the other direction.) | 10 |
| (Word meaning) | 5. What is an aeronaut? (Someone who navigates in the air, especially a balloon) | 10 |
| (Inference) | 6. What was needed to keep the balloon afloat? (The force of the wind) | 10 |
| (Inference) | 7. What did the young people have to be able to do to pull down the balloon? (Follow the aeronaut's directions) | 10 |

[21]David Fulton, "Through Skies Never Sailed," Level 13, *Star Walk* (Needham, MA: Silver Burdett & Ginn, 1989), pp. 353–54.

| | | |
|---|---|---|
| (Inference) | 8. What kind of person was Monsieur Santos-Dumont? State four characteristics. Give proof for your answer. (Creative—the story said he was an inventor; reckless, adventurous—it said he was a daredevil; well-known—it said he was famous; rich—it said he was wealthy.) | 10 |
| (Literal) | 9. What did Monsieur Santos-Dumont predict people would someday be able to do? (Fly like birds) | 10 |
| (Main idea) | 10. What is the main idea of the story? (A courageous girl and her brothers rescue an aeronaut by helping to bring his flying balloon safely to the ground.) | 10 |

Scoring Scale

| Levels | Word Recognition Errors | Comprehension Errors |
|---|---|---|
| Independent | 0–3 | 0–10 points |
| Instructional | 4–13 | 11–25 points |
| Frustration | 26 or more | 50 points or more |

*SILENT READING*[22]

**Introduction: Monsieur Santos-Dumont is very grateful to the children for saving his life. Read the story to see why he comes to the children's home. Then I will ask you questions about the story. Read it carefully.**

"The purpose of my visit in fact is related to the events of this afternoon. I came to invite your family for an excursion in one of my balloons."

Silence filled the Cote parlor as all eyes turned to Sara's father, awaiting his reply. "I don't wish to seem overly conservative or closed minded, Monsieur Santos-Dumont, but I wouldn't consider air travel sufficiently safe to risk my whole family. This afternoon's events are evidence of that."

"I certainly wouldn't ask you to endanger your family, but flying in a balloon, which is merely a big bag filled with hydrogen, has long been demonstrated to be a safe sport.

"I wouldn't suggest taking you in a craft such as the one I was flying this afternoon. That was a 'dirigible.' Its design is the latest breakthrough in the attempt to control the direction of flight. It's a balloon that has a gasoline engine suspended beneath it to direct its movement. Unfortunately, my colleagues and I have yet to work out all the problems. But we will. In any case, the dirigible may soon be obsolete. I recently heard a report at a meeting of the Aero Club, and I understand that some Americans have actually built a glider of some sort that is heavier than the air, and it is said they use a gasoline engine to power it. Now, that is really incredible."

Comprehension Questions

| | | Points |
|---|---|---|
| (Literal) | 1. What was the purpose of Monsieur Santos-Dumont's visit to the children's family? (To invite them on an excursion in one of his balloons) | 10 |
| (Word meaning) | 2. What is an excursion? (A short pleasure trip) | 10 |
| (Literal) | 3. How does the children's father feel about air travel? (He feels it is not safe.) | 10 |
| (Inference) | 4. What evidence does the children's father give to back up his feelings? (The afternoon's events) | 10 |
| (Literal) | 5. What does Monsieur Santos-Dumont claim is safe? (Flying in a balloon filled with hydrogen) | 10 |
| (Literal) | 6. What kind of machine was Monsieur Santos-Dumont flying in the afternoon? (A dirigible, which has a gasoline engine suspended beneath it to direct its movement) | 10 |
| (Inference) | 7. How do we know Monsieur Santos-Dumont is not working alone on developing the dirigible? (The story says that he and his colleagues have yet to work out the details.) | 10 |
| (Literal) | 8. What does Monsieur Santos-Dumont feel is incredible? (The glider that the Americans have built, which is heavier than air and uses a gasoline engine to power it) | 10 |
| (Inference) | 9. What does Monsieur Santos-Dumont feel the Americans' flying machine will do to the dirigible? (Make the dirigible obsolete, that is, no longer useful or in use) | 10 |

[22]Ibid., p. 356.

(Main idea)      10. What is the main idea of the story? (Monsieur Santos-Dumont tries to      10
persuade the children's father to allow his family to go on a short
trip in a balloon Monsieur Santos-Dumont insists is safe.)

Scoring Scale

| *Levels* | *Comprehension Errors* |
|---|---|
| Independent | 0–10 points |
| Instructional | 11–25 points |
| Frustration | 50 points or more |

# Level 8

*ORAL READING (275)*[23]

**Introduction: Read this story aloud to find out why Lo Tung came to America. Then I will ask you questions about the story.**

Lo Tung leaned against the rattling wall of the freight car. Beneath him the floor moved as the wheels cracked over the rails. It was a long time since he'd sat or walked on anything steady. First there had been the long days and nights on the Pacific Mail Steamship that had brought him from China, then the riverboat from San Francisco to Sacramento, then the train, waiting on the levee.

He hadn't had time for more than a glimpse of the strange, iron monster belching smoke before the boss man had hustled them aboard. It was hard to believe that he was here now, in this freight car along with other Chinese workers, rolling eastward across America.

Lo Tung looked sideways at his friend, Wei. Wei was fifteen years old, too, and as small and thin as Lo Tung.

"Not more than a hundred pounds, either of you," the agent had said in disgust. "You two will not be able to do the heavy railroad work."

"Don't worry. We are strong," Lo Tung had said. He had not added, "Ho Sen was strong, the strongest man in our village. And he was killed building the American railway." Now Ho Sen's bones lay somewhere in this strange country. And Chen Chi Yuen. He had gone and never been heard from again.

Sitting now in the freight car, thinking about the work, Lo Tung flexed his muscles. Strong for the work. Of course, strong and fearless.

It was growing dark. They had been closed in here together for hours, so many of them from the ship. The air was used up and the smells were bad.

## Comprehension Questions

|  |  | Points |
|---|---|---|
| (Literal) | 1. What kind of car was Lo Tung in? (A freight car) | 10 |
| (Inference) | 2. How do we know Lo Tung has never seen a train before? (Lo Tung thought the locomotive was a strange, iron monster. It wouldn't have been strange if he had seen it before.) | 10 |
| (Inference) | 3. How do we know it has been a long time since Lo Tung was on land? (The story states that it was a long time since he was on anything steady.) | 10 |
| (Literal) | 4. What means of transportation was used to get Lo Tung to his destination? (Steamship, riverboat, and train) | 10 |
| (Inference) | 5. How long did Lo Tung have between getting off the riverboat and boarding the train? (Not long; he only had time to catch a glimpse of the train before he was hustled aboard.) | 10 |
| (Literal) | 6. What was the agent concerned about? (That Lo Tung and his friend were too thin to work on the railroad) | 10 |
| (Literal) | 7. What had happened to Ho Sen? (He had been killed working on the American railroad.) | 10 |

---

[23]Eve Bunting, "It's Not the Great Wall, But It Will Last Forever," Level 14, *Worlds Beyond* (Needham, MA: Silver Burdett & Ginn, 1989), pp. 238–39.

| (Inference) | 8. Why were the smells on the freight bad? (There was not much air, and there were many people crowded together.) | 10 |
| (Literal) | 9. In what direction was the train rolling across America? (Eastward) | 10 |
| (Main idea) | 10. What is the main idea of the story? (Lo Tung's journey from China to America to work on the American railroad has been long and hard.) | 10 |

Scoring Scale

| Levels | Word Recognition Errors | Comprehension Errors |
|---|---|---|
| Independent | 0–3 | 0–10 points |
| Instructional | 4–14 | 11–20 points |
| Frustration | 28 or more | 50 points or more |

*SILENT READING*[24]

**Introduction: Agents had advertised in Lo Tung's village for laborers to help build the railroad in California. They offered houses to live in, plenty of food, and thirty dollars a month. The passage to go was fifty-four dollars. Read the story to find out why Lo Tung signed on. Then I will ask you questions about the story. Read it carefully.**

Fifty-four dollars was a fortune, and impossible for his mother! The agent had allowed them to borrow from him. That was when he'd complained of Lo Tung's size.

"Not a penny of your wages will be yours till you pay me back," he had warned.

Lo Tung had agreed. He would have agreed to almost anything. Not that he wanted to go to America. The thought of leaving his home brought tears to his eyes. But it was clearly his duty. He was, after all, the eldest son. Since his father's death the family responsibility had been his. If he went, his debt to the agent would be cleared in two months. Then he could begin sending money home for his mother and his sisters, and his little brother. He had to believe that he could save enough to go home himself some day.

Thinking of home here in the heat of the freight car made loneliness rise in him like water in a swamp. Fear was bad, but loneliness was worse. He would not allow himself to remember.

"We are slowing," Wei said. "I can see through a crack."

Someone else announced, "We are here."

Tired men and boys staggered up, swaying, hoisting their bedrolls. As the train chugged to a stop they waited quietly for what was to come.

When the doors opened Lo Tung saw that it was night outside, the sky filled with a million crystal stars.

"American stars," he whispered to Wei, pointing upward.

"Are they the same that shine over China or . . . "

"Out! Everyone out!" Men waited beside the train, big, bulky men who cast massive shadows.

"Hurry! Get a move on!"

The words were not in Lo Tung's language but he understood the tone.

Comprehension Questions

*Points*

| | | |
|---|---|---|
| (Literal) | 1. How were Lo Tung and his mother able to get enough money to go to America? (The agent had allowed them to borrow from him.) | 10 |
| (Inference) | 2. Why was Lo Tung going to America? (Because his family needed the money; he couldn't earn the money they needed in his village.) | 10 |
| (Inference) | 3. Why did he feel he had to support his family? (Because his father was dead and he was the eldest son) | 10 |
| (Literal) | 4. How long would it take to clear his debt to the agent? (Two months) | 10 |
| (Inference) | 5. Does Lo Tung expect to stay in America? Explain. (No, the story states that he had to believe that he could save enough to go home himself some day.) | 10 |

[24]Ibid., p. 240.

| | | |
|---|---|---|
| (Literal) | 6. What does Lo Tung feel is worse than fear? (Loneliness) | 10 |
| (Inference) | 7. What simile is used to describe Lo Tung's loneliness? Explain the simile. (Loneliness rose in him like water in a swamp; when it rains, water in a swamp rises very quickly, and that's how fast his loneliness rose.) | 10 |
| (Inference) | 8. How do we know it was a clear night when they arrived at their destination? (The sky was filled with a million crystal stars.) | 10 |
| (Literal) | 9. What kind of men were waiting beside the train? (Big, bulky men who cast massive shadows) | 10 |
| (Main idea) | 10. What is the main idea of the story? (Even though Lo Tung does not want to leave his family, he goes to America so he can earn money for his family in China.) | 10 |

Scoring Scale

| Levels | Comprehension Errors |
|---|---|
| Independent | 0–10 points |
| Instructional | 11–20 points |
| Frustration | 50 points or more |

# Teacher's Resource Guide of Language Transfer Issues for English Language Learners

## GRAMMAR TRANSFER ISSUES FOR TEN LANGUAGES

The following chart identifies areas in which speakers of various primary languages may have some difficulty in acquiring English grammar (syntax). The type of transfer error and its cause is outlined for each grammatical category.[1]

**NOUNS**

| Grammar Point | Type of Transfer Error in English | Language Background | Cause of Transfer Difficulty |
|---|---|---|---|
| **Plural forms** | omission of plural marker –s<br>*I have 5 book.* | Cantonese, Haitian Creole, Hmong, Khmer, Korean, Tagalog, Vietnamese | Nouns do not change form to show the plural in the primary language. |
| **Possessive forms** | avoidance of *'s* to describe possession<br>*the children of my sister* instead of *my sister's children* | Haitian Creole, Hmong, Khmer, Spanish, Tagalog, Vietnamese | The use of a prepositional phrase to express possession reflects the only structure or a more common structure in the primary language. |
| | no marker for possessive forms<br>*house my friend* instead of *my friend's house* | Haitian Creole, Khmer, Vietnamese | A noun's owner comes after the object in the primary language. |
| **Count versus noncount nouns** | use of plural forms for English noncount nouns<br>*the furnitures, the color of her hairs* | Haitian Creole, Russian, Spanish, Tagalog | Nouns that are count and noncount differ between English and the primary language. |

## ARTICLES

| Grammar Point | Type of Transfer Error in English | Language Background | Cause of Transfer Difficulty |
|---|---|---|---|
| | omission of article<br><br>*He has job.*<br>*His dream is to become lawyer, not teacher.* | Cantonese, Haitian Creole, Hmong, Khmer, Korean, Russian, Tagalog, Vietnamese | Articles are either lacking or the distinction between *a* and *the* is not paralleled in the primary language. |
| | omission of articles in certain contexts such as to identify a profession<br><br>*He is teacher.* | Spanish | The article is not used in Spanish in this context, but it is needed in English. |
| | overuse of articles<br><br>*The honesty is the best policy.*<br>*This food is popular in the Japan.*<br>*I like the cats.* | Arabic, Haitian Creole, Hmong, Spanish, Tagalog | The article is used in the primary language in places where it isn't used in English. |
| | use of *one* for *a/an*<br><br>*He is one engineer.* | Haitian Creole, Hmong, Vietnamese | Learners sometimes confuse the articles *a/an* with *one* since articles either do not exist in the primary language or serve a different function. |

## PRONOUNS

| Grammar Point | Type of Transfer Error in English | Language Background | Cause of Transfer Difficulty |
|---|---|---|---|
| **Personal pronouns, gender** | use of pronouns with inappropriate gender<br><br>*He is my sister.* | Cantonese, Haitian Creole, Hmong, Khmer, Korean, Tagalog | The third person pronoun in the primary language is gender free. The same pronoun is used where English uses masculine, feminine, and neuter pronouns, resulting in confusion of pronoun forms in English. |

(*continued*)

**PRONOUNS** (*continued*)

| Grammar Point | Type of Transfer Error in English | Language Background | Cause of Transfer Difficulty |
|---|---|---|---|
| | use of pronouns with inappropriate gender<br><br>*He is my sister.* | Spanish | In Spanish, subject pronouns are dropped in everyday speech and the verb conveys third-person agreement, effectively collapsing the two pronouns and causing transfer difficulty for subject pronouns in English. |
| | use of inappropriate gender, particularly with neuter nouns<br><br>*The house is big. She is beautiful.* | Russian, Spanish | Inanimate nouns have feminine and masculine gender in the primary language, and the gender may be carried over into English. |
| **Personal pronoun forms** | confusion of subject and object pronoun forms<br><br>*Him hit me.*<br>*I like she.*<br>*Let we go.* | Cantonese, Hmong, Khmer | The same pronoun form is used for *he/him, she/her,* and in some primary languages for *I/me* and *we/us.* |
| | use of incorrect number for pronouns<br><br>*I saw many yellow flowers. It was pretty.* | Cantonese, Korean | There is no number agreement in the primary language. |
| | omission of subject pronouns<br><br>*Michael isn't here. Is in school.* | Korean, Russian, Spanish | Subject pronouns may be dropped in the primary language and the verb ending supplies information on number and/or gender. |
| | omission of object pronouns<br><br>*That man is very rude, so nobody likes.* | Korean, Vietnamese | Direct objects are frequently dropped in the primary language. |
| | omission of pronouns in clauses<br><br>*If not have jobs, they will not have food.* | Cantonese, Vietnamese | A subordinate clause at the beginning of a sentence does not require a subject in the primary language. |

**PRONOUNS** (*continued*)

| Grammar Point | Type of Transfer Error in English | Language Background | Cause of Transfer Difficulty |
|---|---|---|---|
| | use of pronouns with subject nouns<br><br>*This car, it runs very fast.*<br><br>*Your friend, he seems so nice.*<br><br>*My parents, they live in Vietnam.* | Hmong, Vietnamese | This type of redundant structure reflects the popular "topic-comment" approach used in the primary language: The speaker mentions a topic and then makes a comment on it. |
| | avoidance of pronouns by repetition of nouns<br><br>*Sara visits her grandfather every Sunday, and Sara makes a meal.* | Korean, Vietnamese | It is common in the primary language to repeat nouns rather than to use pronouns. |
| **Pronoun *one*** | omission of the pronoun *one*<br><br>*I saw two nice cars, and I like the small.* | Russian, Spanish, Tagalog | Adjectives can be used on their own in the primary language, whereas English often requires a noun or *one*. |
| **Possessive forms** | confusion of possessive forms<br><br>*The book is my.* | Cantonese, Hmong, Vietnamese | Cantonese and Hmong speakers tend to omit final *n,* creating confusion between *my* and *mine.* |

**ADJECTIVES**

| Grammar Point | Type of Transfer Error in English | Language Background | Cause of Transfer Difficulty |
|---|---|---|---|
| | position of adjectives after nouns<br><br>*I read a book interesting.* | Haitian Creole, Hmong, Khmer, Spanish, Vietnamese | Adjectives commonly come after nouns in the primary language. |
| | position of adjectives before certain pronouns<br><br>*This is interesting something.* | Cantonese, Korean | Adjectives always come before words they modify in the primary language. |
| **Comparison** | omission of markers for comparison<br><br>*She is smart than me.* | Khmer | Since there are no suffixes or inflections in Khmer, the tendency is to omit them in English. |

(*continued*)

## ADJECTIVES (*continued*)

| Grammar Point | Type of Transfer Error in English | Language Background | Cause of Transfer Difficulty |
|---|---|---|---|
| | avoidance of -*er* and -*est* endings<br><br>*I am more old than my brother.* | Hmong, Khmer, Korean, Spanish | Comparative and superlative are usually formed with separate words in the primary language, the equivalent of *more* and *most* in English. |
| **Confusion of -*ing* and -*ed* forms** | confusion of -*ing* and -*ed* forms<br><br>*The movie was <u>bored</u>.*<br><br>*I am very <u>interesting</u> in sports.* | Cantonese, Khmer, Korean, Spanish | The adjective forms in the primary language that correspond to the ones in English do not have active and passive meanings. In Korean, for many adjectives, the same form is used for both active and passive meanings *boring* versus *bored*. |

## VERBS

| Grammar Point | Type of Transfer Error in English | Language Background | Cause of Transfer Difficulty |
|---|---|---|---|
| **Present tense** | omission of *s* in present tense, third person agreement<br><br>*She <u>go</u> to school every day.* | Cantonese, Haitian Creole, Hmong, Khmer, Korean, Tagalog, Vietnamese | There is no verb agreement in the primary language. |
| | problems with irregular subject-verb agreement<br><br>*Sue and Ed <u>has</u> a new house.* | Cantonese, Hmong, Khmer, Korean, Tagalog | Verbs forms do not change to indicate the number of the subject in the primary language. |
| **Past tense** | omission of tense markers<br><br>*I <u>study</u> English yesterday.*<br><br>*I <u>give</u> it to him yesterday.* | Cantonese, Haitian Creole, Hmong, Khmer, Korean, Tagalog, Vietnamese | Verbs in the primary language do not change form to express tense. |
| | confusion of present form and simple past of regular verbs<br><br>*I <u>give</u> it to him yesterday.* | Cantonese, Spanish | Speakers of the primary language have difficulty recognizing that merely a vowel shift in the middle of the verb, rather than a change in the ending of the verb, is sufficient to produce a change of tense in irregular verbs. |

**VERBS** (*continued*)

| Grammar Point | Type of Transfer Error in English | Language Background | Cause of Transfer Difficulty |
|---|---|---|---|
| | incorrect use of present for the future<br>*I come tomorrow.* | Cantonese, Korean | The primary language allows the use of present tense for the future. |
| **In negative statements** | omission of helping verbs in negative statements<br>*I no understand.*<br>*I not get in university.* | Cantonese, Korean, Russian, Spanish, Tagalog | Helping verbs are not used in negative statements in the primary language. |
| **Perfect tenses** | avoidance of present perfect where it should be used<br>*I live here for two years.* | Haitian Creole, Russian, Tagalog, Vietnamese | The verb form either doesn't exist in the primary language or has a different function. |
| | use of present perfect where past perfect should be used<br>*Yesterday I have done that.* | Khmer, Korean | In the primary language a past marker, e.g., *yesterday,* is inserted to indicate a completed action and no other change is necessary. In English when a past marker is used, the verb form must change to past perfect instead of present perfect. |
| **Past continuous** | use of past continuous for recurring action in the past<br>*When I was young, I was studying a lot.* | Korean, Spanish, Tagalog | In the primary language, the past continuous form can be used in contexts in which English uses the expression *used to* or the simple past. |
| **Main verb** | omission of main verb<br>*Criticize people not good.* | Cantonese | Unlike English, Cantonese does not require an infinitive marker when using a verb as a noun. |
| | use of two or more main verbs in one clause without any connectors<br>*I took a book went studied at the library.* | Hmong | In Hmong verbs can be connected without *and* or any other conjunction (serial verbs). |
| **Linking verbs** | omission of linking verb<br>*He hungry.* | Cantonese, Haitian Creole, Hmong, Khmer, Russian, Vietnamese | The verb *be* is not required in all sentences. In some primary languages, it is implied in the adjective form. In others the concept is expressed as a verb. |

(*continued*)

**VERBS** (*continued*)

| Grammar Point | Type of Transfer Error in English | Language Background | Cause of Transfer Difficulty |
|---|---|---|---|
| **Passive voice** | omission of helping verb *be* in passive voice<br>*The food finished.* | Cantonese, Vietnamese | Passive voice in the primary language does not require a helping verb. |
| | avoidance of passive constructions<br>*They speak Creole here.*<br>*One speaks Creole here.*<br>avoiding the alternate<br>*Creole is spoken here.* | Haitian Creole | Passive constructions do not exist in Haitian Creole. |
| **Transitive verbs versus intransitive verbs** | confusion of transitive and intransitive verbs<br>*He married with a nice girl.* | Cantonese, Korean, Russian, Spanish, Tagalog | Verbs that do and do not take a direct object differ between English and the primary language. |
| **Phrasal verbs** | confusion of related phrasal verbs<br>*I look after the word in the dictionary.*<br>instead of *I look up the word in the dictionary.* | Korean, Russian, Spanish | Phrasal verbs do not exist in the primary language. There is often confusion over their meaning in English. |
| ***have* versus *be*** | use of *have* instead of *be*<br>*I have hunger.*<br>*I have right.* | Spanish | Some Spanish constructions use *have* where English uses *be*. |

**ADVERBS**

| Grammar Point | Type of Transfer Error in English | Language Background | Cause of Transfer Difficulty |
|---|---|---|---|
| | use of adjective form where adverb form is needed<br>*Walk quiet.* | Haitian Creole, Hmong, Khmer | There are no suffix-derived adverb forms in the primary language, and the adjective form is used after the verb. |
| | placement of adverbs before verbs<br>*At ten o'clock this morning my plane landed.*<br>avoiding the alternate, *My plane landed at ten o'clock this morning.* | Cantonese, Korean | Adverbs usually come before verbs in the primary language, and this tendency is carried over into English. |

## PREPOSITIONS

| Grammar Point | Type of Transfer Error in English | Language Background | Cause of Transfer Difficulty |
|---|---|---|---|
| | omission of prepositions<br><br>*Money does not grow trees.* | Cantonese | There are no exact equivalents of English prepositions in Cantonese although there are words to mark location and movement. |

## COMPLEX SENTENCES

| Grammar Point | Type of Transfer Error in English | Language Background | Cause of Transfer Difficulty |
|---|---|---|---|
| **Relative clauses** | omission of relative pronouns<br><br>*My grandfather was a generous man helped everyone.* | Vietnamese | Relative pronouns are not required in Vietnamese. |
| | incorrect pronoun used to introduce a relative clause<br><br>*the house <u>who</u> is big* | Hmong | Hmong used the same forms of relative pronouns for both personal and inanimate antecedents. |
| **Adverbial clauses** | inclusion of additional connecting word<br><br>*Because he was reckless, <u>so</u> he caused an accident.*<br><br>*Although my parents are poor, <u>but</u> they are very generous.* | Cantonese, Korean, Vietnamese | The primary language sometimes uses a "balancing word" in the main clause. |
| | use of incorrect tenses in time clauses<br><br>*She <u>speaks</u> French before she studied English.*<br><br>*After she <u>comes</u> home, it was raining.*<br><br>*We will go to the beach if the weather <u>will be</u> nice.* | Cantonese, Hmong, Tagalog, Vietnamese, | The primary language lacks tense markers so that matching the tenses of two verbs in one sentence correctly can be difficult. Learners may also try to analyze the tense needed in English according to meaning, which in some cases can result in the use of an incorrect tense. |
| ***If* versus *when*** | Confusion of *if* and *when*<br><br>*If you get there, call me!*<br><br>instead of *When you get there, call me!* | Korean, Tagalog | The primary language has one expression that covers the use of English *if* and *when* for the future. |

(*continued*)

## INFINITIVES AND GERUNDS

| Grammar Point | Type of Transfer Error in English | Language Background | Cause of Transfer Difficulty |
|---|---|---|---|
| | use of present tense verbs in places where gerunds or infinitives are used in English<br><br>*Stop walk.*<br><br>*I want go there.* | Haitian, Creole, Khmer, Korean | Either the *–ing* form does not exist in the primary language, or learners tend to use present tense verbs instead of gerunds even if they do exist [Haitian Creole]. |
| | use of *for* in infinitive phrases<br><br>*They went for to see the movie.* | Spanish | Spanish uses a prepositional form in similar constructions, which is carried over into English and translated as *for*. |

## SENTENCE STRUCTURE

| Grammar Point | Type of Transfer Error in English | Language Background | Cause of Transfer Difficulty |
|---|---|---|---|
| | omission of object<br><br>*He dyed [his hair].*<br><br>*Yes, I want [some].* | Korean | Korean tends to omit objects and noun phrases after verbs. |
| | lack of variety in the position of clauses<br><br>*Because you weren't at home and I couldn't find [you], I left.*<br><br>avoiding the alternate, *I left because you weren't at home and I couldn't find [you].* | Korean | Since main clauses always come last in Korean, there is a tendency to put the main clause last in English. This is not an error in English, but it leads to a lack of sentence variety. |
| | clauses that describe earlier actions come first<br><br>*After I finish my homework, I will watch TV.*<br><br>avoiding the alternate, *I will watch TV after I finish my homework.* | Cantonese, Korean | The pattern in the primary language is to describe what happens first while later occurrences follow. This is not an error in English, but it leads to a lack of sentence variety. |
| | placement of phrase with the indirect object before the direct object<br><br>*They gave to the girl the book.* | Spanish | The phrase with the indirect object can come before the direct object in Spanish. |

## SENTENCE STRUCTURE *(continued)*

| Grammar Point | Type of Transfer Error in English | Language Background | Cause of Transfer Difficulty |
|---|---|---|---|
| | placement of modifiers between verb and direct object *She speaks <u>very well</u> English.* | Korean, Spanish | Word order, including the placement of adverbials, is freer in the primary language than in English. |
| | use of double negatives *I <u>no</u> see <u>nobody</u>.* | Spanish | Spanish requires double negatives in many sentence structures. |
| | use of clauses for other structures *I want <u>that you help me</u>.* | Russian, Spanish | Verbs that take direct objects versus those that require clauses differ in the primary language and English. |

## QUESTIONS

| Grammar Point | Type of Transfer Error in English | Language Background | Cause of Transfer Difficulty |
|---|---|---|---|
| | avoidance of English inverted question forms in yes/no questions in favor of tag questions or intonation *You come tomorrow, OK?* *He goes to school with you?* | Cantonese, Haitian Creole, Khmer, Korean, Russian, Tagalog, Vietnamese | The primary language doesn't use subject-verb inversion in questions. |
| | lack of subject-verb inversion in questions with helping verbs *When she will be home?* *Where you are going?* | Cantonese, Hmong, Russian, Tagalog | In the primary language, word order is the same in some questions and statements, depending on the context. |
| | omission of *do* or *did* in questions *Where you went?* | Haitian Creole, Hmong, Khmer, Korean, Russian, Spanish, Tagalog | In the primary language, there is no exact counterpart to the *do/did* verb in questions. |

*(continued)*

**QUESTIONS** (*continued*)

| Grammar Point | Type of Transfer Error in English | Language Background | Cause of Transfer Difficulty |
|---|---|---|---|
| **Yes/no questions** | incorrect answer form for yes/no questions<br><br>*A: Do you want more food?*<br>*B: I want.*<br>*A: Do you have a pen?*<br>*B: I not have.* | Cantonese, Hmong, Khmer, Korean, Russian | In the primary language, learners tend to answer yes by repeating the verb in the question. They tend to say no by using *not* and repeating the verb. |
| | positive answer to negative question<br><br>*A: Aren't you going?*<br>*B: Yes.* when the person is not going | Cantonese, Korean, Russian | The appropriate response pattern differs between the primary language and English. |
| **Tag questions** | incorrect tag questions<br><br>*You want to go home, are you?* | Cantonese, Khmer, Korean, Vietnamese | The primary language has no exact counterpart to a tag question, forms them differently, or does not add *do/did* to questions. |

# PHONICS TRANSFER ISSUES FOR SEVEN LANGUAGES

*Sound Transfer (Phonology)*

The symbol • identifies areas in which these primary language speakers may have some difficulty pronouncing and perceiving spoken English. The sound may not exist in the primary language, may exist but be pronounced somewhat differently, or may be confused with another sound. Sound production and perception issues impact phonics instruction.

**CONSONANTS**

| Sound | Spanish | Vietnamese | Hmong | Cantonese | Haitian Creole | Korean | Khmer |
|---|---|---|---|---|---|---|---|
| /b/ as in bat | | | • | • | | • | |
| /k/ as in cat and kite | | | • | | | | |
| /d/ as in dog | | | | • | | • | |
| /f/ as in fan | | | | | | • | |
| /g/ as in goat | | | • | • | | • | • |
| /h/ as in hen | | | | | • | | |
| /j/ as in jacket | • | • | • | • | | • | |
| /l/ as in lemon | | | | | | • | |
| /m/ as in money | | | | | | | |

## CONSONANTS (*continued*)

| Sound | Spanish | Vietnamese | Hmong | Cantonese | Haitian Creole | Korean | Khmer |
|---|:---:|:---:|:---:|:---:|:---:|:---:|:---:|
| /n/ as in nail | | | | | | | |
| /p/ as in pig | | | • | | | | |
| /r/ as in rabbit | • | | • | • | • | • | |
| /s/ as in sun | | | • | | | | |
| /t/ as in teen | | • | • | | | | |
| /v/ as in video | • | | | • | | • | • |
| /w/ as in wagon | • | | • | | | | • |
| /y/ as in yo-yo | | | | | | | |
| /z/ as in zebra | • | | • | • | | • | • |
| /kw/ as in queen | | | • | | | | |
| /ks/ as in Xray | | | • | • | | | |

## SHORT VOWELS

| Sound | Spanish | Vietnamese | Hmong | Cantonese | Haitian Creole | Korean | Khmer |
|---|:---:|:---:|:---:|:---:|:---:|:---:|:---:|
| short *a* as in hat | • | • | | • | | • | |
| short *e* as in set | • | | • | • | • | • | |
| short *i* as in sit | • | • | • | • | • | • | |
| short *o* as in hot | • | | • | | | • | |
| short *u* as in cup | • | | • | • | • | • | |

## LONG VOWELS

| Sound | Spanish | Vietnamese | Hmong | Cantonese | Haitian Creole | Korean | Khmer |
|---|:---:|:---:|:---:|:---:|:---:|:---:|:---:|
| long *a* as in date | | | • | • | | | |
| long *e* as in be | | | | • | | • | |
| long *i* as in ice | | | | • | | | |
| long *o* as in road | | | • | • | | | |
| long *u* as in true | | | | • | | • | |

## VOWEL PATTERNS

| Sound | Spanish | Vietnamese | Hmong | Cantonese | Haitian Creole | Korean | Khmer |
|---|:---:|:---:|:---:|:---:|:---:|:---:|:---:|
| *oo* as in book | • | • | • | | • | • | • |
| *aw* as in saw | • | | | | | • | |

(*continued*)

## DIPHTHONGS

| Sound | Spanish | Vietnamese | Hmong | Cantonese | Haitian Creole | Korean | Khmer |
|---|---|---|---|---|---|---|---|
| *oy* as in b<u>oy</u> | | | • | | | | |
| *ow* as in h<u>ow</u> | • | | | | | | |

## R-CONTROLLED VOWELS

| Sound | Spanish | Vietnamese | Hmong | Cantonese | Haitian Creole | Korean | Khmer |
|---|---|---|---|---|---|---|---|
| *ir* as in b<u>ir</u>d | • | • | • | • | • | • | • |
| *ar* as in h<u>ar</u>d | • | • | • | • | • | • | • |
| *or* as in f<u>or</u>m | • | • | • | • | • | • | • |
| *air* as in h<u>air</u> | • | • | • | • | • | • | • |
| *ear* as in h<u>ear</u> | • | • | • | • | • | • | • |

## CONSONANT DIGRAPHS

| Sound | Spanish | Vietnamese | Hmong | Cantonese | Haitian Creole | Korean | Khmer |
|---|---|---|---|---|---|---|---|
| *sh* as in <u>sh</u>oe | • | • | | • | | | • |
| *ch* as in <u>ch</u>ain | | • | • | | | | |
| *th* as in <u>th</u>ink | • | • | • | • | • | • | • |
| *ng* as in si<u>ng</u> | • | | • | | • | | |

## CONSONANT BLENDS

| Sound | Spanish | Vietnamese | Hmong | Cantonese | Haitian Creole | Korean | Khmer |
|---|---|---|---|---|---|---|---|
| *bl*, *tr*, *dr*, etc, (start of words) as in <u>bl</u>ack, <u>tr</u>ee, <u>dr</u>ess | | • | • | • | • | • | |
| *ld*, *nt*, *rt*, etc. (end of words) as in co<u>ld</u>, te<u>nt</u>, sta<u>rt</u> | | • | • | • | • | • | • |

# SOUND-SYMBOL TRANSFER (PHONICS)

The following chart identifies sound-symbol transfer issues for four languages that use the roman alphabet. (The remaining three do not). The symbol • identifies symbols which do not represent the corresponding sound in the writing system of the primary language.

## CONSONANTS

| Sound-Symbols | Spanish | Vietnamese | Hmong | Haitian Creole |
|---|---|---|---|---|
| *b* as in bat | | | • | |
| *c* as in cat | | • | • | • |
| as in cent | | • | • | |
| *d* as in dog | | | | |
| *f* as in fish | | | | |
| *g* as in goat | | | • | |
| as in giant | • | | • | |
| *h* as in hen | • | | | |
| *j* as in jacket | • | • | • | |
| *k* as in kite | | | • | |
| *l* as in lemon | | | | |
| *m* as in moon | | | | |
| *n* as in nice | | | | |
| *p* as in pig | | | | |
| *qu* as in queen | • | | • | • |
| *r* as in rabbit | • | | • | |
| *s* as in sun | | | • | |
| *t* as in teen | | | • | |
| *v* as in video | • | | | |
| *w* as in wagon | | • | • | |
| *x* as in Xray | | • | • | • |
| *y* as in yo-yo | | | | |
| *z* as in zebra | • | • | • | |

## CONSONANT DIGRAPHS

| Sound-Symbols | Spanish | Vietnamese | Hmong | Haitian Creole |
|---|---|---|---|---|
| *sh* as in shoe | • | | | |
| *ch* as in chair | | | | • |
| *th* as in think | • | | | • |
| as in that | | | | |

(*continued*)

## VOWELS AND VOWEL PATTERNS

| Sound-Symbols | Spanish | Vietnamese | Hmong | Haitian Creole |
|---|:---:|:---:|:---:|:---:|
| *a* as in b<u>a</u>t | • | | • | |
| *aCe* as in d<u>a</u>te | • | • | | |
| *ai* as in r<u>ai</u>n | • | • | • | • |
| *ay* as in d<u>ay</u> | • | | • | • |
| *au* as in <u>au</u>thor | • | • | • | • |
| *aw* as in s<u>aw</u> | • | • | • | • |
| *e* as in b<u>e</u>t | • | | • | • |
| *ee* as in s<u>ee</u>d | • | • | • | • |
| *ea* as in t<u>ea</u> | • | • | • | • |
| *ew* as in f<u>ew</u> | • | • | • | • |
| *i* as in s<u>i</u>t | • | | • | • |
| *iCe* as in p<u>i</u>pe | • | • | • | • |
| *o* as in h<u>o</u>t | • | | • | • |
| *o* as in r<u>o</u>de | • | • | • | • |
| *oo* as in m<u>oo</u>n | • | • | • | • |
| *oo* as in b<u>oo</u>k | • | | • | • |
| *oa* as in b<u>oa</u>t | • | • | • | • |
| *ow* as in r<u>ow</u> | • | • | • | • |
| *ow* as in h<u>ow</u> | • | • | • | • |
| *ou* as in s<u>ou</u>nd | • | • | • | • |
| *oi* as in b<u>oi</u>l | | | • | • |
| *oy* as in b<u>oy</u> | | • | • | • |
| *u* as in c<u>u</u>p | • | • | • | • |
| *uCe* as in J<u>u</u>ne | • | • | | |
| *ui* as in s<u>ui</u>t | • | • | • | • |
| *ue* as in bl<u>ue</u> | • | • | • | • |
| *y* as in tr<u>y</u> | • | • | • | • |
| *ar* as in st<u>ar</u> | | | • | • |
| *er* as in f<u>er</u>n | • | | • | • |
| *ir* as in b<u>ir</u>d | • | | • | • |
| *or* as in t<u>or</u>n | • | | • | |
| *ur* as in b<u>ur</u>n | • | | • | |

# Glossary

**Accommodation.** The individual's developing of new categories rather than integrating them into existing ones—Piaget's cognitive development.

**Affective domain.** Includes the feelings and emotional learnings that individuals acquire.

**Affixes.** Prefixes that are added before the root word and suffixes that are added to the end of a root word.

**Alternative assessment.** Use of evaluations other than standardized tests to achieve direct assessment of student performance on important learning tasks.

**Analogies.** Relationships between words or ideas.

**Analysis.** Breaking down something into its component parts.

**Analytic phonics.** Same as implicit phonics instruction.

**Anecdotal record.** A record of observed behavior over a period of time.

**Antonyms.** Words opposite in meaning.

**Appendix.** A section of a book containing extra information that does not quite fit into the book but that the author feels is important enough to be presented separately.

**Appraisal.** Part of diagnostic pattern: a student's present reading performance in relation to his or her potential.

**Assessment.** A broad term that covers various types of tests and measurement.

**Assimilation.** A continuous process which helps the individual to integrate new incoming stimuli to existing concepts—Piaget's cognitive development.

**Association.** Pairing the real object with the sound of the word.

**Astigmatism.** A defect of vision that causes blurred vision.

**At-risk students.** Those students who because of their backgrounds or other factors are in danger of failing in school.

**Attention deficit disorder without hyperactivity (ADD) and attention deficit disorder with hyperactivity (ADHD).** Difficulty sustaining concentration at a task.

**Attitude.** Exerts a directive and dynamic influence on an individual's behavior.

**Auding.** Highest level of listening, which involves listening with comprehension.

**Audiometer.** An instrument used for measuring hearing acuity.

**Auditory acuity.** Physical response of the ear to sound vibration.

**Auditory discrimination.** Ability to distinguish differences and similarities between sound symbols.

**Auditory fatigue.** Temporary hearing loss due to a continuous or repeated exposure to sounds of certain frequencies.

**Auditory memory span.** Amount of information able to be stored in short-term memory for immediate use or reproduction.

**Authentic Assessment.** Helps teachers to measure students' important abilities using procedures that simulate the application of these abilities to real-life situations.

**Basal reader approach.** An approach involving a basal reader series. This approach is usually highly structured; it generally has a controlled vocabulary, and skills are sequentially developed.

**Bibliotherapy.** The use of books to help individuals to cope better with their emotional and adjustment problems.

**Big books.** Enlarged versions of regular children's books; known for their repetitive patterns which lend to their predictability; they are usually children's favorites.

**Bilingual.**   Using or capable of using two languages.

**Bilingual education.**   Instruction in both the student's native language and English.

**Binaurality.**   The ability of listeners to direct both ears to the same sound.

**Binocular vision.**   The ability to focus both eyes on a similar point of reference and see one object.

**Bottom-up reading models.**   Models which consider the reading process as one of grapheme-phoneme correspondences; code emphasis or subskill models.

**Breve.**   The short vowel mark (ˇ)

**Buffer zone.**   The area that falls between the instructional and frustration levels (Betts reading levels).

**Capacity level.**   See **Listening capacity level.**

**Categorizing.**   A thinking skill involving the ability to classify items into general and specific categories.

**Central idea.**   The central thought of a group of paragraphs, an article, or a story. All the paragraphs develop the central idea of a group of paragraphs, an article, or a story. See **Main idea.**

**Chapter 1.**   Renamed Title I in 1994.

**Checklist.**   A means for systematically and quickly recording a student's behavior; it usually consists of a list of behaviors that the observer records as present or absent.

**Classroom tests.**   Teacher-made tests; also called informal tests.

**Cloze procedure.**   A technique that helps teachers gain information about a variety of language facility and comprehension ability skills.

**Cloze test.**   Reader must supply words which have been systematically deleted from a passage.

**Clusters.**   Clusters represent a blend of sounds.

**Cognitive development.**   Refers to development of thinking.

**Cognitive domain.**   Hierarchy of objectives ranging from simplistic thinking skills to the more complex ones.

**Combining forms.**   Usually defined as roots borrowed from another language that join together or that join with a prefix, a suffix or both to form a word, for example, *aqua/naut.*

**Communication.**   Exchange of ideas.

**Comparison.**   A demonstration of the similarities between persons, ideas, things, and so on.

**Compound word.**   Separate words that combine to form a new word, for example, *grandfather, stepdaughter, sunlight.*

**Comprehension.**   Understanding; the ability to get the meaning of something.

**Computer-assisted instruction.**   Instruction using computers.

**Concentration.**   Sustained attention. It is essential for both studying and listening to lectures.

**Concept.**   A group of stimuli with common characteristics.

**Consonant clusters (blends).**   A combination of consonant sounds blended together so that the identity of each sound is retained.

**Consonants.**   One speech sound represented by one letter.

**Consonant digraph.**   Two consonants that represent one speech sound.

**Construct.**   Something which cannot be directly observed or directly measured—such as intelligence, attitudes, and motivation.

**Content domain.**   Term that refers to subject matter covered.

**Context.**   The words surrounding a particular word that can shed light on its meaning.

**Context clue.**   An item of information from the surrounding words of a particular word in the form of a synonym, antonym, example, definition, description, explanation, and so on, that helps shed light on the particular word.

**Contrast.**   A demonstration of the differences between persons, ideas, things, and so on.

**Creative reading.** Uses divergent thinking skills to go beyond the literal comprehension, interpretation, and critical reading levels.

**Creativity.** Difficult to define; one definition that has been given: a combination of imagination plus knowledge plus evaluation.

**Criterion-referenced tests.** Based on an extensive inventory of objectives in a specific curriculum area; they are used to assess an individual student's performance in respect to his or her mastery of specified objectives in a given curriculum area.

**Critical reading.** A high-level reading skill that involves evaluation; making a personal judgment on the accuracy, value, and truthfulness of what is read.

**Cross-age tutoring.** Students from upper grades work with children from lower grades.

**Crossed dominance.** The dominant hand on one side and the dominant eye on the other.

**Decoding.** Listening and reading are decoding processes involving the intake of language.

**Deductive teaching.** Students are given a generalization and must determine which examples fit the rule, going from general to specific.

**Derivatives.** Combinations of root words with either prefixes or suffixes or both; for example, prefix (*re*) plus root word (*play*) = *replay*.

**Developmental reading.** All those reading skills and strategies that are systematically and sequentially developed to help students become effective readers throughout their schooling.

**Developmental spelling.** Learning to spell is ongoing and based on the cognitive development of the child.

**Diacritical marks.** Marks that show how to pronounce words.

**Diagnosis.** The act of identifying difficulties and strengths from their signs and symptoms, as well as the investigation or analysis of the cause or causes of a condition, situation, or problem.

**Diagnostic pattern.** Consists of three steps: identification, appraisal and diagnosis.

**Diagnostic-reading and correction program.** Reading instruction interwoven with diagnosis and correction.

**Diagnostic reading test.** Provides subscores discrete enough so that specific information about a student's reading behavior can be obtained and used for instruction.

**Diagnostic teaching.** The practice of continuously trying a variety of instructional strategies and materials based on the needs of students.

**Dialect.** A variation of language sufficiently different to be considered separate, but not different enough to be classified as a separate language.

**Dictionary.** A very important reference tool that supplies word meanings, pronunciations, and a great amount of other useful information.

**Digraph.** Usually consisting of either two consonants or two vowels which represent one speech sound, for example, *ch, ai.*

**Diphthongs.** Blends of vowel sounds beginning with the first and gliding to the second. The vowel blends are represented by two adjacent vowels, for example, *oi*. For syllabication purposes, diphthongs are considered to be one vowel sound.

**Directed listening/thinking approach.** Requires teachers to ask questions before, during, and after a talk; consists of a number of steps; requires students to be active participants.

**Directed Reading-Thinking Activity (DRTA).** Requires teachers to nurture the inquiry process and students to be active participants and questioners; includes prediction and verification.

**Direct instruction.** Instruction guided by a teacher, who uses various strategies to help students understand what they are reading.

**Divergent thinking.** The many different ways to solve problems or to look at things.

**Dyslexia.** Severe reading disability.

**Ebonics.** A combination of *ebony* and *phonics*. A variation of standard English; in the class of nonstandard English.

**Educational factors.** Those factors that come under the domain or control of the educational system and influence learning.

**Egocentric speech.** Child speaks in a collective monologue or primarily in parallel, that is, speech is not directed to another's point of view; concerned with own thoughts.

**Emergent literacy.** That stage in literacy which is concerned with the young child's involvement in language and his or her attempts at reading and writing before coming to school or before conventional or formal reading and writing begin.

**Emergent writing.** Nonconventional writing that includes scribbling and nonphonetic letterings.

**Environmental psychology.** Focuses on behavior in relation to physical settings.

**English language learners (ELL).** Teaching that concentrates on helping children who speak a language other than English or who speak nonstandard English to learn standard English as a language.

**Equilibrium.** According to Piaget, a balance between assimilation and accommodation in cognitive development.

**Evaluation.** A process of appraisal involving specific values and the use of a variety of instruments in order to form a value judgment; goes beyond test and measurement.

**Example.** Something representative of a whole or a group.

**Experience story.** A basic teaching technique in reading founded on experiences of students.

**Explicit instruction.** Instruction guided by a teacher, who uses various strategies to help students understand what they are reading.

**Explicit phonics instruction.** Each sound associated with a letter in the word is pronounced in isolation, and then the sounds are blended together; synthetic phonics.

**Eye movements.** How the eyes appear to move in the act of reading.

**Fact.** Something that exists and can be proved true.

**Finding inconsistencies.** Finding statements that do not make sense.

**Fixations.** Stops readers make in the act of reading continuous text.

**Frustration reading level.** The child reads with many word recognition and comprehension errors. It is the lowest reading level and one to be avoided.

**Full inclusion.** All children with disabilities receive all instruction in regular education classes with their nondisabled peers; all support services take place in the regular education classroom.

**Functional reading.** Includes all reading in which the primary aim is to obtain information.

**Grade equivalents.** Description of year and month of school for which a given student's level of performance is typical.

**Grapheme-phoneme correspondences.** Letter-sound relationships.

**Graphemes.** The written representation of phonemes.

**Graphemic base.** Same as phonogram.

**Graphic organizer.** Same as semantic mapping.

**Group instruction.** A number of students are taught at the same time; helps make instruction more manageable.

**Group tests.** Administered to a group of people at the same time.

**Halo effect.** A response bias that contaminates an individual's perception in rating or evaluation.

**Hearing.** The lowest level in the hierarchy of listening; the physical perception of sound.

**High-stake tests.** Used to determine whether students should be promoted to the next grade. Also, may be used to either reward or penalize teachers based on students' performance on such tests.

**Home environment.** Socioeconomic class, parents' education, and the neighborhood in which children live are some factors that shape children's home environment.

**Homographs.** Words that are spelled the same but have different meanings.

**Homonyms.** Words that sound alike, are spelled differently, and have different meanings.

**Homophones.** Same as homonyms.

**Hypermetropia.** Farsightedness; difficulty with close-up vision.

**Identification.** Part of diagnostic pattern; the act of determining the student's present level of performance in word recognition and comprehension for screening purposes.

**Immersion.** Complete exposure of a nonnative English speaker to English as soon as he or she enters school.

**Implicit phonics instruction.** Does not present sounds associated with letters in isolation. Children listen to words that begin with a particular sound; then they state another word that begins with the same sound; analytic phonics.

**Independent reading level.** Level at which child reads on his or her own without any difficulty.

**Individualized instruction.** Student works at own pace on material based on the needs, interests, and ability of the student.

**Individual tests.** Administered to one person at a time.

**Inductive teaching.** Students discover generalizations by being given numerous examples which portray patterns; going from specific to general.

**Inference.** Understanding that is not derived from a direct statement but from an indirect suggestion in what is stated; understanding that is implied.

**Informal diagnostic reading tests.** Teacher-made tests to help determine students' specific strengths and weaknesses.

**Informal interviews.** Teachers converse with students to learn about their interests and feelings.

**Informal reading inventory (IRI).** A valuable aid in helping teachers determine a student's reading levels and his or her strengths and weaknesses. It usually consists of oral and silent reading passages selected from basal readers from the preprimer to the eighth-grade levels.

**Informal tests.** Teacher-made tests.

**Instructional reading level.** The teaching level.

**Intake of language.** Listening and reading.

**Intelligence.** Ability to reason abstractly; problem-solving ability based on a hierarchical organization of two things—symbolic representations and strategies for processing information.

**Interactive instruction.** The teacher intervenes at optimal times to enhance the learning process.

**Interactive reading models.** The top-down processing of information is dependent on the bottom-up processing, and vice versa.

**Interest inventory.** A statement or questionnaire method that helps teachers learn about likes and dislikes of students.

**Interpretation.** A reading level that demands a higher level of thinking ability because the material it involves is not directly stated in the text but only suggested or implied.

**IPA.** International Phonetic Alphabet.

**Junior Great Books Program.** Program in which parent-teacher teams work together to plan reading discussions for students; sessions take place in regular classrooms during the reading period and are led by both parent and teacher.

**Language.** A learned, shared, and patterned arbitrary system of vocal sound symbols with which people in a given culture can communicate with one another.

**Language arts.** The major components are listening, speaking, reading, and writing.

**Language-experience approach.** A nonstructured emerging reading program based on students' experiences, which incorporates all aspects of the language arts into reading.

**Laterality.** Refers to sidedness.

**Learning center.** An integral part of the instructional program and vital to a good individualized program. An area is usually set aside in the classroom for instruction in a specific curriculum area.

**Listening.** Middle of hierarchy of listening in which the individual becomes aware of sound sequences, and is able to identify and recognize the sound sequences as words.

**Listening capacity level.** The highest level at which a learner can understand material when it is read aloud to him or her.

**Listening capacity test.** Given to determine a child's comprehension through listening. Teacher reads aloud to child and then asks questions about the selection.

**Listening comprehension test.** Given to assess a child's comprehension through listening; teacher reads aloud to child and then asks questions about the selection. Same as listening capacity test.

**Listening vocabulary.** The number of different words one knows the meaning of when they are said aloud.

**Literal comprehension.** The ability to obtain a low-level type of understanding by using only information that is explicitly stated.

**Literature webbing.** A story map technique to help guide children in using predictable trade books.

**Locator test.** Used to determine at what level a student should begin testing.

**Macron.** The long vowel mark ( ˉ )

**Main idea.** The central thought of a paragraph. All the sentences in the paragraph develop the main idea. The term *central idea* is usually used when referring to a group of paragraphs, an article, or a story.

**Mainstreaming.** The placement of disabled children in the least restrictive educational environment that will meet their needs.

**Masking.** Factor inhibiting hearing as sounds interfere with the spoken message.

**Measurement.** Part of the evaluative process; broader than test; involves quantitative descriptions.

**Memory span.** The number of discrete elements grasped in a given moment of attention and organized into a unity for purposes of immediate reproduction or immediate use; synonym for digit span.

**Metacognition.** Thinking critically about thinking; refers to individuals' knowledge about their thinking processes and ability to control them.

**Miscue.** Unexpected response to print.

**Miscue analysis.** A process that helps teachers learn how readers get meaning from language.

**Mixed dominance.** No consistent preference for an eye, hand, or foot.

**Modeling strategy.** Thinking out loud; verbalizing one's thoughts to help students gain understanding.

**Morpheme.** The smallest individually meaningful element in the utterances of a language.

**Motivation.** Internal impetus behind behavior and the direction behavior takes; drive.

**Myopia.** Nearsightedness; difficulty with distance vision.

**Newbery Award books.** The books that have received the Newbery Medal, which is given annually to the book in the United States that has been voted "the most distinguished literature" for children.

**Noneducational factors.** Supposedly those factors that do not come under the domain or control of the educational system and cannot be influenced by it.

**Nonstandard English.** A variation of standard English in the United States.

**Normal curve.** Bell-shaped symetrical curve in which the majority of scores fall near the mean (average) of distribution, and the minority of scores fall above or below the mean.

**Norm-referenced tests.** Standardized tests with norms so that comparisons can be made to a sample population.

**Norms.** Average scores for a given group of students, which allow comparisons to be made for different students or groups of students.

**Notetaking.** A useful study and paper-writing tool.

**Objective.** Desired educational outcome.

**Objectivity.** The same score must result regardless of who marks the test.

**Observation.** A technique that helps teachers collect data about students' behavior.

**Open syllable.** A syllable having a single vowel and ending in a vowel. The vowel is usually long, for example, *go.*

**Opinions.** Based on attitudes or feelings; they can vary from person to person, but cannot be conclusively proved right or wrong.

**Oral reading.** Reading aloud.

**Overlearning.** Helps persons retain information over a long period of time; occurs when individuals continue to practice even after they think they have learned the material.

**Paired reading.** The child reads aloud simultaneously with another person.

**Pay for performance.** The giving of pay increments or bonuses if students' test scores rise.

**Peer tutoring.** A student helps another student gain needed skills.

**Percentile.** A point on the distribution below which a certain percentage of the scores fall.

**Perception.** A cumulative process based on an individual's background of experiences. It is defined as giving meaning to sensations or the ability to organize stimuli on a field.

**Perceptual domain.** Part of the reading process that depends on an individual's background of experiences and sensory receptors.

**Performance assessment.** Involves actual demonstrations by students of their knowledge or skills in a particular area; a synonym for authentic assessment.

**Phoneme.** Smallest unit of sound in a specific language system; a class of sounds.

**Phonemic awareness.** Ability to recognize that a word is composed of a sequence of individual sounds.

**Phonetics.** The study of the nature of speech sounds.

**Phonic analysis.** The breaking down of a word into its component parts.

**Phonics.** The study of the relationships between letter symbols of a written language and the sounds they represent.

**Phonic synthesis.** The building up of the component parts of a word into a whole.

**Phonogram (graphemic base).** A succession of graphemes that occurs with the same phonetic value in a number of words (*ight, ake, at, et,* and so on); word family.

**Physical environment.** Refers to any observable factors in the physical environment that could affect the behavior of an individual.

**Portfolio.** A storage system that represents samples of students' reading and writing over a period of time.

**Portfolio assessment.** Material in portfolio is evaluated in some way.

**Practice test.** Ensures that the actual test measures what students know rather than test-taking ability; it familiarizes students with the test.

**Prefix.** An affix; a letter or a sequence of letters added to the beginning of a root word that changes its meaning, for example, *re* plus *play = replay.*

**Pre-reading.** Precursor to reading; before formal reading begins.

**Pre-reading test.** Usually given in Kindergarten before formal reading begins; actually a reading readiness test.

**Principle.** Refers to a rule or a guide.

**Projective technique.** A method in which the individual tends to put himself or herself into the situation and reveal how he or she feels.

**Propaganda.** Any systematic, widespread, deliberate indoctrination or plan for indoctrination.

**Proximodistal development.** Muscular development from the midpoint of the body to the extremities.

**Question Answer Relationships (QARs).** Helps students distinguish between "what they have in their heads" and information that is in the text.

**Questions.** A good way for students to gain a better insight into a subject; questioning also gives the instructor feedback and slows the instructor down if he or she is going too fast.

**Rating scale.**   An evaluative instrument used to record estimates of particular aspects of a student's behavior.

**Raw score.**   The number of items that a student answers correctly on a test

**Readiness.**   An ongoing, dynamic process which teachers use to prepare students for various learning activities throughout the school day.

**Reading.**   A dynamic, complex act that involves the bringing of meaning to and the getting of meaning from the written page.

**Reading autobiography.**   Students write or tell about their feelings and attempt to analyze their reading problems.

**Reading comprehension.**   A complex intellectual process involving a number of abilities. The two major abilities involve word meanings and reasoning with verbal concepts.

**Reading Olympics programs.**   Programs vary; however, most include a contest to challenge students to read the most books they can and the sharing of these books in some way with parents.

**Reading process.**   Concerned with the affective, perceptual, and cognitive domains.

**Reading readiness.**   Preparing students for the reading lesson by taking into account their maturation, past experiences, and desire to learn.

**Reading readiness test.**   Supposed to predict those children who are ready to read. If used, it must be used with great caution and never as a "waiting period." It is now generally called a pre-reading test.

**Reading Recovery program.**   An early individualized, one-on-one intervention program for first-graders who are experiencing difficulty in learning to read.

**Reading taxonomy.**   A hierarchy of reading comprehension skills ranging from the more simplistic to the more complex ones; a classification of these skills.

**Reciprocal Reading Instruction.**   A four-step teacher-directed reading technique that consists of summarizing, questioning, clarifying, and predicting.

**Recite or recall.**   The process of finding the answer to a question in one's memory without rereading the text or notes.

**Recreational reading.**   Reading primarily for enjoyment, entertainment, and appreciation.

**Regressions.**   Eyes move backward; they move back to reread material while in the act of reading continuous text.

**Reinforcement.**   Any stimulus, such as praise, which usually causes the individual to repeat a response.

**Reliability.**   The extent to which a test instrument consistently produces similar results.

**Remedial reading program.**   Takes place outside the regular classroom and is handled by special personnel.

**Repeated reading.**   Similar to paired reading; child reads along (assisted reading with model or tape) until he or she gains confidence to read alone.

**Reversals.**   Confusion of letters and words by inverting them; for example, $b = d$, *was = saw,* and vice versa.

**Role playing.**   A form of creative drama in which dialogue for a specific role is spontaneously developed.

**Root.**   Smallest unit of a word that can exist and retain its basic meaning, for example, *play.*

**Rubric.**   A scoring system used to determine if students have achieved certain standards; it places a value on students' performance in certain areas.

**Running record.**   Documentation of a child's reading.

**Saccades.**   Quick, jerky movements of the eyes as they jump from one fixation to another in the reading of continuous text.

**Scale score.**   Used to derive other scores.

**Schemata.**   These structured designs are the cognitive arrangements by which the mind is able to categorize incoming stimuli.

**Schema theory.**   Deals with relations between prior knowledge and comprehension.

**Schwa.** The sound often found in the unstressed (unaccented) syllables of words with more than one syllable. The schwa sound is represented by an upside-down e (ə) in the phonetic (speech) alphabet.

**Second-language learners.** Refers to those children whose parents have usually been born in another country and who speak a language other than English; it may also refer to a child who is born in the United States, but English is not the dominant language spoken in the child's home.

**Self-fulfilling prophecy.** Teacher assumptions about children become true, at least in part, because of the attitude of the teachers, which in turn becomes part of the children's self-concept.

**Semantic clue.** Meaning clue.

**Semantic mapping (graphic organizer).** A graphic representation used to illustrate concepts and relationships among concepts such as classes, properties, and examples.

**Silent consonants.** Two adjacent consonants, one of which is silent, for example, *kn (know), pn (pneumonia).*

**Silent reading.** Reading to oneself; not saying aloud what is read.

**Skimming.** Reading rapidly to find or locate information.

**Slow learners.** Children whose IQs usually range from approximately 70 to 85.

**Social promotion.** Promotion of students based on chronological age rather than achievement.

**Sociogram.** A map or chart showing the interrelationships of children in a classroom and identifying those who are "stars" or "isolates."

**SQ3R.** A widely used study technique that involves five steps: survey, question, read, recite or recall, and review.

**Standard.** Describes or defines what students should have learned in order to achieve certain levels of competency in subjects.

**Standard deviation (SD).** Measures that define a range of scores around the mean.

**Standard English.** English in respect to spelling, grammar, vocabulary, and pronunciation that is substantially uniform, though not devoid of regional differences. It is well established by usage in the formal and informal speech and writing of the educated and is widely recognized as acceptable wherever English is spoken and understood.

**Standardized oral reading test.** Individually administered test that helps teachers analyze the oral reading performance of students.

**Standardized reading achievement test.** Usually part of a standardized achievement survey test battery that includes other curriculum areas besides reading; measures general reading achievement.

**Standardized reading survey test (single-subject-matter test).** Measures general reading achievement; similar to a reading achievement test in a standardized achievement survey test battery.

**Standardized tests.** Tests that have been published by experts in the field and have precise instructions for administration and scoring.

**Standard scores.** Used to compare test takers' assessment scores. They are presented in terms of standard deviations.

**Stanine.** A score in educational testing on a nine-point scale, ranging from a low of 1 to a high of 9, of normalized standard scores.

**Story sense.** The understanding that there is a structure used to tell stories and that stories are written to be understood.

**Structural analysis.** A technique for breaking a word into its pronunciation units; the breaking down of a word into word parts such as prefixes, suffixes, roots, and combining forms.

**Structural synthesis.** A technique for building up of word parts into a whole.

**Study procedures.** (1) Build good habits, (2) devise a system that works for you, (3) keep at it, (4) maintain a certain degree of tension, and (5) concentrate.

**Suffix.** An affix; a letter or a sequence of letters added to the end of a root word, which changes the grammatical form of the word and its meaning; for example, *prince* plus *ly* = *princely.*

**Suitability.**   The appropriateness of a test for a specific population of students.

**Summary.**   A brief statement of the essential information in a longer piece.

**Supporting details.**   Additional information that supports, explains, or illustrates the main idea. Some of the ways that supporting details may be arranged are as cause and effect, examples, sequence of events, descriptions, definitions, comparisons, or contrasts.

**Survey.**   To gain an overview of the text material.

**Survey batteries.**   A group of tests in different content areas.

**Sustained silent reading (SSR).**   Practice in independent silent reading.

**Syllable.**   A vowel or a group of letters containing one vowel sound, for example, *blo.*

**Synonyms.**   Words similar in meaning.

**Syntax.**   Refers to word order or position of the word in a sentence.

**Synthesis.**   Building up the parts of something, usually into a whole.

**Synthetic phonics.**   Same as explicit phonics instruction.

**Teacher-made tests.**   Tests prepared by the classroom teacher for a particular class and given by the classroom teacher under conditions of his or her own choosing.

**Test.**   An assigned set of tasks to be performed.

**Thinking.**   Covert manipulation of symbolic representations.

**Top-down reading models.**   These models depend on the reader's background of experiences and language ability in constructing meaning from the text.

**Topic sentence.**   This sentence states what the paragraph will be about by naming the topic.

**Underachievement.**   Achievement below one's ability level.

**Validity.**   The degree to which certain inferences can be made from test scores or other measurements; the degree to which a test instrument measures what it claims to measure (nontechnical definition).

**Visual discrimination.**   The ability to distinguish differences and similarities between written symbols.

**Vocabulary consciousness.**   An awareness that words may have different meanings based on their context and a desire to increase one's vocabulary.

**Vowel digraph.**   Two vowels that represent one speech sound.

**Whole word or "look and say."**   A word recognition technique in which a child's attention is directed to a word and then the word is said.

**With-in Class Ability Grouping.**   The grouping of students in a class to two, three, four, or more groups according to ability in order to accommodate students' individual differences.

**Word recognition.**   A twofold process that includes both the identification of printed symbols by some method so that the word can be pronounced and the association of meaning to the word after it has been properly pronounced.

# Index